Humanitarian Assistance and State Sovereignty in International Law
Towards a Comprehensive Framework

SCHOOL OF HUMAN RIGHTS RESEARCH SERIES, Volume 76.

The titles published in this series are listed at the end of this volume.

Humanitarian Assistance and State Sovereignty in International Law

Towards a Comprehensive Framework

Emilie Ellen Kuijt

Intersentia Ltd
Sheraton House | Castle Park
Cambridge | CB3 0AX | United Kingdom
Tel.: +44 1223 370 170 | Fax: +44 1223 370 169
Email: mail@intersentia.co.uk
www.intersentia.com | www.intersentia.co.uk

Emilie Ellen Kuijt
Humanitarian Assistance and State Sovereignty in International Law: Towards a Comprehensive Framework

ISBN 978-1-78068-366-9
D/2015/7849/156
NUR 828

Cover image © Denise Rosenboom – 'Source'

A thesis edition of this book has also been published by Intersentia.

in loving memory of my grandfather hans b kuijt
auschwitz survivor ▽ 126054

we must never again stand idly by when a humanitarian crisis unfolds

ACKNOWLEDGEMENTS

It has been a privilege to complete my Ph.D. research with the support of so many wonderful people.

My gratitude first and foremost goes out to Prof. Nico Schrijver, my 'promotor'. You have expressed faith in me and supported me in every step of this process, as well as in my personal voyage. Nico, I thank you: both for this support, and for always managing to challenge me on the content of the thesis. This appreciation similarly goes out to Dr. Robert Heinsch. Your critical comments and willingness to always discuss my questions and thoughts have improved my work and kept me going through various stages of the research: thank you.

Next to Leiden University, this thesis was written at various stages while visiting Tel Aviv University. I am grateful for the support of Prof. Eyal Benvenisti in giving me an academic home away from home, and for his insightful comments on my manuscript as a member of the Ph.D. committee.

Many thanks of course also go to the other members of the committee: Prof. Willem van Genugten, Prof. Cedric van Ryngaert, Dr. Heike Spieker, Prof. Horst Fischer and Prof. Carsten Stahn for their perceptive comments. You have given me the opportunity to improve myself.

My sincere recognition also goes to the people behind the Gieskes-Strijbis Fund, for their continuous interest in the protection of those in need, resulting in their generous support of this Ph.D. research.

At a personal level, my deep, deep thanks go out to my parents, both of whom have spent many an hour supporting the positive outcome of this project. Parental love is immeasurable. Similarly Steffi, I want to thank you for your steadfast faith in me, and always reminding me of that of opa. Robert Jan: thank you for your brotherly advice and technical support, often supplemented of course by Niene. Our discussions have always helped shape my thoughts.

Words cannot express how honoured I am to have so many wonderful friends, my 'adoptive family', who have always cheered me on and believed in the outcome of this project. I am a better friend, researcher and person because of you. I thank you from the bottom of my heart for being there for the hope, the despair and all the chapters in between. In particular my appreciation goes out to Lotte, as well as to Marianne, Jessica, Lisa, Pauline, Rogier, Tali, Ranish, Olga, Denise, Jorrit, Tess and Esther. Many thanks also of course to all those I do not name as space is running out – you know who you are!

I would furthermore especially like to thank my dear colleagues at Leiden University. My two roommates Daniëlla and Hanna made me look forward to coming to work every day in the otherwise often lonely process of writing a Ph.D. thesis. The rest of the group has also always made my days in Leiden joyful and only upon leaving did I truly realise what I had: thanks to all and in particular Vid, Ruben, Cecily, Erik, Helen, Niels, Andrea, Luca, Mette and of course the ladies across the hall from my office, Esther, and Wendy for her editorial work! Stefanie: I am glad you jumped on board when I brainstormed the idea of organising a conference together. It was one of the most fulfilling experiences I have had whilst working on my Ph.D., and I am happy we had the opportunity to share it. Thanks also of course to those who have shared my lunches and coffees at TAU, especially Keren, Mirjam, Masua and Myriam – it has been a pleasure sharing my days working on the thesis with you.

And so, it comes to an end. The thesis has been completed. I am grateful to have been surrounded by so many wonderful people during this process. I thank you all.

October 2015

CONTENTS

Chapter 8
Legal Consequences of the Denial of Humanitarian Assistance: Methods of Enforcement 411

List of Abbreviations

ACHR	American Convention for Human Rights
ACHPR / African Charter	African Charter on Human and Peoples Rights
AP I / II	Additional Protocol I / II to the Geneva Conventions
Bruges Resolution	the Institute of International Law Resolution 2003, Bruges
CEDAW	Convention on the Elimination of Discrimination Against Women
CESCR	Committee on Economic, Social and Cultural Rights
CRED	Centre for Research on the Epidemiology of Disasters
CRB	The Commission for Relief in Belgium
CRC	Convention on the Rights of the Child
EC	European Community
ECHO	European Community Humanitarian Office
ECHR	European Convention for Human Rights
ECtHR	European Court of Human Rights
ECOSOC	UN Economic and Social Council
EU	European Union
FAO	Food and Agriculture Organization
Fourth Geneva Convention	Convention (IV) relative to the Protection of Civilian Persons in Time of War
Friendly Relations Declaration	Declaration on Principles of International Law Concerning Friendly Relations and Cooperation among States in Accordance with the Charter of the United Nations
GC I / II / III / IV	Geneva Convention I / II / III / IV
Guiding Principles on IDPs	UN Guiding Principles on Internal Displacement 1998
High-Level Panel Report	Report of the Secretary General's High Level Panel on Threats, Challenges and Change
HRC	Human Rights Committee
IACtHR	Inter-American Court on Human Rights
IASC	Inter-Agency Standing Committee
ICC	International Criminal Court
ICC Statute	Rome Statute of the International Criminal Court
ICCPR	International Covenant on Civil and Political Rights

ICERD	International Convention on the Elimination of All Forms of Racial Discrimination
ICESCR	International Covenant on Economic, Social and Cultural Rights
ICJ	International Court of Justice
ICRC	International Committee of the Red Cross
ICTY	International Criminal Tribunal for the former Yugoslavia
ICTR	International Criminal Tribunal for Rwanda
IDPs	Internally Displaced Persons
IDRL Guidelines	IFRC Guidelines for the domestic facilitation and regulation of international disaster relief and initial recovery assistance'
IDRL Programme	International Disaster Relief Laws, Rules and Principles Programme
IFRC	International Federation of the Red Cross
ILA	International Law Association
ILC	International Law Commission
IRO	International Refugee Organization
IRU	International Relief Union
Kampala Convention	African Union Convention for the Protection and Assistance of Internally Displaced Persons in Africa
Maastricht Principles	Maastricht Principles on Extra-Territorial Obligations (ETOs) of States in the area of Economic, Social and Cultural Rights
Mohonk Criteria	Mohonk Criteria for Humanitarian Assistance in Complex Emergencies
NATO	North Atlantic Treaty Organization
NGO	non-governmental organisation
OCHA	Office for the Coordination of Humanitarian Affairs
Refugee Convention	Convention Relating to the Status of Refugees
RtoP	Responsibility to Protect
San Remo Institute	The International Institute of Humanitarian Law in San Remo
San Remo Principles	Guiding Principles on the Right to Humanitarian Assistance
UDHR	Universal Declaration of Human Rights
UN	United Nations
UNDHA	United Nations Department of Humanitarian Affairs
UNDRO	United Nations Disaster Relief Organisation
UNHCR	United Nations High Commissioner for Refugees

UN HRC	United Nations Human Rights Council
UNRRA	United Nations Relief and Rehabilitation Administration
Vienna Declaration	1993 Vienna Declaration and Programme of Action
1907 Hague Convention	1907 Hague 'Convention respecting the Laws and Customs of War on Land'
1907 Hague Regulations	Convention (IV) respecting the Laws and Customs of War on Land', 'Regulations concerning the Laws and Customs of War on Land'
1984 Draft Convention	UN Draft Convention on Expediting the Delivery of Emergency Relief

Part I

Setting the Framework

CHAPTER 1
INTRODUCTION

'Humanitarian assistance' has increasingly been brought to the attention of the international community over the past years. The United Nations General Assembly declared in the Spring of 2009 that it:

> "*Decides* to designate 19 August as World Humanitarian Day in order to contribute to increasing public awareness about humanitarian assistance activities worldwide and the importance of international cooperation in this regard, as well as to honour all humanitarian and United Nations and associated personnel who have worked in the promotion of the humanitarian cause and those who have lost their lives in the cause of duty, and invites all Member States and the entities of the United Nations system, within existing resources, as well as other international organizations and non-governmental organizations, to observe it annually in an appropriate manner".

What are the rights and duties under international law involved in the provision of humanitarian assistance? Which actors are involved, and how can the provision of assistance be enforced? This thesis addresses the legal framework on the provision of humanitarian assistance in a humanitarian crisis.[1]

1.1 Introduction

In the 21st century, whenever a humanitarian crisis[2] unfolds, the entire world watches closely. With today's media and global communication methods, the crisis can unravel before our very eyes. As a result, we are confronted with humanitarian crises on an almost daily basis. As the images of persons in need of emergency aid appear in our newspapers, on our television screens and through social and online media sources, these crises cannot but become of global concern.

In 2013, the Centre for Research on the Epidemiology of Disasters (CRED) reported a total of 330 disasters, affecting over 96 million people worldwide.[3] These reported disasters do not include the humanitarian emergencies arising from conflict situations around the globe, but only refer to natural disasters such as droughts, earthquakes and floods, and technological disasters. Indeed, the past

---

[1] United Nations General Assembly (UNGA) Res 63/139 (5 March 2009) UN Doc A/RES/63/139 'Strengthening of the coordination of emergency humanitarian assistance of the United Nations' §26.
[2] All legal concepts relevant to this research will be fully defined in Chapters 2 and 3. A full definition of a 'humanitarian crisis' will therefore be discussed in Section 3.3.3. Defining a Humanitarian Crisis.
[3] Debarati Guha-Sapir, Philippe Hoyois and Regina Below *Annual Disaster Statistical Review 2013: The numbers and trends* (CRED 2014) 21.

decade has shown a wide array of circumstances that may warrant the delivery of humanitarian assistance. Several of these circumstances quickly spring to mind, such as the devastating tsunami in the South Pacific Ocean in 2004, the earthquake in Pakistan in 2005 in the conflict area of Kashmir, and the earthquakes in l'Aquila (Italy) and Haiti in 2009 and 2010, respectively. More recently the world has seen the disastrous effects of the earthquakes in Japan in March 2011 (including the ensuing tsunami) and Nepal in 2015, as well as the consequences of the on-going droughts in east Africa, particularly in Somalia.

Adding to the millions of people affected by (natural) disasters, over 30 severe crises involving the use of massive force were counted by the Heidelberg Institute for International Conflict Research.[4] Of these crises, the vast majority can be classified as *intra*state conflicts, often resulting in a non-international armed conflict, as opposed to *inter*state conflicts, which may lead to an international armed conflict.[5] Indeed, over the past century, a change in the nature of conflicts has taken place, as the traditional interstate 'war' has increasingly come to be replaced by circumstances of non-international armed conflicts. Examples over the past few years include the recent 'Arab Spring', resulting in conflicts in Libya and Syria, but may also include the more complex situation in the Sudan. In fact, when considering the provision of humanitarian assistance, often an overlap is found between circumstances of conflict and natural disaster, resulting in more complex emergencies. Humanitarian assistance is not provided in a legal vacuum: conflicts, (natural) disasters, complex emergencies and other potential crises warrant legal regulation, as does the provision of assistance within these circumstances. Indeed, natural disasters and non-international armed conflicts are two circumstances in which the provision of aid is increasingly needed, whilst regulation is lacking.

Standing idly by in the face of devastation is challenging for many people. When images of hungry, thirsty and distraught people come into our homes through modern media, cries for the provision of humanitarian assistance to these persons in need become louder and with time, more organised. Indeed, the second half of the 20th century, in the aftermath of World War II and with a proliferation of natural disasters and non-international armed conflicts, has witnessed growing international concern for the protection of persons in crisis, increasingly resulting in international attention.[6] Humanitarian assistance cannot *make* peace, nor can it *prevent* disasters. Yet, it can *contribute to the survival of millions during a crisis or emergency*, as well as in its immediate aftermath. The prompt delivery of emergency assistance can furthermore assist in the mitigation of displacement issues and the creation of refugees. Failing to provide humanitarian assistance to those in need can result in starvation and death.

---

[4] Heidelberg Institute for International Conflict Research, *Conflict Barometer 2009: Crises - Wars - Coups d'État Negotiations - Mediations - Peace Settlements*, (University of Heidelberg 2009) 1.
[5] Ibid. 4. For a definition of these concepts, see Section 3.2.1 Defining an Armed Conflict.
[6] Heike Spieker, 'The Right to Give and Receive Humanitarian Assistance', in HJ Heintze & A Zwitter (eds), *Humanitarian Assistance and International Law* (Springer 2011) 7.

As such, the United Nations (UN) Charter calls upon states to cooperate in solving problems of amongst others a 'humanitarian character'.[7] This call has been translated into action over the years, especially following the end of the Cold War, upon which many international actors have become involved in the delivery of humanitarian assistance.[8] When various actors in the international community wish to participate in the alleviation of human suffering resulting from a variety of emergencies such as conflicts or natural disasters and provide humanitarian assistance, international law becomes a factor of major importance. The roles of the affected state, on whose territory the crisis is occurring, and other potential third parties must be legally ascertained. Indeed, recent crises such as in Iraq and Syria demonstrate the need to determine the legal boundaries of the state sovereign in the legal framework pertaining to the delivery of humanitarian assistance. The concepts of state sovereignty and humanitarian assistance must be brought into balance.

In light of the abovementioned changes in circumstances in which humanitarian assistance is needed, as well as the proliferation of actors involved in its provision, international law regulating humanitarian assistance is in need of clarity and potentially development. This need for clarity (and development) of the law follows from these factual changes: the protection granted by the law to persons in times of a crisis must be adapted to encompass these new movements in the world concerning humanitarian assistance. What rights do persons have to receive assistance? Which duties do states have to provide aid? What role do third parties have in the delivery of assistance, and how might access to a territory be obtained? Can humanitarian assistance be enforced? Such questions are raised through the increase and developments in crises over the past decades, whilst international law has also continued to develop. Determining which rights and obligations the current legal framework encompasses and whether improvements are necessary, is therefore particularly relevant. The current international law issues in the field of humanitarian assistance are in essence fourfold and cumulative.

Firstly, the need for humanitarian assistance may exist in a variety of *circumstances*, such as international and non-international armed conflicts, occupation and (natural) disasters, resulting in fragmented legal regimes and a risk of fragmented protection.[9] In each of these various circumstances, there are indeed different applicable legal regimes and as a result, also different legal regulations that exist for the provision of humanitarian assistance. For example, the legal regime applicable to an international armed conflict is not the same as the regime applicable in times of a natural disaster, resulting in disparate and divergent

[7] Article 1(3) UN Charter states: "To achieve international co-operation in solving international problems of an economic, social, cultural, or humanitarian character, and in promoting and encouraging respect for human rights and for fundamental freedoms for all without distinction as to race, sex, language, or religion".

[8] Kate Mackintosh, 'The Principles of Humanitarian Action in International Humanitarian Law: Study 4 in: The Politics of Principle: the principles of humanitarian action in practice', *Humanitarian Policy Group* Report 5 (March 2000) 1.

[9] For a definition of these concepts, see Section 3.2 The Circumstances that may Require Humanitarian Assistance.

regulations for the provision of humanitarian assistance in both circumstances. Thus, to what extent an individual may be provided with humanitarian assistance is today commonly determined by the nature of the humanitarian crisis, which determines the applicable regime and the available law. The bulk of existing legal regulations concern international armed conflicts, given the developments following World War II. As seen above however, in today's world victims of natural disasters or of non-international armed conflicts greatly outnumber the victims of international armed conflicts and are in need of legal protection.

Secondly, the provision of humanitarian assistance is subject to a variety of *actors,* resulting in a variety of potential rights-holders and duty-bearers. Major roles in the provision of humanitarian assistance are played by the affected states, international organisations, other (coalitions of) states, non-governmental organisations (NGOs) and individuals.[10] All these actors have different responsibilities in international law with regard to the provision of humanitarian assistance. These responsibilities may vary according to the nature of the crisis. In the event of a natural disaster the assumption will often exist that the affected state will take charge in assisting those individuals affected by said disaster and may welcome foreign assistance, contrary to conflict situations where this may not regularly be the case. However, cyclone Nargis, hitting Myanmar in 2008, sadly demonstrated that governments may not always be *willing* to allow for the provision of humanitarian assistance from abroad, even in the event of natural disasters.[11] Thus, the various actors are not only rights-holders or duty-bearers, in turn, they are also stakeholders in the (non-)provision of humanitarian assistance.

Particularly poignant is therefore the third issue of *state sovereignty* in relation to the provision of humanitarian assistance. State sovereignty issues are related to both the first issue of 'circumstances' as these issues may arise in all three situations (occupation, conflict and (natural) disaster) that are addressed in this research concerning legal regulations affecting the provision of humanitarian assistance. The notion of sovereignty however is also related to the rights and duties third actors may potentially have within this legal framework. A study into the rights and obligations with regard to the provision of humanitarian assistance by all potential actors therefore always also includes the relationship with the state sovereignty of the affected state, more particularly with regard to the boundaries of this notion. Given the variety of actors and circumstances relevant to the provision of humanitarian assistance, the eventual problems with sovereignty will also vary according to the specific situation. It has been stressed by various states that humanitarian crises, non-international armed conflicts and the influx of refugees may be more readily addressed if and when underlying political crises in a territory

[10] For a definition of these concepts and a discussion of their role see Section 2.3 Actors Involved in Humanitarian Assistance. In referring to 'international organisations' throughout this research, inter-governmental organisations are interchangeably meant.

[11] Rebecca Barber, 'The Responsibility to Protect Survivors of Natural Disaster: Cyclone Nargis, a Case Study' (2009) 14 *Journal of Conflict and Security Law* 4.

were also to be addressed.[12] Sovereignty-related issues such as the offering and refusal of humanitarian assistance can indeed often be politically motivated, which will also be addressed, as part of the study into legal obligations concerning humanitarian assistance.

Proliferation of regulations is a fourth and final problem that has arisen regarding the legal framework concerning the provision of humanitarian assistance, as a result of the three abovementioned problems. The fourth issue is not only related to both the variety of circumstances in which humanitarian assistance may be relevant and legal regulations pertaining to this such as humanitarian law and human rights. It is also related to the variety of actors involved in the provision of assistance that have mushroomed in recent years, resulting in the application of fields such as refugee law and provisions concerning internally displaced persons (IDPs). Many actors have, in attempting to regulate issues concerning state sovereignty and the circumstances in which they operate, established their own set of applicable (soft law) regulations.[13] Unfortunately, proliferation of regulations often leads to ambiguity rather than legal clarity. In the case of the scope of rights and obligations relevant to the provision of humanitarian assistance, this is no different.

As this research will show, the variety of legal regimes, actors and applicable legal regulations has resulted in gaps and overlaps concerning the rights and obligations related to the provision of humanitarian assistance in various circumstances and particularly related to the notion of state sovereignty. With the lack of one common, comprehensive, overarching international legal framework regulating rights and obligations pertaining to humanitarian assistance in today's world, combined with the growing number of emergencies and actors, it is apparent that a thorough study into the *entire* current legal framework on humanitarian assistance, encompassing armed conflict, occupation and (natural) disasters, is demanded. Comprehensive and coherent international regulation of the provision of humanitarian assistance is desperately needed, to ensure adequate and equal protection for all individuals suffering during or after a humanitarian crisis. Clarity regarding the body of law to serve all circumstances and actors would be a relevant contribution to the existing legal regulations currently in place concerning the provision of humanitarian assistance. In other words, in this particular area of law, further clarification of the *lex lata* is necessary.

---

[12] Repertoire of the Practice of the Security Council (1996-1999), Chapter VIII, 'Consideration of questions under the responsibility of the Security Council for the maintenance of international peace and security', Section 37 Protection for humanitarian assistance to refugees and others in conflict situations, Initial proceedings Deliberations of 21 May 1997 (3778th meeting) 1023-1024.

[13] Examples include the UN International Law Commission's study on the protection of persons in the event of disaster, including Draft Articles on the protection of persons in the event of disaster currently in the making; the 1993 San Remo 'Guiding Principles on the Right to Humanitarian Assistance' of the International Institute of Humanitarian Law; and the Bruges 2003 Resolution on 'Humanitarian Assistance' of the Institut de Droit International. All will be discussed more in depth at a later stage throughout this research.

1.2 Aim of the Research and Research Questions

From the above, the topicality of the research can be easily discerned. There is no question that the notion of humanitarian assistance plays and will continue to play a role in international law given the various circumstances in which it may be relevant, and the various legal actors involved in its provision. The role of international law however remains somewhat undetermined, as there appears to be a lack of consistency and clarity with regard to the rights and obligations surrounding humanitarian assistance in all its relevant circumstances; namely armed conflict, occupation and natural disaster, as well as all actors in this particular international legal arena concerning humanitarian assistance. Due to the vast amount of actors and the proliferation of (soft law) regulations, a necessity arises to establish the core of the binding legal regulations applicable to the provision of humanitarian assistance, to enhance both legal certainty and practical applicability on the ground.

1.2.1 Aim of the Research

The aim of this research is to determine *what* the status and scope of the existing legal framework regarding humanitarian assistance is, and to discern *whether* clarification of and improvements to the current legal framework are necessary or desirable. Answering these questions will enhance the embedding and enforcement of humanitarian assistance in international law through the creation of a comprehensive legal framework. If such improvements are indeed necessary or desirable, the research in this thesis will have provided the background to make recommendations towards that end. In order to reach this aim, it will be relevant to firstly examine what the current existing legal framework is concerning the rights and obligations surrounding the provision of humanitarian assistance. Issues concerning sovereignty form a large part of the examination of this framework and they will be addressed in relation to the potential improvements. To this end, this thesis will examine what the prevailing law is, and what potential obstacles to the provision of assistance must be overcome in the current framework. The purpose is to analyse the existing international law with regard to the provision of humanitarian assistance in times of humanitarian emergencies and crises. Only upon establishment of the current legal regime, can the possible problems and need for improvement be discerned. Furthermore, only upon the establishment of such a possible need, can an endeavour be made towards finding improvements and proffering suggestions for new regulations. As part of this thesis, such improvements and suggestions are offered in Chapter 9. These potential improvements will contribute to the notion of a singular legal framework for the provision of humanitarian assistance. Meeting the aim of this research will contribute to the clarification of an aspect of international law – the law related to humanitarian assistance – and possibly help towards its development. Eventually this will then also aid persons in the midst of a humanitarian crisis to receive the assistance they desperately need, which is the ultimate goal of this legal research.

The approach of this research to such a framework will be comprehensive and will consider the provision of humanitarian assistance in all circumstances in which it may take place, namely in times of armed conflict, occupation and (natural) disaster if and when these circumstances amount to a humanitarian crisis. This *inclusive* approach of the research, taking into account the various circumstances, is a novel method and approach in itself – as opposed to existing legal research dealing usually with one of the respective fields – thereby providing added value. Given the fact that, as stated above, the (legal) circumstances of armed conflict, occupation and (natural) disaster are quite dissimilar, so are the legal regimes applicable to each situation. As a result, most research projects have focused on their *separate* legal frameworks, studying humanitarian assistance either in natural disasters, or occupation and conflicts.[14] Yet, a need for food, water, shelter and medicine remains a need for food, water, shelter and medicine in any humanitarian crisis, regardless of the legal differentiation between a natural disaster, a conflict or a situation of occupation. A person in need is a person in need, regardless of whether a cyclone, tsunami or armed attack has taken place, and the loss of a human life due to a lack of humanitarian assistance should not be categorised.

As relevant as a legal distinction therefore may be to determine whether or not the law of war is applicable in a certain situation, such a distinction should not be as pertinent to the rights and obligations amounting to the legal framework regarding humanitarian assistance. If the needs of a person in a humanitarian crisis or emergency are always similar; namely food, water, shelter and medicine, so then should the rights and obligations regarding the provision of humanitarian assistance be equal in all circumstances, rather than being dependent on the legal qualification of the circumstances.[15] This research will therefore determine in an *inclusive* manner what the current rights and obligations in the international legal framework are upon which the provision of humanitarian assistance is built, looking into armed conflict, occupation and circumstances of disaster in a truly comprehensive manner to establish an overview in its entirety, rather than separately. It is important to find

[14] Examples include the International Federation of the Red Cross' International Disaster Relief Law Programme; the International Law Commission's study on the protection of persons in the event of disaster, including draft articles currently in the making; the 1993 San Remo 'Guiding Principles on the Right to Humanitarian Assistance'; and the Bruges 2003 Resolution on 'Humanitarian Assistance'.

[15] For a similar approach with regard to the qualification of a person as 'protected person' in the sphere of Article 4 of the Geneva Convention (IV) relative to the Protection of Civilian Persons in Time of War, 12 August 1949, see *Prosecutor v. Tadić* IT-94-1A (ICTY Appeals Chamber 15 July 1999) § 164-168. In this instance, the Appeals Chamber stated that a nationality-nexus could not be argued as a manner to avoid application of Article 4 of the Geneva Convention (IV), as its applicability should be seen in light of its object and purpose, rather than be made dependent on formalities and purely legal relations. The object and purpose of this Article is the establishment of the largest degree of protection possible for a civilian population. As such, according to the Appeals Chamber, the Article intends to look not to legal characterisations of relations, but rather their substance. In a similar manner, rights and obligations pertaining to humanitarian assistance should not be made dependent on legal qualifications, but rather on the suffering of persons the assistance attempts to alleviate.

synchronisation between the legitimate needs of persons facing a crisis, and the realities on the ground, at the times of such a crisis. These practical issues will also guide the solutions sought in the existing legal framework and contribute to the new insights offered.

An inclusive approach will also create more clarity on the status of the law in any given situation, and provide a comparison of the rights and obligations in the various circumstances relevant to the provision of humanitarian assistance. From such a comparison, insights can be gained into possible gaps and overlaps in the existing framework. Regulations existing in one area may be absent in another domain, or *vice versa*. For example, circumstances such as 'internal disturbances' not meeting a threshold of armed conflict, often lack specifically tailored regulation whilst they may amount to a humanitarian crisis. This holds particularly true for the abovementioned increase of non-international armed conflicts where the state sovereign is often unwilling to recognise the conflict as such, in an attempt to avoid the application of humanitarian law. With a comprehensive approach to the provision of aid, these circumstances can also be incorporated and it can be determined what law is applicable in *all* potential circumstances warranting the provision of assistance. As a result of this comprehensive approach, a possible need for improvements can be established, and suggestions can be made for the development of such improvements to the entire legal regime concerning humanitarian assistance. Ultimately, legal rights and obligations relevant to the provision of humanitarian assistance may be seen as the body of 'law of humanitarian assistance' rather than several provisions dispersed over various legal fields. From this research, a *core* set of regulations will then be derived in Chapter 9, upon which actors involved can base themselves with regard to legal rights and legal responsibilities in the provision of humanitarian assistance.

1.2.2 General Research Questions and Boundaries

The general research question posed in this legal research is: *what are the existing rights and obligations concerning the receipt, provision, denial and enforcement of humanitarian assistance, and is development or improvement of international law necessary for the creation of a comprehensive legal framework?* This question can be broken down into several more narrow research questions, each to be addressed in various parts of this research to eventually reach the general aim of the research.[16] In a general sense, this question can be divided into three separate issues. Firstly, this research will address what the current rights and obligations regarding the receipt, provision and denial of humanitarian assistance are. In doing so, this research will discern what gaps and/or overlaps may emanate from this assessment. This will secondly enable the identification of areas of development and/or improvement, to enhance the embedding and enforcement of humanitarian assistance in international law should withholding or denial of assistance be wrongful. Lastly, and resulting from the former two, the creation of a

[16] See Section 1.3 Research Structure.

comprehensive, synchronised core legal framework will be discussed that may function as a basis in all circumstances of humanitarian crisis.

As a result of the general research question, the various sub-questions discussed in the following chapters are addressed in a tiered manner. These questions will include amongst others *what* the various legally delimited circumstances are in which emergency aid is necessary, and *how* the matter of state sovereignty can be incorporated as part of the provision of humanitarian assistance. Furthermore, the question *whether* a possible human right to humanitarian assistance exists is addressed, to determine the applicability of human rights law. Research is needed to determine on which legal grounds a claim for assistance can be made by those enduring a humanitarian crisis. Subsequently, the matter whether an obligation to provide assistance exists, as well as alternatively a right to receive assistance, is considered in the various specific circumstances. Following on from this, addressing the possible right to access for its provision and a possible obligation to allow such access is relevant. Lastly, the research questions warrant a closer look at enforcement options, consequential to the possible withholding or denial of the provision of assistance.

Having discussed the questions that are addressed within this research, it remains relevant to establish what will *not* be addressed in order to clearly establish boundaries. This research into the legal framework regarding the provision of humanitarian assistance is *international* by nature. As a result, the domestic legal frameworks of various states will not be specifically addressed. Such frameworks vary, and this research seeks to establish a core, overarching baseline and framework from which may not be deviated and upon which may be relied in all circumstances. An aspect of such domestic variations pertain to practical issues relating to the delivery of aid, such as placing search and rescue dogs into quarantine, visa issues for persons from a variety of nationalities, etc. It is not possible as part of this research into the international legal rights and responsibilities relating to the provision of assistance to address these matters in depth. As such, a focus will be placed upon sources of international law like treaties and customary norms that have a broader scope.[17] This approach also aligns with the practical circumstances that both conflicts and disasters often have cross-border effects, warranting binding international regulation.

This research is furthermore built on two distinct premises. As a point of departure, it is presumed in this research that in the discussion of sovereign duties or third party rights and responsibilities to provide assistance, the affected persons indeed wish to *receive* such aid. Whereas in certain instances persons affected by emergencies are indeed not willing to engage with authorities or third parties, this is not the common denominator in circumstances of crisis. Thus, this research assumes the position that the delivery of assistance is not in fact only *necessary* for the immediate survival of persons in crisis, but also *desired* by those in need. Secondly, this research accepts that the provision of humanitarian assistance may in reality at times also have a negative impact on the ground, due to conflicting

[17] See Section 1.4.1 Primary Sources.

interests of sovereign authorities, third parties, international organisations and persons in need. Indeed, there is no singular solution in times of crisis, and this research cannot provide all the answers needed to resolve humanitarian emergencies. This research attempts to provide legal clarity regarding the existing framework, and to assist those affected by humanitarian crises through such legal means. Thus, from the outset, it is assumed in this research that the positive effects of the provision of humanitarian assistance to persons in need outweigh the potential occasional negative effects.

1.3 Research Structure

In order to determine the existing legal framework in the provision of assistance, this research is separated into three distinct parts. Part I addresses the delimitations and boundaries of the framework, and establishes the relevant legal definitions. Part II then discusses the current rights and duties of involved actors in the provision of assistance, and Part III lastly examines the rights and duties of third parties in the delivery of aid when such initial provision is absent. These three parts are explained in more detail below to portray the structure of this research.

Given the aim of this research, namely to establish in a comprehensive manner which rights and obligations regarding humanitarian assistance and international law are currently in place, a structure divided according to the various rights and obligations is necessary. Only in this manner will it be possible to adequately establish what differences and similarities exist in the three circumstances relevant to the law regarding humanitarian assistance: armed conflict, occupation and (natural) disaster and possibly synchronise them. A distinct choice has been made with this structure, so as to approach the legal framework of humanitarian assistance per legal question, in order to contribute to the aim of the research, as a situational structure (according to the law in each circumstance, rather than according to the rights and duties per actor cumulatively) would have provided a more fractioned overview of the framework that is currently in place. Reduction of fragmentation and enhancement of unification of protection is a distinct aim of this legal research.

To realise the first aim of this research; namely examining and establishing the scope of the current legal framework concerning humanitarian assistance, delimitation of the framework is necessary, which is the subject of Part I. This research therefore commences in Chapter 2 with a historical overview of the framework and of definitions of the concepts relevant to this framework. These include the definition of humanitarian assistance itself, as well as a discussion of the principles by which it is provided. Furthermore, the various actors involved in its provision are addressed. Subsequently, Chapter 3 provides the scope of application of the legal framework; namely the circumstances in which humanitarian aid is generally provided. These circumstances include armed conflict, occupation and (natural) disaster. As a result, whilst proffering the notion of a 'humanitarian crisis' in this Chapter, the research will subsequently address the rights and obligations under international law according to these three distinct circumstances. In this regard, Chapter 3 concludes with a discussion of the applicable law in times of crisis, and the relationship between these *corpora juris* to provide a basis for more in depth analysis of individual provisions relating to the delivery of humanitarian aid in further Chapters. Chapter 4, the final Chapter of Part I, discusses the notion of state sovereignty as a contextual concept in relation to the legal framework on the delivery of humanitarian assistance. The concept of sovereignty plays a distinct role throughout the discussion of the legal framework on humanitarian assistance, and is therefore critically examined at the outset. Chapter 4 provides a historical overview of the developments of the concept, its reconceptualisation following the development of the 'Responsibility to Protect' doctrine, and its current status in international law.

Having established the (legal) definitions to be used within this research, as well its scope of application, Part II addresses the legal rights and duties in the provision of assistance. Part II commences with Chapter 5 concerning the possible (human) right to *receive* humanitarian assistance, as well as corresponding *obligations* of the affected state under human rights law. This Chapter considers whether a possible (human) right to receive humanitarian assistance exists independently in human rights law or results from existing human rights. Human rights law, as discussed in Chapter 5, maintains applicability in times of crisis, warranting a discussion of the protection it offers to those in need of assistance. With the approach taken by this research; namely a structure according to rights and obligations that are applicable in this framework, Chapter 6 subsequently addresses the existing duties of the sovereign authorities to provide assistance and the rights of persons to receive it in the three circumstances of armed conflict, occupation and (natural) disaster, whilst differentiating between international armed conflicts and non-international armed conflicts. This Chapter provides an overview of the current rights and duties of the primary actors involved, as well as revealing gaps in protection that may exist.

Having established what rights and duties initially exist for the persons in need and their sovereign authorities under the current legal framework, Part III examines the role of third parties in the provision of assistance, as well as enforcement mechanisms. Thus, Part III addresses the aspects of the legal framework that become relevant when the initial provision of aid remains absent. Chapter 7 in this regard addresses the provision of humanitarian assistance from the perspective of third parties wishing to deliver aid. This Chapter considers the rights and obligations of external actors, such as states and international organisations, to offer and provide humanitarian assistance. Related to this is the possible right to access of those providing assistance in the aforementioned three circumstances of armed conflict, occupation and (natural) disaster as well as the potential duty of the affected state to allow such access. With an assessment of whether access to a territory can be obtained through existing rights and obligations under international law, a completion of the comprehensive framework regarding the provision of humanitarian assistance will have been put in place, laying bare the potential problems in the provision of aid. Having established what rights and obligations exist, Chapter 8 examines the possibility of enforcement of these rights and obligations, should assistance remain lacking. Enforcement options exist at various levels, varying from the use of force to legal enforcement before international courts or other bodies, both at the inter-state level and at the level of individual responsibility. This Chapter adds to the existing legal framework in the assessment of manners in which humanitarian assistance may be enforced, when aid is not delivered.

With the described structure and method of research, the current legal framework will be established in a truly comprehensive manner. These Chapters, in establishing the existing framework, will simultaneously have led this research towards its second aim. It will thus also have become clear what gaps, problems and/or overlaps exist in the law between the various circumstances, and therefore also if potential developments are necessary for the clarification and possible improvement of the law, in order to enhance the embedding and enforcement of humanitarian assistance in international law. These conclusions regarding the overarching, comprehensive legal framework in times of humanitarian crises are offered in Chapter 9. This Chapter addresses the foundations available in international law *at all times*, explicating the existing rights and duties upon which can be relied in times of armed conflict, occupation and (natural) disaster amounting to a humanitarian crisis. The Chapter furthermore addresses potential synchronising developments and improvements applicable to the legal framework that may be necessary and practically achievable.

1.4 Methodology

This legal research makes use of a variety of sources of international law. The broad topic of humanitarian assistance, which can be needed in a variety of legally delimited circumstances, warrants the applicability of multiple bodies of law. Furthermore, the developments as described above in Section 1.1 concerning the proliferation of regulations warrant a discussion of both primary sources of law and secondary sources of law, both discussed in more detail below. The generally accepted primary sources of public international law are stated in Article 38(1) of the Statute of the International Court of Justice (ICJ) and include treaties, customary international law and general principles of law.[18] The subsidiary sources of international law, mentioned in Article 38 (1)(d) the ICJ Statute, namely case law and legal scholarship, remain relevant to this research related to humanitarian assistance, in particular in consideration of the potential gaps in protection. Other suggested subsidiary sources of international law include unilateral acts and

[18] Article 38(1) of the ICJ Statute states: "The Court, whose function is to decide in accordance with international law such disputes as are submitted to it, shall apply: a. international conventions, whether general or particular, establishing rules expressly recognized by the contesting states; b. international custom, as evidence of a general practice accepted as law; c. the general principles of law recognized by civilized nations; d. subject to the provisions of Article 59, judicial decisions and the teachings of the most highly qualified publicists of the various nations, as subsidiary means for the determination of rules of law".

resolutions of UN bodies such as those of the Security Council and General Assembly, as well as soft law.[19] In the subsequent Sections, a more in-depth perspective is provided regarding the specific sources that are of particular relevance to the legal framework concerning the delivery of humanitarian assistance.

First however, the manner in which the abovementioned sources are studied must also be briefly clarified. Different methods of interpretation may lead to different outcomes in research. Articles 31 and 32 of the 1969 Vienna Convention on the Law of Treaties set out the general methods of interpretation. The primary method according to the Vienna Convention is to interpret according to a treaty term's ordinary meaning, in light of its object and purpose.[20] This approach, which can be considered to reflect customary international law, encompasses aspects of the three main interpretation techniques accepted in international law.[21] A first technique is the grammatical or objective method, where the factual text and analysis of the words is emphasised. A second technique is the subjective approach in which the intention of parties to an agreement is underlined. Finally, the teleological interpretation stresses the object and purpose in its determination of the meaning of an agreement.[22] All abovementioned manners of interpretation play a role in this research in order to ensure the proper interpretation of the sources at hand. In the discussion of the various sources relevant to the legal framework relating to the provision of assistance, the factual text primarily provides means for analysis, yet upon a need for clarity the subsequent methods are utilised. The *travaux préparatoires* of various international treaties provide a source for the subjective approach, whilst available public statements or treaty reservations by states as well as official *Commentaries* allow for a teleological interpretation.

---

[19] Hugh Thirlway, 'The Sources of International Law' in Malcolm Evans (ed) *International Law* (Oxford University Press 2010) 115-118.

[20] Article 31 of the Vienna Convention on the Law of Treaties states: "1. A treaty shall be interpreted in good faith in accordance with the ordinary meaning to be given to the terms of the treaty in their context and in the light of its object and purpose. 2. The context for the purpose of the interpretation of a treaty shall comprise, in addition to the text, including its preamble and annexes: (a) any agreement relating to the treaty which was made between all the parties in connection with the conclusion of the treaty; (b) any instrument which was made by one or more parties in connection with the conclusion of the treaty and accepted by the other parties as an instrument related to the treaty. 3. There shall be taken into account, together with the context: (a) any subsequent agreement between the parties regarding the interpretation of the treaty or the application of its provisions; (b) any subsequent practice in the application of the treaty which establishes the agreement of the parties regarding its interpretation; (c) any relevant rules of international law applicable in the relations between the parties. 4. A special meaning shall be given to a term if it is established that the parties so intended". Article 32 of the same Convention states: "Recourse may be had to supplementary means of interpretation, including the preparatory work of the treaty and the circumstances of its conclusion, in order to confirm the meaning resulting from the application of article 31, or to determine the meaning when the interpretation according to article 31: (a) leaves the meaning ambiguous or obscure; or (b) leads to a result which is manifestly absurd or unreasonable".

[21] Malcolm Shaw, *International Law* (Cambridge University Press 2008) 932-933.

[22] Ibid.

Furthermore, Article 31(3)(c) of the Vienna Convention on the Law of Treaties, states that as a basic interpretative rule, together with the object, purpose and context of a treaty, also 'any relevant rules of international law applicable in the relations between the parties' must be considered. This provision is considered a general rule of interpretation, with a view to the continuous development and evolution of the law and remains equally relevant to the legal framework concerning the provision of humanitarian assistance.[23] Indeed, with developments over the past century in types of crises and the proliferation of actors and regulations as discussed above, each source of international law, as well as each distinct body of law, must be interpreted in consideration of other relevant applicable rules of international law. As discussed in Chapter 3, this method of interpretation is particularly relevant to the consideration of human rights law and humanitarian law that according to Article 31(3)(c) Vienna Convention should also be interpreted with the *other* body of law in mind. Chapter 3 furthermore addresses at a more in depth level the concept of the *lex specialis* principle as a method of interpretation, and its applicability to the various bodies of law relevant in the provision of humanitarian assistance.

Lastly, before addressing the various primary and secondary sources applied in this research, a differentiation must be made between types of obligations in international law, as relevant to the provision of humanitarian assistance. In discussing the existing legal framework, the relevant responsibilities are addressed. Under international law, a distinction is made between 'obligations of result' and 'obligations of conduct' (also called obligations of 'effort'). Chapter 5, exploring human rights law in relation to the provision of humanitarian assistance, and subsequent Chapters address the effects of these two types of obligations in relation to the provision of assistance. At the more theoretical level, it is relevant to note that an obligation of 'result' requires a duty-bearer to ensure a specific *outcome*, whereas an obligation of 'conduct' requires a duty-bearer to *act* in a specific way.

1.4.1 Primary Sources

The primary sources of international law applied in this research include international treaties and customary law, as well as general principles of international law.[24] Within treaty law, at a general level the UN Charter is relevant, but given the fact that humanitarian assistance is addressed in a variety of circumstances, including in times of armed conflict, occupation and (natural) disaster, various treaties within the fields of international law are relevant. Particularly, the focus in Chapters 5, 6, 7 and 8 will lie on international humanitarian law and human rights law. Analysis regarding the field of international humanitarian law centres around the four Geneva Conventions of 1949 and their Additional Protocols. With regard to human rights law, specific

---

[23] Commentary to the Vienna Convention, *Yearbook of the International Law Commission*, Vol. II (1966) 222 (Draft Article 27).
[24] Article 38(1) ICJ Statute.

human rights treaties, such as the International Covenant on Economic, Social and Cultural Rights (ICESCR) and the International Covenant on Civil and Political Rights (ICCPR) will play a role. Specific rights relevant to humanitarian assistance, such as the right to life, the right to food and the right to health, are studied.[25] Next to these major treaties, regional treaties are furthermore considered. Also relevant are the Refugee Convention and the framework concerning internally displaced persons (IDPs). When considering treaty law, the *travaux préparatoires* of the relevant treaties are of importance, as an additional method of interpretation, to assess the intentions of states parties in relation to the provision of assistance. Given the aim of this research, comparative analysis of treaty law and of *corpora juris* takes place throughout the Chapters, in order to establish the overarching applicable legal framework in times of crisis.

With the abovementioned proliferation of regulations and actors in the area of humanitarian assistance, ascertaining the existence of particular rules of customary international law may be invaluable to the determination of existing rights and obligations within the framework of the provision of humanitarian assistance. Due to its characteristics regarding legal developments, customary international law can thus be of specific relevance. As a source of law, Article 38(1)(b) of the ICJ Statute has declared it to entail a 'general practice accepted as law'.[26] Traditional doctrine considers customary rules of international law to result from two particular elements, namely widespread and consistent state practice, and a more normative component '*opinio juris sive necessitatis*'; the conviction that this practice indeed flows from a rule of law.[27] Furthermore, established customary international law is binding upon all states and is therefore particularly relevant to the study of rights and obligations concerning the all-encompassing legal framework pertaining to humanitarian assistance.[28] Throughout the following Chapters, these requirements: state practice and *opinio juris*, are used in the context of various norms under consideration, in order to determine whether a particular norm can be considered to have binding customary international legal status. In this regard, aspects of the abovementioned human rights treaties but also the 1948 Universal Declaration of Human Rights, and humanitarian law provisions that have near universal accession, are considered in particular.

Of the general principles of international law, one in particular is of the utmost importance to this particular field of research regarding the provision of humanitarian assistance. Circumstances in which humans are involved, should be

---

[25] The right to adequate housing is distinctly left outside the realm of this research, as the concept of humanitarian assistance is considered to encompass those aspects of emergency aid needed for the immediate survival in times of a crisis.

[26] See Article 38(1) of the ICJ Statute (n 18).

[27] Thirlway, 'The Sources of International Law' (n19) 102; Military and Paramilitary Activities in and against Nicaragua (Nicaragua v. United States of America), Merits, Judgment 27 June 1986 I.C.J. Reports 1986, p. 14 § 175-177 and 186; as well as more generally the North Sea Continental Shelf cases (Federal Republic Of Germany/Denmark; Federal Republic of Germany/Netherlands) Judgment Of 20 February 1969, I.C.J. Reports 1969, p. 3.

[28] Shaw, *International Law* (n 21) 91.

guided by the principle of humanity.[29] As a general principle, the principle of humanity functions as a baseline throughout this research, given that the provision of humanitarian assistance aims at ensuring basic human dignity for those persons affected by humanitarian crises. The essence of the delivery of humanitarian aid is, after all, the insurance that those affected by crises do not starve and perish.

These three primary sources of law are, as primary sources, of equal standing in international law. Outside of the realm of the ICJ Statute, binding decisions of the Security Council, as discussed in Chapters 6, 7 and 8 are furthermore a source of international law. Such binding decisions, unlike other decisions of a non-binding nature adopted by international organisations and their organs, are not considered secondary sources. As stated in Article 38 ICJ Statute, *subsidiary* sources of law are relevant in consideration to aid the interpretation of the abovementioned primary sources.

1.4.2 Secondary Sources

Secondary sources including case law and legal scholarship, as well as soft law, form a large part of the current available (semi) legal resources regarding humanitarian assistance and are therefore of relevance to this research. Of particular relevance is the jurisprudence of the ICJ, as well as of specific judiciary bodies such as the International Criminal Tribunal for the Former Yugoslavia (ICTY) and regional bodies like the European Court of Human Rights (ECtHR). ICJ judgements such as in the 1986 case concerning Military and Paramilitary in and against Nicaragua, the 2007 case concerning the Application of the Convention on the Prevention and Punishment of the Crime of Genocide (Bosnia and Herzegovina v. Serbia and Montenegro) and the 2011 case concerning the Application of the International Convention on the Elimination of All Forms of Racial Discrimination (Georgia v. Russian Federation) are particularly relevant throughout this research. Numerous ICTY and ECtHR decisions are also considered in the interpretation of various primary sources of international law.

Soft law can then be considered in two distinct categories, both of which are relevant to this research. A first category is that of non-binding actions by states, such as resolutions or declarations in international settings, amongst which the UN. Indeed, UN resolutions of a non-binding character and other documents adopted within the UN framework form another major aspect of available secondary legal resources, especially with regard to humanitarian assistance in the event of natural disasters. Such resolutions are often indicative of developments in the perspectives of states on the law, and can add to the existence of *opinio juris* on a matter, or even state practice in the case of for example General Assembly Resolutions through consistent voting patterns. An example specifically concerning the provision of humanitarian assistance includes the widely known United Nations General

[29] See Section 2.2.3.1 The Principle of Humanity.

Assembly Resolution 46/182 'Strengthening the coordination of humanitarian emergency assistance of the United Nations'.[30]

A second category of soft law instruments is that of international bodies, not compiled of states, attempting to add to the existing hard law and state action by means of standard-setting. With a view to the provision of humanitarian assistance, these include various non-binding decisions and comments of treaty body mechanisms existing in human rights law, as well as the work of the International Law Commission's (ILC).[31] In particular the ILC's current work (in progress) on the 'Protection of persons in the event of disasters' is relevant, and throughout this research, the ILC's Draft Articles of May 2014 are utilised. Furthermore, the ILC's adopted Articles on the Responsibility of States for Internationally Wrongful Acts (ARSIWA) form a major source of law in the discussion of the law on state responsibility, as they are largely an attempt at codification of existing customary international law, as discussed in Chapter 8. Both the Draft Articles on the 'Protection of persons in the event of disasters' and the ARSIWA have not yet been adopted by the UN General Assembly, although their various stages of development are clearly distinct, given that the drafting of the 'protection of persons in the event of disasters' is still ongoing. Furthermore, outside the UN realm, many organisations have created their own semi-legal frameworks with regard to certain aspects of humanitarian assistance, as well as functioning as practical benchmarks for practitioners in the field. Whether they be named guidelines, principles, or rules of procedure, it is clear that they do not form part of the primary sources that shape the hard body of law concerning humanitarian assistance. The various documents of these organisations discussed within this research furthermore differentiate in their goal, which is of relevance to their potential consideration as a secondary source. Within this context of particular importance are the 'International Disaster Response Law Guidelines' (IDRL Guidelines) of 2007, reviewed at length in Chapters 6 and 7. Whilst these Guidelines are of great relevance, they are not a codification attempt, and merely attempt to be of practical use; therefore within this legal research, they must be treated as such. Various other organisations, such as the UN and the European Union (EU) concerning their member states, *do* attempt to create legislation, or at least binding regulations. As discussed in the above, the work of NGOs, given their contested status in international law and the fact that they do not create legal norms themselves, falls largely outside the scope of this research into the international legal framework pertaining to the delivery of humanitarian assistance.

---

[30] UNGA Res 46/182 (19 December 1991) UN Doc A/RES/46/182 'Strengthening the coordination of humanitarian emergency assistance of the United Nations'.

[31] The work of the ILC will be discussed at length in later Chapters, but it is relevant to note that the purpose of the Commission is "the promotion of the progressive development of international law and its codification"; Article 1 of the 1947 Statute of the International Law Commission (Adopted by the General Assembly in resolution 174 (II) of 21 November 1947, as amended by resolutions 485 (V) of 12 December 1950, 984 (X) of 3 December 1955, 985 (X) of 3 December 1955 and 36/39 of 18 November 1981).

These relevant secondary sources – namely case law, UN documents and frameworks from other organisations – form the bulk of materials available for additional legal analysis for the purpose of this thesis, next to the primary sources of international law. Whereas the existing hard law may be sufficient for the establishment of an overarching framework concerning humanitarian assistance, secondary sources and soft law contribute to the further development of this framework. Indeed, soft law contributes to the body of international law in its entirety and can be considered supplementary evidence of existing law, or reflecting one of the formative components of customary international law.[32] As such, these additional sources can be of aid in the determination of potential solutions to the problems within the existing legal framework on the delivery of humanitarian assistance that this research may uncover. However, this research does not consider soft law instruments in any way to be a source containing binding rights and duties in the international legal sphere.[33]

Soft law however can also aid in the explanation and interpretation of existing law.[34] A distinction must furthermore be made between existing soft law and *lex ferenda*. Whilst both are not *lex lata*, a differentiation is possible between soft law and the scope of *lege ferenda*. At which point in creation soft law potentially becomes binding is arguable, and moreover largely dependent on which form of hard law it could eventually take; such as a formal treaty, or development into customary international law.[35] Many soft law instruments however never develop into hard law and as such do not form part of the body of existing law. Yet resolutions, guidelines and principles are often the result of careful drafting and negotiations. The *intent* with which many such documents are created can be seen as evidence towards a commitment to law-making.[36] This holds true in particular when states are party to such negotiations. Indeed, it is these efforts that can be seen as *de lege ferenda*; as what the law ought to be. With greater and widespread commitment towards law-making, opposing positions may be more difficult to legally uphold. As such, these various resources may be invaluable in particular with respect to the analysis of current rights and obligations, as well as the development of a comprehensive legal framework regarding humanitarian

---

[32] Alan Boyle, 'Soft Law in International Law-Making' in Malcolm Evans (ed) *International Law* (Oxford University Press 2010) 122-123.

[33] For a discussion on soft law more in general, see amongst others Alan Boyle & C M Chinkin, *The Making of International Law* (Oxford University Press 2007); Gregory C Shaffer and Mark A Pollack, 'Hard vs. Soft Law: Alternatives, Complements, and Antagonists in International Governance' (2010) 94 *Minnesota Law Review*, 706-799 and with a more objecting perspective Jan Klabbers, 'The Redundancy of Soft Law' (1996) 65 *Nordic Journal of International Law*, 167-182. Whilst being aware of the discussion that exists regarding the inherent value of soft law, this discussion remains outside the scope of this research, as these non-binding documents are merely used in a supplementary manner to form part of a discussion of existing law.

[34] Ulrich Fastenrath, 'Relative Normativity in International Law' (1993) 4 *European Journal of International Law*, 313-314.

[35] C M Chinkin, 'The Challenge of Soft Law: Development and Change in International Law', (1989) 38 *International and Comparative Law Quarterly* 856-857.

[36] Boyle, 'Soft Law in International Law-Making' (n 32) 124-125.

assistance. Thus, although not hard law in itself, these sources will play a role throughout this thesis, as their application will be relevant to all aspects of the research questions.

1.4.3 Character of the Research

Lastly, prior to commencing the discussion of the legal framework concerning the provision of humanitarian assistance, the character of this research needs to be addressed. This character is dual in its nature. The duality of the research holds true at various levels. As such, the main research question holds elements pertaining to the *lex lata*, as well as *de lege ferenda* and furthermore is dual in its addressing of multiple potential rights and duties and their respective rights-holders and duty-bearers.

In this research, a focus is firstly placed on the determination of the existing law, making it descriptive and comparative in nature. With this critical legal analysis, the current legal framework regarding humanitarian assistance will be brought into place. At the same time, a supervisory element will also be present, as part of this research is to uncover whether or not compatibility exists between the law concerning humanitarian assistance in times of armed conflict, occupation and (natural) disaster. This duality furthermore applies to the various right-holders and duty-bearers concerned with the provision of assistance, varying from the affected persons and states, to third parties.

Having established whether or not gaps, overlaps or other potential problems stand in the way of such compatibility, this research then proceeds towards different questions. Fundamental questions, such as how the law may be adapted to better match underlying legal principles concerning humanitarian assistance (such as the principle of humanity) are discussed, as well as how the existing law could be further synchronised in the three circumstances in which humanitarian assistance is potentially relevant, when amounting to a humanitarian crisis. Lastly, the drafting and formulating of recommendations for potential future development is relevant to the research. Therefore, instrumental questions, trying to develop suggestions for the issues encountered in the current framework on the delivery of humanitarian assistance will be raised.

The character of this research is however distinctly geared towards an in-depth discussion of existing *lex lata*. When referring to the determination of 'one singular, comprehensive and overarching framework' this does *not* imply *lege ferenda* or soft law. The purpose remains the demonstration and evincing of the *existing* legal framework as a shared common legal basis in all circumstances in which the need for the provision of humanitarian assistance arises. There is no intention of merging existing legal regimes, or creating an entirely new regime. The character of this research, with a focus on *lex lata*, attempts to demonstrate that within existing international law, a foundation can be found to apply to *all* circumstances warranting the provision of assistance. As such, this framework is distilled from existing hard law. By doing so, an assessment can be made of the existing law governing the provision of humanitarian assistance at all times. Furthermore, with an analysis of *lex lata*, the necessity for and desirability of new developments can be assessed, based upon the potential uncovering of gaps in the existing law.

CHAPTER 2
DEFINING HUMANITARIAN ASSISTANCE, THE PRINCIPLES FOR ITS PROVISION AND DETERMINING THE RELEVANT ACTORS

In the summer of 2014, Russia attempted to bring goods to the Ukraine whilst clashes were ongoing. As was reported:

> "A Russian convoy of trucks carrying tonnes of humanitarian aid left on Tuesday for eastern Ukraine, where government forces are closing in on pro-Russian rebels, but Kiev said it would not allow the vehicles to cross onto its territory […] 'No political or any other objectives must be pursued,' EU humanitarian aid commissioner Kristalina Georgieva told a news conference. 'The content of humanitarian aid must be exactly that, humanitarian aid, and obviously cannot be taken on face value'".

What makes certain goods humanitarian assistance? What makes their providers humanitarian actors? This chapter addresses these questions and provides legal resolutions.[1]

2.1 Introduction

To start an analysis of the legal framework regarding humanitarian assistance, including all relevant rights and obligations, it is necessary to establish and define the legal concepts that form part of this research. To that extent, this Chapter explores and establishes the legal definitions and parameters of relevant concepts related to humanitarian assistance. Firstly, the notion of humanitarian assistance itself is examined, as well as the manner in which it may be provided. Relevant actors are discussed, considering both those who provide assistance and those that may receive it. This examination commences with a brief historical overview of the development of humanitarian assistance, first within the context of armed conflict, where the notion was born, but later in the 20th century also with a discussion of its incorporation in times of (natural) disaster. By assessing the origins of humanitarian assistance, it will be possible to address the notion as a contemporary concept, and make it possible to proffer a working definition of the concept of humanitarian assistance as it is understood today.

---

1 <http://uk.reuters.com/article/2014/08/12/uk-ukraine-crisis-russia-aid-idUKKBN0GC08O20140812> accessed 9 September 2014.

2.2 The Concept of Humanitarian Assistance

Understanding humanitarian assistance as it exists today, also entails understanding its origins and history. Tracing the origins of humanitarian assistance acknowledges its foundation and explains the manner in which it has developed in international law.

2.2.1 Historical Development

The precursors of the modern provision of humanitarian assistance can be found in the efforts throughout history to constrain the use of force in conflict as well as occasional early efforts to spare the lives of prisoners of war.[2] The growth of religions throughout the world furthermore spurred limits to warfare, as well as enhancing humanitarian initiatives.[3] The development of the notion of humanitarian assistance was however not solely confined to religious spheres, as secular humanitarianism developed through natural law notions and the enlightenment of the eighteenth and nineteenth centuries.[4] In 1758, Emer de Vattel argued:

> "[…] si un people est désolé par la famine, tous ceux qui ont des vivres de reste doivent l'assister dans son besoin, sans toutefois s'exposer eux-mêmes à la disette […] L'assistance, dans cette dure extrémité, est si essentiellement conforme à l'humanité, qu'on ne voit guères de Nation un peu civilisée y manquer absolument […] De quelque Calamité qu'un peuple soit affligé, la même assistance lui est dûe".[5]

De Vattel refers to English actions of humanity with regard to calamities in Portugal in the eighteenth century where tens of thousands died, as well as Swiss initiatives at that time towards neighbouring countries.[6] With these initiatives, a period ensued in which further steps were taken in the development of the more contemporary notion of humanitarian assistance. The notion of humanitarian assistance as we understand it today was particularly developed by the Swiss businessman Henri Dunant, upon witnessing the battle of Solferino on June 24, 1859.[7] Dunant shared his experiences of that battle in *Un Souvenir de Solférino*,

---

[2] Frits Kalshoven & Liesbeth Zegveld, *Constraints on the Waging of War: An Introduction to International Humanitarian Law* (Cambridge University Press 2011) 3.

[3] Peter Macalister-Smith, *International Humanitarian Assistance: Disaster Relief Actions in International Law and Organization* (Martinus Nijhoff 1985) 8.

[4] Ibid. 9.

[5] Emerik de Vattel, *Le Droit de Gens: ou Principes de la Loi Naturelle*, Vol. II Chapitre I (1758) 260-261. English translation: "If a people is visited with famine, all those who have provisions enough and to spare should come to its assistance, though not to the extent of exposing themselves to scarcity…Help in such an extremity is so much in accordance with humanity that no civilized nation could altogether fail to respond…Whatever the nature of the disaster that afflicts a nation, the same help is due to it".

[6] Ibid 261.

[7] The battle of Solferino was part of the Italian unification process. It was fought in northern Italy between Austrian and Franco-Italian soldiers, leaving ten thousands dead, injured or missing. For more

first published in 1862.[8] In this book, Dunant related the horrors of the battlefield, in particular the incapacity of the present medical services to deal with the number of victims. Having shared his experience in this publication, Dunant expressed his desire to develop organisations of a neutral and impartial character, to aid those wounded by war:

> "Mais pourquoi avoir raconté tant de scènes de douleur et de désolation, et avoir peut-être fait éprouver des émotions pénibles? Pourquoi s'être étendu comme avec complaisance sur des tableaux lamentables, et les avoir retracés d'une manière qui peut paraitre minutieuse et désespérante? A cette question toute naturelle, qu'il nous soit permit de répondre par cette autre question: N'y aurait-il pas moyen de fonder de Sociétés *volontaires* de secours qui auraient pour le but de donner ou de faire donner, en temps de guerre, des soins aux blessés".[9]

Raising this simple question eventually led to the establishment of the International Committee for the Red Cross (ICRC), while his subsequent question led to the development of the original Geneva Convention for the Amelioration of the Condition of the Wounded in Armies in the Field of 22 August 1864:[10]

> "Dans des occasions extraordinaires, comme celle qui réunissent, par exemple à Cologne ou à Chalons, des princes de l'art militaire, de nationalités différentes, ne serait-il pas à souhaiter qu'ils profitent de cette espèce de congres pour formuler quelque principe international, conventionnel et sacré, lequel, une fois agréé et ratifié, servirait de base à des *Sociétés de secours pour les blessés*, dans les divers pays de l'Europe. Il est d'autant plus important de se mettre d'accord et d'adopter d'avance des mesures, que, lors d'un commencement d'hostilités, les belligérants sont déjà mal disposés les uns envers les autres, et ne traitent plus les questions qu'au point de vue unique de leurs ressortissants".[11]

Here, Dunant raised the idea of creating international standards that parties to a conflict should abide by. With his publication, Dunant wished to raise awareness amongst leaders of his time to create the abovementioned Convention and the ICRC

information on this battle, see Spencer C. Tucker, *Battles That Changed History: An Encyclopedia of World Conflict* (Greenwood Publishing Group 2011) 331-334.

[8] Henri Dunant, *Un Souvenir de Solférino* (self-published 1862); <www.icrc.org/eng/assets/files/other/icrc_002_0361_memory_of_solferino.pdf> accessed 23 June 2011.

[9] Henri Dunant, *Un Souvenir de Solférino* (1863, 3rd ed. Imprimerie de J.G. Flick) 150. English translation: "But why have I told of all these scenes of pain and distress, and perhaps aroused painful emotions in my readers? Why have I lingered with seeming complacency over lamentable pictures, tracing their details with what may appear desperate fidelity? It is a natural question. Perhaps I might answer it by another: Would it not be possible, in time of peace and quiet, to form relief societies for the purpose of having care given to the wounded in wartime by zealous, devoted and thoroughly qualified volunteers?".

[10] François Bugnion, 'From Solferino to the Birth of Contemporary International Humanitarian Law', online publication with the ICRC (April 22nd 2009), 5 <www.icrc.org/eng/assets/files/other/solferino-bugnion-icrc.pdf> accessed 24 June 2011.

[11] Dunant, *Un Souvenir de Solférino* (n 8) 165.

and to that end, he distributed his book free of charge.[12] Thus, the notion of humanitarian assistance as we know it today, was first developed to relieve the wounded and other victims of wars. For his extraordinary achievement, Henri Dunant was the first recipient of the Nobel Peace Prize in 1901.[13] Following the establishment of the Convention and ICRC, National Societies of the Red Cross were created. Returning in greater detail to the ICRC and its specific role as a major actor in this area of international law in Sections 2.2.2.2 and 2.3.2, other developments that have led to the current state of legal rights and obligations concerning humanitarian assistance will first be briefly addressed.

At first, notwithstanding De Vattel's influence, relief assistance remained within the sphere of armed conflict as developed through Dunant's ideas. From the late nineteenth century to the beginning of the twentieth century, the ICRC provided humanitarian assistance during instances such as the Franco-Prussian War, the Boer War and the Russian-Japanese War, reaching a larger scale with its assistance during World War I.[14] With the increase of international awareness, the first civilian oriented assistance action was undertaken during that same war, aimed at the Belgian population that was threatened by famine due to the German occupation. The *Commission for Relief in Belgium* (CRB) was created in 1914 by Herbert Hoover, later president of the United States of America, and operated with a strictly humanitarian mandate to provide relief to civilians during World War I.[15] Having convinced all parties to the conflict that providing relief to Belgian civilians was desirable, the CRB received support from *both* sides to the conflict, to operate while maintaining its neutrality.[16] This particular scheme created a valuable precedent for ensuing attempts of humanitarian assistance, as neutrality, independence and communication towards all parties have continued to remain invaluable to relief organisations today, while subsequent organisations have benefitted from this first experience.[17]

During the *interbellum*, several developments occurred. In 1921, the President of the Italian Red Cross proposed the creation of an organisation focused specifically on assistance to victims of natural disasters, which was taken up by the League of Nations and resulted in the establishment of the International Relief Union (IRU) in 1927.[18] The IRU's goals were the delivery of first aid, the procurement of means to

[12] Bugnion, 'From Solferino to the Birth of Contemporary International Humanitarian Law' (n 10).
[13] Dunant shared the first Nobel Peace Prize in 1901 with Frédéric Passy. For more information, see <http://nobelprize.org/nobel_prizes/peace/> accessed 23 June 2011.
[14] Macalister-Smith, *International Humanitarian Assistance: Disaster Relief Actions in International Law and Organization* (n 3) 10.
[15] Yves Beigbeder, *The Role and Status of International Humanitarian Volunteers and Organizations: the Right and Duty to Humanitarian Assistance* (Martinus Nijhoff Publishers 1991) 22.
[16] Macalister-Smith, *International Humanitarian Assistance: Disaster Relief Actions in International Law and Organization* (n 3) 11.
[17] Ibid 12; see also Beigbeder *The Role and Status of International Humanitarian Volunteers and Organizations: the Right and Duty to Humanitarian Assistance* (n 15) 23. On these principles, see Section 2.2.3 The Principles for the Delivery of Assistance.
[18] Macalister-Smith, *International Humanitarian Assistance: Disaster Relief Actions in International Law and Organization* (n 3) 18-19.

do so and the coordination of other organisations providing relief, and as an organisation it was governed by the principles of non-discrimination and respect for state sovereignty.[19] Yet, as the first meeting of the IRU's General Council was held in 1933, ensuing developments leading up to World War II in Europe prevented it from actually providing the relief it was established for.[20] During this same period, the League of Nations involved itself with the numerous refugees following various revolutions and the aftermath of World War I, and installed a High Commissioner for Russian Refugees.[21] In following years, a High Commissioner for Refugees from Germany was established, but both offices were dissolved in 1938 for the establishment of a general 'Office of the High Commissioner for all Refugees' under the protection of the League of Nations.[22] The outbreak of World War II, however, cut short the further work of this Office. In 1943, still in the midst of the war, the United Nations Relief and Rehabilitation Administration (UNRRA) was created for international cooperation and the provision of humanitarian relief.[23] Interestingly, this organisation was thus created prior to the United Nations itself. UNRRA's main tasks consisted of the provision of relief to, rehabilitation and resettlement of specific groups of victims and displaced persons due to World War II.[24] Although UNRRA based many of its principles on its 'predecessor' the CRB, unlike the CRB it was not an NGO but an intergovernmental organisation, receiving funding from states on a voluntary basis.[25] While the organisation only lasted until 1948 when it was dismantled into several separate organisations, it managed to achieve quite massive relief operations throughout war stricken Europe.[26] Yet, as time went on, states became hesitant to continue with such a large-scale cooperative approach to humanitarian assistance.[27] Thus, although UNRRA was closed down as an organisation, its general goals of cooperation and provision of humanitarian relief were incorporated in the United Nations' fundamental purposes and as such continue to exist today.[28] Upon the closing of UNRRA, the International Refugee

[19] Beigbeder, *The Role and Status of International Humanitarian Volunteers and Organizations: the Right and Duty to Humanitarian Assistance* (n 15) 24.
[20] Ibid 24-25; see also *Law and legal issues in international disaster response: a desk study* (International Federation of Red Cross and Red Crescent Societies 2007) 27.
[21] Beigbeder, *The Role and Status of International Humanitarian Volunteers and Organizations: the Right and Duty to Humanitarian Assistance* (n 15) 23.
[22] Paul Weis, 'Human Rights and Refugees', (1971) 1 *Israel Yearbook for Human Rights* 36.
[23] Macalister-Smith, *International Humanitarian Assistance: Disaster Relief Actions in International Law and Organization* (n 3) 12-13.
[24] Article 1 Agreement for United Nations Relief and Rehabilitation Administration, November 9 1943; see also Beigbeder, *The Role and Status of International Humanitarian Volunteers and Organizations: the Right and Duty to Humanitarian Assistance* (n 15) 25.
[25] Beigbeder, *The Role and Status of International Humanitarian Volunteers and Organizations: the Right and Duty to Humanitarian Assistance* (n 15) 25.
[26] Macalister-Smith, *International Humanitarian Assistance: Disaster Relief Actions in International Law and Organization* (n 3) 13 -14.
[27] Ibid 14.
[28] Ibid. See also Article 1(3) UN Charter.

Organization (IRO) similarly existed for a few years, functioning as a specialised agency for the relief of refugees following from World War II.[29]

2.2.1.1 The Role of the UN in the Development of Humanitarian Assistance

Major organisations currently involved in the provision of humanitarian assistance are the ICRC and the International Federation of the Red Cross (IFRC)[30] and the UN, including its specialised organisations. Both have had a parallel but separate development and warrant discussion. The United Nations as a major actor in the provision of humanitarian assistance will be discussed in Section 2.3.2, yet the development to its current status will be briefly addressed at this stage. Upon cessation of UNRRA, the United Nations did not partake in humanitarian assistance for several years. Rather, it focused in the 1950s and 1960s on promoting development aid.[31]

The Cold War and events surrounding decolonisation further enabled this attitude, but one specific and problematic instance invoked the UN's subsequent active participation in humanitarian assistance.[32] In 1967, the eastern state of the Nigerian Federation, Biafra, declared itself independent, which resulted in a civil war within the Nigerian Federation.[33] As the UN viewed the conflict was an internal strife, it remained silent throughout the evolving humanitarian crisis, and efforts for the provision of humanitarian assistance were initiated through various organisations only at a regional level.[34] The UN had continuously struggled with the decision to involve itself situations of armed conflict. Rather, it laid the focus on situations of providing assistance in cases of natural disaster, doing so for the first time in a General Assembly resolution in 1965.[35] Yet in 1971, a few years after the UN's failure to act in the situation in Biafra, the UN General Assembly adopted a resolution establishing the UN Disaster Relief Organisation (UNDRO).[36] In doing so, the General Assembly set aside the UN Secretariat's position that the United Nations system should lay emphasis on 'good offices' rather than becoming actively involved in humanitarian relief operations. Unfortunately, UNDRO was unable to live up to expectations, and with each new crisis or disaster various specialised agencies mushroomed, making the UN's role in humanitarian assistance

---

[29] Emily Haslam, 'United Nations Relief and Rehabilitation Administration', (2006) *Max Planck Encyclopedia of International Law* 1.
[30] See (n 52) regarding the IFRC.
[31] Ed Tsui & Thant Myint-U, 'The Institutional response: creating a framework in response to new challenges' (2004) II *The Humanitarian Decade: challenges for Humanitarian Assistance in the last decade and into the future* (OCHA) 2.
[32] Ibid.
[33] Henning Lahmann, 'Biafra Conflict', (2009) *Max Planck Encyclopedia of Public International Law* § 1.
[34] Ibid § 20-23.
[35] UNGA Res 2034 (XX) 'Assistance in cases of natural disaster' (7 December 1965).
[36] UNGA Res 2816 (XXVI) (14 December 1971). In the same resolution at § 1, the appointment of a Disaster Relief Coordinator for the UN was also envisaged.

during the following two decades scattered and dispersed, rather than coherent.[37] In 1984, UNDRO attempted to address problems regarding the provision of disaster relief in times of natural or man-made disaster, *excluding* ongoing armed conflict, through the development of the Draft Convention on Expediting the Delivery of Emergency Relief (1984 Draft Convention).[38] Although this initiative had not been requested of UNDRO, the Organisation based itself on a 1977 resolution that instigated UN bodies to look more closely into the expedition of disaster relief.[39] Yet, the Draft Convention, having been presented to the UN Economic and Social Council (ECOSOC), never came beyond discussion by the UN's Second Committee, where no further official action was taken.[40] Although the reasons as to why this Draft Convention never came into existence are somewhat unclear, it has been speculated that the efforts may have been premature.[41] Furthermore, various NGOs in the field, as well as the ICRC, were disappointed to not have been involved in the drafting process and expressed their concern for this new Draft Convention.[42] These organisations argued that such a new convention, placing emphasis on the concept of state sovereignty, would not be beneficial to the provision of humanitarian assistance, and that the emphasis should lie on the further implementation of existing resolutions and instruments.[43] The emphasis on sovereignty however was a reflection of the Cold War time period in which the drafting had taken place. By the end of the Cold War era and with the changing times, the UN General Assembly called for an 'International Decade for Natural Disaster Reduction' in response to the vast increase of disasters occurring throughout the world:

> "Decides to designate the 1990's as a decade in which the international community, under the auspices of the United Nations, will pay special attention to fostering international co-operation in the field of natural disaster reduction [...]".[44]

In subsequent years, the General Assembly followed up on this initiative and emphasised its interest in natural disaster reduction.[45] The culmination of these

---

[37] Tsui and Myint-U, 'The Institutional response: creating a framework in response to new challenges' (n 31) 3; see also UNGA Res 36/225 (17 December 1981) UN Doc A/RES/36/225.

[38] UNGA Res 39/367 (18 June 1984) UN Doc. A/39/367/Add.2 and E/1984/96/Add.2 'Draft Convention on Expediting the Delivery of Emergency Relief'.

[39] ECOSOC Resolution 2102 (LXIII) (3 August 1977) UN Doc E/2102 (LXIII) § 2.

[40] IFRC's 'Law and legal issues in international disaster response: a desk study' (n20) 28. The UN's Second Committee is also known as the Economic and Financial Committee, and deals with economic issues at its meetings. For further information on the Second Committee, <www.un.org/en/ga/second/index.shtml> accessed 4 January 4 2012.

[41] IFRC's 'Law and legal issues in international disaster response: a desk study' (n20) 28.

[42] Beigbeder, *The Role and Status of International Humanitarian Volunteers and Organizations: the Right and Duty to Humanitarian Assistance* (n 15) 378.

[43] Ibid.

[44] UNGA Res 42/169 (11 December 1987) UN Doc. A/42/169 § 3.

[45] UNGA Res 43/202 (20 December 1988) UN Doc A/43/202 and also UNGA Res 44/236 (22 December 1989) UN Doc A/44/236 where the General Assembly in § 1 "Proclaims the International Decade for Natural Disaster Reduction, beginning on 1 January 1990".

efforts can be found in the landmark Resolution 46/182 'Strengthening the coordination of humanitarian emergency assistance of the United Nations', in which the General Assembly laid out a framework of 'Guiding Principles' for humanitarian assistance.[46] This resolution and theme followed the combined efforts of providing relief to southern Sudan by UN agencies and NGOs, which started in 1989 and is known as 'Operation Lifeline Sudan'.[47] Following this resolution a first Emergency Relief Coordinator, Jan Eliasson, was appointed and UNDRO was enveloped into the newly instated UN Department for Humanitarian Affairs (UNDHA).[48] Another drastic change occurred in 1998 when UN reform, under the auspices of then Secretary-General Kofi Annan led to the dissolution of DHA into the newly established Office for the Coordination of Humanitarian Affairs (OCHA), which still exists today.[49] The UN furthermore established its 'International Strategy for Disaster Reduction' followed by the well-known Hyogo Framework for Action, both focused on disaster risk reduction and prevention.[50] With these structural changes also came the UN's realisation that coordination between its various agencies was necessary, as well as cooperation with its partners in the field.[51]

2.2.1.2 The Role of the ICRC and IFRC in the Development of Humanitarian Assistance

One of the UN's major counterparts is the abovementioned ICRC, which similar to the UN has also broadened its focus over the last century. Whereas the UN now also embraces the provision of assistance in times of conflict as part of its work, the ICRC strives to encompass more than its original focus on assistance in times of armed conflict, resulting in often overlapping areas of interest of the two organisations. The development of the ICRC and its founding in 1863 has already been touched upon, but the Red Cross and Red Crescent Movement also comprises the IFRC as the umbrella organisation of the national Red Cross Societies,[52] which

[46] UNGA Res 46/182 (19 December 1991) UN Doc. A/RES/46/182, General Assembly Resolution 'Strengthening the coordination of humanitarian emergency assistance of the United Nations', Annex I.
[47] For more detailed information on Operation Lifeline Sudan, see amongst others Larry Minear *Humanitarianism under siege: A Critical Review of Operation Lifeline Sudan* (The Red Sea Press 1991).
[48] Tsui and Myint-U, 'The Institutional response: creating a framework in response to new challenges' (n 31) 10.
[49] Ibid 11. See also <www.unocha.org/about-us/who-we-are/history> accessed 3 January 2012.
[50] UNGA Res 56/195 (21 January 2002) UN Doc A/RES/56/195, 'International Strategy for Disaster Reduction'. Disaster risk reduction as a topic falls outside the scope of this research. Through risk reduction however, the need for the provision of humanitarian aid can often be greatly reduced.
[51] Tsui and Myint-U, 'The Institutional response: creating a framework in response to new challenges' (n 31) 11-13.
[52] The International Federation of the Red Cross, forming a federation of the various Red Cross National Societies, will be discussed more in depth in Sections 2.2.3 The Principles for the Delivery of Assistance and 2.3.2 Providers of Humanitarian Assistance. At this stage it is relevant to briefly mention the distinction between the ICRC and the IFRC, as well as the National Red Cross and Red Crescent Societies through their separate mandates. This distinction of the three prongs can be found in

since 1919, then known as the 'League of Red Cross Societies', has been involved in the provision of assistance and cooperation between the national Red Cross entities.[53] In the aftermath of World War I, the formation of a federation was proposed, to continue the close cooperation amongst the National Red Cross and Red Crescent Societies that had proven fruitful during that war.[54] In the Statute of the Red Cross and Red Crescent Movement, the combined effort between the ICRC, the IFRC and the National Societies can be found:

> "the National Red Cross and Red Crescent Societies, the International Committee of the Red Cross and the International Federation of Red Cross and Red Crescent Societies together constitute a worldwide humanitarian movement, whose mission is to prevent and alleviate human suffering wherever it may be found, to protect life and health and ensure respect for the human being, in particular in times of armed conflict and other emergencies".[55]

Since 2001 the IFRC has developed its interest in legal issues pertaining to disaster relief. Although the original idea of the International Conference of the Red Cross and Red Crescent had been to develop a comprehensive treaty regarding international disaster response law, the organisation was unable to decide on the matter and initiated the 'International Disaster Relief Laws, Rules and Principles

---

the Article 1 of the 2006 Statute of the International Red Cross and Red Crescent Movement: "The International Red Cross and Red Crescent Movement (hereinafter called "the Movement") is composed of the National Red Cross and Red Crescent Societies recognized in accordance with Article 42 (hereinafter called "National Societies"), of the International Committee of the Red Cross (hereinafter called "the International Committee") and of the International Federation of Red Cross and Red Crescent Societies (hereinafter called "the Federation")". With regard to the ICRC, the Statutes of the Movement declare in Article 5: "The International Committee, founded in Geneva in 1863 and formally recognized in the Geneva Conventions and by International Conferences of the Red Cross, is an independent humanitarian organization having a status of its own. It co-opts its members from among Swiss citizens". Article 5(2) and 5(3) of the Statute proceed to formulate the specific tasks and mandate of the ICRC, particularly relevant for this research is the fact that it is the ICRC that is given tasks under international humanitarian law, as mentioned in the Geneva Conventions and their Protocols. With regard to the IFRC, the Statutes proclaim in Article 6: "The International Federation of Red Cross and Red Crescent Societies comprises the National Red Cross and Red Crescent Societies. It acts under its own Constitution with all rights and obligations of a corporate body with a legal personality". Article 6(4) of the Statutes envisage the task of the IFRC to lie mainly within the area of disaster relief, outside the scope of international humanitarian law. For the purpose of this research, the ICRC and IFRC will be addressed independently. Use of the formulation 'Red Cross' will be done in referral to the umbrella organization of the 'Red Cross Movement'.

[53] See <www.ifrc.org/en/who-we-are/history/> accessed 23 February 2012.

[54] Ibid.

[55] Preamble of the Statutes of the International Red Cross and Red Crescent Movement, (adopted by the 25th International Conference of the Red Cross at Geneva in 1986, amended in 1995 and 2006).

Programme' (IDRL programme).[56] Subsequently in 2003, the goal was set forth at the 28th International Conference of the Red Cross and Red Crescent[57] to:

> "Enhance international disaster response through support for the compilation and application of the laws, rules and principles applicable to international disaster response".[58]

Thus, the possibilities of the *law* as part of disaster response were to be explored, including the identification of gaps, for which the IFRC was designated as coordinator.[59] Accordingly, the IFRC developed 'Guidelines for the domestic facilitation and regulation of international disaster relief and initial recovery assistance', which were adopted by the Red Cross and states parties to the Geneva Conventions in 2007.[60] The UN General Assembly quickly supported this development by encouraging their use in the following year.[61] The IDRL Guidelines function as a non-legal initiative, striving to assist governments in practical ways to ensure the enhanced dissemination of humanitarian assistance in the aftermath of a disaster.[62]

2.2.2 Defining Humanitarian Assistance

The above discussion of the historical development of humanitarian assistance serves as a means to a more thorough understanding of what precisely the notion of humanitarian assistance entails today. With a (legal) definition in place, a more in depth discussion of the current status of various actors in the field of humanitarian assistance and their particular work can be provided, as well as an analysis of the existing international legal framework. The legal framework does not exist in a vacuum and the realities on the ground in various circumstances must be taken into consideration. The concept of humanitarian assistance[63] was developed largely by

---

[56] Red Cross/Red Crescent Council of Delegates Resolution 5 'International Disaster Response Law' (14 November 2001). See also Heike Spieker, 'The Right to Give and Receive Humanitarian Assistance', in HJ Heintze & A Zwitter (eds), *Humanitarian Assistance and International Law* (Springer 2011) 23.

[57] For a discussion on the Red Crescent as part of the Red Cross movement see the Statutes of the International Red Cross and Red Crescent Movement.

[58] XXVIIIth International Conference of the Red Cross and Red Crescent, 'Agenda for Humanitarian Action' (6 November 2003) Final Goal 3.2.

[59] Ibid § 3.2.6.

[60] ICRC Resolution 30IC/07/R4 'Guidelines for the domestic facilitation and regulation of international disaster relief and initial recovery assistance', 30th International Conference of the Red Cross and Red Crescent (30 November 2007).

[61] UNGA Res 63/137 (11 December 2008) UN Doc A/RES/63/137 § 6; UNGA Res 63/139 (11 December 2008) UN Doc A/RES/63/139 § 8; UNGA Res 63/141 (11 December 2008) UN Doc. A/RES/63/141 § 5.

[62] See in this regard <www.ifrc.org/what-we-do/disaster-law/about-disaster-law/international-disaster-response-laws-rules-and-principles/idrl-guidelines/> accessed 1 September 2014.

[63] This research will use the term humanitarian assistance, while acknowledging the use of terms such as humanitarian and disaster relief assistance, emergency (international) assistance, aid, relief actions, etc. For the purposes of this research however, one phrase has been chosen.

Dunant as part of the envisaged relief of victims of war, and thus the definition of this concept will firstly be sought in the law of war. Yet over time, the provision of humanitarian assistance has also developed outside the realm of conflict, in situations of natural disaster; therefore a wide range of sources will be addressed and incorporated in the determination of the content of humanitarian assistance. Naturally, assistance is time- and case specific, and not defining it too strictly can be relevant to its adaptation to various different situations.

Within international humanitarian law,[64] the actual *content* of humanitarian assistance is not defined as such. The 'Convention (IV) relative to the Protection of Civilian Persons in Time of War' (Fourth Geneva Convention or GC IV) of 1949 makes reference to 'relief schemes' that should consist:

> "in particular, [of] the provision of consignments of foodstuffs, medical supplies and clothing".[65]

Additional Protocol I to the Geneva Conventions (Additional Protocol I or AP I) adds to this by stating that such relief schemes are to be 'implemented without delay',[66] emphasising the character of urgency that is attached to humanitarian assistance.[67] No further specificities are mentioned, nor is the (non-exhaustive) list of Article 59 of the Fourth Convention further developed. Importantly however in light of the application of Article 59 GC IV, humanitarian assistance can amongst other things be distinguished by its *urgent* character.

Similarly, the ICRC has not provided much insight into what it includes as humanitarian assistance; referring in a resolution to it as 'providing food, shelter, clothing, health care, first aid, psycho-social support, etc'.[68] This non-limitative approach is reflective of the manner in which the ICRC follows humanitarian law, as well as its desire not to restrict its work.

Within the UN system, in relation to the deliverance of humanitarian assistance, the General Assembly referred in 1970 to:

---

[64] The law of war, or *ius in bello*, is often divided into 'The Hague law', relating to the regulation of hostilities or combat and the 'law of Geneva', also known as international humanitarian law. An in depth discussion of the distinction between 'The Hague law' and 'Geneva law' will remain outside the scope of this research. For further reading on these notions see amongst others Frits Kalshoven & Liesbeth Zegveld, *Constraints on the Waging of War: An Introduction to International Humanitarian Law* (Cambridge University Press 2011); Yoram Dinstein, *The conduct of hostilities under the law of international armed conflict* (Cambridge University Press 2010).

[65] Article 59, Convention (IV) relative to the Protection of Civilian Persons in Time of War, Geneva, 12 August 1949.

[66] Article 69 of the Protocol Additional to the Geneva Conventions of 12 August 1949, and relating to the Protection of Victims of International Armed Conflicts (Protocol I), 8 June 1977.

[67] Yves Sandoz, Christophe Swinarski and Bruno Zimmermann (eds), *Commentary on the Additional Protocols of 8 June 1977 to the Geneva Conventions of 12 August 1949* (International Committee of the Red Cross 1987) Protocol I Article 69, 814.

[68] ICRC Resolution 1 'Together for Humanity', 30th International Conference (Geneva, 26-30 November 2007) 75.

"emergency supplies, including medicines, non-perishable food-stuffs, blankets, tents and clothing, and ... other facilities such as logistical equipment and helicopters".[69]

Quite narrowly, this preliminary list thereby solely includes those supplies necessary for the immediate survival of people, as well as the equipment to ensure the arrival of such supplies. ECOSOC elaborated on this definition, stating in 1971 that aid in emergency situations may include not only food supplies and medicines, but also personnel, transportations and communications".[70] The failed UN 1984 Draft Convention on Expediting the Delivery of Emergency Relief proposed emergency assistance to entail relief consignments such as the abovementioned foodstuffs, medical supplies, blankets and shelter materials, but also vehicles, seeds and agricultural equipment, as well as other goods of prime necessity.[71] The Draft Convention however also considered services such as personnel, equipment, means of transport and necessary action to meet the needs as part of emergency assistance.[72] A few years after this Draft Convention, the UN General Assembly stated in its Resolution 'Strengthening the coordination of humanitarian emergency assistance of the United Nations' that particular focus should lie on the supply of food, medicines, shelter and health care.[73] Although the UN Security Council has referred to the concept of humanitarian assistance frequently in resolutions, it has never defined or elaborated upon the concept as such. Hence, a definition provided by this UN organ is absent. According to the criteria formulated by other UN organs therefore, humanitarian assistance at least encompasses the supply of food, medicines or health care, as well as clothing and shelter. Arguably, certain aspects of transportation necessary for the provision of these items, also form part of this definition. In recent years, the ILC has concerned itself with the study of the 'Protection of persons in the event of disaster', and as such performed in-depth research into humanitarian assistance.[74] Although the ILC study discusses many of the definitions of humanitarian or emergency relief and assistance provided by other organisations, it does not itself provide for a definition of the concept of humanitarian assistance.[75] It also remains uncertain whether the efforts of the ILC

[69] UNGA Res 2717 (XXV) (15 December 1970) UN Doc A/2717 §5(c).
[70] ECOSOC Resolution 1612 (LI) (23 July 1971) UN Doc E/1612 (LI) § 57.
[71] UNGA Res 39/367 'Draft Convention on Expediting the Delivery of Emergency Relief' (n 38) Article 1(c).
[72] Ibid Article 1(d).
[73] UNGA Res 46/182 (19 December 1991) UN Doc A/RES/46/182 §6.
[74] The work of the ILC is not in itself binding by nature, both prior and after the adoption of its work by the General Assembly. However, its draft work is frequently cited, amongst others the ICJ relied on the Draft Articles on the Responsibility of States for Internationally Wrongful Acts numerous times prior to their adoption by the General Assembly in 2001. See in this regard Gabčíkovo-Nagymaros Project (Hungary/Slovakia), Merits Judgment 25 September 1997, I.C.J. Reports 1997, p.7, § 47, 50, 52-53, 79 and 83. As a result, it is submitted that the work of the ILC is highly esteemed and authoritative; in particular upon its adoption by the General Assembly and when referenced by international courts.
[75] 'Protection of persons in the event of disasters' (26 February 2008) Memorandum by the Secretariat (ILC), Addendum, UN Doc A/CN.4/590/Add.1.

pertaining to the protection of persons in the event of disasters will in time evolve into a binding document. In a rather broad manner, the ILC puts forward:

> "assistance can be described as the availability and distribution of the goods, materials and services essential to the survival of the population. The elements of the concept of protection depend largely on the context or area of law in which the concept is employed".[76]

Thus, in the current phase of its study, the ILC has unfortunately decided not to formulate a Draft Article on the concept of humanitarian assistance, rather leaving its definition open to interpretation, without explaining its choice to do so.

Yet not only the UN bodies have concerned themselves with finding a clear definition of what constitutes humanitarian assistance; such attempts can also be found in legal scholarship. In 1991, Peter Macalister-Smith[77] formulated the 'International Guidelines for Humanitarian Assistance Operations'[78] at the Max Planck Institute in Heidelberg, defining humanitarian assistance as including urgent material consignments, which in turn aligns with those goods also listed by the UN.[79] The International Institute of Humanitarian Law in San Remo (San Remo Institute) declared in its 1993 'Guiding Principles on the Right to Humanitarian Assistance' (San Remo Principles) that:

> "Humanitarian assistance may consist of any material indispensable to the survival of victims, such as foodstuffs, water, medication, medical supplies and equipment, minimum shelter, clothing; of services such as medical services, tracing services, religious and spiritual assistance, as well as civil defence, in conformity with the tasks defined in international humanitarian law".[80]

Clearly, this definition is broader than the one formulated by the Geneva Conventions and the UN, as it includes religious and spiritual assistance, 'civil defence' and other services that are more extensive than the preceding definitions have provided for. Subsequently in 2003 the Institute of International Law[81]

---

[76] 'Preliminary report on the protection of persons in the event of disasters' (5 May 2008) International Law Commission UN Doc. A/CN.4/598 § 51.

[77] Peter Macalister Smith is affiliated with the Max Planck Institute for Comparative Law and International Law at Heidelberg, Germany.

[78] The Guidelines were formulated at the request of the Federal Republic of Germany and the study was completed in 1988.

[79] P. Macalister-Smith, 'International Guidelines for Humanitarian Assistance Operations', (Max Planck Institute for Comparative Law and International Law, Heidelberg,1991) Article 2 (a) and (d).

[80] 'Guiding Principles on the Right to Humanitarian Assistance' (April 1993) The International Institute of Humanitarian Law in San Remo, Principle 9. These Principles were adopted by the Council of the Institute after the Institute's 17th Round Table on 'Current Problems of International Humanitarian Law to "The Evolution of the Right to Assistance"' in September of 1992. The International Institute of Humanitarian Law is a non-profit organisation established in 1970 with as main purpose the promotion of humanitarian law, human rights and refugee law.

[81] Founded in 1873, the Institute of International Law aims to contribute to the development of international law, as an independent scientific institution. According to the Institute, the adopted

adopted the 'Bruges Resolution' pertaining to humanitarian assistance, in which it declared the following:

> "1. "Humanitarian assistance" means all acts, activities and the human and material resources for the provision of goods and services of an exclusively humanitarian character, indispensable for the survival and the fulfillment of the essential needs of the victims of disasters.
> a) "Goods" includes foodstuffs, drinking water, medical supplies and equipment, means of shelter, clothing, bedding, vehicles, and all other goods indispensable for the survival and the fulfillment of the essential needs of the victims of disasters; this term never includes weapons, ammunition or any other military material.
> b) "Services" means the means of transport, tracing services, medical services, religious, spiritual and psychological assistance, reconstruction, de-mining decontamination, voluntary return of refugees and internally displaced persons, and all other services indispensable for the survival and the fulfillment of the essential needs of the victims of disasters".[82]

From the above, it is apparent that this definition also elaborates on the formulations of the UN and the San Remo Principles, including not only the basic elements of food, medicine, shelter and logistics, but also such aspects as religious and psychological assistance and the return of displaced persons and refugees. Whilst indeed religious and cultural particularities may be considered, it remains relevant to be aware of the extreme urgency in which humanitarian aid provision operates. In such circumstances of armed conflict or of (natural) disasters, the factual provision of assistance in itself is challenging and recourse must be had to the most urgently needed supplies such as water and food. Interestingly, the 'Bruges' definition explicitly excludes weapons, ammunition or any other form of military material.

Similarly the International Court of Justice determined in the 1986 *Military and Paramilitary Activities in and against Nicaragua Case*, in referral to United States' legislation defining humanitarian assistance as including the provision of food, clothes, medicine and 'other assistance', that humanitarian assistance distinctly *excludes* weapons, ammunition or other material which can be used to inflict bodily harm.[83] The Court argued that in order to be considered humanitarian assistance rather than a breach of the principle of non-intervention, the assistance must be strictly limited to such humanitarian purposes.[84] Indeed, in a more recent example, the carrying of weapons was also put forward by Israel as an argument that the 2010 'Flotilla' towards Gaza was in fact not providing humanitarian assistance, but

---

Resolutions seek to highlight current international law and may sometimes be determinations *de lege ferenda*, so as to contribute to the development of the law and give assistance to progressive codification of international law: <www.idi-iil.org/idiE/navig_history.html> accessed 29 June 2011.

[82] Resolution 'Humanitarian Assistance' (2 September 2003) Institute of International Law, Sixteenth Commission, Bruges Session § 1.

[83] Military and Paramilitary Activities in and against Nicaragua (Nicaragua v. United States of America), Merits, Judgment 27 June 1986 I.C.J. Reports 1986, p. 14 § 242-243.

[84] Ibid § 243.

rather also supplying materials for other purposes.[85] Such an argument may also be applied to the intentions of those providing the assistance, as will be seen in the subsequent Section 2.2.3.

Ascertaining the particularities of humanitarian assistance is relevant to establishing a definition of humanitarian assistance. From the above, it is clear that a single legal definition of the notion of humanitarian assistance is lacking. Although various institutions and resolutions, provided as soft law or secondary sources of international law, hold a rather broad definition of humanitarian assistance, the abovementioned views portray that common ground can at least be found in a more *narrow* definition of humanitarian assistance. Such a more narrow definition also takes into consideration the attempts at definitions made through the UN, ICRC and case law. The definition of humanitarian assistance that is put forward by the author is that it is:

> *Assistance consisting of food, medicine, shelter and logistics for its provision; for urgent purposes and which is indispensable to the survival of the people at whom it is aimed.*

According to the definition suggested here, the provision of humanitarian assistance is restricted to urgent purposes and the qualification that it is to be indispensable to the survival of people during and in the aftermath of a humanitarian crisis, suggests particular boundaries to the timeframe in which humanitarian assistance may be delivered. Arguably, as assistance could and should be provided as long as it is indispensable to the survival of victims of emergencies, such assistance should take place not only in the immediate aftermath of an emergency situation, but rather as long as it may remain necessary.[86] Evidently a crisis-like situation can last for a prolonged period of time and those persons finding themselves in such circumstances may not differentiate between searching for food and searching for a school for children. From a legal perspective however, a clear distinction must be made between humanitarian assistance as defined here and development assistance, although a possible transition from the former to the latter does often occur.[87]

[85] See amongst others: <www.mfa.gov.il/MFA/Government/Communiques/2010/Israel_Navy_warns_flotilla_31-May-2010.htm> accessed 3 December 2012 and <www.jpost.com/Israel/Article.aspx?id=177342> accessed 3 December 2012.

[86] Budislav Vukas, 'Humanitarian Assistance in Cases of Emergency', (2007) *Max Planck Encyclopedia of Public International Law* § 7.

[87] Development assistance is (financial) assistance provided by international organisations or states to aid the development of other states, either economically, socially or politically. It can be distinguished from humanitarian assistance through its long-term perspectives. Development aid is furthermore not necessarily neutral or impartial, as it can be subject to conditions. For the purpose of this research, development assistance will however not be discussed, as it is not part of the scope of the research. See for the distinction between the two concepts amongst others Spieker 'The Right to Give and Receive Humanitarian Assistance' (n 56) 7. With regard to the UN's stance in general, see UNGA Res 46/182 'Strengthening the coordination of humanitarian emergency assistance of the United Nations' Guiding Principle 9: "There is a clear relationship between emergency, rehabilitation and development. In order to ensure a smooth transition from emergency to rehabilitation and development, emergency assistance

Whilst in factual circumstances both notions are often intertwined and recipients may not acknowledge the differentiation between both types of aid, such conceptual boundaries remain relevant to the research into the legal framework on the provision of humanitarian assistance, addressing the relevant rights and duties within this particular framework.

Furthermore, the provision of humanitarian assistance must not be seen as a substitute for otherwise engaging in international efforts that may advance peace or stability in a country or region.[88] Indeed, humanitarian assistance is often provided in conflict areas, where civilians are in dire need of protection from violence. The provision of food, water, medicine and shelter aimed at the survival of persons in these circumstances must therefore be distinctly acknowledged in this light. The provision of assistance is aimed at the survival of persons in circumstances of emergency and crisis, through the provision of supplies that are key to that survival. While various institutions and their resolutions apply a broad definition of humanitarian assistance, the abovementioned perspectives show that common ground can be found in the aforesaid more narrow definition of humanitarian assistance. Importantly, humanitarian assistance can amongst other things be distinguished by its *urgent* character and *indispensible* nature.[89]

2.2.3 The Principles for the Delivery of Assistance

Ascertaining the particularities of humanitarian assistance, generically consisting of food, shelter, basic health care, and personnel and equipment to provide such items, is one part of defining humanitarian assistance. Yet, whether or not an act is humanitarian assistance is not only determined by *what* is provided, but also relates to the *manner* in which such assistance is provided: only when its delivery abides by certain principles of delivery can aid be considered 'humanitarian assistance'.[90]

---

should be provided in ways that will be supportive of recovery and long-term development. Thus, emergency measures should be seen as a step towards long-term development". For an alternative perspective, see the UN Educational, Scientific and Cultural Organization (UNESCO)'s stance with regard to humanitarian assistance in relation to development assistance in 'Contributing to Conflict Prevention and Post-Conflict Peace-Building', Medium-Term Strategy for 1996-2001 (1995) adopted by the General Conference at its 28th session § 190: <www.unesco.org/webworld/fed/temp/communication_democracy/conflict_resolution.htm> accessed 2 November 2011. For further information on development assistance, see also the United Nations Development Programme (UNDP) at <www.beta.undp.org/content/undp/en/home/ourwork/overview.html> accessed 4 January 2012 and the Organisation for Economic Co-operation and development at: <www.oecd.org/pages/0,3417,en_36734052_36734103_1_1_1_1_1,00.html> accessed 4 January 2012.

[88] UNCHR 'Report of the Representative of the Secretary-General, Mr. Francis M. Deng, submitted pursuant to Commission on Human Rights resolution 1995/57: Internally displaced persons' (22 February 1996) UN Doc E/CN.4/1996/52 § 78.

[89] Rohan J Hardcastle & Adrian T L Chua, 'Humanitarian Assistance, Towards a Right of access to victims of natural disaster', (1998) 38 *International Review of the Red Cross* 325, 590.

[90] For the various actors involved in the provision of humanitarian assistance, see Section 2.3.2 Providers of Humanitarian Assistance. The role of the affected state in particular will be dealt with in greater detail in that Section.

Looking to international humanitarian law first, the Geneva Conventions and Additional Protocols of 1977 refer to the deliverance of relief schemes by an impartial humanitarian organisation, or to relief actions that are of an 'exclusively humanitarian and impartial nature'.[91] Such an organisation envisaged by the Conventions may be the ICRC, or any other organisation that acts according to the principles of the ICRC.[92] In order to establish more in depth what humanitarian assistance encompasses, it is relevant to look into these notions of 'humanity' and 'impartiality', as well as specific principles of the ICRC referred to, for the organisation's own characterisation of the delivery of humanitarian assistance. The Statutes of the International Red Cross and Red Crescent Movement declare the Movement *itself* to be guided by its 'Fundamental Principles':

> "1) *Humanity:* The International Red Cross and Red Crescent Movement, born of a desire to bring assistance without discrimination to the wounded on the battlefield, endeavours, in its international and national capacity, to prevent and alleviate human suffering wherever it may be found. Its purpose is to protect life and health and to ensure respect for the human being. It promotes mutual understanding, friendship, cooperation and lasting peace amongst all peoples.
> *2) Impartiality*: It makes no discrimination as to nationality, race, religious beliefs, class or political opinions. It endeavours to relieve the suffering of individuals, being guided solely by their needs, and to give priority to the most urgent cases of distress.
> *3) Neutrality*: In order to continue to enjoy the confidence of all, the Movement may not take sides in hostilities or engage at any time in controversies of a political, racial, religious or ideological nature.
> *4) Independence:* The Movement is independent. The National Societies, while auxiliaries in the humanitarian services of their governments and subject to the laws of their respective countries, must always maintain their autonomy so that they may be able at all times to act in accordance with the principles of the Movement.
> *5) Voluntary Service:* It is a voluntary relief movement not prompted in any manner by desire for gain.
> *6) Unity:* There can be only one Red Cross or one Red Crescent Society in any one country. It must be open to all. It must carry on its humanitarian work throughout its territory.

---

[91] Common Article 3, Articles 10, 59 and 61 Convention (IV) relative to the Protection of Civilian Persons in Time of War; Article 70 Protocol Additional to the Geneva Conventions of 12 August 1949, and relating to the Protection of Victims of International Armed Conflicts (Protocol I), 8 June 1977; Article 18(2) Protocol Additional to the Geneva Conventions of 12 August 1949, and relating to the Protection of Victims of Non-International Armed Conflicts (Protocol II), 8 June 1977.

[92] Article 63 GC IV states: "Subject to temporary and exceptional measures imposed for urgent reasons of security by the Occupying Power: (a) recognized National Red Cross (Red Crescent, Red Lion and Sun) Societies shall be able to pursue their activities in accordance with Red Cross principles, as defined by the International Red Cross Conferences. Other relief societies shall be permitted to continue their humanitarian activities under similar conditions; (b) the Occupying Power may not require any changes in the personnel or structure of these societies, which would prejudice the aforesaid activities. The same principles shall apply to the activities and personnel of special organizations of a non-military character, which already exist or which may be established, for the purpose of ensuring the living conditions of the civilian population by the maintenance of the essential public utility services, by the distribution of relief and by the organization of rescues".

> *7) Universality:* The International Red Cross and Red Crescent Movement, in which all Societies have equal status and share equal responsibilities and duties in helping each other, is worldwide".[93]

Thus, for assistance to be considered 'humanitarian' according to the Geneva Conventions and thereby also customary international humanitarian law,[94] it must fulfill the criteria of humanity and impartiality, whereas the ICRC furthermore refers to the aspect of neutrality.[95] The latter two criteria of 'unity' and 'universality' refer to the Red Cross itself, and therefore fall outside the scope of the principles to be discussed.

2.2.3.1 The Principle of Humanity

Separate to the provision of humanitarian assistance, the principle of humanity has existed in international law for a long period of time. Humanity as a concept can be defined in various ways, but a common denominator can be found in 'the state of being human' or 'humane', as well as treating others with 'benevolence' or kindness.[96] As codified in the well-known 'Martens-clause' in 1899, the minimum requirements for belligerent parties would be those rules of international law as resulting from the practice between states, as well as 'from the laws of humanity, and the requirements of the public conscience'.[97] Today, its equivalent can be found in Article 1(2) of AP I declaring:

> "in cases not covered by this Protocol or by other international agreements, civilians and combatants remain under the protection and authority of the principles of international law derived from established custom, from the principles of humanity and from the dictates of public conscience".

---

[93] Statutes of the International Red Cross and Red Crescent Movement, (adopted by the 25th International Conference of the Red Cross at Geneva in 1986, amended in 1995 and 2006), Preamble. The Fundamental Principles of the Movement were proclaimed in Vienna in 1965. See also Article 2(a) of the Statute which states: "The role of the International Committee, in accordance with its Statutes, is in particular: a) to maintain and disseminate the Fundamental Principles of the Movement, namely humanity, impartiality, neutrality, independence, voluntary service, unity and universality".

[94] To date, 194 states are party to the four Geneva Conventions of 1949, also granting their content the status of customary international humanitarian law. The 1977 Additional Protocols do not have this customary law status, as not all states are party to these treaties. With regard to the customary status of the 1949 Geneva Conventions, see amongst others Theodor Meron, 'The Geneva Conventions as Customary Law' (1987) 81 *American Journal of International Law* 2. For further information on ratification of the Geneva Conventions, see <www.icrc.org/IHL.nsf/(SPF)/party_main_treaties/$File/IHL_and_other_related_Treaties.pdf> accessed 7 November 2011.

[95] Sections 2.2.3.4 An Alternative: The UN Principles Regarding Humanitarian Assistance and 2.2.3.5. Other Perspectives on the Principles for Providing Humanitarian Assistance explore the adoption of the ICRC Principles by other organisations, such as the UN and EU, as well as several resolutions pertaining to humanitarian assistance.

[96] See in this regard the definitions provided by the Oxford Dictionaries and Merriam-Webster.

[97] Hague Convention II with Respect to the Laws and Customs of War on Land of 1899.

The principle of humanity thereby serves as an underlying notion by which parties to a conflict must always abide, to ensure the protection of civilians. As such it also stands in close relation to the principle of distinction. Although codified within the context of international humanitarian law, the principle and concept of humanity can be found throughout history in major world faiths, and has origins also in natural law, with the notion of 'human dignity'. According to Meron, and supported by the above definition of 'humanity', the principle of humanity is equal to the notion of 'elementary considerations of humanity'.[98] These have been recognised by the ICJ as obligations resting upon states both in times of war and in times of peace.[99] The ICJ has furthermore recognised such obligations, amongst which the Martens-clause and thereby also the principle of humanity, as 'fundamental to the respect of the human person' and 'intransgressible principles of international customary law'.[100] In doing so, the Court also relates these principles to the obligation under humanitarian law to prohibit causing unnecessary suffering (to combatants).[101] Indeed, the provision of humanitarian assistance aims to accomplish precisely that goal in relation to the *civilian* population also.

According to the ICRC, the principle of humanity is its supreme principle and the driving force behind its work.[102] Aside from the Geneva Conventions, and the ICRC, the ICJ has also referred to the principles of humanity (and impartiality), declaring in the *Nicaragua* case that in order for the provision of aid to be considered humanitarian, it must be given without any form of discrimination to all those in need of aid and not merely to one party to a conflict.[103] Additionally, the assistance must be limited to those purposes echoed by the practice of the ICRC, namely the alleviation of human suffering and the protection of life, health and the human being:

> "An essential feature of truly humanitarian aid is that it is given "without discrimination" of any kind. In the view of the Court, if the provision of "humanitarian assistance" is to escape condemnation as an intervention in the internal affairs of Nicaragua, not only

[98] Theodor Meron, 'The Martens Clause, Principles of Humanity, and Dictates of the Public Conscience' (2000) 94 *American Journal of International Law* 1, 82.

[99] Corfu Channel Case (UK v Albania) (Merits) 9 April 1949 I.C.J. Reports 4, §67: "The obligations incumbent upon the Albanian authorities consisted in notifying, for the benefit of shipping in general, the existence of a minefield in Albanian territorial waters and in warning the approaching British warships of the imminent danger to which the minefield exposed them. Such obligations are based, not on the Hague Convention of 1907, No. VIII, which is applicable in time of war, but on certain general and well-recognized principles, namely: elementary considerations of humanity, even more exacting in peace than in war; the principle of the freedom of maritime communication; and every State's obligation not to allow knowingly its territory to be used for acts contrary to the rights of other States".

[100] Legality of the Threat or Use of Nuclear Weapons, Advisory Opinion, I.C.J. Reports 1996, p. 226, § 78-79.

[101] Ibid.

[102] 'The International Committee of the Red Cross (ICRC): Its mission and work', Adopted by the Assembly of the ICRC on 19 June 2008, (2009) 91 *International Review of the Red Cross* 874, 404.

[103] ICJ Military and Paramilitary Activities in and against (n 83) § 243. For support in legal scholarship, see also Vincent Chetail, 'The contribution of the International Court of Justice to international humanitarian law', (2003) 85 *International Review of the Red Cross* 850, 265.

> must it be limited to the purposes hallowed in the practice of the Red Cross, namely "to prevent and alleviate human suffering" and "to protect life and health and to ensure respect for the human being"; it must also, and above all be given without discrimination to all in need in Nicaragua, not merely to the *contras* and their dependents.[104]

This stance of the Court also aligns with the above formulated definition of humanitarian assistance which focuses on emergency aid. In this ruling, the ICJ declares these principles applicable to all providers of humanitarian assistance (such as the United Nations), not merely the ICRC itself.[105] This latter take on the principles by the Court echoes Article 63 of the Fourth Geneva Convention that in the same way declared (other) providers of aid to be able to operate under similar conditions as the ICRC.[106] Yet the ICJ's stance that assistance must be given to *all* parties to a conflict is challenged by some. Firstly, it must be noted that the *Nicaragua* case did not concern an international armed conflict,[107] and as such there is no proscription to be found in the Geneva Conventions regarding the provision of assistance to only one side of a conflict by organisations providing humanitarian assistance. Conversely, in an international armed conflict, international organisations providing assistance are permitted to provide relief to civilians in need that are under the control of only one party to the conflict.[108] Frits Kalshoven argued that states often provide assistance to only one side of a conflict, especially in liberation wars, which is still considered by the larger community to be humanitarian in nature.[109] Furthermore, international organisations providing assistance also usually operate in the territory of just one side of the conflict, rather than being able to operate on both or multiple sides.[110] Particularly significant is the fact that the assistance may not *contribute* to one side of a conflict, but pursues the goal of alleviation of human suffering.[111] As long as the *purpose* of the aid is not to support any party to a conflict rather than to alleviate the suffering of a civilian population in need, it can be considered humanitarian.[112] Given the abovementioned definition of humanity, as well as the ICRC's declaration that the

---

[104] Ibid § 243.

[105] Chetail, 'The contribution of the International Court of Justice to international humanitarian law' (n103).

[106] See (n92) for the text of Article 63 GC IV.

[107] For the definition of an international armed conflict, see Section 3.2.1 Defining an Armed Conflict.

[108] Ruth Abril Stoffels, 'Legal Regulation of Humanitarian Assistance in Armed Conflict: Achievements and Gaps', (2004) 86 *International Review of the Red Cross* 855, 541. See for example Article 25 GC II; Article 27 GC IV; and Article 8 of Additional Protocol I.

[109] Frits Kalshoven, 'Impartialité et neutralité dans le droit et la pratique humanitaires', (1989) 71 *International Review of the Red Cross* 780, 543-544.

[110] Kate Mackintosh, 'The Principles of Humanitarian Action in International Humanitarian Law: Study 4 in: The Politics of Principle: the principles of humanitarian action in practice', *Humanitarian Policy Group* Report 5 (March 2000) 7.

[111] Joakim Dungel, 'A Right to Humanitarian Assistance in Internal Armed Conflicts Respecting Sovereignty, Neutrality and Legitimacy: Practical Proposals to Practical Problems', (2004) *Journal of Humanitarian Assistance* § 2.2 <http://sites.tufts.edu/jha/archives/838> accessed 24 November 2014.

[112] Abril Stoffels, 'Legal Regulation of Humanitarian Assistance in Armed Conflict: Achievements and Gaps' (n108) 540.

principle of humanity entails but three main aspects, namely respect for the human being, the prevention and alleviation of human suffering, and the protection of life and health as well as legal debate, providing assistance to both sides of the conflict in order to be deemed humanitarian, as argued by the ICJ, does not appear to be a general consensus under international law.[113]

2.2.3.2 The Principle of Impartiality

Impartiality, the second criterion mentioned not only in the Geneva Conventions but also by the Fundamental Principles of the Red Cross for its own purposes, essentially considers that assistance must be given in a non-discriminatory manner, with a focus on those who most urgently need to be aided.[114] As seen above, the ICJ has echoed this principle in its judgement in the *Nicaragua* case.[115] In his 1979 *Commentary to the Fundamental Principles of the Red Cross*, Jean Pictet divides this principle into three separate elements, namely non-discrimination, proportionality and impartiality itself as distinguished principle.[116] Firstly, regarding non-discrimination, Pictet argues it is the primordial of the Red Cross Principles, and closely related to the principle of humanity.[117] As seen above, the ICJ has echoed the importance of these two concepts within the provision of humanitarian assistance in the *Nicaragua*-case.[118] The Geneva Conventions themselves in Common Article 3 prohibit 'any adverse distinction founded on race, colour, religion or faith, sex, birth or wealth, or any other similar criteria'.[119]

---

[113] Statutes of the International Red Cross and Red Crescent Movement, (adopted by the 25th International Conference of the Red Cross at Geneva in 1986, amended in 1995 and 2006). See also Jean Pictet, '1979 Commentary to the Fundamental Principles of the Red Cross' (Principle of Humanity Commentary (a) (b) and (c)) <www.icrc.org/eng/resources/documents/misc/fundamental-principles-commentary-010179.htm> accessed 24 November 2014.

[114] Statutes of the International Red Cross and Red Crescent Movement, (adopted by the 25th International Conference of the Red Cross at Geneva in 1986, amended in 1995 and 2006) and ibid Pictet, '1979 Commentary to the Fundamental Principles of the Red Cross' (Principle of Impartiality).

[115] ICJ Military and Paramilitary Activities in and against (n 83) §242.

[116] Pictet, '1979 Commentary to the Fundamental Principles of the Red Cross' (n 113) (Principle of Impartiality, I. Non-Discrimination).

[117] Ibid.

[118] ICJ Military and Paramilitary Activities in and against (n 83) § 243.

[119] The full text of Article 3 common to the four Geneva Conventions of 1949 states: "In the case of armed conflict not of an international character occurring in the territory of one of the High Contracting Parties, each Party to the conflict shall be bound to apply, as a minimum, the following provisions: (1) Persons taking no active part in the hostilities, including members of armed forces who have laid down their arms and those placed hors de combat by sickness, wounds, detention, or any other cause, shall in all circumstances be treated humanely, without any adverse distinction founded on race, colour, religion or faith, sex, birth or wealth, or any other similar criteria. To this end the following acts are and shall remain prohibited at any time and in any place whatsoever with respect to the above-mentioned persons: (a) violence to life and person, in particular murder of all kinds, mutilation, cruel treatment and torture; (b) taking of hostages; (c) outrages upon personal dignity, in particular humiliating and degrading treatment; (d) the passing of sentences and the carrying out of executions without previous judgment pronounced by a regularly constituted court, affording all the judicial guarantees which are recognized as indispensable by civilized peoples. (2) The wounded and sick shall be collected and

Clearly, this list is non-limitative in its nature. Yet, considering the fact that assistance is to be provided based on the urgency of the need, non-discrimination does not mean that certain considerations such as age or sex may not be relevant to the determination of whom is to receive the most immediate relief of suffering.[120] As such, Common Article 3 of the Geneva Convention mentioned that no *adverse* distinction was to be allowed. The ICRC itself declares:

> "Impartiality, a principle that rejects any form of discrimination, calls for equal treatment for people in distress, according to their needs. It enables the ICRC to prioritize its activities on the basis of the degree of urgency and the types of needs of those affected".[121]

Evidently, the Red Cross envisages the possibility to distinguish based on need, whilst simultaneously adhering to the principle of non-discrimination. This reasoning also falls in line with Pictet's second element within the principle of impartiality: the notion of proportionality, which entails that the relief is to be accorded in proportion to the degree of suffering and the degree of urgency.[122] Thirdly, Pictet discerns the element of impartiality as a separate notion within the larger scope of the principle.[123] He argues that, once non-discrimination has been accepted as a norm, impartiality becomes secondary, due to the fact that it relates to the 'lesser' action without prejudice, namely not to be partial in one's individual (organisation's) actions.[124] Whereas non-discrimination and proportionality apply to the deliverance of humanitarian assistance, the distinct element of impartiality as noted by Pictet concerns the decision-making process of an organisation such as the ICRC in its entirety.[125] Particularly in situations of non-international conflicts, the notion of partiality can be an issue, as those providing aid, such as National Red Cross Societies, are often very familiar with all parties to the conflict.[126] This also adheres to the above discussion on whether or not aid may be provided to the

---

cared for. An impartial humanitarian body, such as the International Committee of the Red Cross, may offer its services to the Parties to the conflict. The Parties to the conflict should further endeavour to bring into force, by means of special agreements, all or part of the other provisions of the present Convention. The application of the preceding provisions shall not affect the legal status of the Parties to the conflict".

[120] Dungel 'A Right to Humanitarian Assistance in Internal Armed Conflicts Respecting Sovereignty, Neutrality and Legitimacy: Practical Proposals to Practical Problems' (n 111) § 2.2.

[121] 'The International Committee of the Red Cross (ICRC): Its mission and work', Adopted by the Assembly of the ICRC (n 102).

[122] Pictet, '1979 Commentary to the Fundamental Principles of the Red Cross' (n 113) (Principle of Impartiality, II. Proportionality).

[123] Pictet is not alone in distinguishing separate elements in the larger principle of impartiality, see also Abril Stoffels, 'Legal Regulation of Humanitarian Assistance in Armed Conflict: Achievements and Gaps' (n108) 540-541.

[124] Pictet, '1979 Commentary to the Fundamental Principles of the Red Cross' (n 113) (Principle of Impartiality, III Impartiality).

[125] Denise Plattner, 'ICRC neutrality and neutrality in humanitarian assistance', (1996) 36 *International Review of the Red Cross* 311, 171.

[126] Ibid.

civilian population of only *one* party to a conflict as addressed by the ICJ. Furthermore, there is also a different concept of impartiality to consider, where cooperation amongst relief providers may be in order, to ensure that distribution of aid is truly only determined based on need, and that impartiality can be discerned through the equal results of the assistance.[127] However, at this point in time, there is no legal requirement within international humanitarian law for this last concept of impartiality, as it would also impose obligations of cooperation on various relief providers.[128]

2.2.3.3 The Principle of Neutrality

Lastly, the principle of neutrality needs to be addressed. Often confused with, and closely related to, impartiality, this principle relates to the ICRC's position that to be able to provide relief, the organisation needs to enjoy the trust of all sides to a particular conflict and to that extent may itself not take sides in any kind of armed conflict.[129] Importantly, both neutrality and non-participation of non-belligerent states with regard to a conflict are not intended by this principle of neutrality.[130] Neutrality as a principle in humanitarian assistance is furthermore absent from the Geneva Conventions, perhaps also due to this military connotation with regard to the abovementioned non-belligerent states.[131] Yet as a legal concept it does appear in various provisions related to the field of humanitarian assistance,[132] and has been widely described in guidelines relating to the manner in which humanitarian organisations or other actors provide relief. It can be considered an autonomous concept, independent of the entity that is actually providing the assistance: the body providing the assistance may not be neutral, but the assistance itself may still meet the requirements of the principle of neutrality of assistance.[133] Thus, third states and

[127] Dungel, 'A Right to Humanitarian Assistance in Internal Armed Conflicts Respecting Sovereignty, Neutrality and Legitimacy: Practical Proposals to Practical Problems' (n 111) § 2.2; and Abril Stoffels, 'Legal Regulation of Humanitarian Assistance in Armed Conflict: Achievements and Gaps' (n108) 540.

[128] Abril Stoffels, 'Legal Regulation of Humanitarian Assistance in Armed Conflict: Achievements and Gaps' (n108) 541.

[129] Statutes of the International Red Cross and Red Crescent Movement, (adopted by the 25th International Conference of the Red Cross at Geneva in 1986, amended in 1995 and 2006) and 'The International Committee of the Red Cross (ICRC): Its mission and work', Adopted by the Assembly of the ICRC (n 102).

[130] Pictet, '1979 Commentary to the Fundamental Principles of the Red Cross' (n 113) (Principle of Neutrality, (b) military neutrality). For a more in depth discussion of the distinction between neutrality and non-participation in conflicts when applicable to states, as opposed to the neutrality of a relief organisation such as the ICRC, see Plattner, 'ICRC neutrality and neutrality in humanitarian assistance' (n 125) 164-165.

[131] Mackintosh, 'The Principles of Humanitarian Action in International Humanitarian Law' (n 110) 8.

[132] See Chapters 6 and 7. Also, see Plattner, 'ICRC neutrality and neutrality in humanitarian assistance' (n 125) 175.

[133] Plattner, 'ICRC neutrality and neutrality in humanitarian assistance' (n 125) 178. An example provided by Plattner includes the possibility of a non-neutral state providing humanitarian assistance that in itself is neutral.

various international organisations *can* certainly meet these requirements. However, referring back to Article 63 of the Fourth Geneva Convention, any entity wishing to provide humanitarian assistance in accordance with international humanitarian law, must act according to principles similar to those of the ICRC, which has incorporated the notion of neutrality.[134] In their actions, humanitarian organisations or other actors such as third states must convey their neutrality to all sides of a conflict through refraining from any action that may be harmful or helpful to the parties in conflict, and in return, so should the neutrality of these organisations be respected by the parties.[135] Thus, the principle of neutrality obliges duties of abstention.[136] Neutrality as a principle of humanitarian assistance is not merely military, but also political, racial, religious and ideological.[137] Pictet refers to this aspect of neutrality as 'ideological neutrality' but notes that although it is distinct from military neutrality, in today's world politicisation is a grave concern for the Red Cross, considering the change in warfare since the World War II.[138] Publicly voicing an opinion on a certain conflict or supporting one of the parties could be, and has in the past sometimes been, considered a violation of this principle; note in this regard the discussion on the delivery of aid by Russia to the Ukraine in the summer of 2014.[139] Yet there is no legal obligation to abstain from drawing attention to large-scale violations of human rights or humanitarian law, regardless of whether or not this may form part of an organisation's own code of conduct.[140] In relation to this, the Red Cross' perspective on neutrality has thus always been a *means* to provide humanitarian assistance rather than an *end* in and of itself.[141] For an organisation providing humanitarian assistance, like the ICRC, there must be a choice between striving for justice or politics and striving for the provision of assistance to all those in need. To uphold the principle of neutrality, often only the

---

[134] See Article 63 Fourth Geneva Convention (n 92).

[135] Pictet, '1979 Commentary to the Fundamental Principles of the Red Cross' (n 113) (Principle of Neutrality, (b) military neutrality). An example given by Pictet is the neutrality of a hospital: parties to a conflict must never attack such a location and relief providers must for their part not allow the existence of for instance a military observation post on its roof. See also Abril Stoffels, 'Legal Regulation of Humanitarian Assistance in Armed Conflict: Achievements and Gaps' (n108) 543. Abril Stoffels notes examples such as the transportation of weapons, attacking combatants and spreading propaganda.

[136] Plattner, 'ICRC neutrality and neutrality in humanitarian assistance' (n 125) 170.

[137] Statutes of the International Red Cross and Red Crescent Movement, (adopted by the 25th International Conference of the Red Cross at Geneva in 1986, amended in 1995 and 2006) and 'The International Committee of the Red Cross (ICRC): Its mission and work', Adopted by the Assembly of the ICRC (n 102).

[138] Pictet, '1979 Commentary to the Fundamental Principles of the Red Cross' (n 113) (Principle of Neutrality, (c) ideological neutrality).

[139] <http://uk.reuters.com/article/2014/08/12/uk-ukraine-crisis-russia-aid-idUKKBN0GC08O20140812> accessed 9 September 2014; Abril Stoffels, 'Legal Regulation of Humanitarian Assistance in Armed Conflict: Achievements and Gaps' (n108) 543; and Plattner, 'ICRC neutrality and neutrality in humanitarian assistance' (n 125) 171.

[140] Abril Stoffels, 'Legal Regulation of Humanitarian Assistance in Armed Conflict: Achievements and Gaps' (n108) 543 and Plattner, 'ICRC neutrality and neutrality in humanitarian assistance' (n 125) 171.

[141] Plattner, 'ICRC neutrality and neutrality in humanitarian assistance' (n 125) 172.

latter can be chosen.[142] Denise Plattner[143] observes that neutrality as a principle of humanitarian assistance may function as an umbrella under which the principle of impartiality, together with non-discrimination, may also fall.[144] Problematic for the principle of neutrality and in connection to Pictet's views, is that it runs the risk of being compromised in the event where humanitarian assistance is to be delivered in a territory contrary to the will of the party that controls this territory. This particular issue will be dealt with extensively at a later stage, as issues relating to state sovereignty are a continuous thread in the discussion of the legal framework on the provision of humanitarian assistance.[145]

Remaining within the scope of international humanitarian law, the San Remo Institute has also adopted the abovementioned three principles in its 1993 'Guiding Principles on the Right to Humanitarian Assistance', stressing:

> "that humanitarian assistance, both as regards those granting and those receiving it, should always be provided in conformity with the principles inherent in all humanitarian activities, namely the principles of humanity, neutrality and impartiality, so that political considerations should not prevail over these principles".[146]

The Institute furthermore declares that neutrality and impartiality *vis-à-vis* parties to a conflict must always be upheld in the provision of assistance during an armed conflict.[147] Legal scholarship thereby – through such soft law documents – supports this view of the principle of impartiality.

2.2.3.4 An Alternative: The UN Principles Regarding Humanitarian Assistance

The above Sections have addressed the development of the principles for the provision of assistance in times of conflict. The abovementioned principles have also been widely incorporated in humanitarian assistance outside the scope of armed conflict, for example in relation to the regulation of the provision of humanitarian assistance in the aftermath of natural or other disasters, in particular through the work of the UN warranting some further discussion. Both the principle of humanity and impartiality have been extensively referred to, as well as interestingly the principle of neutrality, which clearly finds its origins in conflict.[148] A first mention of such principles within the context of the UN can be found in

---

[142] Pictet, '1979 Commentary to the Fundamental Principles of the Red Cross' (n 113) (Principle of Neutrality, 'other aspects of neutrality'). See also Plattner, 'ICRC neutrality and neutrality in humanitarian assistance' (n 125) 162.

[143] Denise Plattner worked as a longtime legal advisor to the ICRC and in that capacity was also part of several missions for that organisation.

[144] Plattner, 'ICRC neutrality and neutrality in humanitarian assistance' (n 125) 177-178.

[145] For an in depth discussion of the problems relating to the delivery of assistance when a sovereign or other party in control of a territory is reluctant or unwilling to allow entry and access of humanitarian assistance, see Chapters 7 and 8.

[146] 'Guiding Principles on the Right to Humanitarian Assistance' (n 80) preambular § 5.

[147] Ibid Foreword § 3.

[148] Plattner, 'ICRC neutrality and neutrality in humanitarian assistance' (n 125) 175.

some 1970 UN General Assembly Resolutions that declare to be 'mindful' of principles adopted by the Red Cross with regard to humanitarian relief the prior year as well as referring to their applicability.[149] The principles referred to by the General Assembly relate to the provision of relief without discrimination, by an impartial organisation, which is to be considered a humanitarian matter.[150] In fact, the General Assembly asserts that the principles shall apply equally to circumstances of natural disaster and conflict.[151] The (failed) UN 1984 Draft Convention on Expediting the Delivery of Emergency Relief proposed that relief consignments and services be of an 'exclusively humanitarian and non-political character provided to meet the needs of those affected by disasters'.[152] As can be derived from the above, the scope of this Draft Convention lay outside international humanitarian law, focusing on disasters of a natural or other kind.[153] Furthermore, the Draft Convention declared that the provision of assistance should occur without discrimination.[154] In 1988 a clear reference to the principles of humanity, impartiality and neutrality occured for the first time, as the UN General Assembly stated in its Resolution 'Humanitarian Assistance to victims of natural disasters and similar emergency situations':

> "recalling that, in the event of natural disasters and similar emergency situations, the principles of humanity, neutrality and impartiality must be given utmost consideration by all those involved in providing humanitarian assistance".[155]

Following this Resolution, the General Assembly posed in 1990 that efficiency and speed of assistance often depend on organisations working 'in an impartial manner and with strictly humanitarian motives', as well as recognising the important contributions made by this manner of work.[156] Only one year later, the General Assembly fortified its earlier statements and declared:

---

[149] UNGA Res 2675 (XXV) (9 December 1970) 'Basic principles for the protection of civilian populations in armed conflict' § 8 and UNGA Res 2717 (XXV) (15 December 1970) 'Assistance in cases of natural disaster', Preambular § 4.

[150] 'Declaration of principles for international humanitarian relief to the civilian population in disaster situations' XXIst International Conference of the Red Cross, Resolution XXVI (Istanbul September 1969) § 2 and §4.

[151] UNGA Res 2675 (XXV) (9 December 1970) § 8.

[152] UNGA Res 39/367 'Draft Convention on Expediting the Delivery of Emergency Relief' (n 38) Article 1 (a).

[153] Article 1(b) of the Draft Convention on Expediting the Delivery of Emergency Relief states: "'Disaster' means any natural, accidental or deliberate event (not being an ongoing situation or armed conflict) as a result of which assistance is needed from outside the State upon whose territory the event occurred or which has been affected by the consequences of the event". A more in depth discussion of the concept of a natural disaster can be found in Section 3.2.5 Defining a (Natural) Disaster .

[154] UNGA Res 39/367 'Draft Convention on Expediting the Delivery of Emergency Relief' (n 38) Article 5 (c).

[155] UNGA Res 43/131 (8 December 1988) UN Doc A/RES/43/131 'Humanitarian Assistance to victims of natural disasters and similar emergency situations' Preambular § 12.

[156] UNGA Res 45/100 (14 December 1990) UN Doc A/RES/45/100 'Humanitarian Assistance to victims of natural disasters and similar emergency situations', Preambular § 11 and operational § 3.

> "humanitarian assistance must be provided *in accordance with* the principles of humanity, neutrality and impartiality".[157]

During the 1990s several ensuing resolutions affirmed the importance the UN attaches to the principles of humanity, impartiality and neutrality.[158]

Interestingly, in 2004 the General Assembly not only reaffirmed the abovementioned principles, but also addressed a *new* principle relevant to the provision of humanitarian assistance, namely the principle of 'independence':

> "Reaffirming the principles of neutrality, humanity and impartiality for the provision of humanitarian assistance, Recognizing that *independence*, meaning the autonomy of humanitarian objectives from the political, economic, military or other objectives that any actor may hold with regard to areas where humanitarian action is being implemented, is also an important guiding principle for the provision of humanitarian assistance".[159]

In a following resolution, all four principles, including the newly phrased principle of independence, are subsequently reaffirmed by the General Assembly as relevant to the provision of humanitarian assistance.[160] Thus, independence as a principle is related to the provision of humanitarian assistance by the UN General Assembly, whilst the actor providing the actual assistance in question might also be concerned with certain other objectives.

In this sense, the definition is somewhat similar to Plattner's perspective in international humanitarian law that an actor does not necessarily have to be neutral, as long as the humanitarian assistance itself is neutral.[161] This principle of independence as coined by the UN also finds some overlap with the Red Cross' principle of neutrality, whilst the Red Cross' notion of independence is somewhat different.[162] Whereas from the UN's perspective the *objectives* must be independent; the Statutes of the Red Cross Movement state that the National Societies of the Red Cross *themselves* must maintain their autonomy.[163] This refers to political, economic and religious autonomy, which as an essential derivative

[157] UNGA Res 46/182 (19 December 1991) UN Doc. A/RES/46/182 (n 46) § 2. [*Emphasis added EEK*]

[158] UNGA Res 48/57 (14 December 1993) UN Doc A/RES/48/57, 'Strengthening the coordination of humanitarian emergency assistance of the United Nations' § 18; and UNGA Res 49/139 (20 December 1994) UN Doc A/RES/49/139 'Strengthening the coordination of humanitarian emergency assistance of the United Nations' § 3.

[159] UNGA Res 58/114 (5 February 2004) UN Doc A/RES/58/114 'Strengthening the coordination of humanitarian emergency assistance of the United Nations' Preambular § 4 and 5. [*Emphasis added EEK*]

[160] UNGA Res 60/124 (8 March 2006) UN Doc A/RES/60/124 'Strengthening the coordination of humanitarian emergency assistance of the United Nations' Preambular § 4.

[161] Plattner, 'ICRC neutrality and neutrality in humanitarian assistance' (n 125) 178.

[162] See the Statutes of the International Red Cross and Red Crescent Movement, (adopted by the 25th International Conference of the Red Cross at Geneva in 1986, amended in 1995 and 2006) concerning the definition of the principle of Independence.

[163] Ibid.

principle, at the same time guarantees the neutrality of the ICRC.[164] Thus, where neutrality for the Red Cross entails to refrain from any political or otherwise explicit acts or statements, *independence* means that the authorities of the territories in which the National Societies are established must abstain from any interference with the work and functioning of these Societies, to enable them to act impartially without interference.[165] The differences in perspectives of both principles of independence can be derived from the difference in *addressees*. The UN addresses states in its resolutions, whilst the ICRC addresses its own National Societies. Both perspectives are not necessarily contradictory, given the difference in addressees, as well as the fact that the UN's notion of 'independence' is to a certain extent also expressed in the Red Cross principle of neutrality, a principle also adhered to by the UN in its resolutions.[166] However, given the discrepancy between the two definitions of the principle of independence, it is therefore not possible to derive one single definition of the principle of independence, applicable to the provision of humanitarian assistance, as the two major actors, the UN and the Red Cross, both hold different views of what this principle entails. Thus, although the UN commenced by incorporating the principles as defined by the Red Cross, it has continued to develop its own definition of the principle of independence. This development has then lead to proliferation of principles, and more uncertainty as to their content.

Within the UN framework the concept of 'human security' has also been coined, in the United Nations Development Programme's 1994 'Human Development Report', stating that – although related to development – human security is a more narrow, centred and universal concept with an interdependent approach.[167] In 2005, in the World Summit Outcome Document, the UN accepted the concept, with a view to further clarifying it:

> "We stress the right of people to live in freedom and dignity, free from poverty and despair. We recognize that all individuals, in particular vulnerable people, are entitled to freedom from fear and freedom from want, with an equal opportunity to enjoy all their rights and fully develop their human potential. To this end, we commit ourselves to discussing and defining the notion of human security in the General Assembly".[168]

Given this explanation, the notion of human security exists of course in close relationship with the principle of humanity discussed above. It is precisely this

[164] Pictet, '1979 Commentary to the Fundamental Principles of the Red Cross' (n 113) (Principle of Independence).
[165] Ibid.
[166] UNGA Res 43/131 (8 December 1988) UN Doc A/RES/43/131 (n 155) Preambular § 12; UNGA Res 46/182 (19 December 1991) UN Doc. A/RES/46/182 (n 46) § 2; UNGA Res 48/57 (14 December 1993) UN Doc A/RES/48/57 (n 158) § 18; UNGA Res 49/139 (20 December 1994) UN Doc A/RES/49/139 (n 158) § 3.
[167] 'Human Development Report' United Nations Development Programme (UNDP) (Oxford University Press 1994) 22-33.
[168] UNGA Res 60/1 (24 October 2005) UN Doc A/RES/60/1 'World Summit Outcome Document' § 143.

common denominator of humankind that forms the foundation and supports the legal framework on the provision of humanitarian assistance. Furthermore, the principles for the provision of assistance, as recognised not only by the ICRC but also the UN and the ICJ exclude the concept of so-called 'conditional' humanitarian assistance, in which the receipt of aid is based on the fulfillment of certain conditions or obligations. This has also been asserted by the Security Council on recent occasions, where the Council has stressed the need to uphold 'humanitarian principles', whilst condemning the 'politicization', 'misuse' and 'misappropriation' thereof.[169]

2.2.3.5 Other Perspectives on the Principles for Providing Humanitarian Assistance

In his research into the 'Protection of persons in the event of disasters', the Special Rapporteur of the UN International Law Commission has suggested that Draft Article 7 states:

> "Response to disasters shall take place in accordance with the principles of humanity, neutrality and impartiality, and on the basis of non-discrimination, while taking into account the needs of the particularly vulnerable".[170]

With regard to these principles, the ILC's discussion of the Draft Article had noted several different viewpoints on their relationship and their possible applicability to situations of natural disaster, but the Article has remained unchanged to date.[171] Not only has the ILC incorporated these humanitarian principles and included the non-discriminatory basis upon which the provision of humanitarian assistance must take place, the Draft Articles also consider the concept of human dignity, stating in Draft Article 5:

> "In responding to disasters, States, competent intergovernmental organizations and relevant non-governmental organizations shall respect and protect the inherent dignity of the human person".[172]

The ILC Draft Articles are thereby taking an inclusive approach; also incorporating concepts originally from humanitarian law although the Draft Articles themselves are restricted to circumstances other than conflict.

---

[169] See amongst others UNSC Res 2100 (25 April 2013) UN Doc S/RES/2100 preamble § 8; and UNSC Res 2060 (25 July 2012) UN Doc S/RES/2060 § 5.

[170] ILC 'Protection of persons in the event of disasters: Texts and titles of the draft articles adopted by the Drafting Committee on first reading' Draft Article 7 'Humanitarian principles' UN Doc. A/CN.4/L.831 (15 May 2014).

[171] ILC 'Report of the International Law Commission' UN Doc A/65/10 (3 May – 4 June, 5 July – 6 August 2010) § 309-313.

[172] ILC 'Protection of persons in the event of disasters' Draft Articles UN Doc. A/CN.4/L.831 (15 May 2014).

Although the UN is one of the major actors next to the ICRC in the provision of humanitarian assistance, other actors have also incorporated the various abovementioned principles relevant to the provision of humanitarian assistance, as well as many of the available soft law mechanisms and resolutions concerning humanitarian assistance.[173] Such soft law examples include Macalister-Smith's 1991 Guidelines that argue that assistance provided should be of an exclusively humanitarian character, and that its provision should be 'on an impartial basis without any adverse distinction to all persons in urgent need'.[174] Also, the 'Mohonk Criteria for Humanitarian Assistance in Complex Emergencies' (Mohonk Criteria) formulated in 1994 by the 'Task force on Ethical and Legal issues in Humanitarian Assistance',[175] adopt the principles of humanity, impartiality and neutrality as developed by the ICRC, as well as a principle similar to its notion of independence.[176] However, the Mohonk Criteria furthermore add the principle of 'empowerment' to the aforementioned principles, declaring this to entail an effort for local institutions to build on the steps taken with humanitarian assistance to continue with reconstruction and development.[177] Thereby the Mohonk Criteria pursue a wider concept of humanitarian assistance than other organisations or resolutions have envisaged. Interestingly, the 2003 Bruges Resolution of the Institut de Droit International / Institute of International Law is not outspoken in this regard, declaring only that the provision humanitarian assistance must occur with an 'exclusively humanitarian character', as well as stating in general that the resolution is without prejudice to principles of international humanitarian law, yet not naming any specific principles.[178]

Furthermore, the European Community (EC)[179] as an actor also adhered to the principle of impartiality, as well as the provision of aid without discrimination in its 1996 regulation concerning humanitarian assistance.[180] This approach was followed by the European Union (EU) in its 2008 'European Consensus on Humanitarian Aid' declaring the principles of humanity, neutrality and impartiality to be fundamental principles of humanitarian assistance and also adhering to the UN's

[173] For a detailed discussion of the various actors relevant to the provision of humanitarian assistance, see Section 2.3.2 Providers of Humanitarian Assistance.

[174] Macalister-Smith' 'International Guidelines for Humanitarian Assistance Operations (n 79) Article 2(a) and Article 6(a).

[175] The Mohonk Criteria were developed in February 1994 by the 'Task force on Ethical and Legal issues in Humanitarian Assistance', established at the World Conference on Religion and Peace, during the 'Program on Humanitarian Assistance', under the lead of then UN affiliate J.M. Ebersole.

[176] 'The Mohonk Criteria for Humanitarian Assistance in Complex Emergencies', (1995) reprinted in 17 *Human Rights Quarterly* 1, 196-197.

[177] Ibid 197.

[178] Bruges Resolution 'Humanitarian Assistance' (2 September 2003) (n 82) § I.1 and § X.a.

[179] For a more in depth discussion of the role of the European Community and Union as an actor within the provision of humanitarian assistance, see Section 2.3.2.2. International Organisations.

[180] European Council Regulation concerning humanitarian aid (EC) No. 1257/96 (20 June 1996) preambular § 10 and § 11.

abovementioned notion of independence as a principle.[181] However, with the new Treaty on the Functioning of the European Union, Article 214 now stipulates that assistance provided by the EU shall comply with international law and the principles of 'impartiality, neutrality and non-discrimination'.[182] Thus, whilst incorporating 'non-discrimination' similarly to the ILC, the principle of humanity has been left out of this provision, although the final paragraph dictates that the aid provision of the EU shall have to be in conformity with that of the UN, thereby incorporating the principle in a backhand manner.

Most recently, the African Union Convention for the Protection and Assistance of Internally Displaced Persons in Africa (Kampala Convention) declared an obligation for state parties to uphold and ensure respect for the principles of humanity, impartiality and neutrality, as well as independence of the humanitarian actors.[183] In a reciprocal manner, those organisations and actors providing assistance are themselves bound by the abovementioned principles.[184] This Convention, dating from 2009, recently entered into force in 2012.[185] Following from the above, it has become apparent that also outside the sphere of international humanitarian law the principles of humanity, impartiality and neutrality have been

---

[181] 'Joint Statement by the Council and the Representatives of the Governments of the Member States meeting within the Council, the European Parliament and the European Commission' (European Consensus on Humanitarian Aid) (30 January 2008) EU Doc 2008/C/25/01 § 10-14.

[182] The full text of Article 214 of the Treaty on the Functioning of the European Union states: "1. The Union's operations in the field of humanitarian aid shall be conducted within the framework of the principles and objectives of the external action of the Union. Such operations shall be intended to provide ad hoc assistance and relief and protection for people in third countries who are victims of natural or man-made disasters, in order to meet the humanitarian needs resulting from these different situations. The Union's measures and those of the Member States shall complement and reinforce each other. 2. Humanitarian aid operations shall be conducted in compliance with the principles of international law and with the principles of impartiality, neutrality and non-discrimination. 3. The European Parliament and the Council, acting in accordance with the ordinary legislative procedure, shall establish the measures defining the framework within which the Union's humanitarian aid operations shall be implemented. 4. The Union may conclude with third countries and competent international organisations any agreement helping to achieve the objectives referred to in paragraph 1 and in Article 21 of the Treaty on European Union. The first subparagraph shall be without prejudice to Member States' competence to negotiate in international bodies and to conclude agreements. 5. In order to establish a framework for joint contributions from young Europeans to the humanitarian aid operations of the Union, a European Voluntary Humanitarian Aid Corps shall be set up. The European Parliament and the Council, acting by means of regulations in accordance with the ordinary legislative procedure, shall determine the rules and procedures for the operation of the Corps. 6. The Commission may take any useful initiative to promote coordination between actions of the Union and those of the Member States, in order to enhance the efficiency and complementarity of Union and national humanitarian aid measures. 7. The Union shall ensure that its humanitarian aid operations are coordinated and consistent with those of international organisations and bodies, in particular those forming part of the United Nations system".

[183] African Union Convention for the Protection and Assistance of Internally Displaced Persons in Africa (Kampala 22 October 2009) Article 5(8).

[184] Ibid Article 6(3).

[185] In 2014, although all African Union members have signed the Kampala Convention, 22 member states had ratified the Convention. <www.au.int/en/sites/default/files/Convention%20on%20IDPs%20-%20displaced..._0.pdf> accessed 9 September 2014. The Convention entered into force 6 December 2012.

embraced on a large scale, with more recent developments including the notion of non-discrimination.

From the above analysis, a concise and narrow definition of humanitarian assistance can be discerned. Establishing such a definition is not only relevant to the purposes of this research, but can also clarify ambiguities between various actors in this field. Furthermore, clearly establishing the objectives and purpose of humanitarian assistance protects it from 'abuse' by certain actors for other goals.[186] Concluding, for the purpose of this research, humanitarian assistance can be defined as assistance consisting of food, medicine, shelter and logistics for its provision; for urgent purposes and which is indispensable to the survival of the people at whom it is aimed.[187] The main objective of humanitarian assistance can also be established, namely the alleviation of human suffering, and the purpose of saving lives.

Furthermore, the manner in which this assistance is provided must at least be in conformity with the principles of humanity, neutrality and impartiality. The ICRC's definition of the principle of independence is somewhat different from the UN's view of the same principle, preventing the further incorporation of this principle into the above definition of humanitarian assistance that is based purely on common ground amongst all actors. However, the principle of independence remains an equally relevant principle as a whole to most actors in the field. The concept of non-discrimination has been brought to the forefront more recently through the EU and ILC initiatives. As ever, the law does not operate in a vacuum. Whilst these principles are the legal basis upon which assistance may be provided, this unfortunately does not preclude an affected state from sometimes arguing that certain providers of assistance might not satisfy their view of the content of these provisions.

2.3 Actors Involved in Humanitarian Assistance

From the above Section on the manner in which assistance is provided, it becomes clear that the ICRC and other organisations distinguish several principles, amongst which the principle of humanity in their provision of assistance to those in need. When discussing humanitarian assistance, it is relevant to establish clearly to whom this assistance is provided. Although many may automatically assume that assistance is provided to certain victims, or a civilian population, it is necessary to briefly establish on what basis such an assumption is made.

2.3.1 Recipients of Humanitarian Assistance

With regard to humanitarian assistance in times of armed conflict or occupation, the Geneva Conventions and their Additional Protocols stipulate that the provision of

---

[186] Frances Stevenson & Joanna Macrae, 'Legislating for humanitarian aid', (2002) 21 *Humanitarian Exchange Magazine*, 34-35.

[187] See Section 2.2.2 Defining Humanitarian Assistance.

humanitarian assistance must occur to a 'civilian population'.[188] This excludes prisoners of war from the receipt of humanitarian assistance, as many tailored provisions exist within humanitarian law for their specific protection.[189] The civilian population must furthermore be distinguished from civilians as 'protected persons' as mentioned in the Geneva Conventions, for which the Conventions also provide specifically.[190] A distinction must also be made between the civilian population and 'internees', although such internees may be civilians.[191] According to Article 50 AP I:

> "1. A civilian is any person who does not belong to one of the categories of persons referred to in Article 4 A (1), (2), (3) and (6) of the Third Convention and in Article 43 of this Protocol. In case of doubt whether a person is a civilian, that person shall be considered to be a civilian. 2. The civilian population comprises all persons who are civilians. 3. The presence within the civilian population of individuals who do not come within the definition of civilians does not deprive the population of its civilian character".[192]

Thus, within the Geneva Conventions and their Protocols, a presumption exists to consider a population as a 'civilian population' unless it can be otherwise defined. Furthermore, if individuals within that population cannot be considered civilians, humanitarian assistance can still be provided as the population in general is not deprived of its civilian character. As the abovementioned Section 2.2.3 has discussed, humanitarian assistance may only be provided in accordance with the principles of humanity, neutrality and impartiality. The distinction between

---

188 See amongst others Articles 10 and 55 GC IV; Article 69 AP I; Article 18 AP II.

189 Note in particular GC III: Geneva Convention relative to the Treatment of Prisoners of War, 75 U.N.T.S. 135, entered into force Oct. 21, 1950.

190 Article 4 GC IV states in regard to protected persons: "Persons protected by the Convention are those who, at a given moment and in any manner whatsoever, find themselves, in case of a conflict or occupation, in the hands of a Party to the conflict or Occupying Power of which they are not nationals. Nationals of a State which is not bound by the Convention are not protected by it. Nationals of a neutral State who find themselves in the territory of a belligerent State, and nationals of a co-belligerent State, shall not be regarded as protected persons while the State of which they are nationals has normal diplomatic representation in the State in whose hands they are. The provisions of Part II are, however, wider in application, as defined in Article 13. Persons protected by the Geneva Convention for the Amelioration of the Condition of the Wounded and Sick in Armed Forces in the Field of August 12, 1949, or by the Geneva Convention for the Amelioration of the Condition of Wounded, Sick and Shipwrecked Members of Armed Forces at Sea of August 12, 1949, or by the Geneva Convention relative to the Treatment of Prisoners of War of August 12, 1949, shall not be considered as protected persons within the meaning of the present Convention". For a discussion on the categories of 'protected persons' mentioned in Article 4 of GC IV, see Jean Pictet, *Commentary on the Geneva Conventions of 12 August 1949 Volumes I-IV* (International Committee of the Red Cross 1952-1959), Volume IV Commentary GC IV Article 4, 46-51.

191 The Geneva Conventions provide specifically for internees, amongst others in Articles 108-111 GC IV.

192 Article 43 AP I refers to those persons who are members of the armed forces, and the persons in Article 4 A (1), (2), (3) and (6) refer to several categories of prisoners of war.

civilians and combatants therefore remains relevant to date in relation to the principle of neutrality, as well as to specifically defining a civilian population.[193]

Clearly, this distinction between civilians and combatants is only relevant to the situation of an international armed conflict or occupation, whereas the provision of humanitarian assistance is broader; also encompassing circumstances outside of conflict, such as man-made or natural disasters. Arguably, today the distinction made by the Geneva Conventions regarding 'categories' of civilians is not as relevant, due to the changing nature of conflict increasingly towards non-international armed conflicts, which results in less distinct groups of civilians.[194] Yet, Article 50 AP I regarding international armed conflicts also acknowledges this changing nature, as its final paragraph refers to the possible presence of combatants among the civilian population, something occurring more and more frequently in modern warfare. The provision of humanitarian assistance to the civilian population thereby remains protected under international law and the provider of assistance must do everything in its power to respect the principle of neutrality.[195]

The United Nations refers to a variety of subjects of humanitarian assistance, although all can be considered part of a civilian population. As such, UN resolutions refer to 'victims' or 'affected populations' of natural disasters or of other emergencies,[196] as well as 'civilians' or 'civilian populations' which should include 'refugees and internally displaced persons'.[197] This line of reasoning by the UN follows the Guiding Principles on Internal Displacement that, although non-binding, are implemented by key actors in the field and provide that IDPs are subjects of the provision of humanitarian assistance when affected by a natural or man-made disaster.[198] Refugees and IDPs can be considered a distinct category of

[193] Abril Stoffels, 'Legal Regulation of Humanitarian Assistance in Armed Conflict: Achievements and Gaps' (n108) 542.

[194] Mackintosh, 'The Principles of Humanitarian Action in International Humanitarian Law' (n 110) 5

[195] Abril Stoffels, 'Legal Regulation of Humanitarian Assistance in Armed Conflict: Achievements and Gaps' (n108) 542

[196] UNGA Res 46/182 (19 December 1991) UN Doc. A/RES/46/182 (n 46) § 1 and 4.

[197] UNSC Res 1265 (17 September 1999) UN Doc S/RES/1265 § 7; UNGA Res 52/167 (18 February 1998) UN Doc A/RES/52/167 'Safety and security of humanitarian personnel' § 3; UNGA Res 53/87 (27 January 1999) UN Doc A/RES/53/87 ' Safety and security of humanitarian personnel and protection of United Nations personnel' § 11; UNGA Res 60/124 (8 March 2006) UN Doc A/RES/60/124 (n 160) § 2; UNGA res 61/133 (1 March 2007) UN Doc A/RES/61/133 'Safety and security of humanitarian personnel and protection of United Nations personnel' § 4; UNGA Res 62/94 (25 January 2008) UN Doc A/RES/62/94 'Strengthening of the coordination of emergency humanitarian assistance of the United Nations' § 24; UNGA Res 63/139 (5 March 2009) UN Doc A/RES/63/139 'Strengthening of the coordination of humanitarian and disaster relief assistance of the United Nations, including special economic assistance: strengthening of the coordination of emergency humanitarian assistance of the United Nations' § 25.

[198] 'Report of the Representative of the Secretary-General, Mr. Francis M. Deng, submitted pursuant to Commission resolution 1997/39', Addendum 'Guiding Principles on Internal Displacement' (Guiding Principles on IDPs) (11 February 1998) UN Doc E/CN.4/1998/53/Add.2, Principle 3. The Guiding Principles are supported by the United Nations offices UNHCR and OHCHR, and furthermore the UN General Assembly declared in § 7 of UNGA Res 58/177 (12 March 2004) UN Doc A/RES/58/177 'Protection of and assistance to internally displaced persons' that it 'Expresses its appreciation of the Guiding Principles on Internal Displacement as an important tool for dealing with situations of internal

persons in international law, but are included in the recipients of humanitarian assistance.[199] The inclusion of IDPs as the recipients of humanitarian assistance flows from the increase of many internal disturbances and non-international armed conflicts during the 1990s, in which affected persons, although in need of aid, could not be granted the status of refugees as there was no crossing of borders involved.[200] Furthermore, their situation often arises both from an ongoing situation, and in the aftermath of an event such as a natural disaster. To avoid gaps

displacement'. The former UN Special Rapporteur on the Human Rights of Internally Displaced Persons Walter Kälin has furthermore declared in his final 'Report of the Representative of the Secretary-General on the human rights of internally displaced persons', UN Doc A/HRC/13/21 (5 January 2010) § 10 that: "The Guiding Principles reflect and are consistent with international human rights and humanitarian law, restating existing norms and tailoring them to the needs of the displaced". Furthermore the General Assembly has continued to embrace the Guiding Principles, amongst others in UNGA Res 60/1 (24 October 2005) UN Doc A/RES/60/1 'World Summit Outcome Document' § 132 where the General Assembly recognises the Principles as an "important international framework for the protection of internally displaced persons", a phrasing that is echoed by UNGA Res 60/124 (8 March 2006) UN Doc. A/RES/60/124 (n 160) § 6; UNGA Res 60/168 (7 March 2006) A/RES/60/168 'Protection of and assistance to internally displaced persons' § 8; and UNGA Res 62/153 (6 March 2008) UN Doc. A/RES/62/153, 'Protection of and assistance to internally displaced persons' § 10; as well as UN HRC Res 6/32 (14 December 2007) A/HRC/6/32 § 5.

[199] Article 1 of the 1951 Convention Relating to the Status of Refugees (Refugee Convention) declares anyone to be a refugee who: "(1) Has been considered a refugee under the Arrangements of 12 May 1926 and 30 June 1928 or under the Conventions of 28 October 1933 and 10 February 1938, the Protocol of 14 September 1939 or the Constitution of the International Refugee Organization; Decisions of non-eligibility taken by the International Refugee Organization during the period of its activities shall not prevent the status of refugee being accorded to persons who fulfil the conditions of paragraph 2 of this section; (2) As a result of events occurring before 1 January 1951 and owing to wellfounded fear of being persecuted for reasons of race, religion, nationality, membership of a particular social group or political opinion, is outside the country of his nationality and is unable or, owing to such fear, is unwilling to avail himself of the protection of that country; or who, not having a nationality and being outside the country of his former habitual residence as a result of such events, is unable or, owing to such fear, is unwilling to return to it. In the case of a person who has more than one nationality, the term "the country of his nationality" shall mean each of the countries of which he is a national, and a person shall not be deemed to be lacking the protection of the country of his nationality if, without any valid reason based on well-founded fear, he has not availed himself of the protection of one of the countries of which he is a national". A thorough discussion of the notion of a refugee falls outside the scope of this research. For further reading, see Guy S Goodwin-Gill and Jane McAdam, *The Refugee in International Law* (Oxford University Press 2007) and Erika Feller, Volker Türk, Frances Nicholson (eds), *Refugee Protection in International Law: UNHCR's Global Consultations on International Protection* (Cambridge University Press, 2003). Currently, no legal binding definition of IDPs exists, nor any legal binding document governing their status. The 'Guiding Principles on Internal Displacement' (11 February 1998) UN Doc E/CN.4/1998/53/Add.2 (n 198) declare in Preambular § 2 that: "For the purposes of these Principles, internally displaced persons are persons or groups of persons who have been forced or obliged to flee or to leave their homes or places of habitual residence, in particular as a result of or in order to avoid the effects of armed conflict, situations of generalized violence, violations of human rights or natural or human-made disasters, and who have not crossed an internationally recognized State border". Furthermore, the African Union Kampala Convention on IDPs echoes this definition by the 'Guiding Principles on Internal Displacement' in its Article 1(k). For further reading, see Catherine Phuong, *The International Protection of Internally Displaced Persons* (Cambridge University Press 2004).

[200] Roberta Cohen, 'Humanitarian Imperatives are Transforming Sovereignty', (2008) 9 *Northwestern Journal of International Affairs* 1, 3-4.

in the protection of such affected persons the UN High Commissioner for Refugees (UNHCR), followed by the Security Council, commenced incorporating the protection of IDPs in their mandate and actions.[201] The Guiding Principles on IDPs interestingly refer specifically to women, children and other vulnerable groups, stating that their special needs entitle them to protection that takes this status into account.[202]

Like the UN, the International Law Association (ILA) adopted a position with regard to IDPs.[203] The ILA asserted in 2000 that all IDPs have the right to seek and receive humanitarian assistance.[204] For the purpose of this research, refugees and IDPs will like other civilians be considered the subjects of humanitarian assistance, unless a separate discussion is warranted and relevant to the legal rights and obligations specific to their status. It remains to be noted however that the provision of humanitarian assistance is aimed at such a stage in a crisis so as to prevent large-scale displacement and refugees, thereby not warranting an in depth discussion of many particular provisions of refugee law and other bodies of law specific to IDPs and refugees.

The ILC, in its study into the protection of persons in the event of disasters also studied the recipients of humanitarian assistance in order to assess which category of persons should fall within its scope of application. The ILC noted that being affected by natural disasters is not considered a criterion for the attribution of the status of refugee, although it is precisely such disasters that result in the generation of large numbers of refugees and IDPs.[205] As the ILC notes, being affected by a disaster at this point in time does not represent a separate legal category in international law.[206] With this consideration, the ILC concludes that the current study and the draft articles it is developing shall 'apply to the protection of persons in the event of disasters'.[207] Thereby the ILC chooses not to distinctly define which categories of persons fall within these 'persons' who may be protected through humanitarian assistance. Certainly, this broad approach will enable the widest array of persons to be eligible to fall under the ILC's scope of protection.

---

201 Ibid 4-5, and Roberta Cohen & Francis Mading Deng, *Masses in Flight: The Global Crisis of Internal Displacement* (Brookings Institution Press 1998) 120.

202 'Guiding Principles on Internal Displacement' (11 February 1998) UN Doc E/CN.4/1998/53/Add.2 (n 198) Principle 18(3) and 19(2).

203 The International Law Association, founded in 1873 in Brussels is an NGO founded with the purpose to further the understanding and respect of (public and private) international law, as well as its study, clarification and development. For more information, see <www.ila-hq.org/index.cfm> accessed 5 January 2012.

204 ILA Declaration of International Law Principles on Internally Displaced Persons (29 July 2000) Article 3 (2). The possible right to receive humanitarian assistance will be discussed more in depth in Chapter 6.

205 ILC 'Preliminary report on the protection of persons in the event of disasters' UN Doc. A/CN.4/598 (n 76) § 27-28.

206 Ibid § 50.

207 ILC 'Protection of persons in the event of disasters' Draft Articles UN Doc. A/CN.4/L.831 (15 May 2014) Draft Article 1: "The present draft articles apply to the protection of persons in the event of disasters".

Likewise, the European Community also makes reference to victims and vulnerable groups, declaring that assistance shall be provided to:

> "people in third countries, particularly the most vulnerable among them, and as a priority those in developing countries, victims of natural disasters, man-made crises, such as wars and outbreaks of fighting, or exceptional situations or circumstances comparable to natural or man-made disasters".[208]

Similar to the European Community before it, the EU stated in 2008 that civilians are the main victims of humanitarian crises, in particular the 'most vulnerable among them' as well as generating large numbers of refugees and IDPs.[209]

Furthermore with a view to soft law initiatives, like the early UN resolutions, the Institute of International Law, in its 2003 Bruges Resolution also refers to the notion of victims, as a group of persons 'whose fundamental human rights or whose essential needs are endangered'.[210]

It can be concluded that the subjects and recipients of humanitarian assistance, regardless of the specific circumstances they may find themselves in (such as conflict or natural disaster) are civilians, including particularly vulnerable groups such as refugees and IDPs. Although the Guiding Principles on IDPs make a separate reference to groups with special needs, such as women and children, this is not common to the discussion of the subjects of humanitarian assistance.

2.3.2 Providers of Humanitarian Assistance

In previous Sections, various organisations involved in the provision of humanitarian assistance have already been touched upon, as well as the manner in which humanitarian assistance must be provided. At this stage, it is important to look into these organisations in more depth, including the particular roles they fulfill in the delivery of humanitarian assistance. In this Section a basic overview of the various relevant actors in the *provision* of humanitarian assistance will be provided in a more comprehensive manner, namely the 'affected state', international organisations and NGOs, and third states. As such, this Section shall commence by addressing the actor that is often considered the primary responsible provider of assistance: the 'affected state'. The affected state holds a particularly special and delicate position and therefore a greater focus will be placed on its specific responsibilities and duties in the following Chapters as an in depth analysis of an affected states' duties and rights will not be pursued at this stage.

---

[208] European Council Regulation concerning humanitarian aid (EC) No. 1257/96 (20 June 1996) Article 1.

[209] 'Joint Statement by the Council and the Representatives of the Governments of the Member States meeting within the Council, the European Parliament and the European Commission' (European Consensus on Humanitarian Aid) (30 January 2008) EU Doc 2008/C/25/01, § 2.

[210] Bruges Resolution 'Humanitarian Assistance' (2 September 2003) (n 82) §3.

2.3.2.1 The Affected State

Whether humanitarian assistance is provided or not, is often directly related to the possibilities and willingness of the affected state to do so itself. As the sovereign authority in the particular area where the assistance is needed, its role cannot be overlooked or surpassed. In fact, the affected state can be both a vehicle and an obstacle in the provision of assistance.[211] The Geneva Conventions do not make use of the particular phrasing 'affected state', as it is mostly derived from situations of (natural) disaster, but by analogy it can be applicable to circumstances of conflict too, as the sovereign over a territory in which a conflict takes place shall be the primary 'affected' actor, for a variety of reasons amongst which simply the matter of vicinity and sovereign responsibility.[212] Although no specific mention is made of the 'affected state', the Geneva Conventions did foresee a role for authorities in territories dealing with a situation of potential crisis, where assistance may be needed. Article 59 GC IV mentions for example that an 'Occupying Power' is to allow for assistance in the occupied territories, as well as facilitate such assistance.[213] Staying within the realm of occupation, the Geneva Conventions furthermore provide a role for the delivery of humanitarian assistance for many other actors:

> "The distribution of the relief consignments referred to in the foregoing Articles shall be carried out with the cooperation and under the supervision of the Protecting Power. This duty may also be delegated, by agreement between the Occupying Power and the Protecting Power, to a neutral Power, to the International Committee of the Red Cross or to any other impartial humanitarian body [...]".[214]

As such, the Conventions acknowledge the possibility of the provision of assistance by third states, the ICRC or another neutral organisation.

Returning to the 'affected state', the Geneva Conventions' Common Article 3 lays an obligation on all 'parties to the conflict' to take certain minimum

---

[211] See Chapter 4 State Sovereignty as a Contextual Concept regarding Humanitarian Assistance, for a discussion of sovereignty as such an obstacle or vehicle.
[212] For considerations into primary responsibility, see Chapter 6.
[213] Article 59 GC IV states: "If the whole or part of the population of an occupied territory is inadequately supplied, the Occupying Power shall agree to relief schemes on behalf of the said population, and shall facilitate them by all the means at its disposal. Such schemes, which may be undertaken either by States or by impartial humanitarian organizations such as the International Committee of the Red Cross, shall consist, in particular, of the provision of consignments of foodstuffs, medical supplies and clothing. All Contracting Parties shall permit the free passage of these consignments and shall guarantee their protection. A Power granting free passage to consignments on their way to territory occupied by an adverse Party to the conflict shall, however, have the right to search the consignments, to regulate their passage according to prescribed times and routes, and to be reasonably satisfied through the Protecting Power that these consignments are to be used for the relief of the needy population and are not to be used for the benefit of the Occupying Power". See also Section 6.5.3 Duties of the Affected State (Occupying Power) in Times of Occupation for the particular duties of an occupier.
[214] Article 61 GC IV.

requirements.[215] For the purpose of this Section, it is relevant to note that these parties include not only states, but also armed groups and other forces involved in a non-international armed conflict.[216] Additional Protocol I, relating to international armed conflicts, similarly mentions a role for 'the Parties to the conflict' as well as 'each High Contracting Party', wording also used by the Additional Protocol II in relation to non-international armed conflicts.[217] Although not hard law, but voicing international legal scholarship, the San Remo Principles formulated:

> "The primary responsibility to protect and assist the victims of emergencies is that of the authorities of the territory in which the emergency causing urgent humanitarian needs occurs".[218]

Thus, like the Geneva Conventions, in particular their 1977 Protocols, the San Remo Principles envisaged that not only a state sovereign may function as the highest authority within a certain territory, but in certain territories this role may be taken by some other form of authority.

Outside the realm of international humanitarian law and focusing more on situations of (natural) disaster, the UN General Assembly has also reaffirmed the primary role of the affected state in many of its resolutions, with a view to its tasks as a sovereign.[219] In more recent years, the ILC has also considered the 'affected state' as holding a primary position in the provision of humanitarian assistance in the event of disasters and as such has drafted:

> "1. The affected State, by virtue of its sovereignty, has the duty to ensure the protection of persons and provision of disaster relief and assistance on its territory. 2. The affected State has the primary role in the direction, control, coordination and supervision of such relief and assistance".[220]

Thereby the ILC, in line with the UN General Assembly, maintains this primary role for the affected state, as well as granting it a coordinating role, thus acknowledging the possibility of assistance from the exterior.[221] This viewpoint had

[215] For the full text of Common Article 3 of the Geneva Conventions see (n 119).

[216] See Section 3.2.1 Defining an Armed Conflict on the definition of a non-international armed conflict and actors involved therein.

[217] Article 70 AP I and Article 18 AP II.

[218] 'Guiding Principles on the Right to Humanitarian Assistance' (n 80) Principle 4.

[219] Amongst others in UNGA Res 36/225 (17 December 1981) UN Doc A/RES/36/225 'Strengthening the Capacity of the United Nations system to respond to natural disasters and other disaster situations' § 2; UNGA Res 45/100 (14 December 1990) UN Doc A/RES/45/100 (n 156) Preambular § 2 and Operative § 2; and UNGA Res 46/182 (19 December 1991) UN Doc. A/RES/46/182 (n 46) Guiding Principle 4. See for more specific duties Section 6.3.3 Duties of the Affected State under General Assembly Resolutions.

[220] ILC 'Protection of persons in the event of disasters' Draft Articles UN Doc. A/CN.4/L.831 (15 May 2014) Draft Article 12.

[221] See for more specific duties Section 6.3.3 Duties of the Affected State under General Assembly Resolutions. In further Sections, an in depth discussion of the relationship between sovereignty and the

already been adopted by the ILC at an earlier stage of its research, as it argued that 'outside actors' could play a considerable role in the provision of assistance.[222]

The IFRC has, unlike the UN General Assembly and the ILC, opted to provide a definition of such an affected state, and has declared it to be:

> "The State upon whose territory persons or property are affected by a disaster".[223]

As discussed, it may be assumed that the affected state undertakes its allotted role and task in the event of a (natural) disaster more willingly, as opposed perhaps to an unwilling attitude in a situation of armed conflict or occupation in which assistance may be necessary, but further Sections will show that such an assumption must not be made lightly.[224] A well-known recent example is that of cyclone Nargis, where the authorities in Myanmar were unwilling to allow the provision of humanitarian assistance for a prolonged period of time.[225]

Most other institutions and actors have attempted to abstract the concept of the affected state from a particular situation such as conflict or natural disaster and rather apply the role of primary responsible actor to a range of situations. In doing so, these institutions attempt to provide more regulation for the practical circumstances on the ground, that have proven that humanitarian assistance is certainly not always provided when it is in fact needed. As such, the Institute for International Law declared in its 2003 Bruges Resolution that an affected state is 'the State or the territorial entity where humanitarian assistance is needed', without specifying the particular circumstance.[226] The Bruges Resolution emphatically places a primary responsibility on the affected state in the provision of humanitarian assistance, or on another authority that may be exercising jurisdiction in a certain area.[227] Similarly, the Mohonk Criteria envisage the task for the

---

provision of humanitarian assistance will take place, as well as a more in depth view of the responsibilities of the affected state.

222 ILC 'Protection of persons in the event of disasters, Memorandum by the Secretariat' UN Doc A/CN.4/590 (11 December 2007) § 250.

223 IFRC 'Guidelines for the domestic facilitation and regulation of international disaster relief and initial recovery assistance' (IDRL Guidelines) (30 November 2007), adopted at the 30th International Conference of the Movement, Section 2, § 8 .

224 See in particular Chapter 4 State Sovereignty as a Contextual Concept regarding Humanitarian Assistance.

225 Reports of the Myanmar government refusing external delivery of aid can be found at: <www.hrw.org/news/2010/04/29/burma-after-cyclone-repression-impedes-civil-society-and-aid-0>; <http://reliefweb.int/report/myanmar/myanmar-cyclone-nargis-ocha-situation-report-no-6> accessed 2 October 2013.

226 Bruges Resolution 'Humanitarian Assistance' (2 September 2003) (n 82) Section I.4.

227 Bruges Resolution 'Humanitarian Assistance' (2 September 2003) (n 82) Section III on the primary responsibility of the affected State declares "1. The affected State has the duty to take care of the victims of disaster in its territory and has therefore the primary responsibility in the organization, provision and distribution of humanitarian assistance. As a result, it has the duty to take the necessary measures to prevent the misappropriation of humanitarian assistance and other abuses. 2. Any other authority exercising jurisdiction or de facto control over the victims of a disaster (for example in case of disintegration of the governmental authority) has the duty to provide them with the necessary

provision of humanitarian assistance to lie firstly with the authorities in the affected state, declaring also that 'insurgent groups and militias' should be held to equal standards.[228] Furthermore, Macalister-Smith also noted the primary role as lying with the affected state, keeping in mind that the state may however be limited in its possibilities:

> "Primary responsibility for providing humanitarian assistance within the limits of the resources available rests with the national authorities of the State where persons are in need".[229]

In relation to the assistance of the specific category of IDPs, the recently effective 2009 Kampala Convention and the ILA Declaration on IDPs of 2000 both see a primary role for the national authorities of the affected territories, but also include a role for international organisations providing relief.[230] This position can also be seen with the abovementioned Geneva Conventions and the Institute for Humanitarian Law. The latter envisaged with its San Remo Principles that national and international organisations mandated with the provision of humanitarian assistance should in fact be *able* to provide it.[231] Furthermore the Institute for International Law also envisages multiple actors involved in the provision of assistance, other than the affected state or another authority in that territory:

> "Assistance may be sought on behalf of the victims, by the members of the group, by local and regional authorities, the government of the affected State, and national or international organizations".[232]

Thus, most institutions realise that designating a primary role for the affected state in itself is not enough to *ensure* the provision of humanitarian assistance, thereby acknowledging important roles for other actors, such as international organisations and NGOs. This approach in itself hints at a need for *international* assistance in the provision of assistance as is addressed in Chapter 7. Indeed, whilst a primary role for the affected state remains crucial, the changing notion of state sovereignty in the 21st century addresses the difficulties faced in circumstances where an affected state

---

humanitarian assistance, and also has all the other duties and rights of the affected State provided for in this Resolution".

228 'The Mohonk Criteria for Humanitarian Assistance in Complex Emergencies', (1995) (n 176) Section II 'Responsibility to provide assistance during complex emergencies': "1. Primary responsibility for the protection and wellbeing of civilian populations rests with the government of the state or the authorities in control of the territory in which the endangered persons are located. 2. Insurgent groups and militias should be held to the same standards of responsibility as governments".

229 Macalister-Smith' 'International Guidelines for Humanitarian Assistance Operations (n 79) Principle 6(b).

230 African Union Kampala Convention Article 5(1) and 5(7); ILA Declaration of International Law Principles on Internally Displaced Persons (29 July 2000) Article 10.

231 Guiding Principles on the Right to Humanitarian Assistance' (n 80) Principle 5.

232 Bruges Resolution 'Humanitarian Assistance' (2 September 2003) (n 82) Section II.2.

does not provide assistance or provide for its citizens in a broader sense.[233] The specific legal framework pertaining to the legal rights and duties of the affected state in the provision of humanitarian assistance will be discussed further in Chapter 6. Given the struggles and difficulties states face in times of conflict, as well as the fact that authorities in times of natural disaster are often either overwhelmed or occasionally unwilling to provide assistance, it is indeed logical to turn to providers of humanitarian assistance from either outside the territory that is affected, or national organisations without ties to the affected state.[234] These institutions provide alternative manners for the provision of humanitarian assistance to those in need.

2.3.2.2 International Organisations

The previous Sections have already touched upon various organisations involved in the provision of humanitarian assistance. Furthermore, from the above it has become apparent that, although a primary role is envisaged for the affected states or other authorities acting as such, the ICRC, the UN and other organisations and institutions also play a large role in the provision of such assistance.[235] A distinction must be made between international organisations such as the UN and EU, with both inter-governmental and supranational characteristics, as subjects of international law, and non-governmental organisations with a different standing in the international legal arena. Specifically in circumstances of (non-) international conflict, the Geneva Conventions consider a large role for the ICRC, an organisation with a very particular status, as it is neither intergovernmental nor non-governmental.[236] Given the character of this research into the legal framework on the rights and duties under international law in the provision of humanitarian assistance, a focus will be placed upon those organisations with a particular standing or enforcement possibility in international law, in order to assess potential rights and duties that they might have. This is not to say that local NGOs do not play an important role on the ground in the factual distribution of food, water and medicine to those in need of assistance.

The Geneva Conventions and their Additional Protocols refer to the ICRC or another organisation that follows its principles of humanity and impartiality for the provision of humanitarian assistance.[237] In its Articles, the Geneva Conventions and

---

233 The following Chapters will provide an in depth discussion of the relationship between humanitarian assistance and sovereignty.

234 See UNGA Res 59/141 (25 February 2005) UN Doc A/RES/59/141 'Strengthening of the coordination of emergency humanitarian assistance of the United Nations' § 11-12 referencing the central role played by civilian organisations.

235 This research will not provide an overview of all organisations involved in the provision of humanitarian assistance. It will merely portray that organisations are involved in humanitarian assistance, and in what manner their involvement is codified in treaties, resolutions or other relevant documents.

236 See Section 2.3.2.2 International Organisations.

237 Common Article 3, Articles 10, 59 61 and 63 GC IV; Article 70 AP I; Article 18(2) AP II.

Protocols declare that the ICRC or a comparable humanitarian and impartial organisation may be involved in the provision of humanitarian assistance in times of conflict or occupation amounting to a crisis.[238] Outside the realm of occupation and conflict, resort must be had to sources other than international treaties, to determine the roles laid out for international organisations.

A clear distinction has been made between the work of the ICRC and the IFRC,[239] which also becomes apparent in determining the role of the latter as a provider of humanitarian assistance. The IFRC itself declares:

> "The IFRC carries out relief operations to assist victims of disasters [...]. The IFRC's work focuses on four core areas: promoting humanitarian values, disaster response, disaster preparedness, and health and community care".[240]

Although the IFRC is the largest humanitarian organisation in the world, with 187 national societies in countries around the globe,[241] a central role is also played by the UN in the coordination of humanitarian assistance for those in need in the international community. Such a leading and coordinating role was already envisaged by the UN General Assembly in its 1991 Resolution 46/182.[242] The Inter-Agency Standing Committee (IASC) was created in 1992, following a call thereto in this prominent Resolution on 'Strengthening the coordination of humanitarian emergency assistance of the United Nations'.[243] Its envisaged task of being primary coordinator for the UN and other organisations delivering international humanitarian assistance, was confirmed in a subsequent General Assembly Resolution.[244] Following the structural changes within the UN in the 1990s, the IASC falls within the larger framework of the Office for the Coordination of

238 Ibid. Further Chapters will discuss the exact status of the rights of such organisations in the provision of humanitarian assistance.

239 See (n 52) on the tasks and mandate of the ICRC and IFRC, as well as their mutual relationship.

240 For more information on the role and tasks of the IFRC: <www.ifrc.org/en/who-we-are/vision-and-mission/> accessed 3 January 2011.

241 Ibid.

242 UNGA Res 46/182 (19 December 1991) UN Doc. A/RES/46/182 (n 46) Annex I, Guiding Principles 5 and 12, and Section VI 'Coordination, Cooperation and Leadership'.

243 UNGA Res 46/182 (19 December 1991) UN Doc. A/RES/46/182 (n 46) Annex I Section VI 'Coordination, Cooperation and Leadership' § 38.

244 UNGA Res 48/57 (14 December 1993) UN Doc A/RES/48/57 (n 158). For more information on the IASC, see <www.humanitarianinfo.org/iasc/pageloader.aspx?page=content-about-default> accessed 24 October 2011. Members and Invitees to the IASC include the Food and Agriculture Organization (FAO), OCHA, the United Nations Development Programme (UNDP), the United Nations Population Fund (UNFPA), the United Nations Human Settlements Programme (UNHABITAT), the United Nations High Commissioner for Refugees (UNHCR), the United Nations Children's Fund (UNICEF), the World Food Programme (WFP), the World Health Organization (WHO), the ICRC, the International Council of Voluntary Agencies (ICVA), the IFRC, InterAction, the International Organization for Migration (IOM), the UN Office of the High Commissioner for Human Rights (OHCHR), the Steering Committee for Humanitarian Response (SCHR), the UN Office of the Special Rapporteur on the Human Rights of Internally Displaced Persons and the World Bank.

Humanitarian Affairs created in 1998,[245] and carries out OCHA's coordination task of providing effective humanitarian assistance through combined efforts of humanitarian organisations. OCHA is mandated as a whole to function as part of the UN Secretariat, and is responsible for the coordination of all humanitarian actors involved in the provision of assistance during and in the aftermath of humanitarian crises, including policy and advocacy work.[246] Both the IASC and OCHA are headed by the Emergency Relief Coordinator.[247] With OCHA and the IASC, the UN has created a large coordinating framework for the provision and delivery of humanitarian assistance, encompassing many organisations involved in the delivery of humanitarian assistance such as the ICRC and UNHCR.[248] Within the European continent, the EU holds a central organisational role with regard to the provision of humanitarian assistance by European countries. The European 'counterpart' of OCHA is the European Community Humanitarian Office (ECHO), also created in 1992. In more recent years, ECHO has undergone changes; becoming first the Directorate-General for Humanitarian Aid and since 2010 also encompassing Civil Protection.[249] Unlike the UN, which had initially focused its humanitarian assistance on situations of natural disaster, the European Civil Protection Mechanism does not distinguish between the circumstances in which it comes into action.[250] The EU has furthermore instated a special commissioner for 'International cooperation, humanitarian aid and crisis response'.[251] Efforts are underway for the development of a European Humanitarian Aid Voluntary Corps. In practice, all the above-mentioned organisations cooperate in the delivery of humanitarian assistance. Besides these three large institutions: the Red Cross, the UN and the EU, actors such as NGOs and private organisations play an extremely large role in the provision of humanitarian assistance. Given the fact that this research focuses on the international legal framework, and such organisations do not have a crystallised status within this body of law, they shall remain outside the scope of this research, which focuses more on the role of international organisations. Furthermore, it is beyond the scope of this research to address all

---

245 Section 2.2.1 Historical Development. See also <http://ochanet.unocha.org/p/Documents/UNOCHA%20Organigramme%202011.pdf> accessed 3 January 2012.

246 For more information on the work and mandate of OCHA: <www.unocha.org/about-us/who-we-are> accessed 3 January 2012.

247 For more information on the Emergency Relief Coordinator, Ms. Valerie Amos: <www.unocha.org/about-us/headofOCHA> accessed 3 January 2012.

248 Regarding the IASC's Members and Invitees see (n 244). Furthermore, although outside the scope of this research, it is relevant to mention that the UN is also active in the arena of disaster risk reduction, through its International Strategy for Disaster Reduction and the Hyogo Declaration and Hyogo Framework for Action of 2005.

249 For more information on ECHO, operating under the EU Commissioner for Humanitarian Aid and Crisis Management, see: <http://ec.europa.eu/echo/who/about-echo_en> accessed 21 May 2015.

250 Ibid: "CPM interventions cover all types of major emergencies, including natural and man-made disasters, acts of terrorism and technological, radiological and environmental accidents, including accidental marine pollution".

251 The current Commissioner for 'Humanitarian Aid & Crisis Management' is Christos Stylianides: <http://ec.europa.eu/commission/2014-2019/stylianides_en> accessed 15 December 2014.

these private organisations and NGOs, and suffice to mention that when in conformity with the principles of humanity, neutrality and impartiality, these organisations too are considered as part of the providers of humanitarian assistance.[252]

2.3.2.3 Third States

Lastly, it is relevant to mention the role of third states as providers of humanitarian assistance. In the event of a humanitarian crisis, not only the affected state, international organisations and NGOs have a large role in the provision of assistance. Individual third states, or sometimes coalitions of third states, may be needed or called upon to provide assistance to people in need. As seen above in Section 2.2.3, it is relevant that the manner of provision of assistance is neutral, and in accordance with the principles of humanity and impartiality. Thus, although states may not always be neutral, they are quite capable of providing humanitarian assistance in conformity with these principles and can therefore be considered providers of humanitarian assistance. As seen above, the Geneva Conventions also make reference to such a potential role for third states (in particular relation to circumstances of occupation), mentioning in Article 61 GC IV 'Protecting Powers' or 'Neutral Powers'.[253] The UN also counts on third states to participate in the provision of humanitarian assistance, calling upon them as early as 1970 to offer:

> "[...] emergency assistance to meet natural disasters, including stand-by relief units or the earmarking of similar units for the service in foreign countries".[254]

This line of reasoning was continued by the UN, as the 1984 Draft Convention also envisaged the possibility of an 'Assisting State' for the provision of humanitarian assistance.[255] Furthermore, the UN has called upon and urged 'the international community' on several occasions with regard to IDPs, refugees or other persons protected by international humanitarian law over the past decades to provide

---

[252] The role of international organisations as well as NGOs in relation to the possible right to provide assistance, as well as the possible right to access for such provision will be addressed further in Chapters 6 and 7.

[253] Article 61 GC IV states: "The distribution of the relief consignments referred to in the foregoing Articles shall be carried out with the cooperation and under the supervision of the Protecting Power. This duty may also be delegated, by agreement between the Occupying Power and the Protecting Power, to a neutral Power, to the International Committee of the Red Cross or to any other impartial humanitarian body. Such consignments shall be exempt in occupied territory from all charges, taxes or customs duties unless these are necessary in the interests of the economy of the territory. The Occupying Power shall facilitate the rapid distribution of these consignments. All Contracting Parties shall endeavour to permit the transit and transport, free of charge, of such relief consignments on their way to occupied territories".

[254] ECOSOC 'Assistance in cases of natural disaster' Res 1546 (XLIX) (30 July 1970) § 6.

[255] UNGA Res 39/367 'Draft Convention on Expediting the Delivery of Emergency Relief' (n 38) Article 1(f).

humanitarian assistance to those within affected states.[256] From this choice in word use, it is also apparent that not only individual third states provide assistance, but that (ad hoc) coalitions of third states are also called upon to aid the affected state. The ILC for its part, in its study of the protection of persons in the event of disaster, has also considered the possibility of third states partaking in emergency assistance.[257] Tasks for an assisting third state are also considered by Macalister-Smith in his International Guidelines for Humanitarian Assistance Operations,[258] as well as seen in the San Remo Principles[259] and the 2003 Bruges Resolution.[260] The Mohonk Criteria on the other hand use the UN formulation of the 'international community' as a whole,[261] while the IFRC in its 2007 IDRL Guidelines considers that the assisting state may make use of civil or military components for its humanitarian assistance, although the military component is recommended to be limited in use.[262] Given the variety and proliferation of actors involved in the provision of humanitarian assistance, the IFRC also considers the quite effective formulation of 'assisting actor', in order to encompass all possible contributors to the provision of humanitarian assistance.[263]

Thus, from the above it is clear that amongst the providers of humanitarian assistance, several distinct actors can be discerned. First and foremost, the affected state has a large and primary role in the provision of assistance. Furthermore, international organisations amongst which primarily the ICRC and IFRC, the UN and the EU play a large role, as well as (national) NGOs. Lastly, third states either individually, through an (ad hoc) coalition or the international community as a whole can be considered, and are on occasion also called upon, for the provision of

---

[256] See for instance UNGA Res 49/169 (23 December 1994) UN Doc A/RES/49/169 § 11; and UNSC Res 1674 (28 April 2006) UN Doc S/RES/1674 § 13. For the current rights and duties of third states in the provision of humanitarian assistance, see Chapter 7.

[257] ILC Doc A/CN.4/590, Protection of persons in the event of disasters, Memorandum by the Secretariat, § 250, 11 December 2007.

[258] Macalister-Smith' 'International Guidelines for Humanitarian Assistance Operations (n 79) Article 2(c): "'Assisting State or organization' means the State or organization providing humanitarian assistance at the request or with the consent of the receiving state".

[259] Guiding Principles on the Right to Humanitarian Assistance' (n 80) Principle 5.

[260] Bruges Resolution 'Humanitarian Assistance' (2 September 2003) (n 82) Article I(5): "'Assisting State or organization' means the State or intergovernmental organization, or impartial international or national non-governmental organization which organizes, provides or distributes humanitarian assistance".

[261] 'The Mohonk Criteria for Humanitarian Assistance in Complex Emergencies', (1995) (n 176) II.4: "Where the government or other authority is unable or manifestly unwilling to provide life-sustaining aid, the international community has the right and obligation to protect and provide relief to affected and threatened civilian populations in conformity with the principles of international law".

[262] IFRC IDRL Guidelines (2007) (n 223) Article 2(9): "'Assisting State' means a State providing disaster relief or initial recovery assistance whether through civil or military components". See also the Annotations to the IDRL Guidelines, 26 October 2007, comments to Article 2(9) at p. 11.

[263] Ibid Article 2(14): "'Assisting actor' means any assisting humanitarian organization, assisting State, foreign individual, foreign private company providing charitable relief or other foreign entity responding to a disaster on the territory of the affected State or sending in-kind
or cash donations". See also the Annotations to the IDRL Guidelines, 26 October 2007, comments to Article 2(14) at p. 13.

humanitarian assistance. The legal framework of the exact rights and duties of such third parties in the provision of humanitarian assistance will be discussed in Chapters 7 and 8.

2.4 Conclusion

This Chapter has served the purpose of providing the foundation upon which an analysis of the current legal framework regarding humanitarian assistance can be based. Before the analysis can take place, it has been relevant to look into the historical development of humanitarian assistance, from Henri Dunant's efforts following the battle at Solferino, to the large-scale efforts today of many international organisations.[264] From this historical overview, the original division and separation of the provision of assistance in times of conflict or occupation and the provision of assistance in times of natural disaster was put in perspective.[265] Following the brief historical overview, a discussion of the notion of humanitarian assistance has taken place, taking into account the various definitions provided by a large variety of (legal) sources, primarily flowing from several institutions and soft law resolutions. A clear, legally binding definition is currently still lacking. For the purpose of this research, a definition of humanitarian assistance has been proposed, which will be used throughout. This definition determines that such assistance, in order to be categorised as humanitarian, must 'consist of food, medicine, shelter and logistics for its provision; for urgent purposes and which is indispensable to the survival of the people at whom it is aimed'.[266] Important elements of this definition of humanitarian assistance are the *urgency* of the need and the *indispensable* nature of the assistance.

Having defined humanitarian assistance, the manner in which it may be provided to be considered 'humanitarian' in nature has also been explored, upon which it has been concluded that such assistance must at least be in conformity with the principles of humanity, neutrality and impartiality.[267] These three principles are embraced by not only the ICRC and the UN, but also various other relevant actors in the field. In particular the ICJ has contributed to the reinforcement of the notion of humanity, as well as the assertion that the provision of assistance must occur in a non-discriminatory manner. The principle of independence remains an important aspect of the deliverance of humanitarian assistance, yet its definition and content vary amongst actors in the field.[268]

With clearer picture of the notion of humanitarian assistance and the manner in which it should be provided set in place, this Chapter has proceeded to discuss the various actors involved in the provision and receipt of humanitarian assistance. The subjects, or recipients, of such assistance have been found to be civilians, including

[264] Section 2.2.1 Historical Development.
[265] Ibid.
[266] Section 2.2.2 Defining Humanitarian Assistance.
[267] Section 2.2.3 The Principles for the Delivery of Assistance.
[268] Section 2.2.3.5. Other Perspectives on the Principles for Providing Humanitarian Assistance.

vulnerable groups such as refugees and IDPs.[269] Providers of humanitarian assistance can be divided into several categories. Firstly, a primary role can be discerned for the 'affected state' or authorities in the affected territory. Other actors include international organisations such as the ICRC and IFRC, the UN and the EU. Furthermore, whilst NGOs are of great importance to the deliverance of assistance, they are too numerous to be discussed independently. Lastly, third states, be it individually or through an (ad hoc) coalition are recognised as providers of assistance to those in need.[270] It remains relevant to note that although many of these actors (in particular NGOs) have developed instruments, such as guidelines and resolutions that have been used in this Chapter with regard to certain definitional issues, these instruments do not have independent legal standing.[271] Yet, as they are reflective of the perspective of the various actors in the field, they have proven relevant in the discussion of these actors and the manner in which these actors perceive humanitarian assistance and its provision. The legal framework to be discussed in this research will however not lean upon such instruments.

Having provided an overview of the history of the provision of humanitarian assistance and the development of the involvement of various actors, as well as having offered a new definition of humanitarian assistance and discussed the manner in which it must be provided, the subsequent Chapter will address the various circumstances in which humanitarian assistance may be needed. Following on from this, the assessment of the scope of application also warrants a discussion on the applicable law in these circumstances.

---

[269] Section 2.3.1 Recipients of Humanitarian Assistance.
[270] Section 2.3.2 Providers of Humanitarian Assistance.
[271] See Section 1.4.2 Secondary Sources for a more in depth discussion of the concept of 'soft law' and legal scholarship, as well as their role as potential source of law.

CHAPTER 3
HUMANITARIAN ASSISTANCE: ITS SCOPE OF APPLICATION AND THE APPLICABLE LAW

The conflict in Syria (starting 2011) has often been labeled a 'humanitarian crisis' by the international media. OCHA provides shocking figures, stating that half the population of Syria; 10.8 million, out of 21.4 million citizens, are in need of aid. A further 6.4 million are classified as IDPs. OCHA states:

> "An estimated 2.5 million people in Aleppo City continue to be affected by water shortages since the breakdown of the main water network on 2 June. Despite negotiations, technical experts and humanitarian actors have not gained access to the site near the Suleiman al Halabi pumping station to conduct necessary repairs".

Yet, what circumstances make a humanitarian crisis, and which don't qualify as such? When a crisis is established, what law must be applied? This chapter will address the applicable legal framework upon ascertaining the notion of a humanitarian crisis.[1]

3.1 Introduction

Humanitarian assistance as a concept has been defined to include the provision of food, medicine, shelter and logistics, for urgent purposes and aimed at the survival of those in need. Thus, humanitarian assistance is confined to *emergency* situations, in which civilians are in need of receiving such aid. This Chapter will address which particular circumstances can be considered such emergency situations, warranting the provision of assistance. As such, the circumstances of armed conflict, occupation and (natural) disaster in which humanitarian assistance becomes a factor, are explored. Furthermore, the 'umbrella' notion of a 'humanitarian crisis' is addressed, as a concept to encompass these individual circumstances. Indeed, whilst situations of conflict or disaster are factual, they invoke legal consequences through the applicability of several fields of law containing provisions regarding the delivery of humanitarian assistance. In the event of a natural disaster, general public international law and human rights law are of relevance, yet in times of armed conflict and occupation, international humanitarian law will also have to be considered. Thus, the scope of application of humanitarian assistance must be complemented with an analysis of the relationship between the various applicable fields of law that are of relevance in the event of a humanitarian crisis.

[1] 'Humanitarian Bulletin Syria' Issue 49, UN OCHA (19 Jun – 16 July 2014) 1-2.

3.2 The Circumstances that may Require Humanitarian Assistance

This Section addresses the various circumstances in which the delivery of humanitarian assistance can be necessary, given their magnitude, grave nature or overwhelming impact. The international legal regulation of humanitarian assistance commenced with its regulation in times of occupation, leading to its regulation in other circumstances too.[2] Given the change in warfare over the past decades resulting in a vast increase of non-international armed conflicts, as well as keeping in line with chronology where conflict often precedes occupation, this Section firstly addresses armed conflict. Subsequently the circumstance of occupation will be addressed, to determine in which situations humanitarian assistance may be necessary and lastly (natural) disasters are discussed. To consider the scope of application of the legal framework concerning humanitarian assistance, the various circumstances in which it takes place must be considered. The regulation *of the provision of humanitarian assistance* has followed the *general* legal regulation of the various circumstances such as conflict and disaster, in which aid is provided. Indeed, humanitarian assistance need only be provided when it has been ascertained that a humanitarian crisis is taking place as part of the factual circumstances of conflict, occupation or natural disaster. Upon such an assessment, no international legal dispute will exist concerning the status of the situation and thereby the legality of the provision of humanitarian assistance.[3] Such establishments are furthermore of relevance in relation to the role of the affected state sovereign, that has the primary role in the provision of assistance when such aid may be needed. The determination of such a crisis is often assessed by the sovereign itself but, as seen below, can also be established in other manners should the affected state be dismissive with regard to the provision of aid.

3.2.1 Defining an Armed Conflict

A primary circumstance potentially warranting the provision of humanitarian assistance, is traditionally an armed conflict.[4] The legal qualification of this immediately enables the provision of assistance to take place within two distinct circumstances; namely an *international* armed conflict and a *non-international* armed conflict.[5] Although increasingly the legal distinction between the two types

[2] Heike Spieker, 'The Right to Give and Receive Humanitarian Assistance', in HJ Heintze & A Zwitter (eds), *Humanitarian Assistance and International Law* (Springer 2011) 12.

[3] See in this regard Section 8.2.1 Circumstances of Denial or Obstruction: Determining a Humanitarian Crisis.

[4] It is relevant to note that each law has its scope of applicability, divided into *ratione materiae, ratione personae, ratione loci and ratione temporis*. For the purposes of this research however, these notions will not be examined individually. In so far as the scope of application of a certain law is relevant to the application of provisions of humanitarian assistance, this research will address them *ad hoc* in the following Sections.

[5] Much has been written on the concept of armed conflict. Therefore, this research will only briefly establish the legal concepts of an 'international armed conflict' and a 'non-international armed

of conflict is being discussed,[6] both will be defined separately for the purpose of this research. Firstly, regarding the concept of an international armed conflict, Common Article 2 of the Geneva Conventions notes:

> "In addition to the provisions which shall be implemented in peacetime, the present Convention shall apply to all cases of declared war or of any other armed conflict which may arise between two or more of the High Contracting Parties, even if the state of war is not recognized by one of them. The Convention shall also apply to all cases of partial or total occupation of the territory of a High Contracting Party, even if the said occupation meets with no armed resistance. Although one of the Powers in conflict may not be a party to the present Convention, the Powers who are parties thereto shall remain bound by it in their mutual relations. They shall furthermore be bound by the Convention in relation to the said Power, if the latter accepts and applies the provisions thereof".

With the Geneva Conventions, a declaration of war is no longer necessary for the rules of international humanitarian law, as laid down in these Conventions, to become applicable.[7] To avoid states' arguments that international humanitarian law is not applicable in certain instances due to the fact that the state of war has not been recognised, the Conventions become applicable from the very moment that hostilities take place.[8] However, the Conventions do not define this notion of 'armed conflict', nor does any other treaty, and Pictet notes in the *Commentary* that any intervention of armed forces between two states can be considered an armed conflict, regardless of length or intensity.[9] Additional Protocol I has furthermore elaborated that an armed conflict may include those situations in which a people fight against 'colonial domination, alien occupation and racist régimes' in the

conflict'. For further reading, see amongst others Robert Kolb and Richard Hyde, *An Introduction to the International Law of Armed Conflicts* (Hart 2008); Anthony Cullen, *The Concept of Non-International Armed Conflict in International Humanitarian Law* (Cambridge University Press 2010); and Sylvain Vité, 'Typology of armed conflicts in international humanitarian law: legal concepts and actual situations', (2009) 91 *International Review of the Red Cross* 873, 69 – 94. See also the International Law Association, 'Final Report on the Meaning of Armed Conflict in International Law' of the Committee on the Use of Force (Hague Conference 2010).

[6] Ibid ILA 'Final Report on the Meaning of Armed Conflict in International Law' 8-9. As this research will focus for a large part on the *lex lata*, it remains important to distinguish both types of armed conflict, and the relevant provisions regarding humanitarian assistance related thereto.

[7] Jean Pictet, *Commentary on the Geneva Conventions of 12 August 1949 Volumes I-IV* (International Committee of the Red Cross 1952-1959), Volume IV Commentary GC IV Article 2, 20. See also Frits Kalshoven & Liesbeth Zegveld, *Constraints on the Waging of War: An Introduction to International Humanitarian Law* (Cambridge University Press 2011) 30-31.

[8] Pictet, *Commentary on the Geneva Conventions of 12 August 1949* (n 7).

[9] Ibid Article 2, 20-21. The Commentary states: "Any difference arising between two States and leading to the intervention of armed forces is an armed conflict within the meaning of Article 2, even if one of the Parties denies the existence of a state of war. It makes no difference how long the conflict lasts, or how much slaughter takes place. The respect due to human personality is not measured by the number of victims. Nor, incidentally, does the application of the Convention necessarily involve the intervention of cumbrous machinery. It all depends on circumstances".

exercise of their right to self-determination, as opposed to viewing them as a non-international armed conflict.[10]

For a definition of a non-international armed conflict, Common Article 3 of the Geneva Conventions is a starting point. Common Article 3 notes that its provisions are applicable:

> "In the case of armed conflict not of an international character occurring in the territory of one of the High Contracting Parties".[11]

Article 3 follows with the declaration that it is applicable to 'each party' to the conflict, thereby encompassing non-state actors fighting against the sovereign. From this text, it is clear that Common Article 3 distinguishes itself from the abovementioned international conflicts, as well as that it presupposed the existence of an armed conflict. A clear definition of such a conflict was not to be reached during the drafting phase on 1949. The Commentary, while considering that Common Article 3 should receive the widest possible scope of application, submits a list of conditions that may be considered for a non-international armed conflict.[12]

---

[10] Article 1 AP I states: "The High Contracting Parties undertake to respect and to ensure respect for this Protocol in all circumstances. In cases not covered by this Protocol or by other international agreements, civilians and combatants remain under the protection and authority of the principles of international law derived from established custom, from the principles of humanity and from the dictates of public conscience. This Protocol, which supplements the Geneva Conventions of 12 August 1949 for the protection of war victims, shall apply in the situations referred to in Article 2 common to those Conventions. The situations referred to in the preceding paragraph include armed conflicts in which peoples are fighting against colonial domination and alien occupation and against racist régimes in the exercise of their right of self-determination, as enshrined in the Charter of the United Nations and the Declaration on Principles of International Law concerning Friendly Relations and Co-operation among States in accordance with the Charter of the United Nations".

[11] The full text of Common Article 3 of the Geneva Conventions states: "In the case of armed conflict not of an international character occurring in the territory of one of the High Contracting Parties, each Party to the conflict shall be bound to apply, as a minimum, the following provisions: (1) Persons taking no active part in the hostilities, including members of armed forces who have laid down their arms and those placed ' hors de combat ' by sickness, wounds, detention, or any other cause, shall in all circumstances be treated humanely, without any adverse distinction founded on race, colour, religion or faith, sex, birth or wealth, or any other similar criteria. To this end, the following acts are and shall remain prohibited at any time and in any place whatsoever with respect to the above-mentioned persons: (a) violence to life and person, in particular murder of all kinds, mutilation, cruel treatment and torture; (b) taking of hostages; (c) outrages upon personal dignity, in particular humiliating and degrading treatment; (d) the passing of sentences and the carrying out of executions without previous judgment pronounced by a regularly constituted court, affording all the judicial guarantees which are recognized as indispensable by civilized peoples. (2) The wounded and sick shall be collected and cared for. An impartial humanitarian body, such as the International Committee of the Red Cross, may offer its services to the Parties to the conflict. The Parties to the conflict should further endeavour to bring into force, by means of special agreements, all or part of the other provisions of the present Convention. The application of the preceding provisions shall not affect the legal status of the Parties to the conflict".

[12] Pictet, *Commentary on the Geneva Conventions of 12 August 1949* (n 7) Common Article 3, 35-36 stating: "1. That the Party in revolt against the de jure Government possesses an organized military force, an authority responsible for its acts, acting within a determinate territory and having the means of respecting and ensuring respect for the Convention. 2. That the legal Government is obliged to have

Furthermore, Additional Protocol II (AP II) must be considered, which states in its primary Article:

> "This Protocol, which develops and supplements Article 3 common to the Geneva Conventions of 12 August 1949 without modifying its existing conditions of application, shall apply to all armed conflicts which are not covered by Article 1 of the Protocol Additional to the Geneva Conventions of 12 August 1949, and relating to the Protection of Victims of International Armed Conflicts (Protocol I) and which take place in the territory of a High Contracting Party between its armed forces and dissident armed forces or other organized armed groups which, under responsible command, exercise such control over a part of its territory as to enable them to carry out sustained and concerted military operations and to implement this Protocol. 2. This Protocol shall not apply to situations of internal disturbances and tensions, such as riots, isolated and sporadic acts of violence and other acts of a similar nature, as not being armed conflicts".[13]

This text is considered to set a higher threshold than Common Article 3, which unlike large parts of AP II has a customary international law status.[14] It must be noted that (internal) disturbances or clashes that do not meet the threshold of an armed conflict,[15] can be distinguished based on their intensity and level of organisation.[16] Protocol II has, both due to its higher threshold and applicability only to state parties, excluded more instances than Common Article 3 which holds customary status.[17] AP II is applicable, as stated in Article 1, only to those non-international armed conflicts that take place between a state party and 'dissident

---

recourse to the regular military forces against insurgents organized as military and in possession of a part of the national territory. 3. (a) That the de jure Government has recognized the insurgents as belligerents; or (b) That it has claimed for itself the rights of a belligerent; or (c) That it has accorded the insurgents recognition as belligerents for the purposes only of the present Convention; or (d) That the dispute has been admitted to the agenda of the Security Council or the General Assembly of the United Nations as being a threat to international peace, a breach of the peace, or an act of aggression. 4. (a) That the insurgents have an organization purporting to have the characteristics of a State.(b) That the insurgent civil authority exercises de facto authority over persons within a determinate portion of the national territory. (c) That the armed forces act under the direction of an organized authority and are prepared to observe the ordinary laws of war. (d) That the insurgent civil authority agrees to be bound by the provisions of the Convention. The above criteria are useful as a means of distinguishing a genuine armed conflict from a mere act of banditry or an unorganized and short-lived insurrection". It must be noted that these conditions are not considered to be comprehensive or ultimate, see in that regard outside of the *Commentary* itself also *Prosecutor v. Fatmir Limaj, Haradin Bala, Isak Musliu*, (Judgment Trial Chamber II) IT-03-66-T (30 November 2005) § 85-86 and ILA 'Final Report on the Meaning of Armed Conflict in International Law' (n 5)20.

[13] Article 1 Additional Protocol II to the Geneva Conventions, 1977 (Additional Protocol II or AP II)

[14] Yves Sandoz, Christophe Swinarski & Bruno Zimmermann (eds) *Commentary on the Additional Protocols of 8 June 1977 to the Geneva Conventions of 12 August 1949, Protocol I and II (*International Committee of the Red Cross 1987*)* Protocol II Article 1, 1348. See also ILA Committee on the Use of Force final report p12.

[15] Ibid *Commentary to the Additional Protocols*.

[16] *Prosecutor v. Tadić a.k.a "Dule"* (Judgment Trial Chamber) IT-94-1-T (7 May 1997) § 562. See also ILA 'Final Report on the Meaning of Armed Conflict in International Law' (n 5) 28.

[17] Sandoz, Swinarski & Zimmermann *Commentary to the Additional Protocols* (n 14) Protocol II Article 1, 1349.

armed forces or other organised armed groups which, under responsible command, exercise such control over a part of its territory as to enable them to carry out sustained and concerted military operations and to implement this Protocol'. This allows for a second category of non-international armed conflicts to be discerned, namely when a level of 'control' is reached by the armed groups within a state.

More recently the International Criminal Tribunal for the former Yugoslavia (ICTY) has also given a concrete definition of an armed conflict in the well-known *Tadić*-decision, stating that:

> "*An armed conflict exists whenever there is a resort to armed force between States or protracted armed violence between governmental authorities and organized armed groups or between such groups within a State.* International humanitarian law applies from the initiation of such armed conflicts and extends beyond the cessation of hostilities until a general conclusion of peace is reached; or, in the case of internal conflicts, a peaceful settlement is achieved. Until that moment, international humanitarian law continues to apply in the whole territory of the warring States or, in the case of internal conflicts, the whole territory under the control of a party, whether or not actual combat takes place there".[18]

With regard to an international armed conflict, the ICTY considered the length and intensity of such a conflict, deliberating that the Geneva Conventions contain language that suggests their application beyond strictly during the existence of armed violence.[19] Such is of relevance to the provision of assistance: aid may be needed for a civilian population that is itself not subject to hostilities, but may have been cut off from the outside world, or fled to remote areas. The ICTY furthermore considered the 'geographical scope' of international armed conflicts, with regard to the application of the Conventions. The Chamber concluded that a distinction can be made between certain provisions of the Geneva Conventions that can be limited to areas of direct hostilities, whilst other provisions, amongst which those pertaining to the protection of civilians are not as limited and may apply to the entire territory of the states that are in conflict.[20] Indeed, the provisions pertaining to the provision of humanitarian assistance relate to the protection of civilians. The ICTY reasoned so in referral to Article 6(2) of GC IV, which declares that the Convention remains applicable until the 'general close of military operations'[21] and

---

[18] *Prosecutor v. Tadić a.k.a "Dule"* (Appeals Chamber Decision on the Defence motion for Interlocutory Appeal on Jurisdiction) IT-94-1-AR72 (2 October 1995) §70 [*Emphasis added EEK*].

[19] Ibid § 67.

[20] Ibid § 68.

[21] Article 6 GC IV states: "The present Convention shall apply from the outset of any conflict or occupation mentioned in Article 2. In the territory of Parties to the conflict, the application of the present Convention shall cease on the general close of military operations. In the case of occupied territory, the application of the present Convention shall cease one year after the general close of military operations; however, the Occupying Power shall be bound, for the duration of the occupation, to the extent that such Power exercises the functions of government in such territory, by the provisions of the following Articles of the present Convention: 1 to 12, 27, 29 to 34, 47, 49, 51, 52, 53, 59, 61 to 77, 143. Protected persons whose release, repatriation or re-establishment may take place after such dates shall meanwhile continue to benefit by the present Convention".

argued that a stricter reading of the Article and similar ones, would defeat the very rationale behind GC III and GC IV.[22] The Geneva Conventions after all, as part of humanitarian law, aim to protect those caught in conflict, which is also what the provision of humanitarian assistance attempts to do. Article 6 of the Fourth Geneva Convention furthermore notes that the Convention shall apply 'from the outset of any conflict'.[23] The line of reasoning of the ICTY also follows the official *Commentary*, which remarks in relation to the protection of civilians, that the Fourth Convention should be applied immediately once a civilian population comes into contact with foreign armed troops.[24] Thus, the application of the Geneva Conventions can be considered to commence with the *establishment* of an international armed conflict, and the application of provisions in relation to the civilian population can be established in regard to an entire territory. Thus, humanitarian law provides different levels of protection to those in need according to the specific category of armed conflict in which persons in need of aid find themselves.

Yet whereas the application of AP II requires for one of the *parties* to be a state party to the Conventions and Common Article 3 alternatively requires for the *territory* to be that of a state party, in recent years armed conflicts amongst armed groups in so-called 'failed' states have provided *another* type of non-international armed conflict. With a lack of sovereign authority, these conflicts often do not meet the threshold of AP II (also AP II does not have universal application, as discussed above), nor do they sometimes fit the framework of Common Article 3. Indeed in internal strife, a common defence for the non-application of international humanitarian law is the argument that no armed conflict exists, or that no responsible sovereign may be in place. Such circumstances, regardless of their classification, however may warrant the provision of assistance, as a crisis for a civilian population may be taking place. Humanitarian assistance however continues to be a need for all those in circumstances of crisis, regardless of the classification of the conflict. Whether or not a sovereign authority in a territory has indeed declared the existence of a conflict is therefore not necessary for the application of humanitarian law, and therefore also for the application of the provisions related to the delivery of humanitarian aid. This enhances the protection of those persons caught in circumstances where the affected state sovereign is unwilling or unable to provide aid.

---

[22] *Prosecutor v. Tadić a.k.a "Dule"* IT-94-1-AR72 (n 18) § 68. The Appeals Chamber here also referred to Article 3(b) of AP I, which states that: "Without prejudice to the provisions which are applicable at all times: (...) (b) the application of the Conventions and of this Protocol shall cease, in the territory of Parties to the conflict, on the general close of military operations and, in the case of occupied territories, on the termination of the occupation, except, in either circumstance, for those persons whose final release, repatriation or re-establishment takes place thereafter. These persons shall continue to benefit from the relevant provisions of the Conventions and of this Protocol until their final release, repatriation or re-establishment".

[23] Article 6 GC IV (n 21).

[24] Pictet, *Commentary on the Geneva Conventions of 12 August 1949* (n 7) Article 6, 59.

3.2.2 Armed Conflicts and the Provision of Humanitarian Assistance

When applied to the provision of assistance, the immediate application of the Conventions and their Protocols means that those provisions within humanitarian law related to the provision of emergency aid, become applicable upon establishment of the armed conflict. The mere existence of armed violence reaching the threshold of an armed conflict leads to the applicability of international humanitarian law and thereby also the Geneva Conventions. From the above, it can be concluded that the actual establishment of the existence of an armed conflict remains a factual determination.

Although the *Commentary* suggests a wide application of Common Article 3, with regard to non-international armed conflicts, the *Tadić* judgment is stricter in its interpretation. In its much-cited definition of a non-international armed conflict, the ICTY considers the need for a certain intensity and duration as well as a certain organisation of armed groups, for a situation to amount to a non-international armed conflict. The ICTY confirmed this to be an exhaustive list, as it declared the purpose of the armed forces' violence to be irrelevant.[25] As with an international armed conflict, the Trial Chamber in the *Tadić* case equally observed a broad scope of application with regard to time and territory. In referral to Article 2 of AP II, the ICTY concluded that the application should not be limited to the 'actual hostilities', nor to a limited geographical scope.[26] Article 2 of Additional Protocol II itself reads equally broad that it is applicable to all persons 'affected by an armed conflict'.[27] Thus, with regard to the provision of humanitarian assistance, it can be concluded that once the threshold set by AP II of a situation of non-international armed conflict is met, all people *affected* by the conflict are to be protected by the provisions of AP II, for the purposes of the delivery of humanitarian aid.

From the above, it remains clear that establishing what entails an armed conflict, be it international or non-international, remains a factual, objective determination. As such, establishing whether a situation amounts to an armed conflict, thereby invoking the application of international humanitarian law; amongst which the provisions in relation to humanitarian assistance, remains to be done on a case-by-case basis. Yet, once this conflict is established, it can be said that for an international armed conflict, the provisions regarding the protection of civilians

---

[25] *Prosecutor v. Fatmir Limaj, Haradin Bala, Isak Musliu*, (Judgment Trial Chamber II) IT-03-66-T (30 November 2005) § 170: "the determination of the existence of an armed conflict is based solely on two criteria: the intensity of the conflict and organisation of the parties, the purpose of the armed forces to engage in acts of violence or also achieve some further objective is, therefore, irrelevant".

[26] *Prosecutor v. Tadić a.k.a "Dule"* IT-94-1-AR72 (n 18) § 69.

[27] Article 2 AP II states: "1. This Protocol shall be applied without any adverse distinction founded on race, colour, sex, language, religion or belief, political or other opinion, national or social origin, wealth, birth or other status, or on any other similar criteria (hereinafter referred to as "adverse distinction") to all persons affected by an armed conflict as defined in Article 1. 2. At the end of the armed conflict, all the persons who have been deprived of their liberty or whose liberty has been restricted for reasons related to such conflict, as well as those deprived of their liberty or whose liberty is restricted after the conflict for the same reasons, shall enjoy the protection of Articles 5 and 6 until the end of such deprivation or restriction of liberty".

through the provision of humanitarian assistance can be considered applicable as soon as an armed conflict exists, even if said civilians are not in the direct vicinity of hostilities. The absence of hostilities from a specific area does indeed not automatically lead to the inference that persons may not be suffering from the consequences of the armed conflict and be in need of humanitarian assistance. Furthermore, regarding a non-international armed conflict, the temporal scope is equally wide, as well as the geographical scope, with Article 2 of AP II referring to all those 'affected' by the armed conflict.[28] Problematic to the provision of assistance in times of non-international armed conflict however remains the fact that a level of control by armed groups is needed in the conflict, for the application of AP II, which contains further protection of civilians and their access to humanitarian assistance than the framework of Article 3. A subsequent issue remains the lack of universal applicability of AP II. Furthermore, although international humanitarian law may not be applicable in circumstances that do not amount to armed conflicts, such as instances of civil unrest, these circumstances may warrant the provision of humanitarian assistance. As such, this research recommends that it is necessary to regard the provision of humanitarian assistance from one overarching perspective, rather than looking into the various circumstances separately.[29] When addressing the provision of assistance from the needs of persons, rather than from the perspective of the factual circumstances, greater protection may be provided.

3.2.3 Defining Occupation

Whereas conflict and natural disaster make up the majority of circumstances in which humanitarian assistance is needed, the law pertaining to such assistance is well developed in times of occupation, due to the creation of the Geneva Conventions in the aftermath of World War II. As a result of this existing framework, it is necessary to also address occupation as a legal concept. 'Occupation' was first elaborately regulated in the 1907 Hague 'Convention respecting the Laws and Customs of War on Land' (1907 Hague Convention).[30] A first definition was provided by the Institute of International Law,[31] which in 1880 stated in its 'Laws of War on Land':

> "Territory is regarded as occupied when, as the consequence of invasion by hostile forces, the State to which it belongs has ceased, in fact, to exercise its ordinary authority therein, and the invading State is alone in a position to maintain order there. The limits

[28] For further reading on the notion of a non-international armed conflict, see Lindsay Moir, *The Law of Internal Armed Conflict* (Cambridge University Press 2002).
[29] See Section 3.3.3. Defining a Humanitarian Crisis for the definition of a humanitarian crisis as overarching concept.
[30] 1907 Hague 'Convention respecting the Laws and Customs of War on Land' (opened for signature 18 October 1907, entered into force 26 January 1910).
[31] See for information on the Institute of International Law Chapter 2 (n 81).

> within which this state of affairs exists determine the extent and duration of the occupation”.[32]

The first actual codification of the concept of occupation was provided in Article 42 of the annex to the 1907 Hague Convention, ‘Regulations concerning the Laws and Customs of War on Land’ (1907 Hague Regulations):

> “Territory is considered occupied when it is actually placed under the authority of the hostile army. The occupation extends only to the territory where such authority has been established and can be exercised”.[33]

Over time, the Regulations annexed to the 1907 Hague Convention have become accepted as norms of customary international law.[34] Two cumulative conditions can be determined from this definition: namely that an authority has been established, and that the actual exercise of such an authority can take place.[35] With two World Wars still in mind at the time of drafting, Common Article 2(2) of the 1949 Geneva Conventions, although not providing a definition, adds to the aforementioned by stating that the Geneva Conventions are applicable in cases of partial or total occupation of a territory of a High Contracting Party, even if such occupation is not met with armed resistance.[36] Article 154 of the Fourth Geneva Convention furthermore states that the Geneva Convention is ‘supplementary’ to the Hague Regulations, and thereby also to its definition of the notion of occupation.[37] The Additional Protocols, adapting to the developments in the past few decades, do not focus on occupation but rather on forms of armed conflict. As such, the Geneva

---

[32] Article 41 of ‘The Laws of War on Land’ (9 September 1880) Institute of International Law.

[33] Article 42 ‘Regulations concerning the Laws and Customs of War on Land’ of the Hague ‘Convention respecting the Laws and Customs of War on Land’.

[34] ‘International Military Tribunal Nuremberg Judgment and Sentences’ (1947), 41 *American Journal of International Law,* 1, 248-249. This acknowledgement was also reiterated by the ICJ in its Legal Consequences of the Construction of a Wall in the Occupied Palestinian Territory, Advisory Opinion, I.C.J. Reports 2004, p. 136, § 78 and 89.

[35] Yoram Dinstein, *The International Law of Belligerent Occupation* (Cambridge University Press 2009) 42.

[36] Article 2 common to the four Geneva Conventions of 1949 provides: “(1)In addition to the provisions which shall be implemented in peacetime, the present Convention shall apply to all cases of declared war or of any other armed conflict which may arise between two or more of the High Contracting Parties, even if the state of war is not recognized by one of them. (2) The Convention shall also apply to all cases of partial or total occupation of the territory of a High Contracting Party, even if the said occupation meets with no armed resistance. (3) Although one of the Powers in conflict may not be a party to the present Convention, the Powers who are parties thereto shall remain bound by it in their mutual relations. They shall furthermore be bound by the Convention in relation to the said Power, if the latter accepts and applies the provisions thereof”.

[37] Article 154 of the Fourth Geneva Convention states: “In the relations between the Powers who are bound by the Hague Conventions respecting the Laws and Customs of War on Land, whether that of July 29, 1899, or that of October 18, 1907, and who are parties to the present Convention, this last Convention shall be supplementary to Sections II and III of the Regulations annexed to the above-mentioned Conventions of The Hague”. See also *Prosecutor v. Mladen Naletilić, aka Tuta & Vinko Martinović, aka “Štela* (Trial Judgment) IT-98-34-T (31 March 2003) § 215.

Conventions – created in the aftermath of World War II – remain the last codifications relating to the concept of occupation.

From the compilation of the abovementioned definitions, several elements can be derived. Firstly, some form of authority must be established which can be exercised, secondly this authority must cover parts of or the whole territory and lastly, occupation is not dependent on having met armed resistance.[38] The notion of the 'exercise of authority or control', which is relevant in the discussion of the provision of humanitarian assistance, has been subject to multiple distinct interpretations.[39] The ICJ has furthermore clarified in its *Case Concerning Armed Activities on the Territory of the Congo* that authority not only 'can be exercised' as intended by the Hague Regulations but that it in fact *be* exercised.[40] The Court furthermore noted that in order to establish the exercise of authority, it is necessary for groups or movements to be placed 'under the control' of the intervening state, whereas the establishment of administrative control in a certain area – *in casu* the Kisangani Airport – does not suffice to be considered an occupying power in the sense of Article 42 of the 1907 Hague Regulations.[41] The actual amount of control necessary to determine whether occupation indeed is established has been addressed on various occasions by the ICTY, which like the ICJ in later years, concluded that the law of occupation only applies to those areas actually under control of the occupying power.[42] Indeed, the establishment is subject to a factual determination and it is suggested that the commencement of occupation at least requires a level of control that is indeed 'actually exercised'. The theoretical viewpoint that authority 'can be exercised' is problematic, as it will be very difficult to establish after the fact, whereas the factual 'exercise' of control can be subjected to proof.

---

[38] Daniel Thürer, 'Current challenges to the law of occupation', Speech delivered to the International Committee of the Red Cross, 6th Bruges Colloquium, 20-21 October 2005, p. 4.

[39] For a further discussion on the beginning of occupation and the element of control, see Eyal Benvenisti, *The International Law of Occupation* (Oxford University Press 2012) and Dinstein, *The International Law of Belligerent Occupation* (n 35). See for an alternative view also Michael Siegrist, 'The Functional Beginning of Belligerent Occupation' (2011) 7 *eCahiers de l' Institut* (Graduate Institute Geneva). For the purpose of this research, a focus will lie on the establishment of a certain level of control, also relevant to the provision of humanitarian assistance.

[40] *Armed Activities on the Territory of the Congo* (Democratic Republic of the Congo v. Uganda), Judgment, I.C.J. Reports 2005, p. 168, § 173. See also, ibid, Siegrist.

[41] Ibid, *Armed Activities on the Territory of the Congo* § 177.

[42] *Prosecutor v. Mladen Naletilić, aka Tuta & Vinko Martinović, aka "Štela* IT-98-34-T (n 37) § 214-218. The Trial Chamber provided the following guidelines for the determination of the establishment of authority: "[...] the occupying power must be in a position to substitute its own authority for that of the occupied authorities, which must have been rendered incapable of functioning publicly; the enemy's forces have surrendered, been defeated or withdrawn. In this respect, battle areas may not be considered as occupied territory. However, sporadic local resistance, even successful, does not affect the reality of occupation; the occupying power has a sufficient force present, or the capacity to send troops within a reasonable time to make the authority of the occupying power felt; a temporary administration has been established over the territory; the occupying power has issued and enforced directions to the civilian population".

3.2.4 Occupation and the Provision of Humanitarian Assistance

The determination of commencement of occupation remains relevant in order to ascertain the applicability of the law containing provisions related to the delivery of emergency aid, as seen with regard to the start of an armed conflict. Other than in circumstances of conflict however, circumstances of occupation are fewer and further between. Moreover, when occupation *is* established, the need for humanitarian assistance today, as opposed to during World War II, may well be far less than its immediate need during conflict or in the aftermath of a (natural) disaster. In order to address this transition period from the law of conflict to the law of occupation, the ICTY determined that 'actual authority' of the occupying power may not be necessary, rather 'a state of occupation exists upon the falling of civilians into "the hands of the occupying power"'.[43] Similarly, according to the official *Commentary*, the protection of individuals under the Fourth Geneva Convention does not depend on the establishment of a state of occupation as defined in Article 42 of the 1907 Hague Regulations, but is immediately applicable as soon as these individuals are in contact with the Occupying Power.[44]

Yet, the Commentary's determination does not also assume that *all* obligations relating to occupation under the Geneva Convention become applicable at this early stage. Several provisions in the Geneva Conventions, amongst which relevantly those provisions related to humanitarian assistance, presuppose a certain duration of occupation before amounting to obligations for the occupier, rather than arising within the initial stages of invasion.[45] How long such a duration may be, is left unanswered. Thus, whereas the ICTY considers the Convention immediately applicable with regard to the protection of civilians, the Commentary distinguishes immediate applicability among certain provisions whilst others, relating to

---

[43] *Prosecutor v. Mladen Naletilić, aka Tuta & Vinko Martinović, aka "Štela* IT-98-34-T (n 37) § 221.

[44] Pictet, *Commentary on the Geneva Conventions of 12 August 1949* (n 7) Article 6, 60: "In all cases of occupation, whether carried out by force or without meeting any resistance, the Convention becomes applicable to individuals, i.e. to the protected persons, as they fall into the hands of the Occupying Power. It follows from this that the word "occupation" (…) has a wider meaning than it has in Article 42 of the Regulations annexed to the Fourth Hague Convention of 1907. So far as individuals are concerned, the application of the Fourth Geneva Convention does not depend upon the existence of a state of occupation within the meaning of the Article 42 referred to above. The relations between the civilian population of a territory and troops advancing into that territory, whether fighting or not, are governed by the present Convention. There is no intermediate period between what might be termed the invasion phase and the inauguration of a stable regime of occupation. Even a patrol which penetrates into enemy territory without any intention of staying there must respect the Conventions in its dealings with the civilians it meets. When it withdraws, for example, it cannot take civilians with it, for that would be contrary to Article 49 which prohibits the deportation or forcible transfer of persons from occupied territory. (…) The Convention is quite definite on this point: all persons who find themselves in the hands of a Party to the conflict or an Occupying Power of which they are not nationals are protected persons. No loophole is left."

[45] Ibid. See 6.5.4 Rights of Persons to Receive Assistance in Times of Occupation for a more in depth discussion with regard to provisions relating to a possible right to humanitarian assistance in times of occupation.

humanitarian assistance, may not be immediately invoked.[46] Similarly, this distinction was reiterated by the Eritrea-Ethiopia Claims Commission that stated:

> "The Commission also recognizes that not all of the obligations of Section III of Part III of Geneva Convention IV (the section that deals with occupied territories) can reasonably be applied to an armed force anticipating combat and present in an area for only a few days. Nevertheless, a State is obligated by the remainder of that Convention and by customary international humanitarian law to take appropriate measures to protect enemy civilians and civilian property present within areas under the control of its armed forces. Even in areas where combat is occurring, civilians and civilian objects cannot lawfully be made objects of attack".[47]

Although slightly more vague, this interpretation follows along the line of distinction suggested by Pictet, as it mentions 'a few days' presence as being insufficient for the application of all provisions. Furthermore, a more restrictive approach is put forward by several military manuals, suggesting that occupation can only exist if the occupying power has the level of authority and control needed to be able to fulfil all the obligations required of it by the law of occupation.[48] From the above, different approaches can be discerned with regard to the moment of commencement of occupation. This moment then determines the level of authority involved that is necessary for the establishment of the application of the law of occupation and the obligations resting upon the occupying power.[49] Again, whilst the determination of the state of occupation results in the applicability of legal rights and obligations, it remains factual and shall often occur after its establishment by for example the International Court of Justice.

For the purpose of this research centred around humanitarian assistance, it remains relevant to consider the approaches to the level of authority necessary to establish obligations upon the occupying power discussed above and to establish rights of civilians in the provision of humanitarian assistance. Whereas the provision of humanitarian assistance *could* be essential from the earliest possible stage, should persons be in such need, the Commentary's restrictive line of interpretation also concurs with the ICJ's *Armed Activities in Congo* Judgment, where the Court declared that the law of occupation becomes applicable upon the establishment *and exercise* of authority in a certain area.[50] Thus, it appears possible to suggest that some form of distinction can be considered between the application of the law of occupation in general, and the specific application of provisions relating to humanitarian assistance, amongst which Article 59 GC IV. Yet, legal uncertainty remains with such conclusions, as 'longer presence' or 'a few days' do

---

[46] Ibid.

[47] Eritrea-Ethiopia Claims Commission, *Western Front, Aerial Bombardment and Related Claims - Eritrea's Claims 1, 3, 5, 9-13, 14, 21, 25 & 26* (Partial Award of 19 December 2005), § 27.

[48] Thürer, 'Current challenges to the law of occupation' (n 38), 5.

[49] See 2.3.2 Providers of Humanitarian Assistance for an in depth discussion on the various actors involved in the provision of humanitarian assistance.

[50] ICJ, *Armed Activities on the Territory of the Congo* (n 40).

not clearly state at which point *exactly* the obligations arise for the occupying power to commence providing assistance if the situation calls for this.

In the past decades, states have been hesitant to be designated as occupying power, and not many circumstances are legally established as such to draw from.[51] The ICRC has – with a pragmatic view – therefore established that it adopts the 'maximalist' approach to factual circumstances on the ground which although risking a premature qualification of occupation, aims to extend the greatest protection possible to civilians.[52] Although pragmatic, the legal basis appears to be somewhat more confined, as a result of which it is questionable to what extent the ICRC's position finds legal support from others. If the definition of humanitarian assistance is taken into consideration, especially also considering the fact that its provision is connected to a situation of 'crisis', the viewpoint that immediate application of Article 59 occurs once the beginning of occupation is established, may be somewhat premature. Not only must the situation of occupation be thus, that it amounts to a humanitarian crisis, but an occupier can furthermore only be called upon to comply with Article 59 GC IV concerning assistance in times of occupation, if and when the amount of control established suffices. This threshold of control must be carefully distinguished from the amount of control necessary to establish the state of occupation, as less time may indeed be required for this latter establishment. Two distinct thresholds therefore exist. For the application of the provisions relevant to the supply of humanitarian assistance, a second threshold of control must be established, and a longer timeframe can be determined. Unfortunately the law remains somewhat unclear as to at which point in time precisely obligations under Article 59 GC IV arise for an occupying power to start with the provision of humanitarian assistance, and clarification would enhance legal certainty. Yet, as suggested above, the stricter approach of both Pictet and the ICJ hold a broader support than the more maximalist approach of the ICRC. Therefore, this former approach will be taken as premise for future Chapters, in relation to humanitarian assistance.[53]

3.2.5 Defining a (Natural) Disaster

Where the above Sections focus largely on treaty provisions in international humanitarian law, the definition of a (natural) disaster has not been regulated by treaty law, nor is it of course specifically part of international humanitarian law. The transition from the use of force in times of armed conflict (and occupation) to forces of nature entails a transition away from the legal regime of international humanitarian law discussed above. As done in the above Sections, an attempt will be made to define the factual circumstance in which humanitarian assistance may

---

[51] Dinstein, *The International Law of Belligerent Occupation* (n 35) 10-11.
[52] Thürer, 'Current challenges to the law of occupation' (n 38), 5-6.
[53] For a more in depth discussion on the law of occupation and its beginning, see Benvenisti, *The International Law of Occupation* (n 39); Dinstein, *The International Law of Belligerent Occupation* (n 35); and also Siegrist, 'The Functional Beginning of Belligerent Occupation' (n 39).

be necessary, in order to establish more precisely *when* this provision in fact takes place.

For a definition of a natural disaster, it is necessary to turn to various soft law regulations, as a legal definition that is generally accepted in international law seems to be absent.[54] Some first indications of what a natural disaster requiring the provision of humanitarian assistance entails can be sought in the context of the UN 'International decade for natural disaster reduction'.[55] At the end of the 1980s, as part of the establishment of this 'Decade for natural disaster reduction',[56] the UN proclaimed natural disasters to include:

> "earthquakes, windstorms (cyclones, hurricanes, tornadoes, typhoons), tsunamis, floods, landslides, volcanic eruptions, wildfires and other calamities of natural origin".[57]

Contrary to the previous definitions of armed conflict and occupation, the approach to defining a natural disaster is of a more immediate and practical nature. A few years later the UN furthermore included 'grasshopper and locust infestations, drought and desertification' in its definition of a natural disaster.[58] The Tampere Convention relates the notion of 'natural hazard' to its potential of creating a disaster in a more general sense:

> "'Natural hazard' means an event or process, such as an earthquake, fire, flood, wind, landslide, avalanche, cyclone, tsunami, insect infestation, drought or volcanic eruption, which has the potential for triggering a disaster".[59]

Although most of the soft law principles concerning humanitarian assistance do not define a natural disaster as such, the 2003 Institut de Droit International's Bruges Resolution does note that a disaster of natural origin includes amongst others those natural hazards as also mentioned above, but also cites torrential rains, epidemics and interestingly, famine.[60] The latter, and arguably also epidemics, does not necessarily have a 'natural' origin.

---

[54] Preliminary report on the protection of persons in the event of disasters' (5 May 2008) International Law Commission, UN Doc. A/CN.4/598 § 46.

[55] UNGA Res 42/169 (11 December 1987) UN Doc A/RES/42/169 'International decade for natural disaster reduction' § 3; UNGA Res 44/236 (22 December 1989) UN Doc A/RES/44/236 'International decade for natural disaster reduction' §1.

[56] See 2.2.1 Historical Development.

[57] UNGA Res 42/169 (11 December 1987) UN Doc. A/42/169 (n 55) Preambular § 3.

[58] UNGA Res 44/236 (22 December 1989) UN Doc A/RES/44/236 (n 55) Annex § 1.

[59] Tampere Convention on the Provision of Telecommunication Resources for Disaster Mitigation and Relief Operations, 18 June 1998, Article 1(9).

[60] Resolution 'Humanitarian Assistance' (2 September 2003) Institute of International Law, Sixteenth Commission, Bruges Session § 2.

One of the main organisations primarily involved with relief for the disaster-stricken, the IFRC,[61] envisages a very broad range of disasters that can be included within the 'umbrella-phrase' of natural disaster:

> "Natural hazards are naturally occurring physical phenomena caused either by rapid or slow onset events which can be geophysical (earthquakes, landslides, tsunamis and volcanic activity), hydrological (avalanches and floods), climatological (extreme temperatures, drought and wildfires), meteorological (cyclones and storms/wave surges) or biological (disease epidemics and insect/animal plagues). Technological or man-made hazards (complex emergencies/conflicts, famine, displaced populations, industrial accidents and transport accidents) are events that are caused by humans and occur in or close to human settlements. This can include environmental degradation, pollution and accidents".[62]

As can be seen, the IFRC categorises the various types of natural hazards that fall within the wider notion of a disaster. Particularly focusing on such natural disasters, the IFRC developed the 'Guidelines for the domestic facilitation and regulation of international disaster relief and initial recovery assistance' (IDRL Guidelines). These Guidelines, although a non-legal initiative, are intended to provide assistance to enable States to facilitate humanitarian assistance by international organisations.[63] The IFRC's initiative has been supported by the UN General Assembly, which encourages individual states to make use of the Guidelines.[64] OCHA on the other hand takes a more abstract and theoretical approach, with a definition of natural disaster which does not actually include any examples. As such, OCHA envisages that a disaster will:

> "[...] seriously affect the society, economy and/or infrastructure of a region. Depending on population vulnerability and local response capacity, natural disasters will pose challenges and problems of a humanitarian nature".[65]

OCHA furthermore echoes the definition provided by the IASC that although the term is coined as a 'natural' disaster, the magnitude of its consequences are

---

[61] See Chapter 2 (n 50) on the mandate of the IFRC and Section 2.3.2.2 International Organisations for its particular role.

[62] <www.ifrc.org/en/what-we-do/disaster-management/about-disasters/definition-of-hazard/> accessed 10 November 2011.

[63] For more information on the IFRC's IDRL Programme: <www.ifrc.org/en/what-we-do/idrl/idrl-guidelines/> accessed 29 December 2011.

[64] UNGA Res 63/137 (11 December 2008) UN Doc A/RES/63/137 § 6; UNGA Res 63/139 (5 March 2009) UN Doc A/RES/63/139 'Strengthening of the coordination of humanitarian and disaster relief assistance of the United Nations, including special economic assistance: strengthening of the coordination of emergency humanitarian assistance of the United Nations' § 8; UNGA Res 63/141 (10 March 2009) UN Doc A/RES/63/141 'International cooperation on humanitarian assistance in the field of natural disasters, from relief to development' § 5.

[65] OCHA/ReliefWeb, *Glossary of Humanitarian Terms* (2008): "Natural Disaster".

determined by human (in)action.[66] The IASC had stated previously that a natural *disaster* is a consequence of a natural hazard which overwhelms local capacity to respond as well as seriously affecting the development of a region.[67]

The International Law Committee has the opportunity to provide a more legal definition through its current study into the 'protection of persons in the event of disasters'.[68] Considering the absence of such a legal definition of a disaster, the ILC has formulated in its Draft Article 3 in relation to disasters:

> "'Disaster' means a calamitous event or series of events resulting in widespread loss of life, great human suffering and distress, or large-scale material or environmental damage, thereby seriously disrupting the functioning of society".[69]

Although not formulating any particular examples of such an event, the ILC does provide some criteria, such as a certain severity, which disrupts society. The ILC itself has noted that three elements are relevant; namely that an international component is not a prerequisite for the qualification as a natural disaster, that a threshold of disturbance to the society in which it takes place must be considered and furthermore that a degree of suffering of those affected must be reached.[70] From an international legal perspective, a state or region's capacity, or willingness to manage the circumstances, are then relevant.[71] Indeed this approach allows for the notion of 'disaster' to also contain man-made components, as well as being of natural origin and exacerbated by human (in)action.

3.2.6 Disasters and the Provision of Humanitarian Assistance

From the above, it is clear that rather large-scale, severe and intense (natural) phenomena, with a disrupting influence on the society in which they take place, can be classified as a (natural) disaster. No particular distinction with regard to duration seems to be discernible, or whether such a disaster may be sudden or slow in its development. For the purpose of this research it is however not necessary to create an exhaustive list of all those natural circumstances that may amount to a natural disaster. Relevant to the provision of assistance is whether or not the occurrence of a disaster results in a need for the provision of emergency aid to those persons suffering from the destructive forces of the disaster; regardless of which specific type of natural phenomenon it was. Indeed, it is an occurrence of a crisis that results

---

[66] Ibid and IASC, 'Protecting Persons Affected by Natural Disasters, IASC Operational Guidelines' (2006), 8.
[67] Ibid, 'Protecting Persons Affected by Natural Disasters, IASC Operational Guidelines'.
[68] ILC Report to the General Assembly UN Doc A/62/10 (7 May-5 June and 9 July-10 August 2007) § 375.
[69] ILC 'Protection of persons in the event of disasters' Draft Articles UN Doc. A/CN.4/L.831 (15 May 2014) Draft Article 3.
[70] ILC 'Preliminary report on the protection of persons in the event of disasters' UN Doc. A/CN.4/598 (n 54) § 47.
[71] Ibid § 47.

in the need for the affected sovereign authorities to address the provision of humanitarian assistance.

It must furthermore be noted that the notion of 'man-made' disasters[72] is sometimes discerned from the concept of natural disasters. Such man-made disasters may include nuclear accidents, chemical spills, or the breaking of dams.[73] The relationship and overlap between both is quite clear, as they are sometimes interrelated or follow from one another.[74] It is often not possible to clearly distinguish between a man-made disaster, or one truly flowing from natural causes.[75] Thus, a drought may cause a famine, but other components may also attribute to such a result. Similarly, a natural disaster, such as a wildfire can be caused by human beings with matches. Although many of the above sources mainly note examples of natural disasters, a more abstract definition of the notion of a disaster can be proffered, namely:

> *a sudden or slow-onset (natural) occurrence or course of events that may include a variety of environmental origins (including biological, climatological, geophysical, hydrological, etc.), resulting in an overwhelming of the local or national capacity and an immediate need for assistance to a civilian population.*

From the above, it is clear that ascertaining exactly what level of severity determines a natural disaster is quite difficult, especially in practice. Furthermore, it is not a legal term in and of itself, as opposed to the concept of occupation or armed conflict. Yet, it is also less relevant to determine the exact commencement or the 'intensity' as determining the existence of a natural disaster does not invoke a new particular set of applicable rules. Whereas the determination of an armed conflict or situation of occupation invokes the applicability of international humanitarian law, this is not the case for the determination of a natural disaster. In that event, (merely) human rights law and general customary international law remain applicable for provisions relating to humanitarian assistance.[76] The determination of the situation therefore does not have legal consequences related to the applicability of a body of law.

---

[72] The question of responsibility for certain man-made disasters falls outside the scope of this research and will thus not be addressed. This research focuses on the provision of assistance upon the existence of a crisis, and the legal rights and duties related thereto.

[73] Carlo Focarelli, 'Duty to Protect in Cases of Natural Disasters', (2010) *Max Planck Encyclopedia of International Law* § 5.

[74] Ibid § 5-6.

[75] ILC 'Preliminary report on the protection of persons in the event of disasters' UN Doc. A/CN.4/598 (n 54) § 49. See also Elisabeth Ferris, 'Humanitarian Perspectives on "Protection of Persons in the Event of Disasters', Brookings Project, at Roundtable on ' Canada and International Law, Department of Foreign Affairs and International Trade', April 2009, p. 1.

[76] See Section 3.4 The Relationship between Human Rights Law and International Humanitarian Law on the relationship between international humanitarian law and human rights law (as well as general customary international law).

Interestingly the ILC also recognises, as has been suggested in this research that a need for protection of persons 'can be said to be equally strong in *all* disaster situations'.[77] Persons requiring food, water and shelter do not have a choice concerning which circumstances instigated their need. Their legal protection should therefore in fact be equal, as their needs are equal. However, crucial to the ILC study and attempt at codification is the fact that it is not applicable to situations in which international humanitarian law is applicable, and can therefore in the future not aid persons needing humanitarian assistance as a result of, for example, a non-international armed conflict.[78] Despite the developments that the ILC will make in its study on the protection of persons, it remains closed to those persons affected by armed conflict or occupation. An overarching study into those circumstances in which humanitarian assistance is needed remains essential, to expose the current rights and obligations, under international humanitarian law or other *corpora juris*, pertaining to humanitarian assistance in *all* circumstances requiring the provision of assistance.

3.3 Providing Assistance: Establishing the Existence of a Humanitarian Crisis

Having established what humanitarian assistance entails, it becomes relevant to define the precise circumstances in which humanitarian assistance may be provided. From the above, it is clear that humanitarian assistance, when provided, occurs mainly in three circumstances, namely armed conflict, occupation and (natural) disaster.[79] Yet humanitarian assistance may not be *necessary* every time such a situation arises. For instance, not every natural disaster may lead to states reverting to the provision of (external) humanitarian assistance.[80] Only if and when such a circumstance leads to an actual humanitarian crisis or emergency with a level of severity warranting the provision of aid, does humanitarian assistance become a relevant factor. Also, circumstances of (prolonged) occupation may lead to a situation in which emergency aid is not needed, as the occupier may allow for a society to function normally to a large extent. Furthermore, a humanitarian crisis may develop in circumstances that may not be solely qualified as either a natural disaster or an armed conflict, but a combination of both, such as severe droughts occurring in non-international armed conflicts on the African continent. Their legal qualification remains relevant to the provisions determined by applicable law, such as international humanitarian law in times of armed conflict. Therefore, a definition of an overarching and all-encompassing situation in which humanitarian assistance is necessary must be provided.

---

[77] ILC 'Preliminary report on the protection of persons in the event of disasters' UN Doc. A/CN.4/598 (n 54) § 49. [*Emphasis added EEK*].

[78] ILC 'Protection of persons in the event of disasters' Draft Articles UN Doc. A/CN.4/L.831 (n 69) Article 21.

[79] Section 1.1 Introduction.

[80] Ed Tsui, 'Analysis of Normative Development in Humanitarian Resolutions since the Adoption of 46/182', independent review for OCHA (2009), 11.

3.3.1 An Over-Arching Approach to the Provision of Humanitarian Assistance

Given the fact that humanitarian assistance has been researched mostly from the perspective of the various (legally qualifiable) circumstances in which it takes place, namely occupation, armed conflict and (natural) disaster, an overarching definition of such a crisis or emergency has not often been provided. Whilst the majority of legal provisions can be read as tailored to specific circumstances, not always was such a clear distinction held in practice and by actors in the field. The UN has previously referred to 'natural disasters and other emergency situations'.[81] A separation of all situations in which humanitarian assistance is needed seems artificial, and it is therefore the purpose of this Section to develop an overarching definition of the concept of a 'humanitarian crisis'. The artificiality of distinguishing between such situations must be lifted from the perspective that people in need of assistance should be receiving such assistance regardless of whether their need stems from the effects of an armed conflict or a natural disaster.

Viewing the provision of humanitarian assistance from such an overarching perspective is advantageous for several reasons. Not only does it allow for equal protection of persons in need of aid, but such an encompassing view of the legal framework also deliberately goes against fragmentation of the law, allowing for more coherence. To have one singular approach to the framework on the provision of assistance and assessing the basic legal rights and duties for all actors defragments the whole notion of humanitarian assistance. Advantages can be found in providing a legal definition of a humanitarian crisis as an umbrella-notion also because upon establishing a legal definition, legal regimes can become applicable, granting greater protection to those needing assistance. Ultimately, such protection is the purpose of the provision of assistance and its legal framework. Thus, an overarching approach also falls in line with the principle of humanity and the notion of human dignity as discussed in Section 2.2.3.1. A human being's need for food or shelter is no different in times of conflict or following an earthquake, and should therefore be addressed with the same manner of importance and protection. Furthermore, providing a singular definition of a circumstance that results in a need to provide assistance provides more clarity for the state sovereign functioning as the affected state.

Various actors in the field adhere to a variety of terms such as 'crisis', 'emergency' and 'disaster'; further distinguished for example as 'slow-onset emergencies', 'man-made disasters', or 'complex emergencies'.[82] For the purpose

---

[81] See for example UNGA Res 46/182 (19 December 1991) UN Doc. A/RES/46/182, General Assembly Resolution 'Strengthening the coordination of humanitarian emergency assistance of the United Nations', § 33 as well as UNGA Res 43/131 (8 December 1988) UN Doc A/RES/43/131 'Humanitarian Assistance to victims of natural disasters and similar emergency situations' § 1.

[82] In Section 2.3.2 Providers of Humanitarian Assistance and beyond, various actors in the field of humanitarian assistance are addressed. For the purpose of example, several actors' definitions are mentioned here. For the terminology used by the IFRC see <www.ifrc.org/en/what-we-do/disaster-management/about-disasters/definition-of-hazard/> accessed 21 October 2011; for OCHA see the *Glossary of Humanitarian Terms in relation to the Protection of Civilians in Armed Conflict* (2004) as

of this research it thus becomes important to determine a working definition of a humanitarian crisis,[83] that may serve as a common notion for the circumstances in which invoking the provision of humanitarian assistance is relevant, namely in the above defined situations of conflict, (natural) disaster and occupation. Such an overarching definition may eventually also be of use to and applicable in such situations that lead to a call for humanitarian assistance, such as for instance internal disturbances, but that cannot be qualified as armed conflicts, thereby not invoking the protective clauses of international humanitarian law.[84]

3.3.2 The Material Scope of Application

In situations of occupation or conflict, support for the determination of circumstances when humanitarian assistance may be required can be sought in certain relevant treaty provisions.[85] As such, Article 59 of the Fourth Geneva Convention succinctly declares that relief schemes are necessary if a population of an occupied territory is 'inadequately supplied'.[86] Yet the determination of this inadequacy is left entirely open-ended and Article 59 does not mention what level of 'inadequacy' must be reached for relief schemes to be started, which leads to uncertainty as to who will be making such a determination. Determining whether or

---

well as OCHA/ReliefWeb, *Glossary of Humanitarian Terms* (2008); for the World Health Organization, see: <www.who.int/hac/about/definitions/en/index.html> accessed 21 October 2011.

83 Although both 'humanitarian crisis' and 'humanitarian emergency' can be, and are used, in this research the phrase 'humanitarian crisis' will be mainly used. Given the fact that both the Oxford and Merriam-Webster dictionaries consider unforeseeability as an element of an emergency, a choice has been made to use 'crisis' when referring to a situation in which a need may exist for humanitarian assistance, as not all situations in which humanitarian assistance becomes necessary are unforeseen. The Oxford dictionary provides that an emergency is: "a serious, unexpected, and often dangerous situation requiring immediate action". Similarly, the Merriam-Webster dictionary provides: "an unforeseen combination of circumstances or the resulting state that calls for immediate action" although in second instance also considers "an urgent need for assistance or relief". Rather, when defining a crisis, the Oxford dictionary defines this as "a time of intense difficulty or danger" and the Merriam Webster dictionary declares it to be "an unstable or crucial time or state of affairs in which a decisive change is impending; *especially*: one with the distinct possibility of a highly undesirable outcome […]; a situation that has reached a critical phase".

84 See Section 6.5.2 Rights of Persons to Receive Assistance in Times of Conflict on the possible right to receive humanitarian assistance in times of armed conflict.

85 In further Chapters, these provisions will be dealt with in depth and more intensively. At this stage, they are for illustrational purposes.

86 Article 59 of GC IV states: "If the whole or part of the population of an occupied territory is inadequately supplied, the Occupying Power shall agree to relief schemes on behalf of the said population, and shall facilitate them by all the means at its disposal. Such schemes, which may be undertaken either by States or by impartial humanitarian organizations such as the International Committee of the Red Cross, shall consist, in particular, of the provision of consignments of foodstuffs, medical supplies and clothing. All Contracting Parties shall permit the free passage of these consignments and shall guarantee their protection. A Power granting free passage to consignments on their way to territory occupied by an adverse Party to the conflict shall, however, have the right to search the consignments, to regulate their passage according to prescribed times and routes, and to be reasonably satisfied through the Protecting Power that these consignments are to be used for the relief of the needy population and are not to be used for the benefit of the Occupying Power".

not a territory is adequately supplied will then have to be determined on a case-by-case basis.[87] From the *Commentary* to the corresponding Article 70 of Additional Protocol I a similar 'case-by-case' observance can be deduced in times of international armed conflict, in relation to the urgency of the provision of assistance and the lack of specific legal qualification of the term 'inadequacy'.[88] Likewise, pertaining to non-international armed conflicts, Article 18 of Additional Protocol II provides for humanitarian assistance in the event 'the civilian population is suffering undue hardship owing to a lack of the supplies essential to its survival'.[89] Also in this instance, the *Commentary* argues the impossibility of providing exact criteria for the determination of 'undue hardship', and relates this to a comparison with a more generally accepted standard of living.[90] Obviously, this may lead to problematic circumstances in which an occupying force may consider territory adequately supplied, whilst (parts of) the international community may not agree.[91] And, more topical, it may result for example in circumstances of non-international armed conflict where the sovereign does not wish to allow third parties to provide assistance in territory over which it has lost control.

It should however be possible to establish a minimum degree for which common ground can be found. The nature of 'relief schemes' as seen above in the discussion on the definition of humanitarian assistance, is related to the delivery of those supplies urgently needed for immediate survival.[92] Thus, it must be assumed that the level of 'inadequacy' should therefore be comparable to such a level of urgency that one can speak of amounting to a 'humanitarian crisis'.[93] Whether or not access to a territory can then be established, dependent on the (in)adequacy of the supply, will be discussed in Chapter 8 Section 3. Equally, such difficulties may exist in relation to (natural) disaster, where a State may claim that it is in fact not overwhelmed by the disaster, and local capacity is equipped for an appropriate response.[94] Such difficulties in the determination of the adequacy of supply to a

---

[87] See in this regard Chapter 8.

[88] Sandoz, Swinarski & Zimmermann *Commentary to the Additional Protocols* (n 14) Protocol I Article 70, 817.

[89] The full text of Article 18 AP II states: "Relief societies located in the territory of the High Contracting Party, such as Red Cross (Red Crescent, Red Lion and Sun) organizations, may offer their services for the performance of their traditional functions in relation to the victims of the armed conflict. The civilian population may, even on its own initiative, offer to collect and care for the wounded, sick and shipwrecked. If the civilian population is suffering undue hardship owing to a lack of the supplies essential for its survival, such as foodstuffs and medical supplies, relief actions for the civilian population which are of an exclusively humanitarian and impartial nature and which are conducted without any adverse distinction shall be undertaken subject to the consent of the High Contracting Party concerned".

[90] Sandoz, Swinarski & Zimmermann *Commentary to the Additional Protocols* (n 14) Protocol II Article 18, 1479.

[91] See, likewise, Article 55 GC IV. Thus, some possibilities lie with the Protecting Power to safeguard the access to emergency supplies of the population. See on the possible right to access in times of occupation Section 7.5.4 The Potential Right to Access and the Law of Occupation.

[92] Section 2.2.2 Defining Humanitarian Assistance.

[93] The exact definition of a 'crisis' is addressed in Section 3.3.3 Defining a Humanitarian Crisis.

[94] See Section 7.5.6 The Potential Right to Access in Times of (Natural) Disaster.

civilian population in times of conflict and disaster stress the importance of research into the various rights and obligations currently existing under international law in relation to humanitarian assistance. Furthermore, in relation to armed conflict, as will be seen in Chapters 6 and 7, the provisions concerning the rendering and deliverance of humanitarian assistance are quite dispersed and particular.[95]

These difficulties in ascertaining the moment in time, circumstance and severity of suffering of the affected civilian population highlight the connection between the concept of humanitarian assistance and the concept of state sovereignty. Assessing 'who' or 'what' determines the threshold for the need of the provision of humanitarian assistance is closely related to the rights and duties of a state sovereign in international law.[96] This Section focuses on the scope of application of a humanitarian crisis as a concept, whereas these junctions between the rights of those in need of assistance and the rights of sovereigns will be addressed in subsequent Chapters.

Aside from matters of occupation, thoroughly codified with the horrors of World War II in mind, international humanitarian law as such does not state at which level of severity an (international or non-international) armed conflict can be considered a humanitarian crisis, thereby ensuring the provisions with regard to humanitarian assistance become operable.[97] Yet, determining which instances may result in the deliverance of humanitarian assistance would provide more legal certainty. Thus, in the absence of a clear statement concerning the moment at which the provision of 'relief' becomes applicable under international humanitarian law, its application must be derived from the fact that relief is directly related to the event of its *necessity* as seen above in regard to the definition of humanitarian assistance: it only entails the essential elements for a persons' survival.[98] The San Remo Principles also acknowledge that not every situation of occupation or conflict may lead to the involvement of humanitarian assistance because, although not defining the concept of 'emergency', the Principles do apply that specific term in addressing humanitarian assistance.[99] From the discussion of the application of humanitarian assistance to situations of occupation, it is apparent that lack of legal clarity may lead to attempts to deter the deliverance of assistance in such times. Thus by

---

[95] The Geneva Conventions contain very specific provisions with regard to the rights of civilians and other protected persons, which will be discussed more in depth in Chapter 6. These include amongst others those cited in Article 27 of GC IV.

[96] See in this regard Chapters 4 and 8.

[97] Pictet, *Commentary on the Geneva Conventions of 12 August 1949* (n 7) Article 10, 98-99. Pictet argues that given the unforeseeability of future warfare, choices have been made to leave certain situations open, as at the time of the drafting of the Convention, it was unclear what needs may be given rise to in future times. Furthermore, Article 23 of GC IV only mentions 'essential foodstuffs' that are to be distributed as rapidly as possible without a corresponding clarification at which point in time such foodstuffs do indeed become 'essential'.

[98] Section 2.2.2 Defining Humanitarian Assistance. See also Pictet, *Commentary on the Geneva Conventions of 12 August 1949* (n 7) Article 23, 180-181.

[99] 'Guiding Principles on the Right to Humanitarian Assistance' (April 1993) The International Institute of Humanitarian Law in San Remo, Principle 2 and Principle 3.

analogy, aspects of *willingness* to cope with the inadequacy of supply become a relevant criterion in the consideration of the determination of a humanitarian crisis.

As the provisions in the law of occupation and international humanitarian law are rather limited, an analogous view to natural disaster must be considered in order to distinguish more clearly at which point one can speak of a situation warranting the provision of humanitarian assistance. Operating outside the scope of humanitarian law, the UN General Assembly recognised that many emergencies' dimensions and durations are often beyond the capacity of the affected state, making international assistance of cardinal importance.[100] Thus, the General Assembly connected the existence of an 'emergency' to the *capacity* of the affected state to deal with the occurring event. A few years before, the UN 1984 'Draft Convention on expediting the delivery of emergency assistance' had already formulated that a:

> "'Disaster' means any natural, accidental or deliberate event (not being an ongoing situation of armed conflict) as a result of which assistance is needed from outside the State upon whose territory the event occurred or which has been affected by the consequences of the event".[101]

Following the Draft Convention and the UN General Assembly, the UN Department of Humanitarian Affairs defined an emergency to be a 'sudden and usually unforeseen event that calls for immediate measures to minimise its adverse consequences'.[102] Given the fact that the phrase 'emergency' is often linked to a certain degree of unexpectedness,[103] other terms are used too. As such, the UN International Strategy for Disaster Reduction stated a 'disaster' to be a:

> "serious disruption of the functioning of a community or a society causing widespread human, material, economic or environmental losses which exceed the ability of the affected community or society to cope using its own resources".[104]

A clear link can thus be established between the unfolding of an event and the (local) capacity to deal with this, for the determination of the existence of a humanitarian crisis. Similarly, also with regard to the notion of a disaster the IFRC also considers the relationship between a state's own capacities in relation to the

---

[100] UNGA Res 46/182 (19 December 1991) UN Doc. A/RES/46/182 (n 81) Annex I § 5: "The magnitude and duration of many emergencies may be beyond the response capacity of many affected countries. International cooperation to address emergency situations and to strengthen the response capacity of affected countries is thus of great importance […]".

[101] UNGA Res 39/367 (18 June 1984) UN Doc. A/39/367/Add.2 and E/1984/96/Add.2 'Draft Convention on Expediting the Delivery of Emergency Relief' Article 1(b).

[102] OCHA/ReliefWeb, *Glossary of Humanitarian Terms* (2008), 24.

[103] See (n 83) on definitions of emergency.

[104] OCHA/ReliefWeb, *Glossary of Humanitarian Terms* (2008), 22. The UN International Strategy for Disaster Reduction is the UN Secretariat overseeing the implementation and development of disaster reduction policy. For further information: <www.unisdr.org/who-we-are> accessed 21 October 2011.

extent of its vulnerability when a 'hazard' occurs.[105] Most of these analyses pertain to the notion of 'emergency' or 'disaster' within a non-conflict or -occupation setting. Yet, a humanitarian crisis may not only unfold due to a lack of a state's *capacity* to handle a certain situation, since a state itself may be at the root cause of the crisis, as previously discussed. Thus, *local* capacity may be unable to cope with a certain crisis situation, due to conflict or occupation. The CRED defined a disaster to be a:

> "Situation or event, which overwhelms local capacity, necessitating a request to national or international level for external assistance [...] An unforeseen and often sudden event that causes great damage, destruction and human suffering. Though often caused by nature, disasters can have human origins. Wars and civil disturbances that destroy homelands and displace people are included among the causes of disasters".[106]

Furthermore, the Tampere Convention states that a disaster, which may be caused by 'accident, nature or human activity' is any sudden or long-term serious disruption of a functioning society posing a serious threat to human life, health, property or the environment.[107] *Capacity* and *willingness* to handle the emergency at hand can therefore be deduced as continuous variables in the state's ability to provide assistance.

The various definitions above consider that a humanitarian crisis may unfold itself not only in a situation of (natural) disaster, but also in conflict or occupation, thus providing an overlap of various fields of law. Indeed, as argued before: persons in need of food, water and shelter should not be dependent on the nature of the crisis for the actual provision of aid. Such considerations also support the suggestion made in this research that the approach to the legal framework of humanitarian assistance must occur through an *overarching* perspective. Indeed, such situations in which assistance is necessary are furthermore not always separate and a 'complex emergency' is a notion of particular relevance in the discussion of humanitarian assistance. Disasters, both man-made and natural, often occur in regions already suffering from crises such as internal disturbances or conflict. Interestingly, the notion of a 'complex emergency' has been subject to various definitions, perhaps connected to the fact that it is a situation in which various fields of law come together, as a result of the fact that such a situation can be a combination of both conflict and natural disaster. The UN Inter-Agency Standing Committee defines a complex emergency as:

---

105 <www.ifrc.org/en/what-we-do/disaster-management/about-disasters/what-is-a-disaster/> accessed 14 July 2011. The IFRC views a disaster to be: "a sudden, calamitous event that seriously disrupts the functioning of a community or society and causes human, material, and economic or environmental losses that exceed the community's or society's ability to cope using its own resources".

106 <www.emdat.be/glossary/9#term81> accessed 14 July 2011. EM-DAT is the 'International Disaster Database' of CRED, see Chapter 1 (n 3).

107 Tampere Convention on the Provision of Telecommunication Resources for Disaster Mitigation and Relief Operations, 18 June 1998, Article 1(6).

> "A humanitarian crisis in a country, region or society where there is total or considerable breakdown of authority resulting from internal or external conflict and which requires an international response that goes beyond the mandate or capacity of any single agency and/or the ongoing United Nations country program".[108]

From this definition, a need for 'international response' can be considered, if the turn of events results in national capacities being overwhelmed, or results from national inadequate authorities. Referring back to the IASC's definition, the IFRC also considers complex emergencies, as opposed to single disasters, as a type of disaster that is the result of a combination of causes, both man-made and natural.[109]

Outside the UN or Red Cross context, the Bruges Resolution also refers in its definition of disaster to the endangerment of 'life, health, physical integrity, the right not to be subjected to cruel, inhuman or degrading treatment, or other fundamental human rights, or the essential needs of the population', which may occur through a variety of circumstances either of natural origin or caused by armed conflicts or violence.[110] The Mohonk Criteria also focus on complex emergencies, elaborately stating:

> "[...] a "complex emergency" is a humanitarian crisis which may involve armed conflict and which may be exacerbated by natural disasters. It is a situation in which prevailing conditions threaten the lives of a portion of the affected population who, for a variety of

[108] IASC, 10th meeting, December 1994. The IASC was established in June 1992, following the call thereto in the UNGA Res 46/182 (19 December 1991) UN Doc. A/RES/46/182 (n 81). See for the IASC's task as primary coordinator for organisations delivering international humanitarian assistance Section 2.3.2 Providers of Humanitarian Assistance.

[109] The IFRC also provides examples of possible complex emergencies: "Some disasters can result from several different hazards or, more often, to a complex combination of both natural and man-made causes and different causes of vulnerability. Food insecurity, epidemics, conflicts and displaced populations are examples [...] Such "complex emergencies" are typically characterized by: extensive violence and loss of life; displacements of populations; widespread damage to societies and economies; the need for large-scale, multi-faceted humanitarian assistance; the hindrance or prevention of humanitarian assistance by political and military constraints; significant security risks for humanitarian relief workers in some areas. On a national level, conflict may involve warlike encounters between armed groups from the same country which take place within the borders. Such outbreaks of war may pose large-scale medical problems such as epidemics, lack of water, accumulation of rubbish, displaced persons, refugees, food shortage, hunger etc. Internationally, war may break out between two or more armies from different countries. Similarly such conflict may cause large scale mass movements of refugees and displaced persons." See for further examples <www.ifrc.org/en/what-we-do/disaster-management/about-disasters/definition-of-hazard/complex-emergencies/> accessed 24 October 2011.

[110] Bruges Resolution 'Humanitarian Assistance' (2 September 2003) (n 60) § 2: "Disaster" means calamitous events which endanger life, health, physical integrity, or the right not to be subjected to cruel, inhuman or degrading treatment, or other fundamental human rights, or the essential needs of the population, whether of natural origin (such as earthquakes, volcanic eruptions, windstorms, torrential rains, floods, landslides, droughts, fires, famine, epidemics), or man-made disasters of technological origin (such as chemical disasters or nuclear explosions), or caused by armed conflicts or violence (such as international or internal armed conflicts, internal disturbances or violence, terrorist activities)".

> reasons, are unable to obtain the minimum subsistence requirements and are dependent on external humanitarian assistance for survival".[111]

Therefore, similar to previous definitions, according to this set of criteria, the *overwhelming* nature of the emergency requires external or international help, whereas this emergency may originate from a variety of sources. Although the EC in 1996 did not define a humanitarian crisis in its 'Council Regulation concerning humanitarian aid', and confined itself solely to the purposes of aid,[112] in 2008 the EU clearly defined:

> "Humanitarian crises include both man-made and natural disasters. Their impact is increasingly severe, linked to a number of factors, such as the changing nature of conflict, climate change, increasing competition for access to energy and natural resources, extreme poverty, poor governance and situations of fragility".[113]

Thus, the EU also acknowledges an overlap in various circumstances that may warrant the provision of assistance. Indeed, although the approach to the legal provisions pertaining to the provision of assistance has occurred through *separate* regimes, the organisations involved in its actual provision all recognise the circumstance that a crisis can occur in a more *overarching* manner. Such support can also be found in the above secondary sources that have developed the various guidelines and principles discussed. Therefore, it becomes necessary to indeed approach the legal framework of the provision of assistance in such a manner also. The law often follows practice, and there is no reason for the law pertaining to the delivery of humanitarian assistance to be any different.

3.3.3 Defining a Humanitarian Crisis

From the above, in the determination of the situation in which humanitarian assistance becomes necessary, several criteria or common factors can be considered in relation to the definition of a humanitarian crisis.[114] Clearly, the legal value of these criteria must be seen in light of the fact that most of the abovementioned sources attempting to explicitly define elements of a crisis are considered secondary sources in international law.[115] Yet, common factors can be deduced in determining

---

[111] 'The Mohonk Criteria for Humanitarian Assistance in Complex Emergencies', (1995) reprinted in 17 *Human Rights Quarterly* 1, 196-197, specifically at footnote 7 of their text.

[112] European Council Regulation concerning humanitarian aid (EC) No. 1257/96 (20 June 1996) Article 1.

[113] 'Joint Statement by the Council and the Representatives of the Governments of the Member States meeting within the Council, the European Parliament and the European Commission' (European Consensus on Humanitarian Aid) (30 January 2008) EU Doc 2008/C/25/01 § 2.

[114] For further reading on definitions of disaster, see for example 'Protection of persons in the event of disasters' 26 February 2008) Memorandum by the Secretariat (ILC), Addendum, UN Doc A/CN.4/590/Add.1.

[115] See Sections 1.4.1 Primary Sources and 1.4.2 Secondary Sources concerning the relationship between primary and secondary sources.

the definition of a humanitarian crisis for the purpose of this research. As seen, these criteria can be and indeed are, applied to the general notion of a humanitarian crisis, not distinguishing this crisis into separate (factual) circumstances of application. It is clearly relevant from both a practical and legal perspective to establish a definition of a humanitarian crisis which can be applicable to a situation of conflict, disaster, and of occupation in order to assess the current legal regime for the provision of humanitarian assistance. Such importance exists factually because often such circumstances overlap, and legally because the rights of persons needing food, shelter and the like should not differ according to their actual circumstances. These needs are so closely related to the essence of humanity and human dignity that they warrant protection in *all* situations persons may find themselves in. Furthermore, one overall approach would align with the notion of state sovereignty, which entails constant responsibilities for the sovereign authority as discussed in Chapter 4. Based upon the analysis of the statements above, it is suggested by this research that a humanitarian crisis can be defined as:

> *a situation deriving from a variety of origins, including natural or man-made disaster, armed conflict and occupation, causing grave damages of a personal or material nature to persons, where (national/external) assistance is needed as the local capacity is either overwhelmed, unable or sometimes unwilling to manage the circumstances.*

The above definition is a proposition, rather than an exhaustive list of potential crises. For this purpose, it is not defined how many persons should be 'affected', as this may vary according to the specific circumstance at hand. Such a number of persons furthermore stands in close relation to the affected state or local authority being 'overwhelmed'; a state of being which may differ in various circumstances.

Within this Chapter, the three most common (legally qualifiable) situations that may lead to a humanitarian crisis, namely occupation, armed conflict and (natural) disaster, have been explored. This research will address the provision of assistance equally, as all three circumstances can potentially lead up to a humanitarian crisis, at which point humanitarian assistance becomes relevant to all three situations. As stated above,[116] if persons are suffering and in need of emergency assistance, the legal qualification of the situation should not be decisive or crucial in the possibility to provide aid. Indeed, all persons in need of assistance should be entitled to receive such assistance on an equal legal basis. Therefore, the legal protection of these persons should be equal. Currently however, the viewpoint is often held that the legal qualification of the circumstance in which a person may be requiring assistance, namely either occupation, armed conflict or disaster, is extremely relevant to the legal regulations concerning the provision of relief – or lack thereof. As such, these three circumstances have been defined. Ascertaining which qualifications exist for the various circumstances, will allow for the determination of the applicable rules of humanitarian assistance. Therefore, having established the

[116] Section 1.1 Introduction.

various circumstances in which provision may be relevant, as well as exploring the concept of a 'humanitarian crisis' it becomes relevant to address the interrelationship of the various fields of law that are applicable in times of occupation, conflict and natural disaster.

3.4 Scope of Application: The Relationship between Human Rights Law and International Humanitarian Law

This Section addresses the particular fields of human rights law and humanitarian law that play a distinct role in the analysis of the legal framework pertaining to the provision of humanitarian assistance.[117] This research attempts to set out the current existing legal framework, and ascertain the minimum rights and duties of actors in a circumstance of crisis. When multiple fields of law apply simultaneously, it is relevant to assess their relationship in order to establish the applicable law in a given circumstance. Whilst general international law is certainly relevant to the legal framework on the provision of emergency aid, that body of law does not contain *specific* rights and duties tailored to crisis-situations.[118] Other bodies of law, such as for example environmental law, play a role in disaster prevention, and thereby fall outside the scope of this research. Similarly, another specific *corpus juris*, namely refugee law, only becomes applicable in cross-border situations where refugees require protection by a host state, often in a stadium beyond the provision of emergency aid. The timeframe in which humanitarian assistance takes place thereby lays a focus on two fields of law that both contain specific provisions pertaining to rights and duties involved in the delivery of humanitarian assistance; humanitarian law and human rights law. As Coupland puts it, their names already show that these *corpora juris* are 'traditionally associated with humanity'.[119] Whilst the IFRC has developed IDRL Guidelines, these guidelines are not a legislative initiative, and similarly, whilst many states have adopted international disaster response laws, such laws operate at a national level, falling outside the scope of this research. Humanitarian assistance, provided in times of conflict and peace, is however at the heart of human rights law and humanitarian law, and operates at the intersection of these fields of law, in particular in times of a complex emergency.

These two fields of law both contain a variety of provisions that will prove relevant throughout the following Chapters in this research into the legal framework pertaining to the provision of humanitarian assistance. Indeed, many of the following Chapters analyse the particular provisions of human rights law and humanitarian law in order to establish the current legal regime of the various rights

[117] Indeed, while it remains beyond the scope of this research to provide an in -depth analysis of all fields of law that may be touched upon throughout this research, such as general public international law, or particular provisions of refugee law, the fields of international humanitarian law and human rights law must be addressed more at length.
[118] See in this regard Chapters 6 and 7.
[119] Robin Coupland, 'Humanity: What is it and how does it influence international law?' (2001) 83 *International Review of the Red Cross* 844, 986.

and obligations in relation to the provision of humanitarian assistance. The delivery of humanitarian assistance is in fact dependent on the provisions relating to this in these two particular fields of law. The premise of this research that the provision and receipt of humanitarian assistance in any circumstance (be it occupation, conflict or disaster) should be equally provided for to the greatest extent possible under international law, regardless of whether it be through human rights law or humanitarian law, results in the need to explore the interrelationship between the two fields of law. This exploration must occur at a more abstract level to ascertain this interrelationship at the outset of this research prior to delving into the individual provisions of the bodies of law. Much has been written on the interplay between these two fields of law, in particular in recent years on the convergence of both fields.[120] This potential convergence, given the mutual goal of a greater protection of persons at all times, indeed concurs with the viewpoint of an overarching approach to the provision of humanitarian assistance that is put forward in this research.

3.4.1 Development of the Interaction between both Fields of Law

While the initial development of humanitarian assistance within the framework of international humanitarian law has been addressed in Chapter 2, the entrance of human rights into the international legal arena has prompted a further development of the legal framework on the provision of humanitarian assistance. As such, the development of the interaction between human rights law and humanitarian law is of relevance considering their application to the framework within which the delivery of humanitarian assistance takes place. Understanding the manner in which these fields of law have developed will enhance the understanding of the actual provisions contained within both bodies of law pertaining to the delivery of emergency aid. Human rights law as relevant to the provision of humanitarian assistance will be addressed in Chapter 5, with a specific view to the 'right to receive humanitarian assistance' as a human right. The interaction of humanitarian law and human rights law however can be explored at this stage from a more theoretical viewpoint, prior to the assessment of the various specific rights and duties, and is key to the assessment of the issues that may arise in the consideration of the 'right to receive humanitarian assistance' as a human right, and the consequences thereof, as well as the provisions related to the delivery of emergency assistance as incorporated in humanitarian law. For this reason, a brief overview of their joint development is provided prior to the discussion of their legal interaction in light of the provision of humanitarian assistance. Understanding the development of both fields of law and their interaction will enhance the discussion of the factual interaction of the bodies of law in circumstances of crisis today.

In the immediate aftermath of World War II, when human rights entered the international arena, both fields of law did not interact immediately. Human rights

[120] See Sections 3.4.1 Development of Interaction between both Fields of Law and 3.4.3 Hierarchy or Convergence of International Legal Norms?

law and humanitarian law were considered 'separate and distinct' as they had clearly developed independently from one another.[121] For several decades, although both fields of law envisaged the protection of human beings, the perception was that the two areas of law did not have ideological similarities, amongst others due to the divergence in their addressees.[122] Indeed, whereas human rights are an individual's claims against the state (or another individual),[123] humanitarian law sought to govern the relations between entities in conflict, as well as the protection of those caught in such conflicts.[124] The lack of convergence between both *corpora juris* was furthermore largely inspired by the viewpoints of two main institutions concerned with their maintenance and implementation: the UN and the ICRC.[125] The United Nations, which emphasised its stance against the use of force, did not want to deal with or acknowledge the law of war any more than the ICRC wished to lose its well-preserved neutrality and therefore chose to stay away from the political agenda of the UN, which included human rights.[126] Intermittently, statements did emerge that placed human rights and international humanitarian law within the same context, such as the closing statement of the President of the 'Diplomatic Conference for the Establishment of International Conventions for the Protection of War Victims' of 1949, Max Petitpierre, who commented:

> "[...] we shall celebrate the anniversary of the Universal Declaration of the Rights of Man which was adopted by the General Assembly of the United Nations on December the 10th, 1948. It is (...) interesting to compare that Declaration with the Geneva Conventions. Our texts are based on certain of the fundamental rights proclaimed in it – respect for the human person, protection against torture and cruel, inhuman or degrading punishments or treatment. (...) The Universal Declaration of the Rights of Man and the Geneva Conventions are both derived from one and the same ideal (...) namely that of freeing human beings and nations from the suffering of which they are often at once the authors and the victims [...]".[127]

---

121 Noelle Quénivet, 'The History of the Relationship Between International Humanitarian Law and Human Rights law' in R Arnold & N Quénivet (eds) *International Humanitarian Law and Human Rights Law: Towards a New Merger in International Law* (Martinus Nijhoff Publishers 2008) 2; Heike Krieger, 'A Conflict of Norms: The Relationship Between Humanitarian Law and Human Rights Law in the ICRC Customary Law Study', (2006) 11 *Journal of Conflict and Security Law*, 2, 266.

122 Ibid Quénivet, 5.

123 See Section 5.2 The Development of Human Rights Relevant to Humanitarian Assistance.

124 See for a more in depth discussion Sections 2.2.1 Historical Development, 3.2.1 Defining an Armed Conflict and 3.2.3 Defining Occupation.

125 Krieger, 'A Conflict of Norms' (n 121), 267. See also Katharine Fortin, 'Complementarity between the ICRC and the United Nations and international humanitarian law and international human rights law, 1948–1968', (2012) 94 *International Review of the Red Cross*, 888, 1-22.

126 Robert Kolb, 'The Relationship between international humanitarian law and human rights law: A brief history of the 1948 Universal Declaration of Human Rights and the Geneva Conventions', (1998) *International Review of the Red Cross*, 324, 409-410.

127 Final record of the Diplomatic Conference for the Establishment of International Conventions for the Protection of War Victims (Geneva, 21 April - 12 August 1949) Vol. II-B, 536.

Such comments, although indicative of the mindset of some, were certainly not representative for the majority of the viewpoints of states involved in the preparatory works of the 1948 'Universal Declaration of Human Rights' (UDHR) and the Geneva Conventions.[128] As a result, the UDHR did not address the matter of human rights in times of conflict, nor do these human rights receive proper attention in the *travaux préparatoires* of the 1949 Geneva Conventions.[129] The subsequent *Commentaries* by Pictet follow suit, making only cautious references to human rights, most frequent in relation to GC IV and Common Article 3.[130] Although wary of the notion that international humanitarian law should be applicable between a state and its nationals, the *Commentaries* cling to the accepted idea at that time that the application of humanitarian law is between the belligerent state and 'enemy nationals'.[131]

The discussion on the true interaction between human rights and humanitarian law did not occur until the late 1960s at the 'International Conference on Human Rights' in Teheran, due to many ongoing conflicts at the time such as those in Vietnam, Nigeria and the Middle East, resulting in an increase in interest.[132] The 1968 Teheran Conference marked the beginning of contact through UN means, specifically as the Conference adopted a Resolution entitled 'Human Rights in Armed Conflict'.[133] The Resolution was subsequently adopted by the UN General Assembly, urging the Secretary General to take up studies into the codification needs of international humanitarian law, specifically tailored towards the protection of civilians, prisoners and combatants.[134] The ensuing Secretary General reports of 1969 and 1970, equally using the phrasing 'human rights in armed conflict',[135] signalled the UN's choice of placing the discussion on human rights within the context of armed conflict.[136] Indeed, the General Assembly continued in this line, adopting several resolutions in subsequent years on the topic of human rights in

[128] Kolb, 'The Relationship between international humanitarian law and human rights law: A brief history of the 1948 Universal Declaration of Human Rights and the Geneva Conventions' (n 126) 412.
[129] Ibid 411.
[130] Jean Pictet, *Commentary on the Geneva Conventions of 12 August 1949 Volumes I-IV* (International Committee of the Red Cross 1952-1959), Volume I Commentary GC I Article 7, 78-85; Volume III Commentary GC III Article 7, 87-92 and Article 99, 472-473; Volume IV Commentary GC IV Article 8, 73-80 (inalienable rights), Article 27, 201-204 (treatment of protected persons), Article 32, 221-224 (prohibition of corporal punishment), Article 71, 353-355 (penal procedure), Article 80, 374-376 (civil capacity) and Article 101, 433-435 (complaints and petitions from internees).
[131] Ibid Volume IV Commentary GC IV Article 79, 373.
[132] Quénivet, 'The History of the Relationship Between International Humanitarian Law and Human Rights law' (n 121) 4.
[133] Resolution XXIII '*Human Rights in Armed Conflict*', adopted by the International Conference on Human Rights in Teheran, 12 May 1968 (UN Doc. A/Conf.32/41).
[134] UNGA Res 2444 (XXIII) 'Respect for Human Rights in Armed Conflicts' (19 December 1968) §2(b).
[135] UN Secretary General Report 'Respect for Human Rights in Armed Conflict', UN Doc A/7720 (20 November 1969) and UN Secretary General Report 'Respect for Human Rights in Armed Conflict', UN Doc A/8052 (18 September 1970).
[136] Quénivet, 'The History of the Relationship Between International Humanitarian Law and Human Rights law' (n 121) 5.

armed conflict, one of which specifically refers to the Third Geneva Convention.[137] Equally, the UN commenced to envisage a more active role for itself as an organisation, asserting the need for the development of more substantive rules of procedure for the implementation of humanitarian law, as existing rules according to the UN could not adequately meet all present-day situations of armed conflict.[138] The 1968 Teheran Conference can thus be seen as a pivotal catalyst for the branching out of the UN's vision on human rights, to the point where the organisation sees their possible applicability in times of armed conflict. In fact, the UN General Assembly declared with regard to the provision of humanitarian assistance that:

> "The provision of international relief to civilian populations is in conformity with the humanitarian principles of the Charter of the United Nations, the Universal Declaration of Human Rights and other international instruments in the field of human rights. The Declaration of Principles for International Humanitarian Relief to the Civilian Population in Disaster Situations, as laid down in resolution XXVI adopted by the twenty-first International Conference of the Red Cross, shall apply in situations of armed conflict, and all parties to a conflict should make every effort to facilitate this application".[139]

In this statement, the General Assembly clearly recognises the *role of humanitarian assistance* in transcending the boundaries between both fields of law. Still faced with the common viewpoint that human rights law and humanitarian law operated in different contexts, which could result in a vacuum of protection for individuals, several efforts were made during the 1980s to bridge this gap.[140] One of the well-known soft law results is the 1990 Turku 'Declaration of Minimum Humanitarian Standards'.[141] Hereinafter, the UN Commission on Human Rights declared in 1998 that 'irrespective of their historical roots' both international humanitarian law and human rights law both focus on the dignity of the human person and respect for human values, from which logically follows that:

---

[137] UNGA Res 2674 (XXV) 'Respect for human rights in armed conflicts' (9 December 1970); UNGA Res 2675 (XXV) 'Basic principles for the protection of civilian populations in armed conflict' (9 December 1970); UNGA Res 2676 (XXV) 'Respect for human rights in armed conflicts' (9 December 1970) and referencing GC III in the final preambular §; and UNGA Res 2677 (XXV), 'Respect for human rights in armed conflicts', (9 December 1970).

[138] UNGA Res 2677 (XXV), 'Respect for human rights in armed conflicts', (9 December 1970) preambular § 4.

[139] UNGA Res 2675 (XXV) 'Basic principles for the protection of civilian populations in armed conflict' (9 December 1970) § 8.

[140] Marco Odello, 'Fundamental Standards of Humanity: A Common Language of International Humanitarian Law and Human Rights Law' in R Arnold & N Quénivet (eds) *International Humanitarian Law and Human Rights Law: Towards a New Merger in International Law* (Martinus Nijhoff Publishers 2008) 30.

[141] Turku 'Declaration of Minimum Humanitarian Standards', (2 December 1990) adopted by an expert meeting convened by the Institute for Human Rights, Åbo Akademi University, Turku/Åbo Finland.

> "There is thus no reason why certain acts which may be unlawful in normal times and in situations of internal armed conflict should be lawful in situations of internal violence".[142]

This declaration is a confirmation of earlier statements made by both the ICJ and ICTY with regard to the belief that both areas of law are not entirely separate. The ICJ had acknowledged in its 1996 Advisory Opinion on the *Legality of the threat or use of nuclear weapons* that a large part of humanitarian law is fundamental to the respect of the human person and 'elementary considerations of humanity' as discussed in Section 2.2.3.1 The Principle of Humanity, as well as noting that the law of armed conflict is permeated with an 'intrinsically humanitarian character'.[143] Through such a declaration, the Court indeed acknowledged the common foundation of both fields of law in the notion of 'humanity'. In the Case of *The Prosecutor v. Anto Furundzija*, the ICTY Trial Chamber recognised:

> "The essence of the whole corpus of international humanitarian law as well as human rights law lies in the protection of the human dignity of every person, whatever his or her gender. The general principle of respect for human dignity is the basic underpinning and indeed the very *raison d'être* of international humanitarian law and human rights law; indeed in modern times it has become of such paramount importance as to permeate the whole body of international law".[144]

This position was subsequently reiterated in the ICTY's *Celebici*-judgment.[145] Following the UN's 'change of heart', and both the ICJ and ICTY's recognition of the interplay of both fields of law, other actors in the international arena have also acknowledged that although their development may have been pronged, both *corpora juris* base themselves on the notion of human dignity and equally envisage greater protection for humanity.[146] As a result, it is well established today by the ICJ, other Tribunals, and international organisations that the two bodies of law share a common basis on which they both rely. In particular such declarations by the ICJ and the international tribunals hold international legal value in this regard

---

[142] UNCHR Report of the Secretary General "Promotion and Protection of Human Rights: Fundamental Standards of Humanity" (18 December 1998) UN Doc E/CN.4/1999/92 § 25. See also subsequently UNCHR Report of the Secretary General "Promotion and Protection of Human Rights: Fundamental Standards of Humanity" (12 January 2001) UN Doc. E/CN.4/2001/91; and UNCHR Report of the Secretary General "Promotion and Protection of Human Rights: Fundamental Standards of Humanity" (25 February 2004) UN Doc E/CN.4/2004/90.

[143] Legality of the Threat or Use of Nuclear Weapons, Advisory Opinion, I.C.J. Reports 1996, p. 226, § 79 and 86.

[144] *Prosecutor v. Furundzija* (Trial Judgment) IT-95-17/1-T (ICTY 10 December 1998), § 183.

[145] *Prosecutor v. Zejnil Delalic, Zdravko Mucic (aka "Pavo"), Hazim Delic and Esad Landžo (aka "Zenga") (Celebici - Case)* (Appeals Chamber) IT-96-21-A (20 February 2001) § 149: "Both human rights and humanitarian law focus on respect for human values and the dignity of the human person. Both bodies of law take as their starting point the concern for human dignity, which forms the basis of a list of fundamental minimum standards of humanity".

[146] Quénivet, 'The History of the Relationship Between International Humanitarian Law and Human Rights law' (n 121) 7.

and contribute to this research's perspective that an overarching perspective can be held towards the legal framework on the provision of humanitarian assistance.

Two points of critique relevant to the provision of humanitarian assistance must lastly be briefly addressed with regard to the growing merger and simultaneous application of human rights law and international humanitarian law. It has been argued that this simultaneous application of both fields of law can have the effect of firstly not only exacerbating conflicts, but secondly also affecting the neutrality of humanitarian law. With regard to the first argument, Meron notes that 'humanization' of armed conflict; namely the greater protection of individuals' rights in times of conflict, may have the unwanted side-effect of prolonging hostilities or even making conflicts more acceptable.[147] Nonetheless, Meron does argue that convergence of the two branches of law may be an 'enrichment' to both human rights law and international humanitarian law.[148] Concerning the second aspect, namely the neutrality of humanitarian law and especially the neutrality of organisations operating within this sphere such as the ICRC, it must be noted that the ICRC itself has indeed emphasised that there is no merger of the two *corpora juris*.[149] Historical differences, namely that humanitarian law developed through notions of chivalry and reciprocity, whereas human rights law is based on the premise that individuals must be protected from abuse of power by authorities, continue to also form arguments against their joint interpretation.[150] As such, the ICRC held in its 2005 study into the current status of customary international humanitarian law that although human rights law does 'support, strengthen and clarify analogous principles' of humanitarian law, they remain two separate and distinct branches of law.[151] Yet, Henckaerts and Doswald-Beck do acknowledge that both *corpora juris* reinforce each other 'in all situations', not limited to times of armed conflict.[152] Indeed, while a neutral humanitarian law will provide for the greatest chance of parties to a conflict respecting this law,[153] human rights law in and of itself is not 'coloured' or 'biased' in any way. Human rights law as a legal body must be separated from their incorporation into the mandates of various organisations. Concerns for the neutrality of humanitarian assistance, with a view to a 'rights-based' approach many organisations have adopted are however valid.[154] It must be noted that humanitarian assistance can only be considered *that*, if and when the principles of humanity, neutrality and impartiality are respected.[155] Both concerns therefore, although understandable, do not interfere with the perspective

[147] Theodor Meron, 'The Humanization of Humanitarian Law', (2000) 94 *American Journal of International Law* 2, 241-242.
[148] Ibid 266.
[149] Jean-Marie Henckaerts & Louise Doswald-Beck (eds), *Customary International Humanitarian Law (ICRC Study)* (Cambridge University Press 2006), Volume I: Rules, xxxvii.
[150] Quénivet, 'The History of the Relationship Between International Humanitarian Law and Human Rights law' (n 121) 10-11.
[151] Henckaerts & Doswald-Beck, ICRC Customary International Humanitarian Law Study (n 149).
[152] Ibid, 302 (Fundamental guarantees).
[153] David Rieff, 'Humanitarianism in Crisis', (2002) 81 *Foreign Affairs* 6, 120-121.
[154] Ibid 112, 120-121.
[155] See Section 2.2.3 The Principles for the Delivery of Assistance.

that indeed these two fields of law have developed parallel to one another, and converge in the foundation that humanity and human dignity are of the essence; both fields of law attempt to protect exactly that concept. Humanitarian assistance strives to achieve that same goal, and therefore this research stipulates that civilians finding themselves in a humanitarian crisis must be treated equally in their protection by the law, regardless of the circumstance they find themselves in: a need for humanitarian assistance can be equally great in the aftermath of a cyclone as during a non-international armed conflict, and the law should offer equal protection to persons regardless of these circumstances. In fact, the law should be developed in the *interest* of the victims of such circumstances. In the following Sections, the particular interrelation between and interaction of these fields of law is addressed in further detail, to ascertain in which manner the law protects such victims to the greatest extent.

3.4.2 Applicability of Human Rights in Armed Conflict and Occupation

Determining that both human rights law and humanitarian law have a shared goal and common denominator does not determine whether both *corpora juris* can indeed be simultaneously applicable and thus whether they do indeed interact. It has been clearly established that international humanitarian law is applicable in the event of an occupation or (non-)international armed conflict.[156] However, the applicability of human rights in times of occupation or armed conflict has not been as clearly established, considering the late 'arrival' of this body of law to the international scene post World War II. As discussed in Section 3.3, international human rights law provisions may provide a distinct basis for the provision of humanitarian assistance. As such, exploring their continued application in times of occupation or armed conflict is relevant to establishing which rights and obligations may exist with regard to the provision of assistance in such times. This assessment supports the premise of this research that a common, overarching approach must be taken in the provision of humanitarian assistance. Establishing which provisions may be applicable *at all times* shall contribute to providing clarity with regard to the rights of recipients of humanitarian assistance and moreover to the duties and responsibilities of the state sovereign as affected state.

3.4.2.1 Relevance of Continued Applicability and Acceptance Thereof

When both human rights law and humanitarian law are applicable simultaneously, the rights and duties pertaining to the provision of humanitarian assistance (discussed in Chapters 6 and 7) can be sought in both fields of law equally, should assistance be necessary in times of conflict or complex emergency. Enhanced protection for those persons in need of aid is thereby provided. The previous Section has noted that interaction between both fields of law did not really

[156] Sections 3.2.1 Defining an Armed Conflict and 3.2.3 Defining Occupation.

commence until the late 1960s. In a 1970 Report, the UN Secretary General noted that:

> "United Nations instruments already in force and those which still require ratifications in order to become fully operative, may be invoked to protect human rights at all times and everywhere and thus complete in certain respects and lend support to the international instruments especially applicable in conditions of war or armed conflicts."[157]

From this Report follows an assisting role for human rights in armed conflict, clarified and confirmed by the General Assembly's Resolution 2675 (XXV) of that same year, declaring that indeed in light of the protection of civilians in times of armed conflict, fundamental human rights as encompassed in international instruments 'continue to apply fully in situations of armed conflict'.[158] More momentum was gained in the 1990s, both in jurisprudence and in soft law. The 1993 Vienna Declaration on Human Rights expressed concern for human rights violations in times of armed conflicts and called upon all parties to such conflicts to not only observe humanitarian law, but to also observe 'as minimum standards for protection of human rights, as laid down in international conventions'.[159]As noted previously, the ICTY declared in its Furundžija-case that the notion of human dignity forms the basis and 'the very raison d'être of international humanitarian law and human rights law'.[160] The ICJ has somewhat simultaneously ascertained in several *Advisory Opinions* that the ICCPR and in particular the human right to life has continued applicability in times of armed conflict, as well as in more recent years subsequently broadening this to encompass 'human rights conventions' more generally.[161] In fact, in the binding judgment in the *Case Concerning Armed*

---

[157] UN Secretary General Report "Respect for Human Rights in Armed Conflict" (18 September 1970) UN Doc A/8052 § 16.

[158] UNGA Res 2675 (XXV) (9 December 1970) 'Basic principles for the protection of civilian populations in armed conflict' § 1.

[159] 'Vienna Declaration and Programme of Action' UN Doc A/CONF.157/23, (12 July 1993) § 29.

[160] *Prosecutor v. Furundzija* (Trial Judgment) IT-95-17/1-T (ICTY 10 December 1998), § 183.

[161] Legality of the Threat or Use of Nuclear Weapons, Advisory Opinion, I.C.J. Reports 1996, p. 226, § 25. With regard to the aspect of derogability in general, see Section 5.2.2 Derogability, Human Rights and the Provision of Humanitarian Assistance. However, particularly in relation to the applicability of human rights in times of armed conflict and their derogability, the Human Rights Committee has declared in its General Comment 29 pursuant to Article 4 'States of Emergency' UN Doc. CCPR/C/21/Rev.1/Add.11 § 3, 9 and 11 (31 August 2001) that: "During armed conflict, whether international or non-international, rules of international humanitarian law become applicable and help, in addition to the provisions in article 4 and article 5, paragraph 1, of the Covenant, to prevent the abuse of a State's emergency powers. The Covenant requires that even during an armed conflict measures derogating from the Covenant are allowed only if and to the extent that the situation constitutes a threat to the life of the nation. (…) Furthermore, article 4, paragraph 1, requires that no measure derogating from the provisions of the Covenant may be inconsistent with the State party's other obligations under international law, particularly the rules of international humanitarian law. (…) States may in no circumstances invoke article 4 of the Covenant as justification for acting in violation of humanitarian law". Thus, although derogation from human rights law is permitted, such derogation may not violate international humanitarian law in the process. In particular in relation to humanitarian assistance however, as discussed in Section 5.2.2 Derogability, Human Rights and the Provision of Humanitarian

Activities on the Territory of the Congo the Court recalled its earlier findings on the relationship between human rights and international humanitarian law, confirming with regard to the conflict situation at hand that:

> "both branches of law, namely international human rights law and international humanitarian law, would have to be taken into consideration".[162]

Whilst the ICJ may be valued for setting a standard in today's world lacking a 'world supreme court', Higgins has rightfully addressed the appropriateness of the General Assembly asking *Advisory Opinions* from the Court on one state's *compliance* with human rights treaty obligations as they are 'monitored, in much greater detail, by a treaty body established for that purpose', given the amount of states within that Assembly 'not in compliance with their obligations' under various human rights treaties.[163] The Human Rights Committee established in a (non-binding) General Comment in this regard that the ICCPR 'applies also in situations of armed conflict to which the rules of international humanitarian law are applicable'.[164] Regional human rights courts, including the European Court of Human Rights (ECtHR) and the Inter-American Court on Human Rights (IACtHR), have also determined the continued applicability of the human rights treaties under their jurisdiction in times of armed conflict.[165] The IACtHR herein focused in particular on the right to life, and personal integrity.[166] Derogability of certain clauses in human rights treaties fall outside the scope of this particular discussion on the interrelation of these two bodies of law, as they pertain to specific clauses in specific treaties, and will be addressed in relation to the provision of humanitarian assistance in Chapter 5.[167]

Assistance, the relevant human rights treaty provisions are non-derogable. See also Legal Consequences of the Construction of a Wall in the Occupied Palestinian Territory, Advisory Opinion, I.C.J. Reports 2004, p. 136, § 106: "More generally, the Court considers that the protection offered by human rights conventions does not cease in case of armed conflict, save through the effect of provisions for derogation of the kind to be found in Article 4 of the International Covenant on Civil and Political Rights".

162 ICJ *Armed Activities on the Territory of the Congo* (n 40) § 216.

163 Separate opinion Judge Higgins § 27 in the Legal Consequences of the Construction of a Wall in the Occupied Palestinian Territory, Advisory Opinion, I.C.J. Reports 2004, p. 136. Higgins was herein commenting on the singling out of Israel's compliance with the ICCPR and ICESCR as one state within the General Assembly.

164 Human Rights Committee, General Comment No. 31 (26 May 2004) on the nature of the general legal obligation imposed on States parties to the Covenant (art. 2) UN Doc. CCPR/C/21/Rev.1/Add.13 § 11.

165 *Isayeva, Yusupova and Bazayeva v.* Russia (App nos 57947/00, 57948/00 and 57949/00) ECHR 24 February 2005; Inter-American Court of Human Rights, *Case of Bámaca-Velasquez v. Guatemala* (November 25 2000) (Merits), Series C No. 70 § 207.

166 Ibid *Bámaca Velasquez v Guatamala.*

167 See in this regard also 'Draft articles on the effects of armed conflicts on treaties, with commentaries', Yearbook of the International Law Commission (2011) Vol. II Part Two, 33-34.

3.4.2.2 The Potential Extraterritorial Scope of Application of Human Rights Treaties

The developments regarding the potential extraterritorial scope of application of human rights treaties remain a matter of continued debate, and are clearly more contested than the applicability of human rights in times of armed conflict. In relation to the provision of humanitarian assistance, extraterritorial application of human rights obligations are particularly relevant in the circumstances of international armed conflicts and occupation. As discussed, increasingly non-international armed conflicts and (natural) disasters dominate the situations requiring a need for the provision of humanitarian assistance to persons in need of aid, where extraterritoriality of human rights application is not a relevant matter for the continued application of this body of law. Yet, international armed conflicts and circumstances of occupation still occur, sometimes also resulting in a need for the provision of humanitarian assistance, and as such the notion of the extraterritorial application of human rights obligations must be addressed.

As a result of the evolution in international practice, and in particular relation to the 'war on terror', some of the legal discussion is currently shifting from the matter of *whether* human rights law is indeed directly applicable in times of armed conflict, to *how* this law is applicable in relation to international humanitarian law.[168] This 'how' includes the potential extraterritorial application of human rights law. It must be noted that multiple states have continued to reiterate their objection to the possible extraterritorial application of the various human rights covenants in general, as well as distinguishing between continued application over *persons* abroad, versus continued application in *areas* where a state may exercise a certain level of authority or control.[169]

---

[168] Noam Lubell, 'Challenges in applying human rights law to armed conflict', (2005) 87 *International Review of the Red Cross* 860, 738.

[169] Karen da Costa, *The Extraterritorial Application of Selected Human Rights Treaties* (Martinus Nijhoff Brill Leiden 2013) 60. See for example the United States that has asserted (Concluding Observations of the Human Rights Committee: United States of America UN Doc CCPR/C/79/Add.50, A/50/40 (1995) § 284) and continued to reaffirm its "long-standing position that the Covenant does not apply extraterritorially. States Parties are required to ensure the rights in the Covenant only to individuals who are (1) within the territory of a State Party and (2) subject to that State Party's Jurisdiction" in *United States Responses to Selected Recommendations of the Human Rights Committee* October 10, 2007. See also UN Doc CCPR/C/ISR/2001/2 (4 December 2001) § 8 and the Human Rights Committee's Concluding Observations on the Second Periodic Report of Israel, UN Doc CCPR/CO/78/ISR (21 August 2003), § 11, where Israel argues that the pending armed conflict bars any such application; as well as CESCR 'Concluding observations of the Committee on Economic, Social and Cultural Rights – Israel', (23 May 2003) UN Doc E/C.12/1/Add.90 § 15. See furthermore the perspective of the Netherlands in UN Doc CCPR/CO/72/NET/Add.l, (2003) § 19 that argued with regard to the fall of Srebrenica and the applicability of Article 2 ICCPR that: "the Government disagrees with the Committee's suggestion that the provisions of the International Covenant on Civil and Political Rights are applicable to the conduct of Dutch blue helmets in Srebrenica (para. 8). Article 2 of the Covenant clearly states that each State Party undertakes to respect and to ensure to all individuals "within its territory and subject to its jurisdiction" the rights recognized in the Covenant, including the right to life enshrined in article 6. It goes without saying that the citizens of Srebrenica,

The ICJ has assessed that human rights instruments have continued application 'in respect of acts done by a State in the exercise of its jurisdiction outside its own territory'.[170] In particular relation to the International Convention on the Elimination of Racial Discrimination (ICERD), the Court determined that the treaty does not contain a general restriction pertaining to territorial application and that in fact its provisions 'generally appear to apply' – as is the case with other similar instruments – 'to the actions of a State party when it acts beyond its territory'.[171] Such wording, although somewhat more hesitant, does align with the earlier assertion in the *Congo v. Uganda*-case.

As mentioned above, this determination is of particular relevance to situations of international armed conflict and occupation; as in the event of a non-international armed conflict the determination of continued simultaneous application of human rights law in times of conflict suffices to ascertain the latter's application in that particular territory. Indeed, establishing extraterritorial application of human rights law will allow human rights provisions to function as a basis upon which duties may exist to provide humanitarian assistance outside of a state's territory. As such, an obligation to provide humanitarian assistance and a right to receive it outside of a state's territory may not only be sought in humanitarian law, but could then be sought directly in human rights law also, as a second source in times of international armed conflict or occupation. The continued applicability of human rights law may potentially provide for a broader protection of persons in need of humanitarian assistance in these circumstances, through the applicability of a wider legal framework. In Section 3.2.4 it has already been noted that certain provisions, amongst which those related to the delivery of humanitarian assistance, may only be required of an occupying force when a certain level of control has been established. Such an assessment stands in relation to the acts required of the occupying power in the provision of such assistance. In that regard, the ICJ indeed found that human rights law is applicable to such acts that a state performs in the 'exercise of its jurisdiction'.[172] Thus, the ICJ similarly connects the extraterritorial applicability of human rights law to the exercise of *control* by a state.

With regard to the ICCPR, the HRC noted in its 2004 *General Comment* pertaining to 'The Nature of the General Legal Obligation Imposed on States Parties to the Covenant' that a theory of 'power or effective control' equally applies.[173] Rather early on in the debate, the Inter-American Commission on

---

vis-à-vis the Netherlands, do not come within the scope of that provision. The strong commitment of the Netherlands to investigate and assess the deplorable events of 1995 is therefore not based on any obligation under the Covenant".

[170] ICJ *Armed Activities on the Territory of the Congo* (n 40) § 216.

[171] Application of the International Convention on the Elimination of all Forms of Racial Discrimination (Georgia v. Russian Federation), Provisional Measures, Order of 15 October 2008, I.C.J. Reports 2008, p. 353 § 109.

[172] ICJ *Armed Activities on the Territory of the Congo* (n 40) § 216.

[173] Human Rights Committee, General Comment No. 31 (26 May 2004) UN Doc CCPR/C/21/Rev.1/Add. 13 § 10: "[…] the enjoyment of Covenant rights is not limited to citizens of States Parties but must also be available to all individuals, regardless of nationality or statelessness, such as asylum seekers, refugees, migrant workers and other persons, who may find themselves in the

Human Rights stated that such applicability rests upon the 'authority and control' of a state, rather than a 'particular geographic area'.[174] Similarly, the ECtHR determined in its *Loizidou v. Turkey* judgement concerning Northern Cyprus that the provisions of the ECHR remain applicable in the event a state exercises extraterritorial 'effective control'.[175] Clearly, such extraterritorial application may be of relevance to the duties and rights in times of an international armed conflict or occupation, and favourable arguments find their logic in the common goal of both human rights law and international humanitarian law; namely the protection of persons. Legally however, it must be established what such a level of 'control' entails to establish whether human rights law may function as a source for the determination of a right to receive assistance in times of international armed conflict or occupation or a duty to provide such assistance for the sovereign authority.

What precisely can be determined as 'effective' control or authority has not yet definitively crystallised in international law with regards to this extraterritorial human rights application. Nevertheless, certain determinations with regard to temporal and personal scope can be derived from (regional) case law, as these issues have been addressed in more detail by various human rights courts. The *Loizidou*-case before the ECtHR concerned a situation of rather prolonged occupation, which according to the ECtHR can lead to the continued applicability of human rights law.[176] Furthermore, the ECtHR found in *Ilascu and others v. Moldova and Russia* that Russia was responsible for certain violations although the presence of Russian troops in Moldova was for a restricted time.[177] Therefore, the *temporal* scope according to the ECtHR can be quite broad, ranging from a relatively short period of time to prolonged occupation, but the ECtHR has been known to only allow for extraterritorial application of the Convention as a matter of exception.[178] Therefore, the personal scope should also be assessed, as effective control or authority is divided between *territory* outside the own state and *individuals* outside the territory but remaining under the state's control.[179] As such, the Inter-American Commission on Human Rights asserted in *Coard et al v. USA* that agents of a state in another territory may continue to be under the control of the

territory or subject to the jurisdiction of the State Party. This principle also applies to those within the power or effective control of the forces of a State Party acting outside its territory, regardless of the circumstances in which such power or effective control was obtained, such as forces constituting a national contingent of a State Party assigned to an international peace-keeping or peace-enforcement operation".

174 Inter-American Commission on Human Rights, *Coard et al v USA* (Report No 109/99 Case 10.951) (29 September 1999) § 37.

175 *Loizidou v Turkey (Preliminary Objections)* (App no 15318/89) ECHR 23 March 1995, § 62.

176 *Loizidou v Turkey (Preliminary Objections)* (App no 15318/89) ECHR 23 March 1995.

177 *Ilascu and others v Moldova and Russia* (App no 48787/99) ECHR 8 July 2004, 318.

178 Cedric Ryngaert, 'Clarifying the Extraterritorial Application of the European Convention on Human Rights (Al-Skeini v the United Kingdom)' (2012) 28 *Merkourios - International and European Security Law* 74, 59.

179 Lubell, 'Challenges in applying human rights law to armed conflict' (n 168) 740.

country of origin.[180] Similarly, the ECtHR also found such control to exist, although distinguishing between effective control over 'ground operations' whereby a state exercises extraterritorial jurisdiction as opposed to aerial attacks, thereby adhering to a more 'effective territorial control' approach.[181] The ECtHR elaborated that the entire range of rights under the ECHR must be observed by States Parties when exercising control over a particular area, while it is not necessary to establish whether 'detailed control over the policies and actions of the subordinate local administration' is exercised.[182] Consequently, although the extra-territorial applicability of human rights law is increasingly discussed and addressed in jurisprudence,[183] as seen above the extent of the notion of 'effective' control or authority remains a matter of continued debate and courts are continuing to be restrictive in their application of the concept.

Furthermore, for a large part the discussion through jurisprudence has concentrated itself around the ICCPR and ECHR, whereas the provision of humanitarian assistance can also be placed within the range of rights found in the ICESCR. As such, the assessment of the potential extraterritorial application of these rights is of particular relevance also. Although the ICJ, ECtHR and IACtHR did not determine that the assessment of extraterritorial application of human rights was solely pertinent to civil and political rights, they have not positively and bindingly established extra-territorial obligations for states with regard to economic, social and cultural rights. The ICJ has merely noted that 'it is not to be excluded' that such rights may also apply extraterritorially should a state exercise its territorial jurisdiction, but safeguarded this statement by addressing the fact that the ICESCR may be lacking a provision on its scope of application as it 'guarantees rights which are essentially territorial'.[184] Indeed, it has been argued that there are no indications that the drafters of the ICESCR ever intended such an extraterritorial

---

[180] Inter-American Commission on Human Rights, *Coard et al v USA* (Report No 109/99 Case 10.951) (29 September 1999) § 37.

[181] See amongst others *Bankovic and others v. Belgium and 16 Other Contracting States* (Decision as to the Admissibility) (App no 52207/99) ECHR 12 December 2001 § 67-73 and in particular § 80; and *Öcalan v Turkey* (App no. 46221/99) ECHR 12 May 2005. The Court determined in the latter (§ 91) that "(…) It is common ground that, directly after being handed over to the Turkish officials by the Kenyan officials, the applicant was effectively under Turkish authority and therefore within the "jurisdiction" of that State for the purposes of Article 1 of the Convention, even though in this instance Turkey exercised its authority outside its territory. It is true that the applicant was physically forced to return to Turkey by Turkish officials and was under their authority and control following his arrest and return to Turkey". As such, in the *Öcalan* case, effective authority could be established.

[182] *Al-Skeini and Others v The United Kingdom* (App No 55721/07) ECHR 7 July 2011 § 137-138.

[183] Henckaerts & Doswald-Beck, ICRC Customary International Humanitarian Law Study (n 149), 305-306 (Fundamental Guarantees).

[184] Legal Consequences of the Construction of a Wall in the Occupied Palestinian Territory, Advisory Opinion, I.C.J. Reports 2004, p. 136, § 112. In soft law recently the 'Maastricht Principles on Extra-Territorial Obligations (ETOs) of States in the area of Economic, Social and Cultural Rights' of 28 September 2011 in Geneva, at a UN side-event were adopted with a view to furthering the acceptance of such extraterritorial application. They are co-sponsored by the International Commission of Jurists and Maastricht University.

application of the convention.[185] However, the Committee on Economic Social and Cultural Rights (CESCR) itself declared that a state party's obligations under the ICESCR 'apply to all territories and populations under its effective control', referring also to the obligations of actors 'under the jurisdiction' of States Parties.[186] Furthermore, the 'Maastricht Principles on Extra-Territorial Obligations (ETOs) of States in the area of Economic, Social and Cultural Rights' (Maastricht Principles) were recently adopted with a view to furthering the acceptance of such extraterritorial application.[187]

As mentioned, the potential extraterritorial application of human rights provisions relevant to the provision of humanitarian assistance remains limited to circumstances of international armed conflict or occupation which amount to a humanitarian crisis. Should a humanitarian crisis occur in times of an international armed conflict or during occupation, the extraterritorial application of human rights may be of relevance. In particular the potential application of economic, social and cultural rights is of relevance, as such rights place a positive obligation upon states to perform an active function (such as the provision of food).[188] Indeed, providing humanitarian assistance is such a positive obligation that pertains to the fulfilment of certain human rights by the affected state in a circumstance such as a humanitarian crisis.[189] However it is precisely this category of rights that has not seen as much extraterritorial recognition by courts, compared to human rights such as the right to life, enshrined in the ICCPR and ECHR. Yet, as will be addressed in Chapter 6, the duties of the affected state in times of occupation and international armed conflict are quite well-developed in humanitarian law with regard to the provision of humanitarian assistance. Whilst it remains relevant to reaffirm that human rights do not cease to exist in times of conflict or occupation, the need to rely on the so far contested notion of extraterritorial application of certain human rights, is therefore not immediately necessary for the protection of persons in need of aid. Even with the acceptance that indeed human rights *do* find continued extraterritorial application, the level of 'effective control' or authority necessary for their fulfilment remains to be determined on a case-by-case basis, potentially in

---

185 Michael J Dennis, 'Application of Human Rights Treaties Extraterritorially in Times of Armed Conflict and Military Occupation', (2005) 99 *American Journal of International Law* 1, 127.

186 CESCR 'Concluding observations of the Committee on Economic, Social and Cultural Rights – Israel', (23 May 2003) UN Doc E/C.12/1/Add.90 § 31 and CESCR General Comment 20 (Article 2 ICESCR) UN Doc E/C.12/GC/20 'Non-discrimination in economic, social and cultural rights' (2 July 2009) § 14.

187 The 'Maastricht Principles on Extra-Territorial Obligations (ETOs) of States in the area of Economic, Social and Cultural Rights' of 28 September 2011 in Geneva, at a UN side-event. They are co-sponsored by the International Commission of Jurists and Maastricht University, and have been signed by over 40 distinguished jurists, thereby clearly adding to the *opinio juris* in this area. The final version of the Principles was adopted 29 February 2012. See for a further discussion also Fons Coomans, 'Application of the International Covenant on Economic Social and Cultural Rights in the Framework of International Organisations', (2007) *Max Planck Yearbook of United Nations Law* 11, 359–390.

188 See Section 3.4.2.2 The Potential Extraterritorial Scope of Application of Human Rights Treaties.

189 See Chapter 5 The Potential Human Right to Receive Humanitarian Assistance, regarding the specific human rights related to humanitarian assistance.

court. Should such a control then be definitively established, a primary right to be observed in particular relation to the provision of emergency aid would then potentially be the right to life, as the category of economic, social and cultural rights is challenged with additional difficulties regarding potential extraterritorial application.

3.4.3 Hierarchy or Convergence of International Legal Norms?

Having established that human rights law finds continued applicability in times of armed conflict and occupation and that their application is also continued in times of natural disaster and non-international armed conflict, the simultaneous and reciprocal relationship between human rights law and international humanitarian law must be assessed.[190] Such an assessment may determine which provisions that may invoke a right or duty relating to humanitarian assistance, to be discussed in subsequent Chapters, would perhaps receive precedence over another provision relating to humanitarian assistance. Determining which theories are applicable in the assessment of such a relationship will allow for the more practical determination of the existing specific rights and duties in subsequent Chapters. As just established, human rights law has a general application, whereas humanitarian law is tailored specifically to circumstances of armed conflict. Thus, the doctrine of 'lex specialis derogat lex generalis', which is generally accepted in national law, immediately springs to mind. Yet, given the decentralised structure of the international legal body, applying this domestic regime to the international field does not necessarily immediately resolve the relationship between human rights law and humanitarian law.[191] How to balance the possible conflicting norms must however be addressed, as this may be the case in the provision of humanitarian assistance.[192]

The ICJ has as such not only declared affirmatively that human rights remain applicable in times of armed conflict, it has also addressed the particular relationship between both fields of law. Doing so firstly in its 1996 *Nuclear Weapons*-Opinion, the Court focused in particular on the right to life:

> "The Court observes that the protection of the International Covenant of Civil and Political Rights does not cease in times of war, except by operation of Article 4 of the Covenant whereby certain provisions may be derogated from in a time of national

[190] This Section is an updated version of earlier work published: 'A humanitarian crisis: reframing the legal framework on humanitarian assistance', in Zwitter A et al (eds) *Humanitarian Action: Global, Regional and Domestic Legal Responses* (Cambridge University Press 2014) 54-80.

[191] Krieger, 'A Conflict of Norms' (n 121), 269.

[192] A discussion of conflicting norms in general international law remains outside the scope of this research. See however amongst others Articles 53 and 64 of the Vienna Convention on the Law of Treaties; Article 103 UN Charter; Military and Paramilitary Activities in and against Nicaragua (Nicaragua v. United States of America), Merits, Judgment 27 June 1986 I.C.J. Reports 1986, p. 14, § 177-179, 186; and 'Fragmentation Of International Law: Difficulties Arising From The Diversification And Expansion Of International Law', Report of the Study Group of the International Law Commission (13 April 2006) UN Doc A/CN.4/L.682.

emergency. Respect for the right to life is not, however, such a provision. In principle, the right not arbitrarily to be deprived of one's life applies also in hostilities. The test of what is an arbitrary deprivation of life, however, then falls to be determined by the applicable *lex specialis,* namely, the law applicable in armed conflict which is designed to regulate the conduct of hostilities. Thus whether a particular loss of life, through the use of a certain weapon in warfare, is to be considered an arbitrary deprivation of life contrary to Article 6 of the Covenant, can only be decided by reference to the law applicable in armed conflict and not deduced from the terms of the Covenant itself"[193]

In its analysis, the ICJ asserts that whilst human rights law continues to be applicable, the notion of 'arbitrary deprivation of life' in relation to the use of particular weapons must be determined by humanitarian law as the *lex specialis* in times of hostilities. At a more abstract level, the Court elaborated on its position in the ensuing *Legal Consequences of the Construction of a Wall in the Occupied Palestinian Territory* Advisory Opinion stating:

"As regards the relationship between international humanitarian law and human rights law, there are thus three possible situations: some rights may be exclusively matters of international humanitarian law; others may be exclusively matters of human rights law; yet others may be matters of both these branches of international law. In order to answer the question put to it, the Court will have to take into consideration both these branches of international law, namely human rights law and, as lex specialis, international humanitarian law".[194]

The Court herein evolves its position in the *Nuclear Weapons*-Opinion where it addressed the law of conduct of hostilities to be the 'lex specialis', but now also recognises the potential of matters falling exclusively within the domain of human rights law, while broadening its stance to include *all* human rights as opposed to the right to life. Thus the ICJ takes a somewhat more conciliatory approach.[195] In the above assessment, the ICJ provides three possible scenarios to which the 'lex specialis'-doctrine may be applicable. These scenario's then depend on the content of the rights involved. The ICJ confirmed this approach in its subsequent ruling (as opposed to the previous two being Advisory Opinions) in the *Armed Activities on the Territory of the Congo*-case and thereby appears – at least for the time being – to have taken the abovementioned approach towards the relationship between human rights law and humanitarian law.[196] In this approach by the Court

[193] Legality of the Threat or Use of Nuclear Weapons, Advisory Opinion, I.C.J. Reports 1996, p. 226, § 25.

[194] Legal Consequences of the Construction of a Wall in the Occupied Palestinian Territory, Advisory Opinion, I.C.J. Reports 2004, p. 136, § 106.

[195] Jean d'Aspremont & Elodie Tranchez, 'The quest for a non-conflictual existence of international human rights law and humanitarian law: which role for the lex specialis principle?' in Robert Kolb and Gloria Gaggioli (eds) *Research Handbook on Human Rights and Humanitarian Law* (Edwar Elgar 2013), 241.

[196] ICJ *Armed Activities on the Territory of the Congo* (n 40) § 216. For a different reading see Krieger, 'A Conflict of Norms' (n 121), 271, who argues in reference to the Nuclear Weapons-case that the ICJ

humanitarian assistance, taking place both in times of conflict and peace and finding regulation in both fields of law, would then fall into the third category proposed by the ICJ. The approach in which international humanitarian law functions as *lex specialis* is found equally in the work of the Inter-American Commission.[197] The specific rights and obligations with regard to the provision of humanitarian assistance can however be found in both *corpora juris*, and furthermore provide for a disparate protection of persons depending on the specific circumstance, such as conflict or natural disaster.[198] This, and a broader need for conflict resolution, therefore leads to the need for a more comprehensive solution to conflicts between the law.

An alternative approach can be seen in the practice of the Human Rights Committee that stated regarding the ICCPR:

> "[...] the Covenant applies also in situations of armed conflict to which the rules of international humanitarian law are applicable. While in respect of certain Covenant rights, more specific rules of international humanitarian law may be especially relevant for the purpose of the interpretation of the Covenant rights, both spheres of law are complementary, not mutually exclusive".[199]

The HRC is hereby taking the approach of complementarity, declaring that the rights enshrined in the ICCPR must be interpreted in light of humanitarian law principles in times of armed conflict. This approach is also embraced amongst others by Philip Alston in his role as UN Special Rapporteur on extrajudicial, summary or arbitrary executions, declaring that humanitarian law must be examined for the interpretation of human rights law in times of armed conflict.[200] Such an approach appears to suggest humanitarian law as a *lex specialis*, as it is argued that this body of law must be examined for the interpretation of a human rights principle in times of armed conflict. While indeed human rights law and humanitarian law continue to complement each other, such a haphazard interplay will result in a rather non-homogenous development of norms. This approach furthermore deviates somewhat from the ICJ's approach, as it does not necessarily view humanitarian law firmly as the *lex specialis* obtaining preference over human

restricts itself to specific instances, and does not consider international humanitarian law to override human rights law 'en bloc'.

197 Inter-American Commission on Human Rights, *Coard et al v USA* (Report No 109/99 Case 10.951) (29 September 1999) § 42.

198 See Chapters 6 and 7 in more detail.

199 Human Rights Committee, General Comment No. 31 on the nature of the general legal obligation imposed on States parties to the Covenant (art. 2), UN Doc. CCPR/C/21/Rev.1/Add.13 (26 May 2004) § 11.

200 UN Doc A/HRC/4/20/Add.1, Report of the Special Rapporteur on extrajudicial, summary or arbitrary executions, Philip Alston – Addendum -Summary of cases transmitted to Government and replies received , 12 march 2007 p. 348: "Thus, under current international law, human rights law is applied alongside international humanitarian law during armed conflict, and the interpretation of human rights law requires examination of international humanitarian law". See furthermore for a discussion of various authors Quénivet, 'The History of the Relationship Between International Humanitarian Law and Human Rights law' (n 121) 8-10.

rights law in times of armed conflict, but rather would see human rights law interpreted in light of humanitarian law. The complimentarity-based approach however does align with the notion that both human rights law and humanitarian law find their basis in the concept of human dignity, and as such share a common goal.

Yet another method is taken by Marco Sassòli, who argues that it remains somewhat unclear which body of law is the 'lex specialis' in situations where both are applicable.[201] As Sassòli states, the relationship between human rights law and humanitarian law must in case of conflict indeed be examined according to the 'lex specialis'-doctrine, but humanitarian law is not necessarily the more specialised law in each particular circumstance:

> "The principle does not indicate an inherent quality in one branch of law, such as humanitarian law, or of one of its rules. Rather, it determines which rule prevails over another in a particular situation. Each case must be analysed individually".[202]

How then such a determination must be made, should according to Sassòli be done through a formal observation of which law in the particular circumstance has the most interfaces with the situation; the norm which has a more precise content, and/or with a more 'personal scope of application'.[203] Thus, depending on the particular circumstances, either human rights law, or humanitarian law, may be the *lex specialis* at a particular time. Yet, the *lex generalis* always remains present in the background.[204] This practice has indeed also been established in the ILC's Report of the 'Study group on the fragmentation of international law', that argues the relational character of the special and the general rule.[205] Such an approach could also be read into the HRC's above comment with regard to 'specific' humanitarian rules. Concurring with Sassòli, Doswald-Beck and Krieger both note that especially in circumstances such as non-international armed conflicts the general prevalence of humanitarian law would not seem fitting, despite it being a situation of armed conflict, as human rights law is often more specific.[206] Such a gap-filling method by human rights law has also been the approach of the ECtHR in the situation of non-international armed conflicts.[207] In some specific instances, the

---

[201] Marco Sassòli and Laura M Olson, 'The relationship between international humanitarian and human rights law where it matters: admissible killing and internment of fighters in non-international armed conflicts', (2008) 90 *International Review of the Red Cross* 871, 600.
[202] Ibid 603-604.
[203] Ibid 604.
[204] Ibid 605.
[205] 'Fragmentation Of International Law: Difficulties Arising From The Diversification And Expansion Of International Law', Report of the Study Group of the International Law Commission (13 April 2006) UN Doc A/CN.4/L.682 § 104 and 112.
[206] Louise Doswald-Beck, 'The right to life in armed conflict: does international humanitarian law provide all the answers?' (2006) 88 *International Review of the Red Cross* 864, 903; and Krieger, 'A Conflict of Norms' (n 121), 273.
[207] *Isayeva, Yusupova and Bazayeva v.* Russia [Isayeva I] (App nos 57947/00, 57948/00 and 57949/00) ECHR 24 February 2005 § 167 and 169; *Isayeva v. Russia* [Isayeva II] (App no 57950/00) ECHR 24

inverse has even been argued; where with regard to the right to food in conflict situations, human rights law has been considered the *lex specialis*.[208]

Without concurring with this latter perspective *per se*, as it is all dependent on specific circumstances, this more converging, harmonious approach would indeed be more befitting the developments that have taken place in the evolution of the relationship between international human rights and humanitarian law over the past few decades. Indeed, where international humanitarian law began as strictly addressing states, and human rights law did not apply in times of armed conflict, it is now clear that both *corpora juris* pursue the same goal: the greater protection of persons. In fact, perhaps the time has come to affirmatively declare that both are cast along the same lines and share a common denominator. As such, Krieger suggests the 'most favourable principle' as an interpretative method, through which the norm that grants the greatest protection to the individual would be applied.[209] This would also align with Doswald-Beck's argument to take into consideration the

February 2005, § 173; and *Ilascu and others v Moldova and Russia* (App no 48787/99) ECHR 8 July 2004, 318. The debate whether or not (regional) human rights courts or other bodies *should* be applying humanitarian law remains outside the scope of this research. However, it is relevant to note the self-restriction imposed by the ECtHR in *Bankovic and others v. Belgium and 16 Other Contracting States* (Decision as to the Admissibility) (App no 52207/99) ECHR 12 December 2001 § 75: "[...] had the drafters of the Convention wished to ensure jurisdiction as extensive as that advocated by the applicants, they could have adopted a text the same or similar to the contemporaneous Articles 1 of the four Geneva Conventions of 1949". Compare in this regard the more forward approach of the Inter-American Commission on Human Rights, *Juan Carlos Abella v Argentina* ('Tablada Case') (Case no 11.137) (18 November 1997) § 161: "[...] But the Commission's ability to resolve claimed violations (...) arising out of an armed conflict may not be possible in many cases by reference to (...) the American Convention alone. This is because the American Convention contains no rules that either define or distinguish civilians from combatants and other military targets, much less, specify when a civilian can be lawfully attacked or when civilian casualties are a lawful consequence of military operations. Therefore, the Commission must necessarily look to and apply definitional standards and relevant rules of humanitarian law as sources of authoritative guidance in its resolution of this and other kinds of claims alleging violations of the American Convention in combat situations". However, this decision has been subsequently overturned by the Inter-American Court of Human Rights, *Case of Las Palmeras v Colombia* (4 February 2000) (Preliminary Objections) Case no 67, Series C, § 33; and Inter-American Court of Human Rights, *Case of Bámaca-Velasquez v. Guatemala* (November 25 2000) (Merits), Series C No. 70 § 209: "Indeed, there is a similarity between the content of Article 3, common to the 1949 Geneva Conventions, and the provisions of the American Convention and other international instruments regarding non-derogable human rights (such as the right to life and the right not to be submitted to torture or cruel, inhuman or degrading treatment). This Court has already indicated in the Las Palmeras Case (2000), that the relevant provisions of the Geneva Conventions may be taken into consideration as elements for the interpretation of the American Convention".

[208] 'The Right to Food – Note by the Secretary-General' (23 July 2001) UN Doc A/56/210 § 114: "[...] International human rights law must be complemented by international humanitarian law that protects the right to food in situations of armed conflict. This must include the prohibition of starvation of civilians as a method of warfare and forced displacement, as well as respect for the rules on relief and humanitarian assistance, so that relief is not blocked, diverted or delayed. The right to food, along with other economic, social and cultural rights, must be treated as equal in status and implementation to civil and political rights [...]".

[209] Krieger, 'A Conflict of Norms' (n 121), 274.

object and purpose of international humanitarian law, as both this body of law and human rights law aim to protect persons and prevent the loss of life.[210]

It is precisely for this specific purpose that humanitarian assistance is provided in times of a humanitarian crisis, and such an interpretative method would indeed not only be relevant, but also find ground in the approach common to international humanitarian law to interpret provisions 'protectively'; to err on the side of caution.[211] For this reason it has indeed been necessary to establish the current relationship between humanitarian law and human rights law, in order to apply the theory behind this relationship to practical circumstances on the ground where humanitarian assistance may be necessary and a determination must be made as to which rights and duties exist. Furthermore, this method of interpretation falls in line with Article 31(3)(c) of the Vienna Convention on the Law of Treaties, stating that as a basic interpretative rule, jointly with the object, purpose and context of a treaty, also other relevant applicable rules of international law must be considered.[212] This clause comes as a general rule of interpretation, and was created with a view to the evolution of the law.[213] Thus, given the joint evolution of human rights law and humanitarian law over the past decades, with an enhanced focus on the protection of persons both in times of conflict and peace, a proper interpretation of provisions in either field of law relating to the provision of humanitarian assistance should be interpreted with the other body of law in mind also. In this regard, human rights law can furthermore play a vital role as individuals are provided with more direct means of redress, as opposed to humanitarian law in case of violations.[214]

Furthermore, as humanitarian assistance takes place in times of peace *and* in times of war, such a converging approach is necessary to ensure that the same rights and duties in relation to the receipt and provision of humanitarian assistance exist in *all* circumstances. Equally, the UN Special Rapporteur on the protection of persons in the event of disasters has argued that several regimes are applicable to the protection of persons, and that such bodies of law are necessarily dependent upon each other:

> "[...] the regimes of protection of persons are international humanitarian law, international human rights law and international law relating to refugees and internally displaced persons. These regimes may apply simultaneously to the same situation because they essentially complement each other. In addition, they are guided by a basic

[210] Doswald-Beck, 'The right to life in armed conflict: does international humanitarian law provide all the answers?' (n 206).
[211] Kuijt (n 190), 78-79.
[212] Article 31(1) and (3)(c) Vienna Convention state: "1. A treaty shall be interpreted in good faith in accordance with the ordinary meaning to be given to the terms of the treaty in their context and in the light of its object and purpose. [...] 3. There shall be taken into account, together with the context: [...] (c) Any relevant rules of international law applicable in the relations between the parties".
[213] Commentary to the Vienna Convention, (1966) *Yearbook of the International Law Commission*, Vol. II, 222 (Draft Article 27).
[214] Krieger, 'A Conflict of Norms' (n 121), 289.

identity of purpose: the protection of the human person in all and any circumstances. The three areas of law underscore the essential universality of humanitarian principles".[215]

Such an approach is precisely the premise put forward in this research: the protection of persons should be provided for to the greatest extent possible, regardless of the legally qualifiable situation these persons may be situated in. This holds especially true for circumstances such as complex emergencies, where an overlap of multiple bodies of law is inevitable. Thus, the provision of humanitarian assistance must be sought on the basis of those provisions of humanitarian law and human rights law that are most specific and provide the utmost protection in a given circumstance. It is precisely this approach to the *lex specialis*-rule, which in fact departs from the original notion of the rule, that will be applied throughout this research pertaining to the various rights and obligations applicable to the provision of humanitarian assistance. This interdependence, and growing realisation that a common minimum standard should exist that is applicable at all times has already been asserted earlier.[216] Indeed, such a common standard could assist in the joint interpretation of human rights law and humanitarian law, especially in the event of doubt as to the preferred application of either.

3.5 Conclusion

With a view to establishing the scope of application of humanitarian assistance, the *circumstances* in which such assistance may be of need have been explored. In this context, this Chapter has discussed and defined the notions of international and non-international armed conflict, occupation and (natural) disaster.[217] As this research is based on the premise that a person *in need* should receive assistance, regardless of whether that person finds themselves in the aftermath of a natural disaster, in the midst of a conflict or occupation, it has been relevant to define an overarching concept of a 'humanitarian crisis'. Indeed, this overarching notion is relevant from two specific perspectives. Not only does this concept build forth on the premise that the legal framework with regard to the provision of humanitarian assistance must be viewed in its totality, it furthermore establishes a determination of a certain level of severity that may be warranted in order for humanitarian

---

215 ILC 'Preliminary report on the protection of persons in the event of disasters' UN Doc. A/CN.4/598 (n 76) § 52.

216 See amongst others the Turku 'Declaration of Minimum Humanitarian Standards' (n 141), UNCHR Report of the Secretary General "Promotion and Protection of Human Rights: Fundamental Standards of Humanity" (25 February 2004) UN Doc E/CN.4/2004/90; *Prosecutor v. Furundzija* (Trial Judgment) IT-95-17/1-T (ICTY 10 December 1998) and *Prosecutor v. Zejnil Delalic, Zdravko Mucic (aka "Pavo"), Hazim Delic and Esad Landžo (aka "Zenga") (Celebici-case)* (Appeals Chamber) IT-96-21-A (20 February 2001); see also HJ Heinzte, 'Convergence Between Human Rights Law and International Humanitarian Law' in HJ Heintze & A Zwitter (eds) *Humanitarian Assistance and International Law: A Crosscut Through Legal Issues Pertaining to Humanitarianism* (Springer 2011) 85, regarding the fact that such a convergence is welcome.

217 Sections 3.2.1 Defining an Armed Conflict, 3.2.3 Defining Occupation and 3.2.5 Defining a (Natural) Disaster.

assistance to be needed. Not every situation of occupation, conflict or disaster warrants the provision of humanitarian assistance, but in fact a certain threshold must be met in order for the delivery of emergency assistance to be necessary. As such, it has been put forward that such a humanitarian crisis is 'a situation deriving from a variety of origins, including natural or man-made disaster, armed conflict and occupation; causing grave damages of a personal or material nature to persons, where (national/external) assistance is needed as the local capacity is either overwhelmed, unable or sometimes unwilling to manage the circumstances'.[218] The notion of a humanitarian crisis functions as a basis upon which the further development of the legal framework concerning the rights and obligations relating to the provision of humanitarian assistance may take place.

Such rights and obligations relating to humanitarian assistance primarily find their legal base in international humanitarian law and human rights law. As such, it has been relevant to discuss the relationship between the two *corpora juris*, assessing their pronged development and subsequent interaction over the past decades.[219] Establishing that both fields of law find a common denominator in the greater protection of humanity, the primary goal of humanitarian assistance, and that especially the ICJ and several other international courts and tribunals as well as the UN have a positive perspective on their interaction, the broad applicability of human rights was further examined. Indeed over the past years, and particularly since the ICJ's addressing of the matter, the concept of the potential extra-territorial application of human rights law has been widely discussed. On several occasions regional bodies such as the ECtHR and IACtHR have expressed their (restrained) approach to the matter.[220] The extent of the concept of 'effective' control in the extra-territorial application of human rights law however remains under debate. The extra-territorial applicability of human rights is particularly relevant to the provision of humanitarian assistance in times of international armed conflict and occupation, as this may result in state obligations beyond the national territory.[221] Yet, for the provision of humanitarian assistance, such extraterritorial application is not necessarily relevant. Also, the discussion on the existence of the extra-territorial application of human rights law lead to a renewed discourse on the relationship and possible hierarchy between human rights and humanitarian law, which has subsequently been addressed.[222]

Discussion remains regarding the relationship between the two fields of law as the ICJ, other courts, UN bodies and legal scholars do not always concur on the manner in which both *corpora juris* interact, and a development has taken place over the past decades. Indeed, the *lex specialis*-principle can be interpreted in various ways, such as the tiered approach of the ICJ, recognising a different body of law to be applicable at various times; with humanitarian law as the *lex specialis*,

[218] Section 3.3.3 Defining a Humanitarian Crisis.
[219] Section 3.4.1 Development of the Interaction between both Fields of Law.
[220] Section 3.4.2 Applicability of Human Rights in Armed Conflict and Occupation.
[221] See Chapter 5 The Potential Human Right to Receive Humanitarian Assistance.
[222] Section 3.4.3 Hierarchy or Convergence of International Legal Norms?

whereas the UN takes a more complementary approach. Lastly in scholarship amongst others Sassòli recognises the *lex specialis*-principle to not necessarily imply humanitarian law as the specific law in times of armed conflict *per se*, but that the rule applies the more specific law *in a particular given circumstance*.[223] This could then result in the application of a stand-alone provision of human rights law in times of international armed conflict if such a provision would be more specific than a particular rule of humanitarian law on that topic. Sassòli's approach has been furthermore embraced by the ILC's Report of the 'Study group on the fragmentation of international law', the UN Special Rapporteur on the protection of persons in the event of disasters and other scholars. Indeed, with a view to the above established pursuance of a similar common goal that can be found between human rights and humanitarian law, namely the greater protection of persons at all times, it is submitted that the *lex specialis*-principle must be read accordingly: in times of potential conflicting norms between human rights law and humanitarian law, the most specific provision allowing for the greatest protection of persons must be applied. Such a converging approach also concurs with the viewpoint that the provision and receipt of humanitarian assistance in any circumstance should be equally protected to the greatest extent possible under international law, regardless of whether it be through human rights law or humanitarian law. Indeed, as will be addressed in Chapter 4, such protection also flows forth from the notion of state sovereignty, which is a constant throughout all circumstances in international law.

With this Chapter, the scope of application of humanitarian assistance has been assessed, as well as the applicable fields of law. Therefore, the proceeding Chapters can provide a more substantive analysis of the rights and duties relating to the provision of assistance, such as addressing the question whether a possible (human) right to receive humanitarian assistance exists. In doing so, several individual human rights will be explored. Given the fact that human rights law remains applicable in times of (natural) disaster, armed conflict and occupation, this field of law needs to be assessed first, before examining the various rights and obligations *specifically* pertaining to the provision of humanitarian assistance in times of occupation, armed conflict or disaster. Prior to discussing 'Part II Rights and Duties in Humanitarian Crises' of this research, the following Chapter will address the concept of state sovereignty, which plays a continuous role throughout the legal framework on the provision of humanitarian assistance.

[223] Section 3.4.3 Hierarchy or Convergence of International Legal Norms?

CHAPTER 4
STATE SOVEREIGNTY AS A CONTEXTUAL CONCEPT REGARDING HUMANITARIAN ASSISTANCE

Over the past decades, the Sudan has been faced with a vast array of conflicts, natural disasters, internal uprisings and the creation of a new, independent state. The international community has at various points in time provided humanitarian assistance, amongst which most recently following the creation of the Republic of South Sudan:

"The Republic of South Sudan faces considerable humanitarian challenges, which have increased substantially since the outbreak of violence across the country in mid-december 2013".

In the face of so many problems, the international community is debating whether or not to provide more robust assistance. However, such a role for the international community might face issues relating to the sovereignty of a state. What exactly does the notion of state sovereignty entail? How does this notion relate to concepts such as 'humanitarian intervention' or 'the responsibility to protect'? This Chapter will assess the concept of state sovereignty as it exists in the international legal order today, in particular in relation to the provision of humanitarian assistance.[1]

4.1 Introduction

The previous Chapters have set out the framework in which humanitarian assistance operates. Chapter 2 has addressed the concept of humanitarian assistance, as well as the principles by which it is provided, and the actors involved in receipt and provision. Chapter 3 discussed the legal boundaries of the framework; ascertaining the notion of a humanitarian 'crisis' and addressing the interplay of various fields of law related to the provision of assistance. As the rights and duties involved in the provision of humanitarian assistance are incorporated into various bodies of law, these will be addressed in depth in Part II of this research. To close Part I however, the concept of state sovereignty must be addressed. The notion of state sovereignty is intrinsically linked to the legal rights and duties pertaining to the delivery of emergency aid as addressed in this research. In the instances in which humanitarian assistance is provided, the sphere of state sovereignty is touched upon, given the role of the particular sovereign in allowing the delivery of assistance. The notion of

[1] <www.unocha.org/south-sudan/crisis-overview> accessed 17 September 2014.

sovereignty is extremely relevant to the legal rights and obligations involved in the provision of humanitarian assistance, as the affected state plays a primary role in the delivery of aid, as well as playing a role in the provision of aid by third parties. State sovereignty as a concept in relation to the provision of humanitarian law can be both an obstacle, and a vehicle in the provision of emergency aid. Sovereignty forms an obstacle in the event an external actor wishes to gain access to a territory and is obstructed, and functions as a vehicle in the event a government implements all options to provide assistance. In the recent conflict in Syria and the difficulties gaining access for the purpose of the provision of humanitarian assistance, such effects can be seen.[2] Prior to the subsequent Chapters' discussion of the various international legal rights and obligations existing under international law in the provision of humanitarian assistance in times of a humanitarian crisis, the notion of sovereignty *in relation* to the provision of humanitarian assistance must be addressed as part of this research. Over the past decades, the notion of state sovereignty has furthermore been subject to intense legal debate, due to the emergence of concepts such as 'humanitarian interventions' and the 'Responsibility to Protect' (RtoP).[3] The fact that the notion of state sovereignty functions as a thread throughout the discussion of the existing rights and obligations relating to the provision of assistance, as well as the fact that it is currently a debated topic, therefore warrants a more in depth analysis of the concept, prior to devoting the following Chapter to the various rights and duties in the provision of humanitarian assistance in times of a humanitarian crisis. Indeed, the notion of state sovereignty and the current debate on its changing character influence the possibilities of providing humanitarian assistance, as will be seen below. However, as discussed more in depth in Chapters 7 and 8, the increased need for the provision of humanitarian assistance is – vice versa – also influencing the concept of state sovereignty.

4.2 Sovereignty as a Concept in International Law

The international legal order has embraced the concept of an egalitarian division of nation states since the peace of Westphalia in 1648.[4] Resulting from this approach to the international legal order, the concept of state sovereignty has been embedded in political and legal relations between states for many centuries. From the peace of

[2] See in this regard UNSC Res 2139 (22 February 2014) UN Doc S/RES/2139.
[3] Section 4.2.2 Reconceptualising Sovereignty?
[4] This research will not discuss the formation of sovereign states as such nor the creation of the international division according to such sovereign states, but rather take this as a premise for further discussion of the notion of state sovereignty in so far as it relates to the concept of humanitarian assistance. For an in-depth view on the coming into existence of the world into such sovereign states see amongst others: Nico J Schrijver, 'Begrensde Soevereiniteit: 350 jaar na de vrede van Munster', Oration for the acceptance of the Professorship in international law at the Law Faculty of the Free University of Amsterdam (15 May 1998); T Jacobsen, C Sampford & R Thakur (eds) *Re-envisioning Sovereignty: The End of Westphalia?* (Ashgate 2008); and Malcolm Shaw, *International Law* (Cambridge University Press 2003) 13-20.

Westphalia until well into the nineteenth century, the 'sacred' concept of state sovereignty was not to be tampered with.[5] Today, state sovereignty is increasingly considered restricted, in relation to a sovereign's actions towards those within its jurisdiction.[6] Prior to assessing the current state of international law and state sovereignty, with its embracement of the notion of the 'Responsibility to Protect', a brief overview of developments in the past century is given, for the purpose of contextualisation in relation to the provision of humanitarian assistance.

4.2.1 Historical Context and Relevant Principles in Relation to Humanitarian Assistance

As put by Robert Jackson, prosecutor at the Nuremberg Tribunals in 1949, the notion of sovereignty at the beginning of the twentieth century could be phrased as:

> "each state is sovereign, its right absolute, its will unrestrained, and free to resort to war at any time, for any purpose".[7]

This egalitarian approach to states' mutual relations can be seen as the *external* aspect of state sovereignty: *par in parem non habet imperium*, as laid down in Article 2(1) UN Charter,[8] as well as expressed by the ICJ in the *Corfu Channel* case:

> "Between independent States, respect for territorial sovereignty is an essential foundation of international relations".[9]

---

[5] Jackson Nyamuya Maogoto, 'Westphalian Sovereignty in the Shadow of International Justice? A Fresh Coat of Paint for a Tainted Concept' in T Jacobsen, C Sampford & R Thakur (eds) *Re-envisioning Sovereignty: The End of Westphalia?* (Ashgate 2008) 211.

[6] Section 4.2.2 Reconceptualising Sovereignty?

[7] Robert H Jackson, 'Nuremberg In Retrospect: Legal Answer To International Lawlessness' (1949) 35 *American Bar Association Journal* 813.

[8] The full text of Article 2 UN Charter states: "The Organization and its Members, in pursuit of the Purposes stated in Article 1, shall act in accordance with the following Principles. 1.The Organization is based on the principle of the sovereign equality of all its Members. 2.All Members, in order to ensure to all of them the rights and benefits resulting from membership, shall fulfill in good faith the obligations assumed by them in accordance with the present Charter. 3.All Members shall settle their international disputes by peaceful means in such a manner that international peace and security, and justice, are not endangered. 4.All Members shall refrain in their international relations from the threat or use of force against the territorial integrity or political independence of any state, or in any other manner inconsistent with the Purposes of the United Nations. 5.All Members shall give the United Nations every assistance in any action it takes in accordance with the present Charter, and shall refrain from giving assistance to any state against which the United Nations is taking preventive or enforcement action. 6.The Organization shall ensure that states which are not Members of the United Nations act in accordance with these Principles so far as may be necessary for the maintenance of international peace and security. 7.Nothing contained in the present Charter shall authorize the United Nations to intervene in matters which are essentially within the domestic jurisdiction of any state or shall require the Members to submit such matters to settlement under the present Charter; but this principle shall not prejudice the application of enforcement measures under Chapter VII".

[9] Corfu Channel Case (UK v Albania) (Merits) 9 April 1949 I.C.J. Reports 4, p. 35.

As such, a state cannot be subjected to the authority of another state in the international legal order.[10] Conversely, Article 2(7) of the UN Charter stipulates that within the boundaries of international law, sovereign states are entitled to determine the *domaine reservé*; their domestic jurisdiction, freely and without interference from the United Nations.[11] Implied here is also the fact that such domestic jurisdiction is to remain free from interference from other states. This aspect is considered the flip-side of the same coin of sovereignty, namely the *internal* aspect of state sovereignty.[12] It is both this *domaine reservé* and the permeability of the external aspect of sovereignty which is subject to debate, as the international legal order has begun to redefine the boundaries of sovereignty. Such discussion aligns with the increase of non-international conflicts and the so-called 'war on terror' in recent years that have attracted international concern. The need to provide humanitarian aid in such circumstances indeed contributes to this discussion.

These boundaries to the notion of state sovereignty are both instated and confined by international law, making international law the sphere in which the discussion on the definition and content of state sovereignty takes place. Several principles interconnected with the notion of state sovereignty in international law are of particular importance in relation to the concept of humanitarian assistance, amongst which the above mentioned principle of 'non-intervention', as well as the principle of 'respect for the domestic jurisdiction' and the principle of 'consent'. These three principles will be addressed further in this Section, as the legal content of the concept and the consequences deriving from these principles must be discussed prior to the development of sovereignty into the 21st century. Whilst it has been established that the provision of humanitarian assistance must occur in accordance with the principles of humanity, neutrality and impartiality, gaining access to a territory is key in the actual delivery of *external* aid. The rights and duties involved in the provision of aid by third parties form a large part of the legal framework, in the event the affected state is unable or unwilling to provide assistance. As such the changing notion of sovereignty and its principles are essential in the establishment of the content of the law regarding the rights and duties in the provision of assistance.

4.2.1.1 The Principle of Non-Intervention

The principle of non-intervention is widely recognised in international law as one of the basic premises upon which the international legal order is framed, amongst others laid down in Article 2(4) UN Charter.[13] Closely related is the somewhat

[10] See Schrijver, 'Begrensde Soevereiniteit: 350 jaar na de vrede van Munster' (n 4) 11; and Shaw, *International Law* (n 4) 1013.
[11] See (n 8) for the full text of Article 2 UN Charter.
[12] R Jennings, 'Sovereignty and International Law' in G Kreijen (ed), *State, Sovereignty and International Governance* (Oxford University Press 2002) 32.
[13] See (n 8) for the text of Article 2. See also ILC 'Protection of persons in the event of disasters' Memorandum by the Secretariat, UN Doc A/CN.4/590 (11 December 2007) § 20.

'softer' principle of non-interference. In the second half of the 20th century, sovereignty indeed remained defined as 'let's leave each other alone'.[14] In particular in relation to the provision of assistance, the principle of non-intervention is relevant in two regards. Firstly, as mentioned above, it is relevant to address the differentiation between delivering humanitarian assistance, and forcefully gaining access to a territory; thereby violating the principle of non-intervention. Secondly, should lawful access be established, a differentiation must be made between those 'intervening' by forceful measures, and those providing emergency aid. As such, addressing the content of this principle is relevant to the establishment of the legal framework on the provision of humanitarian assistance.

With the establishment of the UN, the Security Council and the notion of collective security, measures taken by the Security Council under Chapter VII of the UN Charter to remedy violations of international peace cannot be considered to be a breach of the principle of non-intervention.[15] This was indeed confirmed by the UN General Assembly in its 1965 'Declaration on the Inadmissibility of Intervention in the Domestic Affairs of Sates and the Protection of their Independence and Sovereignty'.[16] The General Assembly furthermore declared the prohibition of intervention in any form in the 'internal or external affairs' of another State, condemning any such action of its Member States.[17] Although the Declaration can be placed in the political realities of the Cold War at that time, and dealing largely with decolonisation issues, it does reflect the mindset of the then 117 UN Members. Subsequently in 1970, the General Assembly reaffirmed this take in its 'Declaration on Principles of International Law Concerning Friendly Relations and Cooperation among States in Accordance with the Charter of the United Nations' (Friendly Relations Declaration), declaring that both the principle of non-intervention as well as the principle of sovereign equality remain pillars of international law.[18] Yet again in 1981, the General Assembly adopted a 'Declaration on the Inadmissibility of Intervention and Interference in the Internal Affairs of States' once more reaffirming the relevance of the principles of non-intervention and non-interference in international law, and furthermore providing for an extensive deliberation of what these principles entail.[19]

---

[14] Louis Henkin, 'That "S" Word: Sovereignty, and Globalization, and Human Rights, Et Cetera', (1989) 68 Fordham Law Review 1, 3.

[15] Vincent Chetail, 'The contribution of the International Court of Justice to international humanitarian law', (2003) 85 *International Review of the Red Cross* 850, 265-266. The role of the UN Security Council and its stance on non-intervention in relation to the provision of humanitarian assistance will be discussed in Chapters 7 and 8

[16] UNGA Res 2131 (XX) (21 December 1965) 'Declaration on the Inadmissibility of Intervention in the Domestic Affairs of Sates and the Protection of their Independence and Sovereignty' §8.

[17] Ibid § 1.

[18] UNGA Res 2625 (XXV) (24 October 1970) 'Declaration on Principles of International Law Concerning Friendly Relations and Cooperation among States in Accordance with the Charter of the United Nations', Annex.

[19] UNGA Res 36/103 (9 December 1981) UN Doc A/RES/36/103 'Declaration on the Inadmissibility of Intervention and Interference in the Internal Affairs of States', Annex. The Declaration distinctly sets

Whereas the *Nicaragua*-case has been seen to be relevant in the discussion of the principles pertaining to the delivery of humanitarian assistance (discussed in Chapter 2), the ICJ also notes generally in regard to the content of the principle of non-intervention that:

> "the principle forbids all States or groups of States to intervene directly or indirectly in internal or external affairs of other States. A prohibited intervention must accordingly be one bearing on matters in which each State is permitted, by the principle of State sovereignty, to decide freely. One of these is the choice of a political, economic, social and cultural system, and the formulation of foreign policy. Intervention is wrongful when it uses methods of coercion in regard to such choices, which must remain free ones. The element of coercion, which defines, and indeed forms the very essence of, prohibited intervention, is particularly obvious in the case of an intervention which uses force."[20]

The importance of access to a territory for the purpose of providing aid almost goes without saying, and although the ICJ refers back to the 1965 'Declaration on the Inadmissibility of Intervention in the Domestic Affairs of Sates and the Protection of their Independence and Sovereignty', the Court unfortunately foregoes the opportunity to settle the debate on the possible right to intervene on humanitarian grounds, as it does not clearly address the principle of consent or the principle of non-intervention in that context.[21] However, the ICJ *did* deal with the provision of humanitarian assistance itself as a potential unlawful intervention within the territory of a state, rather than intervening *for the purpose of* assistance. Given the fact that the Court noted in the *Nicaragua*-case that the United States Congress had restricted assistance to 'contras' in Nicaragua, the Court argued that:

> "There can be no doubt that the provision of strictly humanitarian aid to persons or forces in another country, whatever their political affiliations or objectives, cannot be regarded as unlawful intervention, or as in any other way contrary to international law (...) In the view of the Court, if the provision of "humanitarian assistance" is to escape condemnation as an intervention in the internal affairs of Nicaragua, not only must it be limited to the purposes hallowed in the practice of the Red Cross, namely "to prevent and alleviate human suffering", and "to protect life and health and to ensure respect for the human being"; it must also, and above all, be given without discrimination to all in need in Nicaragua, not merely to the *contras* and their dependents."[22]

Thus, although the ICJ does not address the possibility of an intervention for humanitarian purposes, it *excludes* the strict provision of humanitarian assistance

---

forth several rights and duties resting upon states in the compliance with the principle of non-intervention.

[20] Military and Paramilitary Activities in and against Nicaragua (Nicaragua v. United States of America), Merits, Judgment 27 June 1986 I.C.J. Reports 1986, p. 14, § 205. The Court furthermore concluded (§ 209) that: "The Court therefore finds that no such general right of intervention, in support of an opposition within another State, exists in contemporary international law".

[21] Ibid § 203.

[22] Ibid § 242-243.

from being a violation of the principle of non-intervention and thereby being an infringement on state sovereignty. Furthermore, not only the *offer* of assistance is considered lawful by the ICJ, the *provision* itself is also considered to not infringe upon the principle of non-intervention as the Court declares 'the provision of strictly humanitarian aid to persons or forces in another country, (...) cannot be regarded as unlawful intervention, or as in any other way contrary to international law'. Indeed, the *offer* of assistance must be distinguished from the *manner* in which it is delivered.[23] Yet, unfortunately, the notion of an intervention by means of force, for possible humanitarian purposes and indeed the concrete provision of aid, and thereby foregoing the principles of non-intervention and consent, is not addressed by the Court.[24] In fact, the Court asserts that the provision of assistance by a third state is lawful and must not be considered an intervention, without addressing *how* this assistance reaches the territory of provision. This leaves the international community somewhat in limbo as to how the neutral, impartial and humanitarian assistance could reach the needy recipients.

Following the ICJ's 1986 *Nicaragua* Judgement, the General Assembly maintained in several resolutions pertaining to the delivery of humanitarian assistance that such delivery should not interfere with state sovereignty or violate the principle of non-intervention.[25] Where the General Assembly 'reaffirms the sovereignty of affected states' and declares that assistance should be delivered with the consent of the affected state,[26] the ICJ has avoided such declarations. In subsequent Chapters, this relationship between the provision of assistance and access to a territory for such assistance will be addressed in further detail.[27]

4.2.1.2 The Principle of Consent

Historically, international law is founded on the principle of consent. This principle was affirmed by the Permanent Court of International Justice declaring in the 1927 *Lotus case*:

> "International law governs relations between independent States. The rules of law binding upon States therefore emanate from their own free will as expressed in conventions or by usages generally accepted as expressing principles of law and established in order to regulate the relations between these co-existing independent

[23] Carlo Focarelli, 'Duty to Protect in Cases of Natural Disasters', (2010) *Max Planck Encyclopedia of International Law* § 15. See Chapter 7 Third Parties and the Provision of Assistance: The Right to Offer Assistance and the Related (Potential) Right to Access.

[24] See Chapters 7 and 8.

[25] UNGA Res 43/131 (8 December 1988) UN Doc A/RES/43/131 'Humanitarian Assistance to victims of natural disasters and similar emergency situations' § 2; UNGA Res 46/182 (19 December 1991) UN Doc. A/RES/46/182, General Assembly Resolution 'Strengthening the coordination of humanitarian emergency assistance of the United Nations', Annex I, Principle 3; and UNGA Res 45/100 (14 December 1990) UN Doc A/RES/45/100 'Humanitarian Assistance to victims of natural disasters and similar emergency situations', § 2.

[26] Ibid UNGA Res 43/131 § 2; UNGA Res 46/182 Annex I, Principle 3, and UNGA Res 45/100 § 2.

[27] See Chapter 6.

> communities or with a view to the achievement of common aims. Restrictions upon the independence of States cannot therefore be presumed".[28]

Even today, international law continues to build on the ideas set out in the Lotus case, although it has been argued that the notion of sovereignty is changing.[29] With regard to the provision of humanitarian assistance, the outset has been no different, although the absence of consent for the delivery of assistance is increasingly seen to become an issue sparking legal debate regarding enforcement options and the boundaries of sovereignty. In theory and in practice, a state is only bound by those aspects of international law to which it freely consents, with the exception of course of principles of *jus cogens*.[30] As such, a state may accede to a human rights treaty, yet in doing so leans heavily on state sovereignty in its decision to accede, the moment to accede, and even with regard to the extent to which it accedes, through a choice in reservations.[31]

Although the principle of consent is particularly relevant in relation to international treaty law, states have chosen not to invoke this aspect of their sovereignty in relation to their accession to both the four 1949 Geneva Conventions and their 1977 Additional Protocols, forming the basis of international humanitarian law, as well as the relevant provisions of human rights law relating to humanitarian assistance.[32] Treaty law formation is however different from customary international law, where objecting, as opposed to consciously consenting, is the manner in which a state may avoid being bound by newly formed international law.[33] As will be seen in Part II, existing customary international law pertaining to humanitarian assistance has generally also been codified in major human rights treaties and the Geneva Conventions and their Protocols; to which states, as just mentioned, have not made reservations relevant to this research into the framework on humanitarian assistance.

Shaw argues that the principle of consent underlies the entire spectrum of international law, without which the system would not be operable.[34] Thus, although the principle of consent is to be considered one of the cornerstones of international law, with regard to international law and humanitarian assistance, *this*

---

[28] S.S. Lotus (France. v. Turkey.), 1927 P.C.I.J. (ser. A) No. 10 (Sept. 7), The Case of the S.S. Lotus France v. Turkey Judgment September 1927, § 44 – 47.

[29] See Section 4.2.2 Reconceptualising Sovereignty?.

[30] Articles 11-15 Vienna Convention on the Law of Treaties (23 May 1969). Entered into force on 27 January 1980. United Nations, Treaty Series, vol. 1155, p. 331; Shaw, *International Law* (n 4), 9; Dinah Shelton, 'International Law and "Relative Normativity"' in Malcolm Evans (ed), *International Law* (Oxford University Press 2010) 144-145. See Section 8.3.1 The ARSIWA, Peremptory Norms and the Denial of Humanitarian Assistance.

[31] Henkin, 'That "S" Word: Sovereignty, and Globalization, and Human Rights, Et Cetera' (n 14), 5 and Robert McCorquodale, 'The Individual and the International Legal System' in Evans, International Law (n 30) 295.

[32] See infra Chapters 5 and 6 for a more elaborate discussion.

[33] Shaw, *International Law* (n 4), 85. Shaw (p. 9) also points out the situation where newly existing states that are formed in international law clearly do not blindly adopt the existing body of customary international law without the option of objecting to it as part of its formation.

[34] Ibid 10.

aspect of the principle of consent does not form a barrier in the provision of aid, as generally states have acceded to the relevant treaties codifying rights and duties in the provision of assistance. Yet a related notion of the principle of consent remains crucial throughout the entire legal framework regarding the provision of humanitarian assistance. Whilst states may have acceded to treaties regulating such provision of aid, their *accession* cannot be construed as an automatically implied consent to the *factual* provision itself. Indeed, such specific consent to individual acts of assistance must be determined on a case-by-case basis and are directly related to the specificities found in the particular provisions in human rights treaties and humanitarian law as related to the delivery of emergency aid. These will be addressed further in Part II of this research and in particular Chapter 8 Section 3. However, given that this form of consent concerns allowing external assistance into the territory of a sovereign state, it is closely related to the last principle that is discussed in this Section, namely the principle of domestic jurisdiction.

4.2.1.3 The Principle of Domestic Jurisdiction

The final principle, the principle of domestic jurisdiction is directly related to the notion of territorial integrity and non-intervention, as discussed above. It entails that international law cannot perforate with authority into the state's territory, regardless of the 'justness' of the cause.[35] Codification of the principle can be found in Article 2(7) of the UN Charter, clearly stating that its member states shall abide by the fact that certain matters remain outside the international realm and are solely governed by national jurisdiction.[36] According to the UN Charter, the only exceptions to the principle of non-intervention and the duty not to intervene in matters essentially within domestic jurisdiction, are Article 51 relating to the notion of self-defence, and the provisions laid down in Chapter VII of the UN Charter whereby the Security Council may allow for the use of force through collective security.[37] The latter option was quite advanced at the time, as states relinquished parts of their sovereignty to the 'permanent five' of the Security Council for decision-making. Furthermore, although Article 2 UN Charter considers the respect for sovereignty and for the domestic jurisdiction of all member states as part of the foundational

[35] Henkin, 'That "S" Word: Sovereignty, and Globalization, and Human Rights, Et Cetera' (n 14), 10.
[36] See (n 8) for the full text of Article 2 UN Charter.
[37] Article 51 UN Charter states: "Nothing in the present Charter shall impair the inherent right of individual or collective self-defence if an armed attack occurs against a Member of the United Nations, until the Security Council has taken measures necessary to maintain international peace and security. Measures taken by Members in the exercise of this right of self-defence shall be immediately reported to the Security Council and shall not in any way affect the authority and responsibility of the Security Council under the present Charter to take at any time such action as it deems necessary in order to maintain or restore international peace and security". See furthermore Articles 39, 41 and 42 of the UN Charter for the matters concerning collective security. Although an in-depth discussion of this concept falls beyond the scope of this research, it will be addressed in relation to the provision of humanitarian assistance in Chapter 8 Legal Consequences of the Denial of Humanitarian Assistance: Methods of Enforcement.

principles of its Organization, the words remain absent in the rest of the Charter, with the exception of a brief reference to sovereignty in Article 78.[38]

In relation to the delivery of humanitarian assistance, in particular, it becomes clear that as sovereign, the state has a role in determining access to the *domaine reserve*, as well as determining within its jurisdiction matters concerning such provision. The extent of these sovereign rights specifically pertaining to the duties involved in the provision of emergency aid will be further addressed in Chapters 7 and 8. A relevant question remains however who the sovereign is in a domestic jurisdiction that appears to be a vacuum? What of failed states with no clear authority, or an authority helpless to deal with terrorism or other threats? Such 'failed' states find themselves in the midst of humanitarian crises, where the international community is willing to provide assistance. What respect for sovereignty and domestic jurisdiction must the international legal world have for an exploding or imploding state, and what are the consequences for the existence of sovereignty?[39] Henkin posed this question also in relation to the existence of humanitarian crises, asking:

> "who is responsible for the devastating consequences of natural disasters- floods, hurricanes and earthquakes that have devastated economies and blighted hopes for economic and social development, and economic and social rights for hundreds of millions of people seeking human dignity?"[40]

If the domestic jurisdiction is absent, or the sovereign unwilling to assist in such circumstances of grave humanitarian emergencies, what does the notion of sovereignty entail but a hollow phrase? Yet, as Crawford argues, sovereignty is an *attribute* of the state rather than a *precondition*, and the (temporary) absence of a functioning government does not immediately deprive an entity of its statehood and thereby also of its sovereignty.[41] With statehood remaining in place, a primary responsibility continues to exist for the provision of humanitarian assistance, despite a potential lack of government to carry out such responsibilities. It follows from this, that in the absence of such provision due to a possible inability to provide, the international community may and could step in. Indeed, the provision of assistance from the exterior may be a vehicle in the diminishment of state failure.[42] Such a role for the international community follows from the changes in the international legal order with regard to the concept of state sovereignty as it is recognised today, in the beginning of the 21st century. As such, the provision of

---

[38] Article 78 UN Charter declares in relation to the Trusteeship: "The trusteeship system shall not apply to territories which have become Members of the United Nations, relationship among which shall be based on respect for the principle of sovereign equality".

[39] Henkin, 'That "S" Word: Sovereignty, and Globalization, and Human Rights, Et Cetera' (n 14), 8. See Chapter 6.

[40] Henkin, 'That "S" Word: Sovereignty, and Globalization, and Human Rights, Et Cetera' (n 14), 9.

[41] James Crawford, *The Creation of States in International Law* (Oxford University Press 2006) 32, 55-57.

[42] The Netherlands Advisory Council on International Affairs (AIV), Report 'Failing States A Global Responsibility' No. 35 (May 2004) 51.

humanitarian assistance plays a role in this principle of state sovereignty too. While the principles of non-intervention, consent and respect for domestic jurisdiction form an essential part of state sovereignty, a concept in itself that has consistently been considered a fundamental right of the nation-state, their absoluteness has changed with the passing of time since the peace of Westphalia.[43] These changes in legal perspective have followed a practice in which not only 'failed' states have appeared in the international arena, but also increasingly non-international armed conflicts take place where a sovereign is hesitant or unwilling to allow access to third parties for the provision of assistance.[44] The need for the provision of humanitarian assistance indeed influences such changes. The enforcement of the delivery of humanitarian assistance must be differentiated from its provision, as the role of the international community in such circumstances can be twofold: on the one hand the provision of assistance, and on the other hand the use of (military) force to create an environment that enables those providing humanitarian aid to access a territory. The legal rights and obligations with regard to the possible provision of humanitarian assistance by third states or international organisations will be addressed further in Chapters 6 and 7, whereas enforcement issues will be discussed in Chapter 8. To properly understand the concept of sovereignty as it stands today, a brief overview of the debate pertaining to the notion, and several international initiatives that have added to this discussion must be addressed.

4.2.2 Reconceptualising Sovereignty?

In the 21st century, more than 350 years after Westphalia, the international legal order no longer looks the same as the international legal order of 1648. A wide variety of actors has arrived on the international scene, most notably international organisations and individuals that now form part of the discourse alongside sovereign states, in particular in relation to the field of human rights law.[45] The embracement of international human rights law following World War II has most certainly altered the view of state sovereignty and the relationship of a sovereign to those within its jurisdiction. Interestingly however, the notion that sovereignty and the State's power is related to the collective agreement of the individuals comprising this State can be dated as far back as Grotius.[46] Thus, although more emphasis has come to lay on new actors and their direct role in international law today, the collective agreement of the individuals and their influence on the powers

[43] Maogoto, 'Westphalian Sovereignty in the Shadow of International Justice? A Fresh Coat of Paint for a Tainted Concept' (n 5), 212.
[44] See Chapters 7 and 8.
[45] Schrijver, 'Begrensde Soevereiniteit: 350 jaar na de vrede van Munster' (n 4), 25. and A van Staden and H Vollaard, 'The Erosion of State Sovereignty: Towards a Post-territorial World?' in Kreijen, *State, Sovereignty and Internatioinal Governance* (n 12), 171 and Henkin, 'That "S" Word: Sovereignty, and Globalization, and Human Rights, Et Cetera' (n 14), 8; Anne Marie Slaughter, 'Intervention, Libya, and the Future of Sovereignty', *The Atlantic* (4 September 2011).
[46] Schrijver, 'Begrensde Soevereiniteit: 350 jaar na de vrede van Munster' (n 4) 11 and Jennings, 'Sovereignty and International Law' (n 12) 29.

of a state and its actions in the international legal field is many centuries old. A primary reference to this concept can in fact be found in the 1581 Dutch Act of Abjuration: 'Plakkaat van Verlantinghe', considered the Netherlands' declaration of independence and dismissal of the Spanish king.[47] With the division of the international legal order in 1648 also came the theories on such a division between sovereign and society, amongst which most notably Hobbes, Locke and Rousseau in the 16th and 17th centuries, discussing the concept of a 'social contract'.[48] At the heart of this discussion lies the consideration of which bond actually governs the relationship between sovereign and society. Given the primary role of the affected state in the provision of humanitarian assistance to those within its jurisdiction that may be in need, following a humanitarian crisis, such a relationship between sovereign and society warrants discussion.

Argued by some, the relationship between society and sovereign is one of mutual reinforcement, as both are dependent on each other to exist.[49] Indeed this too is the position of Hobbes, Locke and Rousseau, as they deny the 'natural' powers of a sovereign, arguing that if all humans are born free, the relationship with a government or sovereign is one of agreement or contract.[50] An agreement or contract commonly brings forth rights and obligations for both parties. Certainly, this take on the bond between sovereign and society would imply that it is a reciprocal relationship; a so-called two-way street. Building on this premise, and relating this in particular to the provision of humanitarian assistance, arguably the provision of such assistance can be considered a duty in the fulfillment of the reciprocal relationship of state sovereignty. Indeed, if a duty to provide humanitarian assistance can be found in international law, such a duty could fall within the scope of state sovereignty. Conversely, this duty may invoke a right of individuals to receive such assistance based on this provision in international law, as part of the reciprocal relationship between sovereign and society.[51] This notion of reciprocity, whereby a population has handed over certain responsibilities to the sovereign then conversely includes the population's right to expect fulfillment of such duties in return. In relation to the provision of humanitarian assistance, this would then indeed include the responsibility of the sovereign to provide for those

---

[47] The 'Plakkaat van Verlatinghe' of 1581 is considered the declaration of independence of the Netherlands, dismissing the Spanish king Filips II whose family had reigned over the territory for years, by the Netherlands 'Staten Generaal' on behalf of the entire population. It would be the first step in the creation of the Dutch Republic. For the text of the Plakkaat van Verlatinghe: <www.let.rug.nl/~usa/D/1501-1600/plakkaat/plakkaat.htm> accessed 5 July 2012.

[48] See Thomas Hobbes' *Leviathan* (1651), John Locke's *Second Treatise of Government* (1689) and Jean-Jacques Rousseau's *Du contrat social* (1762). Although an in-depth discussion of these treatises falls outside the scope of this research, their considerations remain relevant today for the discussion of the relationship between sovereign and society.

[49] Francesca Piccin & Elia Pusterla, 'Defending eroded states' sovereignty: the European Union humanitarian aid policy' *GARNET Conference* 'The European Union in International Affairs' (22 April 2010) 5.

[50] Christopher Morris (ed), *The Social Contract Theorists: Critical Essays on Hobbes, Locke and Rousseau* (Rowman & Littlefield 1999) ix.

[51] See Chapter 6.

within its jurisdiction, as will also be further established in Chapter 5 pertaining to humanitarian assistance and human rights law. This reciprocal relationship is often referenced also in the more contemporary notion of sovereignty, to which we have gradually progressed over the past century, while redefining the boundaries of the concept of sovereignty.[52]

4.2.2.1 The Post-World War II Era

Although the Westphalian concept of state sovereignty rested firmly in international relations between states until well into the nineteenth century, World War I and the excesses that took place at the hands of sovereign states became the first challenge for this well-established notion of sovereignty.[53] Subsequently, the effects of World War II 'pierced the veil' of sovereignty further, especially considering the impact of the Nuremberg and Tokyo Trials.[54] These Trials, which for the first time subjected the classic notion of sovereignty to the newly developing international perspectives on peace and human rights, would prove to be a true turning point, as it was during these Trials that individual criminal responsibility at an international level was established for those in positions of authority; representing the sovereign state.[55] These developments have been seconded by the continued creation of various human rights treaties. The notion of sovereignty as a 'shield and sword' towards the rest of the international world is no longer tenable, especially with the developments that have taken place over the last decades since the establishment of the UN. With the UN Charter, the Nuremberg and Tokyo Trials, also came greater attention for individual rights and human rights law.[56] At the same time, an enhanced perspective on (individual) responsibility under international law was seen. Such an approach to international law logically affected and corroded the 'old' concept of state sovereignty in international law. With a focus on individual and human rights, placing 'human beings' and their protection at the centre of the international legal discourse, the Nuremberg and Tokyo Trials proved that sovereign states could no longer 'hide' behind the shield of sovereignty. The international community no longer stood idly by watching atrocities take place, as states acted under their 'shield' of sovereignty. The firmly held grip on sovereignty that had lasted until World War II, began to wrench. The subsequent ratification of

[52] See Section 4.2.3 The Responsibility to Protect, the UN and Humanitarian Assistance.
[53] Maogoto, 'Westphalian Sovereignty in the Shadow of International Justice? A Fresh Coat of Paint for a Tainted Concept' (n 5) 213.
[54] See 'The Charter and Judgment of the Nürnberg Tribunal: history and analysis' Memorandum submitted by the Secretary General (3 March 1949) UN Doc. A/CN.4/5; see for the Tokyo International Military Tribunal N. Boister & R. Cryer (eds.) Documents on the Tokyo International Military Tribunal: Charter, Indictment and Judgments 2008 Oxford / New York. See also J Maogoto & K Kindiki, 'A people Betrayed – the Darfur Crisis and International Law: Rethinking Westphalian Sovereignty in the 21st Century', (2007) 19 *Bond Law Review* 2, 108-109.
[55] Jackson, 'Nuremberg In Retrospect: Legal Answer To International Lawlessness' (n 7); and Maogoto, 'Westphalian Sovereignty in the Shadow of International Justice? A Fresh Coat of Paint for a Tainted Concept' (n 5) 215.
[56] See Section 5.2 The Development of Human Rights Relevant to Humanitarian Assistance.

the various international and regional human rights treaties indeed also expresses the willingness of many states to adhere to these standards, imposed upon them by international law.[57] Furthermore, this shifted focus had a moral connotation, perhaps influenced by the recent horrors of World War II. It is precisely this moral aspect, rooted in the principle of humanity, which also plays a role in the provision of humanitarian assistance.

Although the UN Charter indeed eradicated the sovereign right to wage wars and resort to violence, as well as fuelling an embracement of international human rights law, the following decades also embraced a positive notion of sovereignty in relation to the Cold War and concurrent period of the de-colonisation and birth of many new independent states in Africa and Asia during the 1960s and 1970s.[58] These new and sometimes weak states logically sought to strengthen their sovereignty after struggling to free themselves from colonial imperialism.[59] Evidence hereof can be found in the 1970 General Assembly's 'Declaration on Principles of International Law concerning Friendly Relations and Co-operation among States', which elaborates on the principle of 'sovereign equality' amongst states, asserting amongst others the territorial integrity and 'political independence' of all states.[60] Similarly, and conceived in the same era, Article 3 of Additional Protocol II regarding non-international armed conflicts asserts the principle of non-intervention. The Article declares that the provisions of AP II may not be invoked to affect the sovereignty of another state, nor may they be invoked as a 'justification for intervening, directly or indirectly, for any reason whatever, in the armed conflict or in the internal or external affairs' of a state party to the Protocol.[61] Such declarations fit within the abovementioned timeframe of decolonisation, but at the same time in legal scholarship the realisation of the protection of persons, following

[57] Henkin, 'That "S" Word: Sovereignty, and Globalization, and Human Rights, Et Cetera' (n 14), 4.
[58] Jennings, 'Sovereignty and International Law' (n 12), 29; Henkin, 'That "S" Word: Sovereignty, and Globalization, and Human Rights, Et Cetera' (n 14), 1-2.
[59] Maogoto & Kindiki, 'A people Betrayed – the Darfur Crisis and International Law: Rethinking Westphalian Sovereignty in the 21st Century' (n 54) 110-111.
[60] UNGA Res 2625 (XXV) (24 October 1970) 'Declaration on Principles of International Law Concerning Friendly Relations and Cooperation among States in Accordance with the Charter of the United Nations', Annex, The principle of sovereign equality of States: "All States enjoy sovereign equality. They have equal rights and duties and are equal members of the international community, notwithstanding differences of an economic, social, political or other nature. In particular, sovereign equality includes the following elements: a. States are judicially equal; b. Each State enjoys the rights inherent in full sovereignty; c. Each State has the duty to respect the personality of other States; d. The territorial integrity and political independence of the State are inviolable; e. Each State has the right freely to choose and develop its political, social, economic and cultural systems; f. Each State has the duty to comply fully and in good faith with its international obligations and to live in peace with other States".
[61] Article 3 AP II states: "1. Nothing in this Protocol shall be invoked for the purpose of affecting the sovereignty of a State or the responsibility of the government, by all legitimate means, to maintain or re-establish law and order in the State or to defend the national unity and territorial integrity of the State. 2. Nothing in this Protocol shall be invoked as a justification for intervening, directly or indirectly, for any reason whatever, in the armed conflict or in the internal or external affairs of the High Contracting Party in the territory of which that conflict occurs".

the developments in humanitarian and human rights law in the post-World War II era was not lost. As put by Elihu Lauterpacht:

> "to give effect, through appropriate limitation and international supervision of the internal sovereignty of States, to the principle that the protection of human personality and of its fundamental rights is the ultimate purpose of all law, national and international".[62]

It is precisely such a perspective that furthers the legal framework on the provision of humanitarian assistance. Indeed, towards the 1980s and in a shift towards the end of the Cold War, a renewed focus on various humanitarian crises around the globe can be seen. Solutions were sought for the provision of humanitarian aid to those in circumstances warranting the receipt of food, water and shelter, whilst without immediately clear legal means to obtain such aid. In the 1980s the phrase 'humanitarian intervention' was formulated by Mario Bettati and Bernard Kouchner taking stance against the 'old' notion of state sovereignty; on occasion used as a shield against international criticism on mass atrocities.[63]

4.2.2.2 Humanitarian Interventions and Humanitarian Assistance

The concept of humanitarian intervention entails the use of *force* by one or more states (as a group) *intervening* in the territory of another state for humanitarian purposes, either directly related to gross human rights violations, or other violations of human dignity sometimes related to internal conflict or strife.[64] A clear differentiation must be made between humanitarian *assistance* and humanitarian *intervention* and is set out here. The use of force in the context of a humanitarian intervention falls distinctly outside the scope of the UN Security Council's concept of 'collective security' under Chapter VII of the UN Charter. The timeframe of this concept must be seen within the context of the Cold War, where the Security Council was often paralysed and unable to find common ground for resolutions in crisis-situations.[65] The notion of a humanitarian *intervention* must be juxtaposed with the concept of humanitarian *assistance* in this research, which in itself does not encompass the use of force. Although a humanitarian intervention aspires to ameliorate circumstances of people within a certain territory, as such having a

---

[62] Elihu Lauterpacht (ed), *International Law: Being the Collected Papers of Hersch Lauterpacht* (Cambridge University Press 1975) Vol. II, part 1, 47.

[63] Mario Bettati & Bernard Kouchner (eds) *Le devoir d'ingérence: Peut-on les laisser mourir?* (Denoël 1987); Ben Kioko, 'The right of intervention under the African Union's Constitutive Act: From non-interference to non-intervention', (2003) 85 *International Review of the Red Cross* 852, 809-810.

[64] Justin Conlon, 'Sovereignty vs. Human Rights or Sovereignty and Human Rights?', (2004) 46 *Race & Class* 75, 76-77. Francis Deng, 'Frontiers of Sovereignty: A Framework of Protection, Assistance and Development for the Internally Displaced', (1995) 8 *Leiden Journal of International Law* 2, 249-286 at 279; Gelijn Molier, 'De Soevereine Staat en het Internationaal Recht: Een ongemakkelijke Symbiose' (2009) in G Molier, T J M Slootweg (eds), *Soevereiniteit en Recht. Rechtsfilosofische beschouwingen* (Boom Juridische uitgevers) 147.

[65] See Section 7.3.2 Security Council Resolutions and the Right to Access.

humanitarian *purpose*, it is certainly not the same as humanitarian assistance. In Chapter 2, such assistance has been defined as restricted to the provision of emergency facilities, provided in a manner that abides by principles of humanity, impartiality and neutrality.[66] This definition inevitably *excludes* the access to a territory by means of *force* as *part of* the provision of humanitarian assistance. Yet, in subsequent Chapters the use of force as a manner in which access may be gained to a territory *in order to* provide assistance will be discussed.[67] The notion of a humanitarian intervention operates outside the realm of unambiguously accepted usage of force in international law, whilst humanitarian assistance does not 'use' force itself. It is of paramount importance to clearly distinguish the differences between the concept of humanitarian assistance and that of humanitarian intervention, whilst remaining aware that humanitarian interventions were argued by Kouchner and Bettati as a *means* to (amongst others) *provide* humanitarian assistance. Its development in relation to the concept of state sovereignty and humanitarian assistance warrant a discussion within this research.

The development of a 'humanitarian intervention' as a concept must be noted against the backdrop of conflicts over the past four decades, which have increasingly developed from *inter*state conflicts, to *intra*state conflicts such as Rwanda and the former Yugoslavia.[68] Defenders of humanitarian interventions argue that human rights violations cannot be protected with the veil of sovereignty, resulting in the fact that the latter should subside for the protection of the former, as the international legal protection of human rights must be considered at least as important as the norm of protection of state sovereignty.[69] The development of this concept gave rise to fierce debate over the legality of humanitarian interventions, with proponents like Kouchner on one side, and on the other side those like Ian Brownlie, who argued strongly against its legality on grounds such as the embedment of state sovereignty in the UN Charter.[70] This debate relevantly puts

66 See Sections 2.2.2 Defining Humanitarian Assistance and 2.2.3 The Principles for the Delivery of Assistance.

67 See Chapter 8.

68 Christopher Joyner, 'The responsibility to protect: humanitarian concern and the lawfulness of armed intervention', (2007) 47 *Virginia Journal of International Law*, 704; and Gareth Evans, 'From humanitarian intervention to the responsibility to protect', (2006) 24 *Wisconsin International Law Journal* 3, 706. For an in-depth discussion of various interventions, whether for humanitarian reasons or not, over the past decades since the end of the Cold War, see Conlon, 'Sovereignty vs. Human Rights or Sovereignty and Human Rights?' (n 64) 90-96.

69 '*The Responsibility to Protect*', Report of the International Commission on Intervention and State Sovereignty (ICISS) 2001, p 15-16; See also Conlon, 'Sovereignty vs. Human Rights or Sovereignty and Human Rights?' (n 64) 81-82; and Nicholas J Wheeler, 'Legitimating humanitarian intervention: principles and procedures', (2001) 2 *Melbourne Journal of International Law* 2, 550-567.

70 Ian Brownlie, *Principles of Public International Law* (Oxford University Press 2008) 742-745; Bettati & Kouchner *Le devoir d'ingérence: Peut-on les laisser mourir?* (n 63); *See* also Joyner, 'The responsibility to protect: humanitarian concern and the lawfulness of armed intervention' (n 68) 697; Evans, 'From humanitarian intervention to the responsibility to protect' (n 68) 706; and William J Magnuson, 'The Responsibility to Protect and the Decline of Sovereignty: Free Speech Protection under International Law', (2010) 43 *Vanderbilt Journal of Transnational Law* 2, 271-272; Joakim Dungel, 'A Right to Humanitarian Assistance in Internal Armed Conflicts Respecting Sovereignty,

forward the tension that arose between the concept of state sovereignty, and the growing international concern for large-scale human rights violations and mass atrocities.[71] Indeed, it has been argued that the international protection of human rights inevitably clashes with the concept of state sovereignty.[72] Alternatively, Slaughter has argued that there is not so much a *loss* of power of the sovereign, but a *change* over time in the manner in which the sovereign can exercise such a power.[73] Furthermore Tesón, one of the earliest proponents of a right to humanitarian intervention, argues that grounds for such an intervention can be found within the view of sovereignty as a contract with a population. As such, the large-scale human rights violations that lead up to the intended intervention must be seen as the government not fulfilling its sovereign duties to its population.[74] Conversely, it has been argued that the concept of humanitarian intervention was doomed from the start, by attempting to forego the role of state sovereignty, inevitably frustrating and exasperating many states.[75]

Semantics may even have played a role, as a term containing 'intervention' will not sit well with most sovereign powers in the world, clinging tightly to the age-old principle of non-intervention. Furthermore, the unilateral or group aspect that forms part of the notion of humanitarian intervention, rather than the embracement of the initiative by the entire international community of states through Security Council action, clearly form their own objections,[76] as a risk of (greater) conflict arises through the misuse of such interventions on humanitarian grounds when they are not properly defined, or regulated through international channels.[77]

Yet, following the end of the Cold War era, combined with the steady rise of conflicts such as those in the Former Yugoslavia, Afghanistan, Rwanda and Somalia, state sovereignty is deemed by some to be declining.[78] As discussed

---

Neutrality and Legitimacy: Practical Proposals to Practical Problems', (2004) *Journal of Humanitarian Assistance*, 11 <http://sites.tufts.edu/jha/archives/838> accessed 24 November 2014; see also (n 8) for the full text of Article 2 UN Charter; 'A more Secure World: Our Shared Responsibility', UN Report of the Secretary General's High Level Panel on Threats, Challenges and Change (2004) §199; Molier, 'De Soevereine Staat en het Internationaal Recht: Een ongemakkelijke Symbiose' (n 64).

[71] Henkin, 'That "S" Word: Sovereignty, and Globalization, and Human Rights, Et Cetera' (n 14), 4.

[72] Conlon, 'Sovereignty vs. Human Rights or Sovereignty and Human Rights?' (n 64) 78. The author himself however proposes a different view, whereby sovereignty may aid in the protection of human rights.

[73] Anne Marie Slaughter, 'Sovereignty and Power in a Networked World Order', (2004) 40 *Stanford Journal of International Law*, 288.

[74] Fernando R Tesón, 'Humanitarian Intervention: Loose Ends', (2011) 10 *Journal of Military Ethics* 3, 194. See also earlier publications such as Tesón's *Humanitarian Intervention: An Inquiry into Law and Morality* (Transnational Publishers, Inc 2005).

[75] Heraldo Muñoz, 'The Responsibility to Protect: Three Pillars and Four Crimes', (2009) *human rights & human welfare working papers*, 53, 5.

[76] Henkin, 'That "S" Word: Sovereignty, and Globalization, and Human Rights, Et Cetera' (n 14), 10.

[77] Dungel, 'A Right to Humanitarian Assistance in Internal Armed Conflicts Respecting Sovereignty, Neutrality and Legitimacy: Practical Proposals to Practical Problems' (n 70) § 4.3.

[78] Jennings, 'Sovereignty and International Law' (n 12), 30. Jennings himself however argues the contrary, pointing to the exclusive roles still held by states in the international sphere, such as the possibility of appearing before the ICJ and eligibility of membership of the UN, 34-35. See also A van

above, the continued rise of the role of international human rights law in the international field has also contributed to this viewpoint. Indeed, for the first time in 1991, the Security Council placed international human rights at the centre of a resolution, holding the nation-state more and more responsible at the international level for the (domestic) treatment of its individuals.[79] The Security Council clearly stated it:

> "Condemns the repression of the Iraqi civilian population in many parts of Iraq, including most recently in Kurdish-populated areas, the consequences of which threaten international peace and security in the region; [...] Demands that Iraq, as a contribution to removing the threat to international peace and security in the region, immediately end this repression and in the same context expresses the hope that an open dialogue will take place to ensure that the human and political rights of all Iraqi citizens are respected".[80]

Thus, in direct relation to a humanitarian issue, the Security Council altered its view from the position that such matters fall solely within the domestic jurisdiction of a state, and brought the matter to the international sphere. The change in political climate within the Security Council upon the ending of the Cold War has furthermore been a catalyser in such developments, as also seen with the creation of *ad hoc* tribunals such as the ICTY and ICTR that once again reaffirmed that certain excesses of sovereign power can no longer be shielded and now fall within the protected sphere of international law.[81] From solely entailing rights for the nation-state, the concept of sovereignty has slowly begun its alteration towards entailing obligations which may be enforced at the international level. With regard to the provision of humanitarian assistance, such a shift means a greater opportunity for those in need of assistance to have their needs met, as the international community increasingly acknowledges restraints on sovereignty and a related role for the community itself to contribute to the protection of persons. The provision of humanitarian aid itself is clearly a means to provide such protection in humanitarian crises.

The four major developments discussed above; namely (1) the greater international interdependence and globalisation, (2) the participation of new actors in the international legal world, most notably individuals, (3) the proliferation of human rights treaties and the ensuing embracement of human rights law, as well as (4) the development of more and more international tribunals or courts have all contributed to the systematical erosion of the Westphalian concept of sovereignty.

Staden and H Vollaard, 'The Erosion of State Sovereignty: Towards a Post-territorial World?' in Kreijen, *State, Sovereignty and Internatioinal Governance* (n 12), 165.

[79] Nico J Schrijver, 'Sovereignty versus Human Rights? A Tale of UN Security Council Resolution 688 (1991) on the Protection of the Kurdish People', in: M Castermans, F van Hoof and J Smith (eds), *The Role of the Nation-State in the 21st Century: Human Rights, International Organizations and Foreign Policy. Essays in Honour of Peter Baehr* (Brill Nijhoff 1998), 355-6.

[80] UNSC Res 688 (5 April 1991) UN Doc S/RES/688 § 1-2. Of the 5 permanent members of the Security Council, China abstained.

[81] Maogoto, 'Westphalian Sovereignty in the Shadow of International Justice? A Fresh Coat of Paint for a Tainted Concept' (n 5) 219.

In fact, increasingly, sovereignty is considered the 'capacity to participate in cooperative regimes' pursuing the collective interest of all states operating in the world.[82] However, what can then be considered to 'fill the gap' left by a possible departure from our centuries-old division of the international legal order? If the Westphalian concept of sovereignty is eroded, yet the *concept of sovereignty itself* remains intact within the international legal framework, a 'newer' idea or notion of this concept must have been developed alongside the erosion of the Westphalian concept of sovereignty to ensure its continued applicability in international law.

In 1995, the then Representative of the United Nations Secretary-General on Internally Displaced Persons Francis Deng suggested:

> "The very notion of sovereignty implies both responsibility and an international system which imposes accountability on the state in the mutual interest of the state and the international community".[83]

Former UN Secretary General Kofi Annan noted the influence of globalisation and international cooperation on sovereignty, as he attempted to reformulate the concept, by noting two distinct aspects of sovereignty: that of the state, and that of the individual.[84] At that time a regional attempt was made by the African Union, which in 2000 overturned the non-interference principle of the Organization of African Unity and declared that the Union has the right to interfere with a Member State in the event of 'grave circumstances', which specifically include war crimes, genocide and crimes against humanity.[85] That same year Annan again called for an answer to the problem inherent to the notion of humanitarian intervention:

---

[82] Anne Marie Slaughter, 'Disaggregated Sovereignty: Towards Public Accountability of Global Government Networks', (2004) 39 *Government and Opposition* 2, 189; Eyal Benvenisti 'Sovereigns as Trustees of humanity: The Concept and its Normative Implications', (2012) *SSRN* accessed 24 January 2012, 1.

[83] Deng, 'Frontiers of Sovereignty: A Framework of Protection, Assistance and Development for the Internally Displaced' (n 64) 260.

[84] Kofi Annan, 'Two concepts of sovereignty', *The Economist* (18 September 1999) 49-50.

[85] Article 4 of the Constitutive Act of the African Union lays down the principles of the Union, and although declaring sovereign equality of Member States and abiding by the principle of non-interference, it also allows for the right of the Union to intervene in the event of war crimes, genocide or crimes against humanity: "The Union shall function in accordance with the following principles: (a) sovereign equality and interdependence among Member States of the Union; (b) respect of borders existing on achievement of independence; (c) participation of the African peoples in the activities of the Union; (d) establishment of a common defence policy for the African Continent; (e) peaceful resolution of conflicts among Member States of the Union through such appropriate means as may be decided upon by the Assembly; (f) prohibition of the use of force or threat to use force among Member States of the Union; (g) non-interference by any Member State in the internal affairs of another; (h) the right of the Union to intervene in a Member State pursuant to a decision of the Assembly in respect of grave circumstances, namely: war crimes, genocide and crimes against humanity; (i) peaceful co-existence of Member States and their right to live in peace and security; (j) the right of Member States to request intervention from the Union in order to restore peace and security; (k) promotion of self-reliance within the framework of the Union; (l) promotion of gender equality; (m) respect for democratic principles, human rights, the rule of law and good governance; (n) promotion of social justice to ensure balanced economic development; (o) respect for the sanctity of human life, condemnation and rejection of

> "if humanitarian intervention is, indeed, an unacceptable assault on sovereignty, how should we respond to a Rwanda, to a Srebrenica—to gross and systematic violations of human rights that offend every precept of our common humanity? We confront a real dilemma. Few would disagree that both the defence of humanity and the defence of sovereignty are principles that must be supported. Alas, that does not tell us which principle should prevail when they are in conflict. (…) The protection of fundamental human rights, once considered the province of sovereign states alone, is now a universal concern transcending both governments and borders.[86]

In a humanitarian crisis with a sovereign unwilling to provide humanitarian assistance and allow access to the international community for that purpose, it is precisely this dilemma between the conflict of the protection of humanity and the protection of state sovereignty that is faced. As humanitarian assistance is of relevance in the relief of those facing a humanitarian crisis for which a humanitarian intervention is proposed, Annan argued through this 'Millennium Report' that the notion of sovereignty and the protection of human rights needed to be reconciled, and Annan continued to place the topic at the forefront of the international debate. Following this UN Millennium Report, the Canadian government-sponsored International Commission on Intervention and State Sovereignty (ICISS) attempted such a possible framework, 'reconceptualising' sovereignty.[87] The ICISS efforts resulted in a study on a new approach to the topic of humanitarian intervention, from the perspective of responsibility for individual states and the international community. This indeed initiated the process which would become the birth of the doctrine of 'Responsibility to Protect', a phrase coined by the ICISS in its 2001 report.[88]

4.2.3 The Responsibility to Protect, the UN and Humanitarian Assistance

Trying to find an answer to the questions raised in the many debates following the humanitarian intervention in Kosovo in 1999, as well as the situations in Rwanda and Somalia, the ICISS report of 2001 has attempted, through use of the phrase 'Responsibility to Protect' (RtoP), to address humanitarian intervention in a different light, and also notes that it is far broader than a narrow military intervention.[89] Rather than using the much criticised term of 'right of humanitarian

impunity and political assassination, acts of terrorism and subversive activities; (p) condemnation and rejection of unconstitutional changes of governments".

[86] Kofi Annan, '"We the peoples": the role of the United Nations in the 21s century' (United Nations, 2000), 48 &68. The Report is also known as the 'Millennium Report' prepared by Annan in his role of Secretary General prior to the UN Millennium Summit of March 2000.

[87] 'The Responsibility to Protect', Report of the International Commission on Intervention and State Sovereignty (ICISS 2001); see also Evans, 'From humanitarian intervention to the responsibility to protect' (n 68) 707.

[88] See Section 4.2.3 The Responsibility to Protect, the UN and Humanitarian Assistance for a more in depth discussion.

[89] ICISS Report 'The Responsibility to Protect' (n 87) 2, 11.

intervention', the ICISS approaches the matter from the notion that sovereignty includes a *responsibility* on the part of the sovereign.[90] Although arguably a 'rhetorical trick',[91] the ICISS posits that sovereignty as responsibility is not only a change in terminology but also a 'change in perspective', as the notion of humanitarian intervention is not only 'tainted' in language, but furthermore narrow in scope, and focuses on the rights of the interveners, rather than those of the beneficiaries.[92] In fact, the ICISS states that the new perspective on sovereignty as responsibility could add to the realisation that the notion must be considered from the perspective of those beneficiaries, placing primary responsibility with the affected state, and trying to broaden the scope:

> "the responsibility to protect means not just the "responsibility to react, but the responsibility to prevent" and the "responsibility to rebuild" as well".[93]

When focusing on the aspect of the doctrine relevant to the provision of humanitarian assistance, namely the phase in which the international community may play a role in the provision of such assistance, the ICISS notes that coercive measures, which may include 'political, economic or judicial measures' may be required from the international community and in extreme cases even military measures, thereby limiting the principle of non-intervention.[94] Such extreme cases however are limited to cases of such gravity that they 'genuinely shock the conscience of mankind' or which present 'a clear and present danger to international security'.[95] The principle of RtoP attempts to address responsibility for individual states to protect their citizens, as well as for international organisations, civil society and the international community in general if the state cannot, and encompasses the responsibility to prevent atrocities through diplomatic, economic, political and, if need be, forceful measures.[96] As such, the doctrine would fit the purpose of the provision of humanitarian assistance in times of a humanitarian crisis. Its development has indeed altered the discourse on the provision of humanitarian assistance through a renewed look towards the existing rights and duties within the legal framework, as discussed in Chapter 7 and 8.

The ICISS has furthermore elaborately set out the doctrine of RtoP through the use of core principles and various criteria, and finally made recommendations to the UN General Assembly, Security Council and Secretary General.[97] While the ICISS

---

[90] Ibid 8-9, 11.
[91] Carsten Stahn, 'Responsibility to Protect: Political Rhetoric or Emerging Legal Norm?' (2007) 101 *American Journal of International Law* 1, 102.
[92] ICISS Report 'The Responsibility to Protect' (n 87)16.
[93] Ibid 17.
[94] Ibid 29.
[95] Ibid 31.
[96] Lee Feinstein, 'Darfur and Beyond: What is Needed to Prevent Mass Atrocities', (2007) *Council on Foreign Relations* Special Report No 22, 17.
[97] ICISS Report 'The Responsibility to Protect' (n 87) 32 and further. Discussing the ICISS Report to a greater extent is beyond the scope of this research. For further discussion, see amongst others Alex Bellamy, *Responsibility to Protect: the Global Effort to End Mass Atrocities* (Polity Press 2009);

Report with regard to this notion of sovereignty as responsibility can certainly not be seen as a source of international law upon which a new principle can be built, the Report has fostered the debate, and brought the concept within the parameters of the UN discourse on the subject matter. Furthermore, phrasing the notion of sovereignty in such a 'positive' sense as to entail responsibilities of the state to ensure protection of its civilians implies not only the inclusion and facilitation of international efforts but furthermore an *accountability* for the state to care for its population.[98]

4.2.3.1 UN Endorsement of the Responsibility to Protect

Given the fact that the ICISS Report was published in the wake of the events of 11 September 2001, the Report stood somewhat in the shadow of the ensuing focus of the international world on this event and its consequences; the 'war on terror'. It was only a few years later in 2004 that the UN's 'Report of the Secretary General's High Level Panel on Threats, Challenges and Change' (High-Level Panel Report) of 2004, argued that indeed a growing acceptance exists within the international community to fill the vacuum of a 'continuum' spanning both prevention and reaction, as well as rebuilding, in the event a state affected by catastrophe is unable or unwilling to do so itself following a crisis,[99] and furthermore stated to:

> "endorse the emerging norm that there is a collective international responsibility to protect, exercisable by the Security Council authorizing military intervention as a last resort, in the event of genocide and other large-scale killing, ethnic cleansing or serious violations of international humanitarian law which sovereign Governments have proved powerless or unwilling to prevent"[100]

With this endorsement, following the words of the ICISS, a primary reference to the Responsibility to Protect lingo is found in a UN context. Thus, the idea that an intervention – within the context of Security Council action – for the purpose of relieving a people of large-scale human rights law or humanitarian law violations might be justified was considered within the UN. As with the provision of humanitarian assistance, a primary responsibility lies with the affected government, and only as a last resort does the High-Level Panel Report envisage UN intervention by means of the use of force. Distinct from the ICISS however is the UN High-Level Panel Report's position that such a responsibility to protect through

Ramesh Thakur, *The United Nations, Peace and Security: from Collective Security to the Responsibility to Protect* (Cambridge University Press 2006); Stahn, 'Responsibility to Protect: Political Rhetoric or Emerging Legal Norm?' (n 91); and as major drafter also Evans, 'From humanitarian intervention to the responsibility to protect' (n 68) 703-722.

[98] 'Specific Groups and Individuals: Mass Exoduses and Displaced Persons', Report of the Representative of the Secretary-General on internally displaced persons, Francis M Deng, UN Doc E/CN.4/2004/77 (4 March 2004) § 62.

[99] 'A more Secure World: Our Shared Responsibility', UN Report (n 70) § 201.

[100] Ibid § 203.

military measures is only to be carried out by the Security Council, as opposed to a coalition of the willing and able or regional organisations.[101] However, the High-Level Panel Report places the concept of Responsibility to Protect in direct relation to the strengthening of the UN's collective security system, as well as its institutional reform.[102] This approach opened the door to subsequent embracement by other UN organs. Indeed, while noting the sensitivities surrounding the issue, Kofi Annan's Report of March 2005 entitled 'In Larger Freedom' endorses the principle of RtoP; thereby foregoing his own notion of 'two concepts of sovereignty' introduced a few years before.[103] That same year the World Summit Outcome Document also endorsed the notion, declaring:

> "Each individual State has the responsibility to protect its populations from genocide, war crimes, ethnic cleansing and crimes against humanity. This responsibility entails the prevention of such crimes, including their incitement, through appropriate and necessary means. We accept that responsibility and will act in accordance with it. The international community should, as appropriate, encourage and help States to exercise this responsibility and support the United Nations in establishing an early warning capability. The international community, through the United Nations, also has the responsibility to use appropriate diplomatic, humanitarian and other peaceful means, in accordance with Chapters VI and VIII of the Charter, to help to protect populations from genocide, war crimes, ethnic cleansing and crimes against humanity. In this context, we are prepared to take collective action, in a timely and decisive manner, through the Security Council, in accordance with the Charter, including Chapter VII, on a case-by-case basis and in cooperation with relevant regional organizations as appropriate, should peaceful means be inadequate and national authorities are manifestly failing to protect their populations from genocide, war crimes, ethnic cleansing and crimes against humanity. We stress the need for the General Assembly to continue consideration of the responsibility to protect populations from genocide, war crimes, ethnic cleansing and crimes against humanity and its implications, bearing in mind the principles of the Charter and international law. We also intend to commit ourselves, as necessary and appropriate, to helping States build capacity to protect their populations from genocide, war crimes, ethnic cleansing and crimes against humanity and to assisting those which are under stress before crises and conflicts break out".[104]

Through the World Summit Outcome Document, adopted by the General Assembly at its 2005 follow-up summit to the UN's Millenium Summit in 2000, the acceptance of the notion of RtoP is brought to a new level within the UN. It is furthermore indicative of its development and evolving status towards greater acceptance in international law. Both the High-Level Panel Report and Kofi Annan's perspective as Secretary General are indicative of a willingness within the

---

[101] Ibid. Compare in this respect the ICISS Report 'The Responsibility to Protect' (n 87) 54-55.

[102] Stahn, 'Responsibility to Protect: Political Rhetoric or Emerging Legal Norm?' (n 91) 105.

[103] 'In larger freedom: towards development, security and human rights for all', Secretary General Report UN Doc. A/59/2005 (21 March 2005) § 132-135. See also Stahn, 'Responsibility to Protect: Political Rhetoric or Emerging Legal Norm?' (n 91) 107.

[104] UNGA Res 60/1 (24 October 2005) UN Doc A/RES/60/1 'World Summit Outcome Document' § 138-139.

UN to endorse this principle. Yet, it remains up to the UN Member States to indeed endorse the notion, as well as the Security Council as executive organ. Clearly, the World Summit Outcome Document, voicing the approval of the 193 Member States is not of equal standing to the previous Reports, but surpasses it in international legal relevance. The endorsement of the Member States in the General Assembly indicated a new era for the principle of RtoP, towards its use in practice. As such, from this point onwards the concept has continued to influence the actions taken by UN organs and as such is relevant to the discussion of the legal framework on the provision of humanitarian assistance. From here, a 'trickle down' effect can be observed into the work of other organs of the UN. It has become apparent through the embracement of RtoP within the UN context that indeed sovereignty and non-intervention remain cornerstone principles in international law, but that with a view to the protection of persons and humanity, these principles should 'constitute a starting point for the analysis, not a conclusion'.[105]

Yet, from these various approaches prior to the embracement by the World Summit Outcome Document, it also becomes apparent that each time the principle of RtoP is endorsed, it is rephrased. In the World Summit Outcome Document, the latest refinements entail an adaptation to the situations in which the UN considers the principle of RtoP to be applicable: the four core crimes of genocide, war crimes, ethnic cleansing and crimes against humanity. Arguably this alteration and restriction to four crimes chafes at the essence of the principle, and also may impede its potential application to humanitarian crises that do not amount to these four core crimes. In particular, the enforcement of the provision of humanitarian assistance in circumstances of natural disasters will be more difficult to frame within this context, as several of the elements of these four core crimes presuppose the existence of an armed conflict.[106] But, this is indeed the slimmed down notion that has been accepted in relation to the notion of sovereignty by the UN and therefore what international legal practice must deal with.

Eventually in 2006, the Security Council formally reaffirmed the World Summit Outcome Document's text on RtoP, retaining the application to the four core crimes as proposed by the World Summit.[107] Responses have been positive, as continued identical endorsement of the principle enhances its clarity and its possible incorporation as an international norm.[108] The UN Security Council has started to endorse the principle, amongst others in its Resolution 1706 of August 2006 pertaining to the Sudan and Resolution 1894, pertaining thematically to the

[105] 'Third report on the protection of persons in the event of disasters', ILC Special Rapporteur Eduardo Valencia-Ospina, UN Doc A/CN.4/629 (31 March 2010) § 75.

[106] See in further detail Chapter 8.

[107] UNSC Res 1674 (28 April 2006) UN Doc S/RES/1674 § 4: "Reaffirms the provisions of paragraphs 138 and 139 of the 2005 World Summit Outcome Document regarding the responsibility to protect populations from genocide, war crimes, ethnic cleansing and crimes against humanity".

[108] Noha Shawki, 'Responsibility to Protect: The Evolution of an International Norm', (2011) 3 *Global Responsibility to Protect* 2, 172–196 at 187-188.

protection of civilians in times of armed conflict.[109] In these resolutions, the Council 'recalls' the statements made in the World Summit Outcome Document, but has neglected to elaborate on the content of RtoP or provide further clarifications.

The principle of RtoP, though currently still developing within UN organs, is an indication of the continued debate with regard to the notion of state sovereignty. With initial UN endorsement through the World Summit Outcome Document and the successive Security Council affirmation thereof, the question arises: where to from here? What does the principle of RtoP 'do' for or with the concept of sovereignty? Can the principle of responsibility to protect be considered an emerging international (legal) norm, and is this relevant for the current understanding of the international legal concept of state sovereignty or a state's existing responsibilities under international law? And following on from this, in what way is it therefore relevant to this research pertaining to humanitarian assistance? Certainly the concepts have undergone changes over the past decades, and the appearance of RtoP in the international arena must be considered. Given the fact that the principle of RtoP suggests the potential use of force in circumstances where humanitarian crises amount to the selected four core crimes, it is relevant to the discussion of the legal framework concerning the provision of humanitarian assistance. When matters of humanitarian access will be discussed, the developing principle of Responsibility to Protect will be taken into consideration also.[110] Indeed, the notion of RtoP is closely associated with the idea of 'responsible sovereignty', namely that sovereigns have duties towards those within their jurisdiction.[111] Such duties include the provision of humanitarian assistance, as will be discussed in Part II of this research, in particular in Chapter 6.

4.2.3.2 Humanitarian Assistance and the Development of RtoP in Practice

Determining whether RtoP has evolved from a 'political catchword' to a legal norm is relevant to the determination of the boundaries of both sovereignty and other relevant obligations, in relation to the provision of humanitarian assistance.[112] As Stahn argues, RtoP is testimony of a shift in international law, where the principle of state sovereignty is now confined by the protection of 'human security'.[113] In 2007 UN Secretary General Ban Ki Moon appointed Edward Luck as a Special Advisor, tasked with 'conceptual development and consensus building' within the UN, to assist the General Assembly with the notion of RtoP.[114] Furthermore, Ban continued his predecessor's support for the principle, and in 2009 his report 'Implementing the responsibility to protect' attempts to set the tone for

---

[109] UNSC Res 1706 (31 August 2006) UN Doc S/RES/1706 preamble § 2; UNSC Res 1894 (11 November 2009) UN Doc S/RES/1894 preamble § 1 and 7.

[110] See Chapters 7 and 8.

[111] Focarelli, 'Duty to Protect in Cases of Natural Disasters' (n 23) § 27.

[112] Stahn, 'Responsibility to Protect: Political Rhetoric or Emerging Legal Norm?' (n 91) 120.

[113] Ibid 100-101.

[114] <www.un.org/en/preventgenocide/adviser/edwardluck.shtml> accessed 10 July 2012.

operationalising RtoP, acknowledging respect for human rights as an essential element of 'responsible sovereignty'.[115] Ban follows the four central crimes of genocide, war crimes, ethnic cleansing and crimes against humanity, as set out by the World Summit Outcome and considers their protection in three pillars.[116] In subsequent years, Ban has continued to report on the principle of RtoP, thereby addressing its relevance in UN context.[117] Interestingly, considering the aftermath of a conflict, the Secretary General calls upon greater endorsement of the International Criminal Court as part of RtoP.[118] The Report was recognised by the first General Assembly resolution on RtoP, which after a thorough debate, limited itself to 'continue its consideration' of the principle, a fairly meagre stance.[119]

The questions at hand remained however whether RtoP can be operationalised, whether this is desirable, and what (legal) benefits regarding the enhanced provision of humanitarian assistance in crises it would introduce. While RtoP is attempting a shift towards responsibility for protection of populations, it inevitably asserts the possibility for military intervention if and when a state does not live up to its responsibilities and refuses assistance through 'pillar two' of RtoP, thereby involving sovereignty-related issues.[120] Much can be said in favour of the comprehensive attitude of the RtoP doctrine. Yet from the humanitarian perspective, a fear has been expressed that justifying military intervention when a state does not cooperate with international assistance under pillar two, compromises the neutrality of such assistance.[121] However, in the absence of the provision of humanitarian assistance, enforcement may be necessary to ensure delivery of aid to those in need, as discussed in Chapter 8. As always, assistance must be provided in accordance with the principles of humanity, neutrality and impartiality in order to be considered truly 'humanitarian assistance'.[122] Over the past decade since the launch of the concept, RtoP has generated debate amongst scholars and

[115] 'Implementing the responsibility to protect', Secretary General Report UN Doc A/63/677 (12 January 2009) §16.
[116] Ibid § 11. The first pillar concerns 'The protection responsibilities of the State', the second pillar regards 'International assistance and capacity-building' and pillar three discusses 'Timely and decisive response', which includes military action through Security Council authorization. Responses to the 'three pillars' approach have been diverse, as some argue this to be a logical step in the progression of human rights protection, whilst others fear problems with the third pillar, considering the role it grants the Security Council. See in this regard Magnuson, 'The Responsibility to Protect and the Decline of Sovereignty: Free Speech Protection under International Law' (n 70) 267; and Susan Harris Rimmer, 'New Issues in Refugee Research: Refugees, internally displaced persons and the 'responsibility to protect'', (2010) *UNHCR Policy Development and Evaluation Service* Research Paper No. 185, 4.
[117] 'Early Warning, Assessment, and the Responsibility to Protect', Secretary General Report UN Doc A/64/864 (14 July 2010); 'The Role of Regional and Sub-regional Arrangements in Implementing the Responsibility to Protect', Secretary General Report UN Doc A/65/877–S/2011/393 (27 June 2011) and 'Fulfilling our collective responsibility: international assistance and the responsibility to protect' Secretary General Report UN Doc A/68/947–S/2014/449 (11 July 2014).
[118] 'Implementing the responsibility to protect' UN Doc A/63/677 (n 115) § 18-19.
[119] UNGA Res 63/308 (7 October 2009) UN Doc A/RES/63/308.
[120] 'Implementing the responsibility to protect' UN Doc A/63/677 (n 115) § 56.
[121] 'Implementing the responsibility to protect' UN Doc A/63/677 (n 115) § 29 and 56; and Feinstein, 'Darfur and Beyond: What is Needed to Prevent Mass Atrocities' (n 96) 17.
[122] See Section 2.2.3 The Principles for the Delivery of Assistance.

practitioners: viewed by some as the answer to the problem of the concept of 'humanitarian intervention' and by others as overstepping the legal boundaries of sovereignty.[123] As the doctrine of RtoP is growing from infancy into greater maturity, its true test will come in the following years: can the doctrine be translated from words on paper into practice on the ground? RtoP may prove to have great benefits when the protection of populations is at stake, but it may also prove to have unforeseen downsides, as a proliferation of new 'norms' must be cautioned against. Risks of a possible narrow scope of RtoP include 'classifying' humanitarian crises, and possibly leaving some on the back-burner because they do not fall within the scope of RtoP. In particular considering the legal framework on the delivery of humanitarian assistance, such risks exist for crises not amounting to the four 'core crimes'; as mentioned above. The elements of the crimes restrict certain instances to armed conflict, while in practice complex emergencies or natural disasters may equally result in situations where sovereigns are unwilling or hesitant to provide assistance and allow aid into the territory from external sources. It has been argued that the high threshold of the four crimes should be restricted to the 'third pillar' of RtoP concerned with possible military intervention, to allow more leeway to broader preventive international (humanitarian) assistance in the second pillar.[124] This thought is definitely relevant to the further development of international assistance under the cloak of RtoP, and the maintenance of broad civil society support for the doctrine of RtoP, but may be too forward for the UN's position in this regard. Given the restriction of RtoP within UN context to the four core crimes of 'genocide, war crimes, ethnic cleansing and crimes against humanity', the role that the Responsibility to Protect can play with regard to the humanitarian assistance is limited from the outset. Circumstances of natural disaster, which often lead to a humanitarian crisis and a need for humanitarian assistance, are excluded from the 'third pillar' military benefits of RtoP, unless it may be argued that a crime against humanity could be committed by a government against its own population, should it deny the provision of assistance in the aftermath of a natural disaster.[125] A clear attempt to argue this already took place in 2008, when initiatives led by Kouchner were made to apply RtoP to access the victims of a cyclone in Myanmar, yet failed.[126]

[123] Some have even argued that a state 'forfeits its sovereignty' when the international community condemns its actions. Sovereignty is then passed to the international community. See in this regard Maogoto & Kindiki, 'A people Betrayed – the Darfur Crisis and International Law: Rethinking Westphalian Sovereignty in the 21st Century' (n 54) 118 and 122; as well as Roberta Cohen, 'Humanitarian Imperatives are Transforming Sovereignty', (2008) 9 *Northwestern Journal of International Affairs* 1, 4.

[124] Harris Rimmer, 'New Issues in Refugee Research: Refugees, internally displaced persons and the 'responsibility to protect' (n 116) 15.

[125] See Chapter 8.

[126] Jarrod Wong, 'Reconstructing the Responsibility to Protect in the Wake of Cyclones and Separatism', (2009) 84 *Tulane Law Review*, 244-245; and Katherine Iliopoulos, 'UN Debates the Responsibility to Protect', (12 August 2009) Crimes of War Project < www.crimesofwar.org/commentary/un-debates-the-responsibility-to-protect/> accessed 25 December 2014.

Although much of the legal debate concerning the doctrine of RtoP has been on the changing notion of sovereignty, the doctrine is also attempting to establish more clear boundaries concerning humanitarian assistance and the invocation of military force for this purpose. Indeed, whereas the notion of humanitarian intervention argued a right to intervene in the event of gross human rights violations, the principle of RtoP only warrants the use of military force in the event of genocide, war crimes, ethnic cleansing and crimes against humanity, within the context of Security Council action. Thus, access by force as a manner of enforcement in the provision of humanitarian assistance, which in itself needs to remain neutral as discussed above, shall only be permitted under the cloak of RtoP in the event of the four core crimes. This view is also accepted by Ban Ki Moon, as the Secretary General's 2009 report denounces the extension of RtoP to cover grounds such as HIV/AIDS or natural disasters, arguing this would undermine the 2005 World Summit Outcome, which only entails the four abovementioned crimes for which states already have existing legal obligations.[127] As such, RtoP is not extending into new grounds, but embracing the existing notions of genocide, crimes against humanity, war crimes and ethnic cleansing. The sovereignty-related issues surrounding UN (in)action relating to Libya and Syria are fuelling the fierce debate, necessitating cautiousness about the meaning and limits of RtoP. In order to be considered as a new *legal* principle, the application of RtoP as a concept must be continued: consistently, identically and as a result, internationally accepted. Yet, as the Security Council faced the threats to international peace and security during the uprisings related to the 'Arab Spring' starting in 2011, and ensuing threats related to the forces of 'the Islamic State (IS)', it became apparent that the principle so warmly endorsed in 2005, was sometimes difficult to apply in practice.[128] Whilst Chapter 7 and 8 address Security Council action in relation to the provision of humanitarian assistance in more detail, the following paragraphs address the general incorporation of the principle, to establish its relevance in practice and as related to the concept of humanitarian assistance.

In the spring of 2011, responding to the serious human rights violations and strife in Libya, the UN Security Council, in a unanimously adopted resolution, made its primary reference to RtoP in practice, calling upon the 'Libyan authorities responsibility to protect its population'.[129] Subsequently only one month later the Security Council once again reiterated its stance, calling upon the:

> "responsibility of the Libyan authorities to protect the Libyan population and reaffirming that parties to armed conflicts bear the primary responsibility to take all feasible steps to ensure the protection of civilians".[130]

---

[127] 'Implementing the responsibility to protect' UN Doc A/63/677 (n 115) § 10(b).

[128] See Section 7.3.2 Security Council Resolutions and the Right to Access for a more detailed discussion.

[129] UNSC Res 1970 (26 February 2011) UN Doc S/RES/1970 'Peace and security in Africa' preamble.

[130] UNSC Res 1973 (17 March 2011) UN Doc S/RES/1973 'The situation in Libya' preamble.

In both resolutions the Security Council acted under Chapter VII of the UN Charter, imposing sanctions and in the latter authorising member state action, which was followed by the NATO operation.[131] The Security Council followed suit that same month in a resolution concerning Côte d'Ivoire, reiterating the RtoP 'lingo' used for the Libyan authorities, as well as referring back to its resolutions embracing the RtoP principle.[132] Both Resolution 1973 and 1975, where the Security Council acted under Chapter VII, are considered evidence of the Council's proactive attitude, considering the choice to use force for the protection of civilians and framing such force within the context of the Responsibility to Protect.[133] As such, the Security Council authorised its member states:

> "to take all necessary measures (...) to protect civilians and civilian populated areas under threat of attack in the Libyan Arab Jamahiriya, including Benghazi".[134]

Thus, the principle of RtoP was connected *in practice* to the use of military force in the protection of civilians.

A subsequent resolution concerning Libya, as well as several resolutions focusing on Yemen and Sudan, have shown the Security Council to initially be quite prone to the incorporation of RtoP in its practice.[135] In these ensuing resolutions, the Council reiterated its earlier perspective on a government's 'responsibility to protect civilians' or 'responsibility to protect its population'.[136] Unfortunately, the situation in Syria throughout the following years until 2014 has shown that the Security Council's action was dependent on the political will of its

[131] Ibid § 4.

[132] UNSC Res 1975 (30 March 2011) UN Doc S/RES/1975 'The situation in Côte d'Ivoire' preamble §: "reaffirming the primary responsibility of each State to protect civilians and reiterating that parties to armed conflicts bear the primary responsibility to take all feasible steps to ensure the protection of civilians and facilitate the rapid and unimpeded passage of humanitarian assistance and the safety of humanitarian personnel, recalling its resolutions 1325 (2000), 1820 (2008), 1888 (2009) and 1889 (2009) on women, peace and security, its resolution 1612 (2005) and 1882 (2009) on children and armed conflict and its resolution 1674 (2006) and 1894 (2009) on the protection of civilians in armed conflicts".

[133] A J Bellamy & P D Williams, 'The new politics of protection? Côte d'Ivoire, Libya and the responsibility to protect', (2011) 87 *International Affairs* 4, 826.

[134] UNSC Res 1973 (17 March 2011) UN Doc S/RES/1973 'The situation in Libya' § 4.

[135] UNSC Res 1996 (8 July 2011) UN Doc S/RES/1996 § 3(b)(iv) "Advising and assisting the Government of the Republic of South Sudan, including military and police at national and local levels as appropriate, in fulfilling its responsibility to protect civilians, in compliance with international humanitarian, human rights, and refugee law"; UNSC Res 2014 (21 October 2011) UN Doc S/RES/2014 'The situation in the Middle East' § preamble: "*Recalling* the Yemeni government's primary responsibility to protect its population"; UNSC Res 2016 (27 October 2011) UN Doc S/RES/2016 'The situation in Libya' § 3: "underscores the Libyan authorities' responsibility for the protection of its population, including foreign nationals and African migrants"; UNSC Res 2040 (12 March 2012) UN Doc S/RES/2040 'The situation in Libya' § 4: "*underscores* the Libyan authorities' primary responsibility for the protection of Libya's population, as well as foreign nationals, including African migrants".

[136] Ibid.

member states, faltering in the creation of a similar clear-cut resolution for Syria.[137] Subsequent resolutions that were passed by the Security Council with regard to Syria, fail to incorporate RtoP language.[138] Indeed, whilst with the passing of time the Security Council asserted the need for the provision of humanitarian assistance, the use of force to implement such assistance has not been addressed.[139] Arguably, use of the phrase was cautioned against as some member states felt that the lingo in the Libyan resolutions enabled a rather too robust response.[140] The Security Council's stance with regard to RtoP cannot at this stage be unambiguously asserted.

The Secretary General also seems to take a step back from the enthusiastic embracement of RtoP following the 2005 World Outcome, voicing concern in May 2012 about the continuous joint discussion of the 'protection of civilians' and the 'responsibility to protect'. Ban argues that although they may serve a common purpose, the two notions must not be confused:

> "First, the protection of civilians is a legal concept based on international humanitarian, human rights and refugee law, while the responsibility to protect is a political concept, set out in the 2005 World Summit Outcome (see General Assembly resolution 60/1). Second, there are important differences in their scope. The protection of civilians relates to violations of international humanitarian and human rights law in situations of armed conflict. The responsibility to protect is limited to violations that constitute war crimes or crimes against humanity or that would be considered acts of genocide or ethnic cleansing. Crimes against humanity, genocide and ethnic cleansing may occur in situations that do not meet the threshold of armed conflict".[141]

Indeed, this sentiment is reflected by others concerned with the legal value of the principle of RtoP as a parallel discourse may not be helpful for the further development of the protection of persons in a situation of crisis. Considering the provision of humanitarian assistance, it is however relevant to note that Ban has argued in his discussion of the 'protection of civilians' that the four core crimes that can set the military component of RtoP into motion, *may* occur outside of an armed conflict. Thus, the Secretary General argues that these crimes *can* indeed take place in a crisis-like circumstance that does not necessarily meet the threshold for applicability of international humanitarian law. As such, some argue that regardless

---

[137] Security Council SC/10403 (4 October 2011) 6627th Meeting (Night). Russia and China vetoed the pending resolution. Similarly: Security Council SC/10536 (4 February 2012) 6711th Meeting (AM).

[138] UNSC Res 2042 (14 April 2012) UN Doc S/RES/2042 'The situation in the Middle East' and UNSC Res 2043 (21 April 2012) UN Doc S/RES/2043 'The situation in the Middle East'. Furthermore, several resolutions subsequently failed to pass in the Security Council due to China and Russia's veto, such as on 18 July 2012: <www.un.org/apps/news/story.asp?NewsID=42513&Cr=Syria&Cr1=> accessed 19 July 2012.

[139] See Section 7.3.2 Security Council Resolutions and the Right to Access for a more detailed discussion. See also UNSC Res 2165 (14 July 2014) UN Doc S/RES/2165.

[140] Edward C Luck, 'The Responsibility to Protect: The First Decade' (2011) 3 *Global Responsibility to Protect*, 395.

[141] 'Report of the Secretary-General on the protection of civilians in armed conflict' (22 May 2012) UN Doc S/2012/376 § 21.

of whether or not consensus can be reached on the normative and legal value of the notion of RtoP and its acceptance by the international legal community, it can definitively be established that the principle, focusing on the four crimes of genocide, war crimes, ethnic cleansing and crimes against humanity, reflects widely accepted 'core principles' of both human rights and international humanitarian law.[142]

Thus, with a view to the provision of humanitarian assistance, it remains helpful to look to the development of the principle of RtoP with regard to possible increasing responsibilities of governments for the provision of humanitarian assistance, and ensuing possible international responsibilities that may arise should a national government not comply with its responsibilities under international law. These specific individual responsibilities and circumstances will be discussed in subsequent Chapters and remain outside the more theoretical application of the concept of sovereignty in relation to the legal framework of humanitarian assistance that this Chapter addresses.

4.2.3.3 Towards a new Definition of Sovereignty

The development of the principle of RtoP has not occurred in a legal vacuum. Indeed, the principle of RtoP did not develop as a stand-alone concept, but reflects an overall development in international law over the past decades.[143] As a result, the content of RtoP engages with other well-established notions of international law, thereby possibly providing for a favourable continuance of its incorporation in international law, resulting also in a development of its legitimacy.[144] As such, the development of RtoP and its subsequent embracement by the UN has placed the discussion on the definition of 'state sovereignty' back to the forefront of the international legal discourse, with renewed vigour.[145] Both concepts interact, develop simultaneously and influence each other. As argued by Ryngaert, the 'moral-political notion' of the principle of RtoP echoes today's concept of 'relative sovereignty' where a state in fact would forfeit its sovereign rights under the principle of non-intervention and domestic jurisdiction in the event it fails to comply with the most basic norms of international law.[146] In particular relation to

[142] Shawki, 'Responsibility to Protect: The Evolution of an International Norm' (n 108), 191; and Julia Hoffmann & Andre Nollkaemper, 'Concluding observations' in J Hoffmann & A Nollkaemper (eds), *Responsibility to Protect: from Principle to Practice* (Pallas Publications 2012) 356.

[143] Ibid Hoffmann & Nollkaemper.

[144] Shawki, 'Responsibility to Protect: The Evolution of an International Norm' (n 108), 191-192; and Luck, 'The Responsibility to Protect: The First Decade' (n 140) 391.

[145] See amongst others Hoffmann & Nollkaemper, 'Concluding Observations' in *Responsibility to protect: from Principle to Practice* (n 142); Bellamy, *Responsibility to Protect: the Global Effort to End Mass Atrocities* (n 97); Thakur, *The United Nations, Peace and Security: from Collective Security to the Responsibility to Protect* (n 97); see also Nico J Schrijver, 'The Changing Nature of State Sovereignty', (1999) 70 *British Year Book of International Law*, 65-98 for an earlier discussion on the dynamic notion of sovereignty.

[146] Cedric Ryngaert, 'Humanitarian Assistance and the Conundrum of Consent: A Legal Perspective', (2013) 5 *Amsterdam Law Forum* 2, 11-12.

the provision of humanitarian assistance, Ryngaert argues that as a result of this notion of relative sovereignty, a state can thus not prohibit third parties from asserting 'their 'international' responsibility vis-à-vis populations in need on the territory of the former state, and from overriding the absence of state consent to provide humanitarian assistance'.[147] Tomuschat had also already asserted along these lines that consequences exist when a state abuses its sovereign rights by engaging in 'gross atrocities, such as genocide and ethnic cleansing', as the result may be that a state forfeits the protection granted to it under the principles that sovereignty encompasses in international law.[148] As such, Tomuschat poses that when tension exists between the principle of sovereignty and that of respect for human rights, one of the two must yield, and the international community is increasingly affirming the potential to pierce the veil of the principle of sovereignty:

> "Sovereignty is not a natural, inherent quality of any entity recognized as a state. Rather, it is a distinction conferred on that entity by the international community as a recognition of its ability and willingness to take care of law and order and to administer justice within the group of human beings organized under its roof. Inevitably, failure to discharge the general function which legitimates the existence of a government must entail certain consequences".[149]

Indeed, Tomuschat echoes the words of Elihu Lauterpacht a few decades earlier, but today the practice of the international community seems to have caught up with legal theory, through the development of the Responsibility to Protect.[150] As Annemarie Slaughter argues, it is now necessary to:

> "understand sovereignty as at once a government's control of a defined territory and population and as a particular relationship between a government and its citizens. International law still upholds and safeguards a government's power and control over its citizens, including its right to invoke states of emergency and use force to maintain domestic order. But it also now protects the citizens of a particular state when their government fails grossly in its obligations toward them".[151]

This premise that human rights exist as inalienable rights of persons, in concurrence with a state's primary responsibility for the fulfillment thereof, is indeed consistent with the UN Charter. Precisely how far international law will go in the protection of civilians through the provision of humanitarian assistance when a government fails in its obligations towards them, will be discussed in subsequent Chapters.[152] Benvenisti has in this regard already taken the premise that sovereigns must be seen

---

[147] Ibid.
[148] Christian Tomuschat, *Human Rights: Between Idealism and Realism* (Oxford University Press 2008) 277.
[149] Ibid 277-278.
[150] Section 4.2.2.1 The Post-World War II Era.
[151] Slaughter, 'Intervention, Libya, and the Future of Sovereignty' (n 45).
[152] See Chapters 7 and 8.

as 'trustees of humanity' that are 'embedded within a more encompassing global order', as the international community has developed increasingly into a global order of interdependency and multiple stakeholders, which must be realigned with sovereigns' original authorities.[153] As such trustees, Benvenisti argues that sovereigns have obligations to not only do no harm, but to in fact contribute to global welfare, and in the event this is not done, the sovereign must be subjected to an 'external accountability review' with a view to the relevant stakeholders.[154]

This discussion on and rephrasing of the notion of sovereignty might prove a practical solution in pleasing both the protagonists of greater human rights protection, and those that hold on to the principles of non-intervention, consent and domestic jurisdiction. After all, both aspects continue to be two sides of the same coin of sovereignty. This indeed follows the idea that RtoP is, amongst other factors, contributing to the manner in which the international legal community identifies and even defines these principles on which traditional sovereignty is built.[155] Indeed, bringing the notion of the social contract into the 21st century and following Slaughter's argument, if a government fails to protect its citizens, it does not uphold its end of the contract. As international law now directly recognises individuals as subjects, the civilian should then perhaps indeed be free to request and receive protection, for the purpose of this research: humanitarian assistance, from sources outside its own government. Humanitarian assistance can thus not only be seen as a tool for governments in the fulfillment of their sovereign responsibilities, but also as a vehicle through which the international community can provide a population in need with facilities a government is failing to do. Thus, like sovereignty, humanitarian assistance can too be perceived through an internal and an external lens.

4.3 Conclusion

In the above Chapter, the relationship between the concept of state sovereignty and the provision of humanitarian assistance has been addressed. The three core principles of state sovereignty, namely non-intervention, consent and domestic jurisdiction, each have their own particular relationship with the delivery of humanitarian assistance, and thereby with the rights and duties involved in the legal framework on humanitarian assistance.

Regarding the relationship between the principle of non-intervention and the provision of humanitarian assistance, it must be noted that particularly 'intervention' must be distinguished from the provision of assistance, as assistance can only be considered humanitarian if provided in a neutral manner, excluding the use of force. Although the ICJ in the *Nicaragua*-case touched upon the matter, it

---

[153] Benvenisti 'Sovereigns as Trustees of humanity: The Concept and its Normative Implications' (n 82) 5-6.
[154] Ibid, 17 & 35.
[155] Hoffmann & Nollkaemper, 'Concluding Observations' in *Responsibility to protect: from Principle to Practice* (n 142) 363.

unfortunately did not address the notion of intervention by force for a possible *facilitation* of the provision of aid.[156] Indeed, the potential use of force as an enforcement method for the provision of humanitarian assistance – although related – must be clearly distinguished from the *sec* provision itself. The subsequently discussed principle of consent as related to treaty law does not play a large role in this particular research concerning humanitarian assistance. Yet, as will be discussed in subsequent Chapters, this cornerstone in international law remains relevant when considering the various rights and duties of states as they relate to the provision of assistance in general, within international law as based upon the specific provisions in human rights and humanitarian law concerning the potential delivery of aid by third parties. Lastly, the principle of domestic jurisdiction was addressed, in particular in relation to the circumstance of a 'failed state' as can be relevant in the provision of humanitarian assistance which only takes place in a humanitarian crisis. Indeed, while a failed state may not be able to take charge in a crisis, statehood remains in place. Therefore, the primary responsibility for the provision of assistance continues to lie with the affected state. However, the provision of assistance from third parties may be a tool or vehicle through which state failure can be diminished.

Following the three valued principles in relation to the concept of sovereignty and humanitarian assistance, this Chapter has focused on the concept of sovereignty itself and what it entails today. Through a brief historical analysis of the birth of the concept, and its development in recent decades following World War II, it has been possible to address the realities in the international legal order that led to the development of the much plagued notion of humanitarian intervention, and the more recent developments surrounding the principle of responsibility to protect.[157]

It has been observed that the notion of a 'social contract' as posited by Hobbes, Locke and Rousseau, with a relationship of mutual reinforcement between society and sovereign brings forth rights and duties for both parties, and with regard to humanitarian assistance, it can then be argued that the provision of such assistance could be seen as a duty for the sovereign in fulfilling its part of the agreement with society. Subsequently, if international law should encompass a duty to provide assistance, state sovereignty would then oblige a government to provide assistance. Equally, individuals may then claim the right to receive assistance from a sovereign based on such a provision in international law. Indeed, the development of human rights law following World War II and the role of this body of law in international law today has furthermore increasingly supported the view that sovereignty is 'permeated' and that the sovereign must protect and fulfil the rights of those within its jurisdiction. This relationship of mutual enforcement is also viewed in both the concepts of 'humanitarian intervention' and 'responsibility to protect' as both notions address the permeability of state sovereignty, envisaging rights for the

[156] See Section 4.2 Sovereignty as a Concept in International Law.
[157] See Sections 4.2.2 Reconceptualising Sovereignty? and 4.2.3 The Responsibility to Protect, the UN and Humanitarian Assistance.

international community to assert the protection of a population should the sovereign not do so.

While common ground can be found in the rationale of both principles, the notion of humanitarian intervention, clearly distinguishable if not essentially different from humanitarian assistance, did not find general acceptance in international law, given the unilateral use of force (outside the realm of the Security Council) that is incorporated in the doctrine. Thus, the international community turned to a new principle, in the hope that redefining the rationale might prove a more constructive solution to the barriers of state sovereignty. Indeed, while RtoP is currently still developing, the principle does reflect the larger adaptation that the concept of state sovereignty has undergone through changes in international law in general over the past decades, and the renewed attention it receives from international legal scholars and practitioners. Changes in warfare, including the rise of non-international armed conflicts leading to humanitarian crises, as well as the asymmetrical warfare have been conducive to this. Whilst the incorporation of RtoP in general does not have to be a negative development; indeed allowing for a broader international responsibility, for the purpose of the assessment of the legal framework on the provision of assistance, some obstacles remain. Next to obstacles that can be seen in bringing RtoP into practice through Security Council resolutions; leading to doubts as to its practical efficacy, in particular for this research it is relevant to note the restriction of RtoP application by the UN to the four core crimes of genocide, war crimes, crimes against humanity and ethnic cleansing. This restriction is relevant to a discussion in subsequent Chapters concerning the use of force in obtaining access to a territory for the provision of aid, as it distinctly excludes such enforcement for humanitarian crises that do not encompass such four crimes.

It can however be concluded that for the purposes of this research into humanitarian assistance, the Westphalian notion of sovereignty must be reconsidered, to not only retain the old notion of governmental jurisdiction and control but to also encompass a greater protection of civilians, through sovereign responsibilities. In particular in the event a government fails to comply with its obligations towards these civilians, such as in the fulfillment of the provision of humanitarian assistance, such responsibilities must be enforceable at an international level.[158] Both aspects *together* form the two-sided coin of sovereignty. Thus sovereignty can indeed be both a vehicle and an obstacle in the provision of humanitarian assistance, dependent on the perspectives of the particular sovereign. It is therefore crucial to examine the current rights and obligations resting on both states and the recipients of assistance under international law, to more clearly define these sovereign responsibilities. Assessing the state of the law will enable those dependent on humanitarian assistance to truly enforce the receipt of assistance, should a government not be inclined to provide assistance. Holding up the 'shield' of sovereignty will no longer be possible if it can be established that the non-provision of humanitarian assistance can amount to a clear breach of an

[158] See Chapter 8.

international obligation. In fact, such a revision of the concept of sovereignty aligns with the old notion of the 'social contract' allowing individuals to perhaps indeed request and receive humanitarian assistance from the exterior. The following Chapters in Part II of this research will determine the exact extent of the protection of civilians through the provision of humanitarian assistance and shall commence with a discussion of human rights law, as the development of these rights have been instrumental in the increased provision of humanitarian assistance.

Part II

Primary Rights and Duties in Humanitarian Crises

CHAPTER 5
THE POTENTIAL HUMAN RIGHT TO RECEIVE HUMANITARIAN ASSISTANCE

Over the past decades, human rights law has proliferated. In many disaster situations, international organisations express concern for violations of the affected population's human rights. The provision of humanitarian assistance has been connected to this body of law for a long time. As the General Assembly asserted in 1970:

> "The provision of international relief to civilian populations is in conformity with the humanitarian principles of the Charter of the United Nations, the Universal Declaration of Human Rights and other international instruments in the field of human rights".

But how did the provision of humanitarian assistance edge into this body of law? Moreover and more relevantly, in what way does human rights law in fact incorporate the provision of humanitarian assistance? This Chapter addresses specifically which rights to receive assistance and duties to provide it exist in current human rights law.[1]

5.1 Introduction

Part II of this research focuses on the analysis of the *lex lata* pertaining to the legal framework on the delivery of humanitarian assistance. In this light, Chapter 6 addresses the rights and duties in international law of the various stakeholders, such as the affected persons and the affected state. These various rights and obligations are codified for a large part in human rights law and humanitarian law, as Section 3.4 has addressed. The nature of these bodies of law and the provision of humanitarian assistance share a common denominator in the concept of human dignity, as also addressed in Section 2.2.3.1. In fact, this notion of dignity is the opening address of the 1948 'Universal Declaration of Human Rights', as it states that the 'recognition of the inherent dignity and of the equal and inalienable rights of all members of the human family is the foundation of freedom, justice and peace in the world'.[2] Other early referrals to the general relationship between

[1] UNGA Res 2675 (XXV) (9 December 1970) 'Basic principles for the protection of civilian populations in armed conflict' § 8.
[2] UDHR Preamble § 1. Full text of the Universal Declaration of Human Rights (10 December 1948) available at <www.un.org/en/documents/udhr/> accessed 19 July 2012.

humanitarian assistance and human rights law can be found in the work of the General Assembly.[3]

Crucial to the more in-depth analysis of the legal framework on the provision of humanitarian assistance is the assessment of the incorporation of this concept into human rights law. Chapter 2 has provided the historical overview of the birth of humanitarian assistance in humanitarian law, but with a view to this research's more encompassing approach to the provision of humanitarian assistance, human rights law must be addressed as well. An approach through this body of law will allow for applicability in all circumstances of crisis.[4] Given the very essence of humanitarian assistance: ensuring the survival of persons in emergency situations, through the provision of food, water and shelter, the concept itself allows for a placement within the human rights framework. The question whether a potential human right to *receive* humanitarian assistance exists can then only be answered through the establishment of what this right entails. This Chapter therefore assesses the background of the potential human right to receive humanitarian assistance, and examines which established human rights it may build upon or emerge from. These rights include the right to life, food, health and water.[5] A focus is placed on these four rights as opposed to potential other human rights such as the right to housing with a view to this research's definition of humanitarian assistance.[6] The timeframe and nature of the concept (related to emergency situations) distinguishes humanitarian assistance from broader concepts such as development assistance, as a result of which a choice has been made to focus on those rights that directly and distinctly stand in relation to the provision of food, water, shelter and emergency supplies for the survival of persons in times of a humanitarian crisis. Following the examination of the potential independent existence of the receipt of humanitarian assistance as a human right, the right to life, food, health and water are discussed to determine whether they in themselves provide for a right to receive humanitarian assistance under existing human rights law.

Through an analysis of the history and development of human rights in general, as well as the content of the specific rights to life, food, health and water, this Chapter will determine whether or not a human right to receive humanitarian assistance is currently emerging in international law. This Chapter addresses the issue of a potential human right to humanitarian assistance in a two-tiered manner: firstly the question whether an independent *human* right to humanitarian assistance exists is addressed through an analysis of human rights law; secondly, upon the assessment of such potential existence, the potential existing basis in the already established body of individual human rights is addressed. With a view to the continuous proliferation of human rights, a restrained view is taken on the development of 'new' rights, when existing rights may suffice in the protection of

---

[3] UNGA Res 2675 (XXV) (9 December 1970) (n 1) § 8.

[4] See Section 3.4.2 Applicability of Human Rights in Armed Conflict and Occupation.

[5] The notion of humanitarian assistance as adopted in this research focuses on the initial provision of emergency aid. In this regard, the 'human right to housing' is left outside the scope of this research.

[6] See Section 2.2.2 Defining Humanitarian Assistance.

persons in times of humanitarian crises. Given the nature of the provision of assistance, the matter of derogability from human rights treaties is taken into account.

The assessment of the existence of a potential human right to receive assistance is relevant at the beginning of Part II of this research as subsequent Chapters deal with the specific rights and duties in the provision of humanitarian assistance in times of occupation, conflict and natural disaster amounting to a humanitarian crisis. Although various sources in international law other than human rights law may provide for a right to receive such assistance and a duty to provide it in several circumstances, determining the level of protection under human rights law is of crucial relevance to the legal protection of those affected by humanitarian crises. The continued application of human rights law in times of applicability of humanitarian law as discussed in Section 3.4.2 evidences and highlights this crucial nature: it is the body of law that is applicable in *all* circumstances that may amount to a humanitarian crisis, both in times of conflict and peace. It is for this reason that this Chapter assesses the status of protection under human rights law *prior* to the examination of the possible specific rights and duties involved in the provision of assistance through various other sources of international law, in times of a humanitarian crisis.

5.2 The Development of Human Rights Relevant to Humanitarian Assistance

Although Chapters 2 and 3 have addressed the longstanding origins of humanitarian assistance as a concept, placing this assistance within a human rights context makes a transition to the 21st century. Following the atrocities witnessed by the international community during World War II, the United Nations have been crucial to the development of these rights and their embedding in the international legal world. This embedding commences with the organisation's Charter stating in Article 1(3) that one of the purposes of the UN is to promote and encourage fundamental freedoms for all, as well as achieving international cooperation in 'solving international problems of a humanitarian character'.[7] Furthermore, articles 55 and 56 of the UN Charter, calling upon the UN as an organisation and its Member States individually to take action to achieve the promotion of universal respect for, and observance of human rights, have also contributed to the internationalisation of these rights.[8] Indeed, as an obligation resting upon society is

[7] Michael Palumbo, *Human Rights: Meaning and History* (Krieger 1982) 11-12; Lori Damrosch (ed), *International Law: Cases and Materials* (West Group 2001) 650.

[8] The full text of Article 55 of the UN Charter states: "With a view to the creation of conditions of stability and well-being which are necessary for peaceful and friendly relations among nations based on respect for the principle of equal rights and self-determination of peoples, the United Nations shall promote: a. higher standards of living, full employment, and conditions of economic and social progress and development; b. solutions of international economic, social, health, and related problems; and international cultural and educational cooperation; and c. universal respect for, and observance of, human rights and fundamental freedoms for all without distinction as to race, sex, language, or religion"; Article 56 of the UN Charter states:" All Members pledge themselves to take joint and

implied in order to meet the demands of these rights,[9] the international community has sought the reassurance that these concepts would no longer remain within the national domain through the adoption of the well-known and major human rights declarations and treaties, amongst which most importantly the Universal Declaration of Human Rights, the 1965 'International Convention on the Elimination of all forms of Racial Discrimination'[10] (ICERD), the 'International Covenant on Economic Social and Cultural Rights'[11] (ICESCR) and the 'International Covenant on Civil and Political Rights'[12] (ICCPR), both of 1966. Various provisions in the 'International Bill of Rights' (encompassing the UDHR, ICESCR and ICCPR) are considered to have become customary international law.[13] Where the UDHR is widely recognised for establishing a universal and equal basis for all human rights,[14] the European Convention for Human Rights (ECHR), adopted in 1950, has been widely recognised for its similar influence at a regional level.[15] Both the American and African continent have subsequently developed regional human rights treaties, namely the American Convention for Human Rights (ACHR / Pact of San José) and the African Charter on Human and Peoples' Rights (ACHPR / African Charter).[16]

---

separate action in co-operation with the Organization for the achievement of the purposes set forth in Article 55". See also Thomas Buergenthal, 'Human Rights' in *Max Planck Encyclopedia of Public International Law* (March 2007) § 7; Christian Tomuschat, *Human Rights: Between Idealism and Realism* (Oxford University Press 2008) 69-96. For a discussion on the extraterritorial application of human rights, see Section 3.4.2 Applicability of Human Rights in Armed Conflict and Occupation.

[9] Louis Henkin, *The Age of Rights* (Columbia University Press 1990) 3.

[10] Full text of the ICERD (21 December 1965) available at <http://www2.ohchr.org/english/law/cerd.htm> accessed 19 July 2012.

[11] Full text of the ICESCR available at <http://www2.ohchr.org/english/law/cescr.htm> accessed 19 February 2012.

[12] Full text of the ICCPR available at <http://www2.ohchr.org/english/law/ccpr.htm> accessed 19 July 2012.

[13] Erica-Irene Daes, *Freedom of the Individual under Law: A Study on the Individual's Duties to the Community and the Limitations of Human Rights and Freedoms under Article 29 of the Universal Declaration of Human Rights* (1990) 5; Tomuschat, *Human Rights: Between Idealism and Realism* (n 8) 4; Buergenthal, 'Human Rights' (n 8) § 9; and Thomas Buergenthal, 'The Evolving International Human Rights System', in (2006) 100 *American Journal of International Law* 790. Not all rights included in the ICESCR and ICCPR can be found in the UDHR and *vice versa*. An example is the abolition of the death penalty, provided for in the Second Optional Protocol to the ICCPR (UNGA Res 44/128 of 15 December 1989) which was not provided for as part of the right to life in the UDHR. Also, many rights declared in the UDHR have been elaborated upon in the subsequent treaties, to include more specificities.

[14] The preamble to the UDHR itself declares in its final paragraph the UDHR to be a: "a common standard of achievement for all peoples and all nations, to the end that every individual and every organ of society, keeping this Declaration constantly in mind, shall strive by teaching and education to promote respect for these rights and freedoms and by progressive measures, national and international, to secure their universal and effective recognition and observance, both among the peoples of Member States themselves and among the peoples of territories under their jurisdiction".

[15] Full text of the ECHR available at <www.echr.coe.int/NR/rdonlyres/D5CC24A7-DC13-4318-B457-5C9014916D7A/0/CONVENTION_ENG_WEB.pdf> accessed 19 July 2012. See also Tomuschat, *Human Rights: Between Idealism and Realism* (n 8) 31.

[16] Full text of the ACHR ("Pact of San José, Costa Rica") available at <www.oas.org/en/iachr/mandate/Basics/convention.asp> accessed 19 July 2012. The Convention was

The 'Vienna Declaration and Programme of Action'[17] that was adopted by the world conference on the occasion of the 45th anniversary of the UDHR in 1993, states that:

> "All human rights are universal, indivisible and interdependent and interrelated. The international community must treat human rights globally in a fair and equal manner, on the same footing, and with the same emphasis".[18]

The Vienna Declaration thus not only reaffirms the UDHR, but furthermore reaffirms the interdependency and interrelation of human rights, which is of relevance to their analysis in consideration of the provision of humanitarian assistance as such provision simultaneously addresses various human rights. In essence therefore, all rights must be considered to be coherent rather than assuming friction amongst them.[19] Granted, whilst this Declaration must be seen in the context of its time, as it was developed in the wake of the end of the era of communism, this perspective has however been adopted within the UN, and continues to be reaffirmed by the General Assembly.[20]

The various regional human rights courts assist in the progressive interpretation of existing rights, as do the 'treaty bodies' such as the committees pursuant to the ICERD, ICESCR and ICCPR that monitor the proper implementation and regard or compliance for their respective treaties.[21] Yet these committees also provide for interpretation of the content of the specific provisions of these treaties, thereby providing insight into these international standards which are relevant for the evaluation of their content, as well as relevant for the determination of the specific obligations resting upon State Parties to the treaties.[22] Outside this treaty-based system, such interpretations may also be provided with regard to specific individual human rights by so-called 'Special Rapporteurs', instated by the former UN Human

---

adopted November 22, 1969 and entered into force July 18, 1978. Full text of the ACHPR (Banjul Charter) is available at <www.achpr.org/files/instruments/achpr/banjul_charter.pdf> accessed 19 July 2012. The Charter was adopted 27 June 1981 and entered into force 21 October 1986.

[17] Full text of the Vienna Declaration and Programme of Action is available at <www.unhchr.ch/huridocda/huridoca.nsf/(symbol)/a.conf.157.23.en> accessed 19 July 2012.

[18] 'Vienna Declaration and Programme of Action' UN Doc A/CONF.157/23 (12 July 1993) § 5.

[19] Tarlach McGonagle, 'International and European Legal Standards for Combating Racist Expression: Selected Current Conundrums', *Expert Seminar: Combating Racism while respecting Freedom of Expression* (2007) 40. For a perspective on the need to combine the current pronged human rights treaties and monitoring bodies into one single comprehensive approach, see Nico J Schrijver, 'Paving the Way Towards...One World Wide Human Rights Treaty', (2011) 29 *Netherlands Quarterly of Human Rights* 3, 257-260.

[20] UNGA Res 63/176 (20 March 2009) UN Doc A/RES/63/176 'Globalization and its impact on the full enjoyment of all human rights', preamble.

[21] See more in detail Chapter 8. Official statement concerning the purpose of the CERD is available at <http://www2.ohchr.org/english/bodies/cerd/index.htm> accessed 19 July 2012 and the purpose of the HRC at <http://www2.ohchr.org/english/bodies/hrc/index.htm> accessed 19 July 2012; and see for the CESCR <http://www2.ohchr.org/english/bodies/cescr/> accessed 19 July 2012.

[22] The ICJ has followed the authoritative interpretation of the HRC of the ICCPR, amongst others in its Legal Consequences of the Construction of a Wall in the Occupied Palestinian Territory, Advisory Opinion, I.C.J. Reports 2004, p. 136, § 109-11.

Rights Commission or now the Human Rights Council, on thematic issues.[23] Thus, the UN 's Charter-based system and the treaty-based mechanisms are both relevant to the determination of the rights and duties concerning the provision of humanitarian assistance.[24] Through these various developments and interpretative mechanisms, international human rights law develops simultaneously at the regional and international level, also at the same time giving rise to the development of certain rights into customary international law.

5.2.1 'Generations' of Human Rights in Relation to Humanitarian Assistance

Given the nature of the concept of humanitarian assistance, the emergence of a potential human right to receive humanitarian assistance can only be considered within the context of the general developments of the various human rights that are acknowledged today, and which can be roughly divided into three sections. It is widely recognised that the Cold War has influenced the division of the ICESCR and ICCPR into two treaties with two distinct characters: the ICESCR holds rights of an economic, social and cultural nature, whereas the ICCPR holds many civil and political rights. Several ensuing regional human rights instruments have followed this division, such as the ECHR and ACHR that both focus on rights of a mostly civil and political nature. The more recent African Charter encompasses a wider spectrum of human rights, as well as so-called 'peoples' rights'.

Legal discourse has also concentrated these themed rights into categories or 'generations', a phrase first coined by Vasak in the late 1970s.[25] Civil and political 'negative' rights were considered to entail that the state *refrain* from action, whereas economic social and cultural 'positive' rights *impose* a positive obligation upon states. Such an obligation is often seen as a tiered approach consisting of three levels; namely the obligation to respect, the obligation to protect, and the obligation to fulfill the right.[26] With a particular view to the four human rights selected in specific relation to the provision of humanitarian assistance, the right to life is included in the 'civil and political rights' spectrum, warranting the state to *refrain*

---

[23] See for a current list of thematic mandates <www.ohchr.org/EN/HRBodies/SP/Pages/Themes.aspx> accessed 19 July 2012.

[24] See Section 2.2.1.1 The Role of the UN in the Development of Humanitarian Assistance.

[25] Karel Vasak, "Human Rights: A Thirty-Year Struggle: the Sustained Efforts to give Force of law to the Universal Declaration of Human Rights", *UNESCO Courier 30:11* (Paris: UNESCO, November 1977).

[26] CESCR General Comment 12 (Article 11 ICESCR) UN Doc E/C.12/1999/5 'The right to adequate food' (12 May 1999) § 15. Especially developed by Asbjorn Eide and used particularly in relation to economic, social and cultural rights. See in this regard also Asbjorn Eide, 'State Obligations Revisited' in Wenche Barth Eide & Uwe Kracht (eds) *Food and Human Rights in Development* (Volume II) (Intersentia 2005) 137-157; Wenche Barth Eide & Uwe Kracht, 'The Right to Adequate Food in Human Rights Instruments: Legal Norms and Interpretations' in Eide Wenche Barth & Kracht Uwe (eds) *Food and Human Rights in Development* (Volume II) (Intersentia 2005) 106-107. See also Thorsten Kiefer & Catherine Brölmann, 'The Human Right to Water', (2005) 5 *Non-State Actors and International Law*, at 192 (2005).

from the arbitrary deprivation thereof, whereas the rights to food, health and water demand positive action of the affected state.

So-called 'third generation rights' – which would include the potential individual human right to receive humanitarian assistance – came to the international plane during the 1970s, often supported by (newly) developing countries.[27] According to Vasak, a parallel could be drawn between the French Revolution's motto 'liberté, egalité, fraternité' and the content of various types of human rights, as a result of which 'fraternité' refers to a third generation of solidarity rights.[28] This later notion of solidarity rights also concurs with the new concept of collective- or group rights,[29] which the possible right to receive humanitarian assistance could form part of.[30] Although humanitarian assistance is by nature indeed delivered to a group of people as a whole due to the existence of a humanitarian crisis affecting a larger amount of persons, and it may therefore be considered by some a 'group' right; invoking a human right must still occur on an individual basis. Solidarity rights as a whole may be divided into two distinct sections, both tied to the political developments of the final decades of the twentieth century.[31] Within the first section, these rights are said to include the right to self-determination, the right to development and the right to participate in the benefits from the common heritage of humankind, whereas the second section includes the right to peace, the right to a sustainable environment, the right to communication and relevant to this research, the right to humanitarian assistance.[32] Prior to the

[27] 'Report of the independent expert on human rights and international solidarity (Mr. Rudi Muhammad Rizki)' UN Doc A/HRC/4/8 (7 February 2007) § 9.

[28] Vasak, "Human Rights: A Thirty-Year Struggle: the Sustained Efforts to give Force of law to the Universal Declaration of Human Rights" (n 25); see also Zehra F Kabasakal Arat, *Human Rights Worldwide: A Reference Handbook* (ABC Clio 2006) 35-36; and Richard Pierre Claude & Burns H Weston (eds), *Human Rights in the World Community: Issues And Action* (University of Pennsylvania Press 2006) 21.

[29] See Section 5.3 A Human Right to Receive Humanitarian Assistance in International Law?.

[30] It is relevant to note that there are two concepts of 'solidarity' in the context of human rights. Firstly, the term is used as an umbrella for several rights, but secondly is also considered a narrow right in and of itself. Note the UN High Commissioner for Human Rights in 'Promotion and Protection of Human Rights: Human rights and international solidarity' UN Doc E/CN.4/2006/96 (1 February 2006) § 16.

[31] Claude & Weston *Human Rights in the World Community: Issues And Action* (n 28) 22.

[32] Vasak, "Human Rights: A Thirty-Year Struggle: the Sustained Efforts to give Force of law to the Universal Declaration of Human Rights" (n 25); 'Report of the independent expert on human rights and international solidarity (Mr. Rudi Muhammad Rizki)' UN Doc A/HRC/4/8 (7 February 2007) § 41; and 'Promotion and Protection of Human Rights: Human rights and international solidarity' (Note by the UN High Commissioner for Human Rights) UN Doc E/CN.4/2006/96 (1 February 2006) § 29. See also Claude & Weston *Human Rights in the World Community: Issues And Action* (n 28) 22 and Rohan J Hardcastle & Adrian T L Chua, 'Humanitarian Assistance, Towards a Right of access to victims of natural disaster', (1998) 38 *International Review of the Red Cross* 325, 592. See furthermore Articles 19, 20, 22 and 23 of the ACHPR as well as Common Article 1 of the ICCPR and ICESCR on the right to self-determination. The right to Development has been declared in UNGA Res 41/128 (4 December 1986) UN Doc A/RES/41/128 Annex 'Development Declaration' although it has not been affirmed later in legally binding documents; the Right to Peace firstly was called for in the UN Human Rights Commission's Resolution 5 (XXXII) (27 February 1976) and later in UNGA Res 33/73 (15 December 1978) UN Doc A/RES/33/73 'Declaration on the preparation of Societies for Life in Peace', but both times was afflicted by abstentions and rejections from member states. The Right to a Healthy

discussion of this potential human right to receive humanitarian assistance under treaty law and customary international law, as well as a reflection on its duty bearers and right holders a more general discussion on the derogability of human rights in times of crisis is needed.

5.2.2 Derogability, Human Rights and the Provision of Humanitarian Assistance

The existence of a humanitarian crisis, when humanitarian assistance is needed, is *by nature* a time of emergency for a state. However, legally such emergency circumstances are also provided for. Most of the international and regional human rights treaties focusing on civil and political rights include so-called 'derogation clauses', allowing for the derogation from certain rights in times of emergency.[33] Approaching the delivery of humanitarian assistance from a human rights perspective can thus only be possible if derogation of such relevant human rights, such as the right to life, food, health and water in times of a humanitarian crisis is *not* possible. Indeed, should it be possible to derogate from such rights, an approach to humanitarian assistance through human rights would not be possible.

The ICCPR declares in Article 4 that 'in time of public emergency which threatens the life of the nation' derogation from certain rights is possible, yet Article 4(2) ICCPR states that under no circumstances derogation from the right to life, relevant to this research, is possible.[34] The fact that no derogation is possible does not thereby mean that 'conceptually' no limitations or restrictions could be considered justified, as this is to be determined independently from derogability.[35] Yet, the Human Rights Committee considers the non-derogability of the right to life as an expression of this right's peremptory nature in international law, thereby implicitly indicating that justifying limitations or restrictions upon this right will be challenging for states parties.[36]

Both the ECHR and ACHR regionally contain derogation clauses. Similar to the ICCPR, the ECHR allows for derogation from certain rights in times of public emergency, but excludes the right to life from such derogability.[37] The ACHR has the lowest threshold with regard to its derogation clause, allowing for the possibility to derogate from certain rights within the ACHR not only in times of public emergency threatening the life of the nation, but also in times of any *other*

Environment was mentioned in the Stockholm Declaration of 16 June 1972, UN GA Res 45/94 (14 December 1990) UN Doc A/RES/45/94 and Article 24 AChHPR as well as Article 11 of Additional protocol to the American Convention on Human Rights in the Area of Economic, Social and Cultural Rights.

[33] Article 4 ICCPR, Article 15 ECHR and Article 27 ACHR.

[34] See in support of this CCPR General Comment 5: 'Derogation of rights (Art. 4)' (31 July 1981) and General Comment 29 pursuant to Article 4 'States of Emergency' UN Doc. CCPR/C/21/Rev.1/Add.11 (31 August 2001), as well as the General Comments on Article 4: CCPR General Comment 6: 'The right to life (art. 6)' (30 April 1982) § 1 and CCPR General Comment 14 'Nuclear weapons and the right to life (Art. 6)' (9 November 1984) § 1.

[35] Ibid General Comment 29: State of Emergency (Art. 4) § 7-8.

[36] Ibid §11.

[37] Article 15(1) and (2) ECHR.

emergency that may threaten 'the independence or security of the State Party'.[38] However, despite its more lenient derogation clause, the ACHR restricts its scope by listing far fewer rights than the ICCPR and ECHR and in particular relevance to this research, excludes the right to life from derogation.[39] Lastly, the AChHPR, containing relevant references to the right to life and health, does not contain a derogation clause.[40] Thus, for the purpose of this research with regard to humanitarian assistance and to the obligations state parties might have under the right to life as incorporated in human rights instruments in relation thereto, derogability is not relevant.

With a view to economic, social and cultural rights, it has on occasion been argued that the nature of these rights does not allow for a derogation clause in international treaties, although the European Social Charter contains such a clause.[41] Yet the nature of these rights, requiring positive action from the state; as an obligation of 'conduct' rather than 'result', results in a different approach to their fulfilment. Such a different approach then also exists in times of emergencies. Indeed, the ICESCR which contains relevant provisions regarding the right to food and health does not contain a derogation clause. Article 4 ICESCR only allows for states to limit the rights in the treaty on certain occasions, if and when:

> "(…) such limitations as are determined by law only in so far as this may be compatible with the nature of these rights and solely for the purpose of promoting the general welfare in a democratic society".[42]

Thus, in order to *limit* a right under the ICESCR, a state must comply with this tripartite enumeration, namely that (1) the limitation be determined by law, (2) it be compatible with the nature of the rights as enshrined in the ICESCR and (3) it be only for the promotion of the general welfare in a democratic society. Clearly, this is not as far-reaching as a general derogation clause which would allow for states to entirely suspend their obligations towards the fulfilment of a certain right. This strict limitation clause again flows from the nature of the rights enshrined in the ICESCR: following a situation of conflict or disaster amounting to a humanitarian crisis, it will be expected that the affected state shall not be able to provide *as fully* in such rights as the right to food or health as it had been able to do before the crisis-situation, due to a severe change in circumstances.

Furthermore, the criteria as set out in Article 4 ICESCR must also be seen as distinct from measures taken in conformity with Article 2 of the ICESCR, dedicated

---

[38] Article 27(1) ACHR.
[39] Article 27(2) ACHR.
[40] Article 4 AChHPR concerns the right to life; Article 16 AChHPR concerns the right to health.
[41] Stefanie Jansen-Wilhelm, 'A duty to accept humanitarian assistance under the ICESCR' in Zwitter A et al (eds) *Humanitarian Action: Global, Regional and Domestic Legal Responses* (Cambridge University Press 2014) 174-201. See Part V Article F of the ESC.
[42] Article 4 ICESCR.

to the progressive realisation of human rights.[43] Indeed, Article 2 is more relevant to the analysis of the rights enshrined in the ICESCR and their specific relationship to the provision of humanitarian assistance. The scope of Article 2 ICESCR is particularly relevant to the provision of humanitarian assistance, an act which by nature takes place in circumstances of crisis, rather than circumstances in which the full width and breadth of a human right may be explored. The lack of a derogation clause in the ICESCR does not imply complete *and progressive* fulfilment in times of crisis, as explored in Article 2 ICESCR. Whilst the relevant rights to the provision of humanitarian assistance therefore do not allow for derogation, the law must take the practical matters in times of a humanitarian crisis into account.

5.2.3 Progressive Realisation in the ICESCR

Article 2 ICESCR explores the depth of the economic, social and cultural rights and the manner in which they must be fulfilled. As such Article 2 of the ICESCR envisages a positive obligation resting upon state parties to undertake steps and guarantee the rights laid down in the ICESCR:

> "1. Each State Party to the present Covenant undertakes to take steps, individually and through international assistance and co-operation, especially economic and technical, to the maximum of its available resources, with a view to achieving progressively the full realization of the rights recognized in the present Covenant by all appropriate means, including particularly the adoption of legislative measures. 2. The States Parties to the present Covenant undertake to guarantee that the rights enunciated in the present Covenant will be exercised without discrimination of any kind as to race, colour, sex, language, religion, political or other opinion, national or social origin, property, birth or other status. 3. Developing countries, with due regard to human rights and their national economy, may determine to what extent they would guarantee the economic rights recognized in the present Covenant to non-nationals".

From this text, arguably the rights enshrined in the ICESCR can be considered layered, as opposed to absolute. Certainly Article 2(3) provides a corridor for the non-fulfilment with regard to non-nationals. However, it is not so clear-cut, as Article 2(1) provides for several notions to be considered, amongst which 'progressive development' and the requirement of seeking international cooperation when national resources fall short, such as in times of a humanitarian crisis.[44] Indeed, whilst 'progressive development' may not be expected from the affected state in times of emergencies, Article 2 and Article 4 establish that the rights as enshrined in the ICESCR continue to be applicable and must therefore be fulfilled by the affected state in a more basic manner.

The CESCR has in this regard elaborated and assessed in what way the rights and related obligations for the affected state within the ICESCR can be realised in

[43] Amrei Müller, 'Limitations to and Derogations from Economic, Social and Cultural Rights' (2009) 9 *Human Rights Law Review* 4, 584 -585.

[44] The aspect of international cooperation will be addressed further in Chapter 7.

such circumstances. As such the CESCR differentiates between 'progressive realization' as incorporated within Article 2 ICESCR and so-called 'minimum core obligations'. This differentiation is of particular relevance to the provision of humanitarian assistance, in relation to the right to food and health within the ICESCR. As such the CESCR observes that:

> "[...] a State party in which any significant number of individuals is deprived of essential foodstuffs, of essential primary health care, of basic shelter and housing, or of the most basic forms of education is, prima facie, failing to discharge its obligations under the Covenant".[45]

Clearly, a 'significant number' as mentioned by the Committee is not a fixed amount and shall vary depending on circumstances, but shall certainly be reached in the event of a humanitarian crisis, considering that such a crisis 'overwhelms' a State's local capacity.[46] Thus in the event of a crisis 'essential foodstuffs', 'essential primary health care' and 'basic shelter' must continuously be provided by the affected state in order to fulfil its duties under the ICESCR, despite being in an emergency situation. The Committee envisages that indeed the full realisation of rights as incorporated in the ICESCR are meant to be achieved progressively, yet the undertaking 'to take steps' in this regard, is an obligation which is of *immediate* effect, and therefore must be taken relatively soon upon the ICESCR's entry into force for a particular State Party.[47] Such steps must be taken 'by all appropriate means', which must be considered fully without limit and in its natural meaning.[48] Furthermore, the notion of 'progressive realization' must, according to the Committee, be read in light of the *objective* of the ICESCR: namely to establish clear obligations for all State Parties to enable the full realisation of all rights as formulated in the Convention.[49] This objective includes the obligation to actively move towards the fulfilment of these rights in the most effective and prompt manner possible, and emphatically *excludes* any conscious 'retrogressive measures' unless these were to be justified in light of the entire set of rights as incorporated in the ICESCR.[50] Whilst it is therefore understandable that 'progressive development' may *not* occur in times of a humanitarian crisis, 'retrogressive' measures touching upon the *core* content of rights are *excluded*. Article 2(1) in this regard differentiates between the economic circumstances of the States Parties, but has the

[45] CESCR General Comment 3 on Article 2 (14 December 1990) § 10.
[46] See Section 3.3.3 Defining a Humanitarian Crisis where the notion of a humanitarian crisis has been defined.
[47] CESCR General Comment 3 (n 45) § 1 and § 2.
[48] Ibid § 4.
[49] Ibid § 9. See in this regard also Principles 32-35 of the 'Maastricht Principles on Extraterritorial Obligations of States in the area of Economic, Social and Cultural Rights', discussed in more detail in Section 3.4.2 Applicability of Human Rights in Armed Conflict and Occupation.
[50] CESCR General Comment 3 (n 45) § 9. In further detail CESCR General Comment 8 (12 December 1997) UN Doc E/C.12/1997/8 'The relationship between economic sanctions and respect for economic, social and cultural rights' § 3-7 and 10.

intention of functioning as a binding obligation upon all parties to the Convention, despite existing differences between obligations of result and of conduct.[51]

Furthermore and particularly relevant to the provision of humanitarian assistance, although Article 2 ICESCR speaks of 'progressive realization', a 'minimum core obligation' can be discerned according to the CESCR within the fulfilment of the economic, social and cultural rights as encompassed by the ICESCR. Such a 'minimum core obligation' incorporates at least the fulfilment of certain 'minimum essential levels' of each of the rights as otherwise the ICESCR would indeed be deprived largely of its essence, as seen above.[52] Indeed, the fulfilment of the obligations in the Convention must be considered to the 'maximum available resources' of a particular state party.[53] Naturally, not all states have an equal amount of resources at their disposal and to that extent the Committee notes that especially vulnerable members of society ought to be particularly protected, through the use of not only those resources available to the state through its own particular sources, but most certainly also those as available through international cooperation and assistance, by way of the international community at large.[54] Although the considerations of the CESCR are not binding, this stance indeed is a reflection of the text of Article 2(1) ICESCR that calls upon international cooperation in the fulfilment of these rights. From such comments it may be inferred that the CESCR envisages a protection of those vulnerable members of society, in the event of a humanitarian crisis, and an obligation to prevent hunger that goes beyond the individual state and reaches a certain level of international cooperation.[55]

5.3 A Human Right to Receive Humanitarian Assistance in International Law?

From the above follows the pertinent question: is a 'human right to receive humanitarian assistance' acknowledged in international law? And if so, does it exist independently, or does it follow from other human rights such as the human rights to life, food, health and water? It has already been established that a potential human right to humanitarian assistance can arguably be ranked in the category of so-called 'solidarity rights' or 'third generation rights', also considered by some to be 'group rights'.[56] Also, the provision of humanitarian assistance, as has been established, occurs with respect for the principles of humanity, neutrality and impartiality.[57] When relating these principles to human rights law at an abstract level from the outset of human rights law, rather than focusing on the individual

[51] Philip Alston & Gerard Quinn, 'The Nature and Scope of State Parties' Obligations under the International Covenant on Economic, Social and Cultural Rights' (1987) 9 *Human Rights Quarterly* 1, 172.
[52] CESCR General Comment 3 (n 45) § 10.
[53] See Article 2(1) ICESCR.
[54] CESCR General Comment 3 (n 45) § 11-12. See also Article 2(1) ICESCR. See Chapter 7.
[55] Jansen-Wilhelm, 'A duty to accept humanitarian assistance under the ICESCR' (n 41).
[56] See Section 5.2.1 'Generations' of Human Rights in Relation to Humanitarian Assistance.
[57] See Section 2.2.3 The Principles for the Delivery of Assistance.

rights to food or health for example, the provision of humanitarian assistance must occur in a non-discriminatory manner, as is incorporated within these principles themselves.[58] This holds true regardless of whether or not an actual individual human right to receive humanitarian assistance exists, as obligations for states regarding non-discrimination exist separately and independently. Whilst the right to be exempt from (racial) discrimination is not a substantive norm in and of itself with regard to the provision of humanitarian assistance, it forms the *basis* for the existence of such a right in general. In particular in circumstances of non-international armed conflict, but also in international armed conflict or natural disasters in complex emergencies, (racial) discrimination may serve as an underlying factor in the non-delivery of humanitarian assistance. Racial discrimination is considered the violation of a norm of *jus cogens*, and accession to the ICERD has been near universal.[59] Article 5 ICERD determines that states party to the treaty must undertake to 'prohibit and to eliminate' all forms of racial discrimination and in particular – relevant to the provision of humanitarian assistance – in the enjoyment of (amongst others) the right to security of person and the 'protection against bodily harm', economic, social and cultural rights; including the right to health.[60]

The ICJ has also acknowledged that the delivery of humanitarian assistance must occur on the basis of non-discrimination in its well-known *Nicaragua*-judgment, stating that 'an essential feature of truly humanitarian aid is that it is given "without discrimination" of any kind'.[61] Furthermore, in a more recent case concerning Georgia and Russia, the Court had the opportunity to address the provision of assistance specifically within the context of the ICERD, upon Georgia's claim that Russia obstructed assistance based on ethnicity.[62] The Court ordered both parties to:

[58] See in this regard Article 1 ICERD.

[59] See Section 8.2.2 The ARSIWA, Peremptory Norms and the Denial of Humanitarian Assistance for a more in depth analysis of current norms of *jus cogens* and responsibility for violation thereof. The status of ratification of the ICERD on 20 September 2014 was 177 State Parties.

[60] The relevant text of Article 5 ICERD states: "In compliance with the fundamental obligations laid down in article 2 of this Convention, States Parties undertake to prohibit and to eliminate racial discrimination in all its forms and to guarantee the right of everyone, without distinction as to race, colour, or national or ethnic origin, to equality before the law, notably in the enjoyment of the following rights: [...] (b) The right to security of person and protection by the State against violence or bodily harm, whether inflicted by government officials or by any individual group or institution; [...] (e) Economic, social and cultural rights, in particular: [...] (iii) The right to housing; (iv) The right to public health, medical care, social security and social services".

[61] See Military and Paramilitary Activities in and against Nicaragua (Nicaragua v. United States of America), Merits, Judgment 27 June 1986 I.C.J. Reports 1986, p. 14 § 243.

[62] Application of the International Convention on the Elimination of all Forms of Racial Discrimination (Georgia v. Russian Federation), Provisional Measures, Order of 15 October 2008, I.C.J. Reports 2008, p. 353 § 80.

"facilitate, and refrain from placing any impediment to, humanitarian assistance in support of the rights to which the local population are entitled under the International Convention on the Elimination of All Forms of Racial Discrimination".[63]

In doing so, the ICJ asserted that the provision of humanitarian assistance forms the fulfilment of substantive human rights. The duty to refrain from racial discrimination in the provision of humanitarian assistance can therefore be seen as underlying substantive human rights and forming the basis for the incorporation of humanitarian assistance within the human rights discourse relating to more substantive rights. Indeed, both the ILC and the EU for example have included 'non-discrimination' as part of the principles by which humanitarian assistance must be delivered.[64]

5.3.1 Humanitarian Assistance as a Potential Human Right in International Treaty Law

In order to determine whether indeed an international human right to receive humanitarian assistance exists, it is therefore necessary to determine whether this right is incorporated in various internationally legally binding documents or customary international law, laying clear rights upon individuals to resolve the aspirational character of the right and issues relating to enforcement possibilities. Thus, it must be determined whether an international legal framework exists supporting the independent existence of the human right to humanitarian assistance, existing separately from the right to life, food, health or water.

Looking solely to the international and regional treaties, the 'human right to humanitarian assistance' has quite clearly *not* been independently incorporated on a large scale. The UDHR, ICESCR and ICCPR do not explicitly mention the notion of humanitarian assistance at all. The specific 'Convention on the Elimination of Discrimination Against Women' (CEDAW) and ICERD neither reference the notion, despite the ICJ's assertion concerning the ICERD as a basis through which the provision of humanitarian assistance needs to be fulfilled.[65] However, several other specific human rights treaties do acknowledge the concept of humanitarian assistance. As such, the Convention on the Rights of the Child (CRC)[66] stipulates in

[63] Ibid § 149.

[64] See Section 2.2.3.5 Other Perspectives on the Principles for Providing Humanitarian Assistance.

[65] The Convention on the Elimination of Discrimination Against Women, full text available at <www.un.org/womenwatch/daw/cedaw/cedaw.htm> accessed August 2, 2012, adopted 18 December 1979 and entered into force 3 September 1981. Currently the CEDAW has parties 187. Application of the International Convention on the Elimination of all Forms of Racial Discrimination (Georgia v. Russian Federation (n 62) § 149.

[66] The Convention on the Rights of the Child, full text available at <http://www2.ohchr.org/english/law/crc.htm> accessed 19 July 2012, adopted 20 November 1989 and entered into force 2 November 1990. Currently the CRC has 193 parties, thereby making the content of the rights enshrined in the treaty almost universally applicable.

Article 22 that a child that is considered a refugee or that is seeking such a status has the right to receive:

> "appropriate protection and humanitarian assistance in the enjoyment of applicable rights set forth in the present Convention".[67]

Such a right must be ensured by states parties according to the CRC. However, as can be seen in the text of the article, the concept of humanitarian assistance has been linked distinctly to the *fulfillment of the other rights* in the Convention, and is not phrased individually as an independent right. Thus, although the CRC recognises the need of a refugee (seeking) child to receive humanitarian assistance, such receipt is solely acknowledged *as part of the enjoyment* of the rights enshrined in the Convention, rather than being separately incorporated. Secondly, the Convention on the Rights of Persons with Disabilities declares that States Parties have the duty to ensure the proper protection of persons with disabilities *in situations* like humanitarian emergencies, armed conflict or natural disaster.[68] Thus, this inclusion of 'protection' in the Convention does not entail a particular human right to receive humanitarian assistance, but merely notes their *protection* in situations like a humanitarian crisis, given the particular needs that may be relevant for this group. Such a determination falls short of declaring a right to humanitarian assistance for persons with disabilities. It can however be compared to the manner in which the CRC incorporates humanitarian assistance within its framework.

At the international level therefore, humanitarian assistance is only considered in a human rights context as related to children seeking a refugee status, or already considered to be refugees, as well as in relation to persons with disabilities, although neither treaty incorporating this notes a *distinct* right to receive humanitarian assistance. Furthermore, the concept is absent as a distinct human right in the three main regional treaties ACHR, ECHR and ACHPR, as well as in the European Social Charter, the Additional Protocol to the ACHR in the area of Economic, Social and Cultural Rights and the Protocol to the ACHPR on the Rights

[67] Article 22 CRC notes: "1. States Parties shall take appropriate measures to ensure that a child who is seeking refugee status or who is considered a refugee in accordance with applicable international or domestic law and procedures shall, whether unaccompanied or accompanied by his or her parents or by any other person, receive appropriate protection and humanitarian assistance in the enjoyment of applicable rights set forth in the present Convention and in other international human rights or humanitarian instruments to which the said States are Parties. 2. For this purpose, States Parties shall provide, as they consider appropriate, co-operation in any efforts by the United Nations and other competent intergovernmental organizations or non-governmental organizations co-operating with the United Nations to protect and assist such a child and to trace the parents or other members of the family of any refugee child in order to obtain information necessary for reunification with his or her family. In cases where no parents or other members of the family can be found, the child shall be accorded the same protection as any other child permanently or temporarily deprived of his or her family environment for any reason, as set forth in the present Convention".

[68] Article 11 of the Convention on the Rights of Persons with Disabilities states: "States Parties shall take, in accordance with their obligations under international law, including international humanitarian law and international human rights law, all necessary measures to ensure the protection and safety of persons with disabilities in situations of risk, including situations of armed conflict, humanitarian emergencies and the occurrence of natural disasters".

of Women in Africa. Thus, both in the civil and political rights arena, as in the economic, social and cultural rights arena, the right is not recognised independently in the major treaties.

Conversely, the African Charter on the Rights and Welfare of the Child contains a provision that echoes the CRC, declaring the right of children that are refugees or seeking such a status to receive humanitarian assistance 'in the enjoyment of the rights set out in this Charter and other international human rights and humanitarian instruments to which the States are Parties'.[69] Thus, the African Charter on the Rights and Welfare of the Child envisages such receipt of humanitarian assistance not only in the enjoyment of the rights that may be laid out within its own Charter, but also in the enjoyment of the rights set out in any other instrument that a state party to the African Charter on the Rights and Welfare of the Child may be a state party to. Consequently, a state party to the African Charter on the Rights and Welfare of the Child that is also a party to the ICCPR must ensure the receipt of humanitarian assistance in the enjoyment of the rights in the ICCPR for the refugee child. The African Charter on the Rights and Welfare of the Child adds to this provision that:

> "The provisions of this Article apply mutatis mutandis to internally displaced children whether through natural disaster, internal armed conflicts, civil strife, breakdown of economic and social order or howsoever caused".[70]

Thus, the African Charter on the Rights and Welfare of the Child envisages a broader protection, not only for those children that may be considered refugees or seeking that status, but also internally displaced children, in a crisis-like situation that may be caused by a variety of factors. Consequently, as both the African Charter on the Rights and Welfare of the Child as well as the CRC contain provisions pertaining to the right of the child to receive humanitarian assistance albeit as part of the enjoyment of their rights, it may be argued that the 'refugee child' or 'internally displaced child' has a certain right to humanitarian assistance under (regional) international law.

Furthermore, in the context specifically of IDPs, states on the African continent do envisage more protection of humanitarian assistance through international law, declaring in Article 5(9) of the 2009 Kampala Convention that states must respect the right of IDPs to request humanitarian assistance in accordance with international law.[71] Yet, the Kampala Convention does not specifically place such a right to request assistance within the context of human rights law, but phrases it within the context of *general* international law. This recent Kampala Convention's

[69] Article 23 African Charter on the Rights and Welfare of the Child.
[70] Ibid.
[71] African Union Convention for the Protection and Assistance of Internally Displaced Persons in Africa (Kampala 22 October 2009) Article 5(9) states: "States Parties shall respect the right of internally displaced persons to peacefully request or seek protection and assistance, in accordance with relevant national and international laws, a right for which they shall not be persecuted, prosecuted or punished".

incorporation indeed aligns with the abovementioned similar incorporation of such protection under the African Charter on the Rights and Welfare of the Child. It cannot be concluded that therefore an *independent, human* right to humanitarian assistance for refugee children in international or regional African treaty law has crystallised as the incorporation of humanitarian assistance both in the CRC and in the African Charter on the Rights and Welfare of the Child remains directly linked and consequential to the 'enjoyment of human rights' and in the Kampala Convention it is placed under the umbrella of general international law. This phrasing in itself must lead to the conclusion that within these two former treaties, although they make mention of the notion, the concept of a 'right to receive assistance' is not considered an independent human right. However, from the phrasing it can be inferred that 'humanitarian assistance' is placed within the human rights discourse, as its provision must be conceived through other human rights and stands in relation to the fulfilment of these rights. This also aligns with the stance taken by the ICJ in the 2008 *Georgia v. Russia* case. Thus, although the less than plentiful independent incorporation of humanitarian assistance into the binding international and regional codified human rights framework may lead to the inferable suggestion that an independent 'right to receive' does not exist in treaties today, the concept has been placed within the human rights discourse by two treaties. However, as the international human rights framework is comprised of not only treaty law, but also of customary international law, the necessity exists to determine whether the concept of humanitarian assistance has been embraced in that context.

5.3.2 Humanitarian Assistance as a Potential Human Right in Customary International Law

Determining the existence of a human right to humanitarian assistance requires the establishment of both *opinio juris* and state practice on this matter.[72] In recent years, no developments have taken place at the interstate level that can immediately or directly be related to evidence of such an emerging right in customary international law. Much of the reference to a human right to receive humanitarian assistance in international law flows from interpretative documents and soft law: international and regional organisations and various instruments have often asserted the existence of a 'right to receive humanitarian assistance'.

Within the UN framework, the UN General Assembly and Security Council have to date *not* declared a view on the existence of such a human right.[73] Such an expression, in particular from the General Assembly as the largest UN body, would have provided a useful (although not necessary) indication of potential state

[72] See Section 1.4.1 Primary Sources on the requirements for the determination of customary international law.

[73] The two UN bodies have however, outside a human rights context, often referred to the concept of humanitarian access with a view to states' obligations relating to facilitating the provision of assistance or allowing access to humanitarian organisations. See for a further discussion Chapter 7.

practice. However, within the UN several Special Rapporteurs on various related thematic issues have proffered the existence of such a right, or at least framed the delivery and receipt of humanitarian assistance within a human rights context. As early as 1993, Francis Deng argued that the existing body of human rights law does not address the access of civilians to humanitarian assistance, and that an entitlement and right to such access and assistance must be advocated, as part of the fulfilment of customary economic, social and cultural rights.[74] At that time Deng submitted that an entitlement could be argued for individuals to 'receive international assistance' when the affected state is 'unwilling' to provide.[75] Also, the Special Rapporteur on internally displaced persons has affirmed that humanitarian assistance is indeed 'intrinsically linked to human rights', while the Independent Expert on human rights and solidarity foresees an imminent recognition of third generation rights due to the 'urgency of the demand from many international actors', possibly even through the obligations laid down in Article 2 ICESCR that could according to some be read as a basis for solidarity rights claims, which the Independent Expert considers humanitarian assistance to form a part of.[76] Likewise, the Food and Agriculture Organization (FAO) reported that such an emerging right to humanitarian assistance is 'increasingly accepted' by the international community.[77] Moreover, the (soft law) Guiding Principles on Internal Displacement, created within the UN context by Francis Deng, envisage a 'right to request and receive' humanitarian assistance from the national authorities specifically for IDPs.[78] Subsequently, the 'Operational Guidelines on Human Rights and Natural Disasters', developed under the auspices of the Representative on human rights of internally displaced persons, declared that persons affected by such disasters have the right to request and receive assistance from their own governments[79].

---

[74] Report of the Representative of the Secretary-General, Mr. Francis Deng, 'Further promotion and encouragement of human rights and fundamental freedoms, including the question of the programme and methods of work of the commission human rights, mass exoduses and displaced persons Internally displaced persons' UN Doc E/CN.4/1994/44 (25 January 1994), § 21-22.

[75] Ibid § 22.

[76] Report of the Representative of the Secretary-General on the human rights of internally displaced persons, Walter Kälin, Addendum Mission to Somalia, UN Doc A/HRC/13/21/Add.2 (21 January 2010) § 34; 'Report of the independent expert on human rights and international solidarity (Mr. Rudi Muhammad Rizki)' UN Doc A/HRC/4/8 (7 February 2007) § 13 and § 43.

[77] FAO Legislative Study 'Right to Adequate Food in Emergencies' (2002) § 2.3.2.

[78] 'Report of the Representative of the Secretary-General, Mr. Francis M. Deng, submitted pursuant to Commission resolution 1997/39', Addendum 'Guiding Principles on Internal Displacement' (Guiding Principles on IDPs) (11 February 1998) UN Doc E/CN.4/1998/53/Add.2 Principle 3. See Chapter 2 (n 198) for the background of these principles. Although they have been embraced by many organisations in the field, including UNHCR and OHCHR, the General Assembly has solely expressed its appreciation of the Principles and noted their importance as an international legal framework for IDPs. See UN GA Resolutions 58/177 (12 March 2004) UN Doc A/RES/58/177 § 7; and UNGA Res 60/1 (24 October 2005) UN Doc A/RES/60/1 'World Summit Outcome Document' § 132; UNGA Res 60/168 (7 March 2006) A/RES/60/168 'Protection of and assistance to internally displaced persons' § 8, and UN GA Res 62/168 (6 March 2008) UN Doc A/RES/62/153, § 10.

[79] 'Operational Guidelines on Human Rights and Natural Disasters' by the Representative on human rights of internally displaced persons, UN Doc A/HRC/4/38/Add.1 (26 January 2006) § 12. See

Taking all these initiatives together, it can be concluded that several pillars within the UN framework are clearly supportive of the establishment of a human right to humanitarian assistance, and in some respects even assert its current existence. Whilst such developments can function as indicators of the existence of a degree of *opinio juris*, the individual member states have continuously refrained from such expressions, as these assertions are absent from both the General Assembly, Human Rights Council and Security Council resolutions. As such, the value of these assertions by other UN bodies in the determination of the establishment of a developing norm of customary international law remains secondary, in particular in the absence of pro-active action by UN member states themselves.

From a European perspective, the Council of the European Union interestingly enough declared rather forwardly in its 1996 Regulation concerning humanitarian aid that:

> "people in distress, victims of natural disasters, wars and outbreaks of fighting, or other comparable exceptional circumstances have a right to international humanitarian assistance where their own authorities prove unable to provide effective relief".[80]

The subsequent 2008 EU Joint Statement however no longer mentions such a right to receive assistance and consequently it appears that the EU now also takes a somewhat more subdued approach with a view to the possible existence of a right to receive humanitarian assistance.[81] Nevertheless, the 1996 Regulation remains binding and applicable upon member states of the EU. The two major international organisations involved in the provision of humanitarian assistance through OCHR and ECHO respectively can at this stage both, though not convincingly, assert state practice and endorse the existence of such an independent right to assistance. Similarly, some early initiatives in this field, such as the (failed) 1984 Draft Convention on Expediting the Delivery of Emergency Relief and the 1991 International Guidelines for Humanitarian Assistance Operations do not place the receipt of such assistance in a human rights context.

That being said, several other (soft law) international declarations, functioning as secondary sources of international law, do perceive the (emerging) existence of this right to receive assistance. A primary reference can be found in the San Remo Guiding Principles on the Right to Humanitarian Assistance that argue a distinct right to request and receive humanitarian assistance. The San Remo Guiding

furthermore the elaborately updated 'Operational Guidelines on Human Rights and Natural Disasters' UN Doc A/HRC/16/43/Add.5 (31 January 2011) which provides more detailed information on various human rights based approaches to the delivery of humanitarian assistance, in particular Group B with regard to rights related to the provision of food, health, shelter and education.

[80] European Council Regulation concerning humanitarian aid (EC) No. 1257/96 (20 June 1996) Preamble § 4.

[81] 'Joint Statement by the Council and the Representatives of the Governments of the Member States meeting within the Council, the European Parliament and the European Commission' (European Consensus on Humanitarian Aid) (30 January 2008) EU Doc 2008/C/25/01.

Principles envisage such a right for those persons affected by emergencies, who may then turn to national or international organisations to receive assistance.[82] Furthermore, the San Remo Principles note the conditions needed for the invoking of such a right:

> "The right to humanitarian assistance may be invoked: (a) when essential humanitarian needs of human beings in an emergency are not being met, so that the abandonment of victims without assistance would constitute a threat to human life or a grave offence to human dignity; (b) when all local possibilities and domestic procedures have been exhausted within a reasonable time, and vital needs are not satisfied or are not fully satisfied, so that there is no other possibility to ensure the prompt provision of supplies and services essential for the persons affected".[83]

Thus, the San Remo Principles connect the right to request and receive assistance to an *international* source, upon the exhaustion of *national* sources. In this manner, the approach somewhat reflects the wording of Article 2(1) ICESCR, in which a duty is codified for a state to seek international assistance in the fulfilment of rights. As the International Institute of Humanitarian Law in San Remo, which brought forth these Principles, is not comprised of certain member states, these Principles cannot be considered to contribute to the notion of state practice. However, they may well contribute to the potential development of *opinio juris* as the Institute represents the ideas of contemporary judicial scholars. Similarly, the Mohonk Criteria, developed through a collaboration of religious communities and under the auspices of (then) UN affiliate J.M. Ebersole, recognise the right to humanitarian assistance as deriving from fundamental human rights, and state that a right to receive such assistance may be requested from the affected authorities, or national and international organisations.[84] More recently, the Bruges Resolution, developed by the renowned Institute de Droit International has declared that withholding assistance to victims of humanitarian crises is a violation of human rights, and that such victims are:

> "entitled to request and receive humanitarian assistance. Assistance may be sought on behalf of the victims, by the members of the group, by local and regional authorities, the government of the affected State, and national or international organizations".[85]

Similar to the San Remo Principles and Mohonk Criteria, the Bruges Resolution sees a 'right to receive' that is connected to a 'right to request' such assistance from a variety of sources, amongst which of course primarily the affected state itself. As can be held for the San Remo Institute, the Institut de Droit International is

[82] 'Guiding Principles on the Right to Humanitarian Assistance' (April 1993) The International Institute of Humanitarian Law in San Remo, Principle 2.
[83] Ibid Principle 3.
[84] 'The Mohonk Criteria for Humanitarian Assistance in Complex Emergencies', (1995) reprinted in 17 *Human Rights Quarterly* 1, 196 (preamble).
[85] Resolution 'Humanitarian Assistance' (2 September 2003) Institute of International Law, Sixteenth Commission, Bruges Session Principle I.1 and I.2.

representative of current legal scholarship and can therefore contribute to the development of the establishment of *opinio juris* on this matter. Lastly, although not framed in a human rights context, the 'Code of Conduct for the International Red Cross and Red Crescent Movement and NGOs in Disaster Relief', developed by several of the largest disaster response agencies, states that the right to receive humanitarian assistance is a 'fundamental humanitarian principle which should be enjoyed by all citizens', clearly with a view to strengthening the receipt of such assistance.[86] Throughout the years therefore, also in legal scholarship, both opponents and proponents of the creation and potential existence of an independent human right to humanitarian assistance continue to debate its existence.[87]

Thus, in many non-binding instruments and through the work of the EU and Special Rapporteurs within the UN system, reference to the receipt of humanitarian assistance as a human right can be found. Such references can be considered evidence of existing, and continuously developing *opinio juris* with regard to the potential establishment of a human right to receive humanitarian assistance. However, the absence of such references in General Assembly, Human Rights Council and Security Council resolutions cannot be neglected. It is through these bodies that states can express their desire to formulate such a right, and the absence of such expressions remains an indication of the absence of state practice as well as further *opinio juris*. Nor can the fact be overlooked that states parties to the international and regional treaties as discussed in Section 5.3.1 have refrained from making statements with regard to humanitarian assistance either through interpretative comments or reservations.[88] Evidence of state practice of the existence of a *human* right to humanitarian assistance is thus clearly lacking. Given the fact that customary international law is dependent on two equal components, and in the case of the potential human right to humanitarian assistance merely one could *potentially* be considered fulfilled, and even that is at quite a stretch, it cannot be satisfactorily concluded as existing in international law today.

[86] 'Code of Conduct for the International Red Cross and Red Crescent Movement and NGOs in Disaster Relief', Annex VI to the resolutions of the 26th International Conference of the Red Cross and Red Crescent, Geneva, 1995 Prepared jointly by the International Federation of Red Cross and Red Crescent Societies and the ICRC, Principle 1. For further information on the Code of Conduct see <www.ifrc.org/en/publications-and-reports/code-of-conduct/> accessed 11 January 2015.

[87] See amongst others Yoram Dinstein, 'The Right to Humanitarian Assistance' (2000) LIII *Naval War College Review* 4, 77 for a negative perspective and for a positive perspective Bosko Jakovljevic, 'Right to Humanitarian Action and State Sovereignty' in (eds) Stefania Baldini & Guido Ravasi, *Humanitarian Action and State Sovereignty; Refugees: a continuing challenge* (Institute of International Humanitarian Law 2000) 99-100; as well as David Fisher, 'Right to Humanitarian Assistance' in Walter Kälin, Rhodri C Williams, Khalid Koser and Andrew Solomon (eds) *Incorporating the Guiding Principles on Internal Displacement into Domestic Law: Issues and Challenges* (American Society of International Law 2008) 50-51.

[88] It must be noted that reservations that are incompatible with the 'object and purpose' of the treaty are prohibited: see in this regard Article 19(c) of the Vienna Convention on the Law of Treaties 1969.

5.3.3 *Humanitarian Assistance and Collective Human Rights: Rights-holders and Duty-bearers*

States' hesitance towards the acknowledgment of a potential human right to humanitarian assistance could be further explained with a view towards the notions of rights-holders and duty-bearers in the specific case of a potential human right to receive humanitarian assistance. Section 5.2.1 has discussed that as an independent human right, the receipt of humanitarian assistance would most likely be categorised as a so-called 'solidarity' or 'group right' by its proponents. A discourse exists on the determination of who may be rights-holders of such collective human rights. Acknowledging the discourse is relevant to the discussion of a potential human right to receive humanitarian assistance, especially as the determination of a 'group' or 'people' may be problematic in the event of invoking the possible human right to humanitarian assistance.

This discourse needs to be addressed to place the potential human right to humanitarian assistance in its proper framework. Henkin has noted the traditional view that international human rights law is primarily concerned with the rights of individuals, as opposed to the rights of groups.[89] Burguenthal on the other hand argues that human rights law today consists of a vast body of 'individual and group rights' as proclaimed in many international human rights instruments,[90] whereas Alston finds middle ground, arguing they do exist, but are rare.[91] Furthermore, the notion of a group right is also considered by some to be inter-changeable with a so-called 'collective right'.[92] Although both approaches to human rights are clearly distinct and the existence of collective or group rights is not acknowledged by all, the approaches are not necessarily mutually exclusive, as an individual must invoke such a group right, thereby calling upon the possible breach of his or her *individual* right.[93]

---

[89] Louis Henkin, 'Group Defamation and International Law' in MH Freedman & EM Freedman (eds) *Group Defamation and Freedom of Speech: The Relationship Between Language and Violence* (Greenwood Press 1995) 124. This research will not address issues regarding the universality of human rights, but will take the premise that human rights are indeed based on universality. See in support of this premise: Alison Dundes Renteln, *International Human Rights: Universalism Versus Relativism* (Sage Publications 1990) 47; Tomuschat, *Human Rights: Between Idealism and Realism* (n 8) 69-96; H Steiner, P Alston & R Goodman, *International Human Rights in Context: Law, Politics, Morals* (Oxford University Press 2007) 517-540.

[90] Buergenthal, 'Human Rights' (n 8) § 10.

[91] Steiner, Alston & Goodman, *International Human Rights in Context: Law, Politics, Morals* (n 89) 153.

[92] 'Report of the independent expert on human rights and international solidarity (Mr. Rudi Muhammad Rizki)' UN Doc A/HRC/4/8 (7 February 2007) § 9; Tomuschat, *Human Rights: Between Idealism and Realism* (n 8) 35; ibid Steiner, Alston & Goodman. See infra further in this Section regarding various collective rights and humanitarian assistance.

[93] See for example article 27 ICCPR.

Some reluctance towards the acceptance of group- or collective rights finds its origin in the uncertainty as to whom the rights-holders of such rights are.[94] In the event of the possible invoking of a human right to receive assistance, a humanitarian crisis must exist.[95] The sheer existence of such a crisis as defined in Chapter 2 in itself determines that a large group of people is affected in the possible fulfilment of their rights. Yet, possibly problematic with regard to the establishment of the right-holder of a human right to humanitarian assistance may be the fact that such a group can often only clearly be discerned *after* the occurrence of a humanitarian crisis. Unlike those 'peoples' for example invoking the right to self-determination,[96] a group that is possibly entitled to receive humanitarian assistance under international law is not always as clearly discernible or previously determined: this will occur *ex post facto* due to the nature of a humanitarian crisis and is thereby a factor in legal uncertainty. The determination of such a 'collective' is furthermore not only temporally challenging for the law, but also dependent on the particular circumstance that amounts to a humanitarian crisis, which may be for example either conflict or natural disaster. As such, its scope will vary from occasion to occasion, should it be bestowed on an ever-changing group. Consider in this regard the recent non-international conflicts in Libya and Syria, with a view to the establishment of rights-holders caught in internal strife. In both circumstances, groups within one nation and population clashed, and civilians on both sides of the conflict were often in need of assistance.[97] Determining a single group to be the right-holder of the collective right would leave the other group without the legal standing to claim the right to assistance. Also, the occurrence of a natural disaster may invoke problems in the determination of rights-holders as the disaster or its direct consequences could be trans-boundary. Such trans-boundary effects may then also result in the circumstance where two or more groups, peoples or collectives of various nationalities may be in need of humanitarian assistance. Difficulties may then arise in applying this right to different 'groups' simultaneously for the same disaster. Thus, a potential human right to receive humanitarian assistance would have to be bestowed upon the group in need of emergency aid *as a whole*, rather than making an artificial distinction between one people (as possibly in the circumstance of a non-international armed conflict) or an unnecessary distinction between two peoples in other situations such as natural disasters with trans-boundary effects. As such, to argue the possible existence of a human right to

[94] N Roht-Arriaza & SC Aminzadeh, 'Solidarity Rights: Development, Peace, Environment, Humanitarian Assistance' in *Max Planck Encyclopedia of Public International Law* (2007) § 18.

[95] See Section 3.3.3 Defining a Humanitarian Crisis on the definition of such a crisis.

[96] See Article 1 ICCPR and Article 1 ICESCR, as well as CCPR General Comment 12: 'The right to self-determination of peoples (Art. 1)' (13 March 1984).

[97] For a declaration of the ICRC regarding the provision of assistance to civilians in various Syrian cities see <www.icrc.org/eng/resources/documents/update/2012/syria-update-2012-10-25.htm> accessed 9 November 2012. See also the WFP's call for the need to provide assistance in Libya <www.reuters.com/article/2011/03/02/us-libya-food-wfp-idUSTRE7214TM20110302> accessed 9 November 2012; and the ICRC's comments on their need to provide continued assistance <www.icrc.org/eng/resources/documents/news-release/2012/23-10-libya-aid-distributed-fighting-drags-bani-walid.htm> accessed 9 November 2012.

receive aid as a collective right, the right-holder would be determined to be the *entire* collective of persons in need of emergency assistance.

Although it is relevant to be aware of possible difficulties with regard to the establishment of the exact rights-holders, the so-called collective rights also face issues with regard to the determination of specific duty-bearers. General acceptance exists with regard to the premise that the corollary of the existence of a right is the subsequent existence of a duty.[98] Furthermore, primary duty-bearers of such rights remain either states (or those exercising sovereign duties) under international law, or alternatively horizontally other individuals.[99] Yet, solidarity or collective rights function on the premise as already laid out in the UDHR that:

> "Everyone is entitled to a social and international order in which the rights and freedoms set forth in this Declaration can be fully realized".[100]

Thus, solidarity or collective rights look to the social and international community for fulfilment.[101] The current 'duties' under international law for the international community as a whole remain unclear, making the discourse on a specific duty-bearer in the context of collective rights highly theoretical. Indeed, previous Chapters have discussed the various actors involved in the provision of humanitarian assistance and in fact concluded that not only the affected state is primarily involved in the provision of assistance: various organisations and third states can and may also be involved. Yet, when placing the receipt of humanitarian assistance within a human rights context, it is relevant to note that international human rights law has *not* recognised such actors as duty-bearers in a general context. Therefore, duty-bearers also within the framework of solidarity rights, and in the context of this research more specifically regarding a potential human right to receive humanitarian assistance, should continue to be first and foremost the affected states. The role allowed for the international community as a whole will be discussed further in Chapters 7 and 8.

Tomuschat has argued with a rather stringent approach that collective rights, looking towards the international community for fulfilment, should not be defined as *human rights* but 'rather as agreed objectives which the international community has pledged to pursue'.[102] Although such a narrow approach does not necessarily reflect the approach of the entire legal scholarship, it signals a clear existing discussion on the place of 'third generation' rights within the human rights discourse. At this stage, both the notion of collective right-holders and collective duty-bearers prove to be not undisputed in international law today. Should a human

---

[98] Tomuschat, *Human Rights: Between Idealism and Realism* (n 8) 58.

[99] Steiner, Alston & Goodman, *International Human Rights in Context: Law, Politics, Morals* (n 89) 505; ibid Tomuschat.

[100] Article 28 UDHR.

[101] For the perspective of the UN Independent Expert on Human Rights and Solidarity Rui Baltazar Dos Santos Alves on 'solidarity' see 'Report of the independent expert on human rights and international solidarity (Mr. Rudi Muhammad Rizki)' UN Doc A/HRC/4/8 (7 February 2007) § 12.

[102] Tomuschat, *Human Rights: Between Idealism and Realism* (n 8) 59.

right to humanitarian assistance therefore be desired and developed, framing it within such a collective will not enhance legal certainty for those in need of assistance. These legal challenges facing the potential declaration of the existence of a human right to receive humanitarian assistance highlight some explanation for the lack of state action in the declaration of such a right.

5.3.4 Preliminary Conclusion

Problematic to the notion of these collective or solidarity rights, remain their fairly novel status, their premise on a collective rather than an individual, as well as from a practical perspective a more difficult enforcement as they have a rather aspirational and general character, specifically with regard to the absence of a clear duty-bearer.[103] As a result, both the existence of the concept as well as the exact content of the possible rights remain a subject of debate to this day. Therefore, considering the sensitivities surrounding the notion of human rights 'generations', many use the concept of 'categories' of rights to avoid implications of an existing hierarchy.[104] Such a statement, that all human rights are indivisible and interdependent, was of course also put forward by the Vienna Declaration of 1993.[105] The determination of what consists as a human right did not halt with the creation of the UDHR in 1948. Throughout the past decades, and naturally in the decades to come, the determination of the content of (new) human rights evolves according to the developments in international society as a whole.[106] Although the discussion regarding the right-holders and duty-bearers of collective rights is topical and must be resolved through progressive development, it is but one aspect of the determination of the existence of such an independent right.

From another perspective, the evidence of the existence of such an independent human right has been sought in existing international law, considering both treaty law and customary international law. Currently, it can only be concluded that states have remained unwilling to bridge the gap and challenge of assessing the rights-holder and the question of the determination of duty-bearing responsibilities. No major international or regional human rights treaties directly make reference to humanitarian assistance as a human right. Furthermore, the CRC and the African Charter on the Rights and Welfare of the Child merely refer to humanitarian

---

[103] Kabasakal Arat, *Human Rights Worldwide: A Reference Handbook* (n 28) 37 and Claude & Weston *Human Rights in the World Community: Issues And Action* (n 28) 22; as well as the 'Report of the independent expert on human rights and international solidarity (Mr. Rudi Muhammad Rizki)' UN Doc A/HRC/4/8 (7 February 2007) § 42-45; and Roht-Arriaza & Aminzadeh, 'Solidarity Rights: Development, Peace, Environment, Humanitarian Assistance' (n 94) § 19.

[104] Ibid 'Report of the independent expert on human rights and international solidarity (Mr. Rudi Muhammad Rizki)' § 41. An example of the notion of human rights 'categories' is the usage in the Report of the Representative of the Secretary-General on the human rights of internally displaced persons, Walter Kälin 'Specific Groups and Individuals Mass Exodus and Displaced Persons' UN Doc E/CN.4/2005/84 (31 December 2004) § 42 and 43, who argues four main categories.

[105] See Sections 5.2 The Development of Human Rights Relevant to Humanitarian Assistance and 5.2.1 'Generations' of Human Rights in Relation to Humanitarian Assistance.

[106] Jakovljevic, 'Right to Humanitarian Action and State Sovereignty' (n 87) 95.

assistance with regard to the refugee or IDP child, and solely *in connection to* the enjoyment of that child's human rights. The Kampala Convention, although incorporating humanitarian assistance, has not referred specifically to the human rights law framework.

Also customary international law cannot provide solace in the determination of an existing independent human right to receive humanitarian assistance, as state practice remains lacking. Indeed, while subsequent Chapters address state practice with regard to the *provision* of humanitarian assistance, the current Chapter has sought to find the basis for this assistance in a human rights context. Specifically within that context, no state practice can be distilled regarding the existence of an individual human right to receive humanitarian assistance. *Opinio juris* does appear to exist within the UN framework and other international and regional initiatives, despite its absence in the work of relevant bodies such as the General Assembly, Human Rights Council and Security Council. However, more crystallisation and development of the law is needed before the potential human right to humanitarian assistance can be established should it be desired. Therefore, protection of those in need of assistance must currently be sought through other rights that are generally accepted as existing in current international human rights law.

5.4 Humanitarian Assistance Within the Context of Existing Human Rights

In a circumstance such as a humanitarian crisis, where humanitarian assistance is needed, several specific existing human rights may be affected, such as the right to life, the right to food, the right to health and the right to water. The latter are often considered together, as the right to an adequate standard of living.[107] Given their distinct discussion in scholarship however, as well as their distinct relevance to the delivery of humanitarian assistance, they will be equally discussed separately in this Chapter.[108] The conceptual boundaries of this research are thereby formed through the scope of the definition of humanitarian assistance as provided in Sections 2.2.2 and 3.3.3. These four independently existing rights: the right to life, food, health and water, form the core of the content of humanitarian assistance, as their fulfilment ensures the survival of persons during and in the aftermath of humanitarian crises. Fisher has argued such rights (including in his view the rights to housing and clothing) to be 'component rights' in relation to the right to receive assistance.[109] These individual rights would then function as 'components' or 'building blocks' in the provision of humanitarian assistance. In order to establish whether or not the right to receive humanitarian assistance may be incorporated and contained within these existing rights, this Section addresses the four abovementioned rights as related to the provision of assistance. The content of their legal protection is addressed, in particular relation to the needs of people in

[107] Article 11 ICESCR.
[108] See Section 2.2.2 Defining Humanitarian Assistance .
[109] Fisher, 'Right to Humanitarian Assistance' (n 87) 53.

humanitarian crises; i.e. needing food, water and medicine for their immediate survival.[110] Elements of treaty and customary international law are examined to establish the current existing legal framework on human rights law as applicable for the protection of persons through the provision of humanitarian assistance, in the absence of an independent human right to that end. As humanitarian assistance is the provision of food, water, medicine and shelter for the immediate survival of persons in emergency situations, such provision can well be derived from the rights to life, food, health and water.[111] With a view to the progressive development of human rights in a changing and developing world, it is relevant to examine the application of existing human rights to newly arising problems or to matters outside the framework for which they were originally intended but might equally be very well suited.

5.4.1 The Right to Life

Of the four individual human rights to be discussed, first and foremost the human right to life must therefore be considered, in order to determine in what way this human right may be connected to the receipt of assistance in times of a humanitarian crisis. In many circumstances, the receipt of humanitarian assistance makes the difference between life and death for those persons in the midst of a humanitarian crisis. As such, the non-provision of assistance stands in close relation to the loss of life and the potential violation of the right to life. Having established that no derogation from this right is possible in times of emergency, the right to life remains to be protected by the state in the event of a humanitarian crisis.[112] Yet, the content of this right must be examined, for the purpose of its possible relevance to those in need of emergency assistance wishing to call upon this human right.

The UDHR states that 'everyone has the right to life, liberty and security of person'.[113] This formulation is clearly from the perspective of the right of the individual, rather than an obligation that may lie upon the state, distinguishing it from several of the rights discussed in subsequent Sections. Although many discussions were held on possibly including other clauses as part of the formulation to this right, none of these are pertinent to the discussion of the right to life in the context of humanitarian assistance.[114] The ICCPR is somewhat more explicit than the UDHR, stating in Article 6(1) that:

---

[110] It remains beyond the scope of this research to fully address these four rights in all their depth. A focus will remain on those aspects of the rights as relevant to the provision of humanitarian assistance.

[111] See also in this regard this author 'A humanitarian crisis: reframing the legal framework on humanitarian assistance', in Zwitter A et al (eds) *Humanitarian Action: Global, Regional and Domestic Legal Responses* (Cambridge University Press 2014) 61.

[112] See Section 5.2.2 Derogability, Human Rights and the Provision of Humanitarian Assistance.

[113] Article 3 UDHR.

[114] Proposals were made amongst others to include the unborn child, abolition of the death penalty, and physical integrity of persons. See for an in depth discussion LA Rehof, 'Article 3', in G Alfredsson & A Eide (eds) *The Universal Declaration of Human Rights: A Common Standard of Achievement* (Martinus Nijhoff Publishers 1999) 91-94.

> "Every human being has the inherent right to life. This right shall be protected by law. No one shall be arbitrarily deprived of his life".

None of the current declarations and reservations to this right made by state parties are relevant to this research into the right to life as related to the provision of humanitarian assistance.[115] The ICCPR bases itself on the premise that each individual has an *inherent* right to life, thus not only granting the right to life to each individual, but also declaring it inherent to each human, thereby placing an obligation on states to facilitate a legal system that protects this right.[116] Such an obligation has also been reiterated by the Human Rights Committee in both its General Comments to Article 6, declaring that the State has a supreme duty to not only prevent wars or similar emergencies which may cause loss of life, but indeed that the State has an obligation to adopt *positive* measures to protect the right to life.[117] Such measures should, according to the HRC, include the reduction or elimination of malnutrition, epidemics and similar situations that may endanger the right to life.[118] These remarks by the HRC on the obligation for States to implement *positive* measures, reducing famine and preventing emergencies that may threaten the right to life can certainly be viewed in light of the provision of humanitarian assistance, as indeed the provision of food, water and shelter enhances the survival of those facing a humanitarian crisis. It may therefore indeed be suggested that according to the HRC, the provision of humanitarian assistance *could* form part of the fulfilment of a state's obligation to ensure the right to life under Article 6 ICCPR. Furthermore, Article 6 of the ICCPR forbids the 'arbitrary' deprivation of life, an issue the HRC considers a matter of the utmost gravity when occurring at the hands of the authorities.[119] This is somewhat distinct from the ECHR which prohibits the 'intentional' deprivation of life in its Article 2, but like the ICCPR also considers the right to life to entail an obligation of protection from the State.[120]

[115] Several European countries, including Finland, Germany, the Netherlands (28 and 29 September 1993), as well as Belgium, France, Norway, Portugal, Spain (4 and 5 October 1993) and Sweden (18 June 1993) have objected to the United States' reservation with regard to the possibility of enforcing the death penalty upon people under 18 years of age. Furthermore, several countries have objected to Thailand's interpretive declaration (the Netherlands, 27 December 1997) and Pakistan's and reservation (Switzerland and the United States, 28 and 29 June 2011). None of these declarations and reservations however impact the possible obligations that may lie on the State Party in the respect and protection of the right to life, as related to the possible right to humanitarian assistance. The full status of declarations and reservations to the ICCPR can be found at <http://treaties.un.org/Pages/ViewDetails.aspx?src=TREATY&mtdsg_no=IV-4&chapter=4&lang=en#EndDec> accessed 24 May 2012.

[116] Rehof 'Article 3' (n 114) 95.

[117] CCPR General Comment 6: 'The right to life (art. 6)' (30 April 1982) § 2 and CCPR General Comment 14 'Nuclear weapons and the right to life (Art. 6)' (9 November 1984) § 2.

[118] Ibid CCPR General Comment 6 § 5.

[119] Ibid § 3. With regard to 'arbitrary deprivation of life' and an armed conflict, see the discussion in Section 6.5.1 Duties of the Affected State and Non-State Actor in Times of Conflict.

[120] Article 2 of the ECHR reads: "1. Everyone's right to life shall be protected by law. No one shall be deprived of his life intentionally save in the execution of a sentence of a court following his conviction

Arguably, 'intentional' deprivation is a lesser threshold than 'arbitrary' deprivation, thus giving those individuals under the ECHR a *greater* protection.[121] Furthermore, the ECHR provides an exhaustive list of the deathly use of force allowed by authorities under the Convention.[122] However, the degree to which the State is held to certain 'positive obligations' similar to those mentioned by the HRC with regard to the ICCPR, has not been dealt with to a detailed extent by the European Court of Human Rights.[123] Although in the case of Budayeva and others v. Russia, concerning possible responsibility of the state following a mudslide, the European Court held in relation to the right to life that:

> "The Court reiterates that Article 2 does not solely concern deaths resulting from the use of force by agents of the State but also, in the first sentence of its first paragraph, lays down a positive obligation on States to take appropriate steps to safeguard the lives of those within their jurisdiction [...] This positive obligation entails above all a primary duty on the State to put in place a legislative and administrative framework designed to provide effective deterrence against threats to the right to life".[124]

The European Court thereby, although not laying down specificities, does envisage a clear and positive obligation to rest upon the state in ensuring that the right to life of persons remains protected.

Other regional instruments containing provisions with regard to the right to life include the ACHR and ACHPR. The ACHR largely follows the ICCPR, declaring a right to life that must be 'respected' and 'protected by law' and may not be arbitrarily deprived, clearly laying an obligation on State Parties to safeguard this right.[125] The ACHPR follows suit, with a brief provision that also includes a respect

---

of a crime for which this penalty is provided by law. 2. Deprivation of life shall not be regarded as inflicted in contravention of this article when it results from the use of force which is no more than absolutely necessary: (a) in defence of any person from unlawful violence; (b) in order to effect a lawful arrest or to prevent escape of a person lawfully detained; (c) in action lawfully taken for the purpose of quelling a riot or insurrection". The reservation made by Malta (23 January 1967) with regard to the defence as referred to in Article 2(2)(a) is not relevant to this current discussion of the right to life in relation to the possible right to humanitarian assistance. A full list of reservations and declarations can be found at <http://conventions.coe.int/Treaty/Commun/ListeDeclarations.asp?NT=005&CM=8&DF=24/05/2012&CL=ENG&VL=1> accessed 24 May 2012.

121 Rehof 'Article 3' (n 114) 95.

122 See Article 2(2) ECHR.

123 Only on several occasions has the former European Commission on Human Rights dealt with this matter, not relating to the context of humanitarian assistance: European Commission X v Ireland, Appl. No. 6040/73 (20 July 1973); and European Commission, Association X v UK Case No. 7154/75 (12 July 1978).

124 *Budayeva And Others v Russia* (App Nos 15339/02, 21166/02, 20058/02, 11673/02 and 15343/02) ECHR 20 March 2008, Final 29 September 2008, § 128-129.

125 Article 4 ACHR. The interpretive declaration of Mexico (March 24, 1981) does also not relate to the possible right to humanitarian assistance. All reservations and declarations can be found at <www.oas.org/juridico/english/sigs/b-32.html> accessed 24 May 2012.

for the personal integrity of all human beings.[126] At the international level, the CRC, specifically geared towards the protection of children, has also declared State Parties to have an obligation to not only recognise the right to life, but envisions a higher threshold, namely that the State Parties have an obligation to 'ensure to the maximum extent possible the survival and development of the child'.[127] No interpretative remarks have been made with regard to this phrasing and the delivery of humanitarian assistance,[128] but such an obligation could be read in conjunction with the obligation in Article 22 of the CRC to protect the refugee child through the delivery of humanitarian assistance.[129]

When considering the above treaties, the affected state therefore would not merely have an obligation to abstain from action; i.e. the arbitrary deprivation of life, but furthermore to ensure positive action; i.e. ensuring the security of persons within its jurisdiction both under the ICCPR and the ECHR. The CRC equally appears to envisage such a more positive obligation of the affected state. With a view to the provision of assistance, such perspectives on the right to life allow for the perspective that the state may indeed be required to provide assistance in certain circumstances as part of the fulfilment of the right to life.

5.4.2 Humanitarian Assistance and the Right to Life

Thus, the main international and regional treaty (bodies) both consider the right to life to entail certain positive obligations which authorities are required to respect.[130] Furthermore, this right is non-derogable, ensuring its full protection in times of emergency or crisis, pre-eminently a time at which the provision of humanitarian assistance comes into play; as assistance is only relevant in the event of a humanitarian crisis. However, no direct or indirect reference to the provision of humanitarian assistance is made in any of the provisions relating to the right to life in both international and regional treaties. Similarly the UN Special Rapporteur on the Right to Life has in recent years not expressed himself in this regard.

---

[126] Article 4 ACHPR states: "Human beings are inviolable. Every human being shall be entitled to respect for his life and the integrity of his person. No one may be arbitrarily deprived of this right". No reservations or declarations of relevance have been deposited with regard to the right to life.

[127] Article 6 CRC. The interpretive declarations of China, Guatemala, Luxembourg and Tunisia with regard to the right to life do not influence the discussion of this right in relation to this research into the possible right to humanitarian assistance. All reservations and declarations can be found at <http://www2.ohchr.org/english/law/crc-reserve.htm> accessed 24 May 2012.

[128] The interpretive declarations of China, Guatemala, Luxembourg and Tunisia with regard to the right to life do not influence the discussion of this right in relation to this research into the possible right to humanitarian assistance. All reservations and declarations can be found at <http://www2.ohchr.org/english/law/crc-reserve.htm> accessed 24 May 2012.

[129] See Section 5.3.1 Humanitarian Assistance as a Potential Human Right in International Treaty Law.

[130] For a more in depth discussion on the right to life, see Christian Tomuschat, Evelyne Lagrange & Stefan Oeter (eds), *The Right to Life* (Brill 2010). See also Katja Luopojärvi, 'Is There an Obligation on States to Accept International Humanitarian Assistance to Internally Displaced Persons under International Law?' (2004) 15 International Journal of Refugee Law 4, 691-692.

Only through the interpretive remarks of the HRC of the ICCPR could the provision of humanitarian assistance be considered as part of a state's obligation to ensure the right to life under Article 6 ICCPR, as the Human Rights Committee envisages an obligation resting upon state parties to reduce or eliminate malnutrition, epidemics and other such situations. Indeed, providing humanitarian assistance – entailing food, water, medical assistance – can contribute and be a vehicle to such reduction or elimination and would then be the fulfilment of the right to life.[131] Rather than functioning as a right in itself, the provision of assistance then contributes to the fulfilment of the right to life. Likewise the CRC's provision with regard to the right to life could be seen in conjunction with Article 22 of that Convention in which an obligation lies upon states to provide humanitarian assistance to the refugee child in the enjoyment of its human rights, which would naturally include the right to life as incorporated in Article 6 CRC. These two interpretative considerations, although relevant to note, are however currently clearly not sufficient to be able to conclude a clear relationship between the concept of humanitarian assistance *as a human right*, and the human right to life. Nonetheless, they are indicative of the relationship between the provision of such assistance in the fulfilment of states' obligations to ensure the respect for the right to life.

With a specific view towards times of conflict, the concept of the prohibition of 'arbitrary deprivation of life' and security of person must be read in conjunction with international humanitarian law, as the protection of life in times of armed conflict is addressed specifically in this body of law too, leading to a more detailed understanding of the notion of 'arbitrary deprivation'. Several provisions must be taken into account jointly with the human right to life, as protection from violence directed at civilians forms a large part of the essentialities necessary for their survival in times of conflict, and will be addressed more specifically in Chapters 6 and 7.

5.4.3 The Right to Adequate Food

Another pre-existing human right possibly containing or contributing to the existence of the right to humanitarian assistance is the human right to adequate food, one of the rights categorised as an economic, social and cultural right. The promotion of these rights was envisaged as early as 1945, as the UN Charter itself called upon Member States separately and jointly to promote amongst others:

> "higher standards of living, full employment, and conditions of economic and social progress and development; solutions of international economic, social, health, and related problems; and international cultural and educational cooperation".[132]

---

[131] Ibid Luopojärvi 692-693.

[132] See Section 5.2 The Development of Human Rights Relevant to Humanitarian Assistance, as well as Articles 55 and 56 UN Charter.

These provisions are arguably considered to behold an obligation upon state parties to realise economic, social and cultural rights, giving states therefore a potential duty to provide in the right to food.[133] Article 25 of the UDHR has translated that original call in the UN Charter into the statement that all persons have a right to an adequate standard of living, including food.[134] Following the UDHR, the ICESCR has developed in its Article 11 a provision relating to such an adequate standard of living, including the right to food, in which it elaborately declares:

> "1. The States Parties to the present Covenant recognize the right of everyone to an adequate standard of living for himself and his family, including adequate food, clothing and housing, and to the continuous improvement of living conditions. The States Parties will take appropriate steps to ensure the realization of this right, recognizing to this effect the essential importance of international co-operation based on free consent. 2. The States Parties to the present Covenant, recognizing the fundamental right of everyone to be free from hunger, shall take, individually and through international co-operation, the measures, including specific programmes, which are needed: (a) To improve methods of production, conservation and distribution of food by making full use of technical and scientific knowledge, by disseminating knowledge of the principles of nutrition and by developing or reforming agrarian systems in such a way as to achieve the most efficient development and utilization of natural resources; (b) Taking into account the problems of both food-importing and food-exporting countries, to ensure an equitable distribution of world food supplies in relation to need".

Interestingly, Article 11(2) includes the right to be *free from hunger*, uniquely formulated in the ICESCR as a 'fundamental right' and clearly of a more narrow scope than the broader formulated 'right to adequate food'. The Committee on Economic, Social and Cultural Rights (CESCR), the treaty body to the ICESCR, has elaborated on the content of the right to food as laid down in Article 11 ICESCR and determined in one of its 'General Comments' that this right is of fundamental importance for the enjoyment and fulfilment of all other rights as protected in the International Bill of Rights, as well as considering it a right that is 'linked to the inherent dignity of the human person'.[135] As such, the CESCR has furthermore established that as part of the right to food, *access* to food is of relevance, and that priority and attention thereto may especially be needed for victims of natural disasters or people living areas that are likely to be prone to such disasters.[136] As seen in relation to the right to life, in the case of the right to food a link is also made between the provision of humanitarian assistance and the fulfilment of a human right. The establishment of 'adequate' food envisages a

[133] CESCR General Comment 3 (n 45) § 14.

[134] The relevant text of Article 25 UDHR states: "(1) Everyone has the right to a standard of living adequate for the health and well-being of himself and of his family, including food, clothing, housing and medical care and necessary social services, and the right to security in the event of unemployment, sickness, disability, widowhood, old age or other lack of livelihood in circumstances beyond his control".

[135] CESCR General Comment 12 (n 26) § 1 and §4.

[136] Ibid, § 13.

broader spectrum of criteria that need to be met than the mere establishment of a minimum intake in order to fulfil the right to food. The Committee has noted that this right to food encompasses such food which is 'sufficient, nutritionally adequate and safe, to ensure their freedom from hunger' and that the right to food is realised when every person has access to adequate food at all times.[137] This definition, although legally non-binding, is considered most widely used and accepted.[138] Although Article 11 ICESCR is formulated as an inherent individual right, emphasis has mostly been placed on the obligation for state parties to realise this right. Moreover, the then UN Special Rapporteur on the Right to Food (Olivier de Schutter) has argued that such an approach based upon obligations to be imposed on various actors can have a positive influence on the realisation of the right to food, with more legal certainty for rights-holders and accountability for the duty-bearers.[139]

In the above Section 5.2.2.1, a distinction has already been made between the notion of 'progressive realization' as meant in Article 2(1) ICESCR, and the so-called 'minimum core obligations' found within the substantive provisions of the ICESCR according to the CESCR. In light of this viewpoint and the provision of humanitarian assistance, it is relevant to note that none of the current reservations or declarations made by states party to the ICESCR can be considered to object to the progressive realisation of the right to food or its minimum core obligation.[140] Considering these minimum core obligations flowing from each provision in the

---

[137] Ibid § 6 and § 14.

[138] Kerstin Mechlem, 'Right to Food, International Protection' in *Max Planck Encyclopedia of Public International Law* (June 2008) § 4. Within the UN context the Special Rapporteur on the Right to Food has elaborated and declared it to entail: 'the right to have regular, permanent and free access, either directly or by means of financial purchases, to quantitatively and qualitatively adequate and sufficient food corresponding to the cultural traditions of the people to which the consumer belongs, and which ensures a physical and mental, individual and collective, fulfilling and dignified life free of fear'; see in this regard the Report submitted by the Special Rapporteur on the Right to Food 'The Right to Food' UN Doc E/CN.4/2001/53 (7 February 2001) § 14; and subsequently also 'The Right to Food', Report submitted by the Special Rapporteur on the Right to Food UN Doc E/CN.4/2004/10 (9 February 2004) § 3; 'The Right to Food', Report submitted by the Special Rapporteur on the Right to Food UN Doc E/CN.4/2005/47 (24 January 2005) § 5; 'The right to food', Report of the Special Rapporteur on the right to food, UN Doc E/CN.4/2006/44 (16 March 2006) § 2; as well as subsequently transmitted to the General Assembly by the Secretary General in UN Docs A/58/330 'The right to food' (, 28 August 2003) § 3; A/60/350 'The right to food' (12 September 2005) §6; and A/62/289 'The right to food' (22 august 2007) §4.

[139] HRC Res 9/23 (8 September 2008) 'Building resilience: a human rights framework for world food and nutrition security', UN Doc A/HRC/9/23, Special Session on the global food crisis § 17.

[140] However, Kuwait has expressed the viewpoint that the rights set forth in the ICESCR are subject to the limits of national law, to which Finland and Germany have objected (1997). Furthermore, Pakistan has declared that the fulfilment of Article 2 shall be subject to its available resources, which has been rejected by France, the Netherlands, Norway, Sweden and Germany (2005). Also, France and Monaco have declared Article 11 not to be interpreted as derogating from those provisions governing certain rights of aliens. Lastly, Belgium, Monaco and Ireland have expressed a declaration with regard to the non-discrimination clause as laid down in Article 2. For the full status of declarations and reservations to the ICESCR, see <http://treaties.un.org/Pages/ViewDetails.aspx?src=TREATY&mtdsg_no=IV-3&chapter=4&lang=en> accessed 31 May 2012. See also Vienna Convention on the Law of Treaties Articles 19-23 with regard to the law on treaty reservations.

ICESCR and laying upon State Parties, the CESCR notes in relation to the right to food as codified in Article 11 that all states have such an obligation to take steps to 'mitigate and alleviate hunger' even in the event of a natural disaster or a disaster of another kind.[141] This also falls in line with the 'fundamental' aspect of the right to be free from hunger, as laid down in Article 11(2) ICESCR. Clearly, no limitation can be made to the obligation resting upon a State Party to take immediate steps to provide food in the event of a humanitarian crisis. This obligation also follows from the three levels in which the obligation to fulfil the right to food can be divided.[142] The obligation to *respect* the right to food entails that states may not take measures to prevent access to food; the obligation to *protect* requires that States ensure that individuals do not lose their access to food; and the obligation to *fulfil* is pronged, entailing both the obligation to facilitate and strengthen the access to food, whilst also including the obligation to actively provide in the right to food if a person or group is unable to enjoy the right to food through their own means.[143] The CESCR lays an obligation on states to actively provide the right to food in the event of a humanitarian crisis, pre-eminently a situation in which individuals or groups cannot enjoy the right to food through their own means, by stating that 'this obligation also applies for persons who are victims of natural or other disasters'.[144]

Thus, the CESCR sees a role for the provision of humanitarian assistance, which indeed includes the provision of food in such circumstances of natural or other disasters, as part of the fulfilment of the minimum core obligation resting upon states as part of the right to food.[145] The UN Special Rapporteur on the Right to Food has furthermore reiterated this position on numerous occasions, also declaring that the distribution of food as aid in emergency situations forms part of the obligation to fulfil the right to food.[146] Thus, the state parties to the ICESCR and (in the view of the Special Rapporteur also UN Member States) have a clear obligation to not only passively facilitate access to food, but furthermore to actively provide in the right to food in the event of a humanitarian crisis.[147] This duty has been supported by the UN Secretary General, who declared that all states under international law have an obligation to not only respect, protect and fulfil the right to food, but that this obligation entails that a state may not take any measures that

[141] CESCR General Comment 12 (n 26) § 6.
[142] See Section 5.2.2.1 on the three 'levels' in which a human rights obligation may be divided, particularly in relation to economic, social and cultural rights.
[143] CESCR General Comment 12 (n 26) § 15. This position is reiterated by the Special Rapporteur on the Right to Food who states in his Report on the Mission to Nicaragua UN Doc A/HRC/13/33/Add.5 (19 February 2010) § 7 and had been considered earlier by the Secretary General's Note 'The right to food - Seed policies and the right to food: enhancing agrobiodiversity and encouraging innovation' UN Doc A/64/170 (23 July 2009) § 6.
[144] Ibid CESCR General Comment § 15.
[145] See in this regard also Section 5.2.2.1. Progressive Realisation in the ICESCR for the discussion of the CESCR on the content of minimum core obligations in the ICESCR.
[146] 'Report of the Special Rapporteur on the right to food, Addendum Mission to Guatemala' UN Doc A/HRC/13/33/Add.4 (26 January 2010) § 66.
[147] CESCR General Comment 12 (n 26) § 28.

may prevent access to adequate food.[148] Such active provision must be done, as seen above, to the maximum of a states' available resources, which according to Article 2 ICESCR includes the use of sources available through international cooperation and assistance.

The right to food and the provision of food to fulfil this right must indeed be seen in light of the joint responsibility of states as considered in Article 56 UN Charter, and the CESCR also considers Article 11 to include a duty for State Parties 'to take steps' to provide the necessary assistance in *other* countries in the event this may be required, through the occurrence of providing humanitarian assistance in times of emergency, to ensure full enjoyment of the right to food.[149] This view aligns with the notion of 'international cooperation' as codified in Article 2(1) ICESCR. Furthermore, the CESCR envisages an important role and 'coordinated efforts' of the UN and other international organisations in the realisation of the right to food.[150] Indeed, although Article 11 declares that international cooperation is based on 'free consent', this cannot be considered to be void of responsibility for the affected state. As a result, Article 11 ICESCR could be violated if a state party prevents access to food in conflicts or other emergencies, or subsequently in the event it is willing to provide food but does not have sufficient independent resources, and does not seek assistance from outside its own territory.[151] Distinguishing between willingness and ability is necessary, although both may lead to a violation of Article 11 ICESCR. Arguably, although the cooperation is not optional, the form it may take can be considered to be determined in cooperation with the affected state.[152] Bearing in mind that the ICESCR does not contain a derogation clause, and that the limitations to the Convention as laid down in Article 4 ICESCR are rather limited,[153] such violations may indeed occur as state parties cannot claim a 'state of emergency' to avoid fulfilling at least the minimum core obligations of the right to food. As a result, not fulfilling at least the minimum core obligations, such as those in particular relevant in relation to humanitarian assistance, the requirement to 'mitigate and alleviate hunger' may result in a violation of the right to adequate food.

Besides the ICESCR, other international treaties have incorporated the right to food to some degree. A second international instrument considering the right to food is the Convention on the Rights of the Child. The CRC notes, in relation to the right to health[154] that states parties to the CRC have an obligation to provide

---

[148] 'The right to food', Note by the Secretary Genera UN Doc A/66/262 (4 August 2011) § 11.

[149] CESCR General Comment 12 (n 26) § 36 and § 38. See concerning the responsibilities under Article 56 UN Charter in more detail Chapter 7.

[150] Ibid § 40.

[151] Ibid § 17 and § 19. See also 'The right to food', Report of the Special Rapporteur, Note by the Secretary General UN Doc A/63/278 (21 October 2008) § 12 and Chapter 8.

[152] P Alston & K Tomaševski (eds), *The Right to Food* (Martinus Nijhoff 1984) 40-41.

[153] See Section 5.2.2 Derogability, Human Rights and the Provision of Humanitarian Assistance for a discussion of derogability and limitations in regard to the ICESCR.

[154] See Section 5.4.6 Humanitarian Assistance and The Right to Health.

adequate and nutritious foods to children.[155] Besides the CRC, other international instruments declaring a right to food are the CEDAW in relation to pregnancy and post-natal care in Article 12(2), and the Convention on the Rights of Persons with Disabilities in Article 28.[156] Whereas the CEDAW views this right primarily as an obligation of State Parties to ensure 'adequate nutrition', the CRPD codifies a right to adequate food, for which the State Parties have to take appropriate steps to safeguard. As such, these three treaties envisage obligations to rest upon states in the fulfilment of this right, as does the ICESCR with its provision.

Regional instruments such as the main ACHR, ECHR or ACHPR contain no specific provisions relating to the right to food. Although the ACHR and ECHR have a greater focus on civil and political rights, there appears to be no clear reason as to why these conventions omit the right to food, although Alston submits the argument that some regional instruments include the 'right to work', which should theoretically enable persons to fulfil the right to food.[157] However, the Additional Protocol to the ACHR in the Area of Economic, Social and Cultural Rights does recognise the right to food in Article 12.[158] Moreover, Article 15 of the Additional Protocol to the ACHPR on the Rights of Women in Africa envisages a right to food security for women as a specific group.[159] Both Protocols contain far-reaching provisions that are of relevance to the provision of humanitarian assistance, and that are absent in their underlying treaties that have a higher status of ratification. The Protocol to the ACHR contains an obligation lying upon states to undertake measures to improve the distribution of food, promote greater international cooperation to this end and eradicate malnutrition.[160] Furthermore, the Additional Protocol to the ACHPR on the Rights of Women in Africa notes that states parties shall take measures to establish supply systems to ensure food security, which can be of relevance to the provision of assistance. Although relatively few states have ratified both Protocols, the provisions are of importance to two continents that have been prone to many natural disasters and conflicts. As such their further implementation may be of assistance to those needing emergency aid on these continents. Although the African Charter itself does not recognise a right to food, the treaty body to the Charter, the African Commission on Human and Peoples Rights established in 2001 in the *Social and Economic Rights Action Center (SERAC) and Center for Economic and Social Rights (CESR) v. Nigeria* (Ogoni

[155] Article 24(2)(c) CRC: "2. States Parties shall pursue full implementation of this right and, in particular, shall take appropriate measures: […] (c) To combat disease and malnutrition, including within the framework of primary health care, through, inter alia, the application of readily available technology and through the provision of adequate nutritious foods and clean drinking-water, taking into consideration the dangers and risks of environmental pollution". See also Article 27(3) CRC and Section 5.4.6 Humanitarian Assistance and The Right to Health for a further discussion of Article 24.

[156] The Convention on the Rights of Persons with Disabilities was adopted 13 December 2006. As one of the more recent international treaties, currently 113 States are party to the convention.

[157] Alston & Tomaševski, *The Right to Food* (n 152) 28-29.

[158] To date, only 16 states have ratified the Additional Protocol to the ACHR in the Area of Economic, Social and Cultural Rights.

[159] To date, 16 of the 27 states of the African Union have ratified the Additional Protocol.

[160] Article 12 Additional Protocol ACHR.

Case) that a right to food can be *implicitly* read in the Charter's rights to life, health and the right of all persons to economic, social and cultural development.[161] Despite lacking codification therefore, efforts are being made in the establishment of such a right by way of jurisprudence.

Following the provisions as laid down in, amongst others, the ICESCR, the UN has expressed itself with regard to the right to food on multiple occasions and through various bodies. As such, the former UN Commission on Human Rights had reaffirmed the right of every person:

> "to have access to safe and nutritious food, consistent with the right to adequate food and the fundamental right of everyone to be free from hunger so as to be able fully to develop and maintain their physical and mental capacities".[162]

The Commission reiterated this, followed by its successor the Human Rights Council, and it has been furthermore adopted by the General Assembly, thereby firmly establishing the UN's human rights bodies' subscription to the right to food.[163] The UN General Assembly has furthermore endorsed the approach based on international cooperation and assistance as envisaged in Article 2 ICESCR, repeatedly stating that it:

> "Stresses the importance of international development cooperation and assistance, in particular in emergency situations such as natural and man-made disasters, diseases and pests, for the realization of the right to food and the achievement of sustainable food security, while recognizing that each country has the primary responsibility for ensuring the implementation of national programmes and strategies in this regard".[164]

Thus, emphasis lies on the primary responsibility which continues to rest with the national government, although the General Assembly does highlight the importance of international assistance for the realisation of the right to food in the event of humanitarian emergencies, including natural and man-made disasters. More recently, the General Assembly has voiced that it recognises a need to strengthen not only national but also international assistance, in particular in relation to

---

161 *Social and Economic Rights Action Center (SERAC) and Center for Economic and Social Rights (CESR) / Nigeria*, African Commission on Human and Peoples Rights Case No 155/96 (27th October 2001) § 64.

162 UNCHR Res 10 (2000) UN Doc E/CN.4/2000/10 'The right to food' (17 April 2000) § 1.

163 UNCHR Res 19 (16 April 2004) UN Doc E/CN.4/2004/19 § 2; UNHRC Res 7/14 (27 March 2008) 'The right to food' § 2; UNHRC Res 10/12 (26 March 2009) 'The right to food' § 2; UNHRC Res 13/4 (24 March 2010) 'The right to food' § 2; UNHRC Res 16/27 (25 March 2011) 'The right to food' § 2; UNGA Res 59/202 (31 March 2005) UN Doc A/RES/59/202 § 2; UNGA Res 60/165 (2 March 2006) UN Doc A/RES/60/165 §2; UNGA Res 61/163 (19 December 2006) UN Doc A/RES/61/163 §2; UNGA Res 62/164 (18 December 2007) UN Doc A/RES/62/164 § 2; UNGA Res 63/187 (18 December 2008) UN Doc A/RES/63/187 § 2; UNGA Res 64/159 (10 March 2010) UN Doc A/RES/64/159 § 2.

164 UNGA Res 60/165 (2 March 2006) UN Doc A/RES/60/165 § 14; also UNGA Res 61/163 (19 December 2006) UN Doc A/RES/61/163 § 18; UNGA Res 62/164 (18 December 2007) UN Doc A/RES/62/164 § 14 and 22; UNGA Res 64/159 (10 March 2010) UN Doc A/RES/64/159 § 17.

humanitarian emergencies affecting people's enjoyment of the right to food.[165] Also, the Human Rights Council has considered that Member States have a primary obligation to provide in the realisation of the right to food, although such realisation must occur also through international cooperation and assistance, by means of all necessary measures to ensure the fulfilment of this right.[166] Similar to the General Assembly, the Human Rights Council furthermore recognises a need to strengthen international assistance in the event people are affected by humanitarian emergencies and their enjoyment of the right to food is jeopardised, to ensure that humanitarian assistance reaches the affected populations.[167] These expressions are not only indicative of the UN as an organisation adhering to the existence of a 'right to adequate food' but are also reflective of such a belief in state practice, given the fact that these UN bodies are expressing themselves through their Member States. The Special Rapporteur on the Right to Food has moreover noted that states may in fact be considered to be under an obligation to *provide food aid* in certain situations, as the positive obligation resting upon states by way of the ICESCR requires them to cooperate internationally in order to ensure that the right to food is not violated in a particular country.[168] Such situations would naturally most likely be in the event of a humanitarian crisis and could be part of the provision of humanitarian assistance as a whole. As such the Special Rapporteur has argued that 'international aid remains an important component of the right to food'.[169] In this light, the General Assembly has moreover expressed its concern with regard to the increasing amount of humanitarian emergencies, and their impact on the realisation of the right to food.[170] In this context, the FAO has developed 'Voluntary Guidelines to support the progressive realisation of the right to adequate food in the context of national food security' in which it includes the provision of assistance and the allowance of such assistance by the affected state.[171] The large number of states endorsing the FAO's Voluntary Guidelines contribute to their acceptance and

---

[165] UNGA Res 63/187 (18 December 2008) UN Doc A/RES/63/187 § 16 and § 24; UNGA Res 64/159 (10 March 2010) UN Doc A/RES/64/159 § 17 and § 25.

[166] UNHRC Res 7/14 (27 March 2008) 'The right to food' § 14 and § 22; UNHRC Res S-7/1 (22 May 2008) Special Session 'The negative impact of the worsening of the world food crisis on the realization of the right to food for all' § 4; UNHRC Res 10/12 (26 March 2009) 'The right to food' § 26; UNHRC Res 12/10 (12 October 2010) § 5; UNHRC Res 13/4 (24 March 2010) 'The right to food' § 11 and § 13; UNHRC Res 16/27 (25 March 2011) 'The right to food' § 11-13.

[167] Ibid UNHRC Res 7/14; UNHRC Res S-7/1 § preamble; UNHRC Res 10/12 § 16; UNHRC Res 13/4 § 20 and § 28; UNHRC Res 16/27 § 20 and § 28.

[168] Report of the Special Rapporteur 'The right to food' (21 October 2008) UN Doc A/63/278 § 12; Report of the Special Rapporteur on the right to food 'Promotion and Protection of all Human Rights, Civil, political, economic, social and cultural rights, including the right to development' (11 February 2009) UN Doc A/HRC/10/5 § 5.

[169] Report of the Special Rapporteur on the right to food (24 January 2014) UN Doc A/HRC/25/57, 28.

[170] UNGA Res 59/202 (31 March 2005) UN Doc A/RES/59/202, preamble.

[171] FAO 'Voluntary Guidelines to support the progressive realization of the right to adequate food in the context of national food security' (Adopted by the 127th Session of the FAO Council November 2004) Guideline 15.3.

relevance.[172] Also, regionally the EU aligns itself with the UN and FAO, expressing its acceptance of a right to food and the right to be free from hunger, arguing a greater protection for persons through such a rights-based approach.[173] Given the widespread acceptance of the most basic form of the right to food, namely to be 'free from hunger', the FAO has asserted that this also forms part of the customary body of international law.[174] With a view to the International Bill of Rights which the (near universal) UDHR and ICESCR form a part of, as well as the general acceptance of UN Member States hereof, such an assertion does indeed form part of international legal reality. This would then amount to the international legal responsibility of states to fulfil such a right to the greatest extent possible.

5.4.4 Humanitarian Assistance and the Right to Food

From the above, it becomes apparent that the CESCR and UN organs such as the General Assembly, Human Rights Council and the Special Rapporteur on the Right to Food see a clear role for the provision of humanitarian assistance, functioning as an umbrella concept within which the provision of food is incorporated, as a vehicle in emergency situations to fulfil a states' obligation with regard to the right to food. Thus, according to these bodies, the right to food entails the distribution of food aid in the event of a humanitarian crisis. The corresponding obligation of this right might even exist with a view to international cooperation according to the CESCR and the Special Rapporteur. Indeed, the CESCR argues a possible violation of Article 11 ICESCR in the event a state party denies access to food in times of conflict or disaster.[175] Clearly the obligation to mitigate and alleviate hunger as part of the fulfilment of the right to food must according to these bodies be understood in relation to the provision of humanitarian assistance. Such a provision can also be found within the specialised treaties such as the CRC and the CRPD that place specific obligations upon state parties. This view has also been endorsed by the regional Additional Protocol to the ACHR and the Additional Protocol to the

---

[172] The FAO Voluntary Guidelines were adopted by the FAO Council and as stems from Article V.1 of the FAO Constitution, that Council consists of 49 member nations.

[173] See in this regard amongst others 'Communication From The Commission To The Council And The European Parliament An EU Policy Framework to assist developing countries in addressing food security challenges' (31 March 2010) Doc SEC(2010)379, 5;
European Parliament Res 'Assisting developing countries in addressing food security challenges' (27 September 2011) on an EU policy framework to assist developing countries in addressing food security challenges Doc (2010/2100(INI)) § 28. See also FAO Legislative Study 'Right to Adequate Food in Emergencies' (2002) "Under international human rights law, every human being has the right to have physical and economic access at all times to adequate food or to the means for its procurement. In order to progressively realize this right, each State has a legal obligation to take steps to the maximum of its available resources, both individually and through international assistance and cooperation. As a fundamental human right, the right to adequate food applies in emergency situations, including both natural disasters and armed conflicts."

[174] FAO Legislative Study 'Right to Adequate Food in Emergencies' (2002) 6.

[175] See Chapter 7 regarding access by third parties and Chapter 8 concerning enforcement mechanisms.

ACHPR on the Rights of Women in Africa, both considering a duty to provide food assistance in some form.

Thus, although some bodies such as the CESCR, the UN Special Rapporteur recognise far-going international obligations resting upon states, more narrowly, the right *to adequate food* as defined in the ICESCR and interpreted by the CESCR to at least entail a freedom from hunger, can be considered to exist in a wide variety of international treaties and furthermore supported by many UN bodies and its Member States. Indeed, considering both the widespread ratification of the ICESCR and the wide support for the right within the international community at large, through (the membership of) the UN and the FAO, the right to adequate food may arguably be considered to have a customary international law status.[176] It is submitted that this obligation would then in fact include the provision of food as part of the provision of humanitarian assistance. Some resistance to the existence of such an obligation however continues, as states fear that the 'obligation to fulfil' might obligate them to provide for *all* those who are hungry in the world.[177] Yet, States Parties to the ICESCR and UN Member States have a clear obligation to not only passively facilitate access to food, but furthermore to *actively provide* food aid *in the event of a humanitarian crisis*. This obligation follows from the right to adequate food as codified in the ICESCR and Articles 55 and 56 UN Charter while, as the CESCR argues, the primary obligation continues to rest upon the affected state:

> "Even where a state faces severe resource constraints, whether caused by a process of economic adjustment, economic recession, climatic conditions or other factors, measures should be undertaken to ensure that the right to adequate food is especially fulfilled for vulnerable population groups and individuals".[178]

Such obligations have been supported in the subsequent adoption of conventions such as the CRC, CEDAW, CRPD and regionally in the Additional Protocol to the

---

[176] For further reading on the topic of the right to adequate food, see amongst others Alston & Tomaševski, *The Right to Food* (n 152); Eide *Food and Human Rights in Development* Volume II (n 26); and Laura Niada, 'Hunger and International Law: The Far-reaching Scope of the Human Right to Food', (2006) 22 *Connecticut Journal of International Law* 1, 131-201.

[177] In this regard, the United States made a reservation with regard to § 10 of the FAO 'Declaration of the World Food Summit: Five Years Later: International Alliance Against Hunger' in the FAO *Report of the World Food Summit: five years later* (2002) declaring that it: "believes that the attainment of the right to an adequate standard of living is a goal or aspiration to be realized progressively that does not give rise to any international obligation or any domestic legal entitlement, and does not diminish the responsibilities of national governments towards their citizens. Additionally, the United States understands the right of access to food to mean the opportunity to secure food, and not guaranteed entitlement".

[178] CESCR General Comment 12 (n 26) § 28; see also UNGA Res 63/187 (18 December 2008) UN Doc A/RES/63/187 §16 and § 24; UNGA Res 64/159 (10 March 2010) UN Doc A/RES/64/159 § 17 and § 25; UNHRC Res 7/14 (27 March 2008) 'The right to food' § 14 and § 22; UNHRC Res S-7/1 (22 May 2008) Special Session § 4; UNHRC Res 10/12 (26 March 2009) 'The right to food' § 26; UNHRC Res 10/12 (26 March 2009) 'The right to food' § 26; UNHRC Res 12/10 (12 October 2010) § 5; UNHRC Res 16/27 (25 March 2011) 'The right to food' § 11-13.

ACHR and the Additional Protocol to the ACHPR on the Rights of Women in Africa. Thus here too the provision of food aid, as a component of humanitarian assistance in a greater scheme, can be considered a vehicle and obligation in the fulfilment of the internationally recognised human right to adequate food.

5.4.5 The Right to Health

Following the discussion of the rights to life and food, with regard to the determination of the content of the right to receive humanitarian assistance, the discussion of the human right to the highest attainable standard of health is relevant.[179] The WHO Constitution first coined 'the highest attainable standard of health' as a fundamental human right in 1946, following the mentioning of the need for solutions to health problems in Article 55 of the UN Charter the previous year.[180] Briefly touched upon in the previous Section with regard to the right to food, the right to the highest attainable standard of health finds its first international declaration in Article 25 of the UDHR.[181] The ensuing Article 12 ICESCR is considered the main international provision concerning this right 'to the enjoyment of the highest attainable standard' of health.[182] The CESCR notes that the content of the right is broader than the right to health care and although it does not entail the right to 'be healthy' it does include:

> "a wide range of socio-economic factors that promote conditions in which people can lead a healthy life, and extends to the underlying determinants of health, such as food

---

[179] As this research focuses on humanitarian assistance, it is beyond its scope to fully analyse all abovementioned rights from all viewpoints and therefore focuses on those aspects relevant to humanitarian assistance. Yet, for an in depth analysis on the right to health, see Brigit Toebes, *The Right to Health as a Human Right in International Law* (Intersentia 1999).

[180] The Constitution of the World Health Organization was adopted by the International Health Conference held in New York from 19 June to 22 July 1946, signed on 22 July 1946 by the representatives of 61 States (*Off. Rec. Wld Hlth Org.*, 2, 100), and entered into force on 7 April 1948. For a further discussion on the origin of the right to health, see Eibe Riedel, 'International Protection of the Right to Health', (April 2011) *Max Planck Encyclopedia of Public International Law*.

[181] With regard to the right to health, Article 25 UDHR states: "(1) Everyone has the right to a standard of living adequate for the health and well-being of himself and of his family, including food, clothing, housing and medical care (...) (2) The steps to be taken by the States Parties to the present Covenant to achieve the full realization of this right shall include those necessary for: (...) (c) The prevention, treatment and control of epidemic, endemic, occupational and other diseases".

[182] Article 12 ICESCR states: "1. The States Parties to the present Covenant recognize the right of everyone to the enjoyment of the highest attainable standard of physical and mental health. 2. The steps to be taken by the States Parties to the present Covenant to achieve the full realization of this right shall include those necessary for: (a) The provision for the reduction of the stillbirth-rate and of infant mortality and for the healthy development of the child; (b) The improvement of all aspects of environmental and industrial hygiene; (c) The prevention, treatment and control of epidemic, endemic, occupational and other diseases; (d) The creation of conditions which would assure to all medical service and medical attention in the event of sickness". None of the States Parties have made declarations or reservations with regard to this Article in the ICESCR.

> and nutrition, housing, access to safe and potable water and adequate sanitation, safe and healthy working conditions, and a healthy environment".[183]

As the right to health encompasses the right to food, this individual right has been discussed first, to be followed by a discussion on the right to water which has a more disputed status in international law. The CESCR asserts that the notion of the 'highest attainable standard' of health as codified in the ICESCR takes various socio-economic factors into account, as well as a state's own resources and must therefore be considered as the right to the enjoyment of all those resources that may be necessary for the enjoyment of such a highest attainable standard.[184] Accordingly, the right to health entails the access to water and sanitation, as well as an adequate supply of food.[185] The CESCR acknowledges the difficulty states may have in the fulfilment of this right, and affirms that the exact application of the right will be dependent on the facilities in a state with regard to availability, accessibility, acceptability and quality.[186] Of particular relevance in relation to humanitarian assistance in this regard is the requirement under Article 12(2)(c) that States Parties have a duty to take steps in 'the prevention, treatment and control of epidemic, endemic, occupational and other diseases', in which the CESCR reads a right to treatment which includes 'the provision of disaster relief and humanitarian assistance in emergency situations'.[187] Thus, a duty for states to provide adequate disaster relief exists according to the CESCR in order for individuals to enjoy the right to the highest attainable standard of health under the ICESCR to the fullest extent. This duty for states to take steps in the prevention, treatment and control of diseases is indeed a clear obligation within the Convention that can be *related* to the provision of humanitarian assistance. Thus, as was concluded in the discussion of the previous human rights, the provision of humanitarian assistance by ensuring access to minimum levels of food, water and health facilities (as also considered for the fulfilment of the right to life) can be a vehicle in the fulfilment of the right to health.

Like the other rights in the ICESCR, the 'progressive realization' of the right to the highest attainable standard of health is envisaged. However, as is the case with the previously discussed rights, several immediate 'minimum obligations' rest upon states: namely to guarantee that the right will be exercised without discrimination and that concrete steps must be taken towards the fulfilment of the right.[188] The provision of humanitarian assistance would then also fall within such a minimum core obligation, given the provision of Article 12(2)(c). Furthermore, the tiered approach with regard to respecting, protecting and fulfilling the right to health entails specific obligations for states. The duty to respect the right to health

[183] CESCR General Comment 14 (11 August 2000) UN Doc E/C.12/2000/4 'The right to the highest attainable standard of health', § 3- 4 and § 8.
[184] Ibid § 9.
[185] Ibid § 11. See Section 5.4.3 The Right to Adequate Food and Section 5.4.7 The Right to Water.
[186] CESCR General Comment 14 (n 183) § 12.
[187] Ibid §16.
[188] Ibid § 30.

obligates states to refrain from denying access to health services and abstain from any discriminatory practices, while the duty to protect requires states to adopt legislation ensuring equal access to such services in view of third parties' provision thereof.[189] Lastly, the duty to fulfil requires states on the one hand to facilitate the taking of such measures that aid and enable persons to enjoy their right to health and on the other hand requires states to promote this right by taking actions with regard to maintaining or restoring the health of their population.[190]

Furthermore, more specifically geared towards international cooperation, the CESCR envisages that states should 'facilitate access' to health products and services in other states and when obliged, provide the necessary aid.[191] Also, the CESCR explicitly refers to the provision of humanitarian assistance, affirming that states have a responsibility to cooperate in the provision of such assistance, elaborating that states parties obligations in regard to the right to health include that:

> "Priority in the provision of international medical aid, distribution and management of resources, such as safe and potable water, food and medical supplies, and financial aid should be given to the most vulnerable or marginalized groups of the population. Moreover, given that some diseases are easily transmissible beyond the frontiers of a State, the international community has a collective responsibility to address this problem".[192]

This obligation to provide aid must be read in correlation to the particular core obligations concerning the right to health with which states parties must comply, in accordance with Article 2 ICESCR.

From the perspective of the CESCR it follows that special emphasis is placed on the provision of health assistance to vulnerable groups within a population; such as for example IDPs following a disaster. In that regard, the CESCR already noted in its 'General Comment' relating to Article 2 ICESCR that a state fails in its obligations under the ICESCR when a 'significant number' of people are deprived of 'essential primary health care'.[193] Such could indeed occur in times of a humanitarian crisis, if assistance is not provided. Especially in relation to the right to health, the CESCR notes that the core obligations arising for states under Article 12 ICESCR entail a duty to ensure access to minimum essential levels of food, access to health facilities, access to basic shelter and access to water and sanitation and that non-compliance with such a duty shall result in a direct violation of Article 12 ICESCR.[194]

---

[189] Ibid § 34-35.
[190] Ibid § 37.
[191] Ibid § 39.
[192] Ibid § 40.
[193] CESCR General Comment 3 (n 45) § 10 and Section 5.2.2.1. Progressive Realisation in the ICESCR.
[194] CESCR General Comment 14 (n 183) § 43.

Although clearly of relevant interpretative value, the enforceability of such an obligation as perceived by the CESCR is more difficult.[195] Furthermore, the CESCR expressly emphasises a duty of states to provide 'international assistance and cooperation' in enabling other countries to fulfil their core obligations.[196] Clearly, through such wording, the CESCR envisages distinct international cooperation and assistance in the responsibility of states to fulfil the right to health; more particularly in their duty to abide by the minimum core obligations. Such 'international cooperation' in this regard could indeed also be considered 'international assistance' in the situation of a humanitarian crisis. Interestingly these minimum core obligations of the right to health include many of the basic provisions of humanitarian assistance. As such, the provision of humanitarian assistance could be considered a fulfilment of the minimum core obligation of the right to health as envisaged by the CESCR.

Furthermore, other possible violations of the right to health occurring through either inability or unwillingness by a state in relation to humanitarian assistance include amongst others a denial of 'access to health facilities'; the adoption of laws that may interfere with the enjoyment of the right to health; the failure to enforce the proper laws to protect this right; or the failure to take necessary protective measures for its population.[197] Lastly, the CESCR foresees a role for international organisations such as the UN and WHO in particular in relation to the provision of humanitarian assistance in the event of a humanitarian crisis, as it reiterates its previous stance that priority must be given in the distribution of medical aid, water and food to the most vulnerable groups of a population.[198] Thus, the CESCR acknowledges that in the event of a humanitarian crisis, realisation of the right to health could be dependent on the involvement of international organisations providing humanitarian assistance, again reinforcing its take on international cooperation, which is to be sought by the affected state.

Other than the widely ratified ICESCR, the ICERD also recognises the right to health, declaring that States Parties are under the obligation to ensure that the 'right to public health and medical care' be provided without any form of racial discrimination.[199] The CERD treaty body has to date not expressed itself on the right to health in relation to non-discrimination.[200] Furthermore, the CRC has asserted in Article 24 that States Parties are obligated to guarantee 'necessary medical assistance and health care to all children' as part of the right to the highest attainable standard of health for children, in particular related to the right to access

---

[195] See Chapter 8.
[196] CESCR General Comment 14 (n 183) § 45.
[197] Ibid § 50-52.
[198] Ibid § 64-65.
[199] Article Art 5(e)(iv) ICERD.
[200] For more information on the Committee against the Elimination of all forms of Racial Discrimination and its General Recommendations, see <http://www2.ohchr.org/english/bodies/cerd/comments.htm> accessed 16 November 2012.

to such facilities.[201] The Committee on the Rights of the Child has however not provided explanatory commentaries to the right to health.[202] At the regional level, both the ECHR and ACHR do not contain provisions relating to the right to health whereas their counterparts focusing rather more on the economic, social and cultural rights, do contain such provisions. Consequently, the European Social Charter incorporates the right to 'protection of health', that obligates states to take measures to prevent diseases or other causes of ill-health.[203] This stipulation related to the prevention of epidemic diseases is in particular relevant following circumstances of natural disaster that may have extremely damaging impacts on living conditions in certain areas. On the other hand, the Additional Protocol to the ACHR in the area of Economic, Social and Cultural Rights stipulates that the right to health must be understood as the 'enjoyment of the highest level of physical, mental and social well-being' and must furthermore be considered as a public good, requiring states to ensure amongst other facilities essential health care and prevention from diseases.[204] The ACHPR declares a right to the 'best attainable state of physical and mental health', to include a duty of states to protect the health of the population.[205] Additionally, the African Charter on the Rights and Welfare of the Child sees a right for children 'to enjoy the best attainable state of physical, mental and spiritual health' providing in many duties resting upon states parties, amongst which the obligation to provide food and water and combat diseases,[206] whilst the Protocol to the ACHPR on the Rights of Women in Africa states a right to health in combination with reproductive rights, focusing rather on the latter.[207] From the above it can be concluded that whilst many international and regional treaties incorporate the right to health, such incorporation has occurred in a somewhat haphazard manner, codifying several different perspectives on the right to health. A common denominator can however be found with a view to the provision of humanitarian assistance, in the duty – an obligation of conduct – to prevent diseases and furthermore prioritise the provision of medical aid to vulnerable populations.

Within the UN system, the former Human Rights Commission has elaborated on the right to health, declaring that, similar to most of the abovementioned treaty provisions, it recognises a universal right to the 'highest attainable standard of

[201] It is relevant to note that although several countries, amongst which Argentina, Ecuador, the Holy See, Kiribati and Poland, have made declarations and reservations to the right to health as incorporated in the CRC, these are not related to the provision of health as pertaining to humanitarian assistance but rather concern family planning, parenthood or the unborn child.

[202] For more information on the Committee on the Rights of the Child and its General Comments, see <http://www2.ohchr.org/english/bodies/crc/comments.htm> accessed 16 November 2012.

[203] Article 11 European Social Charter.

[204] Article 10 Additional Protocol to the American Convention on Human Rights in the Area of Economic, Social and Cultural Rights.

[205] Article 16 ACHPR.

[206] Article 14 African Charter on the Rights and Welfare of the Child.

[207] Article 14 Protocol to the ACHPR on the Rights of Women in Africa.

physical and mental health'.[208] The UN Special Rapporteur on the right of everyone to the enjoyment of the highest attainable standard of physical and mental health[209] has elaborated, like the CESCR, that this right includes safe drinking water, sanitation, adequate food and 'timely and appropriate health care'.[210] The former Human Rights Commission has in relation to the right to health called upon the international community:

> "to enhance relief assistance to populations affected by devastation caused by natural disasters as well as by man-made events in order to ensure their physical and mental health recovery".[211]

Such a direct call to the international community in relation to the provision of humanitarian assistance and the right to health had already been made by the Special Rapporteur who declared that states not only have a duty to cooperate in the fulfilment of the right to health in general, but more specifically also in the provision of humanitarian assistance in the event of a humanitarian crisis, such as through the provision of water and medical aid.[212] Moreover, it has been emphasised by the Special Rapporteur that this shared responsibility in relation to humanitarian assistance and the right to health encompasses amongst others the provision of aid in order to 'facilitate access to essential health facilities'.[213] As such, the Special Rapporteur noted that the occurrence of a conflict or another humanitarian disaster can place a 'particular heavy burden' upon the mental health of a population.[214] Furthermore, the Special Rapporteur has underscored the

---

[208] UNCHR Res 1989/11 (2 March 1989) UN Doc E/CN.4/RES/1989/11 'Non-discrimination in the field of health' § 1.

[209] For an in -depth discussion on the role of the Special Rapporteur in relation to the development of the right to the highest attainable standard of health see Paul Hunt & Sheldon Leader, 'Developing and applying the right to the highest attainable standard of health: the role of the UN Special Rapporteur (2002-2008)', in John Harrington & Maria Stuttaford (eds) *Global Health and Human Rights: Legal and philosophical perspectives* (Routledge 2010) 28-62.

[210] Report of the Chairperson-Rapporteur of the Working Group on Arbitrary Detention, Leila Zerrougui; the Special Rapporteur on the independence of judges and lawyers, Leandro Despouy; the Special Rapporteur on torture and other cruel, inhuman or degrading treatment or punishment, Manfred Nowak; the Special Rapporteur on freedom of religion or belief, Asma Jahangir; and the Special Rapporteur on the right of everyone to the enjoyment of the highest attainable standard of physical and mental health, Paul Hunt (27 February 2006) UN Doc E/CN.4/2006/120 'Situation of detainees at Guantánamo Bay' § 69; Report of the Special Rapporteur on the right of everyone to the enjoyment of the highest attainable standard of physical and mental health (31 January 2008) A/HRC/7/11 § 45.

[211] UNCHR Res 2005/24 (15 April 2005) UN Doc E/CN.4/RES/2005/24 'The right of everyone to the enjoyment of the highest attainable standard of physical and mental health' § 3.

[212] Report of the Special Rapporteur on the right of everyone to the enjoyment of the highest attainable standard of physical and mental health (13 February 2003) UN Doc E/CN.4/2003/58 § 29; Report of the Special Rapporteur (11 February 2005) UN Doc E/CN.4/2005/51 § 62; and Report of the Special Rapporteur (31 January 2008) UN Doc A/HRC/7/11 § 60.

[213] Report of the Special Rapporteur 'The right of everyone to the enjoyment of the highest attainable standard of physical and mental health' (12 September 2005) UN Doc A/60/348 § 60 and § 64.

[214] UN Doc E/CN.4/2005/51, Report of the Special Rapporteur on the right of everyone to the enjoyment of the highest attainable standard of physical and mental health, 11 February 2005 § 22.

interdependence of the right to health with other essential human rights such as amongst others the rights to life and food.[215]

Lastly, the UN General Assembly – and thereby providing a reflection of the current view of UN Member States – has also embraced the right to the highest attainable standard of health on numerous occasions over the past decades, clearly establishing that the UN supports the efforts made by the various regional and international treaty bodies to underscore the right to health.[216] Such a UN-wide embracement and endorsement of the connection between the provision of humanitarian assistance and the fulfilment of the right to health must also be seen as indicative of the general consensus within the UN to this end. Numerous bodies within the organisation clearly view the provision of assistance as a means to ensure the enjoyment of the right to health, and thereby reflect the position of their Member States.

5.4.6 Humanitarian Assistance and the Right to Health

As can be seen from the above, the discussion of the right to health involves many references to the right to adequate food as well as some to the right to water; as both food and water are distinctly necessary in the fulfilment of the right to health. Equally, various references are made and emphasis is placed on the need for states to cooperate internationally. Furthermore, and most importantly, *humanitarian assistance and the right to health* have been distinctly linked, as states have an obligation under the ICESCR in the prevention of diseases and according to the CESCR in the provision of emergency medical aid therefore, relevant to the fulfilment of the right to health in the event of a humanitarian crisis. Such a connection has also been made by the UN bodies in their endorsement of the existence of a human right to health. Thus, here too the provision of assistance has been connected to the fulfilment of the right to health on several occasions, strengthening the viewpoint that such provision can often be necessary to ensure that these particular human rights are fulfilled.

Contrary to the central provisions relating to the rights to life and food that greatly find common ground as can be seen in the above, the content and scope of the provisions concerning the right to health in many international and regional conventions, and states obligations in the fulfilment thereof, differ to a significant extent from each other as well as from the nearly universally ratified ICESCR. Most notably, the degree of elaboration as to what can be considered part of the right to the highest attainable standard of health varies. Thus, it remains difficult to establish *consensus* on the current content of notion of 'health' or the related 'right

[215] Report of the Special Rapporteur (13 February 2003) UN Doc E/CN.4/2003/58 § 31.

[216] See amongst others UNGA Res 46/91 (16 December 1991) UN Doc A/RES/46/91 'Implementation of the International Plan of Action on Ageing and related activities' § 1 and § 11; UNGA Res 46/119 (17 December 1991) UN Doc A/RES/46/119 'The protection of persons with mental illness and the improvement of mental health care'; UNGA Res 48/104 (20 December 1993) UN Doc A/RES/48/104 'Declaration on the Elimination of Violence against Women', Article 3(f) in relation to women's rights and health; and UNGA Res S-26/2 (27 June 2001) 'Declaration of Commitment on HIV/AIDS'.

to health'. What *can* be discerned is that in relation to humanitarian assistance, prevention of diseases and priority of medical aid to vulnerable populations can be considered part of the right to the highest attainable standard of health.

Thus, although a level of uncertainty exists with regard to the wider scope of application of the right to health, a common ground can be found. In particular of importance to this research with regard to humanitarian assistance, from the various treaty provisions it can be discerned that consensus exists as to the fact that part of the right to the highest attainable standard of health is undoubtedly the obligation (of conduct) resting upon states to prevent diseases and give priority to medical aid delivery to vulnerable populations. This would in fact be part of the 'minimum core obligations' to adhere to under the ICESCR.

5.4.7 The Right to Water

Like the right to adequate food and health, the right to water can be considered one of the rights that is relevant and supplies content to the concept of humanitarian assistance. However, unlike the right to food and health, none of the large international instruments such as the UDHR, ICCPR or ICESCR recognise an independent human right to water, nor do the large regional treaties such as the ECHR, ACHR and ACHPR. Yet, some of the more specialised international treaties do, such as the Convention on the Rights of the Child that considers a duty for States Parties to strive to provide through 'appropriate measures' that all children are provided with clean drinking water.[217] Also, the CEDAW lays an obligation upon States Parties to ensure women have an adequate water supply, in relation to the enjoyment of adequate living conditions, as well as the Convention on the Rights of Persons with Disabilities, which proclaims States Parties to have the obligation to ensure equal access to clean water service for persons with disabilities.[218] Likewise, the Additional Protocol to the ACHPR on the Rights of Women in Africa places the obligation upon States Parties in light of the right to food to provide women with 'access to clean drinking water',[219] and the African Charter on the Rights and Welfare of the Child contains the provision that States Parties must provide safe drinking water.[220] Thus, several international and regional instruments *do* contain provisions pertaining to the 'right to water', but in relation to other rights, such as the 'right to the highest attainable standard of health'.[221] Therefore, this possible right to water is not as well-developed or deeply embedded in the various international and regional legal instruments as the right to life, food or health. At most, the incorporation is haphazard, as it is regionally linked both to the right to food and the right to health, whilst at the international level considered

[217] Article 24(1)(c) CRC.
[218] Article 14(2)(h) CEDAW. See also Article 28 CRPD.
[219] Article 15(a) Additional Protocol to the ACHPR on the Rights of Women in Africa.
[220] Article 14(2)(c) African Charter on the Rights and Welfare of the Child. Currently, 45 countries of the 53 States member of the African Union have ratified the African Charter on the Rights and Welfare of the Child.
[221] See Section 5.4.6 Humanitarian Assistance and the Right to Health.

somewhat independently by specialised treaties with a specific scope, such as the CRC, CEDAW and the CRPD.

Thus, whilst codification initiatives do exist, the current status of the right to water in international treaty law is far from comprehensive, and far from covering most countries in the world with independent and specific treaty obligations. The African continent can be considered to have the furthest degree of implementation of the right to water, through the abovementioned specialised and regional treaties. Furthermore, these specific references to the right to water must be seen in the larger framework of these specialised treaties' efforts for equality for women and health for children, and as a result cannot truly be considered universally comprehensive.[222] On the European continent, the Committee of Ministers to the Council of Europe recommended that the right to water be considered *included* in the right to be free from hunger and the right to an adequate standard of living, as expressed in the European Charter on Water Resources.[223] This too is an indication that within the European human rights framework no independent human right to water is currently envisaged or forthcoming.

Although the ICESCR does not contain an independent provision related to the right to water, the CESCR has expressed itself through one of its 'General Comments'. The CESCR declares that the right to water can be derived from Articles 11 and 12 of the ICESCR, concerning the right to an adequate standard of living and to the highest attainable standard of health respectively, as well as being related to the right to life.[224] The fact that Article 11 ICESCR is not exhaustive in its list of provisions needed for an adequate standard of health indeed points in support of this interpretation.[225] Thus, the CESCR has defined the right to water to entitle every person to:

> "sufficient, safe, acceptable, physically accessible and affordable water for personal and domestic uses. An adequate amount of safe water is necessary to prevent death from

---

[222] Eyal Benvenisti, 'International Protection of the Right to Water', (October 2010) *Max Planck Encyclopedia of Public International Law* § 8 and Takele Soboka Bulto, 'The Emergence of the Human Right to Water in International Human Rights Law: Invention or Discovery?', (2011) 12 *Melbourne Journal of International Law* 2, 298.

[223] Recommendation Rec(2001)14 of the Committee of Ministers to member states on the European Charter on Water Resources (17 October 2001): Article 5 of the Charter of 26 May 1967.

[224] CESCR General Comment 15 (20 January 2003) UN Doc E/C.12/2002/11 'The Right to water (arts. 11 and 12 of the International Covenant on Economic Social and Cultural Rights' § 3. Earlier references by the CESCR on the right to water in relation to Article 11 can be found in its General Comment 6 (8 December 1995) 'The economic, social and cultural rights of older persons' § 5 and § 32, as well as General Comment 4 (13 December 1991) 'The right to adequate housing' § 8(b). The CESCR has furthermore referenced to the right to water in relation to Article 12 ICESCR in its CESCR General Comment 14 (n 183) § 4, § 11-12, § 15, § 36, § 40, § 43 (c), § 51.

[225] Kiefer & Brölmann, 'The Human Right to Water' (n 26) 195; and Bulto, 'The Emergence of the Human Right to Water in International Human Rights Law: Invention or Discovery?' (n 222) 300. Article 11 ICESCR declares that the right of all persons to an adequate standard of living is "including adequate food, clothing and housing", thereby leaving possibilities open for additions to this list.

dehydration, to reduce the risk of water-related disease and to provide for consumption, cooking, personal and domestic hygienic requirements".[226]

Although the abovementioned definition does not mention a relation to situations like a humanitarian emergency, the CESCR argues that adequate water includes availability, quality and accessibility, the latter of which should be provided to especially 'vulnerable sections of the population' such as IDPs.[227] Indeed accessibility of water is an aspect that is seen in other interpretations of this right also.[228] However, this 'reading' of a right in the ICESCR where it is clearly not incorporated as an individual right has been criticised and been argued to be somewhat too pro-active of the CESCR.[229] Granted, while the efforts of the CESCR can be considered constructive to the interpretation of existing provisions of the ICESCR, the attempt to establish a fully-fledged 'codified' human right to water through a 'General Comment' where it does not distinctly appear in the treaty itself, appears somewhat premature. While the fact that Article 11 ICESCR does not include an exhaustive list of what may be necessary to enjoy an adequate standard of health does indeed leave the door open to such suggestions, they should be considered in that light: as suggestions.

By establishing a correlation between the right to water, which is not encompassed independently in the ICESCR and the codified rights to an adequate standard of living and to the highest attainable standard of health, the CESCR considers the right to water to have legally binding implications upon States Parties to the ICESCR. For purposes of exploration, this will be discussed here too. The CESCR analyses the right to water in relation to Article 2 ICESCR and considers that although, like the codified rights of the ICESCR, the right to water indeed must be realised progressively, it too is subject to certain legal obligations with immediate effect.[230] With regard to the tiered approach, the CESCR notes that states have an obligation to respect the right to water by non-interference with the 'enjoyment' of this right, whilst obligations to protect require States Parties to the ICESCR to prevent any third parties from interfering with a person's enjoyment of the right to water.[231] Lastly, the obligation to 'fulfil' encompasses the obligations to 'facilitate, promote and provide'.[232] To 'facilitate the right to water' obligates states according to the CESCR to take positive measures in assisting persons in their

[226] CESCR General Comment 15 (n 224) § 2.

[227] Ibid § 12 and § 16. See in support of this also Benvenisti 'International Protection of the Right to Water' (n 222) § 3.

[228] Ibid Benvenisti § 2. See also Kiefer & Brölmann, 'The Human Right to Water' (n 26); and Margret Vidar, 'The Interrelationships between the Right to Food and Other Human Rights' in Wenche Barth Eide & Uwe Kracht (eds) *Food and Human Rights in Development* (Volume I) (Intersentia 2005) 150-151.

[229] Bulto, 'The Emergence of the Human Right to Water in International Human Rights Law: Invention or Discovery?' (n 222) 293-294.

[230] CESCR General Comment 15 (n 224) § 17. See Section 5.2.2.1 Progressive Realisation in the ICESCR for the discussion of Article 2 ICESCR and the notion of 'progressive realization'.

[231] Ibid General Comment 15 § 21 and § 23-24.

[232] Ibid § 25.

enjoyment of this right, while also obligating them to adopt measures for the full realisation thereof.[233] Furthermore, states are required to ensure access to adequate sanitation as part of the fulfilment of the right to water.[234] Such access may be of special relevance in the aftermath of a disaster or in times of conflict, when large groups of people are displaced.

Article 2 and 11 ICESCR furthermore require states to cooperate internationally in the realisation of the right to water, in particular providing aid where this may be needed. The CESCR argues that:

> "In disaster relief and emergency assistance, including assistance to refugees and displaced persons, priority should be given to Covenant rights, including the provision of adequate water. International assistance should be provided in a manner that is consistent with the Covenant and other human rights standards".[235]

Thus, the States Parties to the ICESCR are under the obligation to cooperate internationally in the provision of emergency aid in the event of a humanitarian crisis, and the right to water amongst other rights of the ICESCR is to be prioritised in that context according to the Committee. In particular, relevant to this research regarding humanitarian assistance, the CESCR calls upon states to take steps to ensure that water is provided to victims of natural disasters.[236] In doing so and linking the right to water to the existing rights in the treaty, the Committee arguably attempts to establish that states have a legally binding obligation to provide water to victims of natural disaster as part of the envisaged human right to water.

Several of the obligations flowing from the right to water can be considered 'minimum core obligations' according to the CESCR.[237] It identifies nine such specific obligations resting upon states; most relevant in relation to the provision of humanitarian assistance are the obligations to ensure equitable distribution of and physical access to a minimum amount of water on a non-discriminatory basis, and to take measures in the prevention and controlling of diseases that may be linked to water.[238] Clearly these minimum core obligations are of relevance in the provision of humanitarian assistance, as the existence of any form of a humanitarian crisis can include the absence of sufficient access to (clean) water. Thus, from the fact that the CESCR notes many core obligations of the envisaged right to water that are related to the provision of humanitarian assistance it follows that the provision of humanitarian assistance is indeed a manner to obtain the fulfilment of this right to water, should it be recognised as such.

---

[233] Ibid § 25-26.

[234] Ibid § 29. For further discussion on the right to sanitation as part of the right to water, see CESCR Statement on the Right to Sanitation (19 November 2010) UN Doc E/C.12/2010/1.

[235] CESCR General Comment 15 (n 224) § 34.

[236] Ibid § 16(h).

[237] See Section 5.2.2.1 Progressive Realisation in the ICESCR for the discussion of Article 2 ICESCR and the notion of 'minimum core obligations'.

[238] CESCR General Comment 15 (n 224) § 37.

As seen in the previous Sections regarding the rights to food and health, the minimum core obligations are not subject to 'progressive realization', but are amongst the obligations that require states to take immediate steps upon ratification of the ICESCR. As a result, in the event a state does not abide by these core obligations that are non-derogable according to the CESCR, a violation of the right to water will occur in each instance in the view of the Committee, despite the fact that the right to water is not independently incorporated in the ICESCR.[239] As was discussed in relation to the right to food and health, a state's unwillingness to comply with the duties as set out by these minimum core obligations must be distinguished from its *inability*, although both may equally result in a violation. Especially relevant in relation to the provision of humanitarian assistance is the CESCR's statement that a state's 'failure to adopt mechanisms for emergency relief' is to be considered such a violation.[240] Lastly, also considering the relation to humanitarian assistance, the Committee notes the importance of the role of international organisations, considering that vulnerable groups should be prioritised in the provision of aid and water.[241]

Whereas the above evidences that a distinct right to water is lacking in current treaty law, the proactive stance of the CESCR certainly contributes to the argument that some *opinio juris* exists to recognise such a right. In this regard, the position of the UN and its Member States is considered, with a view to the potential existence of a right to water in customary international law. In 2010 the UN General Assembly declared by consensus that it:

> "recognizes the right to safe and clean drinking water and sanitation as a human right that is essential for the full enjoyment of life and all human rights".[242]

Although a relevant step by state practice in the process towards international legal recognition of the right to water, this resolution does not envisage duties of a legally binding nature to rest upon states. Building forth on this, the Human Rights Council, which had for several years already concerned itself with human rights and the access to water,[243] declared a few months after the General Assembly that it:

> "Affirms that the human right to safe drinking water and sanitation is derived from the right to an adequate standard of living and inextricably related to the right to the highest

[239] Ibid § 40.
[240] Ibis § 44.
[241] Ibid § 60.
[242] UNGA Res 64/292 (28 July 2010) UN Doc A/64/292 'Human Right to Water and Sanitation' § 1.
[243] See in that regard UNHRC Res 7/22 (28 March 2008) UN Doc A/HRC/7/22 'Human rights and access to safe drinking water and sanitation' in which the Council instated an independent expert on the issue of human rights obligations related to access to safe drinking water and sanitation; and UNHRC Res 12/8 (1 October 2009) UN Doc A/HRC/RES/12/8 'Human rights and access to safe drinking water and sanitation'. See also UNHRC Decision 2/104 (27 November 2006) UN Doc A/HRC/DEC/2/104 'Human rights and access to water'.

attainable standard of physical and mental health, as well as the right to life and human dignity".[244]

Linking the right to water and sanitation to the right to the highest attainable standard of health as well as the right to life enables the Human Rights Council, like the CESCR, to place the right to water within the categories of internationally recognised human rights obligations of a binding nature. Thus, the UN has embraced the development of the right to water and sanitation to a greater extent over the last few years as seen in particular by the fact that the above General Assembly Resolution was adopted by consensus.

However, at this time, a crystallised independent human right to water has not been codified in international treaty law. Only to the extent that these instruments do recognise such a right, it is seen as a derivative of, or explicitly linked to the right to the highest attainable standard of health or the right to an adequate standard of living. The UN High Commissioner on Human Rights acknowledges these considerations, but with a more progressive perspective argues that clear obligations for states *can* be found within human rights law relating to access to water, and that the time has come to consider it a human right.[245] A similar approach can be noted by the UN Special Rapporteur on the human right to safe drinking water and sanitation,[246] arguing that although a discussion may still be on-going, the right to sanitation can be considered not only to follow from obligations found in other rights, but that such a right must also be seen as a distinct right on its own account.[247] The Special Rapporteur furthermore emphasises that states are required to abide by their obligations with regard to the respect for the right to sanitation also in time of emergency, including disasters and conflicts.[248] In that regard, the Rapporteur notes an obligation of states to actively provide sanitation services only in certain instances, one of these being the aftermath of a natural disaster.[249] With regard to the provision of humanitarian assistance or aid, the Special Rapporteur has aligned itself with the Human Rights Council, which has merely 'stressed' the important role of international cooperation in the fulfilment of the right to water, with no direct or indirect reference to the notion of humanitarian

244 UNHRC Res 15/9 (30 September 2010) UN Doc A/HRC/RES/15/9 'Human rights and access to safe drinking water and sanitation' § 3. The Human Rights Council reiterated this approach in UNHRC Res 16/2 (8 April 2011) UN Doc A/HRC/RES/16/2 'Human rights and access to safe drinking water and sanitation' § 1; and UNHRC Res 18/L.1 (23 September 2011) UN Doc A/HRC/18/L.1 § 1.

245 'Report of the United Nations High Commissioner for Human Rights on the scope and content of the relevant human rights obligations related to equitable access to safe drinking water and sanitation under international human rights instruments' (16 August 2007) UN Doc A/HRC/6/3 § 46-47, 49 and 66.

246 Originally the UN independent expert 'on the issue of human rights obligations related to access to safe drinking water and sanitation'.

247 'Report of the independent expert on the issue of human rights obligations related to access to safe drinking water and sanitation' (1 July 2009) UN Doc A/HRC/12/24 § 81.

248 Ibid § 81(a).

249 Ibid § 67.

assistance.[250] More recently, the Rapporteur has however noted that a failure of states to 'seek and accept international assistance where needed' is a common cause of violation of the right to water as well as their failure to 'respond promptly' through the provision of assistance in times of emergencies and 'to allow access to humanitarian service providers'.[251] As such the Rapporteur is aligning more with the CESCR, claiming a violation of the right to water should humanitarian assistance not be provided.

5.4.8 Humanitarian Assistance and the Right to Water

It has become apparent that the development of a right to water and sanitation has progressed rapidly over the last decade, following the CESCR's interpretative comments on the right to an adequate standard of living and the highest attainable standard of health.[252] However, given the lack of proper individual implementation in binding international legal documents at this point in time, it is not possible to truly speak of a codified human right to water. As a result, the relationship between the right to water and sanitation and humanitarian assistance, and a state's obligations in that regard, remains ambiguous. The UN's human rights bodies indeed embrace a progressive approach, but do not assertively declare rights or duties with regard to the provision of aid, making it difficult to definitively establish state practice or *opinio juris* amounting to customary international law. It is rather the CESCR that has argued that states have a duty in the provision of humanitarian assistance to cooperate in the fulfilment of the right to water. While the ICESCR itself does not contain an independent right to water, the CESCR has furthermore argued that states are in violation of that right in the event they do not adopt measures for emergency assistance, in particular related to the victims of disaster situations. Both the CESCR and several of the UN bodies therefore take a proactive stance in arguing the existence of a right to water, but take a different approach, with only the CESCR focusing on the right to water *in relation* to the provision of humanitarian assistance.

Thus, with a lack of proper individual implementation of this right through legally binding obligations, a current human right to water is undeniably lacking. Its haphazard implementation in several of the more specific treaties such as the

---

[250] UNHRC Res 15/9 (30 September 2010) UN Doc A/HRC/RES/15/9 'Human rights and access to safe drinking water and sanitation' § 10; UNHRC Res 16/2 (8 April 2011) UN Doc A/HRC/RES/16/2 'Human rights and access to safe drinking water and sanitation' § 7; UNHRC Res 18/L.1 (23 September 2011) UN Doc A/HRC/18/L.1 § 9. See also the Report by the independent expert on the issue of human rights obligations related to access to safe drinking water and sanitation 'Human rights obligations related to access to safe drinking water and sanitation' (6 August 2010) UN Doc A/65/254 § 19.

[251] Report of the Special Rapporteur on the human right to safe drinking water and sanitation 'Common violations of the human rights to water and sanitation' (30 June 2014) UN Doc A/HRC/27/55 § 41 and 53.

[252] See for an in depth discussion on the evolution of the right to water over the past decades. Salman M A Salman and Siobhán McInerney-Lankford, 'The Human Right to Water: Legal and Policy Dimensions', The World Bank *Law, Justice and Development Series* (2004).

CEDAW, CRPD and CRC – given their limited scope – is not sufficient for an unambiguous assertion in this regard. The consensus found within the UN can in fact be considered indicative of a *potential* forthcoming customary international law norm concerning the right to water, yet these bodies – as mentioned above – do not envisage clear obligations for states with regard to this right. Currently, no option rests but to conclude that although developments are continuous, currently no independent human right to water exists. As a result, the lack of such a right prevents its concrete connection to the provision of humanitarian assistance. However, what *can* be established is that through the interpretative remarks of the UN bodies and in particular the CESCR, the provision of humanitarian assistance remains essential to the fulfilment of this possible future right to water.

5.5 Conclusion

This Chapter has analysed the existence of a possible independent human right to receive humanitarian assistance. Placing the provision of humanitarian assistance within the human rights framework will allow for protection through human rights law in circumstances amounting to a humanitarian crisis, regardless of their occurrence in times of peace or conflict. Firstly, a brief discussion of the development of human rights was necessary, creating a historical context and assessing the various categories or generations of human rights.[253] Upon establishing that a potential human right to humanitarian assistance could be categorised as a so-called 'third generation', or 'solidarity' right, while acknowledging the notion of group rights, the content of the possible human right was considered.[254] Hereafter, the provision of assistance as part of the existing legal framework of the rights to life, food, health and water has been considered.

5.5.1 Humanitarian Assistance as an Independent Human Right

From the above Chapter, it becomes clear that certain efforts are being made to establish a right to receive humanitarian assistance, despite its current absence from international treaty law and practice. Indeed, such a right in relation to refugee and IDP-children has been claimed not only internationally in the CRC, but also regionally in Africa through the African Charter on the Rights and Welfare of the Child and the Kampala Convention. These attempts, next to the efforts of various soft law documents, have placed the concept of humanitarian assistance directly within the human rights discourse. However, determining whether there is such an emerging norm in customary international law may be stretching the norm from its current stance.[255] Although the existence of a degree of *opinio juris* can be derived from the various efforts pertaining to establishing a right to receive assistance in the

[253] See Section 5.2 The Development of Human Rights Relevant to Humanitarian Assistance.
[254] See Section 5.2.1. 'Generations' of Human Rights in Relation to Humanitarian Assistance.
[255] See section 5.3.2 Humanitarian Assistance as a Potential Human Right in Customary International Law.

work of international organisations, as well as the previously discussed embracement in literature of a right to such assistance as part of a 'third generation' of human rights,[256] established state practice is currently absent. Given the considerable uniformity and widespread practice needed to be able to consider the formation of customary international law, it is too soon to speak of such a development.[257] Indeed the commitment to recognise responsibility towards the victims of disasters is found in many soft law documents, but is not (yet) legally binding as a human right.[258] States have been hesitant or unwilling to acknowledge the existence of a right to receive humanitarian assistance, as can also be derived from the absence of General Assembly or Security Council resolutions proclaiming the existence of such an independent right. States' lack of interpretative comments regarding potential relevant provisions in the human rights treaties they are party to cannot be seen as such an indication however, as the incorporation of humanitarian assistance into the human rights framework and discourse developed at a later time than the creation of such treaties.

Another possible issue arising is the more material question of the scope and content of the possible right to humanitarian assistance, in relation to the rights-holders and duty-bearers of such a potential right as also concluded in Section 5.3.4 (Preliminary Conclusion). 'Third generation' or solidarity rights often proclaim broad concepts, such as 'development' or 'peace' for which a wide range of government activities could be ranked as part of the state's obligation to fulfil such a right, enhancing the difficulty in establishing what amounts to state practice.[259] However, in the situation of a possible human right to humanitarian assistance, it is submitted that the scope and content of such a right would be confined to the essence of the notion of 'humanitarian assistance' itself, whilst the conditions of its application could be said to be intrinsically linked to the existence of a humanitarian crisis.[260] As such, the potential right to humanitarian assistance would only entail those items necessary for the immediate survival of people, and the right to request such assistance would only be applicable in the situation of an immediate humanitarian emergency. Thus, although the notion of humanitarian assistance is indeed a 'solidarity' or 'group' right by its nature, contrary to the possible right to peace or development with rather aspirational characters, it is clearly confined by well-defined boundaries in content and scope.

However, being able to define said content and scope, as well as the conditions for its application, does not result in the ability to indeed establish the formation of

---

[256] See Section 5.2.2 Derogability, Human Rights and the Provision of Humanitarian Assistance.
[257] North Sea Continental Shelf cases (Federal Republic Of Germany/Denmark; Federal Republic of Germany/Netherlands) Judgment Of 20 February 1969, I.C.J. Reports 1969, p. 3, § 73-74.
[258] 'Report of the Independent Expert on human rights and international solidarity' (22 July 2009) UN Doc A/HRC/12/27 § 35.
[259] Roht-Arriaza & Aminzadeh, 'Solidarity Rights: Development, Peace, Environment, Humanitarian Assistance' (n 94) § 24 and Hardcastle & Chua, 'Humanitarian Assistance, Towards a Right of access to victims of natural disaster' (n 32) 594.
[260] See supra Sections 2.2.2 Defining Humanitarian Assistance and 3.3.3 Defining a Humanitarian Crisis for the proposed definitions of humanitarian assistance and a humanitarian crisis.

a right to humanitarian assistance. Indeed, problematic to the acceptance of a potential right to humanitarian assistance remain the questions that continue to be raised with regard to possible rights-*holders* and the matter of possible duty-bearers (see Section 5.3.4). Key is in particular the fact that a 'humanitarian crisis' must exist for the need for humanitarian assistance to become acute. Such a crisis by its very nature results in the involvement of various rights-holders and potentially more legally problematic, various duty-bearers. Currently indeed, no definitive incorporation can be found of such a right in customary international law or treaty law.

For some, the desirability of developing a (new) human right is questionable, thereby challenging the need for such a right to humanitarian assistance, as well as its viability.[261] Furthermore, it is argued that the enforcement of the *provision* of assistance is more important than its *realisation* as a right.[262] Yet, framing the receipt and delivery of humanitarian assistance in a human rights context is quite possible and logical, considering the UN General Assembly's view in the requirements proposed for the development of new human rights and that these should:

> "(a) be consistent with the existing body of international human rights law; (b) be of fundamental character and derive from the inherent dignity and worth of the human person; (c) be sufficiently precise to give rise to identifiable and practicable rights and obligations; (d) provide, where appropriate, realistic and effective implementation machinery, including reporting systems; (e) attract broad international support".[263]

When applying such requirements to humanitarian assistance, it is indeed given that the content of humanitarian assistance can be found in the rights to life, food, health (and water). It is of fundamental necessity for the survival of persons in the aftermath of a humanitarian crisis, it has a clear and identifiable content and scope, there is a possibility to identify implementation mechanisms and lastly has support in the international community. It may therefore indeed be justifiably developed into an independent human right within the UN context. Whether this development occurs through the possible incorporation in an international human rights treaty or through the further development of state practice in customary international law, however, remains to be seen. Although arguments exist against the development of such an independent human right, it may however also contribute to the progressive development of human rights law and at the same time to the prevention of

---

[261] Hardcastle & Chua, 'Humanitarian Assistance, Towards a Right of access to victims of natural disaster' (n 32) 594.

[262] Joakim Dungel, 'A Right to Humanitarian Assistance in Internal Armed Conflicts Respecting Sovereignty, Neutrality and Legitimacy: Practical Proposals to Practical Problems', (2004) *Journal of Humanitarian Assistance*, 1 <http://sites.tufts.edu/jha/archives/838> accessed 24 November 2014.

[263] UNGA Res 41/120 (4 December 1986) UN Doc A/RES/41/120 'Setting international standards in the field of human rights' § 4.

fragmentation of the law, in order to establish equal protection to all persons regardless of the disaster they have endured.[264]

Whilst it is accepted from the above findings that the way has been freed for the potential development of an individual right to receive humanitarian assistance should the international community so decide, it is by no means argued in this research that such a right *must* in fact be developed. The creation of new law must be cautioned against when existing law can satisfactorily provide in legal protection, as the proliferation of norms often results in legal uncertainty concerning their value and content. Indeed, the existing human rights framework provides ample protection of persons facing humanitarian crises as it *requires* the provision of emergency aid as fulfilment of these existing rights to life, food and health.

Indeed, it is suggested in this research that as international protection of those in need of emergency aid through an individual human right to receive assistance is currently lacking, this protection must be sought through other rights that are generally accepted in international human rights law. It is through the provision of humanitarian assistance that these internationally recognised rights can be fulfilled and persons in the midst of a humanitarian crisis can be protected.

5.5.2 Humanitarian Assistance as a Vehicle in the Fulfilment of Existing Human Rights

From the above Section 5.4, it can be concluded that the provision of humanitarian aid indeed supports the fulfilment of the essential aspects of the right to life, food and health, as has been recognised in the analysis of each of these rights. As such, the notion of 'survival rights' has been coined,[265] and certainly the right to receive humanitarian assistance could be considered to fall within this category of rights. It has been concluded that in order to fully enjoy one's right to life, food and health, it is necessary to receive humanitarian assistance in certain circumstances. The current developments with regard to the potential right to water have been noted, as well as the fact that such a right has not yet been codified to date, despite movements within the UN to accept this right, which would enable its potential development as a norm of customary international law. Given the well-defined provisions and interpretations of the right to food and health as related to the receipt of humanitarian assistance, it is not necessary for the purpose of this research to assert the existence of such a human right to water.

The ICESCR asserts that certain minimum core obligations must be met with regard to the right to food and health, granting persons in times of a humanitarian crisis the entitlement to receive such assistance, in order not to compromise the fulfilment of their rights. The same holds true regarding the right to not be arbitrarily deprived of one's life. Thus, receiving humanitarian assistance

---

264 Report of the independent expert on human rights and international solidarity (5 July 2010) UN Doc A/HRC/15/32 § 54.

265 Kiefer & Brölmann, 'The Human Right to Water' (n 26) 208.

substantially fulfils the right to life, food, health (and water) and may thereby be considered a *subsidiary* or underlying right and manner to realise an individual's right to life, food, health (and water).[266] In this manner, even though consensus with regard to the existence of an independent established human right to receive humanitarian assistance may be absent, both with regard to the issues of enforcement through determination of rights-holders and its codification in treaty law or development in customary international law, the *provision itself* can be seen as a *vehicle* or a *means* to fulfil other existing human rights. In particular, the interpretative comments of the HRC and the CESCR support the stance that certain basic obligations resting upon states with regard to the right to life, food, health (and water) can be translated into the obligation under the ICCPR and ICESCR to provide humanitarian assistance in a situation of crisis.[267]

It remains essential that a people in need of assistance in the aftermath of a natural disaster, during conflict, occupation or other situation potentially amounting to a humanitarian crisis gain access to such humanitarian aid. Indeed, providing humanitarian assistance may be the substantial fulfilment of a states' obligation to ensure a person's right to life, food and health. Such provision must remain in accordance with the principles of humanity, neutrality and impartiality. Within a human rights context, as has also been asserted by the ICJ, such provision must remain in accordance with the International Convention on the Elimination of all forms of Racial Discrimination and occur on the basis of non-discrimination.[268] This latter aspect is of particular relevance in circumstances of non-international armed conflict or disaster where the affected persons form part of a (ostracised) minority group within a nation.

Framing the receipt of such assistance within a human rights context enforces the basis and standards upon which such provision takes place within the concept of human dignity. Furthermore, rather than being considered passive 'beneficiaries', those needing humanitarian assistance become 'individual human rights-holders' with claims against specific duty-bearers.[269] Thus, as currently no *independent* enforceable human right to receive humanitarian assistance exists, the content of this right will have to be further asserted through claiming potential violations of the existing rights to life, food, health (and water), which are at the disposal of those affected by humanitarian crises. Indeed, the absence of such an individual human right by no means implies that no rights or duties with regard to the receipt and provision of humanitarian assistance exist.

As such, the 'right to receive assistance' must be distinctly discerned from the more narrow 'human right to receive assistance'. Whilst it is not likely that the latter will develop in the near future as an independent human right, such a broader 'right to receive assistance' in certain circumstances *has* in fact been established

[266] Jakovljevic, 'Right to Humanitarian Action and State Sovereignty' (n 87) 97.
[267] See Section 5.4 Humanitarian Assistance Within the Context of Existing Human Rights.
[268] Article 5 ICERD and Section 5.3 A Human Right to Receive Humanitarian Assistance in International Law?.
[269] IASC, 'Protecting Persons Affected by Natural Disasters, IASC Operational Guidelines' (2006), 2.

through existing human rights. Such a right to receive emergency aid within a human rights context is in fact the fulfilment of the rights to life, food and health in times of humanitarian crises. In subsequent Chapters, its fulfilment in other *corpora juris* will be further addressed. Such a right to receive may be furthermore found in humanitarian law and other provisions of international law that will be addressed in more detail in particular relation to obligations of the state sovereign and other actors to provide such assistance.

From this Chapter, it can be concluded that *the provision of humanitarian assistance functions as a vehicle in the fulfilment of the rights to life, food and health in times of humanitarian crises*. This conclusion determines that such a right to receive assistance exists at all times of crises; whether peace or conflict, as the rights to life is non-derogable in times of emergency and the rights to food and health contain minimum core obligations that must indeed be implemented. The determination that the receipt of humanitarian assistance is a fulfilment of these human rights therefore actively *supports the approach in this research that the provision of humanitarian assistance must be seen in an all-encompassing manner*, rather than in a fragmented approach. Through the placement of humanitarian assistance within the protection of the framework of human rights law, persons in need of aid can actively claim such a right to aid in the fulfilment of their human rights, regardless of whether they find themselves in a non-international armed conflict or a natural disaster. This conclusion that the provision of humanitarian assistance is the execution of state obligations in the fulfilment of the rights to life, food and health is furthermore supported by the *opinio juris* found in this Chapter on the right to receive assistance, as well as the role asserted for state sovereigns' responsibilities in the twenty-first century, as determined in Chapter 4.

CHAPTER 6
THE DUTY OF THE AFFECTED STATE TO PROVIDE, AND THE RIGHT OF PERSONS TO RECEIVE HUMANITARIAN ASSISTANCE

In the face of the humanitarian crisis in Libya in 2011, the Security Council called upon those involved in the conflict, stating it:

> "Demands that the Libyan authorities comply with their obligations under international law, including international humanitarian law, human rights and refugee law and take all measures to protect civilians and meet their basic needs, and to ensure the rapid and unimpeded passage of humanitarian assistance".

What exactly are these 'obligations under international law' that a state or sovereign may have to provide humanitarian assistance? To what extent does international law place obligations hereto on the affected state, and what rights can the affected persons claim? This chapter addresses these questions within the legal framework on the provision of humanitarian assistance.[1]

6.1 Introduction

Where previous Chapters have assessed the background to the legal framework, such as the parties involved with humanitarian assistance, its scope of application and applicable law, matters of state sovereignty and the current developments in human rights law, this Chapter addresses at a more concrete level the *specific legal rights and duties* concerning the provision of humanitarian assistance in the *various potential circumstances*. The current Chapter focuses on the *lex lata* involved in the actual provision of assistance. As part of this assessment, the current developments in international law are also considered, such as state practice, treaty law and Security Council resolutions, as well as General Assembly resolutions, soft law mechanisms and codification initiatives that are currently on-going. This study approaches the legal framework concerning the provision of humanitarian assistance from an overarching perspective, focusing on the premise that persons in need of food, water and shelter in times of a humanitarian crisis should be able to gain access to such provisions, regardless of what circumstance put them in such a need. This perspective finds support in various areas of international law, as set out below, as well as the contemporary concept of state sovereignty as discussed in Chapter 4. The approach to these rights and duties must be from the perspective of

[1] UNSC Res 1973 (17 March 2011) UN Doc S/RES/1973 'The situation in Libya' § 3.

complementarity and the principle of humanity, which aligns with the fundamental aspects of the concept of humanitarian assistance. The very notion of humanitarian assistance, as has been asserted in previous Chapters, warrants an overarching and inclusive approach. In fact, this approach has also been taken in the law itself on numerous occasions. Therefore, this Chapter commences the assessment of the legal framework from an overall and general legal perspective, reaching the more specific circumstances of provision at the end.

The legal framework regarding the provision of humanitarian assistance can be divided into certain *legal* rights and *legal* duties. Whilst the horrific images that often cross our path through various media sources may cause a desire to provide assistance, such assistance is regulated by specific legal boundaries. The affected state may be held to certain duties to provide assistance under international law, whereas the persons in need of assistance may hold rights to receive such aid under international law, dependent on the various *corpora juris* involved. This Chapter therefore concretely addresses the various potential legal duties of the affected state in the provision of assistance in times of a humanitarian crisis, as well as the rights of the persons in need. A focus lies on the duties of the *affected state* as primary responsible actor; Chapter 7 will address the rights and duties that may be discerned for *international* assistance, which may be provided by third states or international organisations. The potential unwillingness of the affected state to provide assistance will also be addressed in this regard, as the assessment of such a potential gap in the law, taking state sovereignty into account, is crucial to the protection of persons in need of aid.

6.2 Duties and Rights under General International Law

The legal framework pertaining to the delivery of humanitarian assistance bases itself on several bodies of law, as seen in Chapter 3. From a general perspective, the concept of state sovereignty provides a structural guide to the various actors involved in the provision of assistance; internally and externally. Therefore, it is relevant to assess which duties and rights flow directly from the concept of state sovereignty. State sovereignty as a notion must be considered from a more abstract and elevated level, in a different manner than the other bodies of law that contain specific provisions regarding the delivery of emergency aid. The law pertaining to state sovereignty does not contain substantive provisions concerning the provision of emergency aid. The assessment regarding the potential rights and duties therefore are at a more abstract level, but provide the basis upon which the more substantive provisions are founded.

6.2.1 State Sovereignty and the Duty to Provide Humanitarian Assistance

Chapter 4 has addressed the concept of state sovereignty as international society views it today. The premise taken in this research regarding the concept of state sovereignty, and elaborated in Chapter 4 is that in international law today, sovereignty *can* and in fact *must* be seen to include responsibilities and obligations towards citizens by a sovereign.[2] When this concept is applied to the provision of humanitarian assistance, it stands to reason that the primary responsibility and duty to provide humanitarian assistance lies with the affected state on whose territory the humanitarian crisis takes place. This responsibility and duty naturally flows from the understanding of the concept of state sovereignty. Support for an overall and general responsibility of the affected state to provide assistance for persons within its jurisdiction when a humanitarian crisis arises can be found in the current notion of sovereignty, based on international humanitarian law, human rights law and UN Security Council and General Assembly resolutions as elaborated in more depth in this Chapter.[3] In respect of more regional state practice, the EU has equally asserted such a primary responsibility of the affected state.[4] This reasoning also follows from the analysis in Chapter 2 of the actors involved in the provision of assistance, where the affected state plays a primary role.[5] More recently, this notion of responsibility and of the primary role have been supported by the work of the ILC in its development of draft articles on 'Protection of persons in the event of disasters'. In particular Draft Article 12 declares a duty of the affected state 'by virtue of its sovereignty' to ensure those persons on its territory receive assistance.[6]

State sovereignty, as a legal concept, is a continued and constant standard throughout the entire fabric of international law, regardless of whether a (natural) disaster takes place, or a conflict.[7] As stated earlier, humanitarian assistance may be necessary in various (legally qualifiable) circumstances, invoking a wide range of legal regimes, rights and duties. From a general perspective however, state sovereignty is a continuous thread in the discussion and determination of the legal

---

[2] Section 4.2.3.3 Towards a new Definition of Sovereignty.

[3] See the provisions of the Geneva Conventions and multiple human rights treaties in 6.5 Duties and Rights in Specific Circumstances under International Law; UNGA Res 38/202 (20 December 1983) UN Doc A/RES/38/202 § 4; UNGA Res 43/131 (8 December 1988) UN Doc A/RES/43/131 § 2 and UNGA Res 45/100 (14 December 1990) UN Doc A/RES/45/100 § 2, in which the Assembly reaffirmed "the sovereignty of affected States and their primary role in the initiation, organization, coordination and implementation of humanitarian assistance within their respective territories"; UNGA Res 46/182 (19 December 1991) UN Doc A/RES/46/182 Annex § 4 ("Each State has the responsibility first and foremost to take care of the victims of natural disasters and other emergencies occurring on its territory"); ILC 'Protection of persons in the event of disasters' Memorandum by the Secretariat (11 December 2007) UN Doc A/CN/4/590 § 23: "the receiving State has the primary responsibility for the protection of persons on its territory or subject to its jurisdiction or control during a disaster". Such a position can also be derived from the fact that many states have adopted at a domestic level legislation pertaining to the provision of assistance in the event of a crisis occurring on their territory or under their jurisdiction.

[4] 'Joint Statement by the Council and the Representatives of the Governments of the Member States meeting within the Council, the European Parliament and the European Commission' (European Consensus on Humanitarian Aid) (30 January 2008) EU Doc 2008/C/25/01 § 4: "National authorities in countries faced with crisis retain the primary responsibility for protecting populations confronting disaster".

[5] 2.3.2.1 The Affected State and subsequent Sections in this Chapter.

[6] ILC 'Protection of persons in the event of disasters' Draft Articles UN Doc. A/CN.4/L.831 (15 May 2014) Draft Article 12.

[7] Article 2(1) UN Charter provides an example, with one singular concept of sovereignty.

rights and duties in the provision of assistance. The concept of state sovereignty and the responsibilities found therein also support the perspective taken in this research concerning an overarching approach to the provision of humanitarian assistance. As the concept of state sovereignty including its legal responsibilities towards citizens remains one and the same throughout all aspects of international law and adapts as a whole with time, the notion places the same sovereign obligation in that regard upon states throughout the various circumstances in which humanitarian assistance must be provided. As such, the concept of state sovereignty and the legal obligations flowing from this support the overarching manner in which the provision of humanitarian assistance can be approached, focusing on the need to provide assistance regardless of specific circumstances.

The failure of proper execution of state sovereignty and its duties leads to state responsibility in international law, as Chapter 8 addresses. However, relevant to the establishment of the sovereign duties in this Chapter as pertaining to the provision of emergency assistance that might incur state responsibility, it is relevant to note at the outset that such duties are not refrained to the legal sovereigns *per se*. As the ICJ has addressed in its Advisory Opinion on the *Legal Consequences for States of the Continued Presence of South Africa in Namibia*:

> "physical control of a territory, and not sovereignty or legitimacy of title, is the basis of State liability for acts affecting other States".[8]

The duty-bearing responsibility or 'title' of sovereignty is then transferred from the state, to the *de facto* controller of a certain territory. This assessment is relevant to the provision of humanitarian assistance in particular in times of non-international armed conflicts, or for example natural disasters in conflict areas, resulting in complex emergencies. Indeed in such situations a power struggle often affects the potential to receive aid. The assertion that obligations may be transferred to non-state actors such as *de facto* regimes may furthermore be relevant in circumstances of a collapse of state authority. Such humanitarian crises warrant the delivery of humanitarian aid, but the state sovereign may be unable to provide this due to a loss of control in a specific area. Thus, *de facto* regimes or other non-state entities can be held responsible under international law, when adopting such a pragmatic view as done by the ICJ, for the provision of assistance. As such, when considering the obligations towards citizens, it has become more and more accepted in international law that regimes exercising *de facto* control, or non-state actors, must abide by the substantive provisions concerning the delivery of humanitarian aid in general international law, including human rights obligations, *as would* the state sovereign.[9]

---

[8] Legal Consequences for States of the Continued Presence of South Africa in Namibia (South West Africa) notwithstanding Security Council Resolution 276 (1970), Advisory Opinion, ICJ Reports (1971) p. 16, § 118.

[9] See amongst others Andrew Clapham, 'Human rights obligations of non-state actors in conflict situations', (2006) 88 International Review of the Red Cross 863, 522; Christian Tomuschat, 'The Applicability of Human Rights Law to Insurgent Movements', in Horst Fischer, Ulrika Froissart, Wolff Heintschel von Heinegg and Christian Raap (eds), *Krisensicherung und Humanitärer Schutz – Crisis*

Similarly, such entities must abide by international humanitarian law provisions, as for example common Article 3 of the Geneva Conventions and Article 1 of Additional Protocol II assert their applicability to armed forces not belonging to the state sovereign.[10] More specifically the Kampala Convention *directly* addresses the responsibilities of armed forces, indicating a continuous increasing acceptance of the responsibilities of armed forces as acting 'authorities' within a certain territory, thereby taking on the responsibilities bestowed upon sovereigns, such as the provision of humanitarian assistance.[11]

Similarly, it has been increasingly accepted that whilst states are the primary duty-bearers of obligations under human rights law, non-state actors can hold such responsibilities too. Indeed, the Security Council has for many years asserted the responsibility of armed groups as 'parties to a conflict' to abide by duties under human rights law.[12] Clearly, in such instances, the Security Council is addressing non-state actors in a conflict, as opposed to merely addressing states. The Council furthermore addressed the duties of these 'parties' under human rights law and international law in general, rather than confining their duties to those under humanitarian law. Where some believe that non-state actors should only be held accountable under international humanitarian law, Clapham aligns with the Security Council and argues this perspective to be untenable as the application of humanitarian law is often contested in circumstances involving non-state actors, warranting the application of obligations under human rights law.[13] Alston concurs, declaring that although non-state actors may not be signatories to certain human rights treaties, they do remain 'subject to the demand of the international community' as expressed in the UDHR, stating that every organ of the international society should respect human rights.[14] This stance is also supported by the Articles on the Responsibility of States for Internationally Wrongful Acts (ARSIWA), declaring that a successful insurrectional movement shall be held responsible for

Management and Humanitarian Protection: Festschrift für Dieter Fleck, Berliner Wissenschafts-Verlag (Berliner Wissenschafstverlag 2004) 586; and H Steiner, P Alston & R Goodman, *International Human Rights in Context: Law, Politics, Morals* (Oxford University Press 2007) 675, 1420.

[10] See for a more in depth discussion of the applicability of these treaties to non-state actors 3.2.1 Defining an Armed Conflict.

[11] African Union Convention for the Protection and Assistance of Internally Displaced Persons in Africa (Kampala 22 October 2009) Article 7.

[12] See amongst others UNSC Res 1265 (17 September 1999) UN Doc S/RES/1265 § 4; UNSC Res 1863 (9 July 2009) UN Doc S/RES/1863 § 19 and UNSC Res 2036 (22 February 2012) UN Doc S/RES/2036 §16 that provides an example, stating that the Council: "Demands that all parties and armed groups take appropriate steps to ensure the safety and security of humanitarian personnel and supplies, and further demands that all parties ensure full and unhindered access for the timely delivery of humanitarian aid to persons in need of assistance across Somalia, consistent with humanitarian, human rights and refugee law".

[13] Clapham, 'Human rights obligations of non-state actors in conflict situations' (n 9) 505.

[14] 'Civil And Political Rights, Including The Question Of Disappearances And Summary Executions: Extrajudicial, summary or arbitrary executions' Report of the Special Rapporteur Philip Alston Addendum 'Mission to Sri Lanka' UN Doc E/CN.4/2006/53/Add.5 (27 March 2006) § 25. See also August Reinisch, 'The Changing International Legal Framework for Dealing with Non-State Actors' in Philip Alston (ed) *Non-State Actors and Human Rights* (Oxford University Press 2005) 71.

violations of international law incurred *prior* to their evolvement as a new government or state.[15] In relation to the provision of humanitarian assistance and responsibilities of non-state actors, support can also be sought in practice, when factual agreements are considered between states and non-state actors. In many of these agreements, it is stipulated that the recipients of humanitarian assistance are entitled amongst others to the right to receive assistance according to basic needs, the right to live in security and the rights to legal and effective human rights protection.[16] Hence, in practice it appears that non-state actors are also taking voluntarily certain human rights obligations upon themselves, next to the existence of certain obligations under the law.[17] The debate is continuous and on-going as to the extent of potential other obligations, but as Chapter 8 addresses in further detail, when in the exercise of control, armed groups or other non-state actors can be held responsible for violations of international (human rights) law.[18]

It must therefore be concluded at this point, however, that the current understanding of state sovereignty entails an overall and general obligation for the affected state to provide assistance to its population when in a humanitarian crisis. In the absence of such a sovereign, the non-state actor exercising control shall take up such duties (under human rights law). The specificities of such responsibilities will be discussed in more depth throughout this Chapter.

6.2.2 State Sovereignty and the Right to Receive Humanitarian Assistance

The law concerning state sovereignty is geared specifically towards the notion of the responsibilities of the sovereign state, and as such does not immediately spring to mind when considering a potential 'right to receive assistance'. Yet, although much of the law focuses on a duty of the affected state, as *conduct* is required to provide the actual food, water and medicine, state sovereignty has developed to increasingly include rights of citizens. Chapter 4 has discussed that the concept of state sovereignty suggests a reciprocal relationship between the sovereign and society.[19] As the concept of sovereignty is viewed as a 'social contract' between sovereign and citizens, the latter obtain rights in relation to the power they have

[15] Article 10 ARSIWA. See also Article 9 ARSIWA. For a more in depth discussion, see Section 8.2 The Law of State Responsibility and Enforcement of Humanitarian Assistance

[16] Jean-Daniel Vigny and Cecilia Thompson, 'Fundamental Standards of Humanity: What Future?', (2002) 20 *Netherlands Quarterly of Human Rights* 192-194 concerning the codes of conducts in the situations of Burundi, Liberia, Somalia, Sierra Leone, Afghanistan, Sudan, Democratic Republic of the Congo, Angola, East and West Timor, Democratic People's Republic of Korea and the Russian Federation.

[17] See for example the Agreement between the Transitional Federal Government of Somalia (TFG) and the Alliance for the Re-Liberation of Somalia (ARS), (Djibouti 9 June 2008) § 8(a) and the Lome Peace Agreement between the Government of the Republic of Sierra Leone and the Revolutionary United Front of Sierra Leone (RUF/SL), (June 3rd 1999) Article XXVII and Annex 4.

[18] See also Alston (ed) *Non-State Actors and Human Rights* (n 14); Clapham, 'Human rights obligations of non-state actors in conflict situations' (n 9); Sections 7.4.1 Security Council Resolutions and the Right to Offer Assistance and 7.4.2 Security Council Resolutions and the Right to Access.

[19] 4.2.2 Reconceptualising Sovereignty?.

transferred to the sovereign.[20] This reciprocity lies in the fact that sovereign rights, bestowed by the citizens, are not unlimited and therefore are curtailed to include certain responsibilities which those citizens may claim. Thus, the duty which lies upon the state to provide assistance by virtue of its sovereign responsibilities may translate into a right of individuals seeking such assistance. Indeed, the internal aspect of state sovereignty is curtailed and limited by those individuals within its territory that may claim invocation of their rights.[21] These rights that may be claimed are in fact the direct consequence of the reciprocal relationship between sovereign and society. Yet, they are not distinctly formulated as such regarding the provision of humanitarian assistance, given the more abstract and general level upon which state sovereignty operates, allowing for substantive rights in the specific *corpora juris* relevant to the provision of humanitarian assistance. These specific rights therefore can be directly found in the more detailed provisions within the international legal framework that shall be discussed further below.

It must however be noted at the outset that although the enforceable legal provisions are stipulated in more specific fields of law, they flow directly from the reciprocal relationship between sovereign and society, and are the 'other side' of the two-sided coin of state sovereignty, entailing furthermore the rights of the sovereign in relation to third states. As such, the possibility of individuals to claim the receipt of humanitarian assistance also follows the overarching approach that is taken in this research into the legal framework on humanitarian assistance. This overarching approach suggests a common denominator and basis upon which *all* individuals can base themselves, regardless of the typology of the humanitarian crisis they may find themselves in. Indeed, whereas specialisation of the law is of relevance in order for individuals to base themselves on directly enforceable rights, this must not result in fragmentation of the law. Therefore, it is relevant to take into consideration that state sovereignty plays a role both as an aspect regarding duties of the sovereign, and concerning the rights of individuals on the territory of the affected state in the provision of humanitarian assistance.

6.3 Duties and Rights under Human Rights Law

This Section addresses at a more concrete level the various rights and duties under human rights law in the provision of humanitarian assistance, in reflection of the analysis that has taken place in previous Chapters concerning human rights law. A discussion of the current absence of a potential individual human right to humanitarian assistance has already taken place above in Chapter 5. Furthermore, the continued application of human rights law in times of conflict has been asserted, in recognition of the current stance regarding the *lex specialis* doctrine in relation to international humanitarian law, as well as the discussion on the current status of the

[20]Ibid.

[21] Bosko Jakovljevic, 'Right to Humanitarian Action and State Sovereignty' in (eds) Stefania Baldini & Guido Ravasi, *Humanitarian Action and State Sovereignty; Refugees: a continuing challenge* (Institute of International Humanitarian Law 2000) 99.

potential extraterritorial application of human rights law.[22] Whereas the previous Chapter has addressed that the provision of humanitarian assistance functions as a vehicle in the fulfilment of the rights to life, food, health (and water) by the sovereign state or non-state actor upon which such obligations are placed, this Section specifically assesses the various *substantive* rights and duties on the ground in times of a crisis as part of the current existing legal framework on the provision of humanitarian assistance.

At the outset, the consideration that the provision of humanitarian assistance functions on the basis of non-discrimination must be reiterated. As addressed in Chapter 5, Article 5 ICERD codifies that, in particular relation to the provision of humanitarian assistance, states are obliged to 'prohibit and to eliminate' all forms of racial discrimination in the enjoyment of (amongst rights) the right to security of person and the 'protection against bodily harm', economic, social and cultural rights; including the right to health.[23] Thus, the manner in which these substantive rights must be fulfilled, regardless of which human rights are specifically at stake, must be on the basis of non-discrimination. Such provision on the basis of non-discrimination has also been affirmatively held twice by the ICJ. Firstly in its *Nicaragua* Judgment, the Court addressed that 'an essential feature of truly humanitarian aid is that it is given "without discrimination" of any kind'.[24] Secondly, placing it directly in the context of human rights however, the Court held in its 2008 Order in the case concerning the 'Application Of The International Convention On The Elimination Of All Forms Of Racial Discrimination (Georgia v. Russian Federation)' that:

> "Both Parties shall facilitate, and refrain from placing any impediment to, humanitarian assistance in support of the rights to which the local population are entitled under the International Convention on the Elimination of All Forms of Racial Discrimination".[25]

Thus, the ICJ also observed that prior to addressing the substantive norms, the law dictates at a foundational level that the provision of humanitarian assistance must in all circumstances and at all times occur on the basis of non-discrimination, which would otherwise indeed be a violation of a norm of *jus cogens*.

6.3.1 Duties of the Affected State and Non-State Actor under Human Rights Law

Current international human rights law places several distinct obligations upon states which relate to the provision of humanitarian assistance. As such, Articles 55

[22] Sections 3.4.2 Applicability of Human Rights in Armed Conflict and Occupation and 3.4.3 Hierarchy or Convergence of International Legal Norms?.

[23] See Section 5.3 A Human Right to Receive Humanitarian Assistance in International Law?.

[24] Military and Paramilitary Activities in and against Nicaragua (Nicaragua v. United States of America), Merits, Judgment 27 June 1986 I.C.J. Reports 1986, p. 14 § 243.

[25] Application of the International Convention on the Elimination of all Forms of Racial Discrimination (Georgia v. Russian Federation), Provisional Measures, Order of 15 October 2008, I.C.J. Reports 2008, p. 353 § 149. It must be noted that this decision of the Court was taken by 8 votes to 7.

and 56 of the UN Charter imply an obligation to UN Member States to ensure universal respect for human rights.[26] Specifically relating to the provision of humanitarian assistance, the rights to life, food, health and water have been discussed in Chapter 5 as part of this assurance. States have obligations that can be derived from these rights concerning the provision of humanitarian assistance and it has been noted that derogation from these four rights in times of a humanitarian crisis is not permitted.[27] In this regard, Article 2 of the ICESCR concerning the 'progressive development' of human rights as well as the 'minimum core obligations' has been considered in particular.[28]

For the purpose of discussing duties on the ground in times of crisis, the first and foremost obligations relating to the fulfilment of these rights must be sought with the governments of State Parties to human rights treaties.[29] Yet, when translating treaty obligations into obligations in practice, it is relevant to note the status of obligations of human rights protection by non-state actors such as *de facto* regimes, as for example may be the case with the collapse of state authority.[30] Section 6.2.1 has concluded that, when adopting a pragmatic view, these obligations resting upon states as duty-bearers of international human rights can under current international law also be extended to non-state actors exercising a certain level of control over a territory, as for example in non-international armed conflicts.[31] Furthermore, when considering the obligations towards citizens, it has become more and more accepted in international law that regimes exercising *de facto* control, or non-state actors, must abide by general international law, including human rights obligations.[32] Therefore, whereas the following Section will address the obligations of states under international human rights law concerning humanitarian assistance, such obligations must also be considered equally for non-state actors that may be responsible for the provision of humanitarian assistance.

Regarding the right to life, the state has a clear duty to not arbitrarily deprive humans of their life.[33] Furthermore, the HRC has argued that the right to life within the ICCPR includes an obligation to take positive measures with regard to the reduction or elimination of malnutrition, epidemics and other such situations that

[26] Louis Henkin, *The Age of Rights* (Columbia University Press 1990) 3.
[27] Section 5.2.2 Derogability, Human Rights and the Provision of Humanitarian Assistance.
[28] Section 5.4.4 Humanitarian Assistance and the Right to Food.
[29] See in this regard also the 'Vienna Declaration and Programme of Action' UN Doc A/CONF.157/23 (12 July 1993) §1: "Human rights and fundamental freedoms are the birthright of all human beings; their protection and promotion is the first responsibility of Governments".
[30] Although the applicability of human rights standards to international organisations of naturally also of great relevance, it remains beyond the scope of this research and will therefore not be addressed.
[31] Section 6.2.1.; 'Legal Consequences for States of the Continued Presence of South Africa in Namibia' ICJ Advisory Opinion (n 8) § 118; Liesbeth Zegveld, *The Accountability of Armed Opposition Groups in International Law* (Cambridge University Press 2002) 229.
[32] See amongst others Clapham, 'Human rights obligations of non-state actors in conflict situations' (n 9) 522; Tomuschat, 'The Applicability of Human Rights Law to Insurgent Movements' (n 9) 586; Steiner, Alston & Goodman, *International Human Rights in Context: Law, Politics, Morals* (n 9) 675, 1420.
[33] Article 3 UDHR, 6 ICCPR, Article 2 ECHR, Article 4 ACHR, Article 4 ACHPR. See for an in depth discussion Section 5.4.2.

might endanger the right to life.[34] In practice, this may entail the provision of medicine and food in the aftermath of a (natural) disaster or to those fleeing situations of conflict. This stance of the HRC has also been taken by the ECtHR in regard to the right to life.[35] Evidently, such an obligation (as envisaged by the HRC and ECtHR) remains relevant when considering a duty to provide humanitarian assistance. Indeed, it has been argued that this prohibition on the arbitrary deprivation of life as enshrined in the ICCPR must be seen as part of customary *jus cogens*, making the obligation that lies upon the state one of the highest within international law in general.[36] The provision of humanitarian assistance therefore functions as a means to ensure the fulfilment of the right to life. States and acting sovereigns thus have a duty under the right to life to prevent the 'arbitrary' loss of life by way of ensuring the provision of emergency aid.

Furthermore, the right to food must be considered. Article 11 of the ICESCR, and more particularly the General Comment on this by the CESCR, envisages an obligation for states to provide food as part of humanitarian assistance in the event of a humanitarian crisis; as part of the fulfilment of the right to food.[37] Indeed, according to the CESCR a State would have to demonstrate that it has made *every effort* using the resources at its disposal, to in fact fulfil these minimum core obligations.[38] As such, no retrogressive measures concerning *core* food provision may be taken, even in times of emergency, and Article 2 ICESCR provides that international cooperation and assistance should be sought in the fulfilment of the right to food, in the event a state's own available resources should not suffice. Thus, a certain duty can be discerned for the affected state to seek international assistance in the fulfilment of its duties towards those under its jurisdiction based on Articles 11 and 2 ICESCR. Indeed, a distinct obligation lies with the state *to provide in the right to food*, in times of an emergency. In practice this would mean that state parties to the ICESCR have an obligation to seek international assistance in the delivery of emergency supplies of food to their population facing a humanitarian crisis, should they not be capable of fulfilling the right to food satisfactorily themselves. The duty to provide food aid therefore contains an international aspect under the ICESCR that states must abide by. The various other existing legal provisions pertaining to the obligation of states to provide for food, amongst others Article 24(2)(c) CRC, Article 12(2) CEDAW, Article 28 CRPD, Article 12 Additional Protocol to the ACHR in the Area of Economic, Social and Cultural Rights and Article 15 Additional Protocol to the ACHPR on the Rights of Women

---

[34] CCPR General Comment 6: 'The right to life (art. 6)' (30 April 1982) § 2 and CCPR General Comment 14 'Nuclear weapons and the right to life (Art. 6)' (9 November 1984) § 2.

[35] *Budayeva And Others v Russia* (App Nos 15339/02, 21166/02, 20058/02, 11673/02 and 15343/02) ECHR 20 March 2008, Final 29 September 2008, § 128-129.

[36] 'Promotion and protection of human rights: human rights questions, including alternative approaches for improving the effective enjoyment of human rights and fundamental freedoms', Note by the Secretary-General UN Doc A/66/330 (30 August 2011) § 20.

[37] Section 5.4.4 and CESCR General Comment 12 (Article 11 ICESCR) UN Doc E/C.12/1999/5 'The right to adequate food' (12 May 1999) § 28.

[38] Ibid § 17.

in Africa, support the perspective of the ICESCR. Furthermore, the latter two pertain to continents that are prone to natural disasters and conflicts, making their contribution of particular relevance to the provision of humanitarian assistance.

The right to health, enshrined in Article 25 UDHR and specifically in Article 12 ICESCR equally provides a (minimum core) obligation upon States Parties to ensure that persons within their jurisdiction have access to certain minimum essential levels of food, health facilities, basic shelter, water and sanitation. Non-compliance with this obligation according to the CESCR will result in a direct violation of Article 12 ICESCR.[39] In particular Article 12(2)(c) ICESCR, stating the duty of States Parties to take steps in 'the prevention, treatment and control of epidemic, endemic, occupational and other diseases', interpreted by the CESCR as to include the provision of humanitarian assistance in emergency situations, is of relevance with regard to the duty of the affected state to provide emergency relief.[40] This provision in practice would oblige the affected state to actively set up emergency 'camps' where those affected by crisis may find refuge, which includes sanitation facilities, in order to prevent such health epidemics. Therefore, the provision of humanitarian assistance by the duty-bearer fulfils the obligation of states under Article 12(2)(c) ICESCR to provide in the right to health through an obligation of conduct. Other treaty provisions supporting the state's obligation to provide in the right to health, although not referring so explicitly to humanitarian assistance, are Article 5(e)(iv) ICERD, Article 24 CRC, Article 11 European Social Charter, Article 10 of the Additional Protocol to the ACHR in the area of Economic, Social and Cultural Rights, Article 16 ACHPR, Article 14 of the African Charter on the Rights and Welfare of the Child and Article 14 of the Protocol to the ACHPR on the Rights of Women in Africa.[41] In the above Articles, a consensus can be found concerning the obligation for states to prevent diseases and to prioritise vulnerable populations in the provision of medical aid.

Lastly, the right to water is relevant to the provision of humanitarian assistance. Although international treaty law does not consider the right to water independently, separate from the right to health, several more specialised treaties do contain provisions pertaining to the right to water, such as Article 24(1)(c) CRC, Article 14(2)(h) CEDAW, Article 28 CRPD, Article 15(a) Additional Protocol to the ACHPR on the Rights of Women in Africa, Article 14(2)(c) African Charter on the Rights and Welfare of the Child.[42] From these provisions, an obligation can be distilled of a rather general nature, not focused on the provision of humanitarian assistance, resting upon states to provide access to safe drinking water. This obligation, however, is only found on the one hand in several specific treaties, connected to the rights of children, women or persons with disabilities, and on the other hand in regional conventions. As such, the right to water is not yet codified

[39] CESCR General Comment 14 (11 August 2000) UN Doc E/C.12/2000/4 'The right to the highest attainable standard of health', § 43 and Section 5.4.6.
[40] Ibid § 16.
[41] For a more detailed discussion of these articles, see Section 5.4.6.
[42] Section 5.4.8.

properly or uniformly at an international level, and the most far-reaching obligations lying upon states can be found on the African continent. It must be noted that the CESCR has interpreted a right to water to exist, as derived from Articles 11 and 12 ICESCR, but such an interpretation on its own does not hold legal standing.[43] Thus no practical duties can be discerned for sovereigns in the event of a humanitarian crisis under the 'right to water'.

The rights to life, food and health in international law provide for distinct and specific obligations resting upon states. Not only is the right to life arguably part of the *jus cogens* body of law,[44] the rights to food and health also entail certain minimum core obligations for states to fulfil at all times. Moreover, Article 2 ICESCR addresses a duty of the affected state to search for *international* assistance and cooperation in the fulfilment of its obligations under the ICESCR and the rights to food and health enshrined therein. As such, the provision of humanitarian assistance in times of humanitarian crisis will be a *vehicle* or a *means* to fulfil a state's obligation under the right to life, food or health. Indeed, *not* providing emergency assistance may then be considered a violation of a state's duties under human rights law. Thus, the provision of humanitarian assistance in times of a humanitarian crisis is a translation, as made in the interpretative remarks of the HRC and CESCR, from the basic obligations resting upon states concerning the rights to life, food, health (and water). In practice, this amounts to precisely the provision of supplies as defined to be 'humanitarian assistance'.[45]

Besides the rights to life, food, health and water which have been discussed in relation to the provision of humanitarian assistance, other provisions also exist in current human rights law, calling upon states to protect persons in situations such as a humanitarian crisis. As such, the Convention on the Rights of Persons with Disabilities declares:

> "States Parties shall take, in accordance with their obligations under international law, including international humanitarian law and international human rights law, all necessary measures to ensure the protection and safety of persons with disabilities in situations of risk, including situations of armed conflict, humanitarian emergencies and the occurrence of natural disasters".[46]

Thus, an obligation rests upon State Parties to the CRPD to provide for the fulfilment of human rights of such persons, in the event of a humanitarian crisis. Furthermore, the 1993 Vienna Declaration and Programme of Action, although a non-binding document, has emphasised the 'importance of and the need for

[43] Ibid.
[44] Which norms amount to *jus cogens* continues to be a discussion under international law. See amongst others: Rafael Nieto Navia, 'International Peremptory Norms (Jus Cogens) And International Humanitarian Law' in LC Vohrah, F Pocar et al, (eds) *Man's Inhumanity to Man: Essays in Honour of Antonio Cassese* (Kluwer Law International 2003); Alexander Orakhelashvili, *Peremptory Norms in International Law* (Oxford University Press 2006); and Malcolm Shaw, *International Law* (Cambridge University Press 2008) 303, 720-721.
[45] Section 2.2.2 Defining Humanitarian Assistance.
[46] Article 11 CRPD.

humanitarian assistance to victims of all natural and man-made disasters' in the context of human rights.[47]

Considering the above provisions in human rights law, specifically the provisions concerning the right to life, food and health as they relate to the delivery of emergency assistance in the event of a humanitarian crisis, the conclusions of Chapter 5 must therefore be reiterated. The provision of humanitarian assistance by states, and by non-state actors upon which human rights obligations rest under international law, functions as a *vehicle in the fulfilment of the obligations international human rights law places* upon the affected state concerning the rights to life, food, health (and water). This indeed also aligns with the findings as mentioned above by the ICJ in both the *Nicaragua*-case and the 'Application Of The International Convention On The Elimination Of All Forms Of Racial Discrimination (Georgia v. Russian Federation)'-case. Here, the Court observed that the provision of humanitarian assistance may indeed be a manner in which a state fulfils its obligations under human rights law.

6.3.2 Rights of Persons to Receive Assistance under Human Rights Law

The various human rights individuals may invoke to claim a right to the receipt of humanitarian assistance have been scrutinised above from the perspective of the affected state or non-state actor exercising control. Given the fact that no independent human right to receive humanitarian assistance currently exists in human rights law, individuals seeking to receive such assistance shall have to find recourse in the existing human rights to life, food, health (and water).[48] Within the receipt of humanitarian assistance lies the fulfilment of the basic necessities required in the fulfilment of the rights to life, food and health.

The right to life is distinctly formulated in Article 3 UDHR and Article 6 ICCPR, leaving no doubt as to the right of each individual to have his or her life protected.[49] Individuals may base themselves on Article 6 ICCPR, Article 2 ECHR, Article 4 ACHR or Article 4 ACHPR preventing the arbitrary or intentional deprivation of the right to life, when claiming a right to receive emergency aid from their sovereign authorities. Furthermore, the child in international human rights law may also revert to Article 6 CRC, claiming an inherent right to life which can be read in conjuncture with Article 22 CRC relating to the protection of children through the provision of humanitarian assistance. These international human rights treaties do not specifically refer to the provision of humanitarian assistance as related to the right to life, nor do the interpretive remarks of states parties in reservations to these treaties either.[50] As such, the State Parties have distinctly not chosen to *limit* the right to life in relation to the provision of humanitarian assistance, when they did have the opportunity to do so. This lack of restriction

[47] 'Vienna Declaration and Programme of Action' UN Doc A/CONF.157/23, (12 July 1993) § 23.
[48] 5.4 Humanitarian Assistance Within the Context of Existing Human Rights.
[49] Section 5.4.2.
[50] Ibid.

enables individuals to resort to invocation of this right in the event of a humanitarian emergency, with a view to the assertion that the HRC has interpreted the right to life to include such emergency relief, and following the suggestions thereto also by the ICJ, that has addressed the role humanitarian assistance plays in the fulfilment of human rights.

Subsequently, individuals may resort to the human right to (adequate) food in the event of a humanitarian emergency. As set out in Articles 25 UDHR and 11 ICESCR, each individual has a right to "adequate food" which according to the ICESCR includes the right to be free from hunger. As the CESCR has declared access to food to be of relevance to the fulfilment of the right to food,[51] it unambiguously determines a link between the right to food and the receipt of humanitarian assistance. However, as has been established earlier, although Article 11 ICESCR is formulated as an inherent individual right, the emphasis of the provision lies with the obligation for State Parties to realise the right to adequate food, through its conduct.[52] Article 24(2)(c) CRC and Article 28 CRPD envisage a right to adequate food (through the right to health), whereas the CEDAW follows the formulation as found in the ICESCR and bases the right to adequate food in Article 12(2) CEDAW largely on the obligation of the State Party to provide it. Similarly at the regional level, Article 12 of the Additional Protocol to the ACHR in the Area of Economic, Social and Cultural Rights and Article 15 of the Additional Protocol to the ACHPR on the Rights of Women in Africa formulate a right to food, and these Protocols also emphasise the role of the State Party in the obligation to fulfil the right to food. Whilst an individual's right to food is thus codified broadly at the international level, the formulation of the right for the most part underlines the state's obligations in the fulfilment of the right.[53] From a practical perspective, it is therefore more difficult to claim such an obligation of conduct, as no specificities with regard to the receipt of food in times of emergency are formulated from the perspective of the individual. Rather, the individual shall have to assert that the state is not fulfilling its duty to provide an adequate amount of emergency relief in times of crisis.

Equally the right to health, as codified in Article 25 UDHR and Article 12 ICESCR, accentuates the obligation of states to ensure access to certain minimum essential levels of food, health facilities, basic shelter, water and sanitation. In fact, the receipt of humanitarian assistance may fulfil such an obligation according to Article 12(2)(c) ICESCR. Thus, reversely formulated, as states have a duty under this Article to take steps in 'the prevention, treatment and control of epidemic, endemic, occupational and other diseases', individuals would be entitled through their human right to health to receive humanitarian assistance in the assurance that they do not succumb to certain epidemic diseases during, or in the aftermath of, a humanitarian emergency.[54] However, it is distinctly formulated within Article 12

[51] CESCR General Comment 12 (n 37) § 13.
[52] Section 5.4.3 and 5.4.4.
[53] See Section 8.5.1 on the possibilities of individuals enforcing their rights.
[54] See in this regard also CESCR General Comment 14 (n 39) § 16.

ICESCR that State Parties to the ICESCR should 'take steps'. Such a formulation does not appear to fall within the 'minimum core obligations' and it will be difficult for individuals to truly enforce this 'step' in the right to health in the circumstance of a humanitarian crisis. Yet, it remains apparent that the provision of humanitarian assistance *can* be a vehicle in the fulfilment of the right to health as formulated in the ICESCR. Both the interpretive comments of the CESCR and the formulation of Article 12 ICESCR itself allow this. The right to health is furthermore equally recognised in Article 5(e)(iv) ICERD, Article 24 CRC, Article 11 European Social Charter, Article 10 of the Additional Protocol to the ACHR in the area of Economic, Social and Cultural Rights, Article 16 ACHPR, Article 14 of the African Charter on the Rights and Welfare of the Child and Article 14 of the Protocol to the ACHPR on the Rights of Women in Africa. Problematic to the right to health however, as discussed in Chapter 5, is that each treaty holds different formulations to this specific right, thereby making a consensus difficult to find.[55] However, common ground can be found in the more narrow formulation concerning the prevention of diseases by states, which can be interpreted as part of the right to health for individuals. Such diseases, by their very nature, tend to spread more quickly in times of crisis and in circumstances of displacement of persons, leading to a distinct role of the affected state in the fulfilment of the right to health – through the prevention of diseases – in the circumstance of a humanitarian crisis. Individuals therefore have the right to request assistance in setting up proper health and sanitation facilities in the immediate aftermath of a disaster or when having fled their homes in times of conflict.

Lastly, regarding the right to water, it has indeed already been discussed that such a 'right' does not currently exist as a codified individual provision within major international human rights treaty law. Yet, the more specialised conventions do encompass a right to water, such as Article 24(1)(c) CRC, Article 14(2)(h) CEDAW, Article 28 CRPD, Article 15(a) Additional Protocol to the ACHPR on the Rights of Women in Africa, Article 14(2)(c) African Charter on the Rights and Welfare of the Child. As is the case with the right to food and the right to health, these conventions mostly formulate these provisions as obligations of the State Parties.[56] Furthermore, the incorporation is rather haphazard, as protection at the international level is somewhat limited to children and women, while at the regional level limited to the African and American continents. Indeed the CESCR has, through its interpretive remarks, attempted to ascertain that the right to water exists as derived from Articles 11 and 12 ICESCR, but in and of itself, this does not create an actual right in international law.[57] The further acceptance of such a right is

[55] Section 5.4.3.

[56] Section 5.4.4.

[57] CESCR General Comment 15 (20 January 2003) UN Doc E/C.12/2002/11 'The Right to water (arts. 11 and 12 of the International Covenant on Economic Social and Cultural Rights' § 3. Earlier references by the CESCR on the right to water in relation to Article 11 can be found in its General Comment 6 (8 December 1995) UN Doc E/1996/22 'The economic, social and cultural rights of older persons' § 5 and § 32, as well as General Comment 4 (13 December 1991) UN Doc E/1992/23 'The right to adequate housing' § 8(b). The CESCR has furthermore referenced to the right to water in

currently in motion, through various initiatives in this regard within the resolutions of the UN General Assembly, leading to potential customary acceptance, although at this stage the law has not properly crystallised.[58] Yet, for the provision of humanitarian assistance, as well as its protection through human rights law, such individual codification is however not necessary. Given the possibilities for persons to claim provision of assistance in the fulfilment of their rights to life, food and health, which may include the provision of water, such an individual right is not necessary.

The existence of these rights creates a need and an obligation for their fulfilment. Humanitarian assistance can and must be seen as a vehicle through which these existing rights may be fulfilled. Such fulfilment must occur in respect of the principles of humanity, neutrality and impartiality, amongst others incorporated through Article 5 ICERD. Indeed, the receipt of assistance may be claimed by persons in times of a humanitarian emergency, in order to meet the *content* of the provisions relating to the rights to life, food and health. Such a claim could also be considered the meeting of a basic norm within this context. Whereas an independent right to receive assistance is indeed currently absent from human rights law today, the provision of assistance must be considered part of the human rights regime in a larger perspective. Not receiving assistance (i.e. food, water, medicine and shelter) when in need during a humanitarian crisis, could result in the violation of the human rights to life, food and water. Humanitarian assistance as a concept therefore clearly fits within the human rights framework and discourse. Persons in need of food, water, medicine and other facilities related to their immediate survival have the opportunity, under the existing rights to life, food and health, to request the receipt of humanitarian assistance. Framing the provision of humanitarian assistance within this human rights regime is not only legally sound, it furthermore enables persons in need of emergency aid to actively pursue such claims.

6.4 Duties and Rights under the UN Framework: the Security Council and General Assembly

The UN framework also provides a general and comprehensive perspective on the duties that may rest on the affected state in the provision of humanitarian assistance. The UN framework is, as this research's approach is doing, equally capable of approaching the provision of assistance from an overall perspective, addressing the provision of assistance at all times, as does human rights law. As such, the General Assembly is a representation of nearly all states in the world and therefore often reflects indications of *opinio juris* and state practice. Its scope furthermore is wide and covers all matters in international law. The Security Council on the other hand, whilst only encompassing a few member states,

relation to Article 12 ICESCR in its General Comment No 14 (n 39) § 4, § 11-12, § 15, § 36, § 40, § 43 (c), § 51.

[58] Section 5.4.4.

functions at the supranational level in international law, based upon the provisions in Article 25 of the UN Charter.[59] Given that it therefore has the power to adopt binding resolutions, its work influences the entire international legal world. Furthermore, whilst its scope of action may appear limited due to restrictions placed upon it in Article 39 UN Charter declaring a need for a 'threat to the peace', such a limitation falls within the framework of this research. As argued in Section 3.3.3, the need for humanitarian assistance becomes immediate and relevant in the event of a 'humanitarian crisis'. Such a crisis by definition encompasses a potential threat to the peace due to a variety of reasons, dependent on the specific circumstances. Non-international armed conflicts may incur spill-over effects into neighbouring countries, natural disasters may have cross-border effects and induce a large influx of IDPs and refugees and a variety of other possibilities that may result in a threat to the peace.

Thus, both Security Council and General Assembly resolutions, both for their own reasons, are relevant to analyse in relation to the rights and duties involved in the provision of assistance. Furthermore, several soft law instruments also adhere to such a comprehensive approach in the discussion of various duties related to the provision of emergency assistance. These soft law instruments, when in support of Security Council and General Assembly resolutions, are discussed therewith. They supplement the legal sources throughout this research as they often hold an overarching and encompassing approach in their consideration of rights and duties related to the receipt of humanitarian assistance, often taking the approach from the perspective of individuals entitled to receive aid. Considering the binding nature that Security Council resolutions can have regarding the member states of the UN, this category will be addressed first, followed by the General Assembly resolutions that in themselves do not have a binding force in international law.

6.4.1 Duties of the Affected State under Security Council Resolutions

The UN Security Council has expressed itself regarding the obligations of the affected state in the provision of humanitarian assistance on many occasions in recent years, but it got off to a slow start.[60] Whereas the UN General Assembly first addressed the matter of humanitarian assistance and thus the various responsibilities decades ago,[61] the Security Council has for a long time avoided this topic. The more encompassing approach was furthermore not embraced from the outset. Given the Charter-based determination and division of tasks between the two UN organs, the Security Council did not deal with the General Assembly's addressing of humanitarian assistance, considering the latter's focus on natural disasters. Indeed,

---

[59] Article 25 UN Charter states: "The Members of the United Nations agree to accept and carry out the decisions of the Security Council in accordance with the present Charter".

[60] The provision of humanitarian assistance as provided by peacekeeping operations, including their particular mandate, as frequently addressed by the Security Council, shall remain outside the scope of this research.

[61] UNGA Res 2034 (XX) (7 December 1965) 'Assistance in cases of natural disaster' and Section 2.2.1.1.

when adopting resolutions under Chapter VII of the Charter, these binding decisions affect the international legal realm and contribute to the further development of norms. A turning point came a few decades ago, when the Council embraced humanitarian assistance within its scope of work, and within the boundaries of a 'threat to the peace' as codified in Article 39 UN Charter. The Council then commenced addressing the matter of humanitarian assistance thematically in independent resolutions, which will be concentrated on further in this Section. However, the UN Security Council initially dealt with humanitarian assistance on a more *ad hoc* basis. The Council addressed humanitarian assistance increasingly in several of its resolutions pertaining to certain country situations that arose in the early 1990s, most notably amongst others the prolonged conflicts in the Sudan, Somalia, the Former Yugoslavia and the situation in Iraq.[62] To provide a more thorough view of the Security Council's approach, these situations will be addressed and analysed, for the purpose of establishing the potential thread in the work of the Council.

Several primary references to the provision of humanitarian assistance may be found in the Security Council resolutions concerning the situation in Iraq in the early 1990s. However, in these resolutions the Council fails to address Iraq's *own* sovereign responsibility in adhering to this.[63] Yet, considering the situation, the Security Council for the first time directly links the on-going repression of civilians to a threat to the international peace.[64] Indeed, this approach where the responsibilities of the affected state are not addressed can also be seen in subsequent resolutions pertaining to Somalia that requested the international community to assist in the delivery of assistance.[65] The Security Council foregoes Somalia's responsibilities in the provision of assistance, focusing on the facilitation of international assistance (to be addressed in the subsequent Chapter).[66] Only in passing does the Council note that the Somali *people* have the 'ultimate responsibility for national reconciliation and the reconstruction of their own country'.[67] Similarly, and occurring roughly simultaneously, the Security Council focuses on the *external provision* of assistance in the conflict in the Former Yugoslavia,[68] having received calls for assistance in the delivery of aid by amongst

[62] It remains beyond the scope of this research to provide in depth analyses of all country situations in which the UN Security Council addressed the matter of humanitarian assistance, and only several key examples will be used, to illustrate the legal relevance.
[63] UNSC Res 661 (6 August 1990) UN Doc S/RES/661 § 3(c) and 4; UNSC Res 687 (8 April 1991) UN Doc S/RES/687; UNSC Res 688 (5 April 1991) UN Doc S/RES/688 § 3, 5-6 and UNSC Res 706 (15 August 1991) UN Doc S/RES/706 preamble §8 and §2.
[64] Ibid S/RES/688 § 1.
[65] See amongst others UNSC Res 794 (3 December 1992) UN Doc S/RES/794 preamble § 7.
[66] UNSC Res 733 (23 January 1992) UN Doc S/RES/733 § 2, 8-9; UNSC Res 746 (17 March 1992) UN Doc S/RES/746 § 3,5,8; UNSC Res 751 (24 April 1992) UN Doc S/RES/751 § 12 & 14; UNSC Res 767 (27 July 1992) UN Doc S/RES/767 § 3-4, 6; UNSC Res 775 (28 August 1992) UN Doc S/RES/775 § 7&9; UNSC Res 794 (3 December 1992) UN Doc S/RES/794 § 2-3.
[67] Ibid S/RES/794 preamble § 15.
[68] UNSC Res 752 (15 May 1992) UN Doc S/RES/752 § 7&8; UNSC Res 757 (30 May 1992) UN Doc S/RES/757 § 17; UNSC Res 770 (13 August 1992) UN Doc S/RES/770 § 2-3, 6; UNSC Res 776 (14

others the Bosnian President.[69] At a later stage, still concerning the Former Yugoslavia, but related to the conflict in Kosovo, the Security Council does demand:

> "that the authorities of the Federal Republic of Yugoslavia and the Kosovo Albanian leadership take immediate steps to improve the humanitarian situation and to avert the impending humanitarian catastrophe".[70]

Thus, prior to addressing the *thematic* issue of the protection of civilians in armed conflict, the Security Council did not *systematically* address the potential responsibilities of the *affected* states in the provision of humanitarian assistance. It must however be noted that in these resolutions pertaining to specific country situations, the Security Council often *responded to calls from the affected state* to assist in the provision of international assistance, which indicates a willingness from the state-party to acknowledge a need for international support and in theory also implies an acknowledgment of that state that it cannot handle the situation independently. Such international assistance is then subsequently addressed by the Council. Indeed, where the situation in Kosovo was concerned, the Security Council called to parties, *demanded* even, that they improve the humanitarian situation, although the Council still fell short in addressing such matters as the 'responsibility' of the affected state.

The country-specific circumstances opened the door to the more thematic deliberation of the topic within the work of the Council, and by 1999 the Security Council for the first time issued a thematic, non-country specific resolution. In this resolution concerning the protection of civilians in armed conflict the Council urged all parties involved to:

> "comply strictly with their obligations under international humanitarian, human rights and refugee law, in particular those contained in the Hague Conventions of 1899 and 1907 and in the Geneva Conventions of 1949 and their Additional Protocols of 1977, as well as with the decisions of the Security Council".[71]

September 1992) UN Doc S/RES/776; UNSC Res 781 (9 October 1992) UN Doc S/RES/781 preamble & § 1; UNSC Res 786 (10 November 1992) UN Doc S/RES/786; UNSC Res 787 (16 November 1992) UN Doc S/RES/787 § 17-18; UNSC Res 819 (16 April 1993) UN Doc S/RES/819 preamble § 8 and § 8; UNSC Res 824 (6 May 1993) UN Doc S/RES/824 preamble §4 & § 4(b), 7; UNSC Res 836 (4 June 1993) UN Doc S/RES 836 preamble §15 & § 5.

[69] Ibid S/RES/752 preamble § 7.

[70] UNSC Res 1199 (23 September 1998) UN Doc S/RES/1199 § 2.

[71] UNSC Res 1265 (17 September 1999) UN Doc S/RES/1265 [Protection of Civilians in Armed Conflict] § 4. The thematic resolution followed a Secretary General Report on the matter: UN Doc S/1999/957 (8 September 1999). Since 1999, the Secretary General has systematically reported on the matter of the protection of civilians. See in this regard: UN Doc S/2001/331 (30 March 2001); UN Doc S/2002/1300 (26 November 2002); UN Doc S/2004/431 (28 May 2004); UN Doc S/2005/740 (28 November 2005); UN Doc S/2007/643 (28 October 2007); UN Doc S/2009/277 (29 May 2009); UN Doc S/2010/579 (11 November 2010); and UN Doc S/2012/376 (22 May 2012).

Specifically regarding refugees and IDPs, the Security Council noted that the primary responsibility to protect these vulnerable groups lies with states, but fails to mention a primary responsibility in the protection of *all* civilians or the provision of humanitarian assistance.[72] Despite this lacuna, the Security Council took an important step in the greater protection of civilians with this resolution, urging those involved in armed conflict to adhere to the relevant rules of international law, which include those concerning the provision of humanitarian assistance. The Council has on occasion elaborated such matters with a view to specific groups, by stressing amongst others the importance of children's access to basic services such as health care during 'conflict and post-conflict periods'.[73]

Following this thematic resolution, the Security Council has over the past years specifically addressed the matter of civilians in armed conflict more in depth. In subsequent resolutions, the Security Council reiterated its position concerning the adherence to the rule of law, but again did not declare a direct responsibility *in the protection of persons or the provision of humanitarian assistance* for the affected state.[74] However, with time, the Security Council has altered its take on the provision of humanitarian assistance, to not only view this notion from an external position. Indeed the Council has begun to address it rather from the perspective that a *primary* responsibility lies with the affected state. As such, the Council declared in 2006 in the third thematic resolution on the protection of civilians in armed conflict that it:

> "Urges the international community to provide support and assistance to enable States to fulfil their responsibilities regarding the protection of refugees and other persons protected under international humanitarian law".[75]

Thus, whereas the Council urges the international community to take action, it does acknowledge that it is the primary responsibility of states to not only protect refugees and other protected persons in times of conflict, but to protect *civilians in general*.[76] With time, and with the simultaneous incorporation of the concept of the Responsibility to Protect within the UN framework as of 2005,[77] the Security Council has also taken a stronger position in the declaration that the primary responsibility in the protection of civilians lies with the affected state. Such a protection concerns the basic needs of a population and must therefore include the provision of humanitarian assistance.

---

[72] UNSC Res 1265 (17 September 1999) UN Doc S/RES/1265 preamble.

[73] UNSC Res 1314 (11 August 2000) UN Doc S/RES/1314 § 14.

[74] See amongst others UNSC Res 1296 (19 April 2000) UN Doc S/RES/1296 Protection of Civilians in Armed Conflict preamble & § 19.

[75] UNSC Res 1674 (28 April 2006) UN Doc S/RES/1674 § 13.

[76] Ibid preamble stating: "that parties to armed conflict bear the primary responsibility to take all feasible steps to ensure the protection of affected civilians".

[77] Section 4.2.3.1 UN Endorsement of the Responsibility to Protect.

Subsequently in 2009 in its fourth thematic resolution, the Security Council recalled this position.[78] Intermittently, the Security Council also addressed matters concerning humanitarian assistance in other themed resolutions, where it reaffirmed the position taken in the resolutions concerning the protection of civilians in times of armed conflict.[79] Equally, the Council continued to reaffirm its position in country resolutions, calling upon governments to fulfil their 'primary responsibility in the protection of civilians'.[80] In fact, on occasion the Security Council also called upon 'all parties' to a specific conflict to fulfil their responsibilities in such protection, such as concerning Somalia.[81] In doing so, the Security Council reaffirms that it recognises a responsibility of armed groups to protect civilians and adhere to their responsibilities under international law when playing a role in an international or non-international armed conflict.

Rather than being confined to armed conflict and humanitarian law, as was declared in the previously discussed thematic resolutions, the Security Council's perspective today regarding the provision of humanitarian assistance holds a somewhat broader perspective, through the incorporation of the notion of RtoP in the UN framework.[82] Although the 'protection of civilians' as a thematic issue should arguably not be confused with the notion of RtoP,[83] the two concepts share a common denominator in their ideology of protecting populations in need. Indeed, considering the 'Arab Spring' in 2011, the Security Council called upon the Libyan authorities in its resolution 'Peace and security in Africa' with a primary reference to RtoP *in practice* to 'protect its population'.[84] The Council reiterated that stance in its subsequent resolution declaring that such a duty to 'protect and ensure' that the primary needs of the population were met, was the *responsibility of the state*.[85] As discussed more in depth in Chapter 4 above, the Security Council reaffirmed

[78] UNSC Res 1894 (11 November 2009) UN Doc S/RES/1894 preamble "*Recognizing* that States bear the primary responsibility to respect and ensure the human rights of their citizens, as well as all individuals within their territory as provided for by relevant international law, *Reaffirming* that parties to armed conflict bear the primary responsibility to take all feasible steps to ensure the protection of civilians" and § 15: "Expresses its intention to: (a) Call on parties to armed conflict to comply with the obligations applicable to them under international humanitarian law to take all required steps to protect civilians (...)".

[79] See amongst others UNSC Res 1325 (31 October 2000) UN Doc S/RES/1325 on Women and Peace and Security.

[80] See amongst others UNSC Res 1430 (14 August 2002) UN Doc S/RES/1430 on the Situation between Eritrea and Ethiopia; UNSC Res 1861 (14 January 2009) UN Doc S/RES/1861 preamble on the situation in Chad and the Central African Republic; and UNSC Res 1906 (23 December 2009) UN Doc S/RES/1906 preamble on the situation in the Democratic Republic of the Congo.

[81] See for example UNSC Res 1863 (9 July 2009) UN Doc S/RES/1863 § 19.

[82] UNSC Res 1674 (28 April 2006) UN Doc S/RES/1674 § 13 and UNSC Res 1894 (11 November 2009) UN Doc S/RES/1894.

[83] 'Report of the Secretary-General on the protection of civilians in armed conflict' (22 May 2012) UN Doc S/2012/376 § 21 / p5-6.

[84] UNSC Res 1970 (26 February 2011) UN Doc S/RES/1970 'Peace and security in Africa' preamble.

[85] UNSC Res 1973 (17 March 2011) UN Doc S/RES/1973 'The situation in Libya' preamble § 3. For a more in depth discussion of these resolutions see Section 4.2.3.2.

this position concerning the responsibility of the state in successive resolutions concerning Libya:

> "underscores the Libyan authorities' responsibility for the protection of its population, including foreign nationals and African migrants".[86]

The Council has reiterated such wording as well concerning Cote d'Ivoire, Sudan, the Democratic Republic of the Congo and Yemen; 'stressing', 'reaffirming', 'recalling' or 'underscoring' the responsibility of these states in the protection of their populations.[87] In doing so regarding the Libyan situation, the Security Council distinctly referred to the state's *obligations under international law*, including humanitarian law, human rights law and refugee law, as it had done in earlier resolutions pertaining to the protection of civilians in armed conflict.[88] In both instances therefore the Council addressed the states' obligations under international law. Such statements and declarations by the Security Council reaffirm the assertion that it is indeed the affected state that holds the *primary responsibility as a sovereign* to provide humanitarian assistance when (parts of) its population are in need of this due to a humanitarian crisis.

While it is apparent that the embracement of the notion of RtoP has widened the scope of the Security Council's resolutions concerning the responsibility of states to protect their civilians and populations, the Security Council is somewhat ambiguous in its formulations. On the one hand, it calls upon states to protect 'civilians in time of armed conflict', referring to general international law while including particular obligations under humanitarian law, human rights law and refugee law. On the other hand, in situations falling short of a determination of an armed conflict it calls merely for the 'protection of a population' based on the states' 'responsibility', without addressing the specific bodies of law upon which this responsibility is based.[89] As such, the absence of the determination of an armed conflict alters the wording of the Security Council. The 'responsibility' called upon would then lie within general international law, but if interpreted narrowly within the UN's concept of Responsibility to Protect, would consequently only exist in relation to the four core crimes of genocide, war crimes, crimes against humanity and ethnic cleansing. As argued previously by the UN Secretary General, this distinction

---

[86] UNSC Res 2016 (27 October 2011) UN Doc S/RES/2016 'The situation in Libya' § 3. See similarly UNSC Res 2040 (12 March 2012) UN Doc S/RES/2040 'The situation in Libya' § 4.

[87] UNSC Res 1975 (30 March 2011) UN Doc S/RES/1975 preamble; UNSC Res 1996 (8 July 2011) UN Doc S/RES/1996 § 3(b)(iv); UNSC Res 1991 (28 June 2011) UN Doc S/RES/1991 preamble; UNSC Res 2014 (21 October 2011) UN Doc S/RES/2014 preamble.

[88] UNSC Res 1973 (17 March 2011) UN Doc S/RES/1973 'The situation in Libya' § 3; UNSC Res 2016 (27 October 2011) UN Doc S/RES/2016; UNSC Res 2040 (12 March 2012) UN Doc S/RES/2040 § 3, as well as UNSC Res 1674 (28 April 2006) UN Doc S/RES/1674 § 5; UNSC Res 1296 (19 April 2000) UN Doc S/RES/1296 § 8.

[89] See all resolutions discussed in this Section – a.o. UNSC Res 1975 (30 March 2011) UN Doc S/RES/1975 'The situation in Côte d'Ivoire'; UNSC Res 1996 (8 July 2011) UN Doc S/RES/1996; UNSC Res 2014 (21 October 2011) UN Doc S/RES/2014; UNSC Res 2016 (27 October 2011) UN Doc S/RES/2016; UNSC Res 2040 (12 March 2012) UN Doc S/RES/2040.

between the 'protection of civilians in armed conflict' and RtoP should be upheld, as the 'protection of civilians' finds a greater legal basis than the political concept of RtoP.[90] Yet, a parallel discourse may be counterproductive, as the political concept of RtoP certainly adheres to the protection of civilians in a broader sense. And what of the situations such as Sudan, Yemen and Cote d'Ivoire, where the Security Council referred to the legal notion of 'protecting civilians' rather than the political concept of RtoP, while simultaneously also using terminology such as 'protecting its population'?[91] For instance concerning Syria, the Council:

> "Also demands that all parties take all appropriate steps to protect civilians, including members of ethnic, religious and confessional communities, and stresses that, in this regard, the primary responsibility to protect its population lies with the Syrian authorities".[92]

Indeed, in practice, situations will arise in which one the four core crimes warranting action under the scope of RtoP is perhaps occurring, whilst the situation does not meet the threshold of an armed conflict. Consider in this regard in particular the concept of a crime against humanity, where no connection to an armed conflict is needed.[93] While the primary responsibility of the Security Council is the maintenance of international peace and security, the Council will address matters that are often not defined as an 'armed conflict', but may in fact amount to a 'humanitarian crisis', once a 'threat to the peace' under Article 39 UN Charter is established.

It appears that the Security Council is not adhering to a strict distinction between the two notions of 'protection', and opts for a rather broad approach to the protection of persons in need of assistance. Indeed, it is more all-encompassing, similar to the approach of this research, rather than the more abstract divisions. This path of the Security Council may provide a more practical approach to the circumstances it faces. In fact, the Security Council at times refers to 'civilians' and at times refers to 'populations'; a less legal term. However, despite the variety of formulations, the Council does not *specifically* assert what is needed in many circumstances, rather remaining more abstract.

A common denominator in the resolutions of the Security Council relating to the provision of humanitarian assistance can be found in its referral to *general* international law, while including humanitarian law, human rights law and refugee law. Indeed, this approach also aligns with the UN's embracement of the notion of RtoP, and the more contemporary concept of state sovereignty as including a responsibility of the state to ensure the protection of those within its territory and

---

[90] UN Doc S/2012/376 (n 83) §21.

[91] UNSC Res 1975 (30 March 2011) UN Doc S/RES/1975 'The situation in Côte d'Ivoir'; UNSC Res 1996 (8 July 2011) UN Doc S/RES/1996; UNSC Res 2014 (21 October 2011) UN Doc S/RES/2014; UNSC Res 2016 (27 October 2011) UN Doc S/RES/2016; UNSC Res 2040 (12 March 2012) UN Doc S/RES/2040.

[92] UNSC Res 2139 (22 February 2014) UN Doc S/RES/2139 § 9.

[93] See Section 8.6.2.2.

control.[94] Such an approach is for example also seen in the Council's phrasing of the responsibilities of those involved in the conflict in Syria. Whilst the Council has been severely criticised for its indecisiveness and lack of action regarding Syria as compared to Libya, in 2014 it commenced to address in more detail the provision of humanitarian assistance in Syria, asserting that the 'primary responsibility to protect its population lies with the Syrian authorities'.[95] Subsequently in the summer of 2014 the Council reiterated this position:

> "Reaffirming the primary responsibility of the Syrian authorities to protect the population in Syria and reiterating that parties to armed conflict bear the primary responsibility to take all feasible steps to ensure the protection of civilians, and recalling in this regard its demand that all parties to armed conflict comply fully with the obligations applicable to them under international law related to the protection of civilians in armed conflict, including journalists, media professionals and associated personnel".[96]

It can and must therefore be concluded that the Security Council envisages such a primary responsibility for states and parties exercising control under general international law, while referring to more specific fields of law also as sources of such responsibility, but not adhering to a strict distinction as proposed by the Secretary General and rather taking an all-encompassing view to states' obligations in this regard.

Indeed, this conclusion is also supported by several of the 'Aide Memoires' provided by the President of the Security Council; stating on behalf of the Council that the Council reaffirms that primary responsibility is borne by parties to an armed conflict to protect the 'affected civilians'.[97] In the most recent Aide Memoire pertaining to the theme of 'protection of civilians' the Council has in fact incorporated the scope and lingo of RtoP as it stated:

> "The Security Council recalls that States bear the primary responsibility to respect and ensure `the human rights of their citizens, as well as all individuals within their territory as provided for by relevant international law and reaffirms the responsibility of each individual State to protect its populations from genocide, war crimes, ethnic cleansing, and crimes against humanity".[98]

---

[94] See Sections 4.2.3.1 and 4.2.3.2.

[95] UNSC Res 2139 (22 February 2014) UN Doc S/RES/2139 § 9.

[96] UNSC 2165 (14 July 2014) UN Doc S/RES/2165 preamble.

[97] For example 'Aide Memoire Protection of Civilians in Armed Conflict' UN Doc S/PRST/2010/25 (22 November 2010) preamble, and 'Aide Memoire Protection of Civilians in Armed Conflict' UN Doc S/PRST/2014/3 (12 February 2014) 2. These Aide Memoire's follow the previous one UN Doc S/PRST/2002/6 (15 March 2002); as well as the thematic resolutions UNSC Res 1265 (17 September 1999) UN Doc S/RES/1265, UNSC Res 1296 (19 April 2000) UN Doc S/RES/1296, UNSC Res 1674 (28 April 2006) UN Doc S/RES/1674, UNSC Res 1738 (23 December 2006) UN Doc S/RES/1738; and UNSC Res 1894 (11 November 2009) UN Doc S/RES/1894 relating to the protection of civilians in armed conflict.

[98] Ibid UN Doc S/PRST/2014/3, 2.

Furthermore, the Aide Memoires have requested that the Security Council continues to stress the responsibility of parties to an armed conflict to 'respect, protect and meet the basic needs of civilian populations within their effective control'.[99] Clearly, meeting the 'basic needs' of a population involves the provision of food, water and emergency shelter, which can only lead to the conclusion that the Security Council perceives the primary responsibility in the provision of humanitarian assistance to lie with the sovereign state, or other parties involved in a particular conflict acting with a certain degree of control.

Thus, as Presidential Statements are considered (non-binding) decisions of the Council under Article 27 of the UN Charter,[100] the Security Council continues to restate its commitment to emphasising the primary responsibility of states regarding the protection of individuals within their jurisdiction, through a comprehensive approach, in support of its earlier resolutions in this regard. Indeed, the continued reiteration that the Security Council 'recognises that States bear the primary responsibility to protect civilians' as well as reaffirming that parties to an armed conflict bear the primary responsibility to take 'all feasible steps to ensure the protection of civilians' and urging that they meet civilians' basic needs while at the same time reaffirming the 'responsibility to protect populations' in light of the World Summit Outcome Document, reaffirms the Security Council's comprehensive approach to the provision of assistance, in search of broad protection for those in need. This protection appears to be sought both through the original thematic 'protection of civilians' as well as through the more recent concept of RtoP. Furthermore, such a primary responsibility for states is asserted under international law, including humanitarian law, human rights law and refugee law, to protect their civilians and populations in circumstances of armed conflict and other situations that may provide a threat to the peace.

A primary role can therefore be discerned for the sovereign or other party exercising control within the territory where the humanitarian crisis is taking place in the view of the Security Council in the provision of assistance in circumstances threatening the peace. Finally however, it must be noted that although the Security Council appears to be taking an all-encompassing approach to the discussion of the protection of persons, it does not address such protection in situations not amounting to some form of international threat to the peace. In this regard, the General Assembly's resolutions must be considered, to further develop a view of the current UN framework concerning the obligations of the affected state in the provision of humanitarian assistance. Nonetheless, the decisions of the Council do set forth an increasingly consistent line of reasoning regarding the responsibilities

[99] 'Aide Memoire Protection of Civilians in Armed Conflict' UN Doc S/PRST/2010/25 (22 November 2010) 2; 'Aide Memoire Protection of Civilians in Armed Conflict' UN Doc S/PRST/2014/3 (12 February 2014) 1. This has been furthermore reiterated in 'Aide Memoire Protection of Civilians in Armed Conflict' UN Doc S/PRST/2013/2 (12 February 2013) 1 and 3.

[100] S Talmon, 'The Statements of the President of the Security Council', (2003) 2 *Chinese Journal of International Law*, 447-448, 450.

of the affected state, which can be considered to reinforce existing international norms.

6.4.2 Rights of Persons to Receive Assistance under Security Council Resolutions

Prior to discussing the approach of the General Assembly, the Security Council's approach to the duty of the affected state to provide assistance must be set off against its approach to the potential *right to receive* such assistance. Whereas the Security Council considered the duties of the affected state rather thoroughly as discussed in the above Section, it's take on the rights of individuals in the receipt of such assistance cannot be said to be anything more than meagre.

The approach of the Security Council is quite clearly developed from the perspective of the obligation of the affected state and, as will be seen in the subsequent Chapter, also from the perspective of the potential right to the delivery of assistance by third parties, which relates to a state's potential duty to allow access therefore.[101] In fact, in analysing the Security Council resolutions pertaining to humanitarian assistance and related topics such as the protection of civilians in armed conflict, it becomes apparent that the Security Council does *not* in so many words address the rights of individuals receiving assistance. The Council rather approaches the topic from the viewpoint of the responsibilities of the state. Although this approach from the perspective of state's duties is somewhat disappointing given the opportunities the Council has to exercise influence on strengthening the 'right to receive assistance', it can to a certain degree be clarified and understood. Given the fact that the Security Council resolutions in fact bind *states*, it is logical that they are indeed therefore formulated in a manner to indeed address the responsibilities of states. Nonetheless, the opportunity remains for the Security Council to in fact also address the related right of individuals to receive aid as fulfilment of the states' duties to provide such assistance.

6.4.3 Duties of the Affected State under General Assembly Resolutions

Whilst the General Assembly resolutions do not hold binding legal consequences for states, they do contribute to the determination of the position of state practice, given the large number of states represented within the body, in particular when such resolutions are adopted by consensus. Should a distinct thread or line in the work of the Assembly be discerned, this would then contribute to the argument of potential (developing) customary legal norms in this regard.

The pivotal position of the General Assembly in the development of the role of the UN *as an organisation* in the provision of humanitarian assistance has been previously discussed in Section 2.2.1.1. This Section considers the position of the General Assembly concerning the affected state's duties. From the 1960s onwards, the General Assembly has noted the relevance of the provision of humanitarian

[101] Section 7.4.2.

assistance.[102] A clear stance regarding the affected state's responsibility remained lacking during the early decades, as the General Assembly focused on external offers regarding the provision of assistance from the international community.[103] Yet, as early as 1981 the General Assembly noted the primacy of the role of the affected countries 'in caring for the victims of natural disasters and other disaster situations', while also stating that the primary responsibility for administration and relief operations, as well as the majority of the provision of actual material assistance lies with these affected states.[104] The General Assembly reaffirmed its stance in subsequent resolutions throughout the 1980s.[105] Furthermore, gearing up towards its 'International Decade for Natural Disaster Reduction',[106] the General Assembly noted in 1988 and in 1990 that 'it is up to each state first and foremost to take care of the victims of natural disasters and other emergencies occurring on its territory' and asserted the affected state's primary role in this regard.[107] The Assembly thus unequivocally asserts the responsibility of the affected state. Reiterating this position at an early stage during the 'International Decade for Natural Disaster Reduction', the General Assembly determined in its well-known Resolution 46/182 that:

> "Each state has the responsibility first and foremost to take care of the victims of natural disasters and other emergencies occurring on its territory. Hence, the affected State has the primary role in the initiation, organization, coordination, and implementation of humanitarian assistance within its territory".[108]

Thus, almost a decade before the Security Council asserted a primary role for states in the 'the protection of civilians in time of armed conflict', the General Assembly claimed such a *responsibility* to lie with the affected state in times of 'natural disaster and other emergencies'. As has already been argued, such an 'other emergency' may indeed include a wide variety of situations, originating from multiple origins.[109] It is apparent that the wording of the General Assembly

[102] The General Assembly also notes the importance of disaster preparedness, mitigation and prevention in many of its resolutions. A discussion of these matters however remains outside the scope of this research.

[103] Amongst others UNGA Res 2034 (XX) 'Assistance in cases of natural disaster' (7 December 1965); UNGA Res 2435 (XXIII) (19 December 1968) § 5; UNGA Res 2717 (XXV) 'Assistance in cases of natural disaster' (15 December 1970) § 1; UNGA Res 2816 (XXVI) 'Assistance in cases of natural disaster and other disaster situations' (14 December 1971). International assistance is addressed in Chapter 7.

[104] UNGA Res 36/225 (17 December 1981) UN Doc A/RES/36/225 preamble and § 2.

[105] See amongst others UNGA Res 38/202 (20 December 1983) UN Doc A/RES/38/202 preamble and § 4. See also UNGA Res 41/201 (8 December 1986) UN Doc A/RES/41/201 § 2.

[106] Section 2.2.1 Historical Development.

[107] UNGA Res 43/131 (8 December 1988) UN Doc A/RES/43/131 preamble & § 2; UNGA Res 45/100 (14 December 1990) UN Doc A/RES/45/100 preamble and § 2.

[108] UNGA Res 46/182 (19 December 1991) UN Doc A/RES/46/182, General Assembly Resolution 'Strengthening the coordination of humanitarian emergency assistance of the United Nations', Annex Guiding Principles § 4.

[109] Section 3.2.5 Defining a (Natural) Disaster and Section 3.3.3. Defining a Humanitarian Crisis.

resolutions, although non-binding in character, is much clearer and more direct than the Security Council in the declaration that the provision of humanitarian assistance falls within the scope of responsibilities attributable to the affected state. Where the Security Council considers phrases such as the 'protection of civilians' and meeting their 'basic needs', the General Assembly is straightforward in the assessment of the need for humanitarian assistance in the aftermath of a natural disaster and that such a need should be met through the responsibilities of the affected state. Naturally, a state's *responsibility* for the *occurrence* of such a disaster is far more likely to be absent than is often the case in responsibility for instances of armed conflict, with which the Security Council is concerned. Such a determination by the General Assembly is therefore also more likely to be feasible in the political arena of the UN, with less political and legal consequences. Furthermore, although the General Assembly claims a responsibility for the affected state, it does not specify the exact legal basis for such a responsibility, nor do its resolutions have binding legal value.

The abovementioned Resolution 46/182 is considered to be the cardinal resolution concerning the establishment of the UN framework on the provision and coordination of humanitarian assistance, and the Assembly has referred back to it consistently in subsequent resolutions, generally adopted without a vote, by consensus. In such subsequent resolutions, the Assembly reiterates the *Guiding Principles* annexed to Resolution 46/182, and stresses the need for humanitarian assistance to be provided according to these *Principles*.[110] In doing so, the General

[110] See amongst others UN Res 47/168 (22 December 1992) UN Doc A/RES/47/168; UNGA Res 48/57 (14 December 1993) UN Doc A/RES/48/57; UNGA Res 48/188 (9 March 1994) UN Doc A/RES/48/188; UNGA Res 49/139 (20 December 1994) UN Doc A/RES/49/139; UNGA Res 51/194 (10 February 1997) UN Doc A/RES/51/194; UNGA Res 52/167 (18 February 1998) UN Doc A/RES/52/167; UNGA Res 52/168 (18 February 1998) UN Doc A/RES/52/168; UNGA Res 53/87 (27 January 1999) UN Doc A/RES/53/87; UNGA Res 53/88 (29 January 1999) UN Doc A/RES/53/88; UNGA Res 54/95 (28 January 2000) UN Doc A/RES/54/95; UNGA Res 54/192 (21 February 2000) UN Doc A/RES/54/192; UNGA Res 54/233 (25 February 2000) UN Doc A/RES/54/233; UNGA Res 55/163 (7 February 2001) UN Doc A/RES/55/163; UNGA Res 55/164 (7 February 2001) UN Doc A/RES/55/164; UNGA Res 55/175 (7 March 2001) UN Doc A/RES/55/175; UNGA Res 56/99 (31 January 2002) UN Doc A/RES/56/99; UNGA Res 56/103 (5 February 2002) UN Doc A/RES/56/103; UNGA Res 56/107 (7 February 2002) UN Doc A/RES/56/107; UNGA Res 56/217 (19 February 2002) UN Doc A/RES/56/217; UNGA Res 57/150 (27 February 2003) UN Doc A/RES/57/150; UNGA Res 57/152 (3 March 2003) UN Doc A/RES/57/152; UNGA Res 57/153 (3 March 2003) UN Doc A/RES/57/153; UNGA Res 58/25 (29 January 2004) UN Doc A/RES/58/25; UNGA Res 58/114 (5 February 2004) UN Doc A/RES/58/114; UNGA Res 59/141 (25 February 2005) UN Doc A/RES/59/141; UNGA Res 59/212 (3 March 2005) UN Doc A/RES/59/212; UNGA Res 60/123 (24 March 2006) UN Doc A/RES/60/123; UNGA Res 60/124 (8 March 2006) UN Doc A/RES/60/124; UNGA Res 60/125 (15 March 2006) UN Doc A/RES/60/125; UNGA Res 61/131 (22 February 2007) UN Doc A/RES/61/131; UNGA Res 61/133 (1 March 2007) UN Doc A/RES/61/133; UNGA Res 61/134 (1 March 2007) UN Doc A/RES/61/134; UNGA Res 62/92 (1 February 2008) UN Doc A/RES/62/92; UNGA Res 62/94 (25 January 2008) UN Doc A/RES/62/94; UNGA Res 62/95 (29 January 2008) UN Doc A/RES/62/95; UNGA Res 63/138 (5 March 2009) UN Doc A/RES/63/138; UNGA Res 63/139 (5 March 2009) UN Doc A/RES/63/139; UNGA Res 63/141 (10 March 2009) UN Doc A/RES/63/141; UNGA Res 64/76 (2 February 2010) UN Doc A/RES/64/76; UNGA Res 64/77 (8 February 2010) UN Doc A/RES/64/77; UNGA Res 64/251 (30 April 2010) UN Doc A/RES/64/251;

Assembly has continued to repeat its original approach and wording, asserting the primary responsibility of the affected state. However, the Assembly has progressed and developed its perspective, as in subsequent years the Assembly has also addressed the responsibility of the affected state in circumstances *other* than related to natural disaster, noting:

> "the obligation of all States and parties to an armed conflict to protect civilians in armed conflicts in accordance with international humanitarian law, and invites States to promote a culture of protection, taking into account the particular needs of women, children, older persons and persons with disabilities".[111]

Thus, aligning itself with the position of the Security Council, the General Assembly also affirms the duty of states and other parties to armed conflict to protect civilians, in particular the most vulnerable. This stance has then also been reiterated by the General Assembly in subsequent resolutions pertaining to the provision of humanitarian assistance.[112] More recently, the General Assembly has begun to call upon states to 'comply fully with their obligations under international humanitarian law' regarding the respect for and protection of civilians within their jurisdiction.[113]

When considering the General Assembly's perspective on the responsibility of states in the provision of humanitarian assistance, it becomes apparent that the original focus concerned a responsibility regarding the provision of humanitarian assistance in relation to natural disasters. Yet, in more recent years, the General Assembly has begun to complement the Security Council in both its topic and wording, as it has begun to include the responsibility of states to provide assistance *in times of conflict*, as well as mentioning the duties of states in the 'protection of civilians'. Thus, although it may be too soon to state that the two central UN organs

UNGA Res 65/132 (1 March 2011) UN Doc A/RES/65/132; UNGA Res 65/133 (3 March 2011) UN Doc A/RES/65/133; UNGA Res 65/264 (21 June 2011) UN Doc A/RES/65/264; UNGA Res 65/307 (25 August 2011) UN Doc A/RES/65/307; UNGA Res 66/117 (1 March 2012) UN Doc A/RES/66/117; UNGA Res 66/119 (7 March 2012) UN Doc A/RES/66/119; UNGA Res 66/227 (15 March 2012) UN Doc A/RES/66/227; UNGA Res 67/85 (21 March 2013) UN Doc A/RES/67/85; UNGA Res 67/87 (26 March 2013) UN Doc A/RES/67/87; UNGA Res 67/231 (9 April 2013) UN Doc A/RES/67/231; UNGA Res 68/101 (18 February 2014) UN Doc A/RES/68/101; UNGA Res 68/102 (12 February 2014) UN Doc A/RES/68/102; UNGA Res 68/103 (19 February 2014) UN Doc A/RES/68/103. The General Assembly has also recalled this cardinal resolution in subsequent resolutions relating to specific situations such as for example in the Indian Ocean Tsunami UNGA Res 63/137 (11 December 2008) UN Doc A/RES/63/137; and UNGA Res 64/250 (30 April 2010) UN Doc A/RES/64/250 concerning the earthquake in Haiti.

[111] UNGA Res 58/114 (5 February 2004) UN Doc A/RES/58/114 §12.

[112] UNGA Res 59/141 (25 February 2005) UN Doc A/RES/59/141 § 15; UNGA Res 60/124 (8 March 2006) UN Doc A/RES/60/124 § 3; UNGA Res 62/94 (25 January 2008) UN Doc A/RES/62/94 § 19; UNGA Res 63/139 (5 March 2009) UN Doc A/RES/63/139 § 21; UNGA Res 64/76 (2 February 2010) UN Doc A/RES/64/76 § 22; UNGA Res 65/133 (3 March 2011) UN Doc A/RES/65/133 §23; UNGA Res 66/119 (7 March 2012) UN Doc A/RES/66/119 § 29; UNGA Res 67/87 (26 March 2013) UN Doc A/RES/67/87 § 33; UNGA Res 68/102 (12 February 2014) UN Doc A/RES/68/102 § 36.

[113] See amongst others UNGA Res 65/132 (1 March 2011) UN Doc A/RES/65/132 § 12 and UNGA Res 68/101 (18 February 2014) UN Doc A/RES/68/101 § 13.

are perhaps aligning themselves towards one singular perspective, the General Assembly does indeed appear to be embracing the perspective taken by the Security Council with regard to a more all-encompassing and overarching approach concerning the responsibilities of the affected state, without so much distinction as to the specific circumstance leading up to the need for emergency aid.

What remains however, is some lack in clarity with regard to the *specific* obligations that states may have within the 'general responsibility' to provide assistance. With the exception of the recent referrals to humanitarian law, the General Assembly does not declare whether these responsibilities that it recognises may be a duty to provide assistance under a particular body of law, thereby leaving no other source than general international law. Yet, the General Assembly does insist that such obligations exist in international law, and considers potential enforcement mechanisms should a state not provide for humanitarian assistance.[114] Thus, while the UN body itself does not have the means to adopt legally binding resolutions, the resolutions in general are adopted by consensus and indicative of a particular trend within the body of UN member states. As such, it can be concluded that the UN General Assembly resolutions support the stance taken by the Security Council in the sense that here too an assertion is made regarding an overall primary responsibility for the affected state to protect civilians within its jurisdiction under international law, through the provision of humanitarian assistance in the event of a broad range of emergencies. Unlike the Security Council, which includes non-state actors such as armed groups in its deliberations, the General Assembly however focuses on the responsibilities of the affected state.

6.4.4 Rights of Persons to Receive Assistance under General Assembly Resolutions

Similar to the Security Council, the General Assembly approaches the provision of humanitarian assistance from the perspective of the state, rather than from the perspective of the recipient of such assistance. Indeed, the UN's outlook focuses on the duties that may lie with the affected state (or third states in Chapter 7), rather than possible rights of the persons in need of assistance. At an early stage, the General Assembly merely formulated rather broadly that:

> "The provision of international relief to civilian populations is in conformity with the humanitarian principles of the Charter of the United Nations, the Universal Declaration of Human Rights and other international instruments in the field of human rights".[115]

As such, although noting the human rights context within which humanitarian assistance should take place, the General Assembly does not address specific rights-holders. This formulation that the provision of humanitarian assistance is 'in conformity with' the UDHR and other human rights instruments however does

[114] Chapter 8.

[115] UNGA Res 2675 (XXV) (9 December 1970) 'Basic principles for the protection of civilian populations in armed conflict' § 8.

align with the assessment in Chapter 5 that the provision of such aid is a vehicle in the fulfilment of existing human rights.[116]

Also, the General Assembly has considered that the abandonment of victims of natural disasters 'constitutes a threat to human life and an offence to human dignity', although the Assembly has refrained from noting a specific obligation or duty resting upon a certain duty-bearer.[117] Similarly avoiding a distinct responsible actor, the General Assembly has declared to be 'deeply concerned with the victims' of emergency situations and reaffirming the 'cardinal importance of humanitarian assistance' for such victims.[118] The milestone Resolution 46/182 reiterates this perspective in its Guiding Principles.[119] Indeed, subsequent resolutions do not evolve much, only on occasion adding words of sympathy and solidarity with those affected by disasters, but not framing such sentiments in legal rights:

> "Expressing its solidarity with the people and countries that suffer as a result of natural disasters and expressing also the deepest sympathy to all victims of the natural disasters that have struck in various parts of the globe".[120]

The General Assembly herewith foregoes the opportunity to provide those finding themselves in humanitarian crises with stronger tools to assert themselves, as it avoids the formulation of both a potential right to receive aid, as well as a stronger embedding of humanitarian assistance within the current legal framework of (human) rights. Thus, it must be concluded that the General Assembly, although affirming strongly the responsibility of states to provide assistance, does not perceive this obligation to be translated into a right formulated for persons in need of assistance.

6.5 Duties and Rights in Specific Circumstances under International Law

Humanitarian assistance is not provided in a legal vacuum: it must be considered in the context of the realities on the ground. When facing a humanitarian crisis, the affected state cannot be expected to ensure that 'life continues as normal' prior to this crisis. Yet, humanitarian assistance in essence ensures that the basic necessities are provided to those in need. As such, given that the general international legal regulations have been discussed, the more specific regimes applicable in times of crisis need to be addressed. Therefore, this Section addresses the provision of humanitarian assistance from the various legally qualifiable circumstances of conflict, occupation and (natural) disaster. In these circumstances, specific *corpora juris* are applicable, jointly with the application of more general international law and human rights law and their provisions must therefore be addressed accordingly.

---

116 Section 5.5.1.
117 UNGA Res 45/100 (14 December 1990) UN Doc A/RES/45/100 preamble § 6.
118 Ibid § 1.
119 UNGA Res 46/182 (19 December 1991) UN Doc. A/RES/46/182 Annex Guiding Principles 1.
120 UNGA Res 51/185 (11 February 1997) UN Doc A/RES/51/185 preamble § 2.

Furthermore, refugee law is discussed as a separate body of law, as humanitarian assistance may be of relevance to circumstances in which a refugee population exists.

The obligations of states must continuously be considered within the context of the relationship with state sovereignty. As discussed, the current concept of state sovereignty accepts both the right of the sovereign to be free from external interference; based on the principles of consent, non-interference and domestic jurisdiction, and the duty to provide for those within its jurisdiction. In this Chapter, the provision of assistance from external sources is not specifically addressed, as the focus lies on the duty of the affected state (or non-state actor) to provide humanitarian assistance from the perspective of its sovereign duties. As such, this Chapter looks into the specific circumstances in which the latter aspect of sovereignty plays a role.

Relevant to the discussion of the current legal framework regarding the provision of humanitarian assistance, is the differentiation between the various circumstances in which assistance may be necessary. Only having clearly established which duties and rights exist in the various legal circumstances can a common denominator and shared common ground be sought and found. The determination of such a 'minimum standard' will allow for the better protection of *all* persons facing humanitarian crises, rather than accepting the fact that a person facing food shortages in Syria is hypothetically not as well protected as someone needing food in the aftermath of the Sudanese drought. As such, the rights of persons to receive assistance from their sovereign in certain circumstances, namely armed conflict, occupation, natural disaster and other qualifiable circumstances are addressed according to the duties of these states.

6.5.1 Duties of the Affected State and Non-State Actor in Times of Conflict

Whilst the circumstance warranting the need for humanitarian assistance itself results in the application of a specific regime, within humanitarian law a differentiation must be made between international and non-international armed conflicts. Such a differentiation also exists pertaining to the provisions within humanitarian law, relating to the delivery of humanitarian assistance. States and non-state actors, as parties to a conflict, have obligations under international humanitarian law both in international armed conflicts and in non-international armed conflicts.[121] These two factual circumstances result in the application of different legal provisions and the obligations resting upon the parties to a conflict are discussed accordingly.

Particularly poignant to the circumstance of armed conflict is the fact that the provision of humanitarian assistance not only contributes food, water and medicine to those in need, but also substantially adds to the safety on the ground of persons caught up in a conflict. Through the provision of neutral, impartial and

[121] See amongst others Common Article 3 to the 4 Geneva Conventions and Article 1 AP II.

humanitarian assistance, these persons are often reassured in their protection from violence and in their security of person. Although humanitarian assistance itself does not indeed prescribe this in its most literal definition,[122] the provision of such assistance and the presence of such neutral, impartial and humanitarian providers contributes greatly in this regard. Within the context of humanitarian law, the Geneva Conventions and their Protocols supply a variety of legal considerations in the provision of humanitarian assistance, assessed in the following Sections.

6.5.1.1 Duties of the Affected State in Times of an International Armed Conflict

For the regulation of the obligations resting upon parties to an international armed conflict, recourse must be had in first instance to the 1949 Geneva Conventions, forming the basis of international humanitarian law today.[123] The Geneva Conventions differentiate between various categories of persons and duties related thereto, and as the provision of humanitarian assistance concerns a civilian population, the relevant provisions must be determined.[124] Many provisions concern relief schemes, but very few specifically address the duties of parties to an international armed conflict to provide humanitarian assistance *themselves* as the 'affected state' to a civilian population in need. This may well be explained by the time period in which the Geneva Conventions were drafted. As argued in the official Commentary, the Conventions uphold the principle to 'not interfere in a State's relations with its own nationals' which was recognised in international law rather more unlimited at the time of drafting the Conventions in 1949 than it is today.[125] Thus, the four original Geneva Conventions of 1949 do not hold provisions specifically obliging a party to an international armed conflict to provide humanitarian assistance to (their own) civilian populations in need of such aid. Indeed, neither does their predecessor, the Convention (IV) respecting the Laws and Customs of War on Land; containing only brief provisions relating to relief for prisoners of war.[126] In fact, when considering an international armed conflict, parties are in general considered to be inclined to provide for their own civilian populations facing conflict-related hardships.

Yet, with the changing nature of the international legal domain, the 1977 Additional Protocol I *does* address the responsibility of parties to an international armed conflict to provide for its own population, by declaring a prohibition of starvation in Article 54 AP I, which includes a prohibition of parties to destroy objects that are 'indispensable to the survival of the civilian population':

---

[122] Section 2.2.2 Defining Humanitarian Assistance.

[123] Section 3.2.2 Armed Conflicts and the Provision of Humanitarian Assistance.

[124] Section 2.3.1 Recipients of Humanitarian Assistance for a discussion on the various categories of persons.

[125] Jean Pictet, *Commentary on the Geneva Conventions of 12 August 1949 Volumes I-IV* (International Committee of the Red Cross 1952-1959), Volume IV Commentary GC IV Article 4, 46.

[126] Articles 15 and 16 of Convention (IV) respecting the Laws and Customs of War on Land and its annex: Regulations concerning the Laws and Customs of War on Land, 18 October 1907.

> "1. Starvation of civilians as a method of warfare is prohibited. 2. It is prohibited to attack, destroy, remove or render useless objects indispensable to the survival of the civilian population, such as food-stuffs, agricultural areas for the production of food-stuffs, crops, livestock, drinking water installations and supplies and irrigation works, for the specific purpose of denying them for their sustenance value to the civilian population or to the adverse Party, whatever the motive, whether in order to starve out civilians, to cause them to move away, or for any other motive [...] 5. In recognition of the vital requirements of any Party to the conflict in the defence of its national territory against invasion, derogation from the prohibitions contained in paragraph 2 may be made by a Party to the conflict within such territory under its own control where required by imperative military necessity".[127]

States and other parties to an international armed conflict are therefore obliged to refrain from those activities that are incompatible with the general principle of protecting the civilian population.[128] As noted in Article 54 AP 1 and explained in the *Commentary*, certain acts (such as for example the creation of a blockade) are not necessarily prohibited, but rather the object and purpose of the act, i.e. military necessity as opposed to deliberately cutting off the civilian population, must be taken into consideration.[129]

As the concept of state sovereignty presupposes both a right of non-interference and a duty of the state to take care of its civilian population, it is arguable to suggest that specific provisions thereto may be redundant, but practice has taught otherwise. It remains however rather unfortunate that humanitarian law does not address the specific duty of the actual parties to an international armed conflict to actively provide assistance to their own civilian population. Other than the provision of Article 54 AP I, international humanitarian law does *not* assert such duties from the affected state or other parties to an international armed conflict. And indeed, it is quite clear that the duty to refrain from causing starvation as reflected in Article 54 AP I is not as strong as a positive obligation to *provide* assistance would have been.

However, international humanitarian law is not the only body of law applicable to states involved in an international armed conflict. Indeed, human rights law and more general principles of international law remain applicable also, and are particularly relevant in the absence of specific clauses in humanitarian law. As discussed, with regard to the *lex specialis*-doctrine and the provision of humanitarian assistance, the most specific and most protective clause in a given circumstance must be considered, to provide the utmost protection – on humanitarian grounds, in the spirit of the law – to persons needing assistance.[130]

---

[127] See also Yoram Dinstein, 'The Right to Humanitarian Assistance' (2000) LIII *Naval War College Review* 4, 81.

[128] Yves Sandoz, Christophe Swinarski & Bruno Zimmermann (eds) *Commentary on the Additional Protocols of 8 June 1977 to the Geneva Conventions of 12 August 1949, Protocol I and II (*International Committee of the Red Cross 1987*)* Protocol I Article 54, 653 & 657-659.

[129] Ibid 657-659; see also Eyal Benvenisti, 'International Protection of the Right to Water', (October 2010) *Max Planck Encyclopedia of Public International Law* § 20.

[130] Section 3.4.3 Hierarchy or Convergence of International Legal Norms?.

As such, seen within the context of international human rights law, the obligation under Article 54 AP I does align with the obligations of states and other actors concerning the right to life, food, health (and water) under international human rights law.[131] Indeed, it has been argued with regard to the right to life, that the specific prohibition of starvation as enshrined in Article 54 AP I is a reflection of the influence of human rights law on humanitarian law, as prior to the implementation of amongst others this specific provision, the deprivation of the right to life would only be arbitrary if a person died in violation of the rules of war.[132] Also, the CESCR has asserted that part of this obligation under Article 54 to protect objects that are indispensable for the survival of a civilian population includes:

> "drinking water installations and supplies and irrigation works, protection of the natural environment against widespread, long-term and severe damage and ensuring that civilians, internees and prisoners have access to adequate water".[133]

Thus, the CESCR directly links its perspectives on the right to water to obligations under international humanitarian law.[134] Similarly, the right to adequate food can be directly connected to these circumstances in humanitarian law, as the provision prohibiting starvation as a method of warfare can be considered a manner of protecting the right to food, although this right encompasses further positive obligations. In a similar manner, the Special Rapporteur on the right to health has asserted the duty of states to provide humanitarian assistance in conflict situations.[135] Equally, the Security Council has affirmed these duties as discussed above, although not going into great detail; stating the duties of all parties to fulfil their obligations under human rights law in times of conflict.[136] With regard to the rights as enshrined in the ICESCR, a duty of the affected state to seek international cooperation and assistance to fulfil its obligations regarding the rights to food and health is included under Articles 11 and of the Covenant. In this manner, these provisions in human rights law reach a different and higher level of protection for persons caught in conflict than the prohibition to avoid starvation as enshrined in Article 54 AP I. In particular in international armed conflict, where *states* are

---

[131] Section 6.3.1 Duties of the Affected State and Non-State Actor under Human Rights Law.

[132] Fausto Pocar, 'Human Rights Under The International Covenant On Civil And Political Rights And Armed Conflicts', in LC Vohrah, F Pocar et al, (eds) *Man's Inhumanity to Man: Essays in Honour of Antonio Cassese* (Kluwer Law International 2003) 733-735.

[133] CESCR General Comment 15 (20 January 2003) UN Doc E/C.12/2002/11 'The Right to water (arts. 11 and 12 of the International Covenant on Economic Social and Cultural Rights' § 22.

[134] See in this regard also Benvenisti, 'International Protection of the Right to Water' (n 129) § 7: armies must respect civilians' right to water ; no direct attacks on water installations or other such items that supply water is allowed.

[135] 'Right of everyone to the enjoyment of the highest attainable standard of physical and mental health' Report of the Special Rapporteur on the Right to Health UN Doc A/68/297 (9 August 2013) § 52.

[136] Amongst others UNSC Res 1265 (17 September 1999) UN Doc S/RES/1265 § 4; UNSC Res 1863 (9 July 2009) UN Doc S/RES/1863 § 19 and UNSC Res 2036 (22 February 2012) UN Doc S/RES/2036 § 16; and Section 6.3.1 Duties of the Affected State and Non-State Actor under Human Rights Law.

parties to the conflict, there is little doubt as to whom the addressees of the duties are, and both human rights obligations and duties under humanitarian law are simultaneously applicable. As such, it has been argued that the provisions in the ICESCR indeed create a more substantive protection for the receipt of humanitarian assistance.[137]

Thus, the prohibition of starvation as provided for in Article 54 AP I enshrines an obligation for parties to an international armed conflict to provide emergency assistance in the event of a *threat of starvation*. Furthermore, the duties under human rights law of states party to a conflict do not cease to exist, including the obligation to *seek international assistance in the provision of the 'minimum core obligations'*. As such, not providing such assistance would not only violate Article 54 AP I itself, but also related human rights law provisions as the right to food, health and life. In fact, those latter provisions are more concrete with regard to the positive obligations of states party to an international armed conflict to provide humanitarian assistance.

6.5.1.2 Duties of the Affected State and Non-State Actors in Times of a Non-International Armed Conflict

When considering humanitarian law pertaining to non-international armed conflicts, a differentiation must be made regarding the types of non-international armed conflicts and the applicable law. As discussed in Section 3.2.1, a differentiation can be made between those non-international armed conflicts where Common Article 3 is applicable, conflicts meeting the threshold of Article 1 AP II (and where parties to the conflict are also party to the Additional Protocol) and those circumstances that may arguably not meet the threshold of the applicability of humanitarian law but remain classified as 'internal strife' or a similar consideration.[138] A topical situation to consider in that regard is the current situation in the Ukraine, where difficulties exist in the classification of the conflict.

Commencing with the four Geneva Conventions, it becomes immediately apparent that these, similar to the case in an international armed conflict, do not contain a provision placing a duty upon states or other parties to the conflict to provide assistance to their population. In the circumstance of a non-international armed conflict, common Article 3 is applicable, and although Article 3 does not stipulate an obligation to provide assistance, it does consider that persons with no active role in the hostilities must be treated 'humanely, without any adverse distinction founded on race, colour, religion or faith, sex, birth or wealth, or any other similar criteria'. This principle as explained by the ICTY's Trial Chamber in fact entails the obligation to not intentionally, through an act or omission cause 'serious mental or physical suffering or injury or constitute [...] a serious attack on

[137] Rebecca Barber, 'Facilitating humanitarian assistance in international humanitarian and human rights law', (2009) 91 International Review of the Red Cross 874, 395.
[138] Section 3.2.1.

human dignity'.[139] Such assistance would ensure the humane treatment of those civilians finding themselves in a non-international armed conflict, and would furthermore have to be based upon the principle of non-discrimination. Indeed, although considered to reflect 'elementary considerations of humanity', the rules laid out in common Article 3 of the Conventions do not assist in the determination of the duties resting upon parties to a non-international armed conflict when it comes to the provision of humanitarian assistance.[140] Thus, it may be argued that a duty exists for parties to provide a minimum of assistance based upon common Article 3.

Similar to circumstances of international armed conflict, here too the Additional Protocol presents more considerations. With regard to the duties of the parties to a conflict, Article 1 AP II distinctly asserts that the Protocol's applicability extends to those circumstances between a 'State Party' and non-state actors that can be classified as 'dissident armed forces or other organized armed groups' under responsible command.[141] Article 14 of AP II relating to non-international armed conflicts is drafted in a very similar fashion to Article 54 of AP I, declaring:

> "Starvation of civilians as a method of combat is prohibited. It is therefore prohibited to attack, destroy, remove or render useless, for that purpose, objects indispensable to the survival of the civilian population, such as foodstuffs, agricultural areas for the production of foodstuffs, crops, livestock, drinking water installations and supplies and irrigation works".

The Article elaborates on common Article 3 of the four Conventions which merely refers to humane treatment and is thereby as a specific Article quite relevant for the protection of civilians caught in non-international armed conflicts, as AP II does not otherwise specifically protect civilian objects useful to the survival of civilians.[142] Article 14 must furthermore be read in conjunction with Article 18 AP II, which will be discussed further in Chapter 7, as it concerns the provision of relief through *external* sources. Together, these two provisions do not allow for parties to a non-international armed conflict to use the argument of 'military necessity' as failure to provide for the civilian population, when such a civilian population is at risk of starvation.[143] Indeed, whilst the argument that an airstrip or harbour is not immediately available due to operations being carried out may be a valid point, such an argument will not hold over a prolonged period of time. Furthermore, according to the official Commentary, an *omission* to provide for the civilian population, resulting in starvation, may also result in a violation of parties'

---

[139] *Prosecutor v. Zejnil Delalic, Zdravko Mucic (aka "Pavo"), Hazim Delic and Esad Landžo (aka "Zenga") (Celebici - Case)* (Trial Chamber) IT-96-21-T (16 November 1998) § 543.

[140] Military and Paramilitary Activities in and against Nicaragua (Nicaragua v. United States of America), Merits, Judgment 27 June 1986 I.C.J. Reports 1986, p. 14 § 218.

[141] Article 1(1) AP II.

[142] Sandoz, Swinarski & Zimmermann *Commentary to the Additional Protocols* (n 128) Protocol II Article 14, 1456.

[143] Ibid, 1457.

obligations under Article 14.[144] Indeed, the Commentary distinctly argues that a party's decision to deliberately not take 'measures to supply the population with objects indispensable for its survival in a way would become a method of combat by default, and would be prohibited' under Article 14 AP II.[145] Whereas Article 54 of AP I arguably leaves some leeway to a State with regard to its right to destroy parts of its own territory to halt the progress of enemy troops, Article 14 of AP II obliges parties to respect such civilian objects that are indispensable to the survival of the population throughout the entire territory regardless of under whose control a certain part may be.[146] As such, according to the Commentary, the scope of Article 14 AP II is far-reaching: obliging parties to the conflict to prevent the starvation of civilians through active measures, as omissions and 'deliberate decisions' to not supply indispensable relief provisions can both lead to violations of Article 14 AP II.

Similar to the circumstance of international armed conflicts, human rights law continues to be applicable in situations of non-international armed conflict and to armed groups as parties involved in such conflicts, as also assessed by the Security Council.[147] Indeed, as was established above, human rights obligations also rest upon non-state actors, which often play a large role in non-international armed conflicts.[148] As with an international armed conflict, the relevant provisions remain those related to the right to life, food, health (and water). Such has also been reaffirmed for example by the CESCR, declaring in its General Comment pertaining to Article 11 ICESCR that:

> "Violations of the right to food can occur through the direct action of States or other entities insufficiently regulated by States. These include: (…) prevention of access to humanitarian food aid in internal conflicts or other emergency situations".[149]

Thus, the CESCR argues that parties to a non-international armed conflict are obliged to fulfil the right to food through the provision of humanitarian assistance. Indeed, the prevention of access to humanitarian assistance results in a direct violation of Article 11 ICESCR according to the CESCR. The duties of the state and non-state actors in the realisation of the right to health have been asserted also by the Special Rapporteur on the right to health, arguing a 'primary responsibility' for such parties in times of conflict, which can be fulfilled through the provision of humanitarian aid and making 'resources available'.[150] As such, attacks on health care facilities could be considered a violation of the right to health, with a view to

---

[144] Ibid, 1458.
[145] Ibid.
[146] Ibid, 1459.
[147] Amongst others in UNSC Res 1265 (17 September 1999) UN Doc S/RES/1265 § 4; UNSC Res 1863 (9 July 2009) UN Doc S/RES/1863 § 19 and UNSC Res 2036 (22 February 2012) UN Doc S/RES/2036 § 16. See also Sections 3.4.2 and 6.3.1.
[148] Section 6.3.1.
[149] CESCR General Comment 12 (n 37) § 19.
[150] UN Doc A/68/297 (n 135) § 51- 52

the obligation of conduct enshrined in the ICESCR to provide health care. Thus, although the obligations formulated in AP II are somewhat similar to those of AP I when considering the protection of persons in need of humanitarian assistance, the scope of AP II remains restricted to non-international armed conflicts involving armed groups that hold a certain *degree of control and organisation*. The provisions of Article 14 AP II require the prevention of starvation from parties involved in the conflict, which has been explained to include the prevention of deliberate obstruction of humanitarian aid. A positive obligation cannot therefore be construed within the Protocol. Thus, the content of the Protocol is not very far-reaching in the protection of persons. Furthermore, the scope of the Protocol results in many circumstances of non-international armed conflict remaining outside its protection. This situation results in uncertainty as to the obligations concerning the provision of humanitarian assistance to those in need that happen to be in circumstances falling short of a non-international armed conflict falling within the scope of AP II. Yet, human rights law norms remain relevant and applicable. Indeed, as has been seen concerning international armed conflicts, the duties of the parties to a conflict are more protective under the rights to life, food and health. These rights envisage a *positive* obligation resting upon states, especially those of the ICESCR, to provide minimum levels of food and health care.

6.5.2 Rights of Persons to Receive Assistance in times of Conflict

Regarding the rights to *receive* humanitarian assistance in times of conflict, a similar approach as with the obligations to *provide* such assistance in times of conflict must be held. As such not only does a differentiation need to be made between the circumstance of an international armed conflict and a non-international armed conflict, but also a consideration of the various applicable fields of law is relevant.

6.5.2.1 Rights of Persons to Receive Assistance in Times of an International Armed Conflict

When regarding the Geneva Conventions and AP I, neither contain specific formulations providing persons in need of humanitarian assistance with legal rights to claim such assistance from their sovereign under humanitarian law. This indeed once again reflects the timeframe of the Conventions, as can be seen for example through the incorporation of Articles 30 and 38 GC IV. Both Articles consider a right for 'protected persons' to apply for relief or allowing relief to be sent to them, rather than a right for civilians in general, and this right is furthermore not related to the affected state. Article 30 GC IV notes the opportunity for protected persons:

> "for making application to the Protecting Powers, the International Committee of the Red Cross, the National Red Cross (Red Crescent, Red Lion and Sun) Society of the country where they may be, as well as to any organization that might assist them".

As such, a right to claim assistance from the affected state is absent. Furthermore, Article 38 also does not reflect duties of the affected state to provide assistance to its own population, rather noting certain rights of protected persons such as to be:

> "[...] enabled to receive the individual or collective relief that may be sent to them. (2) They shall, if their state of health so requires, receive medical attention and hospital treatment to the same extent as the nationals of the State concerned. (3) They shall be allowed to practise their religion and to receive spiritual assistance from ministers of their faith. (4) If they reside in an area particularly exposed to the dangers of war, they shall be authorized to move from that area to the same extent as the nationals of the State concerned. (5) Children under fifteen years, pregnant women and mothers of children under seven years shall benefit by any preferential treatment to the same extent as the nationals of the State concerned".

Here too the official Commentary is unambiguous, clearly stating that the intention has been to restrict these possibilities to those persons in specific circumstances (such as detention) granting them the status of 'protected persons'.[151] Thus, civilians finding themselves in an international armed conflict do not have the possibility to resort to specific provisions in international *humanitarian* law granting them the right to receive humanitarian assistance from their sovereign state. However, arguably an implicit right to receive such assistance does exist, as can be read in other provisions. As such, certain provisions refer to a right of third parties to *offer* assistance or relief actions which 'shall be undertaken' (to be discussed further in Chapter 7) if and when a civilian population 'is in need'.[152] Such formulations can be construed as an entitlement of the civilian population to be supplied with emergency aid in situations of need.[153]

This changing approach seen in the formulation of the provisions of AP I towards a right to receive assistance, albeit not from the state sovereign, has been supported by the practice of the ICRC and its perspective as laid down in its 'Customary IHL Study'.[154] The ICRC itself has also repeatedly stated it recognises a right of a civilian population to receive humanitarian assistance in circumstances where it should be in need.[155] Furthermore, such a right to seek and receive relief has been explicitly incorporated by several states in their military manuals, evidencing the belief that civilian populations should be entitled to demand

---

[151] Pictet, *Commentary on the Geneva Conventions of 12 August 1949* (n 125) Article 30, 213-214 and Article 38, 244.

[152] Article 70 AP I and to a lesser extent Articles 10 and 23 of GC IV.

[153] Jean-Marie Henckaerts & Louise Doswald-Beck (eds), *Customary International Humanitarian Law (ICRC Study)* (Cambridge University Press 2006) Rule 55.

[154] Henckaerts & Doswald-Beck, ICRC Customary International Humanitarian Law Study.

[155] 'Code of Conduct for the International Red Cross and Red Crescent Movement and NGOs in Disaster Relief', Annex VI to the resolutions of the 26th International Conference of the Red Cross and Red Crescent, Geneva, 1995 Prepared jointly by the International Federation of Red Cross and Red Crescent Societies and the ICRC, Res II, § A(h).

assistance.[156] Yet, as these states are few and far between, as well as the fact that the ICRC's perspective is not *explicitly* formulated in AP II, it remains difficult to assert an actual right of the civilian population to receive assistance from their state under existing humanitarian law.

Alternatively, as seen in Section 6.3.2, such a right can be found in existing human rights law, more specifically the rights to life, food and health. These rights, considering their continued applicability in times of conflict, ensure at a more concrete level the receipt of assistance for persons in need of emergency aid. Indeed, in requesting assistance, persons in need of aid have more direct protection under human rights law, than through the inferred protection of international humanitarian law, when considering rights to receive assistance from the state sovereign.

6.5.2.2 Rights of Persons to Receive Assistance in Times of a Non-International Armed Conflict

Whilst civilians finding themselves in a non-international armed conflict are subject to a different legal regime, granting them other options, than those caught in an international armed conflict, it remains difficult to find clear-cut *rights* enshrined in humanitarian law for them also. As such, in circumstances falling within the scope of a non-international armed conflict as envisaged by AP II, civilians, similar to the lack of provisions in AP I, do not find distinct rights formulated within this Protocol. Articles 14 and 18 AP II do not provide for a right of civilians to demand assistance from the sovereign or other party involved in the conflict, nor do other provisions of the Protocol.

Yet, the ICRC's perspective does not alter from its stance concerning international armed conflicts, and can remain true also for those civilians who are in need of assistance in times of a non-international armed conflict. As such, the ICRC argues a right to receive humanitarian assistance for *all civilians* finding themselves in a conflict situation.[157] However, for the exercise of these rights of civilians in such conflicts, resort will mostly have to be had to other provisions in general international law and human rights law, which remain applicable at all times. Such resort also leads to a greater protection for those caught in conflicts falling outside the scope of AP II due to a lack of organisation or control of the armed group party to the conflict. Whilst in these circumstances it may be more difficult to claim responsibility of such groups in the provision of assistance, such responsibilities will nonetheless continue to remain for the state sovereign. As seen in Section 6.3.2, the rights to life, food and health provide for such protection at a more concrete level. In fact, given the lack of protection provided to civilians under humanitarian law in particular for non-international armed conflicts falling outside

[156] Henckaerts & Doswald-Beck, ICRC Customary International Humanitarian Law Study (n153) Rule 55 for the Military manuals of Germany, the Netherlands, Nicaragua and Switzerland.

[157] 'Code of Conduct for the International Red Cross and Red Crescent Movement and NGOs in Disaster Relief' (n 155), Res II, § A(h).

the scope of AP I, the right to receive humanitarian assistance from the sovereign is more protectively and substantially enshrined in the rights to life, food and health under human rights law. As such, this law may well function as *lex specialis*, given its more specific and protective nature regarding the provision and receipt of humanitarian assistance. The provision of such assistance in fact, as concluded in Chapter 5, functions as the vehicle for the state's fulfilment of those human rights.

6.5.3 Duties of the Affected State (Occupying Power) in Times of Occupation

It remains essential to note that, while a state of war no longer needs to be declared by parties for humanitarian law to be applicable, such a conflict must be factually determined and equally a situation of occupation must be determined to assess an authority as 'occupying power'.[158] Only if and when an occupation is determined, shall the law of occupation enter into force. As such, the law of occupation is only applicable in a circumstance where a sovereign state is involved as an actor, *exercising a degree of control* as discussed in Section 3.2.1. The possibility of application of the law of occupation to circumstances 'other than a state of war or armed conflict between or among High Contracting parties' has also been suggested by some,[159] allowing for the application of the law to armed groups that may control territory without a sovereign's consent, but such a suggestion is not generally accepted.[160]

Similar to the distinction between *jus ad bellum* and *jus in bello*, the law of occupation applies independently of whether or not the occupation was established lawfully, as long as its factual establishment can be determined.[161] As such, the ICJ concluded in 2005 in the *Armed Activities in the Democratic Republic of Congo* case that:

> "Uganda was the occupying Power in Ituri at the relevant time. As such it was under an obligation, according to Article 43 of the Hague Regulations of 1907, to take all the measures in its power to restore, and ensure, as far as possible, public order and safety in the occupied area, while respecting, unless absolutely prevented, the laws in force in the DRC. This obligation comprised the duty to secure respect for the applicable rules of international human rights law and international humanitarian law, to protect the inhabitants of the occupied territory against acts of violence, and not to tolerate such violence by any third party. The Court, having concluded that Uganda was an occupying Power in Ituri at the relevant time, finds that Uganda's responsibility is engaged both for any acts of its military that violated its international obligations and for any lack of vigilance in preventing violations of human rights and international humanitarian law by other actors present in the occupied territory, including rebel groups acting on their own

158 Section 3.2.3 Defining Occupation.

159 Robert B Oakley, Michael J Dziedzic, Eliot M Goldberg (eds), *Policing The New World Disorder: Peace Operations And Public Security* (National Defense University Press 1998) 405.

160 Barber, 'Facilitating humanitarian assistance in international humanitarian and human rights law', (n 137) 384-385.

161 Section 3.2.3 Defining Occupation; see also Eyal Benvenisti, *The International Law of Occupation* (Oxford University Press 2012) 5.

> account. The Court notes that Uganda at all times has responsibility for all actions and omissions of its own military forces in the territory of the DRC in breach of its obligations under the rules of international human rights law and international humanitarian law which are relevant and applicable in the specific situation".[162]

Thus, establishing *who* the occupying power is in a certain situation is the primary step to determining that the law of occupation is applicable, triggering (some of) the duties of the occupier to provide in humanitarian assistance for the civilian population should it be in need. Indeed this caveat of 'need' is of more relevance to the law of occupation, as opposed to the law of armed conflict, given that circumstances of conflict are more likely to result in situations of humanitarian crisis. Occupation on the other hand may not lead to the establishment of a humanitarian crisis, but rather on the contrary serve to prevent or solve such situations, such as for example the role of the United States and United Kingdom in Iraq following the armed conflict in 2003.[163]

Contrary to the law concerning armed conflict, the law of occupation historically contains many provisions prescribing an occupying power to provide in humanitarian assistance to an occupied population. Explanations for this difference with the law of armed conflict can particularly be found in the circumstances of World War II and the German occupation of large parts of Europe, leading up to the creation of the Geneva Conventions. Article 43 of the Regulations Concerning the Law and Customs of War on Land, as the predecessor to the Geneva Conventions dealing with occupation, does not distinctly mention such a duty of the occupier to provide, but succinctly declares that such a power must ensure 'public order and safety'.[164] However, the 1949 Geneva Conventions and their Protocols, following the events of World War II, clearly and more elaborately set forth the duties of the occupying power, starting with Article 55 GC IV which declares:

> "To the fullest extent of the means available to it, the Occupying Power has the duty of ensuring the food and medical supplies of the population; it should, in particular, bring in the necessary foodstuffs, medical stores and other articles if the resources of the occupied territory are inadequate. The Occupying Power may not requisition foodstuffs, articles or medical supplies available in the occupied territory, except for use by the occupation forces and administration personnel, and then only if the requirements of the civilian population have been taken into account. [...] The Protecting Power shall, at any time, be at liberty to verify the state of the food and medical supplies in occupied territories, except where temporary restrictions are made necessary by imperative military requirements".

[162] *Armed Activities on the Territory of the Congo* (Democratic Republic of the Congo v. Uganda), Judgment, I.C.J. Reports 2005, p. 168, § 178-180.
[163] See in this regard the role of the Coalition Provisional Authority, UNSC Res 1483 (22 May 2003) UN Doc S/RES/1483.
[164] Article 43 Regulations Concerning the Law and Customs of War on Land – annex to Convention Respecting the Laws and Customs of War on Land. See also Yoram Dinstein, *The International Law of Belligerent Occupation* (Cambridge University Press 2009), who argues that the 1907 Hague Regulations provide insufficient protection to civilians.

Clearly this is a differentiation from the law applying to parties to an armed conflict in which no occupation exists, as the obligations in the Geneva Conventions and their Protocols do not contain such provisions for parties to a conflict in general. Indeed, the developments in the law of occupation cannot be viewed as separate from the Nazi-occupation of large parts of Europe, in the aftermath of which these provisions were developed. Article 55 GC IV thereby extends the duties of the occupier, as it now has to 'ensure to the fullest extent of the means available' that the population is provided with food and medical supplies. As such, Article 55 GC IV remains aware of the difficulties an occupier may face while doing so at the time of a conflict.[165] The occupying power may furthermore not be relieved from its duties in the event assistance is provided through other, external, sources (to be discussed further in Chapter 7), as Article 60 GC IV stipulates that the responsibility to provide relief remains with the occupying power.[166]

In relation to the provision of relief and duty to ensure that an occupied population receives medical supplies, Article 56 GC IV obliges the occupier furthermore to ensure and maintain hospitals and public health, particularly taking measures concerning the prevention of epidemics.[167] However, this responsibility does not rest solely with the occupying power, as Article 56 provides that such measures should be taken 'with the co-operation of national and local authorities'.[168] While the provisions relating to the duties of an occupier in GC IV already greatly surpass the duties resting upon parties to conflicts in general under the Geneva Conventions, Additional Protocol I has added to these duties as GC IV relates mostly to a responsibility of the occupying power to provide necessary food and medical supplies. Article 69 AP I supplements this obligation by stipulating that the occupier must, again 'to the fullest extent of the means available to it', also ensure clothing, shelter and *other* supplies that may be 'essential to the survival of the civilian population'. AP I thereby creates a non-limitative list through which the occupier is obliged to supply those items that may be necessary specific to a certain situation.[169] However, the text of the Article does recognise that an occupying power may be limited (beyond its control) in its possibilities, as the Protocol stipulates that the occupier shall be limited by the 'extent of the means available to it'.[170] Such limitations indeed reflect the fact that a circumstance of occupation can immediately follow that of conflict, resulting in a situation in which the fulfilment

---

[165] Pictet, *Commentary on the Geneva Conventions of 12 August 1949* (n 125) Article 55, 309-310.

[166] Article 60 GV IV and also Pictet, *Commentary on the Geneva Conventions of 12 August 1949* (n 125) Article 60, 323.

[167] The relevant passage of Article 56 GC IV declares: "To the fullest extent of the means available to it, the Occupying Power has the duty of ensuring and maintaining, with the cooperation of national and local authorities, the medical and hospital establishments and services, public health and hygiene in the occupied territory, with particular reference to the adoption and application of the prophylactic and preventive measures necessary to combat the spread of contagious diseases and epidemics".

[168] Pictet, *Commentary on the Geneva Conventions of 12 August 1949* (n 125) Article 56, 313.

[169] Sandoz, Swinarski & Zimmermann *Commentary to the Additional Protocols* (n 128) Protocol I Article 69, 812.

[170] Dinstein, *The International Law of Belligerent Occupation* (n 164) 150.

of these duties are more difficult. Whereas certain duties apply immediately upon establishment of occupation, other duties, amongst which those stipulated in Articles 55, 56 and 59-62 and related to the provision of assistance through relief such as food and medical supplies, may arise only at a later stage.[171] Thus, interestingly the particular provisions under GC IV *pertaining to the delivery of humanitarian assistance* necessary at the time of a humanitarian crisis only arise upon the *longer* establishment of occupation, whereas such a crisis may then not, or no longer, exist.

However, as established also with regard to times of armed conflict, the law of war, or in this case, the law of occupation is not necessarily the only body of law applicable. As seen above, it is accepted by the ICJ that human rights find continued application in times of occupation.[172] Such application in relation to the duties of the 'affected state' is distinct from its application in times of armed conflict, as in the latter case such application relates to the sovereign's duties regarding its own citizens whilst in times of occupation such obligations would rest upon the occupying force regarding the occupied population. However, for all the obligations of the occupier to enter into force, including relevant human rights obligations, a level of 'effective' control or authority must be established.[173] Therefore it is necessary to establish the exact level of 'control' of the occupying force in order for human rights law to be a source of obligations in the provision of humanitarian assistance for the occupier in a certain circumstance. As noted in more detail in Section 3.4.2.2 however, international law today does not definitively determine the level of 'effective' control or authority needed for the extraterritorial application of human rights.[174] Thus, this leaves the practical application of human rights obligations in times of occupation somewhat uncertain.

Furthermore, the 'progressive development' aspect of the rights incorporated in the ICESCR, such as the right to food and health, as relevant to the provision of humanitarian assistance, may be problematic for an occupying force establishing new control over a certain territory and not necessarily intending to *remain* the occupying force for an extended period of time, and must therefore be taken into account.[175] The 'minimum core obligations' of the ICESCR resting upon states regarding the rights to food and health, which must be fulfilled, however do complement the duties of an occupier under the law of occupation, as this framework can be seen as 'emergency law'.[176] Indeed, these minimum core

[171] See in particular Section 3.2.4 Occupation and the Provision of Humanitarian Assistance regarding the timeframe and level of control necessary for the application of several of the provisions. See also Pictet, *Commentary on the Geneva Conventions of 12 August 1949* (n 125) Article 6, 60.
[172] ICJ *Armed Activities on the Territory of the Congo* (n 162) § 216.
[173] See amongst others for example with regard to the right to water Benvenisti, 'International Protection of the Right to Water' (n 129) § 7 and 20.
[174] Section 3.4.2 Applicability of Human Rights in Armed Conflict and Occupation.
[175] Sylvain Vité, 'The interrelation of the law of occupation and economic, social and cultural rights', (2008) 90 *International Review of the Red Cross* 871, 632.
[176] Ibid 636.

obligations must then be seen in the context of the establishment of control by the occupying power.

Both for the applicability of human rights obligations and for the applicability of the specific provisions in the Geneva Convention relating to the provision of humanitarian assistance, a certain duration and degree of control are therefore necessary to incur responsibilities for the occupying power. Given the fact that humanitarian assistance is of relevance in the immediate existence of a humanitarian crisis such may well not be the case in the establishment of situations of occupation today, as compared to the origins of the elaborations in the Geneva Conventions following World War II. In that regard, it has also been noted by Higgins that whilst the protection of civilians is an 'intransgressible obligation of humanitarian law', such an obligation not only rests upon the occupier, but 'equally for those seeking to liberate themselves from occupation'.[177] Indeed, in such circumstances a humanitarian crisis may once again arise.

6.5.4 Rights of Persons to Receive Assistance in Times of Occupation

Similar to the provisions lacking in humanitarian law concerning an international and a non-international armed conflict, the law of occupation does not provide for a distinct right of individuals to claim humanitarian assistance *from the occupier*. Whereas Articles 59 and 60 GC IV and 69 AP I contain obligations for the occupying power to provide in relief, they do not equally entail a right for individuals during occupation that may be enforced towards the occupier. The obligations resting upon the occupier in fact cannot be 'reversed' into an enforceable right of individuals. Indeed, such a lack in distinct rights for individuals may follow from the related circumstance that a level of control needs to be established prior to which the duties relating to the provision of humanitarian assistance are applicable to the occupying power. In fact, given the need for a certain amount of time to pass in this transitional stage, international humanitarian law in a larger sense may continue to be applicable with the therein-incorporated rights and duties relating to conflict.

Thus, in situations of occupation, individuals wanting to request humanitarian assistance from the occupying power must resort to the above mentioned regulations as enshrined in human rights law, or more general international law regulations. With regard to such possibilities, it must equally be noted that the applicability of human rights law, although acknowledged, has not crystallised yet to the extent of unambiguously determining at what point during an occupation a level of control has been established granting individuals the right to request humanitarian assistance from the occupying force, based on human rights law.

[177] Separate opinion Judge Higgins § 19 in the Legal Consequences of the Construction of a Wall in the Occupied Palestinian Territory, Advisory Opinion, I.C.J. Reports 2004, p. 136.

6.5.5 Duties of the Affected State in Times of (Natural) Disaster

A third circumstance, following armed conflict and occupation, is that of a (natural) disaster. The legal regime applicable to disasters of both man-made and natural origins is not as specific as the legal regime applicable in times of conflict or occupation. Humanitarian law is not applicable, unless the disaster takes place on a territory where an armed conflict is also occurring simultaneously. The general principle of humanity however finds continued application. The ICJ stated as early as the 1949 Corfu Channel-case that indeed

> "certain general and well-recognized principles, namely: elementary considerations of humanity, even more exacting in peace than in war"[178]

exist that are applicable to an even greater detail in times of peace. The principle of humanity has been discussed at length in Section 2.2.3.1. Of course in circumstances of disaster, general international law such as the law of state responsibility and more specifically human rights law are applicable, and in the above Section 6.3.3 in particular the role of the General Assembly in asserting the responsibilities of the affected state has become apparent. The UN body has been concerned with victims of natural disaster for decades, expressing amongst other concerns that:

> "the abandonment of the victims of natural disasters and similar emergency situations without humanitarian assistance constitutes a threat to human life and offence to human dignity".[179]

Given the fact that a particular regime for natural disaster law is absent, efforts have been made to assert the applicability of certain general aspects of international law in the circumstance of a natural or man-made disaster, and the ensuing need for humanitarian assistance when a humanitarian crisis unfolds. As such, the General Assembly has claimed that the primary responsibility in the provision of humanitarian assistance *in the aftermath of a disaster* lies with the affected state, while simultaneously affirming the affected state's sovereignty.[180] This perspective has indeed been reaffirmed by various other organs within the UN framework.[181]

---

[178] Corfu Channel Case (UK v Albania) (Merits) 9 April 1949 I.C.J. Reports 4, 22.

[179] UNGA Res 43/131 (8 December 1988) (n 3) preamble.

[180] For a comprehensive list of GA resolutions see (n 110) and infra Annex. One of the primary affirmations has been in UNGA Res 36/225 (17 December 1981) UN Doc A/RES/36/225 § 2, and a more recent example can be found in UNGA Res 64/251 (30 April 2010) UN Doc A/RES/64/251 preamble.

[181] 'Promotion And Protection Of All Human Rights, Civil, Political, Economic, Social And Cultural Rights, Including The Right To Development Human Rights And International Solidarity' Note By The United Nations High Commissioner For Human Rights UN Doc A/HRC/12/27 (22 July 2009) § 36; 'Promotion And Protection Of All Human Rights, Civil, Political, Economic, Social And Cultural Rights, Including The Right To Development' Report Of The Representative Of The Secretary-General On The Human Rights Of Internally Displaced Persons UN Doc A/HRC/10/13/Add.1 (5 March 2009)

Furthermore, such organs have asserted the importance of states' responsibilities under human rights law in the discourse on the provision of humanitarian assistance, as the provision thereof is a vehicle in, or recognition of, the fulfilment of several essential human rights.[182] Whereas circumstances of disaster may frequently lead to the state asserting a 'state of emergency' which may result in the invocation of certain derogation clauses under international human rights treaties, this does not affect the duty of the affected state in its responsibilities to provide humanitarian assistance. Indeed, as discussed in Section 5.2.2, the relevant rights regarding the provision of humanitarian assistance, i.e. the rights to life, food and health, do not allow for derogation (from minimum core obligations) in times of emergency. As such, the duties of the affected state with regard to the provision of assistance under human rights law continue to be applicable in the aftermath of disasters, and as such Section 6.4.1 has addressed these responsibilities in detail. This Section focuses on the more specific regulations geared towards natural or man-made disasters, *besides* existing obligations in human rights law.

Currently, only a few international (regional) conventions exist concerning the facilitation of humanitarian assistance in the event of a natural disaster. Previously, failed attempts include the 1927 'Convention establishing an International Relief Union'; the first international convention on peacetime disaster relief, and the 1984 'Draft Convention on expediting the delivery of emergency assistance'.[183] Although both initiatives were many years apart, the international community was still unable to positively create legal obligations for the provision of humanitarian assistance in the aftermath of a natural disaster through an international convention.[184] The current binding legal regime as laid down in treaty law is therefore limited and regional. An example includes the 'Inter-American Convention To Facilitate Disaster Assistance' of 1991.[185] Although only very few states have ratified this regional treaty, similar to the stance of the General Assembly, the Convention places the responsibility of the coordination of humanitarian assistance upon the affected state.[186] In 2005, the ASEAN Agreement on Disaster Management and Emergency Response settled with regard to the Asian region that 'each affected Party shall have the primary responsibility to respond to disasters occurring within

§ 38; 'Operational Guidelines on Human Rights and Natural Disasters' by the Representative on human rights of internally displaced persons UN Doc A/HRC/4/38/Add.1 (26 January 2006) General Principle II.

[182] See amongst others 'Report of the independent expert on human rights and international solidarity (Mr. Rudi Muhammad Rizki)' UN Doc A/HRC/4/8 (7 February 2007) § 23; UN Doc A/HRC/10/13/Add.1 (n 181) § 10, 20 and 67; Report of the Special Rapporteur on the Right to Health UN Doc A/HRC/7/11/Add.2 (5 March 2008) § 133.

[183] Convention establishing an International Relief Union Geneva (12 July 1927); UNGA Res 39/367 (18 June 1984) UN Doc A/39/367/Add.2 and E/1984/96/Add.2 'Draft Convention on Expediting the Delivery of Emergency Relief'.

[184] See Ssection 2.2.1 on the reasons behind the failure of this convention.

[185] 'Inter-American Convention To Facilitate Disaster Assistance' (7 June 1991, entry into force 16 October 1996). To date, 6 states have ratified the treaty, namely Colombia, Dominican Republic, Nicaragua, Panama, Peru and Uruguay

[186] Article IV(a) Inter-American Convention To Facilitate Disaster Assistance.

its territory'.[187] The ASEAN Agreement bases this assertion on the concept of state sovereignty. More specifically geared towards nuclear accidents, the 1986 Convention on Assistance in the Case of a Nuclear Accident or Radiological Emergency also places the primary responsibility for 'the overall direction, control, co-ordination and supervision of the assistance' with the affected state.[188]

It becomes apparent that besides rather topic-specific regulations and small regional initiatives, international binding regulation concerning the responsibilities for the provision of humanitarian assistance in the aftermath of a disaster are lacking. Indeed, general international law and human rights law provide a solid basis, upon which responsibility can be asserted for the affected state to provide such assistance. Despite such existing obligations, certain specific soft law regulations as well as regulations currently under development, can be applied to the circumstance of a natural disaster, although they do not (currently) have legally binding force. Despite their non-binding nature, they are of practical value to the provision of assistance, as well as contributing to further development of the current legal framework.

6.5.5.1 The Potential Application of the ILC Study: Protection of persons in the event of disaster

In developing its study on the 'Protection of persons in the event of disaster', the ILC has formulated Draft Articles pertaining to the rights and obligations in the provision of assistance. Although these Articles do not currently have binding legal stature, and it remains uncertain whether they will obtain such standing, the ILC's work is relevant to the development of the law pertaining to humanitarian assistance and international law.[189] Indeed, the Articles themselves are currently very much in the developmental stage, and it remains unclear precisely which form they will obtain if and when adopted. Draft Article 21 clearly defines the scope, stating that the Articles will not be applicable to circumstances in which international humanitarian law is applicable.[190] The ILC Study thereby takes the approach that international humanitarian law as a body of law is the *lex specialis* in times of conflict, and a different regime applies entirely in times of disaster.[191]

---

[187] Article 3, Principle 1 ASEAN Agreement on Disaster Management and Emergency Response 2005. Currently 10 states are party, equal to the number of member states of ASEAN, namely Brunei Darussalam, Cambodia, Indonesia, Lao PDR, Malaysia, Myanmar, Philippines, Singapore, Thailand and Viet Nam.

[188] Article 3(a) of the Convention on Assistance in the Case of a Nuclear Accident or Radiological Emergency (18 November 1986). To date the Convention has 112 state parties.

[189] See Section 2.2.2 on the work of the ILC.

[190] ILC 'Protection of persons in the event of disasters' Draft Articles UN Doc. A/CN.4/L.831 (15 May 2014) Draft Article 21. In subsequent reports, states have addressed the option that the Articles apply in situations where existing international law provisions do not: 'Fourth report on the protection of persons in the event of disasters' by Eduardo Valencia-Ospina, Special Rapporteur (11 May 2011) UN Doc A/CN.4/643 § 10.

[191] 'Preliminary report on the protection of persons in the event of disasters' (5 May 2008) International Law Commission, UN Doc A/CN.4/598 § 49.

Although this follows on from the approach taken by many of the UN organs in the provision of humanitarian assistance during the past decades, the opportunity was missed to approach disaster relief from a more all-encompassing perspective, including all applicable fields of law through one study, namely human rights law, humanitarian law and refugee law; an approach that has been adhered to increasingly in the past years.[192] Indeed such a perspective is held by the ILC Special Rapporteur who has argued for a more simultaneous applicability and complementarity of the various fields of law relevant to disaster situations, including humanitarian law.[193] It is therefore regrettable that the ILC as a whole in drafting these Articles is apparently creating another niche and separate body of law applicable to non-conflict disaster situations, as opposed to embracing a more all-encompassing view.

Addressing more specifically the obligations set out in these Draft Articles, it becomes apparent that a *primary responsibility* is envisaged for the affected state. Draft Article 12 sets out that:

> "1. The affected State, by virtue of its sovereignty, has the duty to ensure the protection of persons and provision of disaster relief and assistance on its territory. 2. The affected State has the primary role in the direction, control, coordination and supervision of such relief and assistance".[194]

Thus, Draft Article 12 clearly expresses the primary duty of the affected state to provide assistance to the population affected by disaster. The term 'protection' reflects the overall theme of study of the ILC.[195] The notion of 'protection of persons' is therefore of a broader view than the more narrow 'protection of civilians' as a concept within international humanitarian law and as also used by the Security Council, although discussion on this topic also exists.[196] The Special Rapporteur has elaborated that the Draft Articles intend to respect state sovereignty within their framework.[197] Interestingly, Draft Article 13 includes another duty of the affected state, namely a *duty to seek assistance* should the disaster not be manageable through its own resources:

> "To the extent that a disaster exceeds its national response capacity, the affected State has the duty to seek assistance from among other States, the United Nations, other

---

[192] See Section 3.4 on the relationship between human rights and humanitarian law.

[193] ILC 'Preliminary report on the protection of persons in the event of disasters' UN Doc A/CN.4/598 (n 191) § 51.

[194] ILC 'Protection of persons in the event of disasters' Draft Articles UN Doc. A/CN.4/L.831 (n 190).

[195] 'Third report on the protection of persons in the event of disasters', ILC Special Rapporteur Eduardo Valencia-Ospina, UN Doc A/CN.4/629 (31 March 2010) § 97.

[196] Amra Lee, 'The Case for Strengthening Protection Frameworks in 'Other Situations of Violence' (2014) *The Journal of Humanitarian Assistance* <http://sites.tufts.edu/jha/archives/2091> accessed 1 March 2015.

[197] UN Doc A/CN.4/629 (n 195) § 67 and further.

competent intergovernmental organizations and relevant non-governmental organizations, as appropriate".[198]

The Draft Articles therefore see an active duty from the perspective of the affected state to not only provide humanitarian assistance individually but to also take up the responsibility to seek such assistance from other states. This duty aligns with the obligations reflected in the ICESCR. When indeed reasoned from a human rights perspective, such a duty would in fact be arguable in line with the obligations resting upon a state under Article 2 ICESCR, in combination with the relevant rights to food, health (and water).[199] Indeed, the ILC Special Rapporteur has also followed this reasoning, elaborating that while this duty to seek assistance by no means diminishes the obligations of the affected state to provide assistance itself, this notion of 'internal sovereignty' also encompasses a duty to seek assistance from other, external, sources in a state's fulfilment of its human rights obligations.[200] Given the fact that the Draft Articles are currently in a state of development, it remains to be seen what the final outcome shall become, and what their influence may be on the law pertaining to the provision of humanitarian assistance in times of natural disaster. Furthermore, given the fact that the Draft Articles distinctly do *not* incorporate circumstances in which humanitarian law is applicable, it is at least commendable that they follow the line of existing human rights law. With a view to the continuous protection of persons in need of assistance, the creation of *another* separate body of law, applicable in specific circumstances, may only add to the fragmentation of the law, as opposed to assisting in the creation of greater protection.

6.5.5.2 The Potential Application of the IDRL Guidelines and Model Act

As a second initiative, the 'Guidelines for the domestic facilitation and regulation of international disaster relief and initial recovery assistance' (IDRL Guidelines), may be considered. The IDRL Guidelines were developed by the International Federation of the Red Cross and were unanimously adopted by all state parties to the 1949 Geneva Conventions in 2007.[201] The IDRL Guidelines aim to aid governments in preparedness at a domestic level with regard to overcoming legal obstacles in the provision of assistance in the aftermath of disaster, but are distinctly *not binding* in their nature. More relevantly, nor are they *intended* to be binding as they merely provide suggestions to adopt, and in this way distinctly differ from for example the General Assembly resolutions which are also non-binding in nature but hold a different standing as they are more reflective of state

[198] ILC 'Protection of persons in the event of disasters' Draft Articles UN Doc. A/CN.4/L.831 (n 190).
[199] Sections 5.2.2.1 and 5.4 and further.
[200] UN Doc A/CN.4/643 (n 190) § 32-40.
[201] ICRC Resolution 30IC/07/R4 'Guidelines for the domestic facilitation and regulation of international disaster relief and initial recovery assistance', 30th International Conference of the Red Cross and Red Crescent (30 November 2007).

practice and contribute to customary developments.[202] The IDRL Guidelines follow the IDRL Programme which was developed in 2001 (as of 2012 called the 'Disaster Law Programme') following a resolution for this purpose by the Red Cross and Red Crescent Council of Delegates, and aimed at a:

> "compilation and publication of existing international laws and regulations, and the evaluation of their actual effectiveness in humanitarian operations".[203]

Therefore initially appearing to have a more international legal approach, the Guidelines themselves however operate as more domestic tools for states. In their creation and methodology, the IFRC did build on domestic examples as well as various existing (soft) law tools.[204] As the Guidelines aim to be a practical tool for governments in their national responses, they will not be discussed in depth as part of the international legal framework concerning humanitarian assistance.[205] Indeed, following their adoption in 2007, only 12 states have reported to have 'drawn language or inspiration' from the Guidelines in their domestic legislation.[206] Even if the intention of the Guidelines therefore had been more legislative they cannot be considered reflective of state practice. For the purpose of this Chapter it is however relevant to note that these IDRL Guidelines also identify the affected state as the primary responsible actor in the provision of assistance in the event of a disaster.[207]

However, the more recently developed 'Model Act for the Facilitation and Regulation of International Disaster Relief and Initial Recovery Assistance', as supplement to the IDRL Guidelines, does indeed attempt to provide more legal regulation, although also operating at a domestic level. This 'Model Act'; which is a model and example for domestic lawmakers, was adopted in March 2013 as an initiative of the IFRC 'intended to assist states to strengthen their legal preparedness for international disaster cooperation' in a manner that would be 'appropriate to their national circumstances'.[208] Similar to the IDRL Guidelines, the Model Act suggests in its Article 2 that the affected state bears primary responsibility for the provision of humanitarian assistance.[209] Given the novel status

---

[202] IFRC 'Guidelines for the domestic facilitation and regulation of international disaster relief and initial recovery assistance' (IDRL Guidelines) (30 November 2007), adopted at the 30th International Conference of the Movement, § 1: "These Guidelines are non-binding. While it is hoped that States will make use of them to strengthen their laws, policies and/or procedures related to international disaster response, as appropriate, the Guidelines do not have a direct effect on any existing rights or obligations under domestic law".

[203] Council of Delegates of the International Red Cross and Red Crescent Movement, (Geneva, Switzerland 11 - 14 November 2001) 'Resolution 5: International Disaster Response Law' §1.

[204] 'International Disaster Response Laws (IDRL) Project Report 2002-2003', 28th International Conference of the Red Cross and Red Crescent (2-6 December 2003), IFRC and Red Crescent Societies Doc 03/IC/11.

[205] IFRC IDRL Guidelines (2007) (n 202) § 3.

[206] <www.ifrc.org/en/what-we-do/idrl/idrl-guidelines/new-legislation-adopted-on-idrl/> accessed 8 February 2015.

[207] IFRC IDRL Guidelines (2007) (n 202) Article 3.

[208] <www.ifrc.org/en/what-we-do/idrl/model-act-on-idrl/> accessed 19 October 2014.

[209] Article 2(a) of the Model Act.

of this Model Act, it has yet to be embraced by states and subsequently incorporated into their domestic regulatory framework.

Thus, contrary to the circumstance of conflict and occupation, *one* particular legal regime pertaining to humanitarian assistance in times of (natural) disaster is missing. As such, no concrete, specific legal provisions relate to the obligations resting upon the affected state to provide in assistance for the population within its territory or control, following such a disaster. However, general international law and most notably human rights law provide the continuous legal basis for such obligations and assertions in times of disaster. Such more general provisions are occasionally supplemented with regional conventions such as on the South American continent and the ASEAN Management Agreement. Although the developments of the ILC and IFRC recognise the responsibility of the affected state, in a similar matter to existing international law, it remains to be seen what their contributions to the existing legal framework will be. On the one hand, the IDRL Guidelines and Model Act operate more at the domestic level, while the ILC initiatives into the protection of persons in the event of a disaster have yet to concretely materialise with more binding status. The latter also problematically limits itself to circumstances distinctly outside the realm of the applicability of international humanitarian law.

6.5.6 Rights of Persons to Receive Assistance in Times of (Natural) Disaster

As a result of the above lacking framework on the specific obligations for the affected state in times of disaster, similarly no particular framework is in place concerning the *rights* of persons to *request* such (international) assistance from their sovereign.[210] General human rights law of course continues to find applicability and individuals shall therefore be able to have recourse to such provisions in the aftermath of disaster. The UN IASC has also asserted this perspective, developing 'Operational Guidelines on Human Rights and Natural Disaster' through which victims of natural disaster 'should enjoy the same rights and freedoms under human rights law as others in their country'.[211] Important as such Guidelines may be for those involved in the practice of humanitarian assistance, from a *legal* perspective additional specific guarantees in the form of specific rights to request humanitarian aid are absent for victims of natural disasters in these Guidelines. However, the work of the ILC in developing its Draft Articles on the Protection of persons in the event of disasters may bring renewed possibilities to the victims of natural disasters that find themselves in need of humanitarian assistance, strengthening their position. Formulating specific legal rights enhances the position of those finding

[210] The Directory of National emergency Response offices, Disaster Emergency Plans and Legislation, and Regional and Sub-Regional Agreements for Disaster Assistance, UNDRO 1992 however states to have documentation on legislation for 64 countries; that apparently entail a right to receive assistance.

[211] 'Operational Guidelines on Human Rights and Natural Disasters' by the Representative on human rights of internally displaced persons UN Doc A/HRC/4/38/Add.1 (26 January 2006) General Principle I. See also in this regard the follow-up thereto, developed in cooperation with the Brookings-Bern Project, 2011.

themselves in the aftermath of disaster, to claim aid from those exercising sovereign duties.

6.5.6.1 The Potential Application of the ILC Study: Protection of persons in the event of disaster

The ILC study, which is currently still in progress, has to date foregone the opportunity to create a Draft Article tailored specifically to the needs of those requesting assistance in the aftermath of a disaster.[212] Until now, the ILC study has merely incorporated a Draft Article 6 stating that 'persons affected by disasters are entitled to respect for their human rights'.[213] As the focus lies on the protection of those in the aftermath of a disaster, it appears that the ILC, like many other initiatives and legal provisions, has taken the approach of the obligation of the *state*, rather than the right of the *individual* to request specific assistance from its sovereign. In doing so, the ILC has opted to focus in its study on those obligations that may rest upon states or rights that may exist for other providers of assistance, rather than attempting to formulate a right to receive assistance for victims of (natural) disasters. Indeed, the ILC study does not break new ground, or depart from the existing degree of protection envisaged under general human rights law. Whilst it is commendable to ensure the protection that may be derived from existing human rights provisions; and these existing human rights do ensure a sufficient level of protection for those in a humanitarian crisis without warranting the development of an individual human right, it remains somewhat disappointing that the ILC study has not asserted a more specific formulation. Indeed, as the Draft Articles appear to attempt to develop a new legal framework specifically tailored for circumstances of disaster, one would expect a more elaborate development of rights of persons finding themselves in such crises. From the perspective of this research however, which takes a more encompassing view of the legal framework of humanitarian assistance, the reliance of the ILC study on the existing legal body of human rights law in fact confirms the assertion made in this research that such a framework adequately represents the rights of persons in need of emergency aid.

6.5.6.2 The Potential Application of the IDRL Guidelines and Model Act

An entirely different stance has been taken by the IFRC/ICRC, in relation to the IDRL Guidelines. Indeed, while the IDRL Guidelines do not hold binding legal status nor formulate a specific right to receive assistance, the ICRC in 2007 recognised that the Movement considers persons to have a fundamental right 'both to offer and receive humanitarian assistance', whilst adopting these Guidelines.[214] Moreover, this stance was a reaffirmation of the 'Principles and Rules of the Red

[212] Spring 2015.
[213] ILC 'Protection of persons in the event of disasters' Draft Articles UN Doc. A/CN.4/L.831 (n 190).
[214] ICRC Resolution 30IC/07/R4 (n 201).

Cross and Red Crescent in Disaster Relief'.[215] Clearly such expressions are not legally binding, but may be seen as the perspective of the ICRC/IFRC on the manner in which humanitarian assistance and its legal framework should be approached. Subsequently, although the 'Model Act for the Facilitation and Regulation of International Disaster Relief and Initial Recovery Assistance' was created to supplement the IDRL Guidelines, it too does not formulate a right of persons to receive assistance. Therefore, whilst such a perspective may be the stance of the ICRC/IFRC as an organisation, it is not reflected in their legislative attempts for the domestic regulation of disaster response.

In times of conflict and occupation many of the legal provisions concern the duties of the state as opposed to the rights of the individuals, resulting in the absence of an individual's right to claim assistance from the sovereign. In times of natural disaster, the end result is indeed similar, whereas the result is reached through a general lack of an existing legal framework, and a lack of implementation of the perspective into the existing initiatives.

6.5.7 Duties of the Affected State under Refugee Law

Although being a 'refugee' or an 'Internally Displaced Person' is not a situational circumstance as for example conflict and natural disaster, being defined as a 'refugee' or as an 'IDP' does warrant the applicability of a specific set of rules, as in certain instances those persons in need of humanitarian assistance may be categorised as refugees or IDPs, independently from other groups of civilians facing for example a conflict or disaster.[216]

The application of refugee law and obligations in this regard concerning the provision of humanitarian assistance is dependent on the qualification of a person as 'refugee' under the 1951 Refugee Convention.[217] As noted above in Section 2.3.1, the provision of humanitarian assistance is aimed at all those in need of emergency aid in the aftermath of a crisis, while refugees mark a distinct category of such persons, and their legal qualification often occurs during a timeframe that may *exceed* the situation of a 'humanitarian crisis' in which humanitarian assistance is necessary. Furthermore, for the purposes of the provision of humanitarian assistance upon which this research is focused, the determination of a 'refugee-status' involves a cross-border movement to the extent that a person no longer is able to turn to the government of its original nationality for assistance.[218] Refugee law therefore has a specific focus on 'protection' which is distinct from emergency assistance with which the legal framework of humanitarian assistance is concerned. With regard to the framework of humanitarian assistance, such simultaneous occurrence will most likely be at the time of a non-international armed conflict

[215] 'Principles and Rules of the Red Cross and Red Crescent in Disaster Relief' as amended by the 26th International Conference of the Red Cross and Red Crescent, 1995.
[216] Section 2.3.1 Recipients of Humanitarian Assistance.
[217] See Section 2.3.1 on the definition of a refugee, as according to the 1951 Refugee Convention.
[218] Article 1 Refugee Convention.

where civilians are fleeing the country, or a (natural) disaster with cross-border effects. As such, refugees form a distinct category of persons in the discussion of obligations under international law resting upon states in the provision of humanitarian assistance. Determining that a person is a 'refugee' almost unequivocally results in the conclusion that the state of origin is (sometimes wilfully) not fulfilling certain duties in accordance with international law.[219] Thus, when discussing the obligations pertaining to the provision of assistance, in refugee law such obligations automatically pertain to *third* states, as these states become the 'affected' state: namely the state with a received refugee population. As such, Article 23 of the 1951 Refugee Convention declares that:

> "The Contracting States shall accord to refugees lawfully staying in their territory the same treatment with respect to public relief and assistance as is accorded to their nationals".

Although the provision itself does not specify what is meant with 'public relief', according to its *Commentary* it was meant to be interpreted widely and includes hospital treatment and emergency relief.[220] Consequently, the state *receiving* refugees shall be under the obligation to provide refugees with the same assistance as they are obliged to provide their own nationals.[221] In the event of a humanitarian crisis that results in the creation of a refugee population, the 'affected' state shall therefore be obliged to apply those rules of humanitarian law and human rights law that may be relevant in the specific circumstance, acting towards the refugees with the same responsibilities it would towards its own civilians. Both the UN Security Council and the General Assembly have indeed also taken the stance that the civilian population, as recipient of humanitarian assistance, includes refugees and IDPs.[222] The UN accordingly acknowledges the need that may incur in certain

---

[219] It remains beyond the scope of this research to address the full range of refugee law in depth. This research will concern itself strictly with those provisions of refugee law that are relevant to the legal regime concerning the provision of humanitarian assistance.

[220] Paul Weis, *The Refugee Convention 1951: The Travaux Preparatoires Analysed With A Commentary* (UNHCR 1995) 125.

[221] It must be noted that several states have placed reservations to Article 23 of the Convention, mainly concerning the fact that this Article shall be interpreted as a recommendation rather than as legally binding. States that have placed reservations are: Austria, Canada, Egypt, Estonia, Iran, Malta, Monaco, Timor Leste, Zimbabwe: Convention Relating To The Status Of Refugees Geneva, 28 July 1951, Entry into Force: 22 April 1954, Signatories: 19. Parties: 144, UNTS, vol. 189, p. 137.

[222] See in this regard amongst others: UNSC Res 1265 (17 September 1999) UN Doc S/RES/1265 § 7; UNGA Res 52/167 (18 February 1998) UN Doc A/RES/52/167 'Safety and security of humanitarian personnel' §3; UNGA Res 53/87 (27 January 1999) UN Doc A/RES/53/87 ' Safety and security of humanitarian personnel and protection of United Nations personnel' § 11; UNGA Res 60/124 (8 March 2006) UN Doc A/RES/60/124 'Strengthening the coordination of humanitarian emergency assistance of the United Nations' § 2; UNGA res 61/133 (1 March 2007) UN Doc A/RES/61/133 'Safety and security of humanitarian personnel and protection of United Nations personnel' § 4; UNGA Res 62/94 (25 January 2008) UN Doc A/RES/62/94 'Strengthening of the coordination of emergency humanitarian assistance of the United Nations' § 24; UNGA Res 63/139 (5 March 2009) UN Doc A/RES/63/139 'Strengthening of the coordination of humanitarian and disaster relief assistance of the

instances to provide humanitarian assistance to refugees and IDPs. However, as refugees are considered civilians, and as the 'affected' state is a third state that has an obligation to provide equal assistance to lawful refugees as to its own nationals, the duties resting upon a state to provide humanitarian assistance must therefore be sought within general international law, human rights law and, on occasion, humanitarian law. Refugee law itself does not offer much support aside from the abovementioned Article 23 of the Refugee Convention with regard to specific obligations resting upon states in the provision of humanitarian assistance. As such, an in-depth look into this body of law is not necessary for the purpose of this research into the legal framework on the provision of humanitarian assistance. Recourse must be had to those provisions the third (recipient) state is obliged to fulfil at all times concerning its own civilian population, which would in essence result in the application of general principles of international law and human rights law.

6.5.8 Rights of Persons to Receive Assistance under Refugee Law

As the 1951 Refugee Convention is almost silent in its consideration of humanitarian assistance, only briefly referring to the duties of states to treat refugees as nationals in their provision of 'public relief' in Article 23, the Convention also does not specifically address a right of refugees to receive or claim humanitarian assistance from the 'affected' state. This affected state continues to be the 'third' state to which they have travelled. The Refugee Convention merely provides in Article 5 that:

> "Nothing in this Convention shall be deemed to impair any rights and benefits granted by a Contracting State to refugees apart from this Convention".

Thus, the Convention declares that refugees remain entitled to all those rights which the State Parties bestow upon them. This must be read in light of the rights and duties existing in international law with regards to human rights, as discussed in the above Section 6.3.2. Two provisions in particular are relevant to the discussion of the human rights of refugees to receive assistance, as the Convention on the Rights of the Child and the African Charter on the Rights and Welfare of the Child stipulate in Article 22 and Article 23 respectively that a *refugee child* is entitled to receive humanitarian assistance within the context of the enjoyment of the rights of the Conventions.[223] Thus, when it comes to the right to receive humanitarian assistance, recourse must be had to other substantial bodies of law, as refugee law in itself does not make provisions in this. Refugees are of course free to claim such assistance from their original authorities based upon existing human rights law. Refugee children, particularly within the African continent, have extra means at

---

United Nations, including special economic assistance: strengthening of the coordination of emergency humanitarian assistance of the United Nations' § 25.

[223] See Section 5.4 and further on the full discussion of these rights.

their disposal through the particular clauses in the Convention on the Rights of the Child and the African Charter on the Rights and Welfare of the Child. More relevantly, once refugees are lawfully within the jurisdiction of another state, they may claim assistance based on human rights provisions that are applicable to them within the jurisdiction of this *third* state. These provisions are applicable to such refugees through the very scope of human rights law itself, as discussed above in Chapter 4.

6.5.9 Duties of the Affected State under the (Potential) IDP Framework

Like refugees, internally displaced persons are a category of persons recognised in the receipt of humanitarian assistance by the UN.[224] Furthermore, like refugees, they are indeed civilians although they are distinctly categorised in international law.[225] However, unlike the case for refugees, no international binding legal framework exists with regard to the duties resting upon states concerning the treatment of IDPs.

Regionally in Africa, however, the Kampala Convention for the 'Protection And Assistance Of Internally Displaced Persons In Africa' declares far-reaching obligations resting upon states regarding the provision of humanitarian assistance to IDPs. Article 3 pertaining to 'general obligations' stipulates in particular relating to the provision of assistance that:

> "1. States Parties undertake to respect and ensure respect for the present Convention. In particular, States Parties shall: (…) j. Ensure assistance to internally displaced persons by meeting their basic needs as well as allowing and facilitating rapid and unimpeded access by humanitarian organizations and personnel; k. Promote self-reliance and sustainable livelihoods amongst internally displaced persons, provided that such measures shall not be used as a basis for neglecting the protection of and assistance to internally displaced persons, without prejudice to other means of assistance; (…)".

---

[224] UNSC Res 1265 (17 September 1999) UN Doc S/RES/1265 § 7; UNGA Res 52/167 (18 February 1998) UN Doc A/RES/52/167 'Safety and security of humanitarian personnel' § 3; UNGA Res 53/87 (27 January 1999) UN Doc A/RES/53/87 ' Safety and security of humanitarian personnel and protection of United Nations personnel' § 11; UNGA Res 60/124 (8 March 2006) UN Doc A/RES/60/124 § 2; UNGA res 61/133 (1 March 2007) UN Doc A/RES/61/133 'Safety and security of humanitarian personnel and protection of United Nations personnel' § 4; UNGA Res 62/94 (25 January 2008) UN Doc A/RES/62/94 'Strengthening of the coordination of emergency humanitarian assistance of the United Nations' § 24; UNGA Res 63/139 (5 March 2009) UN Doc A/RES/63/139 'Strengthening of the coordination of humanitarian and disaster relief assistance of the United Nations, including special economic assistance: strengthening of the coordination of emergency humanitarian assistance of the United Nations' § 25.

[225] See Section 2.3.1 on their inclusion as recipients of humanitarian assistance. See furthermore 'Report of the Representative of the Secretary-General, Mr. Francis M. Deng, submitted pursuant to Commission resolution 1997/39', Addendum 'Guiding Principles on Internal Displacement' (Guiding Principles on IDPs) (11 February 1998) UN Doc E/CN.4/1998/53/Add.2 preamble § 2 and the African Union Kampala Convention Article 1(k).

Clearly, the African Union has wished to place a distinct obligation upon the State Parties to the Kampala Convention to provide assistance to IDPs by meeting their basic needs and respecting their rights, as stated in particular in Article 3(1)(j). The Kampala Convention takes the obligations of States Parties one step further than the general obligations of international law, stating in Article 4 that such States Parties have an obligation to prevent conditions that *may lead to* arbitrary displacement and, 'where necessary, provide immediate protection and assistance to internally displaced persons'. Following this obligation, Article 5 asserts that States Parties shall have the *primary* obligation and responsibility in the provision of humanitarian assistance to all IDPs within their territory or jurisdiction, specifying a duty to 'take necessary steps to effectively organize, relief action that is humanitarian, and impartial in character'. Article 5 explicates that such a duty exists regardless of the origin of the disaster which causes displacement; be it manmade or natural, whilst at the same time recognising respect for the existing principles of sovereignty and territorial integrity under international law.[226] Article 9 of the Kampala Convention reiterates this obligation to protect the rights of IDPs regardless of the cause of the displacement, and sets forth that states, in doing so, must refrain amongst others from 'genocide, crimes against humanity, war crimes and other violations of international humanitarian law' as well as from starvation, which has already been discussed more in detail above, in Section 6.5.1.[227] More specifically concerning humanitarian assistance, Article 9 also sets forth that *during* internal displacement:

> "2. States Parties shall: (…) b. Provide internally displaced persons to the fullest extent practicable and with the least possible delay, with adequate humanitarian assistance, which shall include food, water, shelter, medical care and other health services, sanitation, education, and any other necessary social services, and where appropriate, extend such assistance to local and host communities; c. Provide special protection for and assistance to internally displaced persons with special needs, including separated and unaccompanied children, female heads of households, expectant mothers, mothers with young children, the elderly, and persons with disabilities or with communicable diseases; (…) g. Respect and maintain the civilian and humanitarian character of the places where internally displaced persons are sheltered and safeguard such locations against infiltration by armed groups or elements and disarm and separate such groups or elements from internally displaced persons".

As such, the Kampala Convention has created specific provisions for the various timeframes that may be of relevance, namely assistance in the protection *from* displacement, assistance *during* displacement, as well as in the aftermath thereof. Tailoring to many possible situations and with many specific provisions, the Kampala Convention has also asserted particularly in relation to armed groups participating in conflict that obligations pertaining to the provision of humanitarian

[226] Article 5(4) and 5(12) African Union Kampala Convention.
[227] See in further detail Section 8.6.2 for the consequences of such assertions.

assistance rest upon *them* also and not merely upon the State Parties to the Convention. As such, Article 7 states that:

> "5. Members of armed groups shall be prohibited from: (...) b. Hampering the provision of protection and assistance to internally displaced persons under any circumstances; c. Denying internally displaced persons the right to live in satisfactory conditions of dignity, security, sanitation, food, water, health and shelter; and separating members of the same family; (...) g. Impeding humanitarian assistance and passage of all relief consignments, equipment and personnel to internally displaced persons h. Attacking or otherwise harming humanitarian personnel and resources or other materials deployed for the assistance or benefit of internally displaced persons and shall not destroy, confiscate or divert such materials; and i. Violating the civilian and humanitarian character of the places where internally displaced persons are sheltered and shall not infiltrate such violations".

Although this provision does not contain a positive obligation towards armed groups to provide humanitarian assistance, the Kampala Convention does envisage a *prohibition* for armed groups to *interfere* with the provision of such assistance. The inclusion of this provision adds to the protection of IDPs on the African continent, where complex emergencies often occur, and natural disasters take place in regions afflicted by (often non-international) armed conflict. Given the gaps in protection offered by humanitarian law in times of non-international armed conflict, the enhanced protection provided by the efforts of the Kampala Convention add to the legal framework for IDPs. Clearly, it must be noted that the Kampala Convention is limited as the treaty's scope concerns the African continent, and has only recently entered into force.[228]

It is therefore relevant to note furthermore that, in circumstances of non-international armed conflict, Additional Protocol II to the Geneva Convention holds in Article 17 that displacement of civilians, aside from two exceptional circumstances, is prohibited and that should displacements indeed have to be carried out, all possible measures must be taken to ensure that the IDPs are 'received under satisfactory conditions of shelter, hygiene, health, safety and nutrition'. This provision also includes the conditions *during* displacement itself and not only upon the arrival of IDPs in a new area, and it follows Article 49 of GC IV, as the original 1949 Conventions are silent on the matter of internal displacement and treatment of such IDPs.[229] Thus, in circumstances of non-international armed conflict as covered by the level of control indicated in AP II, a minimum level of protection for IDPs exists, as states have a duty to ensure that no displacement occurs, and in the exceptional circumstance that such displacement does occur, assistance must be provided to the IDPs.

At a more general level, the Guiding Principles on Internal Displacement, developed within and largely embraced by the UN framework, are the current

[228] Currently 22 states are party to the Convention.
[229] Sandoz, Swinarski & Zimmermann *Commentary to the Additional Protocols* (n 128) Protocol II Article 17, 1472 .

existing *soft law* framework with regard to the rights and duties concerning IDPs.[230] Although non-binding in nature, they will be discussed in this Section pertaining to the legal framework as they have been widely embraced by actors in the field.[231] Similar to the Kampala Convention, the Guiding Principles distinguish between provisions concerning protection *from* displacement, *during* displacement *and* thereafter. Specifically concerning the obligation resting upon states in the provision of humanitarian assistance during the prevention of displacement, Guiding Principle 3 stipulates that 'national authorities have the primary duty and responsibility' in this regard.[232] Similar to the provision of Article 17 AP II, Guiding Principle 7 declares that should displacement be inevitable, 'satisfactory conditions of safety, nutrition, health and hygiene' must be met.[233] In the event displacement has occurred, the Guiding Principles prohibit, as do the Geneva and Kampala Conventions, 'starvation as a method of combat'.[234] In fact, according to Guiding Principle 18(2) authorities shall have the obligation to at least provide IDPs with access to:

> "(a) Essential food and potable water; (b) Basic shelter and housing; (c) Appropriate clothing; and (d) Essential medical services and sanitation".

The subsequent Principle explicates what such essential medical services entail, with a specific view to the prevention of contagious diseases.[235] From the above it

[230] See Section 2.3.1 with regard to the development and legal value of these Guiding Principles and (n 231).

[231] Ibid and more specifically also 'Report of the Representative of the Secretary-General, Mr. Francis M. Deng, submitted pursuant to Commission resolution 1997/39', Addendum 'Guiding Principles on Internal Displacement' (Guiding Principles on IDPs) (11 February 1998) UN Doc E/CN.4/1998/53/Add.2, Principle 3. The Guiding Principles are supported by the United Nations offices UNHCR and OHCHR, and furthermore the UN General Assembly declared in § 7 of UNGA Res 58/177 (12 March 2004) UN Doc A/RES/58/177 'Protection of and assistance to internally displaced persons' that it: "Expresses its appreciation of the Guiding Principles on Internal Displacement as an important tool for dealing with situations of internal displacement, welcomes the fact that an increasing number of States, United Nations agencies and regional and non-governmental organizations are applying them as a standard, and encourages all relevant actors to make use of the Guiding Principles when dealing with situations of internal displacement". See also former UN Special Rapporteur on the Human Rights of Internally Displaced Persons Walter Kälin has furthermore declared in his final 'Report of the Representative of the Secretary-General on the human rights of internally displaced persons', UN Doc A/HRC/13/21 (5 January 2010) § 10. Furthermore the General Assembly has continued to embrace the Guiding Principles, amongst others in UNGA Res 60/1 (24 October 2005) UN Doc A/RES/60/1 'World Summit Outcome Document' § 132 where the General Assembly recognises the Principles as an "important international framework for the protection of internally displaced persons", a phrasing that is echoed by UNGA Res 60/124 (8 March 2006) UN Doc. A/RES/60/124 § 6; UNGA Res 60/168 (7 March 2006) A/RES/60/168 'Protection of and assistance to internally displaced persons' § 8; and UNGA Res 62/153 (6 March 2008) UN Doc. A/RES/62/153, 'Protection of and assistance to internally displaced persons' § 10; as well as UN HRC Res 6/32 (14 December 2007) A/HRC/6/32 § 5.

[232] Guiding Principle 3(1).

[233] Guiding Principle 7(2).

[234] Guiding Principle 10(b).

[235] Principle 19(3).

follows that the Guiding Principles have attempted to be as explicit and detailed as possible in their assertion of the duties of states. As such, reiterating Principle 3 (that dealt more particularly with the prevention of displacement), Guiding Principle 25 declares unambiguously that the 'primary duty and responsibility for providing humanitarian assistance' to IDPs lies with national authorities.[236] The creation of the Guiding Principles was primarily to 'fill the gap' in protection for IDPs under existing human rights, refugee and humanitarian law, as many provisions were not tailored to the specific needs of such IDPs.[237] Prior to their development, Francis Deng addressed a problem that unfortunately still exists today, as the Principles are non-binding:

> "Clear gaps in international protection arise in certain areas where no explicit norms exist to address identifiable needs of the internally displaced (…) A norm may exist in human rights law but be lacking in humanitarian law, or vice versa (…) The second category of insufficient coverage results where a general norm exists but a corollary, more specific right has not been articulated that would ensure implementation of the general norm in areas of particular need to internally displaced persons (…) While it may be possible to infer specific legal rights from general norms, the protection of the internally displaced would be strengthened by spelling out the particular corollary of the norm relevant to their needs. There are also inherent shortcomings in the law".[238]

Although these Guiding Principles have been embraced by the UN General Assembly and other organs, they are indeed non-binding and as such do not add to the existing legal framework on the protection of persons in need of humanitarian assistance.[239] Indeed as addressed by Deng himself, the Guidelines build forth on existing law to provide 'gap-filling' for the grey areas in the law concerning IDPs. In their support several organs of the UN themselves have also in recent years called upon the primary responsibility of states to provide in assistance towards IDPs.[240] Not only have UN organs supported the embracement of the Guiding

---

[236] Guiding Principle 25(1). Paragraphs 2 and 3 of Principle 25 shall be dealt with more in depth in Chapter 7.

[237] 'Further Promotion And Encouragement Of Human Rights And Fundamental Freedoms, Including The Question Of The Programme And Methods Of Work Of The Commission Human Rights, Mass Exoduses And Displaced Persons Internally displaced persons' Report of the Representative of the Secretary General UN Doc E/CN.4/1997/43 (4 February 1997) § 2-5.

[238] Ibid § 3-5.

[239] See (n 230 and 231).

[240] See amongst others regarding the General Assembly's support of this position: UNGA Res 49/169 (23 December 1994) UN Doc A/RES/49/169 § 11; UNGA Res 58/177 (12 March 2004) UN Doc A/RES/58/177 preamble; See also the Report of the Representative of the Secretary-General, Mr. Francis Deng, UN Doc E/CN.4/1994/44 (n 74) § 21; 'Further Promotion And Encouragement Of Human Rights And Fundamental Freedoms, Including The Question Of The Programme And Methods Of Work Of The Commission Human Rights, Mass Exoduses And Displaced Persons Internally displaced persons', Report of the Representative of the Secretary-General (22 February 1996) UN Doc E/CN.4/1996/52 § 71; Report of the Representative of the Secretary-General on the human rights of internally displaced persons UN Doc A/HRC/4/38/Add.2 (18 October 2006) § 5; 'Specific Groups And Individuals: Mass Exoduses And Displaced Persons' Report of the Representative of the Secretary-General UN Doc E/CN.4/2002/95/Add.3 (10 December 2001) § 13; and more recently ILC

Principles, their content too has been specifically supported, as several organs have expressed that IDPs at least should enjoy (amongst others) access to essential food and water, shelter and medical services.[241] Such assertions are most relevant, as they can be construed as potential indications of *opinio juris* with regard to legal developments. In fact, with the changing nature of humanitarian crises, focusing more on natural disasters and non-international armed conflicts, the need for clear regulations regarding IDPs is increasing. Such a need is also of a more general level, rather than focusing perhaps more specifically on the receipt of humanitarian aid. Indeed, where persons are displaced as the result of a natural disaster or potential (non-) international armed conflict, the more general applicable law in such circumstances remains appropriate and valid, such as human rights law and humanitarian law.[242] When considering however the *binding* and *specific* legal framework placing obligations upon states to provide humanitarian assistance to IDPs, it must be concluded that such a framework only exists regionally for states that fall within the scope of the Kampala Convention, and rather limited for those circumstances regulated by AP II of the Geneva Conventions, as Article 17 AP II does not allow for much (explicit) protection. In a more general sense therefore, circumstances in which IDP populations arise, such as non-international armed conflicts falling outside the scope of AP II, or outside of the African continent, recourse must be had to the more general protection of the existing human rights to life, food and health, similar to other civilians.

6.5.10 Rights of Persons to Receive Assistance under the (Potential) IDP Framework

Similar to refugees, several specific legally binding provisions detail the rights of IDPs to request humanitarian assistance. In particular, within a human rights context, the African Charter on the Rights and Welfare of the Child stipulates in Article 23 that the rights applicable to the refugee child are equally applicable to the IDP child, entitling it to receive humanitarian assistance within the context of the

'Preliminary report on the protection of persons in the event of disasters' UN Doc. A/CN.4/598 (n 191) § 45; as well as UN Doc A/HRC/13/21 (n 231) § 56.

[241] Report of the Representative of the Secretary-General on the human rights of internally displaced persons, 'Addendum Framework on Durable Solutions for Internally Displaced Persons' UN Doc A/HRC/13/21/Add.4 (9 February 2010) § 65. See also HRC Res 6/32 (14 December 2007) UN Doc A/RES/6/32 § 3 in which the Human Rights Council expresses concern for IDPs not having access to such materials; Commission on Human Rights resolution 2002/56l (25 April 2002) § 10; Report of the Representative of the Secretary-General on the human rights of internally displaced persons (23 December 2005) UN Doc E/CN.4/2006/71/Add.1 § 10.

[242] This perspective has amongst others also been supported by the ILA in its ILA Declaration of International Law Principles on Internally Displaced Persons (29 July 2000) Article 2. See the Commentary to the Declaration for a further discussion on the ILA's perspective that the state is the primary responsible for the provision of assistance to IDPs (Article 10). As this declaration is also non-binding, this research will not discuss it within this section on the legal framework.

enjoyment of the rights of that Charter.[243] Also within the African continent, but more elaborately and unambiguously, the Kampala Convention declares in Article 5(9):

> "States Parties shall respect the right of internally displaced persons to peacefully request or seek protection and assistance, in accordance with relevant national and international laws, a right for which they shall not be persecuted, prosecuted or punished".

Thus, the Kampala Convention very clearly addresses the distinct right to request aid, pertaining to IDPs. Also, the Kampala Convention acknowledges in Article 9(2)(k) that IDPs must be consulted, and more particularly, that they are allowed to participate in the process of receiving assistance.

Furthermore, it has been asserted that IDPs have a right to request assistance based on the existing human rights framework, similar to other civilians in general.[244] The close relationship and complementarity between IDPs' need for humanitarian assistance and the protection offered by general human rights law has indeed frequently been addressed, and an independently existing right to request assistance for IDPs has been asserted by the UN Special Rapporteur.[245] This perspective is also voiced in the Guiding Principles on IDPs, as Principle 3(2) states that IDPs not only have a right to *request* assistance, but that they also have the right to *receive* such assistance. The Guiding Principles therefore hold a dual right for IDPs in relation to their authorities, similar to the Kampala Convention. In circumstances of displacement, Guiding Principle 18 is more elaborate and explicates that:

> "1. All internally displaced persons have the right to an adequate standard of living. 2. At the minimum, regardless of the circumstances, and without discrimination, competent authorities shall provide internally displaced persons with and ensure safe access to: (a) Essential food and potable water; (b) Basic shelter and housing; (c) Appropriate clothing; and (d) Essential medical services and sanitation. 3. Special efforts should be made to ensure the full participation of women in the planning and distribution of these basic supplies".

Thus, the Guiding Principles envisage a right for IDPs to receive and request humanitarian assistance in the fullest possible manner. This viewpoint is echoed by the ILA's Declaration of International Law Principles on Internally Displaced

---

243 See supra Section 4.3.I.A Humanitarian Assistance as a Potential Human Right in International Treaty Law on the full discussion of this right.

244 Section 5.4 Humanitarian Assistance Within the Context of Existing Human Rights.

245 See in this regard amongst others Commission on Human Rights resolution 2003/52 (24 April 2003) preamble § 9; Report of the Representative of the Secretary-General, Mr. Francis Deng, UN Doc E/CN.4/1994/44 (n 74) § 20; 'Further Promotion And Encouragement Of Human Rights And Fundamental Freedoms, Including The Question Of The Programme And Methods Of Work Of The Commission Alternative Approaches And Ways And Means Within The United Nations System For Improving The Effective Enjoyment Of Human Rights And Fundamental Freedoms' Note by the Secretary-General UN Doc E/CN.4/1993/35 (21 January 1993) § 59. For the perspective of the Special Rapporteur: UN Doc A/HRC/4/38/Add.2 (n 240) § 5.

Persons, creating a strong perspective in soft law with regard to the rights of IDPs in relation to humanitarian assistance.[246] Existing binding legal provisions however remain those provisions in general international law and human rights law. Specifically within human rights law, next to the existing rights to life, food and health, tailored provisions exist such as Article 23 African Charter on the Rights and Welfare of the Child and particularly supplemented by the Kampala Convention.

6.6 Ascertaining the Existing Legal Framework in a Humanitarian Crisis

From the above overview of the applicable legal framework, it must be distinctly ascertained in which circumstances the provision of humanitarian assistance is developed most fully, and which circumstance may be lacking proper legal provisions. The relationship of various *corpora juris* is furthermore relevant, to determine the exact level of protection for persons needing emergency aid in a humanitarian crisis, depending on the specific kind of crisis at hand.

The perspective is taken in this research that persons in need of assistance should be able to receive such assistance, regardless of the origin of the humanitarian crisis. The determination of such a crisis in itself warrants the provision of assistance. Yet, various legal regimes are currently applicable in different circumstances, providing for different levels of protection. It has therefore been established that the *lex specialis* principle entails that the more detailed *provision* (as opposed to a whole body of law) is considered the applicable law, while the *lex generalis* remains present in the background.[247] With a more harmonious approach, focus would lay on gap-filling methods and the application of specific provisions, rather than entire bodies of law having prevalence over another body of law.[248] This approach would enhance the level of protection at all times, as provisions can be utilised from various bodies of law, to ensure a greater level of protection for the provision of assistance.

Only upon analysing the interaction of the various applicable rights and duties that have been ascertained above, can it be ascertained precisely which duties the affected state has, and which rights persons in need can claim, in circumstances amounting to a humanitarian crisis. When ascertaining the applicable law, it is relevant to take all provisions of the above *corpora juris* into account.

6.6.1 The Applicable Lex Specialis in Armed Conflict

In times of armed conflict, multiple fields of law are of relevance in the determination of the current legal framework pertaining to the provision of humanitarian assistance. Indeed, armed conflict in particular is a circumstance in

---

[246] Article 3(2) Declaration of International Law Principles on Internally Displaced Persons, which confers the right to seek and receive assistance upon IDPs.
[247] Section 3.4.3 Hierarchy or Convergence of International Legal Norms?.
[248] Ibid.

which the circumstantial field of humanitarian law and the topical fields of refugee law and IDP law are applicable next to the generally applicable bodies of law such as human rights law and the duties under state sovereignty or those derived from the UN Security Council resolutions ascertaining a general primary duty for affected states to provide in humanitarian assistance.

With regard to the relation between human rights law and humanitarian law, a conflict does not necessarily exist concerning the provisions pertaining to the delivery of emergency aid. Indeed, whilst the provisions in the Additional Protocols are quite specific, they are duties to refrain from certain actions, and do not conflict with the duties under human rights law, in particular the rights to food and health, that incorporate obligations of conduct, where the affected state is responsible for meeting the minimum core obligations. Both fields of law are specific, and tailored to the topic of humanitarian assistance. Both fields of law address distinct duties in circumstances of armed conflict that are not necessarily in conflict, in particular given the fact that humanitarian law differentiates between the type of armed conflict and thus does not have a broad scope of protection for those persons in need of assistance, to receive such aid from the affected state.

Sections 6.5.1 and 6.5.2 have addressed that humanitarian law recognises obligations resting upon parties to a conflict to prevent certain circumstances. Besides the existing duty of 'humane treatment' in Common Article 3, Article 54 AP I stipulates an obligation resting upon parties to an international armed conflict to prevent the destruction of objects that are indispensable to the civilian population, whereas Article 14 AP II states a duty for parties to a non-international armed conflict to prevent starvation of civilians: both duties are obligations of result. However, human rights law also provides for various positive obligations of states: obligations of conduct. These duties exist regardless of the typology of the conflict, and include the duty to provide adequate food for the civilian population, which the CESCR has interpretatively ascertained to entail the freedom from hunger, as part of the minimum core obligations under Article 11 ICESCR. The right to health, in particular Article 12(2)(c) ICESCR with regard to the prevention of diseases provides for a right of the population in times of conflict to request assistance from the affected state. Such assistance is then related to the prevention epidemics, common to emergency situations. Furthermore, the right to life in armed conflict continues to encompass the right to not be 'arbitrarily deprived' of one's life.

Should an armed conflict be international and include the development of a refugee population, the refugee child shall also be protected through Article 22 of the CRC. Furthermore, if such conflicts occur within the African continent, Article 23 of the African Charter on the Rights and Welfare of the Child holds specific provisions in this regard. Moreover, in the case of a non-international armed conflict, the protection is increased on the African continent through the provisions of the Kampala Convention. Articles 3(1)(j), 4, 5, 7(5)(b) and (c), 9(1), 9(2)(b) and (c), and 9(2)(k) place detailed obligations upon State Parties with regard to the provision of humanitarian assistance.

Thus, the above shows that international humanitarian law is not in itself *by definition* the *lex specialis* with regard to the provision of humanitarian assistance in times of conflict. Rather, various *corpora juris* contain specific provisions pertaining (mostly) to the obligations resting upon the affected state in the provision of assistance; a positive obligation that is distinctly absent in humanitarian law. All such obligations must be read together, facilitating a harmonious approach through which the affected population shall be able to receive the greatest protection in international law, and the best legal protection for the provision of assistance. Indeed, it will be necessary to apply the various obligations side-by-side, as their simultaneous application does not cause conflict of the law. Furthermore, it remains the essence of both human rights law and humanitarian law to enhance the protection of persons, and as such both bodies work towards the same goal.

6.6.2 The Applicable Lex Specialis in Occupation

A similar converging approach must be had to the law applicable in times of occupation that amounts to a humanitarian crisis. As is the case in times of armed conflict, the constant factor of state sovereignty and the UN framework provide for a primary responsibility that lies with the occupier in the provision of assistance, should it be needed in times of occupation.

As seen in Sections 6.5.3 and 6.5.4, the Fourth Geneva Convention stipulates in Articles 55, 56 and 60 that the occupier has a duty to provide food and medical supplies to its available means, whereas Article 69 AP I elaborates on this to include shelter and other supplies that may be essential to the survival of the occupied population. Although the provisions of GC IV and AP I are rather detailed, they do include the phrasing 'to the fullest extent of the means available', which provides the occupier with the possibility to claim it is not in a position to grant the population such materials. Furthermore, it must be noted that these provisions only become relevant upon the passing of a certain amount of *time* and establishment of a certain amount of *control* by the occupying force, when often a humanitarian crisis may not (or no longer) exist.

The level of control of the occupier is furthermore relevant to the application of human rights law. Whereas the continued application of such law is accepted in times of conflict, its continued application in times of occupation is subject to the discussion of the level of 'effective' control or authority, in extraterritorial situations.[249] Whilst the relevant provisions of human rights law include the obligation of states to respect the right to life of civilians, provide adequate food, and safeguard health (in particular with regard to the prevention of epidemics and diseases), their continued application is not crystal clear. Should a crisis exist, most logically the rather detailed provisions of the Geneva Conventions would be resorted to.

[249] Sections 3.4.2 Applicability of Human Rights in Armed Conflict and Occupation and 3.4.2.2 The Potential Extraterritorial Scope of Application of Human Rights Treaties.

As the provisions in times of occupation allow for a rather far-reaching level of obligations upon states, it has been argued that such duties resemble the duties upon states in peacetime situations to quite a large extent.[250] Indeed, in contrast to a situation of conflict, occupation may be prolonged over time, and the urgency to supply goods may subside or may indeed already have subsided when occupation is established. As such, it would then need to be re-evaluated whether or not a humanitarian crisis exists, to re-evaluate the application of legal provisions concerning humanitarian assistance. Today, the need for humanitarian assistance is more often found in other circumstances, such as (natural) disasters.

6.6.3 The Applicable Lex Specialis in Times of (Natural) Disaster

As has been addressed in Sections 6.5.5 and 6.5.6, a particular encompassing and tailored legal framework is absent in times of disaster not resulting from armed conflict. State sovereignty and the duties expressed through organs in the UN framework such as the General Assembly, however, continue to note the general legal responsibility of the affected state to provide in the delivery of humanitarian assistance to an affected group of persons in the aftermath of such disasters.

Furthermore, human rights law is applicable as only *lex specialis* to provide persons in need of assistance with actual legal rights to claim the receipt such aid from the affected state. Human rights law does so through provisions pertaining to the right to life, food, health (and water). Thus, as in times of conflict, states are obliged to not arbitrarily deprive persons of their life, and fulfil the positive obligations relating to the right to adequate food and health as stipulated in Articles 11 and 12 of the ICESCR as well as in all other specialised treaties discussed above. Furthermore, the topical bodies of refugee and IDP law can be applied. Should children become refugees, Article 22 of the CRC will provide State Parties with specific obligations in light of other obligations they may have under the Convention. The African continent in particular – prone to natural disasters – has developed far-reaching human rights protection for IDPs, as Articles 3(1)(j), 4, 5, 7(5)(b) and (c), 9(1), 9(2)(b) and (c), and 9(2)(k) oblige the affected state to provide in humanitarian assistance for IDPs. Also, Article 23 of the African Charter on the Rights and Welfare of the Child holds specific provisions to this end that are comparable to Article 22 CRC. As seen in the above settings also, the African continent regionally holds the most specific obligations for affected states and specific rights for those in need of humanitarian assistance. This region is furthermore prone to 'complex emergencies' in which a natural disaster may occur in times of armed conflict.

Indeed as addressed in Section 6.6.1, in essence the provisions of the various fields of law that can be applicable in disaster do not conflict with each other. As

[250] Benvenisti, *The International Law of Occupation* (n 161) 87; Flavia Zorzi Giustiniani, 'The Works of the International Law Commission on 'Protection of Persons in the Event of Disasters. A Critical Appraisal' in A de Guttry, M Gestri, G Venturini (eds), *International Disaster Response Law* (TMC Asser Press / Springer 2012) 65-84.

such, no discussion arises on the applicability of fields of law, and the applicable fields complement each other.

6.6.4 Determining the Problems and Gaps in the Provision of Humanitarian Assistance

In addressing the rights of the affected population to request assistance from its sovereign or other authority exercising sovereign control, such as certain armed groups in times of conflict, and addressing the duties of the authorities to provide in this regard, this Chapter has also uncovered the problems and gaps in the current legal framework. Indeed, whereas greatly detailed provisions exist for example with regard to the provision of assistance to children on the African continent falling within the scope of the Kampala Convention, some areas are still very much lacking specific legal protection by the affected state for persons in a humanitarian crisis.

In particular, several situations spring to mind. For example, one might consider situations of non-international armed conflict, outside the realm of the Kampala Convention on the African continent, where one does not look specifically to the IDP population. Both natural disasters and non-international armed conflicts are the types of humanitarian crises most commonly found today. In cases of non-international armed conflict, the civilian population is protected under humanitarian law solely through Additional Protocol II's stipulation that states are obliged to prevent starvation. Such protection is however solely granted to those civilians finding themselves within the scope of AP II's *threshold of 'control'* needed for a non-state party, and furthermore is confined to those states that are party to the Protocol in the first place. Yet, what protection is offered in situations in which a state is not party to the Additional Protocol, or such a threshold is not met?

For all other protection, such civilians must resort to human rights law and the provisions therein that are not necessarily drafted for tailoring to circumstances of conflict. This is equally the law which is applicable in times of natural disaster, as no other detailed provisions exist for the receipt of assistance. Although human rights law offers great protection through the rights to life, food and health, the provisions are not as detailed concerning the delivery of emergency assistance specifically. Despite their lack of detail, the provisions of the ICESCR, in particular due to the notion of 'minimum core obligations' do cast a 'wide net' of protection through their continued applicability and are by some considered to provide greater protection than international humanitarian law.[251] Indeed, human rights law contains positive obligations for the affected state that are lacking in humanitarian law. Whilst it is therefore positive that human rights law provides this protection, it remains regrettable that such duties for the sovereign actor are absent under humanitarian law. Such gaps in the law are particularly poignant in the recent rise

[251] Barber, 'Facilitating humanitarian assistance in international humanitarian and human rights law', (n 137) 395.

in non-international armed conflicts, where populations in need are caught in conflict between state armed forces and non-state actors or armed groups.

Furthermore, complex emergencies are relevant in the determination of gaps in the law, such as those emergencies where a natural disaster takes place in a conflict area. Whilst human rights law remains applicable, consideration must be given to areas where the national authorities may claim not to have sovereignty or control within their state territory due to an on-going conflict. It might be unclear who the sovereign is in a certain area, and therefore upon whom the obligation lies to provide assistance should a sudden natural disaster take place that overwhelms the local authority. The state sovereign may then be unwilling or unable to provide the assistance it is required to provide under existing human rights obligations.

Indeed, the above Chapter has shown that within the current framework, not only do *gaps* exist, but furthermore a lack of *harmony* exists between various *corpora juris*. The implementation of the more detailed provisions tailored specifically to the delivery of assistance has been dispersed: indeed the African continent has the greatest level of protection, in particular for IDPs.[252] Yet even for IDPs not finding themselves within the protection of the new Kampala Convention, a lack of protection from humanitarian law and even human rights law can be argued, as such persons often find themselves displaced due to both natural disasters and non-international armed conflict.[253] To ensure the equal protection of all persons, not merely children on the African continent that happen to fall within the particular scope of the Kampala Convention, the possibilities of ensuring the *external* provision of assistance and potential state duties to *allow access* from abroad must be considered. Enhancing harmonisation of the protection of persons in need will allow for more certainty of that protection, regardless of the particular circumstance in which the humanitarian crisis is taking place.

6.7 Conclusion

The above Chapter has established the current existing legal framework with regard to the specific obligations resting upon affected states and the specific rights for the affected persons to claim such assistance from their national authorities or sovereign. As has become apparent, no 'single' overall duty or right can be discerned. Clarity in the law does not exist concerning the provision of humanitarian assistance. Such lack of clarity is not necessarily only the result of gaps, as it is moreover the result of 'grey areas' in the law and in some circumstances even the result of overlap between multiple human rights as well as humanitarian law provisions. Human rights law acknowledges the right to life, food, health (and water), with the simultaneous acknowledgement of obligations resting upon state parties to human rights treaties to positively provide in the

[252] ICRC Resolution 30IC/07/R4 (n 201) § preambule. See also 'Fragmentation Of International Law: Difficulties Arising From The Diversification And Expansion Of International Law', Report of the Study Group of the International Law Commission (13 April 2006) UN Doc A/CN.4/L.682.
[253] UN Doc E/CN.4/1993/35 (n 245) § 61 & 74.

protection of such rights. Several distinct human rights treaties furthermore cater to the rights of children and IDPs within the scope of the Kampala Convention.

At a general level, the Security Council and General Assembly have asserted the primary responsibility of the affected state in the provision of humanitarian assistance, both in times of conflict and in times of (natural) disaster. Such assertions made by both the Security Council and General Assembly however lack detailed obligations or rights that are *specifically* tailored to the situation of a humanitarian crisis, as the respective resolutions often refer to the affected state's obligations under 'international law', 'human rights law' or 'humanitarian law'.[254] Thus, whilst these resolutions assert general obligations upon states or provide rights for individuals to assistance, they lack specific clarity within their texts. Such grey areas or gaps enhance the difficulties persons may experience in their attempt to receive assistance when in a humanitarian crisis. These assertions must therefore be explicated by human rights law and humanitarian law. Indeed, international humanitarian law contains a variety of very precise and detailed provisions, but lacks the incorporation of more general duties for the affected state and completely foregoes a right of individuals to request assistance from their sovereign or other authorities exercising control. Indeed, no specific duty to provide emergency assistance exists for the affected state.

Such a general obligation is also missing from human rights law, as this body of law was originally of course not specifically designed to protect persons solely in a humanitarian crisis, but more generally at all times. From this general purpose however of the rights to life, food and health, the duty of the affected state to ensure these rights *also in times of crisis* for persons finding themselves in a humanitarian emergency *can* be derived. This particular protection is *essential*, as human rights law finds continued applicability in particular circumstances where protection through other bodies of law is lacking, such as (natural) disasters and non-international armed conflicts.

Furthermore, the African continent has recently expanded its legal framework through the Kampala Convention, allowing for a surge in protection of IDPs in this area of the world. Such enhanced protection must of course be applauded, but it also painfully lays bare the lack of protection for IDPs in other regions of the world. Given the influx of IDPs over the past decades,[255] due to the surge in natural disasters and non-international armed conflicts, this *relative* lack of protection of IDPs (compared to IDPs happening to fall within the scope of the Kampala Convention) exemplifies the need for a more comprehensive, all-encompassing approach to the legal framework protecting those in a humanitarian crisis, rather than haphazard incorporation or geographical protection.

---

[254] Section 6.4 Duties and Rights under the UN Framework: the Security Council and General Assembly.

[255] For some statistics in this regard: <www.unhcr.org/pages/49c3646c23.html> accessed 20 October 2014, where UNHCR states that in 2012 nearly 29 million IDPs existed worldwide, compared to 17 million in 1997.

Another related, and problematic, aspect of the legal framework concerning humanitarian assistance is the fact that the existing detailed provisions are often confined to very specific circumstances, such as IDPs in Africa, or refugee children. Thus, the legal protection provided to persons in need of assistance becomes rather 'sectoral', with different legal obligations resting upon various states and different rights existing for persons depending on the particular category of crisis one finds oneself in, or the particular location on the globe. Such haphazard and disparate protection is rather problematic, as it results in unequal *protection* under the law for persons in need of humanitarian assistance, as well as unequal *obligations* for affected states, depending on their particular region. A person in need of food, water and shelter due to the existence of a humanitarian emergency should have to be able to request and receive such bare necessities and retain human dignity, regardless of country of origin, typology of crisis or age. For this precise purpose, this research takes an overall and encompassing view of the protection of persons in need of humanitarian assistance.

Many soft law documents have sought to solve such problematic situations by developing guidelines and principles with regard to the provision of humanitarian assistance which are applicable to all circumstances. As such, the 1991 Guidelines for Humanitarian Assistance, the 1993 San Remo Principles, the Mohonk Criteria and the well-known Bruges Resolution of 2003 proffer suggestions. These soft law instruments invariably recognise the primary duty of the affected state to provide aid, regardless of the nature or origin of the crisis, and the Mohonk Criteria and Bruges Resolution even explicitly recognise such a duty for other authorities exercising a certain amount of control.[256] Moreover, and quite distinct from the existing law, these instruments almost all acknowledge a right of persons affected by a humanitarian crisis to *request and receive* assistance from their national authorities or sovereign.[257] Clearly, such instruments express a development initiative in the international legal framework regarding humanitarian assistance, as they can be considered to contribute to expressions of *opinio juris*.[258] However, such an all-encompassing approach to the provision of humanitarian assistance is currently lacking in existing law; in particular the recognition of a 'right to request' assistance.

In essence, such an individual right is however not necessary for the protection of persons through human rights law, as argued in Chapter 5, given the sufficient level of protection offered by the existing human rights to life, food and health. Whereas the development of more tailored provisions might theoretically enhance

[256] See in this regard the 1991 Guidelines for Humanitarian Assistance Guideline 6 (6); 'Guiding Principles on the Right to Humanitarian Assistance' (April 1993) The International Institute of Humanitarian Law in San Remo, Principle 4; 'The Mohonk Criteria for Humanitarian Assistance in Complex Emergencies', (1995) reprinted in 17 *Human Rights Quarterly* 1, Principle II; Resolution 'Humanitarian Assistance' (2 September 2003) Institute of International Law, Sixteenth Commission, Bruges Session, Principle III.

[257] Ibid 'Guiding Principles on the Right to Humanitarian Assistance' Principles 1 and 2; ibid 'The Mohonk Criteria'; and ibid the Bruges Resolution § II.2.

[258] See Section 1.4.1 on the components of customary international law.

protection, such development is of greater necessity from the perspective of the duties of the affected state; in particular in circumstances of loss of control of the affected state over areas of its territory, such as in times of non-international armed conflict and complex emergencies.

From the above discussion of the existing legal framework, as well as from the efforts of soft law instruments, a conclusion can be drawn. The international legal framework regarding the provision of humanitarian assistance, although hesitant to affirmatively acknowledge a right of individuals to claim assistance and receive such assistance from their sovereign, *does* view a primary positive, but general, obligation to rest upon the affected state in the provision of humanitarian assistance. Such a duty is furthermore made more concrete through the duties derived from the human rights to life, food and health as well as by the notion of sovereignty as 'responsibility'. Consequently, if an affected state or acting sovereign does not provide in such a duty, the legal framework regarding humanitarian assistance must enlarge its scope, and look to encompass potential rights of *third* parties, such as states and international organisations, in the provision of assistance to persons in need. The subsequent Chapter shall therefore address a potential external right to provide assistance, as well as a potential related right to access for these third parties.

	Duty of Affected State	Right of Affected Population	Source
State Sove-reignty	• Primary duty of affected state to provide assistance based on concept of sovereignty within this research (as responsibility)	• Right to request assistance from affected state based on a reciprocal relationship between the sovereign and society as acknowledged within this research	• 2(1) UN Charter; UNGA Res 38/202 (20 December 1983) UN Doc A/RES/38/202 § 4, UNGA Res 43/131 (8 December 1988) UN Doc A/RES/43/131 § 2, and UNGA Res 45/100 (14 December 1990) UN Doc A/RES/45/100 § 2, UNGA Res 46/182 (19 December 1991) UN Doc A/RES/46/182 Annex § 4
Securi-ty Coun-cil Reso-lutions	• Primary responsibility to protect vulnerable groups lies with states		• UNSC Res 1265 (17 September 1999) UN Doc S/RES/1265 preamble
	• Call to states to comply strictly with their obligations under international humanitarian, human rights and refugee law		• UNSC Res 1265 (17 September 1999) UN Doc S/RES/1265 § 4; UNSC Res 1296 (19 April 2000) UN Doc S/RES/1296 preamble and § 19
	• Primary responsibility of states to protect civilians (in general)		• UNSC Res 1674 (28 April 2006) UN Doc S/RES/1674 § 13; UNSC Res 1894 (11 November 2009) UN Doc S/RES/1894 preamble and § 15. See also amongst others: UNSC Res 1325 (31 October 2000) UN Doc S/RES/1325; UNSC Res 1430 (14 August 2002) UN Doc S/RES/1430; UNSC Res 1906 (23 December 2009) UN Doc S/RES/1906; and UNSC Res 1861 (14 January 2009) UN Doc S/RES/1861
	• 'Responsibility to Protect' population; incorporation of RtoP		• UNSC Res 1970 (26 February 2011) UN Doc S/RES/1970 preamble and UNSC Res 1973 (17 March 2011) UN Doc S/RES/1973 preamble and § 3; UNSC Res 1975 (30 March 2011) UN Doc S/RES/1975 'The

	Duty of Affected State	Right of Affected Population	Source
			situation in Côte d'Ivoir' preamble; UNSC Res 1996 (8 July 2011) UN Doc S/RES/1996 § 3(b)(iv); UNSC Res 2014 (21 October 2011) UN Doc S/RES/2014 § preamble; UNSC Res 2016 (27 October 2011) UN Doc S/RES/2016 § 3; UNSC Res 2040 (12 March 2012) UN Doc S/RES/2040 § 4; UNSC Res 2139 (22 February 2014) UN Doc S/RES/2139 § 9; UNSC 2165 (14 July 2014) UN Doc S/RES/2165 preamble
	• Primary responsibility under general international law to 'take all feasible steps to ensure the protection of affected civilians' as well as responsibility of parties to an armed conflict to 'respect, protect and meet the basic needs of civilian populations within their effective control'		• 'Aide Memoire Protection of Civilians in Armed Conflict' UN Doc S/PRST/2010/25 (22 November 2010) preamble; 'Aide Memoire Protection of Civilians in Armed Conflict' UN Doc S/PRST/2013/2 (12 February 2013) 1 and 3; 'Aide Memoire Protection of Civilians in Armed Conflict' UN Doc S/PRST/2014/3 (12 February 2014) 2; UNSC 2165 (14 July 2014) UN Doc S/RES/2165 preamble
General Assembly Resolutions	• Primacy of the role of the affected countries 'in caring for the victims of natural disasters and other disaster situations'		• UNGA Res 36/225 (17 December 1981) UN Doc A/RES/36/225 preamble and § 2; UNGA Res 38/202 (20 December 1983) UN Doc A/RES/38/202 preamble & § 4; UNGA Res 41/201 (8 December 1986) UN Doc A/RES/41/201 § 2
	• Primary role and responsibility of affected state to take care of the victims of natural disasters and other emergencies		• UNGA Res 46/182 (19 December 1991) UN Doc A/RES/46/182 Annex § 4; UNGA Res 47/168 (22 December 1992) UN Doc A/RES/47/168; UNGA Res

	Duty of Affected State	Right of Affected Population	Source
	occurring on its territory		48/57 (14 December 1993) UN Doc A/RES/48/57; UNGA Res 48/188 (9 March 1994) UN Doc A/RES/48/188; UNGA Res 49/139 (20 December 1994) UN Doc A/RES/49/139; UNGA Res 51/194 (10 February 1997) UN Doc A/RES/51/194; UNGA Res 52/167 (18 February 1998) UN Doc A/RES/52/167; UNGA Res 52/168 (18 February 1998) UN Doc A/RES/52/168; UNGA Res 53/87 (27 January 1999) UN Doc A/RES/53/87; UNGA Res 53/88 (29 January 1999) UN Doc A/RES/53/88; UNGA Res 54/95 (28 January 2000) UN Doc A/RES/54/95; UNGA Res 54/192 (21 February 2000) UN Doc A/RES/54/192; UNGA Res 54/233 (25 February 2000) UN Doc A/RES/54/233; UNGA Res 55/163 (7 February 2001) UN Doc A/RES/55/163; UNGA Res 55/164 (7 February 2001) UN Doc A/RES/55/164; UNGA Res 55/175 (7 March 2001) UN Doc A/RES/55/175; UNGA Res 56/99 (31 January 2002) UN Doc A/RES/56/99; UNGA Res 56/103 (5 February 2002) UN Doc A/RES/56/103; UNGA Res 56/107 (7 February 2002) UN Doc A/RES/56/107; UNGA Res 56/217 (19 February 2002) UN Doc A/RES/56/217; UNGA Res 57/150 (27 February 2003) UN Doc A/RES/57/150; UNGA Res 57/152 (3 March 2003) UN Doc A/RES/57/152; UNGA Res 57/153 (3 March 2003) UN

	Duty of Affected State	Right of Affected Population	Source
			Doc A/RES/57/153; UNGA Res 58/25 (29 January 2004) UN Doc A/RES/58/25; UNGA Res 58/114 (5 February 2004) UN Doc A/RES/58/114; UNGA Res 59/141 (25 February 2005) UN Doc A/RES/59/141; UNGA Res 59/212 (3 March 2005) UN Doc A/RES/59/212; UNGA Res 60/124 (8 March 2006) UN Doc A/RES/60/124; UNGA Res 60/125 (15 March 2006) UN Doc A/RES/60/125; UNGA Res 60/123 (24 March 2006) UN Doc A/RES/60/123; UNGA Res 61/131 (22 February 2007) UN Doc A/RES/61/131; UNGA Res 61/133 (1 March 2007) UN Doc A/RES/61/133; UNGA Res 61/134 (1 March 2007) UN Doc A/RES/61/134; UNGA Res 62/92 (1 February 2008) UN Doc A/RES/62/92; UNGA Res 62/94 (25 January 2008) UN Doc A/RES/62/94; UNGA Res 62/95 (29 January 2008) UN Doc A/RES/62/95; UNGA Res 63/138 (5 March 2009) UN Doc A/RES/63/138; UNGA Res 63/139 (5 March 2009) UN Doc A/RES/63/139; UNGA Res 63/141 (10 March 2009) UN Doc A/RES/63/141; UNGA Res 64/76 (2 February 2010) UN Doc A/RES/64/76; UNGA Res 64/77 (8 February 2010) UN Doc A/RES/64/77; A UNGA Res 64/251 (30 April 2010) UN Doc A/RES/64/251; UNGA Res 65/132 (1 March 2011) UN Doc A/RES/65/132; UNGA Res 65/133 (3 March 2011) UN Doc

	Duty of Affected State	Right of Affected Population	Source
			A/RES/65/133; UNGA Res 65/264 (21 June 2011) UN Doc A/RES/65/264; UNGA Res 65/307 (25 August 2011) UN Doc A/RES/65/307; UNGA Res 66/117 (1 March 2012) UN Doc A/RES/66/117; UNGA Res 66/119 (7 March 2012) UN Doc A/RES/66/119; UNGA Res 66/227 (15 March 2012) UN Doc A/RES/66/227; UNGA Res 67/85 (21 March 2013) UN Doc A/RES/67/85; UNGA Res 67/87 (26 March 2013) UN Doc A/RES/67/87; UNGA Res 67/231 (9 April 2013) UN Doc A/RES/67/231; UNGA Res 68/101 (18 February 2014) UN Doc A/RES/68/101; UNGA Res 68/102 (12 February 2014) UN Doc A/RES/68/102; UNGA Res 68/103 (19 February 2014) UN Doc A/RES/68/103
	• Obligation of all States and parties to an armed conflict to protect civilians in armed conflicts		• UNGA Res 58/114 (5 February 2004) UN Doc A/RES/58/114 § 12; UNGA Res 59/141 (25 February 2005) UN Doc A/RES/59/141 § 15; UNGA Res 60/124 (8 March 2006) UN Doc A/RES/60/124 § 3; UNGA Res 62/94 (25 January 2008) UN Doc A/RES/62/94 §19; UNGA Res 63/139 (5 March 2009) UN Doc A/RES/63/139 §21; UNGA Res 64/76 (2 February 2010) UN Doc A/RES/64/76 §22; UNGA Res 65/133 (3 March 2011) UN Doc A/RES/65/133 § 23; UNGA Res 66/119 (7 March 2012) UN Doc A/RES/66/119 § 29; UNGA Res 67/87 (26 March 2013) UN Doc A/RES/67/87 § 33;

	Duty of Affected State	Right of Affected Population	Source
			UNGA Res 68/102 (12 February 2014) UN Doc A/RES/68/102 §36.
Human Rights Law	• Obligation on UN Member States to ensure universal respect for human rights		• Articles 55 & 56 UN Charter
	• Duty to not arbitrarily deprive persons of their life	• Right to life	• Article 3 UDHR, 6 ICCPR, Article 2 ECHR, Article 4 ACHR, Article 4 ACHPR; Article 6 & 22 CRC
	• Obligation for states to provide food (as part of humanitarian assistance in the event of a humanitarian crisis)	• Right to adequate food	• Article 11 ICESCR (and Article 2 ICESCR); Article 24(2)(c) CRC, Article 12(2) CEDAW, Article 28 CRPD, Article 12 of the Additional Protocol to the ACHR in the Area of Economic, Social and Cultural Rights and Article 15 of the Additional Protocol to the ACHPR on the Rights of Women in Africa, Article 25 UDHR.
	• Obligation upon states parties to ensure that persons have access to certain minimum essential levels of food, health facilities, basic shelter, water and sanitation (more narrowly: prevention of diseases)	• Right to health	• 25 UDHR and Article 12 ICESCR (and Article 2 ICESCR) [*in particular: 12(2)(c) ICESCR*]; Article 5(e)(iv) ICERD, Article 24 CRC, Article 11 European Social Charter, Article 10 of the Additional Protocol to the ACHR in the area of Economic, Social and Cultural Rights, Article 16 ACHPR, Article 14 of the African Charter on the Rights and Welfare of the Child and Article 14 of the Protocol to the ACHPR on the Rights of Women in Africa
	• General obligation resting upon states to provide access to safe drinking water (this obligation is only found in several specific treaties and	• Right to water	• Article 24(1)(c) CRC, Article 14(2)(h) CEDAW, Article 28 CRPD, Article 15(a) Additional Protocol to the ACHPR on the Rights of Women in Africa, Article 14(2)(c)

	Duty of Affected State	Right of Affected Population	Source
	in regional conventions)		African Charter on the Rights and Welfare of the Child
	• Obligation on State Parties to provide for the fulfilment of human rights of persons with disabilities, in the event of a humanitarian crisis		• Article 11 CRPD
Law of Armed Con-flict	*International Armed Conflict* • Prohibition of parties to destroy objects that are 'indispensable to the survival of the civilian population'	*International Armed Conflict*	*International Armed Conflict* • Article 54 AP I
		• (Right of a civilian population to receive humanitarian assistance in circumstances where it should be in need)	• ICRC Customary IHL Study
	Non-International Armed Conflict • Obligation of humane treatment	*Non-International Armed Conflict*	*Non-International Armed Conflict* • Common Article 3 GC
	• Prohibition of starvation of civilians 'as a method of combat'		• Article 14 AP II
Law of Occu-pation	• Occupier must ensure 'public order and safety'		• Article 43 Regulations Concerning the Law and Customs of War on Land – annex to Convention Respecting the Laws and Customs of War on Land
	• Duties of occupier to 'ensure to the fullest extent of the means available' that the population is provided with food and medical supplies		• Article 55 GC IV
	• Responsibility to provide relief		• Article 60 GC IV

	Duty of Affected State	Right of Affected Population	Source
	remains with the occupying power		
	• Obligation to ensure and maintain hospitals and public health, particularly taking measures concerning the prevention of epidemics ('with the co-operation of national and local authorities')		• Article 56 GC IV
	• Occupier must 'to the fullest extent of the means available to it', also ensure clothing, shelter and other supplies that may be 'essential to the survival of the civilian population'		• Article 69 AP I
IDRL / ILC Protec-tion of Per-sons	• Duty of affected state to ensure the protection of persons and provision of disaster relief and assistance on its territory. The affected State has the primary role in the direction, control, coordination and supervision of such relief and assistance		• Inter-American Convention To Facilitate Disaster Assistance • Article 3 (a) Convention on Assistance in the Case of a Nuclear Accident or Radiological Emergency • Draft Article 12 ILC
	• Duty to seek assistance should the disaster not be manageable through States own resources		• Draft Article 13 ILC
	• (Affected state as primary responsible actor in the provision of assistance in the event of a disaster)		• (Article 3 of the IDRL Guidelines)
		• (Right of persons 'both to offer and receive humanitarian assistance')	• (ICRC Conference 2007, Resolution 4, preamble)

	Duty of Affected State	Right of Affected Population	Source
Refugee Law	• Obligation of State Parties to provide same treatment with respect to public relief and assistance as is accorded to their nationals		• Article 23 Refugee Convention
		• Refugee child is entitled to receive humanitarian assistance within the context of the enjoyment of the rights of the Conventions	• Article 22 CRC and Article 23 African Charter on the Rights and Welfare of the Child
IDP Framework	• Obligation for State Parties to provide assistance to IDPs by meeting their basic needs and respecting their rights		• Article 3(1)(j) Kampala Convention
	• Obligation to prevent conditions that may lead to arbitrary displacement and, 'where necessary, provide immediate protection and assistance to internally displaced persons'		• Article 4 Kampala Convention
	• Primary obligation and responsibility in the provision of humanitarian assistance to all IDPs within their territory or jurisdiction, specifying a duty to 'take necessary steps to effectively organize, relief action that is humanitarian, and impartial in character'	• Right of IDPs to peacefully request or seek protection and assistance	• Article 5 Kampala Convention • Article 5(9) Kampala Convention
	• Obligation to protect the rights of IDPs regardless of the		• Article 9(1) Kampala Convention

	Duty of Affected State	Right of Affected Population	Source
	cause of the displacement, and to refrain amongst others from 'genocide, crimes against humanity, war crimes and other violations of international humanitarian law' as well as from starvation		
	• Duty to provide IDPs to the fullest extent practicable and with the least possible delay, with adequate humanitarian assistance, which shall include food, water, shelter, medical care and other health services, sanitation, education, and any other necessary social services	• IDPs allowed to participate in the process of receiving assistance	• Article 9(2)(b) Kampala Convention • Article 9(2)(k) Kampala Convention
	• Prohibition for armed groups of hampering the provision of protection and assistance to IDPs under any circumstances and denying IDPs the right to live in satisfactory conditions of dignity, security, sanitation, food, water, health and shelter		• Article 7(5)(b) and (c) Kampala Convention
	• Obligation in situations of displacement to ensure that all possible measures must be taken to ensure that the IDPs		• Article 17 AP II

	Duty of Affected State	Right of Affected Population	Source
	are 'received under satisfactory conditions of shelter, hygiene, health, safety and nutrition'		
		• IDP child is entitled to receive humanitarian assistance within the context of the enjoyment of the rights of the Convention	• Article 23 African Charter on the Rights and Welfare of the Child
		• IDPs have a right to request assistance, the right to receive such assistance and right to an adequate standard of living	• (Guiding Principles 3 and 18 IDPs)

Part III

Third Party Action When Provision Is Lacking

Chapter 7
Third Parties and the Provision of Assistance: The Right to Offer Assistance and the Related (Potential) Right to Access

In the summer of 2014, OCHA, UNICEF and the World Food Programme declared in a joint statement regarding the humanitarian crisis in Syria:

> "Hungry, homeless children don't know or care whether they are in a government-controlled area or an opposition-controlled area. They just want a safe place to live. Inside Syria, nearly 11 million people need immediate humanitarian aid. We must do everything we can to help them, bringing aid by the most direct routes, whether they are across borders or across conflict-lines".

But what precisely are the rights of third parties to access a territory, from an international legal perspective? What duties does the affected state or acting sovereign have to allow such access? In this Chapter these questions are addressed as part of the legal framework on the provision of humanitarian assistance.[1]

7.1 Introduction

The previous Chapter has established that the affected state is the primary responsible actor for the provision of assistance in the event of crises on its territory or under its control with a corresponding right of persons in such a crisis to request assistance from their sovereign, commonly based on human rights law. In certain instances, the local authorities may be overwhelmed by the nature of the crisis and may be unable to provide in assistance. In other circumstances, the local authorities may even be unwilling to provide assistance, or may have lost the exercise of control over parts of their territory. Examples include the collapse of state authorities which may result in so-called 'failed states'. This circumstance, and the others mentioned above where a lack of *will* or *control* prevents the provision of assistance by the affected state, warrant further examination of the legal framework pertaining to humanitarian assistance from an *external* perspective. In such circumstances, regardless of whether these may factually be conflict or disaster, the right to offer and provide humanitarian assistance through external sources such as

---

[1] <https://docs.unocha.org/sites/dms/Documents/16%20July%202014%20Syria%20SC%20resolution_joint%20statement.pdf> accessed 21 October 2014: joint statement on Security Council Resolution 2165 on humanitarian access in Syria by OCHA, UNICEF and WFP.

third states or international organisations needs to be addressed. Such 'external' provision of assistance is subsidiary to the primary right and duty of the affected state.[2]

The external provision of humanitarian assistance is guided by two legally distinct aspects; namely (1) the right to offer provision of assistance and (2) a related right to access, or, alternatively formulated, a potential duty to allow such access by the affected state. As such, there is a tiered approach to the provision of assistance from external sources. In addressing the current legal framework concerning the *provision* of humanitarian assistance by or through external sources, this Chapter thus also addresses the directly related potential right to *access* the affected territory for such assistance or the duty to allow this access. These external aspects in the provision of humanitarian aid are a vast part of the existing legal framework and will also map out existing gaps in the provision of assistance.

Indeed, given the nature of the provision of humanitarian assistance; namely its taking place in a crisis, external assistance is often needed. This Chapter specifically addresses the provision of assistance *from the perspective of third parties*. Should however the affected state not allow for the provision of assistance, the result may be the denial of humanitarian assistance, which will be further explored in Chapter 8. Chapter 8 addresses the consequences of the denial of humanitarian aid, and the consequences if a state or other duty-bearer does not comply with its existing duties under international law. Part III of this research thus addresses the current legal framework on the provision of humanitarian assistance from an external perspective, looking firstly into the legal possibilities for third parties to provide access, and secondly, in the subsequent Chapter, into enforcement methods should such access and assistance be denied.

In many instances, international organisations themselves have provided for a form of self-regulation and protection in their provision of assistance, through treaties, or soft-law documents. As such, whilst this aspect of regulation remains outside the realm of this research, it is relevant to note amongst others the Convention on the Safety of United Nations and Associated Personnel.[3] In fact, these regulations need only come into place upon the establishment of what precisely the rights (and duties) are of third parties in the provision of humanitarian assistance. It is precisely *this* that is addressed in the current Chapter. As has been the case in previous Chapters, the approach of this research to the legal framework and the rights and duties encompassed therein is overarching. As such, the *lex lata* in general fields of international law shall be addressed first, after which the more specific bodies of law will be concentrated on. A tiered approach is taken; in each field of law firstly addressing the right to offer the provision of assistance, and secondly addressing the related right to access. This access is distinctly entangled with the affected state sovereign's (or other authority's) rights to determine the

[2] Carlo Focarelli, 'Duty to Protect in Cases of Natural Disasters', (2010) *Max Planck Encyclopedia of International Law* § 4.

[3] Convention on the Safety of United Nations and Associated Personnel, New York, 9 December 1994, United Nations, *Treaty Series*, vol. 2051, p. 363.

allowance of such access. Such rights and duties reflect two sides of the same coin, in this aspect of the legal framework. As will be apparent, the political will of the respective actors plays a large role in this area of the legal framework, and Chapter 8 therefore addresses the consequences of the denial of assistance, should the affected sovereign not allow the external provision of aid, in the circumstances that this Chapter *assesses as rightful.*

7.2 The Provision of Humanitarian Assistance by Third Parties under General International Law

The previous Chapter addressed the rights and duties of clear-cut actors: the affected state or authority, and the persons in need of receiving aid. The potential external right to provide aid however extends to a large variety of actors.[4] As such, international organisations and third states in some circumstances may have the right to offer and deliver humanitarian assistance, provided that such assistance is procured according to the principles of neutrality, humanity and impartiality.[5] These potential legal rights will be explored according to various fields of law below, commencing with the general fields of law relating to state sovereignty. Simultaneously, the corresponding duties of the affected state and potential other actors shall be addressed.

7.2.1 State Sovereignty and the Right to Offer Assistance

The notion of state sovereignty continues to be one of the cornerstones upon which the international legal domain is built. Thus, when exploring the potential right of third parties to offer and provide humanitarian assistance, such a discussion cannot forego the concept of sovereignty. Chapter 4 has addressed the various principles which have played a large role in this discussion, amongst which the principle of non-intervention, of consent and of domestic jurisdiction. The 1984 Draft Convention on expediting the delivery of emergency assistance remained unclear regarding the notion of sovereignty and the amount of emphasis the concept should receive in relation to the provision of humanitarian assistance. As such, Article 3(a) of the Draft Convention stated that the assistance as provided under the Draft Convention had to be in accordance with the principle of respect for the 'sovereignty of the receiving state and non-interference in its internal affairs'. Although the Draft Convention never materialised as international law, the ICRC has criticised the document for giving too much leeway to sovereignty.[6] The question of whether a potential right to offer and provide humanitarian assistance may not be consistent with the concept of sovereignty is not new. The ICJ determined only a few years after the failed Draft Convention that:

---

[4] Section 2.3.2 Providers of Humanitarian Assistance.

[5] Section 2.2.3 The Principles for the Delivery of Assistance.

[6] *Law and legal issues in international disaster response: a desk study* (International Federation of Red Cross and Red Crescent Societies 2007) 28.

> "There can be no doubt that the provision of strictly humanitarian aid to persons or forces in another country, whatever their political affiliations or objectives, cannot be regarded as unlawful intervention, or as in any other way contrary to international law (...) In the view of the Court, if the provision of "humanitarian assistance" is to escape condemnation as an intervention in the internal affairs of Nicaragua, not only must it be limited to the purposes hallowed in the practice of the Red Cross, namely "to prevent and alleviate human suffering", and "to protect life and health and to ensure respect for the human being"; it must also, and above all, be given without discrimination to all in need in Nicaragua, not merely to the *contras* and their dependents."[7]

As argued in Chapter 4, in this determination by the ICJ, the Court declares that not only the *offer* of assistance is considered lawful, but that such *provision* can also not be considered to infringe upon the principle of non-intervention.[8] The Court thus emphatically excludes the *sec* provision of assistance from an *infringement* on state sovereignty.

Today, sovereignty however indeed remains a factor in the provision of humanitarian assistance. The foremost explication of this is the fact that as the primary responsibility in the provision of humanitarian assistance lies with the affected state, the (un)willingness of the affected state is expressed through its exercise of sovereign rights to withhold the provision of assistance by external sources. However, the inclusion of sovereign responsibilities also in itself reflects the fact that sovereignty has changed over time. Such change is also effectuated by the fact that failing to oblige with certain duties under international law may lead to a responsibility for the international community to provide assistance, as just mentioned. Indeed, it was already asserted in the early 1990s by the UN General Assembly that the protection of human rights is a matter that concerns the international community *as a whole*.[9] As the previous Chapters have addressed, the provision of humanitarian assistance is a vehicle in the fulfilment of the human rights to life, food, health (and water). As such, it may be argued that the international community is invested also from a human rights perspective in the provision of humanitarian assistance, should a state not uphold its sovereign duties in the provision of humanitarian assistance.[10] On what grounds and with which legal basis the international community shall be able to offer and provide such assistance will be discussed in subsequent Sections through the discussion of various bodies of law.

---

7 Military and Paramilitary Activities in and against Nicaragua (Nicaragua v. United States of America), Merits, Judgment 27 June 1986 I.C.J. Reports 1986, p. 14 § 242-243.

8 Section 4.2.1 Historical Context and Relevant Principles in relation to Humanitarian Assistance.

9 UNGA Res 48/141 (20 December 1993) UN Doc A/RES/48/141 § 3(a): "the promotion and protection of all human rights is a legitimate concern of the international community".

10 'Further Promotion And Encouragement Of Human Rights And Fundamental Freedoms, Including The Question Of The Programme And Methods Of Work Of The Commission Alternative Approaches And Ways And Means Within The United Nations System For Improving The Effective Enjoyment Of Human Rights And Fundamental Freedoms' Note by the Secretary-General UN Doc E/CN.4/1993/35 (21 January 1993) § 84-88.

The international community is often also concerned with the provision of humanitarian assistance in circumstances where a sovereign is lacking. Situations such as failing states and multiple actors claiming sovereignty over a territory influence the potential role of state sovereignty. The factual circumstance of a failing state often coincides with the existence of a severe humanitarian crisis and a need for assistance. Although arguably the provision of humanitarian assistance in the event of a state failure is purely symptomatic, such provision will be necessary nonetheless.[11] It is undeniable that state sovereignty as a concept remains a crucial factor in the provision of humanitarian assistance by external sources, but although state sovereignty as a concept is a constant, the factual circumstances in which provision is necessary may vary, including conflict and disaster. Indeed Ryngaert also argues that given the diversity of situations in which the provision of assistance is necessary, the uniting factor is 'emphasis on state consent' as an exercise of sovereignty.[12] Consent as an aspect of the 'principle of consent' that is relevant to state sovereignty indeed most distinctly factors in the circumstance of a potential right to access.

7.2.2 State Sovereignty and the Right to Access

As recalled above, the ICJ asserted in the *Nicaragua*-case that the *sec* offer and provision of assistance could not be considered an impediment to the notion of sovereignty. An omission in the ICJ's analysis however remains the fact that the Court neglects to address *how* such assistance should reach the affected territory, and thereby avoids addressing the issue of access by means of force or an 'intervention' for humanitarian purposes. Clearly, the principles of consent and non-intervention stand in the way of unlimited and continuous access by third parties to a territory.[13] But, such principles do not always prevent such access to a territory *per se* for the delivery of assistance. Vukas concurs, arguing that the *offer* of assistance cannot be construed as an unlawful interference with a state's domestic affairs.[14] The developments surrounding these principles and the notion of sovereignty over the past decades, including the concept of the 'Responsibility to Protect' and the UNs approach in this regard, result in an approach to sovereignty that *may* allow for access to a territory by third parties under certain circumstances

[11] The Netherlands Advisory Council on International Affairs (AIV), Report 'Failing States. A Global Responsibility' No. 35 (May 2004) 51.
[12] Cedric Ryngaert, 'Humanitarian Assistance and the Conundrum of Consent: A Legal Perspective', (2013) 5 *Amsterdam Law Forum* 2, 5.
[13] Focarelli, 'Duty to Protect in Cases of Natural Disasters' (n 2) § 15. See in this regard also UNGA Res 2131 (XX) (21 December 1965), UNGA Res 2625 (XXV) (24 October 1970) 'Declaration on Principles of International Law Concerning Friendly Relations and Cooperation among States in Accordance with the Charter of the United Nations', Annex; and UNGA Res 36/103 (9 December 1981) UN Doc A/RES/36/103 discussed in Section 4.2.1.
[14] Budislav Vukas, 'Humanitarian Assistance in Cases of Emergency', (2007) *Max Planck Encyclopedia of Public International Law* § 22.

and for specific purposes.[15] Indeed with the development of this concept, the international community may indeed also have responsibilities in the provision of aid to a certain territory. In fact, this was already assessed by the ICJ in its *Nicaragua* judgment, while the Court did not address *how* the provision of such assistance should be provided to the affected territory. Within the RtoP doctrine, the notion of 'access' for humanitarian purposes is furthermore only addressed in the context of state sovereignty as access 'by force'. Such a means of gaining access, although on occasion necessary, does not fall within the scope of a potential 'right to access' for third parties in the provision of assistance itself. Access as discussed within this Chapter maintains the principles of humanity, neutrality and impartiality, in order to fit within the notion of humanitarian assistance. Access by means of force shall be discussed subsequently in Chapter 8 as a means of enforcing the provision of humanitarian assistance. A clear differentiation must therefore be made between access granted by the affected sovereign directly to those providers of aid themselves, and the (forceful) gaining of access by those *creating the necessary conditions* to allow the provision of emergency assistance in the absence of consent.

In subsequent Sections, the potential right to access is linked to the primary responsibility of the affected state to provide assistance. Only if and when the affected state does not fulfil its duties, does the international community act. Therefore, as Chapter 6 has established a primary role of the affected state, this role must be taken into consideration when contemplating the right to access. Through the determination in the following Sections regarding the rights and duties of third parties under the relevant *corpora juris*, it will become apparent in which instances the affected state must consent, and in which instances such consent may be withheld. The premise remains that the provision of humanitarian assistance occurs in a situation of a 'humanitarian crisis'.[16]

7.3 The Provision of Humanitarian Assistance by Third Parties Under Human Rights Law

The relationship between human rights law and humanitarian assistance has been addressed to a large extent in Chapter 5. It has been concluded that currently no independent human right to receive humanitarian assistance exists, whilst the provision of such assistance functions as a vehicle in the fulfilment of the existing human rights to life, food, health (and water). As such, Chapter 6 has assessed the value of this; discussing the rights of persons in need to receive assistance and the duty of the affected state to provide in this regard. Such duties have also been addressed from the perspective of various non-state actors fulfilling the role of 'affected sovereign authority'.

---

[15] Section 4.2.3.2 Humanitarian Assistance and the Development of RtoP in Practice.

[16] Section 3.3.3 Defining a Humanitarian Crisis.

This Section thus subsequently addresses the rights of third parties to provide humanitarian assistance under existing human rights law, followed by an assessment of a potential right to gain access to the affected territory. As this Section pertains to *lex lata*, solely the potential *currently existing* right to provide assistance by third parties under the right to life, food, health (and water) will be evaluated, rather than focusing on the progressive development of the law.

7.3.1 Human Rights Law and the Right to Offer Assistance

In the relationship between human rights law and humanitarian assistance, a focus is placed on the rights to life, food, health (and water). The previous Chapter concerning the *right to life* has shown that the current legal framework places emphasis on the duties of the affected state in securing that a person is not arbitrarily deprived of his or her life, and furthermore that the HRC and ECtHR envisage a certain positive obligation in the prevention of epidemics and similar circumstances.[17] Whereas the right to life entails certain positive obligations for states towards persons within their jurisdiction, most often this right is regarded as a right to 'not interfere, and thereby does not hold many links for the international community to read a 'right or duty to provide' humanitarian assistance into the provisions of the various international treaties.[18] As such, it must be concluded that the current international human rights legal framework cannot be said to entail an *external duty* to provide humanitarian assistance in the fulfilment of the human right to life.

The right to food, health (and water), hold many positive obligations to fulfil, which *could* be attributed to the international community as a whole. Unequivocally, the fulfilment of human rights in general must be seen in light of the joint responsibility states have under Article 56 of the UN Charter. Indeed, the CESCR has argued with regard to Article 2 ICESCR concerning the 'progressive realization' of the rights in the Convention that:

> "the phrase 'to the maximum of its available resources' was intended by the drafters of the Covenant to refer to both the resources existing within a State and those available from the international community through international cooperation and assistance. [...] The Committee wishes to emphasize that in accordance with Articles 55 and 56 of the Charter of the United Nations, with well-established principles of international law, and with the provisions of the Covenant itself, international cooperation for development and thus for the realization of economic, social and cultural rights is an obligation of all States. It is particularly incumbent upon those States which are in a position to assist others in this regard".[19]

[17] Section 6.3.1 Duties of the Affected State and Non-State Actor under Human Rights Law.
[18] Section 5.4.2 Humanitarian Assistance and the Right to Life.
[19] CESCR General Comment 3 on Article 2 (14 December 1990) § 13 and 14 'The Nature of State Parties Obligations'.

Thus, the CESCR envisages not only a duty of the affected state to exceed its national borders in search of international assistance, but also envisages a distinct duty upon those states within the international community that are in a position, to indeed assist when such help is needed.[20] This viewpoint of the Committee aligns with the provisions of Article 2 ICESCR, in which a state party undertakes to:

> "take steps, individually and through international assistance and co-operation […] to the maximum of its available resources, with a view to achieving progressively the full realization of the rights recognized in the present Covenant by all appropriate means".[21]

Whilst this provision allows for the assertion of a duty resting upon the affected state to seek international assistance, the formulation is arguably open to a wider interpretation for the international community, yet shying away from a hard 'obligation'. In fact, during the *travaux préparatoires*, most states argued that such international assistance cannot be seen as a duty under Article 2(1), not accepting wording such as 'to guarantee'.[22] Proposals which were also considered unacceptable for the participating states as part of Article 2 were 'to ensure' and 'to pledge themselves'.[23] International cooperation under the ICESCR is therefore not necessarily meant as an international legal obligation, although the CESCR would argue otherwise.

The CESCR envisages this combined duty of the affected state and the international community not just in general, but also in particular concerning the *right to food*. As such, the treaty body has considered Article 11 ICESCR to contain a duty for State Parties to 'take steps' in the provision of assistance when necessary in *other* countries, in order to ensure the fulfilment of the right to food.[24] Furthermore, the Protocol to the ACHR stresses an obligation resting upon states parties to take measures in cooperating to ensure food security and 'promote greater international cooperation' to this end.[25] Although clearly the Protocol does not encompass worldwide coverage, it does cover a continent which is particularly prone to food emergencies resulting from natural disasters (such as cyclones) and therefore holds significant practical relevance.

Also from a soft law perspective support can be found for international cooperation, although clearly falling short of a binding obligation. As such, the UN Human Rights Council has also stressed the need and importance of international assistance in relation to the right to food and has argued that the international

---

[20] For a further discussion on Article 2(1) see Section 5.4.4 Humanitarian Assistance and the Right to Food.

[21] Article 2(1) ICESCR.

[22] Philip Alston & Gerard Quinn, 'The Nature and Scope of State Parties' Obligations under the International Covenant on Economic, Social and Cultural Rights' (1987) 9 *Human Rights Quarterly* 1, 165.

[23] Ibid.

[24] CESCR General Comment 12 (Article 11 ICESCR) UN Doc E/C.12/1999/5 'The right to adequate food' (12 May 1999) § 36 and § 38.

[25] Article 12 Additional Protocol ACHR.

community 'should provide' such assistance when needed.[26] While the Human Rights Council's resolutions are not of a binding character, the distinct political nature of the body must also be taken into account, compared to the General Assembly as a representation of all UN member states proper. Support for international cooperation can also be found in the Voluntary Guidelines of the FAO, adopted in 2004.[27] Olivier de Schutter, UN Special Rapporteur on the Right to Food, has argued that problematic in the establishment of an *international* duty to provide food is the fact that none of the above treaties, their organs or the UN in general have established 'precise levels at which States should provide aid'.[28] Indeed, while the push towards acknowledgment of such an international duty to cooperate in the provision of food aid appears to exist amongst others in the work of the CESCR, the actual *content* of the duty may currently be in need of clarification. Emerging *opinio juris* is therefore at most to be established with regard to the potential *duty* of third parties, which of course does not prevent the existence of the *right* of third parties to *offer* assistance, as can clearly be read in Article 2(1) and 11 ICESCR.

In relation to the human *right to health*, recourse must equally be had to the provisions of the ICESCR. As in the case of the right to food, Article 2 ICESCR calls upon the international community to provide assistance in the fulfilment of the right to health, should a state not be in the capacity to fulfil its own obligations in this regard. The CESCR has interpreted this as an obligation of states to provide international cooperation and assistance to the affected state in its fulfilment of the core obligations of the convention.[29] The minimum core obligations of the right to health, as assessed in Chapter 5, indeed align for a large part with the basic content of humanitarian assistance and its provision - internationally - will thus aid in the fulfilment of the right to health.[30] In fact the CESCR itself acknowledges that in situations where humanitarian assistance is needed, the realisation of the right to health may be dependent on international cooperation, as it calls in particular on the importance of involvement of UN organs and the WHO.[31] As such, the CESCR has argued, also concerning third states that:

---

[26] See amongst others UNHRC Res 7/14 (27 March 2008) § 14 and § 22; UNHRC Res S-7/1 7th Special Session 'The negative impact of the worsening of the world food crisis on the realization of the right to food for all' (22 May 2008) preamble and §4; UNHRC Res 10/12 'The right to food' (26 March 2009) § 16 & 26; UNHRC Res 13/4 The right to food (14 April 2010) §11, 13, 20 and § 28; UNHRC Res 12/10 (12 October 2010) § 5; UNHRC Res 16/27 (13 April 2011) § 11, 13, 20 and § 28.

[27] FAO 'Voluntary Guidelines to support the progressive realization of the right to adequate food in the context of national food security' (Adopted by the 127th Session of the FAO Council November 2004) § 15 and 16.

[28] Report of the Special Rapporteur on the right to food 'Promotion and Protection of all Human Rights, Civil, political, economic, social and cultural rights, including the right to development' (11 February 2009) UN Doc A/HRC/10/5 § 8. De Schutter refers in this regard to the potential of the Food Aid Convention, which establishes clear volumes and guidelines.

[29] CESCR General Comment 14 (11 August 2000) UN Doc E/C.12/2000/4 'The right to the highest attainable standard of health', § 45.

[30] See in particular Section 5.4.6 Humanitarian Assistance and The Right to Health.

[31] CESCR General Comment 14 (n 29) § 65.

> "States parties have a joint and individual responsibility, in accordance with the Charter of the United Nations and relevant resolutions of the United Nations General Assembly and of the World Health Assembly, to cooperate in providing disaster relief and humanitarian assistance in times of emergency, including assistance to refugees and internally displaced persons [...] Priority in the provision of international medical aid, distribution and management of resources, such as safe and potable water, food and medical supplies, and financial aid should be given to the most vulnerable or marginalized groups of the population. Moreover, given that some diseases are easily transmissible beyond the frontiers of a State, the international community has a collective responsibility to address this problem".[32]

While the CESCR has read such international obligations into the text of Article 12 ICESCR, Chapter 5 has discussed that the right to health is a somewhat more diverse right, due to the various alternative provisions in the international human rights treaty framework.[33] The other existing treaties, or their interpretative bodies, in this instance do not argue an international duty to provide external assistance in the fulfilment of the right to health. The UN Special Rapporteur on the right to health has equally not assessed such a duty, simply stating that the legal framework 'recognizes that international and non-governmental organizations have particular importance in relation to disaster relief and humanitarian assistance'.[34] Thus, similarly to the right to food, it must be concluded that indeed whilst no legal duty exists, a *right to offer* assistance can be found in international law with regard to the right to health.

Lastly, concerning the *right to water*, such an international legally binding obligation is even more difficult to ascertain. Given the current incomplete status of the right to water under international law, ascertaining a duty or right to internationally provide assistance in the fulfilment of the right to water is challenging. The CESCR has derived a right to water from the right of persons to an adequate standard of living and to the highest attainable standard of health as encompassed in Articles 11 and 12 of the ICESCR respectively.[35] Given the commitment to cooperate internationally as enshrined in Article 2 ICESCR, arguably an international right may be found to offer assistance in the provision of the right to water in the aftermath of disasters also, as the CESCR asserts.[36] Yet, due to the haphazard international incorporation of the right to water in and of itself, through its absence as an individual right in the major existing international treaties today despite current UN commitment, establishing an external duty or right to provide water in the fulfilment of the (developing) human right to water is currently not possible. The interpretative comments of the CESCR are to date the

[32] Ibid § 40.
[33] Section 5.4.6 Humanitarian Assistance and The Right to Health.
[34] 'Right of everyone to the enjoyment of the highest attainable standard of physical and mental health' Report of the Special Rapporteur on the Right to Health UN Doc A/68/297 (9 August 2013) § 60.
[35] Section 5.4.8 Humanitarian Assistance and The Right to Water.
[36] CESCR General Comment 15 (20 January 2003) UN Doc E/C.12/2002/11 'The Right to water (arts. 11 and 12 of the International Covenant on Economic Social and Cultural Rights' § 34.

only indication that such an external duty may exist in international law and therefore fall short of creating such an obligation or right.

Furthermore, within the UN context, the Special Rapporteur on IDPs has asserted that a growing acceptance exists that an obligation to 'invite, accept and facilitate' the provision of aid is a part of the obligation to 'respect, protect and fulfil' human rights in general, particularly in the event an affected state is unwilling or unable to provide in such assistance.[37] Yet this assertion is not backed up with legal sources, and whilst admirable, does not in itself add to the above conclusions that indeed a right to offer assistance exists.

Thus, when determining whether an external duty to provide humanitarian assistance under human rights law exists, not much affirmative evidence can be found in existing international law. The most outspoken provisions may be seen within the context of the right to food, and somewhat within the right to health, based on the interpretative remarks of the CESCR. The nature of the right to life does perhaps not allow for such international duties to be read into the existing provisions, and the right to water would be in need of more development, prior to ascertaining whether an external duty may be related to this. However, current international human rights law allows for a right to offer the provision of assistance, in line with Article 2(1) ICESCR. Establishing a potential right to access a territory under human rights law should the affected state not be able to fulfil its obligations shall prove to be challenging, in particular considering the notion of state consent, in the absence of an international legal duty under human rights law to provide assistance. In this regard, third states or other third parties will in certain instances be left to attempt to hold a state *responsible* under international law for certain breaches of *its* duties, rather than being able to act upon their own duties under human rights law to provide assistance.[38]

7.3.2 Human Rights Law and the Right to Access

A distinction must be made between this Section examining the right to gain access under human rights law for the purpose of providing aid, and other enforcement mechanisms – such as access – should flagrant *violations* of human rights take place that will be discussed in Chapter 8. As seen in the above Section, current existing international human rights law does not contain many provisions solidly providing for an external *duty* to provide assistance codified in human rights law. The related 'right to access' for third parties to provide such assistance is then certainly even more difficult to ascertain.

When considering the *right to life*, the previous Section has already shown that the current legal framework pertaining to this particular human right in relation to the provision of humanitarian assistance focuses on the duties which relate to the *affected state*, as duty-bearer. Thus, an external right of third parties to access a territory for the provision of humanitarian assistance can currently not be found in

[37] Report of the UN Special Rapporteur on IDPs UN Doc A/65/282 (11 August 2010) § 77.
[38] See in this regard Chapter 8.

the existing international law relating to the human right to life. The *right to food* however, as seen above, entails a wider scope of potential duty-bearers, as the provision in the ICESCR envisages distinctly that some form of international cooperation takes place in the fulfilment of this right. However, Article 11 (1) ICESCR also notes:

> "The States Parties to the present Covenant recognize the right of everyone to an adequate standard of living for himself and his family, including adequate food, clothing and housing, and to the continuous improvement of living conditions. The States Parties will take appropriate steps to ensure the realization of this right, recognizing to this effect the essential importance of international co-operation based on free consent".

The text of the Article is unambiguous and calls for 'consent' on the part of the involved parties. As explained by the Special Rapporteur on the right to food, the consent of the affected state is necessary, while the Rapporteur argues that in the event a state's unwillingness to consent to aid results in the violation of the right to food, the international community might resort to the 'responsibility to protect'.[39] Thus, while the above Section saw the most far-going provisions within the right to food, current international human rights law does not allow for an external right to access a territory in the fulfilment of a person's right to food without the consent of the affected state. Unlike in the case with the right to food, when considering the *right to health* in Article 12, the ICESCR does not specify a particular form of international cooperation or an affiliated need for consent of the affected state. Although the right to health has been incorporated in numerous international treaty bodies, a related right of third parties to gain access to a territory in order to provide assistance in the event of a crisis, to ensure the fulfilment of the right to health has not been codified. Similarly, as the *right to water* has not been laid down definitively in international law, with haphazard incorporation at the regional level and often in relation to the right to health, it is therefore even more difficult to ascertain a potential right to access.

Indeed, the 'right to access' from a human rights perspective is more logically formulated as a duty to allow access by the affected state: the primary duty-bearer of obligations of conduct in relation to the provision of assistance. This perspective has in fact been taken by the ICJ. In the 2008 case concerning the Application of the International Convention on the Elimination of all Forms of Racial Discrimination (Georgia v. Russian Federation) the ICJ had occasion to express itself on humanitarian access through a human rights context. The Court determined that:

---

[39] 'The right to food', Report of the Special Rapporteur, Note by the Secretary General UN Doc A/63/278 (21 October 2008) § 12 and Chapter 8 on the matter of access by force. This perspective on access for the provision of aid in the fulfilment of the right to food has been reiterated not long ago also by the UN Human Rights Council, in Res S-7/1 (n 26).

> "both parties shall facilitate, and refrain from placing any impediments to, humanitarian assistance in support of the rights to which the local population are entitled under the International Convention on the Elimination of All Forms of Racial Discrimination".[40]

Thus, the Court determined that Georgia and Russia both had an *obligation to allow access* for the provision of humanitarian assistance, on the basis of their obligations under human rights law, as opposed to international humanitarian law.[41] As seen in Section 5.3, the ICERD determines in Article 5 that states parties must undertake to 'prohibit and to eliminate' all forms of racial discrimination, and relevant to the provision of humanitarian assistance, particularly in the enjoyment of (amongst others) the right to security of person and the 'protection against bodily harm', as well as economic, social and cultural rights; including the right to health. A distinct connection is therefore made by the Court between allowing access for humanitarian assistance and the fulfilment of human rights duties. As following logically from the above, the ICJ indeed places this duty upon the state, as duty-bearer, rather than formulating it as a right from the viewpoint of third parties wishing to provide assistance.

In this manner, the fulfilment of the rights to life, food and health would not only be the provision of assistance by the affected state, as discussed in Chapter 6, but would also entail the allowance of access for third parties to provide assistance. From the perspective of the affected state then, *withholding consent* would amount to a violation of the duties of that state under human rights law. Indeed, such an assessment aligns with the perspective of the Security Council also, as will be addressed in Section 7.4.2, assessing that access granted by the affected state amounts in certain cases to the fulfilment of its duties under international law, including human rights law. As argued by Rygnaert, human rights law has not only 'penetrated the legal regimes governing humanitarian assistance' but has also 'eroded, or at least conditioned, the state consent requirement'.[42] It remains to be noted in this regard that in essence, human rights are considered primarily within the context of the state as duty-bearer, and the individuals within their jurisdiction as rights holders. Thus, not much hard law is to be found concerning a potential right to *access* by third parties in order to provide humanitarian assistance from outside the affected territory.[43] Nonetheless, from the perspective of the ICJ and as confirmed by the CESCR following the provision of Article 2 ICESCR, duties may exist under human rights law *for the affected state* to allow access.

Although this Section pertains to *lex lata*, several expressions on the matter of access were given by international organs that contribute to the expression of *opinio*

[40] Application of the International Convention on the Elimination of all Forms of Racial Discrimination (Georgia v. Russian Federation), Provisional Measures, Order of 15 October 2008, I.C.J. Reports 2008, p. 353 § 149 B.

[41] Whilst the outcome of the ICJ ruling was torn (8 against 7), it appears that this finding was not a reason, as none of the dissenting or separate opinions address this assessment.

[42] Ryngaert, 'Humanitarian Assistance and the Conundrum of Consent: A Legal Perspective' (n 12), 8.

[43] Report of the Representative of the Secretary-General, Mr. Francis M. Deng (5 December 1995) UN Doc E.CN.4/1996/52/Add.2 § 391.

juris on the matter. As such, from a human rights perspective, the European Community asserted in 1996 that:

> "[...] people in distress, victims of natural disasters, wars and outbreaks of fighting, or other comparable exceptional circumstances have a right to international humanitarian assistance where their own authorities prove unable to provide effective relief".[44]

Such a formulation suggests the right of third parties to then assist in the fulfilment of this right of such individuals, given the distinct mention of the inability of the affected state. The subsequent EU 2008 Joint Statement on the subject matter has however not reiterated this rather forward position, merely stating that the EU's humanitarian aid amongst other matters aims 'at facilitating or obtaining access to people in need'.[45] Furthermore, the UN Human Rights Council and its predecessor, the Commission on Human Rights have similar to the Security Council and General Assembly on multiple occasions expressed concern for the denial of humanitarian access and called upon the facilitation of 'safe and unhindered access' to a territory.[46] Such indications by EU and UN organs provide some indication of *opinio juris*, or at least states' willingness to consider the necessity of access for the provision of humanitarian assistance from a human rights perspective, but at this point currently cannot amount to an existing right in international human rights law to access for third parties in the provision of emergency aid. The perspective taken by the ICJ, as well as amongst others the Security Council to be discussed subsequently, indeed aligns with the approach that human rights law views the affected state as the original primary duty-bearer in the fulfilment of rights, and therefore in relation to humanitarian assistance considers a *duty to allow access*, rather than a right to obtain access.

An interesting aspect in this discourse, however, is the determining factor of *when* the duty-bearing affected state is violating its duties by not allowing access. In essence, such a violation would occur at the moment that indeed the affected state is not fulfilling its *own* duties in the provision of humanitarian assistance, as required under the rights to life, food and health. Given its role as duty-bearer, this duty would then oblige the affected state to seek international assistance in the fulfilment of these rights, by allowing access to third parties for the provision of humanitarian assistance.

---

[44] European Council Regulation concerning humanitarian aid (EC) No. 1257/96 (20 June 1996) Preamble § 4.

[45] 'Joint Statement by the Council and the Representatives of the Governments of the Member States meeting within the Council, the European Parliament and the European Commission' (European Consensus on Humanitarian Aid) (30 January 2008) EU Doc 2008/C/25/01 § 8.

[46] See amongst others Commission on Human Rights Res 2000/53, (25 April 2000) UN Doc E/CN.4/RES/2000/53 § 11; Commission on Human Rights Res 2000/55 (25 April 2000) UN Doc E/CN.4/RES/2000/55 § 7; Commission on Human Rights Res 2001/54 (24 April 2001) UN Doc E/CN.4/RES/2001/54 § 12; Commission on Human Rights Res 2003/52 (24 April 2003) UN Doc E/CN.4/RES/2003/52 preamble §5; Commission on Human Rights Res 2004/55 (20 April 2004) UN Doc E/CN.4/RES/2004/55 § 10; HRC Res 14/6 (23 June 2010) UN Doc A/HRC/RES/14/6 §5; and HRC Res 23/L.1 (28 May 2013) UN Doc A/HRC/23/L.1 §5.

7.4 The Provision of Humanitarian Assistance by Third Parties Under the UN Framework: the Security Council and General Assembly

Both the Security Council and the General Assembly have on numerous occasions expressed themselves concerning the potential external provision of humanitarian assistance, occurring both by third states and by international organisations. Such a perspective falls in line with Article 1(3) of the UN Charter stating that one of the purposes of the UN is to 'achieve international cooperation in promoting and encouraging respect for human rights and fundamental freedoms for all'. When regarding the resolutions adopted by both the General Assembly and the Security Council, it remains relevant therefore to keep this purpose of the organisation in mind, when it calls upon its Member States to act in the provision of humanitarian assistance.

A distinct differentiation can be made in the legal value of the resolutions of both organs as explained in Chapter 6.[47] Although the General Assembly may have a wider scope, the Security Council can take binding decisions under Chapter VII of the UN Charter, warranting its discussion prior to that of the General Assembly. Indeed, these binding resolutions form a source of law; warranting even more so their assessment as part of the current legal framework on the provision of humanitarian assistance, whereas the resolutions adopted by the General Assembly merely contribute in interpretative value and in the contribution to the formation of *opinio juris* on a given topic. Furthermore, as will be addressed below, the various resolutions themselves can hold different value in the discussion of the legal framework.

7.4.1 Security Council Resolutions and the Right to Offer Assistance

The UN Security Council has concerned itself not only with the duties of the affected state in the provision of humanitarian assistance, but through its resolutions also with the position of the international community in the provision of such assistance. Although it appears in recent resolutions as though the Security Council glosses over the specificities related to the *sec* provision of assistance from external sources and the particular rights of parties to indeed provide assistance, focusing mainly on access of such parties (see following Section), this has not always been the case. Indeed, the Security Council has independently and specifically addressed the role of third states and international organisations in the provision of assistance. Whereas the previous Chapter has shown that the Security Council did not commence addressing the responsibilities of the affected state until the Council's in-depth deliberation of the situation in Iraq in the 1990s (a decade which has shown a proliferation of resolutions in general), it has occasionally expressed its gratitude or called upon third parties and international organisations to contribute to

[47] Section 6.4 Duties and Rights under the UN Framework: the Security Council and General Assembly.

the provision of assistance at an earlier time.[48] As such, as early as 1982, the Security Council addressed all UN member states and the agencies of the UN itself stating in relation to the situation in Lebanon that it:

> "*Appeals* to Member States to continue to provide the most extensive humanitarian aid possible (…) Stresses the particular humanitarian responsibilities of the United Nations and its agencies (…) towards civilian populations".[49]

In doing so, the Security Council addressed the 'humanitarian responsibilities' of the UN and its agencies, distinctly stating that the organisation has a responsibility in the provision of humanitarian assistance. Furthermore, an 'appeal' is made to the international community of states to also provide in such assistance, which although falling short of a responsibility, does portray the intention of the Council to involve third states in the provision of aid.

This choice of wording of the Council, next to choices such as adopting a resolution under Chapter VII, implies a level of commitment for the international community. The latter is an often-cited indication of the level of involvement and binding nature of the decision-making of the Council. As is known, interpretative methods related to wording are often applied to treaty interpretation rather than the interpretation of Council resolutions.[50] Yet, 'appealing' expresses a different sentiment than 'calling', which in turn is different from 'urging' or 'stressing', all commonly utilised by the Council. The Security Council in essence is a political body, but its resolutions potentially have legal effects especially when adopted with binding force.[51] As such, its choices in wording are open to a variety of interpretations. As remarked by the ICJ in its 1971 *Namibia* Advisory Opinion,

> "The language of a resolution of the Security Council should be carefully analysed before a conclusion can be made as to its binding effect. In view of the nature of the powers under Article 25, the question whether they have been in fact exercised is to be determined in each case, having regard to the terms of the resolution to be interpreted, the discussion leading to it, the Charter provisions invoked and, in general, all circumstances that might assist in determining the legal consequences of the resolution of the Security Council".[52]

[48] It remains beyond the scope of this research to provide in depth analyses of all country situations in which the UN Security Council addressed the matter of humanitarian assistance, and only several key examples will be used, to illustrate the legal relevance.
[49] UNSC Res 513 (19 June 1982) UN Doc S/RES/513 'Lebanon' § 2 and 3.
[50] Michael C Wood, 'The Interpretation of Security Council Resolutions', (1998) *Max Planck Yearbook of United Nations Law* 74.
[51] Alexander Orakhelashvili, 'The Impact of Peremptory Norms', (2005) 16 *European Journal of International Law*, 61.
[52] Legal Consequences for States of the Continued Presence of South Africa in Namibia (South West Africa) notwithstanding Security Council Resolution 276 (1970), Advisory Opinion, ICJ Reports (1971) p. 16, § 114.

The ICJ viewed such tests as relevant to interpretation methods. Indeed, a transition in argumentation over the past years has been to view the Security Council as a body that has legally binding effects through decision-making, or to actively assert it as a legislative organ, given the influx of thematic resolutions.[53] In this Section, the Council's resolutions *relevant to the legal framework on the delivery of humanitarian assistance* will be assessed, rather than discussing the status of the organ *per se*. In this assessment, both wording and potential binding nature of adoption will be addressed and interpreted. As will be seen below, many of the Security Council's resolutions addressing the rights of the international community take place within the context of country-specific resolutions. As such, their potential legislative value must be considered within that specific context.

Where the Security Council in 1982 did not adopt this resolution regarding Lebanon under Chapter VII, in 1990 it did choose to adopt such a binding resolution concerning the situation in Iraq. Acting with binding force under Chapter VII of the UN Charter, the Security Council declared in Resolution 661 of 1990 a duty for states to 'not make available' any funds, including by their nationals to the government of Iraq save for the provision of strictly humanitarian aid.[54] In subsequent resolutions the Council reiterated this stance, adding hereto that although no trade with the Government of Iraq is permitted, this ban shall not apply 'to foodstuffs'.[55] These resolutions, instated prior to the UN 'Oil for Food Programme', provide insight into the Security Council's viewpoint that regardless of the other prohibitions it may place upon states, the offering and provision of humanitarian aid by third parties continues to be a global responsibility.[56] Pursuant to the well-known Resolution 661, a special committee was established (only to be terminated in 2003) amongst others to oversee the vast amount of sanctions, the 'Oil for Food Programme' and to determine the needs concerning the provision of humanitarian assistance. Immediately following Resolution 661, in its well-known Resolution 688 the Council used the phrasing it had done earlier regarding Lebanon in 1982 and stated that it:

---

[53] Wood, 'The Interpretation of Security Council Resolutions' (n 50) 77-78; S Talmon, 'The Security Council as World Legislature', (2005) 99 *The American Journal of International Law* 1, 175.

[54] UNSC Res 661 (6 August 1990) UN Doc S/RES/661 § 3(c) and 4. A similar approach and call to Member States was held by the Council concerning Yugoslavia (also acting under Chapter VII) in UNSC Res 757 (30 May 1992) UN Doc S/RES/757 § 5.

[55] UNSC Res 687 (8 April 1991) UN Doc S/RES/687 § 20; UNSC Res 706 (15 August 1991) UN Doc S/RES/706 § 1(c).

[56] The larger concept of the 'Oil for Food Programme' which was instated by the UN following the reports on the humanitarian situation in Iraq in the early 1990s, will not be discussed within this research. For the Security Council's basis for this programme, see amongst others UNSC Res 661 (6 August 1990) UN Doc S/RES/661; UNSC Res 687 (8 April 1991) UN Doc S/RES/687; UNSC Res 688 (5 April 1991) UN Doc S/RES/688; UNSC Res 706 (15 August 1991) UN Doc S/RES/706; UNSC Res 712 (19 September 1991) UN Doc S/RES/712 and in particular UNSC Res 986 (14 April 1995) UN Doc S/RES/986. For the report suggesting the need for immediate humanitarian relief, see UN Doc S/22366 (20 March 1991) § 37.

> "*appeals* to all Member States and to all humanitarian organizations to contribute to these humanitarian relief efforts".[57]

Falling short of an obligation, the Security Council does, however, envision a large role for third states and international organisations in the provision of assistance. Only a year later in similar spirit concerning the situation in Somalia, the Council called upon the Secretary General to see to the increase of the provision of aid by the UN, its specialised agencies and other international organisations and states, as well as calling upon all states and organisations to contribute to the delivery of international aid.[58] The Council followed up on this stance in a subsequent resolution, as it 'welcomes' and 'encourages' the continuous efforts of the various organisations involved in the provision of assistance.[59] Thus, not only does the Council see a role for organisations next to a role for third states, this role is in fact *proactively* engaged by the Council itself. In 1993, regarding the situation in Liberia, the Council goes a step further and:

> "[...] *commends* the efforts of the Member States, the United Nations system and humanitarian organizations in providing humanitarian assistance to the victims of the conflict in Liberia, and in this regard *reaffirms* its support for increased humanitarian assistance".[60]

In this situation, not only are appeals made to states and organisations, they are furthermore commended for providing assistance and receive the full support of the Council.[61] Acting under Chapter VII, the Security Council has also in relation to the situation in Kosovo called upon 'Member States and others concerned to provide adequate resources for humanitarian assistance in the region and to respond promptly and generously', thereby showing the Council's willingness to turn to the international community in a more binding manner.[62] In more recent years, such as regarding the situation in Iraq in 2003, the Security Council has called upon the international community to:

> "[...] provide immediate humanitarian assistance to the people of Iraq, both inside and outside Iraq in consultation with relevant States, and in particular to respond immediately to any future humanitarian appeal of the United Nations, and supports the activities of the International Committee of the Red Cross and of other international humanitarian organizations".[63]

---

[57] UNSC Res 688 (5 April 1991) UN Doc S/RES/688 § 6.
[58] UNSC Res 733 (23 January 1992) UN Doc S/RES/733 § 2 & 9.
[59] UNSC Res 775 (28 August 1992) UN Doc S/RES/775 preamble and § 9.
[60] UNSC Res 813 (26 March 1993) UN Doc S/RES/813 § 14. [Italics EEK]
[61] The Council continues to reiterate such positions over the next years, such as for example concerning assistance to Burundi in UNSC Res 1286 (19 January 2000) UN Doc S/RES/1286 § 13.
[62] UNSC Res 1199 (23 September 1998) UN Doc S/RES/1199 § 12.
[63] UNSC Res 1472 (28 March 2003) UN Doc S/RES/1472 § 2.

In the above it appears that a road is taken in which the Council appeals with more urgency to the UN member states, whilst acting under Chapter VII. Again, the Council has reiterated its support for the provision of assistance by humanitarian organisations, expressing its perspective that such provision forms a part of the larger framework of provision of emergency aid. Whilst Chapter VII resolutions are case-specific, and general assumptions should not be derived too quickly, case-specific conclusions can be drawn. As such, in this particular instance, whilst a general duty cannot be concluded, this particular Resolution was also taken under Chapter VII of the UN Charter, thereby placing a binding 'call' upon states to assist in the provision of aid in Iraq. Specifically tailored towards the international community however, this formulation does not allow for the assertion or interpretation of a right to receive aid for the affected persons.

The Security Council has continued to refer to the possible rights and duties of third states and international organisations in country-specific resolutions, rather than addressing these matters in *thematic* resolutions such as the previously discussed (in Chapter 6) resolutions concerning the 'Protection of Civilians in Armed Conflict'. In this sense, it remains difficult to establish a more general thread in the Council's work.

With regard to country situations, for instance concerning the Democratic Republic of the Congo, the Security Council has continued along its previously set out lines and in 2009 called upon member states to 'continue to provide medical, humanitarian and other assistance to victims' of the conflict in the DRC.[64] Continuing its concern for the Congo, the Council 'urged' the UN and other relevant actors to address the challenges of humanitarian assistance, but has not used the stronger language it engaged with regard to Iraq.[65] Furthermore, more recently with regard to the situation in Yemen, the Security Council equally merely 'encouraged' the whole of the international community to provide humanitarian aid to the country.[66] A comparable approach can be found in the Council's address of the situation in Libya.[67] Even more restrained was the Council's approach to the situation in Syria in its Resolutions 2042 and 2043 of 2012 where the Council did not call upon the international community to act; merely acknowledging their presence in the provision of humanitarian assistance through a call to the *parties in Syria* to:

> "cooperate fully with the United Nations and relevant humanitarian organizations to facilitate the provision of humanitarian assistance".[68]

---

[64] UNSC Res 1906 (23 December 2009) UN Doc S/RES/1906 preamble. Earlier views are expressed amongst others concerning the situation in Lebanon: UNSC Res 1701 (11 August 2006) UN Doc S/Res/1701 § 6.

[65] UNSC Res 1991 (28 June 2011) UN Doc S/RES/1991 preamble.

[66] UNSC Res 2014 (21 October 2011) UN Doc S/RES/2014 § 10.

[67] UNSC Res 1970 (26 February 2011) UN Doc S/RES/1970 Peace and Security in Africa § 26.

[68] UNSC Res 2042 (14 April 2012) UN Doc S/RES/2042 'The situation in the Middle East' § 10 and similarly UNSC Res 2043 (21 April 2012) UN Doc S/RES/2043 § 11.

In Resolution 2043, the Council then also reaffirms the need for *external* humanitarian assistance:

> "Expressing its appreciation of the significant efforts that have been made by the States bordering Syria to assist Syrians who have fled across Syria's borders as a consequence of the violence, and requesting UNHCR to provide assistance as requested by member states receiving these displaced persons (...) Expressing also its appreciation of the humanitarian assistance that has been provided to Syria by other States".[69]

As can be seen, this Resolution addresses the needs of those receiving humanitarian aid after having fled Syria, rather than focusing on the need to provide aid inside the conflict area itself. This perspective however is also indicative of the approach by the Council, as discussed at the beginning of this Section, namely to forego the rights of states to offer assistance and focus on the actual access of a territory. Given the Security Council's primary dealing with situations threatening the international peace, such a focus has its merits.[70] Naturally, as the Security Council is a UN organ comprised of Member States, the wording of the Council is dependent on the political situation it is seized of. It remains however relevant to note that the specific language choices of the Council over the past decades; 'urging' and 'calling' its member states, indicate the *presupposition of a right to offer assistance*. Indeed, such expressions of the Council indicate the *presupposition of a responsibility* of the international community – be it through the various international (humanitarian) organisations or through the involvement of third states – *to provide humanitarian assistance in situations amounting to a humanitarian crisis*. Indeed, such situations must be within the realm of the work of the Security Council in order for the Council to be seized of the matter, and therefore must meet the threshold of an established threat to the international peace.

7.4.2 Security Council Resolutions and the Right to Access

As the above Section has shown, the Council plays a distinct role in ascertaining whether or not the international community may be called upon to provide assistance in the event of a crisis that amounts to a threat to the peace. Yet the Security Council, in its role as primary organ concerned with the maintenance of peace and security, has also often called upon states to comply with their obligations under international law in the provision of humanitarian assistance.[71] Thus, it is relevant to ascertain whether the Council addresses in a consistent manner in what way and on which grounds the international community might have a *right to access a territory as aid provider and for the provision of humanitarian assistance* (to be distinctly differentiated from access by force), should the affected state not comply with its own responsibilities under international law and

[69] Ibid UN Doc S/RES/2043 preamble.
[70] Article 39 UN Charter.
[71] 6.4.1 Duties of the Affected State and Non-State Actor under Security Council Resolutions.

sufficiently provide assistance itself. As many of the Security Council's resolutions are taken under Chapter VII of the UN Charter and therefore are of a binding character pursuant to Article 25 UN Charter, it is of crucial importance to also note the practice of the Security Council in this particular regard. It is unfortunately not always clear which resolutions are taken with such a binding intention, and specific attention must therefore also be given to the exact language and vocabulary in the phrasing of the resolutions, as also addressed in the above.[72] Dinstein rightfully notes the Security Council's trajectory in this regard, often commencing with a non-binding call upon parties and States to allow for free passage of goods and assistance and only subsequently providing for binding measures.[73] Whereas the previous Section saw Security Council resolutions addressing the international community and their possibilities to provide assistance, this current Section discusses the Council's perspective on the duties of the affected state or sovereign actor *in relation to third parties*, as the Council calls upon the *facilitation* of access.

In 1982, regarding the situation in Lebanon discussed above, the Council called upon all parties to the conflict to facilitate 'the dispatch and distribution of aid' provided by relief organisations.[74] Indeed, the call to states to allow free passage of humanitarian aid in 'situations' it is 'seized' with can be seen as a continuous thread throughout the practice of the Security Council in subsequent years with regard to the external provision of assistance by third parties. As such, the wording of the Council has in this particular aspect of its resolutions been especially static over the course of multiple decades. In subsequent country situations with which the Council has been seized, the Council has built on this phrasing, such as the situation in Iraq in 1991 where the Council has for the first time *insisted* that Iraq:

> "allow immediate access by international humanitarian organizations to all those in need of assistance in all parts of Iraq and make available all necessary facilities for their operations".[75]

In this well-known resolution, the Security Council does not explicitly act under Chapter VII, and refers to Article 2(7) of the UN Charter, pertaining to non-intervention in the domestic affairs of a state.[76] However, through its wording, the Council binds Iraq to an obligation to allow for the international community to provide humanitarian assistance. Interestingly in this Resolution for the first time the Security Council also links the assessed human rights violations to the existing threat to international peace and security.[77]

---

[72] Section 7.4.1 Security Council Resolutions and the Right to Offer Assistance; also Yoram Dinstein, 'The Right to Humanitarian Assistance' (2000) LIII *Naval War College Review* 4, 87.
[73] Ibid Dinstein.
[74] UNSC Res 513 (19 June 1982) UN Doc S/RES/513 'Lebanon' § 1.
[75] UNSC Res 688 (5 April 1991) UN Doc S/RES/688 § 3.
[76] Christine Grey, 'The use of force and the international legal order' in Malcolm Evans (ed) *International Law* (Oxford University Press 2010) 621.
[77] UNSC Res 688 (5 April 1991) UN Doc S/RES/688 § 1-2. See also Nico J Schrijver, 'Sovereignty versus Human Rights? A Tale of UN Security Council Resolution 688 (1991) on the Protection of the Kurdish People', in: M Castermans, F van Hoof and J Smith (eds), *The Role of the Nation-State in the*

In many of the subsequent resolutions following equally as many 'country situations' the Security Council continues to reiterate the wording that it *calls* upon or *urges* parties involved to allow immediate access for the external provision of assistance as it:

> "*Calls on* all parties to cooperate with the Secretary-General to this end and to facilitate the delivery by the United Nations, its specialized agencies and other humanitarian organizations of humanitarian assistance to all those in need of it [...] *Urges all* parties to take all the necessary measures to ensure the safety of personnel sent to provide humanitarian assistance, to assist them in their tasks and to ensure full respect for the rules and principles of international law regarding the protection of civilian populations".[78]

As discussed in the above Section, such wording is stronger than an 'appeal' and expresses a higher level of urgency adhered to by the Council. The facilitation of 'unhindered delivery' and 'safe access' specifications of the Security Council can also be found in many resolutions during the 1990s such as those pertaining amongst others to the extended conflicts in Somalia, the Former Yugoslavia, Liberia, the DRC, Burundi and Afghanistan; in which the Security Council in some instances 'demands' these actions from parties.[79] Indeed, intermittently the Security Council has in these same conflicts acted under Chapter VII, while calling upon parties to facilitate the provision of assistance and allow safe and unhindered passage, such as in the Former Yugoslavia where it:

> "*Demands* that all parties and others concerned create immediately the necessary conditions for unimpeded delivery of humanitarian supplies to Sarajevo and other destinations in Bosnia and Herzegovina [...]".[80]

As such, the language in this approach is increasingly forceful and the Council opts to act under Chapter VII. *Demanding* compliance from parties to a conflict, whilst operating under the binding cloak of Chapter VII places a duty under international

---

21st Century: Human Rights, International Organizations and Foreign Policy. Essays in Honour of Peter Baehr (Brill Nijhoff 1998).

[78] UNSC Res 733 (23 January 1992) UN Doc S/RES/733 § 7-8.

[79] See amongst others resolutions regarding Somalia: UNSC Res 746 (17 March 1992) UN Doc S/RES/746 § 3 and 8; UNSC Res 751 (24 April 1992) UN Doc S/RES/751 § 14; UNSC Res 767 (27 July 1992) UN Doc S/RES/767 § 3; UNSC Res 775 (28 August 1992) UN Doc S/RES/775 § 7; UNSC Res 794 (3 December 1992) UN Doc S/RES/794 § 2-3. See also resolutions concerning the Former Yugoslavia such as: UNSC Res 752 (15 May 1992) UN Doc S/RES/752 § 8; UNSC Res 758 (8 June 1992) UN Doc S/RES/758 § 8; UNSC Res 787 (16 November 1992) UN Doc S/RES/787 § 18; See also resolutions such as pertaining to Liberia: UNSC Res 813 (26 March 1993) UN Doc S/RES/813 § 15; UNSC Res 1059 (31 May 1996) UN Doc S/RES/1059 § 7; UNSC Res 1071 (30 August 1996) UN Doc S/RES/1071 § 10; UNSC Res 1083 (27 November 1996) UN Doc S/RES/1083 § 8. See furthermore resolutions relating to the Democratic Republic of the Congo, such as UNSC Res 1258 (6 August 1999) UN Doc S/RES/1258 § 11. Concerning the situation in Burundi: UNSC Res 1286 (19 January 2000) UN Doc S/RES/1286 § 9 and 10; and Afghanistan: UNSC Res 1378 (14 November 2001) UN Doc S/RES/1378 § 2.

[80] UNSC Res 757 (30 May 1992) UN Doc S/RES/757 § 17.

law upon the addressees of this resolution. On the other hand, it also allows for a larger scope of action for the international community in providing humanitarian assistance, given the request for compliance by the Council.

Subsequent resolutions in which the Council acts under Chapter VII equally show a continued request of the affected state to facilitate and ensure safe and unhindered passage of assistance, as well as to ensure the safety of humanitarian personnel.[81] In some instances, specific mention is made of access for the 'International Committee of the Red Cross and other relevant humanitarian agencies'.[82] The Council assesses such facilitation of humanitarian assistance and safety of its providers to be part of the 'fulfillment' of a state's responsibilities.[83] Furthermore, the Security Council asserts that 'impediments' to such delivery constitute violations of international humanitarian law.[84] Whilst the resolutions of the Council are strictly only binding regarding the specific situation they are concerned with, the continued reiteration and repetition of a particular stance is indicative of this body's approach to the provision of humanitarian aid by third parties within the international legal framework pertaining to this.

This perspective of the Security Council regarding access for third parties has progressed over the past decades as the Security Council has shown a continuing stronger stance, appealing to states or parties to a conflict and *demanding* their allowing unhindered passage of humanitarian assistance under binding resolutions of Chapter VII. Indeed, the *thematic* resolutions of the Council concerning the 'Protection of Civilians in Armed Conflict' with which the Council commenced in 1999 reflect this perspective, as the Council:

> "Underlines the importance of safe and unhindered access of humanitarian personnel to civilians in armed conflict, including refugees and internally displaced persons, and the protection of humanitarian assistance to them [...] urges all parties to armed conflicts to respect fully the status of United Nations and associated personnel and, in this regard, condemns attacks and the use of force against United Nations and associated personnel, as well as personnel of international humanitarian organizations [...] Expresses its willingness to respond to situations of armed conflict where civilians are being targeted or humanitarian assistance to civilians is being deliberately obstructed, including through

[81] Relating to the Former Yugoslavia: UNSC Res 770 (13 August 1992) UN Doc S/RES/770 § 2-3 and 6; UNSC Res 819 (16 April 1993) UN Doc S/RES/819 § 8 and 10; UNSC Res 824 (6 May 1993) UN Doc S/RES/824 § 4(b); UNSC Res 1004 (12 July 1995) UN Doc S/RES/1004 § 5; UNSC Res 1199 (23 September 1998) UN Doc S/RES/1199 § 4(c) and 10; as well as resolutions relating to Sierra Leone: UNSC Res 1132 (8 October 1997) UN Doc S/RES/1132 § 2; and UNSC Res 1270 (22 October 1999) UN Doc S/RES/1270 § 13. See furthermore concerning East Timor UNSC Res 1264 (15 September 1999) UN Doc S/RES/1264 § 2; UNSC Res 1272 (25 October 1999) UN Doc S/RES/1272 § 10-11.

[82] For example UNSC Res 770 (13 August 1992) UN Doc S/RES/770 § 3.

[83] UNSC Res 1319 (8 September 2000) UN Doc S/RES/1319 concerning East Timor § 1.

[84] See amongst others UNSC Res 771 (13 August 1992) S/RES/771 preamble; UNSC Res 787 (16 November 1992) UN Doc S/RES/787 § 7; UNSC Res 819 (16 April 1993) UN Doc S/RES/819 § 8; UNSC Res 824 (6 May 1993) UN Doc S/RES/824 preamble. For a discussion of the various rights and duties under humanitarian law: Sections 7.5.1 and 7.5.2.

the consideration of appropriate measures at the Council's disposal in accordance with the Charter of the United Nations".[85]

The Security Council has proceeded with this stance in its subsequent thematic resolutions, reiterating the importance of access for personnel to deliver assistance, and urging parties to respect such personnel.[86] Such thematic resolutions, although not binding in nature, speak more towards a 'legislative' approach of the Council, as it attempts to regulate a topic, rather than a country situation.[87]

Whilst addressing the issue of access to humanitarian assistance in thematic resolutions, the Council has not ceased to also attend to the matter in country-specific situations. It must be noted that the Council's resolutions over the past decade have commenced to contain stronger wording compared to the 1990s, as the Council 'expresses its *condemnation*' of violence against humanitarian personnel and calls upon states to adhere to their 'obligations to comply with international law related to' such personnel, while simultaneously calling for '*unimpeded access*'.[88] Furthermore, the Council has continued to address and 'demand' the need for (rapid and unimpeded) humanitarian access through resolutions taken both under Chapter VII and without the enforcement options of this Chapter in the UN Charter.[89] Such

[85] UNSC Res 1265 (17 September 1999) UN Doc S/RES/1265 preamble and § 7, 9 and 10.

[86] UNSC Res 1296 (19 April 2000) UN Doc S/RES/1296 § 8 and 12; UNSC Res 1674 (28 April 2006) UN Doc S/RES/1674 § 22 where the Council asserts such is reflected in humanitarian law: "Urges all those concerned as set forth in international humanitarian law, including the Geneva Conventions and the Hague Regulations, to allow full unimpeded access by humanitarian personnel to civilians in need of assistance in situations of armed conflict, and to make available, as far as possible, all necessary facilities for their operations, and to promote the safety, security and freedom of movement of humanitarian personnel and United Nations and its associated personnel and their assets"; UNSC Res 1894 (11 November 2009) UN Doc S/RES/1894 § 14, 15(a) and 16(b). The Council has also addressed the matter in other thematic resolutions, such as pertaining to 'Children and Armed Conflict' UNSC Res 1314 (11 August 2000) UN Doc S/RES/1314 §7; and UNSC Res 1379 (20 November 2001) UN Doc S/RES/1379 § 5.

[87] This research will not address the legality of legislature by the Security Council as it falls outside the scope of the research. Merely those resolutions relevant to the legal framework on humanitarian assistance will be addressed. See for a more in depth analysis of the Security Council as a potential legislator and legal problems related thereto amongst others V Popovski and T Fraser (eds), *The Security Council as Global Legislator* (Routledge Global Institutions Series 2014). See also for an earlier perspective Talmon, 'The Security Council as World Legislature' (n 52) 175-193.

[88] See for examples amongst others UNSC Res 1502 (26 August 2003) UN Doc S/RES/1502 'Protection of Personnel in Conflict zones' § 1, 3 -5 and thematic resolutions such as pertaining to Children and Armed Conflict UNSC Res 1882 (4 August 2009) UN Doc S/RES1882 § 1. The Council has done so also in country specific resolutions such as amongst others pertaining to the Sudan UNSC Res 1769 (31 July 2007) UN Doc S/RES/1769 preamble; the DRC: UNSC Res 1794 (21 December 2007) UN Doc S/RES/1794 § 17; UNSC Res 1991 (28 June 2011) UN Doc S/RES/1991 preamble; as well as in Afghanistan UNSC Res 1868 (23 March 2009) UN Doc S/RES/1868 preamble. Furthermore, (although not requesting 'access'): UNSC Res 1860 (8 January 2009) UN Doc S/RES/1860 § 2; and the situation in Georgia, UNSC Res 1866 (13 February 2009) UN Doc S/RES/1866 § 4.

[89] See for resolutions taken under Chapter VII for example those concerning Liberia UNSC Res 1509 (19 September 2003) UN Doc S/RES/1509 § 8; concerning the Sudan UNSC Res 1769 (31 July 2007) UN Doc S/RES/1769 § 19; the DRC: UNSC Res 1794 (21 December 2007) UN Doc S/RES/1794 § 17, UNSC Res 1906 (23 December 2009) UN Doc S/RES/1906 preamble; and Somalia: UNSC Res 1744 (21 February 2007) UN Doc S/RES/1744 § 11, UNSC Res 1772 (20 August 2007) UN Doc

calls by the Council express the perspective that indeed the affected state should be 'condemned' in the event it does not allow access for the provision of assistance or does not protect the safety of humanitarian personnel. A condemnation thus implies a violation of a duty of the affected state to allow such access. The calls furthermore operate with the possibility of future enforcement action through Chapter VII, should the affected state not allow access for international humanitarian assistance.

As has been seen in the previous Chapter, following its embracement within the UN framework, the notion of the Responsibility to Protect enters the Council's resolutions pertaining to the delivery of humanitarian assistance, in particular in relation to the affected state's responsibilities in the provision of assistance.[90] Indeed, Barber has argued that the notion of the 'Responsibility to Protect', its premise that sovereignty implies responsibility, and its embracement by the UN, has certainly strengthened the argument that customary international law imposes an obligation upon states to not only *facilitate* humanitarian assistance, but perhaps even go so far as to *consent* to its delivery.[91] A customary norm deduced at an abstract, non-case specific level, which requires consent and derives from the Security Council's work as Barber argues, is today however a bit of a stretch. Whether or not customary international law imposes such an obligation to consent has not been addressed by the Council in its most recent, relevant resolutions. While the Security Council has addressed RtoP in connection to the responsibilities of the affected state, it has *not* done so in addressing the potential right to access of third parties which might be based on a responsibility to provide assistance. Furthermore, the Council has not actively taken the stance that a failure of the affected state to provide assistance (and thereby fulfil its sovereign duties) *automatically* translates into a potential right to provide assistance externally, including a related right to obtain access to a territory therefore. Indeed, even after the embracement of RtoP as a doctrine, the Security Council is seen to reiterate the (on occasion strong) language it has in fact used over the past decades. As such concerning Libya, the Council, acting under Chapter VII of the UN Charter declares it (is):

> "*Expressing its determination* to ensure the protection of civilians and civilian populated areas and the rapid and unimpeded passage of humanitarian assistance and the safety of humanitarian personnel, [...] 3. *Demands* that the Libyan authorities comply with their

S/RES/1772 § 20, UNSC Res 1801 (20 February 2008) UN Doc S/RES/1801 § 14, UNSC Res 1814 (15 May 2008) UN Doc S/RES/1814 § 12 and UNSC Res 1872 (26 May 2009) UN Doc S/RES/1872 § 4. For resolutions with similar wording but in absence of Chapter VII support: regarding Lebanon UNSC Res 1701 (11 August 2006) UN Doc S/Res/1701 § 6; regarding Iraq UNSC Res 1770 (10 August 2007) UN Doc S/RES/1770 preamble; concerning Afghanistan UNSC Res 1806 (20 March 2008) UN Doc S/RES/1806 preamble. Such wording is also reiterated by the Council in thematic resolutions, amongst others regarding Women and Peace and Security, UNSC Res 1889 (5 October 2009) UN Doc S/RES/1889 § 12.

[90] Section 6.4.1.

[91] Rebecca Barber, 'Facilitating humanitarian assistance in international humanitarian and human rights law', (2009) 91 International Review of the Red Cross 874, 397.

> obligations under international law, including international humanitarian law, human rights and refugee law and take all measures to protect civilians and meet their basic needs, and to ensure the rapid and unimpeded passage of humanitarian assistance.[92]

The Council has repeated this stance in similar wording through subsequent resolutions pertaining to situations like those concerning Côte d'Ivoire, the Republic of South Sudan, the DRC and Somalia (all acting under Chapter VII), as well as Yemen, Syria and Afghanistan, on occasion adding the phrase 'in accordance with the guiding principles of humanitarian assistance'.[93] An example of this latter phrasing can be seen in relation to the situation in Somalia where the Council:

> "Demands that all parties ensure full, safe and unhindered access for the timely delivery of humanitarian aid to persons in need of assistance across Somalia, in accordance with humanitarian principles of impartiality, neutrality, humanity and independence, underlines its concern at the humanitarian situation in Somalia, urges all parties and armed groups to take appropriate steps to ensure the safety and security of humanitarian personnel and supplies [...]".[94]

Although it sometimes remains unclear exactly which principles the Council refers to, when merely referencing 'UN principles' or 'humanitarian principles', it may be assumed that the principles of humanity, impartiality and neutrality (and independence) are meant as it refers to them by name in later resolutions.[95] On other occasions, the Council has continued to add to this phrasing by 'strongly condemning' the obstruction of humanitarian aid.[96]

From this above analysis, an approach by the Security Council can be discerned regarding the body's willingness to address matters concerning humanitarian access. Quite unfalteringly the Council 'calls', 'urges' or 'demands' for parties to 'facilitate', 'allow' or 'ensure' 'safe', 'unhindered', 'timely' and 'unimpeded' access for both humanitarian assistance and personnel. Furthermore, parties are called upon to comply with their obligations under international (humanitarian) law

---

[92] UNSC Res 1973 (17 March 2011) UN Doc S/RES/1973 'The situation in Libya' preamble and § 3. In the primary resolution UNSC Res 1970 (26 February 2011) UN Doc S/RES/1970, also acting under Chapter VII, the Security Council did not use such strong language, as in § 2 it: "*Urges* the Libyan authorities to: (c) Ensure the safe passage of humanitarian and medical supplies, and humanitarian agencies and workers, into the country".

[93] Acting under Chapter VII: UNSC Res 1975 (30 March 2011) UN Doc S/RES/1975 'The situation in Côte d'Ivoir' preamble and § 10; UNSC Res 1996 (8 July 2011) UN Doc S/RES/1996 § 8; UNSC Res 2046 (2 May 2012) UN Doc S/RES/2046 § 4; UNSC Res 2076 (20 November 2012) UN Doc S/RES/2076 § 11; UNSC Res 2127 (5 December 2013) UN Doc S/RES/2127 § 51 and 52. Not acting under Chapter VII: UNSC Res 2014 (21 October 2011) UN Doc S/RES/2014 § 10; UNSC Res 2042 (14 April 2012) UN Doc S/RES/2042 § 10 and also concerning Syria UNSC Res 2043 (21 April 2012) UN Doc S/RES/2043 § 11; and UNSC Res 2096 (19 March 2013) UN Doc S/RES/2096 § 29; UNSC Res 2113 (30 July 2013) UN Doc S/RES/2113 preamble § 14.

[94] UNSC Res 2060 (25 July 2012) UN Doc S/RES/2060 § 6.

[95] See in this regard also UNSC Res 2096 (19 March 2013) UN Doc S/RES/2096 preamble, as well as UNSC Res 2127 (5 December 2013) UN Doc S/RES/2127 § 52.

[96] UNSC Res 2010 (30 September 2011) UN Doc S/RES/2010 preamble § 14.

related to the provision of assistance and the protection of humanitarian personal, as well as to act in accordance with 'the guiding principles of humanitarian assistance'. Particularly relevant is also the fact that the Security Council adheres to similar wording, regardless of whether the situation with which it is seized is an international armed conflict, a non-international armed conflict or any other form of situation, as long as it may be considered 'a threat to the peace'. The Council continuously does so, both under Chapter VII and without such binding force. The latter is relevant to the enforcement mechanisms it might envisage, which of course relates to the political nature of the organ that must always be taken into consideration. Thus, it appears possible to conclude from the Council's approach that it does not differentiate according to the circumstances, as long as the threshold of a 'threat to the peace' is met. As such, the Council, similar to this research, adheres to a more all-encompassing approach in dealing with humanitarian crises.

Of course, not all Security Council resolutions attract equal attention or are equally forceful. The political composition of the Council influences the viability of its actions as was distinctly visible in the aftermath of the Cold War, when resolutions surged and alternatively in Syria where the Council was paralyzed. The situation in Syria has resulted in the Security Council's refraining from Chapter VII action, which has attracted a lot of negative attention. An impasse was broken when the Council adopted Resolution 2118 (although not related to the provision of humanitarian assistance) and progress was made, despite the Resolution not being adopted under Chapter VII.[97] Subsequently, the road was paved for Security Council action concerning the provision of humanitarian assistance in February 2014, after nearly 2 years of crisis. The Council, although still not acting under Chapter VII, 'demanded' that all parties allow 'rapid, safe and unhindered humanitarian access' to all those in need of assistance.[98] Most recently in the summer of 2014 (and renewed in December 2014), the Council has, whilst reminding Syria that UN member states are obliged under Article 25 of the UN Charter to 'accept and carry out the Council's decisions' taken a very novel approach.[99] The Security Council has, whilst steering clear of Chapter VII action, circumvented the consent of the Syrian authorities and authorised so-called 'cross-conflict' delivery of humanitarian aid:

> "Decides that the United Nations humanitarian agencies and their implementing partners are authorized to use routes across conflict lines and the border crossings of Bab al-Salam, Bab al-Hawa, Al Yarubiyah and Al-Ramtha, in addition to those already in use, in order to ensure that humanitarian assistance, including medical and surgical supplies, reaches people in need throughout Syria through the most direct routes, with notification to the Syrian authorities, and to this end stresses the need for all border crossings to be used efficiently for United Nations humanitarian operations; [...] Also decides that all

[97] UNSC Res 2118 (27 September 2013) UN Doc S/RES/2118 more specifically on the prohibition of the use of chemical weapons.
[98] UNSC Res 2139 (22 February 2014) UN Doc S/RES/2139 § 5-7. See subsequently the renewal in UNSC 2191 (17 December 2014) S/RES/2191 § 2.
[99] UNSC 2165 (14 July 2014) UN Doc S/RES/2165 preamble.

> Syrian parties to the conflict shall enable the immediate and unhindered delivery of humanitarian assistance directly to people throughout Syria, by the United Nations humanitarian agencies and their implementing partners, on the basis of United Nations assessments of need and devoid of any political prejudices and aims, including by immediately removing all impediments to the provision of humanitarian assistance".[100]

Although the Council has always continued to reaffirm the affected states' sovereignty in each of its resolutions dealing with humanitarian matters, through binding resolutions and wording, in this Resolution the Council appears to assert that *consent* is possibly *not always a prerequisite* in the provision of humanitarian assistance.[101] This potential acknowledgment must be differentiated from the forceful access as discussed in Chapter 8, where force is used to pave the way for the provision of assistance. It is therefore novel that the Security Council directly addresses access for the provision of assistance itself without referring to the role of the Syrian authorities. Such a novel phrasing appears to search for an intermediate approach to the provision of assistance, as it circumvents Syrian sovereignty, but does not reference the use of force.

Perhaps the decades of Security Council action – and thereby joint international condemnation – suggest the formation of a customary principle which allows access to humanitarian organisations and third states in the provision of humanitarian assistance as argued by Barber? Such adoption and acceptance by states of these resolutions also puts forth arguments that *opinio juris* or state practice (by way of the Member States of the Security Council) may exist on this matter.[102] Yet subsequent state practice in accordance with such a norm continues to remain problematic, as a common practice with regard to 'consent' to access (as required for customary law to exist) cannot be distinguished at this time, with but two resolutions from the Council, both relating to the same country-situation. At this point, it therefore remains to be seen which path is chosen by the Council in subsequent resolutions and circumstances. Suggestions as to the direction of the Council have often been made, such as underlining the importance of access, calling for strict compliance with the law and condemnation of failure to provide access.[103]

As has been noted in the above Section 7.4.1, the Security Council often presupposes a right of the international community to provide assistance, whereas this Section has discussed the potential *duty of the affected state to facilitate and allow access* to the international community in the provision of aid. Certainly, the reverse of such a duty of the affected state can and must be seen as a right to

---

[100] Ibid § 2 and 6.

[101] The phrasing used often by the Security Council in the preambles to its resolutions is: "Reaffirming respect for the sovereignty and territorial integrity of…" or "Reaffirming its strong commitment to the sovereignty, independence, unity and territorial integrity of…". See also Barber, 'Facilitating humanitarian assistance in international humanitarian and human rights law', (n 91) 390.

[102] Ibid Barber, 390.

[103] 'Security Council, Internal Displacement And Protection: Recommendations For Strengthening Action Through Resolutions', *Brookings Institute* (September 2011) 21.

provide humanitarian assistance. The existence of an actual right to *access a territory for the provision of aid* potentially derived from the practice of the Security Council remains somewhat ambiguous.

It is suggested here that such a right may be concluded in the event the Council adopts a resolution under Chapter VII, while using particularly stringent wording such as 'demanding' the affected state to 'ensure' the safe and unimpeded passage of humanitarian assistance and its personnel. Such a conclusion would, however, remain case- or country-specific as this would not occur in thematic resolutions. Indeed, in such specific instances the Council foregoes the stadium in which the international community is called to offer such aid to a state, and presupposes the existence of willingness in this regard. However, this phrasing of the Security Council in itself does *not* imply a right to intervene. A right or duty for third states to intervene forcefully only exists if the Security Council explicitly calls thereto.[104] In one of its 'quasi-judicial' Presidential Statements[105] the Security Council has however recognised the need for humanitarian access as a prerequisite for the effective provision of assistance:

> "The Security Council reiterates that safe, and unhindered access by United Nations humanitarian agencies and national and international organisations to people in need, in accordance with the humanitarian principles of humanity, neutrality, impartiality and independence, and the Guiding Principles of Humanitarian Assistance, is a prerequisite for the effective delivery of humanitarian assistance".[106]

This position is held similarly by the Secretary-General, and can only be reiterated here.[107] Access to a territory is a vital component in the provision of assistance.

7.4.3 General Assembly Resolutions and the Right to Offer Assistance

As seen in the previous Chapter, the General Assembly has noted the importance of the provision of humanitarian assistance from early in the 1960s, and has addressed the international community's role in this assistance from the start. To provide a full overview of the current developments regarding the role of third states and the international community in general, the views of the General Assembly must be juxtaposed with those of the Security Council. Indeed, the General Assembly cannot adopt binding resolutions, nor can these resolutions be considered an

---

[104] With regard to the use of force in general: Articles 2(4) and 39 UN Charter. See in particular in relation to the provision of humanitarian assistance: UN Doc E.CN.4/1996/52/Add.2 (n 43) § 389 and Chapter 8 for a discussion on enforcement through the use of force.

[105] S Talmon, 'The Statements of the President of the Security Council', (2003) 2 *Chinese Journal of International Law*, 441.

[106] 'Aide Memoire Protection of Civilians in Armed Conflict' UN Doc S/PRST/2013/2 (12 February 2013) 4.

[107] 'Report of the Secretary-General on the protection of civilians in armed conflict' (22 May 2012) UN Doc S/2012/376 § 57. See equally the earlier Secretary General Reports on the Protection of Civilians in Armed Conflict: UN Doc S/2009/277 (29 May 2009) § 58 and UN Doc S/2010/579 (11 November 2010) § 43.

independent source of law. As such, these resolutions are of lesser immediate importance in the legal framework. However, the General Assembly's approach to the external provision of humanitarian assistance may well support the perspective of the Security Council and as such add to existing *opinio juris* or state practice. Given the large number of states partaking in the General Assembly as compared to the Security Council, its resolutions are in fact often regarded in this way.

In some of its most early resolutions the General Assembly presupposes offers of assistance from its Member States in the case of a crisis.[108] In other instances, the General Assembly has 'appealed' to states to offer such assistance.[109] In particular, such calls were issued in circumstances of natural disaster, but on occasion also in circumstances of 'war'.[110] Furthermore, the General Assembly has expressed its awareness of the need to strengthen the collective efforts of the international community in the provision of assistance.[111] The General Assembly has indeed asserted that the provision of assistance to those states that have suffered the results of a disaster is an 'expression of the principle of international solidarity' as enshrined in the UN Charter.[112] This notion can also be traced in the views behind the UN Declaration on Principles of International Law concerning Friendly Relations and Co-operation among States in accordance with the Charter of the United Nations and of course international humanitarian law, although the latter also focuses more on the principle of humanity.[113]

In addition, not only the UN Member States but indeed also the UN as an organisation itself is counted on in the provision of assistance, as the General Assembly discusses the Relief Coordinator's possibilities to 'instantly' provide emergency assistance.[114] On the other hand, the General Assembly has also addressed the 'recipient Government' in suggesting practical manners through which it may facilitate international emergency aid.[115] In a general appeal, the

---

[108] UNGA Res 2034 (XX) 'Assistance in cases of natural disaster' (7 December 1965) § 2.

[109] UNGA Res 2435 (XXIII) (19 December 1968) § 5; UNGA Res 2717 (XXV) 'Assistance in cases of natural disaster' (15 December 1970) § 1; UNGA Res 2816 (XXVI) 'Assistance in cases of natural disaster and other disaster situations' (14 December 1971) § 9 (a) and (b); UNGA Res 3244 XXIX (29 November 1974) § 2-3; UNGA Res 34/127 (14 December 1979) UN Doc A/RES/34/127 'Assistance to the Comoros' § 4; UNGA Res 36/225 (17 December 1981) UN Doc A/RES/36/225 § 12 and 19; UNGA Res 49/139 (20 December 1994) UN Doc A/RES/49/139 § 13. See also the range of General Assembly resolutions pertaining to 'Safety and security of humanitarian personnel and protection of United Nations personnel'.

[110] See in this regard amongst others UNGA Res 35/92 B (5 December 1980) UN Doc A/RES/35/92 B 'Emergency Humanitarian Assistance to Chad'.

[111] UNGA Res 2816 (XXVI) 'Assistance in cases of natural disaster and other disaster situations' (14 December 1971) preamble.

[112] UNGA Res 3244 XXIX (29 November 1974) 'Assistance to Bangladesh' preamble.

[113] UNGA Res 2625 (XXV) (24 October 1970) 'Declaration on Principles of International Law Concerning Friendly Relations and Cooperation among States in Accordance with the Charter of the United Nations'.

[114] UNGA Res 3440 XXX (9 December 1975) Assistance in cases of natural disaster and other disaster situations' § 1(a); UNGA Res 36/225 (17 December 1981) UN Doc A/RES/36/225 § 8.

[115] UNGA Res 2816 (XXVI) 'Assistance in cases of natural disaster and other disaster situations' (14 December 1971) § 8.

international community and the affected state are both called upon by the UN General Assembly to continue to provide information regarding the provision and receipt of assistance as the organ:

> "*Calls* upon Governments and international organizations to co-operate with the United Nations Disaster Relief Co-ordinator by furnishing his Office, as expeditiously as possible, with detailed information on their current and intended relief contributions, in cash and in kind, in order to render more effective the provision of assistance to the victims of disasters. *Further calls upon* recipient Governments to co-operate with the United Nations Disaster Relief Co-ordinator by informing his Office of the relief contributions offered and received".[116]

Thus, the General Assembly has from a very early stage assumed a need for the international community to assist in the provision of humanitarian assistance (in circumstances of a natural disaster) and has furthermore envisaged an acceptance thereof by the affected state. Indeed, an active role remains for the affected state, as in subsequent resolutions such as pertaining to the situation in Chad, the Assembly has called upon the international community to provide assistance to the government of Chad, to enable *Chad* to assist the affected persons.[117]

In line with this approach, the General Assembly (as does the Security Council) continues to reaffirm the sovereignty of the affected state.[118] Furthermore, as the thematic resolutions regarding 'Strengthening the capacity of the United Nations system to respond to natural disasters and other disaster situations' progressed, the General Assembly has also reiterated on several occasions that the international provision of assistance shall take place upon the 'request' of the affected state.[119] Yet, the General Assembly has equally stressed the important contribution made through the external provision of assistance to the survival of persons in emergency situations.[120] As such, in its well-known Resolution 46/182, the General Assembly stressed the need to strengthen and effectuate the 'collective efforts of the international community' in the provision of humanitarian assistance.[121] Furthermore, the General Assembly asserted in this cardinal resolution that the

[116] UNGA Res 33/22 (29 November 1978) UN Doc A/RES/33/22 'Office of the United Nations Disaster Relief Co-ordinator' § 1 and 2.

[117] UNGA Res 35/92 B (5 December 1980) UN Doc A/RES/35/92 B 'Emergency Humanitarian Assistance to Chad' § 2.

[118] See in this regard amongst others UNGA Res 36/225 (17 December 1981) UN Doc A/RES/36/225 § 2 and UNGA Res 43/131 (8 December 1988) UN Doc A/RES/43/131 'Humanitarian Assistance to victims of natural disasters and similar emergency situations' § 2; UNGA Res 46/182 (19 December 1991) UN Doc A/RES/46/182 'Strengthening the coordination of humanitarian emergency assistance of the United Nations' Annex § 3.

[119] UNGA Res 36/225 (17 December 1981) UN Doc A/RES/36/225 § 8 and 9.

[120] UNGA Res 43/131 (8 December 1988) UN Doc A/RES/43/131 § 1 and 3; UNGA Res 45/100 (14 December 1990) UN Doc A/RES/45/100 'Humanitarian Assistance to victims of natural disasters and similar emergency situations', § 1 and 3.

[121] UNGA Res 46/182 (19 December 1991) UN Doc A/RES/46/182 preamble. See also subsequently UN Res 47/168 (22 December 1992) UN Doc A/RES/47/168; UNGA Res 48/57 (14 December 1993) UN Doc A/RES/48/57 preamble.

provision of external assistance is of 'great importance' as a disaster may overwhelm national capacity.[122] However, whilst negotiating this Resolution, a number of states reiterated the need to respect the principle of sovereignty, arguing that the provision of humanitarian assistance was dependent on the approval of the affected state.[123] While reiterating the call to the international community to assist in the provision of humanitarian assistance, the General Assembly proceeded – as did the Security Council – and called for 'timely and speedy' provision in subsequent resolutions.[124] In subsequent resolutions, the General Assembly has continued to stress the importance of the provision of assistance by the international community; not only calling upon UN Member States, but also the organs of the UN itself as well as humanitarian organisations.[125] In this sense, its approach is similar to that of the Security Council, which also views a role for both states and international organisations.

A culmination of the viewpoint of the General Assembly, namely that the provision of humanitarian assistance is a *shared international responsibility*, can be found in its Millennium Declaration where the General Assembly asserts that:

> "we have a collective responsibility to uphold the principles of human dignity, equality and equity at the global level. [...] We will spare no effort to ensure that children and all civilian populations that suffer disproportionately the consequences of natural disasters, genocide, armed conflicts and other humanitarian emergencies are given every assistance and protection so that they can resume normal life as soon as possible. We resolve therefore: To expand and strengthen the protection of civilians in complex emergencies, in conformity with international humanitarian law. To strengthen international cooperation, including burden sharing in, and the coordination of humanitarian assistance to, countries hosting refugees and to help all refugees and displaced persons to return voluntarily to their homes, in safety and dignity and to be smoothly reintegrated into their societies".[126]

Indeed, the principle of human dignity itself warrants the provision of humanitarian assistance, and the General Assembly makes a clear statement acknowledging the importance of enhancing the protection of those who are in need of humanitarian assistance. As argued by Vukas, the General Assembly's stance to uphold the principle of human dignity is an answer to some states' reluctance to 'admit the vulnerability of their societies in the face of a disaster and their inability to cope

---

[122] Ibid UNGA Res 46/182 Annex § 5.

[123] ILC 'Protection of persons in the event of disasters' Memorandum by the Secretariat, UN Doc A/CN.4/590 (11 December 2007) *footnote* 75. Amongst others Brazil, Ethiopia, Nicaragua, France, Iran, Mexico, Japan, Pakistan, Tunisia, the Sudan, China, Ghana, Cuba, Iraq, Switzerland and India held various takes on this position, with regard to the development of resolutions UNGA Res 43/131 (8 December 1988) UN Doc A/RES/43/131 and UNGA Res 46/182 (19 December 1991) UN Doc A/RES/46/182.

[124] UNGA Res 49/169 (23 December 1994) UN Doc A/RES/49/169 § 11.

[125] See amongst others UNGA Res 49/174 (24 February 1995) UN Doc A/RES/49/174 § 6 and 12.

[126] UNGA Res 55/2 (18 September 2000) UN Doc A/RES/55/2 'United Nations Millennium Declaration' § 2 and 26.

with the effects thereof'.[127] In later resolutions, the General Assembly has reiterated its stance that the international community (in particular the UN system) bears the task of strengthening and improving the humanitarian response in the aftermath of emergencies.[128] The General Assembly indeed continues to 'encourage efforts' of cooperation and coordination amongst international humanitarian organisations, third countries and the affected state to enhance more effective delivery of assistance.[129] The General Assembly does so not only in its thematic resolutions, but also in more specific circumstances, expressing its appreciation of those states that have aided, amongst others El Salvador in the aftermath of hurricane Ida and Haiti following the earthquake.[130]

Yet, although the General Assembly acknowledges that assistance by external providers is 'essential' and 'necessary', the UN body does not go beyond 'welcoming' effective cooperation amongst states and organisations, nor does the General Assembly use stronger wording than 'urging' its Member States to assist, or 'stressing' a continued need for enhanced cooperation.[131] While 'urging' Member States may come across as an urgent appeal, the General Assembly falls short from actually declaring an international legal *responsibility* or *duty* in the provision of assistance. Whereas both the Security Council and General Assembly stress the importance of adhering to international law, from the above it becomes apparent that the General Assembly emphasises somewhat more the *moral* duty lying with the international community, such as through recalling the principles of solidarity and seen in the above discussed Millennium Declaration. This approach can similarly be found in the 2008 EU Consensus with regard to the stance of the EU.[132] However, as the General Assembly places a fair amount of emphasis on the need for the affected state to *allow access* to external providers of humanitarian

---

[127] Vukas, 'Humanitarian Assistance in Cases of Emergency' (n 14) § 21. Vukas herein also refers to UNGA Res 43/131 (8 December 1988) UN Doc A/RES/43/131 § 8.

[128] UNGA Res 60/124 (8 March 2006) UN Doc A/RES/60/124 'Strengthening the coordination of humanitarian emergency assistance of the United Nations' § 11; and subsequent thematic resolutions such as amongst others UNGA Res 63/139 (5 March 2009) UN Doc A/RES/63/139 'Strengthening of the coordination of humanitarian and disaster relief assistance of the United Nations, including special economic assistance: strengthening of the coordination of emergency humanitarian assistance of the United Nations' § 3; UNGA Res 64/76 (2 February 2010) UN Doc A/RES/64/76 preamble.

[129] UNGA Res 63/139 (5 March 2009) UN Doc A/RES/63/139 'Strengthening of the coordination of humanitarian and disaster relief assistance of the United Nations, including special economic assistance: strengthening of the coordination of emergency humanitarian assistance of the United Nations' § 11; UNGA Res 63/141 (10 March 2009) UN Doc A/RES/63/141 preamble and § 6, 10-11; UNGA Res 64/76 (2 February 2010) UN Doc A/RES/64/76 § 3 and 8. See in this regard also UNGA Res 64/251 (30 April 2010) UN Doc A/RES/64/251 §13; UNGA Res 65/133 (3 March 2011) UN Doc A/RES/65/133 preamble, § 3 and 13.

[130] UNGA Res 64/74 (7 December 2009) UN Doc A/RES/64/74 'Humanitarian assistance, emergency relief and rehabilitation for El Salvador as a result of the devastating effects of Hurricane Ida' § 2-3; UNGA Res 64/250 (30 April 2010) UN Doc A/RES/64/250 § 3-5.

[131] See for example UNGA Res 65/264 (21 June 2011) UN Doc A/RES/65/264 preamble and § 8, 12-13. See also UNGA Res 66/119 (7 March 2012) UN Doc A/RES/66/119 preamble, § 4 and 10.

[132] 'Joint Statement by the Council and the Representatives of the Governments of the Member States meeting within the Council, the European Parliament and the European Commission' (European Consensus on Humanitarian Aid) (30 January 2008) EU Doc 2008/C/25/01, § 1.

assistance, perhaps this shared international *responsibility* to provide aid is somewhat presupposed, as the Assembly focuses on the difficulties with entry into the affected territory upon an offer of assistance.

7.4.4 General Assembly Resolutions and the Right to Access

Following a discussion of the Security Council's approach to the potential right to access a territory for the provision of humanitarian assistance, the General Assembly's perspective must be addressed also. Whereas the General Assembly's initial approach was to address the external provision of humanitarian assistance through the assumption that such provision would be instigated at the request of the affected state, this changed over time.[133] The General Assembly has in fact stated that it:

> "*Invites* all States in need of such assistance to facilitate the work of these organizations in implementing humanitarian assistance, in particular the supply of food, medicines and health care, for which access to victims is essential; *Appeals*, therefore, to all States to give their support to these organizations working to provide humanitarian assistance, where needed, to the victims of natural disasters and similar emergency situations".[134]

This statement, stressing the need for cooperation of the affected state implies the realisation of the General Assembly that indeed the affected state itself is not always willing to welcome international organisations into the territory for the provision of assistance. Moreover, the General Assembly simultaneously calls upon states in the vicinity to facilitate the transit of such emergency aid.[135] Thus, the General Assembly asserts the essential character of humanitarian *access*, which the organ has continued to do in subsequent resolutions and more particularly in its well-known Resolution 46/182 of 1991.[136] In fact, the General Assembly adopts some of the language as seen in the Security Council resolutions, and calls upon 'parties to conflicts' to:

> "take all possible necessary measures to ensure impartial, safe and timely humanitarian access to persons in need of protection and assistance".[137]

In doing so, the Assembly does not only acknowledge the role of non-state actors, but also addresses circumstances of conflict: this is somewhat unfamiliar territory to it. Yet, the General Assembly appears conflicted, as it subsequently falls back on its earlier position and asserts that:

---

[133] UNGA Res 36/225 (17 December 1981) UN Doc A/RES/36/225 § 8 and 9.
[134] UNGA Res 43/131 (8 December 1988) UN Doc A/RES/43/131 § 4 and 5.
[135] Ibid § 6; see for a reiteration UNGA Res 45/100 (14 December 1990) UN Doc A/RES/45/100 § 7.
[136] Ibid UNGA Res 45/100 § 4 and 5; UNGA Res 46/182 (19 December 1991) UN Doc A/RES/46/182 Annex § 6-7. Subsequently, see also UNGA Res 49/174 (24 February 1995) UN Doc A/RES/49/174 preamble.
[137] UNGA Res 49/169 (23 December 1994) UN Doc A/RES/49/169 § 12.

> "humanitarian assistance should be provided with the consent of the affected country and in principle on the basis of an appeal of the affected country".[138]

Indeed, the General Assembly thus unequivocally argues that a right to access does not exist, but that access for third parties for the provision of humanitarian assistance is dependent on the will of the affected state. In the very same Resolution however the General Assembly reiterates the importance of access to provide assistance, and calls upon the international community for such provision.[139]

Nevertheless, despite this occasional diverging in the organ's approach to the provision of assistance from external sources, the General Assembly simultaneously adopted several resolutions in which it once again appears to follow the line set out by the Security Council (sometimes even referring to such resolutions),[140] as it calls to 'parties in complex humanitarian emergencies' to act in conformity with international law and to:

> "[...] ensure the safe and unhindered access of humanitarian personnel in order to allow them to perform efficiently their task of assisting the affected civilian population, including refugees and internally displaced persons".[141]

Indeed, ensuing resolutions of the General Assembly at the beginning of the 21st century reiterate such wording, including the 'delivery of supplies and equipment', while also calling upon states to ensure 'the safety and security of humanitarian personnel'.[142] Such resolutions also portray a willingness of the General Assembly

[138] UNGA Res 51/194 (10 February 1997) UN Doc A/RES/51/194 'Strengthening of the coordination of emergency humanitarian assistance of the United Nations' preamble, and UNGA Res 57/150 (27 February 2003) UN Doc A/RES/57/150 preamble.

[139] Ibid A/RES/51/194 preamble and § 10.

[140] See for example UNGA Res 54/192 (21 February 2000) UN Doc A/RES/54/192 preamble, UNGA Res 55/175 (7 March 2001) UN Doc A/RES/55/175 preamble and UNGA Res 56/217 (19 February 2002) UN Doc A/RES/56/217 preamble, where the General Assembly refers to the thematic resolutions of the Security Council concerning the protection of civilians in times of armed conflict.

[141] UNGA Res 52/167 (18 February 1998) UN Doc A/RES/52/167 'Safety and security of humanitarian personnel' § 3.

[142] UNGA Res 53/87 (27 January 1999) UN Doc A/RES/53/87 ' Safety and security of humanitarian personnel and protection of United Nations personnel' § 11 and see also § 3; UNGA Res 54/192 (21 February 2000) UN Doc A/RES/54/192 § 2-3; UNGA Res 55/175 (7 March 2001) UN Doc A/RES/55/175 § 3-4; UNGA Res 56/217 (19 February 2002) UN Doc A/RES/56/217 § 3, 4 and 12; UNGA Res 58/114 (5 February 2004) UN Doc A/RES/58/114 § 8 and 10; UNGA Res 59/141 (25 February 2005) UN Doc A/RES/59/141 § 18; UNGA Res 60/124 (8 March 2006) UN Doc A/RES/60/124 § 2; UNGA Res 60/123 (24 March 2006) UN Doc A/RES/60/123 § 3-4; UNGA Res 61/133 (1 March 2007) UN Doc A/RES/61/133 'Safety and security of humanitarian personnel and protection of United Nations personnel' § 3 and 4; UNGA Res 61/134 (1 March 2007) UN Doc A/RES/61/134 § 20; UNGA Res 62/94 (25 January 2008) UN Doc A/RES/62/94 'Strengthening of the coordination of emergency humanitarian assistance of the United Nations' § 24; UNGA Res 62/95 (29 January 2008) UN Doc A/RES/62/95 § 3-4; UNGA Res 63/138 (5 March 2009) UN Doc A/RES/63/138 § 3 and 4; UNGA Res 64/76 (2 February 2010) UN Doc A/RES/64/76 §26; UNGA Res 64/77 (8 February 2010) UN Doc A/RES/64/77 § 4; UNGA Res 65/132 (1 March 2011) UN Doc A/RES/65/132 §4; UNGA Res 65/133 (3 March 2011) UN Doc A/RES/65/133 § 27; UNGA Res 66/117 (1 March 2012) UN Doc A/RES/66/117 § 4; UNGA Res 66/119 (7 March 2012) UN Doc

to address not only situations of natural disaster, but to also address more complex and conflict-related circumstances. The General Assembly has continued to reaffirm the stance it has taken, amongst others in its well-known 2005 World Summit Outcome Document.[143] On other occasions, the General Assembly calls upon states to 'facilitate the efforts' of third parties in the provision of relief.[144] Again following the Security Council choice in language, the General Assembly has also in more recent years urged states in the 'proximity to humanitarian emergencies' to facilitate the transit of emergency aid.[145] In an even more converging manner, in 2013 the General Assembly:

> "Calls upon all States and parties in complex humanitarian emergencies, in particular in armed conflict and in post-conflict situations, in countries in which humanitarian personnel are operating, in conformity with the relevant provisions of international law and national laws, to cooperate fully with the United Nations and other humanitarian agencies and organizations and to ensure the safe and unhindered access of humanitarian personnel, as well as the delivery of supplies and equipment, in order to allow such personnel to efficiently perform their task of assisting affected civilian populations, including refugees and internally displaced persons".[146]

In this approach, the General Assembly focuses on the obligations of parties to humanitarian crises *under international law* in ensuring access to providers of aid, a line of reasoning which it has continued subsequently.[147]

From the above analysis and comparison with the approach taken by the Security Council follows that the General Assembly to a certain extent appears to also take the line set out by the Security Council with regard to the potential 'right to access' for third parties in the event of a humanitarian crisis. Such an impression appears from the statements of the General Assembly in adopting the language of the Security Council that preceded it in the vocabulary of certain resolutions. A common perspective, through common language, appears at the least to be that both organs call upon the affected parties to abide by their *duties under international law*

A/RES/66/119 § 33; UNGA Res 66/120 (7 March 2012) UN Doc A/RES/66/120 'Strengthening humanitarian assistance, emergency relief and rehabilitation in response to the severe drought in the Horn of Africa region' § 12; UNGA Res 67/85 (21 March 2013) UN Doc A/RES/67/85 § 4; UNGA Res 67/87 (26 March 2013) UN Doc A/RES/67/87 § 37.

143 UNGA Res 60/1 (24 October 2005) UN Doc A/RES/60/1 'World Summit Outcome Document' § 169.

144 UNGA Res 56/164 (19 December 2001) UN Doc A/RES/56/164 'Protection of and assistance to internally displaced persons' § 10. See also UNGA Res 60/168 (16 December 2005) UN Doc A/RES/60/168 'Protection of and assistance to internally displaced persons' § 12.

145 UNGA Res 59/141 (25 February 2005) UN Doc A/RES/59/141 preamble; UNGA Res 64/251 (30 April 2010) UN Doc A/RES/64/251 § 14. See also UNGA Res 65/264 (21 June 2011) UN Doc A/RES/65/264 § 14; UNGA Res 66/227 (15 March 2012) UN Doc A/RES/66/227 §16; and UNGA Res 67/231 (9 April 2013) UN Doc A/RES/67/231 § 16.

146 UNGA Res 67/87 (26 March 2013) UN Doc A/RES/67/87 § 37.

147 See amongst others UNGA Res 68/102 (12 February 2014) UN Doc A/RES/68/102 § 37 and 41; UNGA Res 68/101 (18 February 2014) UN Doc A/RES/68/101 § 2-4 and 13-14 in which the General Assembly focuses more specifically on duties towards medical personnel.

to allow access in times of a crisis, although the General Assembly resolutions fall short of actually identifying these obligations in greater detail. As argued by Quenivet, the Security Council resolutions indeed prove to be a more 'sound basis' to argue that persons may have a right to humanitarian assistance, and that such assistance indeed must be provided.[148] In fact, the ICRC argues also in its 'Customary International Humanitarian Law Study' that *both* the General Assembly and the Security Council have on occasion 'underlined the obligation' to allow civilians access to emergency aid.[149] While such wording is in reality not strictly purported by the two UN organs, both do assert a need for the affected state to allow access to the affected territory. Such urgent and pressing calls to the affected state may however not be directly translated to a 'right' of third parties to gain access to the affected territory. Barber has argued that the combined stance of the General Assembly and Security Council allow for the assertion that *opinio juris* exists regarding a specific customary norm, namely a duty of states to allow access for the delivery of humanitarian assistance, *should the denial thereof lead to starvation.*[150] The exact threshold of consent and denial, leading to forcible enforcement mechanisms in international law, will be further addressed in Chapter 8.

7.5 The Provision of Humanitarian Assistance by Third Parties Under Specific Circumstances in International Law

In the above Sections, the more general international legal framework pertaining to the right to provide humanitarian assistance from an external perspective has been discussed, and the related potential right to access. Following this discussion, the more specific regimes need to be assessed. This Section therefore addresses the legal framework pertaining to conflict, occupation and (natural) disaster, in relation to the legal possibilities of third parties to provide assistance in an affected territory. The legal framework pertaining to refugees and IDPs shall also be considered, as a sectoral aspect rather than a circumstantial perspective.

In practice, gaining access to a territory for the provision of humanitarian assistance also entails *safety* for such provision. Again, this is to be differentiated from the use of force to create an environment in which assistance can be provided;

[148] Noelle Quenivet, 'Humanitarian assistance: a right or a policy? Case study: the Security Council and the armed conflict in the former Yugoslavia' (1999) *The Journal of Humanitarian Assistance,* 17 < http://sites.tufts.edu/jha/archives/category/noelle-quenivet-2> (online publication) accessed 2 March 2015.

[149] Jean-Marie Henckaerts & Louise Doswald-Beck (eds), *Customary International Humanitarian Law (ICRC Study)* (Cambridge University Press 2006), Rule 55: "The UN Security Council, UN General Assembly and UN Commission on Human Rights have on several occasions underlined the obligation to grant civilians access to relief supplies See, e.g., UN Security Council, Res. 824 (ibid., § 701); UN General Assembly, Res. 55/2 (ibid., § 704); UN Commission on Human Rights, Res. 1995/77 (ibid., § 705)".

[150] Barber, 'Facilitating humanitarian assistance in international humanitarian and human rights law', (n 91) 390-391.

as this form of safety caters specifically to the duties of the affected authority and others to ensure the safety of humanitarian aid providers. In this regard, with a view to such safety, for example the Convention on the Safety of United Nations and Associated Personnel states:

> "1. United Nations and associated personnel, their equipment and premises shall not be made the object of attack or of any action that prevents them from discharging their mandate. 2. States Parties shall take all appropriate measures to ensure the safety and security of United Nations and associated personnel. In particular, States Parties shall take all appropriate steps to protect United Nations and associated personnel who are deployed in their territory from the crimes set out in article 9. 3. States Parties shall cooperate with the United Nations and other States Parties, as appropriate, in the implementation of this Convention, particularly in any case where the host State is unable itself to take the required measures".[151]

States are indeed therefore called upon to act according to the realities on the ground. Access to a territory must naturally include the safety to provide assistance, otherwise such access remains a theoretical perspective rather than a practical reality. Such duties are also reflected in the enforcement mechanisms of international criminal law, discussed in Section 8.6.2.

7.5.1 The Right to Provide Assistance in Times of Conflict

Given the nature of a situation of conflict, the discussion on this shall take place prior to a circumstance of occupation, which, when occurring, often follows an armed conflict. As the legal regimes in an international armed conflict and a non-international armed conflict vary, the potential duty of third parties to provide humanitarian assistance is discussed accordingly. While non-international armed conflicts are increasingly common in this era, the legal framework regarding an international armed conflict is taken as a starting point, therefore reflecting the development in the law pertaining to the provision of assistance and access.

7.5.1.1 The Right to Provide Assistance in Times of International Armed Conflict

To determine whether a possible external right or duty to provide humanitarian assistance in an international armed conflict exists, the 1949 Geneva Conventions and their Additional Protocols must be considered primarily. Article 10 GC IV provides explicitly:

> "The provisions of the present Convention constitute no obstacle to the humanitarian activities which the International Committee of the Red Cross or any other impartial

[151] Article 7 Convention on the Safety of United Nations and Associated Personnel. This Convention specifically relates to humanitarian aid providers, as Article 2, regarding the scope of application, excludes enforcement action under Chapter VII of the UN Charter.

> humanitarian organization may, subject to the consent of the Parties to the conflict concerned, undertake for the protection of civilian persons and for their relief".[152]

Thus, Article 10 GC IV does not prescribe a duty, rather formulating the possibilities of international humanitarian organisations as a 'right to offer' assistance.[153] Reflective of the time of drafting of the Conventions is that such organisations are distinctly mentioned, whilst third states are not. Whereas Pictet describes the Article as 'an invitation to all men of good will' to continue the work of the late Henri Dunant, whose drafting was not in any way disputed, it is indeed not seen as more than *that*: an invitation, certainly not placing a *legal* obligation upon third parties in the provision of assistance.[154]

The ensuing Additional Protocols of 1977 formulate more elaborately the possibilities that lie with third parties to provide a civilian population with humanitarian assistance as Article 70(1) AP I stipulates:

> "If the civilian population of any territory under the control of a Party to the conflict, other than occupied territory, is not adequately provided with the supplies mentioned in Article 69, relief actions which are humanitarian and impartial in character and conducted without any adverse distinction shall be undertaken, subject to the agreement of the Parties concerned in such relief actions. Offers of such relief shall not be regarded as interference in the armed conflict or as unfriendly acts. In the distribution of relief consignments, priority shall be given to those persons, such as children, expectant mothers, maternity cases and nursing mothers, who, under the Fourth Convention or under this Protocol, are to be accorded privileged treatment or special protection [...]".

Although the provision stipulates firmly that such assistance 'shall' be undertaken, rather than 'may' be undertaken, it is unclear who the addressee of this obligation is, and the Commentary does not provide an answer. The level of 'adequacy' is also not elaborated upon, and raises the dilemma that it remains unclear as to whom shall *determine* whether or not the territory is 'adequately' supplied (see Section 8.3 in this regard). As seen above in Chapter 2, the intensity of the situation must amount to a humanitarian crisis in order to warrant the delivery of humanitarian assistance, yet Article 70 AP I does not prescribe the determination of this to a certain actor. Moreover, Article 70(1) AP I importantly reiterates that the relief actions are 'subject to the agreement of the Parties concerned', which according to the Commentary includes the recipient state, and the state(s) from whose territory

---

[152] Although not relating to humanitarian assistance, several other provisions in the Fourth Geneva Convention also consider the delivery of food, such as Article 89 with regard to the rations internees should receive, Article 91 concerning the medical attention due to internees and Articles 108-11 concerning the relief shipments internees might receive.

[153] See Section 7.5.2.1 on the aspect that a state's consent is needed.

[154] Jean Pictet, *Commentary on the Geneva Conventions of 12 August 1949 Volumes I-IV* (International Committee of the Red Cross 1952-1959), Volume IV Commentary GC IV Article 10, 95-97.

the relief is sent.[155] Thus, a *requirement* to consent is not strictly formulated.[156] However, this 'agreement', pertaining to the degree to which the affected state may be obliged to allow humanitarian assistance into its territory was added to the Article to protect the affected state's sovereignty.[157] Yet it was also acknowledged during the negotiations by states, while recalling the importance of state sovereignty, that there was no 'absolute and unlimited freedom' in the denial of an agreement to provide relief schemes, as this provision must also be read in conjuncture with the duty for affected parties in Article 54 AP I concerning the prohibition of starvation of civilians.[158] Indeed, the boundary lies precisely there: the sovereign right to determine the allowance of access by way of consent is curtailed by the sovereign duties to not starve persons within its jurisdiction, as determined in humanitarian law, or to violate their rights to life, food and health, as determined in human rights law.[159]

Thus, although the *addressee* of the obligation to provide assistance according to Article 70(1) AP I may be unclear, it is apparent that this provision may in fact come from external parties, as the second sentence elaborates that such offers of relief may not be considered as hostile acts. From the last sentence of Article 70(1) AP I, calling for a distribution of relief according to necessity, once again the obligatory character of the provision is apparent, through the wording 'shall'. Therefore, taking into consideration the lack of clarity in the formulation of some aspects of Article 70(1), the Article *does* in fact call upon the obligatory provision of assistance, which it considers to include assistance from external sources. This approach taken by the Additional Protocol furthermore aligns with the obligations under human rights law of the affected state or party involved in the conflict that requires an appeal for external assistance, in particular through Article 2 ICESCR.

A discussion however remains as to the level of the obligation of the affected state to accept a *bona fide* offer, the determination of the adequacy by which the civilian population is supplied and the discrepancy states have in the exercise of their sovereignty as they might decide not to consent to the provision of assistance. As such, Dinstein has argued that the widest interpretation of Article 70(1) AP I may only be read as the impediment of a refusal by the affected state to an agreement of external relief for arbitrary reasons.[160] On the other hand, Plattner has argued that an offer meeting the terms of Article 70 AP I, even upon an arbitrary refusal, does not divest from its neutral character and may still be considered within the range of humanitarian assistance as meant by the Additional Protocol, whereas Spieker has argued that if the civilian population is at risk, consent may not be

[155] Yves Sandoz, Christophe Swinarski & Bruno Zimmermann (eds) *Commentary on the Additional Protocols of 8 June 1977 to the Geneva Conventions of 12 August 1949, Protocol I and II (*International Committee of the Red Cross 1987*)* Protocol I Article 70, 819.

[156] Ryngaert, 'Humanitarian Assistance and the Conundrum of Consent: A Legal Perspective' (n 12), 6.

[157] Sandoz, Swinarski & Zimmermann *Commentary to the Additional Protocols* (n 155).

[158] Ibid 819-820. See also Sections 8.3 and further regarding Article 54 AP I and the prohibition of starvation.

[159] See Sections Section7.5.2.1 and 8.3.

[160] Dinstein, 'The Right to Humanitarian Assistance' (n 72) 85.

withheld.[161] Thus, as the provisions of Article 70 AP I are dissected and opinions differ, this Article too must be considered to contain rather a 'right to offer' for third parties than a duty to provide. According to Spieker, although the Protocol does not particularly specify this, such a right to offer exists not only for third states but in particular also for relief organisations.[162] Such an assessment indeed follows Article 10 GC IV and international practice. This right to offer and the related consent of the affected state must then be considered in light of the potential 'right to access' a territory by third parties as shall be addressed in the Section 7.5.2.1.

7.5.1.2 The Right to Provide Assistance in Times of Non-International Armed Conflict

When considering the provision of aid by third parties in a non-international armed conflict, the Geneva Conventions and Protocols have to be considered, similar to the circumstance of an international armed conflict. The well-known common Article 3, also on occasion called a 'miniature convention' regulating non-international armed conflicts, is distinct in its statement as to the role of potential humanitarian organisations, declaring:

> "An impartial humanitarian body, such as the International Committee of the Red Cross, may offer its services to the Parties to the conflict".

The provision that international organisations *may* offer humanitarian assistance is a distinct indication that the drafters envisioned a supplementary role for any outside party, with a responsibility lying first and foremost on the parties to the conflict.[163] This indeed aligns with the assessment in Chapter 6 that the primary responsibility in the provision of assistance lies with the affected state and other parties to the conflict exercising a level of authority. No *duty* for third parties to provide assistance as such exists, under Article 3 and Pictet argues that parties to the conflict may decline such an offer 'if they can do without it'.[164] Again, as seen in previous instances, a difficulty lies in the *determination* of this capacity to fulfill the obligation to provide assistance. It remains unclear from the wording of the Convention who shall determine whether or not the civilian population is adequately supplied.

Following the 1949 Geneva Conventions, the 1977 Additional Protocol II has supplemented Common Article 3, similar to Additional Protocol I supplementing Article 10 GC IV. Article 18 AP II declares:

---

[161] Denise Plattner, 'ICRC neutrality and neutrality in humanitarian assistance', (1996) 36 *International Review of the Red Cross* 311, 177; Heike Spieker, 'Humanitarian Assistance, Access in Armed Conflict and Occupation' (2013) *Max Planck Encyclopedia of Public International Law* § 30.

[162] Ibid Spieker § 33.

[163] Pictet, *Commentary on the Geneva Conventions of 12 August 1949* (n 154) Article 3, 41.

[164] Ibid.

> "1. Relief societies located in the territory of the High Contracting Party, such as Red Cross (Red Crescent, Red Lion and Sun) organizations, may offer their services for the performance of their traditional functions in relation to the victims of the armed conflict. The civilian population may, even on its own initiative, offer to collect and care for the wounded, sick and shipwrecked. 2. If the civilian population is suffering undue hardship owing to a lack of the supplies essential for its survival, such as foodstuffs and medical supplies, relief actions for the civilian population which are of an exclusively humanitarian and impartial nature and which are conducted without any adverse distinction shall be undertaken subject to the *consent* of the High Contracting Party concerned".[165]

Here, AP II provides that during a non-international armed conflict as within the scope of the Protocol (requiring the existence of a non-state actors exercising a degree of control), *local* relief societies 'may' offer assistance, differing from the provision of assistance in the event of an international armed conflict. The external assistance by third parties in times of non-international armed conflicts is considered complementary to the national provision, should the affected authorities be unable to meet the needs of the civilian population.[166] As such, Article 18 AP II must be read in conjuncture with Article 14 AP II concerning the prohibition of starvation as a method of warfare: in order for the affected authorities to respect the obligations under Article 14 AP II, the provision of emergency assistance as formulated under Article 18(2) AP II *should* be authorised.[167] Only in the situation that civilians are experiencing 'undue hardship', does such a right to offer become an *obligation* through the wording of 'shall', as seen in the second paragraph of the Article. Yet, as was seen above in the discussion of Article 70 AP I, again in this instance such an obligation does not have a clear addressee, nor can consent of the affected state be bypassed. As such, the formulation remains problematic.

The formulation of this Article portrays the struggle experienced with regard to balancing the drafting states' concerns for their national sovereignty with the needs of a suffering population.[168] While the wording 'shall' implies an obligation that might be construed as a limitation of the notion of state sovereignty, consent of the affected state continues to be required according to AP II. Yet, as is often the case in circumstances of non-international armed conflict, armed groups or non-state actors operate from certain areas of the territory where the affected state experiences a loss of control. According to the Commentary, in the event it is unclear who the authorities are, *consent must be presupposed* so as to prevent the prolongation of suffering from the affected population.[169] Although the Commentary is widely recognised, such an assertion; declaring the presupposition of consent in the event clarity does not exist concerning the authorities in a

[165] Emphasis added EEK.
[166] Sandoz, Swinarski & Zimmermann *Commentary to the Additional Protocols* (n 155) Protocol II Article 18, 1479.
[167] Ibid Article 14, 1457.
[168] Ibid Article 18, 1476-1477.
[169] Ibid, 1479.

territory, cannot be said to be commonly supported in practice. Dungel has argued that the text of Article 18 AP II in addressing only the affected state has an inherent inequality, which may be explained by the fact that historically obtaining approval from another belligerent party exercising control would be the recognition of this as a government.[170] Yet, as Dungel asserted, as this party indeed exercises *de facto* control, it would be arguable to consider such a party also a 'concerned party' in the sense of Article 18(2) AP II, leading to the requirement of *its* approval, rather than the approval of the affected state, depending on where specifically the assistance is required.[171] Ryngaert has concurred from a practical perspective, but notes that the necessity of the legal requirement of consent by a non-state actor remains unclear, given the silence of the Geneva Conventions and Protocols on this specific matter, whilst the Protocol does impose other obligations on such actors.[172]

Ryngaert furthermore notes that as armed groups increasingly aspire to sovereignty in conflicts with existing authorities, they may be 'bound by exactly the same norms as the state' with regard to the legal framework of humanitarian assistance, which simultaneously implies that such an armed group may not withhold consent arbitrarily, in violation of Article 18 AP II.[173] As is the case in the analysis of the various potential duties or rights to provide assistance in times of an international armed conflict, equal discussion exists with regard to non-international armed conflicts. Whereas Dinstein argues that a decline of an offer of assistance is permissible and that states shall always find plausible arguments to that end, Plattner poses that an offer which meets the terms of Article 18 APII cannot be considered an unlawful interference and may not be arbitrarily refused.[174] Again, semantics remain relevant, as the 'arbitrariness' of the refusal lies in the eye of the beholder. The ILC, in its study on the 'Protection of persons in the event of disasters', has argued that such a determination must be made on a 'case-by-case basis', without elaborating as to who should be the determinant in such circumstances.[175]

Despite the relevance of Article 18 AP II, many of the contemporary non-international conflicts are not governed by the provisions of this particular Protocol, either due to a lack of control of the armed groups, thereby not meeting the threshold of the Protocol, or because the affected stated has not acceded to it. In such circumstances, resort must be had to the general provisions of Common Article 3 of the Conventions, which does not allow for a 'right to access' or even a

[170] Joakim Dungel, 'A Right to Humanitarian Assistance in Internal Armed Conflicts Respecting Sovereignty, Neutrality and Legitimacy: Practical Proposals to Practical Problems', (2004) *Journal of Humanitarian Assistance* § 2.3.1.2 <http://sites.tufts.edu/jha/archives/838> (online publication) accessed 24 November 2014.
[171] Ibid.
[172] Ryngaert, 'Humanitarian Assistance and the Conundrum of Consent: A Legal Perspective' (n 12), 17-18.
[173] Ibid.
[174] Dinstein, 'The Right to Humanitarian Assistance' (n 72) 86; Plattner, 'ICRC neutrality and neutrality in humanitarian assistance' (n 161) 177.
[175] 'Fourth report on the protection of persons in the event of disasters' by Eduardo Valencia-Ospina, Special Rapporteur (11 May 2011) UN Doc A/CN.4/643 § 72.

duty to allow such access. In fact, in these circumstances, relying on the duties of the affected state and non-state actor based on human rights law will provide more protection for persons in need of humanitarian assistance. The rights to life, food and health all warrant the provision of humanitarian assistance by the affected authorities, should a humanitarian crisis take place, as such provision fulfils these human rights as enshrined in the ICCPR, ICESCR and various specific and regional treaties. Therefore, under human rights law, in times of non-international armed conflict – not meeting the threshold of AP II – the affected state and armed groups would still be held to the duty to seek international assistance in the provision of humanitarian assistance. In non-international armed conflicts that *do* fall within the scope of AP II, human rights law of course also continues to apply.

Should such offers of assistance be made, consent continues to be a crucial part of the actual facilitation of assistance. The matter of consent is crucial to the discussion of a potential 'right to access' as needed by third parties in order to factually provide the emergency assistance and shall therefore be further developed in the following Section, whereas the denial of humanitarian assistance (through the denial of consent) leading to a violation of a duty of the affected state shall be subsequently addressed in Section 8.3.

7.5.2 The Potential Right to Access in Times of Conflict

As seen in the previous Sections, the legal rights and duties involved in the provision of assistance are in practice very closely related to the discussion on the potential right to access. Alternatively formulated, the potential duty to allow access facilitates the external provision of assistance. Although the law pertaining to the potential right to access in times of armed conflict must also be discussed according to the type of conflict at hand, an overarching dilemma exists, as the issue of consent exists in circumstances of international armed conflict and non-international armed conflict, as well as for example in times of (natural) disaster. In the following Sections, an assessment is made of whether indeed the obligation resting upon the affected state and other involved parties – at times – can be considered to have evolved into a right of third parties to gain access for the provision of assistance. Again, it must be reiterated that this form of access must be distinguished from access through the use of force, as the provision of humanitarian assistance, in order to be precisely that, must abide by the principles of humanity, neutrality and impartiality.

7.5.2.1 The Potential Right to Access in Times of International Armed Conflict

The main provision of the 1949 Geneva Conventions with regard to the provision of humanitarian assistance, Article 10 GC IV, provides that the offer of assistance – and its provision – is subject to the consent of the affected state. Pictet argues in the *Commentary* that although parties to the conflict cannot be obliged to 'tolerate' the activities of a third organisation or party in its territory and that the states involved in the conflict do not need to provide reasons for the refusal, they may be subjected to some judgment in this regard:

> "The decision is entirely theirs, but since they are pledged to apply the Convention, they alone must bear the responsibility if they refuse help in carrying out their engagements".[176]

Although therefore no 'right to access' can be read into Article 10 GC IV, Pictet suggests an accountability for states that might refuse an offer from third parties to assist in the provision of humanitarian assistance. This responsibility is extended by Pictet to include others that might bear responsibilities, such as those parties involved in controlling a blockade, or facilitating the transit of emergency aid.[177] Subsequently, Article 23 GC IV declares:

> "Each High Contracting Party shall allow the free passage of all consignments of medical and hospital stores and objects necessary for religious worship intended only for civilians of another High Contracting Party, even if the latter is its adversary. It shall likewise permit the free passage of all consignments of essential foodstuffs, clothing and tonics intended for children under fifteen, expectant mothers and maternity cases. The obligation of a High Contracting Party to allow the free passage of the consignments indicated in the preceding paragraph is subject to the condition that this Party is satisfied that there are no serious reasons for fearing: (a) that the consignments may be diverted from their destination, (b) that the control may not be effective, or (c) that a definite advantage may accrue to the military efforts or economy of the enemy through the substitution of the above-mentioned consignments for goods which would otherwise be provided or produced by the enemy or through the release of such material, services or facilities as would otherwise be required for the production of such goods. The Power which allows the passage of the consignments indicated in the first paragraph of this Article may make permission conditional on the distribution to the persons benefited thereby being made under the local supervision of the Protecting Powers".

Thus, Article 23 GC IV imposes an obligation upon states that they 'shall' allow the provision of humanitarian assistance, adding to this that such an obligation may only be set aside if 'serious reasons' as stated above can be argued. Only upon the inclusion of these 'safeguards' were many states willing to agree to the mandatory character of Article 23.[178] Furthermore, Article 23 stipulated that the relief consignments 'shall' be forwarded as speedily as possible, thus placing another obligation upon state parties to not obstruct the distribution of aid. In addition to Article 23, which is specifically tailored to humanitarian assistance for the civilian population, Article 38 of the Fourth Geneva Convention stipulates that protected persons 'shall' be allowed to receive relief that is sent to them. It is therefore a distinct pattern of provisions that show the principle of thought behind the drafting

---

[176] Pictet, *Commentary on the Geneva Conventions of 12 August 1949* (n 154) Article 10, 98. See Chapter 8 on enforcement of violations of the duty to provide assistance.

[177] Ibid.

[178] Pictet, *Commentary on the Geneva Conventions of 12 August 1949* (n 154) Article 23, 183.

of the Convention and the wishes of the drafters, namely that those in need should be able to receive such assistance, implying both a related right to access of third parties and an obligation of the affected state to allow for such access, subject to certain 'control rights'.

Such perspectives are also translated into the Additional Protocol, where Article 70 addresses the provision of humanitarian assistance and, as seen above, the right to offer such assistance. Although attempts were made at a more far-reaching provision during the drafting process; which did not include any restrictions on the obligations of the affected state, the eventually accepted Article 70 AP I follows the general lines of Article 23 GC IV.[179] Concerning the potential right to access, Article 70(2)-(5) AP I declares in line with Article 23 GC IV:

> "2. The Parties to the conflict and each High Contracting Party shall allow and facilitate rapid and unimpeded passage of all relief consignments, equipment and personnel provided in accordance with this Section, even if such assistance is destined for the civilian population of the adverse Party. 3. The Parties to the conflict and each High Contracting Party which allow the passage of relief consignments, equipment and personnel in accordance with paragraph 2: (a) shall have the right to prescribe the technical arrangements, including search, under which such passage is permitted; (b) may make such permission conditional on the distribution of this assistance being made under the local supervision of a Protecting Power; (c) shall, in no way whatsoever, divert relief consignments from the purpose for which they are intended nor delay their forwarding, except in cases of urgent necessity in the interest of the civilian population concerned. 4. The Parties to the conflict shall protect relief consignments and facilitate their rapid distribution. 5. The Parties to the conflict and each High Contracting Party concerned shall encourage and facilitate effective international co-ordination of the relief actions referred to in paragraph 1".

Thus, in first instance only fractional differences exist between the Fourth Convention and the Additional Protocol when considering a potential right to access a territory by third parties in times of international armed conflict. As such, much of the phrasing of Article 70 AP I regarding the content of the rights and duties formulated remains mainly identical, to Article 23 GC IV and including a duty to allow transit of assistance for third states. Yet, several additions and changes have been made, amongst which most notably a broadening of the content of the assistance which shall be allowed. Amongst other matters, the prohibition of *delaying* humanitarian assistance by the affected state is a new addition in Article 70(3)(c) AP I. As such, the obligation to allow the unimpeded passage of assistance is balanced through several 'control rights' of the affected state: to control the emergency aid, to check supplies and cargo or to delay the provision for reasons of necessity. Many examples exist in which a state uses (or abuses) its power to

[179] During the drafting phase, Article 61(1) was proposed for the Additional Protocol I to the Geneva Conventions of August 12, 1949 (1973), "If the civilian population is inadequately supplied, in particular, with foodstuffs, clothing, medical and hospital stores and means of shelter, the Parties to the conflict shall agree to and facilitate those relief actions which are exclusively humanitarian and impartial in character and conducted without any adverse distinction." (Emphasis added EEK).

control the delivery of assistance, such as taking excessive time to search convoys, closing airports, requiring visas or the payment of taxes and even confiscating the aid for other purposes.[180] As the *Commentary* notes, since the affected parties are 'obliged to permit and to facilitate' the passage of relief, they have the right to 'require certain guarantees'.[181] However, Article 70 AP I is less lenient towards the affected state. In fact, the somewhat subjective phrase in Article 23 GC IV allowing it to avert the assistance if it has certain 'fears', is simply omitted in Article 70 AP I.[182] Thus, the 'control rights' are restricted, but do remain part of Article 70 AP I, clearly giving reference to the affected states' sovereignty. Article 70(5) AP I also adds to the existing language, stipulating that international relief shall be encouraged and facilitated, although it is not an international legal obligation as of yet.[183] Indeed, in circumstances in which Additional Protocol I is applicable, Article 70 AP I should be considered to replace the provisions of Article 23 GC IV, given its more recent, detailed nature.[184] With a view to these control rights, the UN Secretary General has recently called upon Member States to facilitate the practicalities of matters such as visas, checkpoints and to ensure aid providers' safety from attacks.[185]

It has also been argued that the discretion of the affected state is limited not only by the provisions in international humanitarian law as referred to in Article 70 AP I, but also by the provisions of existing human rights law and as such, a states' refusal to allow humanitarian assistance must also be in line with the provisions on the right to life and the right to food, health (and water).[186] Indeed, human rights law remains applicable in times of conflict, and thus the duties of states to seek international cooperation (or in the very least, not obstruct international offers) under human rights law, remain relevant.[187] Helpful and contributory to the legal discourse are also statements by international organisations (as seen above through the work of the UN Security Council and General Assembly) that portray a perspective on state practice with regard to the need to abide by existing rules of international humanitarian law and allow access to a territory for the provision of assistance.[188] As such, in particular the Security Council has at times asserted a duty of the affected state to allow unimpeded access to humanitarian aid providers.

---

180 Christa Rottensteiner, 'The denial of humanitarian assistance as a crime under international law', (1999) 81 *International Review of the Red Cross* 835, 560.

181 Sandoz, Swinarski & Zimmermann *Commentary to the Additional Protocols* (n 155) Protocol I Article 70, 822-823.

182 Ibid 827.

183 Spieker, 'Humanitarian Assistance, Access in Armed Conflict and Occupation' (n 161) § 24; and ibid Sandoz, Swinarski & Zimmermann 829.

184 Ibid 827.

185 UN Doc S/2012/376 (n 107) § 79-80.

186 FAO Legislative Study 'Right to Adequate Food in Emergencies' (2002) conclusion.

187 Section 3.4.2 Applicability of Human Rights in Armed Conflict and Occupation.

188 For example comments by regional initiatives, such as the International Conference on Peace, Security, Democracy and Development in the Great Lakes Region 'First Summit of Heads of State and Government' in Dar-Es-Salaam (19-20 November 2004) 'Declaration On Peace, Security, Democracy And Development In The Great Lakes Region' § 8 and 59.

Related to the potential right to access is Article 71(2) AP I, calling upon parties to provide for *safety of humanitarian personnel*.[189] Indeed, this wording has also been seen previously in the discussion of the many Security Council resolutions, and with regard to the UN Convention for the safety of its personnel. Although such a provision does not in itself call for a 'right to access', the safety of such personnel is naturally a prerequisite in the delivery of assistance. The ICRC has argued similarly in its Customary IHL Study, whilst simultaneously arguing the customary international legal status of the obligation to ensure freedom of movement for humanitarian personnel as a 'corollary' to a right to access.[190] Quite understandably, given its particular position, the ICRC as an organisation has for many years asserted such a right to access. However, as seen above, the 'right to access' cannot currently be positively stipulated to exist, despite some trends towards its gradual recognition. As argued by Spieker, this customary right has not been fully established, as both *opinio juris* and state practice have not properly crystallised regarding the abandoning of 'the precondition of consent' concerning a potential arbitrary refusal.[191] The Customary IHL Study has also noted that the broadening of the content of emergency relief within Additional Protocol I (from the original more restricted Article 23 GC IV) has been accepted as customary law.[192] Indeed, the ICRC notes in its Study that state practice (including through national legislation of many states) indicates an obligation of the affected state to not deliberately impede the delivery of humanitarian assistance to civilians under its control.[193] The legality of the offer of assistance is thus not affected, should the provision of humanitarian assistance meet the criteria as mentioned, even if a state refuses to allow assistance and thereby violates its responsibilities by arbitrarily denying access.[194] The provision and offer, however, must at all times abide by the requirements of Article 23 GC IV and 70 AP I regarding the manner in which the assistance should be provided, regardless of whether or not the affected state is consenting and abiding by its obligations under international humanitarian law.[195]

---

[189] See in this regard also Article 81 AP I, setting a duty for parties to a conflict to grant such facilities to the ICRC and similar humanitarian organisations to carry out their tasks.

[190] Henckaerts & Doswald-Beck, ICRC Customary International Humanitarian Law Study (n149) Rule 31 and 56. This same study has also argued the customary status of the notion that 'Objects used for humanitarian relief operations must be respected and protected' (see Rule 32).

[191] Spieker, 'Humanitarian Assistance, Access in Armed Conflict and Occupation' (n 161) § 35-36:

[192] Henckaerts & Doswald-Beck, ICRC Customary International Humanitarian Law Study (n149) Rule 55.

[193] Ibid Rule 55. See in particular the related state practice as provided by the ICRC in its study: <www.icrc.org/customary-ihl/eng/docs/v2_rul_rule55_sectionb> accessed 20 August 2013. The ICRC also references the many Security Council and General Assembly resolutions discussed above in Section7.4 and further.

[194] Kate Mackintosh, 'The Principles of Humanitarian Action in International Humanitarian Law: Study 4 in: The Politics of Principle: the principles of humanitarian action in practice', *Humanitarian Policy Group* Report 5 (March 2000) 11 and see also Chapter 8 with regard to methods of enforcement should a state not abide by its responsibilities under international law.

[195] Ibid Mackintosh 8-9 and 11 for a discussion on the practices of organisations with regard to the principle of humanity, neutrality and impartiality.

7.5.2.2 The Potential Right to Access in Times of Non-International Armed Conflict

The Geneva Conventions do not stipulate precisely whether a right to access exists for third parties in a non-international armed conflict, as common Article 3 is the only source upon which regulations can be sought and it remains silent on the matter, merely stating that assistance 'may' be offered. Thus, for those non-international armed conflicts not reaching the threshold of control required for the application of AP II, as well as those in which the affected state is not a Party to the Protocol, international humanitarian law does not distinctly supply a right to access the affected territory for the purpose of providing assistance. Furthermore, Additional Protocol II itself does not contain a particular provision concerning the access to a territory from abroad, other than the previously discussed provision in Article 18(2) AP II that relief actions 'shall be undertaken' in the event a population is not properly supplied with emergency aid.[196] However, the Commentary to the 1977 Additional Protocol II does consider regarding Article 18 that:

> "Once relief actions are accepted in principle, the authorities are under an obligation to co-operate, in particular by facilitating the rapid transit of relief consignments and by ensuring the safety of convoys".[197]

Indeed, as argued also by the ICRC in its Customary International Humanitarian Law Study, access is a 'conditio sine qua non' for the provision of relief, which in itself is required through the provision 'shall be undertaken' in Article 18 AP II.[198] Such a necessity is according to the Study also incorporated in the national legislation of several states.[199] However, it remains to be noted that Article 18 AP II *itself* does not provide for such a right to access, as it was removed in the final acceptance of the Article, after having been part of earlier draft versions.[200] Such a removal of course is a deliberate act of the drafting State Parties, and at the very least suggests their restraint in the acceptance of such a right. The ICRC has also argued in its Customary IHL Study that the obligation to ensure freedom of movement for humanitarian personnel, consequential to its assertion of the obligation to allow access to civilians, holds customary international legal status also concerning non-international armed conflicts.[201] Yet, as the underlying obligation is absent from AP II, considering the fact that Article 18 does not specifically mention such an obligation, as well as the fact that such a provision is

---

[196] See Section 7.5.2.1.

[197] Sandoz, Swinarski & Zimmermann *Commentary to the Additional Protocols* (n 155) Protocol II Article 18, 1480.

[198] Henckaerts & Doswald-Beck, ICRC Customary International Humanitarian Law Study (n 149), Rule 55.

[199] 55 State Practice (n 193).

[200] See in this regard Article 33 of Draft Additional Protocol II submitted by the ICRC to the Diplomatic Conference (CDDH).

[201] Henckaerts & Doswald-Beck, ICRC Customary International Humanitarian Law Study (n 149), Rule 56.

not codified for non-international armed conflicts falling short of the threshold of AP II, it appears somewhat premature to argue a customary legal norm derived from an obligation which has not been codified, nor unequivocally accepted in state practice.[202]

Yet, an evolution in the law has taken place since the codification of the Protocols in 1977, and the development of the Customary IHL Study in 2005. As reflected in this research, the steady increase of non-international armed conflicts adds to the development of the law. As such, attacks on humanitarian convoys or personnel in a non-international armed conflict have been incorporated as a war crime in the ICC Statute.[203] It has been put forward that this incorporation contributes to the position that the provision of humanitarian assistance within such a conflict is indeed evidential of the continuous further incorporation of such a potential right to access, as it embraces the reality of such provision on the ground.[204]

Furthermore, specific to the character of a non-international armed conflict is the matter of the duty-bearer of the obligation to allow humanitarian assistance into a certain territory, touched upon in the above Section. Whereas consent is a crucial element to the discussion on access to a territory in a variety of circumstances, in a non-international armed conflict, similar to circumstances of failed states, the legal sovereign may not be exercising factual control. Problematic in this respect is the difficulty in establishing contact with such entities, as contact is often considered to reflect a manner of recognition which states may wish to avoid. As discussed above, Dungel and Ryngaert argue the need to perhaps consider the non-state actor the 'concerned party' in the sense of Article 18 AP II, although Ryngaert views this as merely a practical obligation.[205] Consent may in reality be necessary not only of the state, but also of the non-state actor holding control over certain areas or territory. Although Article 18(2) AP II only addresses the consent of the concerned 'High Contracting Party', in reality a non-state actor exercising a certain level of de facto control would also be a 'concerned party' within the meaning of Article 18(2).[206] Schwendimann concurs with Ryngaert, arguing that the consent from such

---

[202] Consider in this regard also Security Council resolutions in which the Council has on multiple occasions referred to the notion of state sovereignty whilst calling upon states to allow for rapid passage of humanitarian assistance. The Council is thus fully aware of the potential international legal barriers that might exist in a non-international legal conflict when considering the potential obligation of states or other parties to a conflict to allow full freedom of movement to humanitarian personnel.
[203] Section 8.6.2 Enforcement through International Criminal Law.
[204] Jelena Pejic, 'The right to food in situations of armed conflict: the legal framework', (2001) 83 *International Review of the Red Cross* 844, 1106. See Chapter 8 on the enforcement of violations of states' obligations in the provision of humanitarian assistance.
[205] Dungel, 'A Right to Humanitarian Assistance in Internal Armed Conflicts Respecting Sovereignty, Neutrality and Legitimacy: Practical Proposals to Practical Problems' (n 170) § 2.3.1.2; and Ryngaert, 'Humanitarian Assistance and the Conundrum of Consent: A Legal Perspective' (n 12), 17-18.
[206] Ibid Dungel also concerning the Tamil / Sri Lanka conflict where, Dungel argues, this line of reasoning could have applied in practice in 1987.

a group does not necessarily imply legal recognition.[207] This approach of non-recognition has also been taken by the states parties to the Kampala Convention, that in a novel manner has incorporated duties of armed groups, declaring that members of such groups are prohibited from impeding humanitarian assistance, attacking humanitarian personnel and violating humanitarian spaces in general.[208] In another attempt to fill the void regarding conflicts that may fall short of such legal qualification, the Turku / Åbo Declaration of Minimum Humanitarian Standards has claimed that the necessary facilities to provide assistance 'shall be granted'.[209]

From the above, a close connection can be distinguished between the right to offer assistance, and the need for access. Such access in times of a non-international armed conflict, however, cannot be legally constructed as a right under international humanitarian law, due to the limitations that are incorporated in both Common Article 3 GC and Article 18 AP II. As analysed by Spieker, indeed the discussion regarding a potential legal obligation to offer and provide humanitarian assistance is divided due to the 'precondition of consent' of the states and parties concerned, which holds true for both international and non-international armed conflicts.[210] Within international humanitarian law, the duty to allow consent balances on the threshold of the affected state's (or acting sovereign's) duty to avoid starvation of the civilian population. Indeed, consent may not be withheld should it lead to a denial of humanitarian assistance that amounts to a violation of international law. Such a violation, also in times of conflict, may perhaps be reached at an earlier stage from a human rights law perspective. Within human rights law, the threshold does not lie with potential starvation, as the rights to life, food and health require the affected state, as a duty-bearer, to take positive action in the fulfilment of these rights towards those within its jurisdiction, as opposed to 'avoiding starvation', as the most meagre requirement of humanitarian law proscribes. A more in-depth analysis of the threshold of consent, denial of humanitarian assistance and violations of the law is provided in Section 8.3.

7.5.3 The Right to Provide Assistance and the Law of Occupation

On occasion, armed conflicts lead to situations of occupation that amount to circumstances of crisis. Should the occupying force in such circumstances not provide assistance, third parties also have possibilities, similar to circumstances of armed conflict, to do so. Within the 1949 Geneva Conventions, the duties of the

---

207 Felix Schwendimann, 'The legal framework of humanitarian access in armed conflict', (2011) *93 International Review of the Red Cross* 884, 1001.

208 Article 7(1) Kampala Convention reflects the position that legal status shall not be conferred onto armed groups. See more specifically Article 7(5)(g-i) from certain actions relating to the delivery of aid.

209 Turku 'Declaration of Minimum Humanitarian Standards', (2 December 1990) adopted by an expert meeting convened by the Institute for Human Rights, Åbo Akademi University, Turku/Åbo Finland, Article 15.

210 Spieker, 'Humanitarian Assistance, Access in Armed Conflict and Occupation' (n 161) § 22.

occupier have been quite extensively addressed as seen above in Chapter 6. Turning to the Geneva Conventions, Article 59 GC IV is considered the primary source for the rights and duties of third parties, stipulating in paragraph (1) and (2):

> "If the whole or part of the population of an occupied territory is inadequately supplied, the Occupying Power shall agree to relief schemes on behalf of the said population, and shall facilitate them by all the means at its disposal. Such schemes, which may be undertaken either by States or by impartial humanitarian organizations such as the International Committee of the Red Cross, shall consist, in particular, of the provision of consignments of foodstuffs, medical supplies and clothing".

Thus, relief schemes 'shall' be agreed upon by the occupying power, which speaks of an obligation for the affected occupier rather than an obligation for third parties. As argued by the *Commentary*, such a duty resting upon the occupier is 'unconditional'.[211] Pictet does subsequently acknowledge that an occupying force may be 'justified' in refusing such assistance which might not be urgently needed for the survival of a population, which is why the final sentence 'foodstuffs, medical supplies and clothing' is added in the wording of Article 59(2).[212] Such materials must be allowed, as they contribute to the survival of civilians. Indeed, Article 59 GC IV may be construed as an inversed right to provide assistance for third parties, but the Article itself is silent on this matter. The *Commentary* elaborates that the third parties – including states – must remain impartial in their provision of assistance.[213] Indeed it is only through impartial provision of relief that such relief can still be qualified as humanitarian assistance, and thereby continue to place the obligation upon the occupying power to agree to its provision.

Related to Article 59 GC IV, Article 55 GC IV provides the *Protecting Power* the right to check the state of provision of assistance by the occupier. A protecting power; a third state that takes care of the interests of the occupied state with the consent of the occupier, has however remained a more theoretical concept in the Conventions, due to the issues relating to its appointment.[214] Indeed, the concept of a 'protecting power' is somewhat out-dated in current international law and is no longer seen much in practice.[215] For purposes of completeness, the concept will be briefly addressed. Pictet argues that the protecting power is not limited to such 'supervision' but may rather be extended to include lending their good offices for the provision of assistance.[216] Although the occupying power has the possibility to restrict the protecting power hereto in case of military necessity, such restrictions are only allowed temporarily. Also related to the role of the protecting power,

---

[211] Pictet, *Commentary on the Geneva Conventions of 12 August 1949* (n 154) Article 59, 320.
[212] Ibid 321.
[213] Ibid.
[214] Eyal Benvenisti, *The International Law of Occupation* (Oxford University Press 2012) 341.
[215] Yoram Dinstein, *The International Law of Belligerent Occupation* (Cambridge University Press 2009) 66; Gabriele Porretto & Sylvain Vité, 'The application of international humanitarian law and human rights law to international organisations' (2006) *UCHL Research Paper Series* 1, 60.
[216] Pictet, *Commentary on the Geneva Conventions of 12 August 1949* (n 154) Article 55, 312.

Article 61 (1) and (2) GC IV provides that the protecting power shall have the duty to supervise the distribution of such assistance (or delegate such a duty to another neutral third party), whereas the occupier must facilitate the rapid distribution of relief:

> "The distribution of the relief consignments referred to in the foregoing Articles shall be carried out with the cooperation and under the supervision of the Protecting Power. This duty may also be delegated, by agreement between the Occupying Power and the Protecting Power, to a neutral Power, to the International Committee of the Red Cross or to any other impartial humanitarian body. Such consignments shall be exempt in occupied territory from all charges, taxes or customs duties unless these are necessary in the interests of the economy of the territory. The Occupying Power shall facilitate the rapid distribution of these consignments".

The protecting power, as a third party, therefore has an *obligation* to cooperate in the distribution of the relief, although the Convention does not elaborate on the manner in which such cooperation or distribution should take place. Furthermore, although the protecting power may delegate its duties to another neutral party, it may only do so in an agreement with the occupying power. Thus, some form of insurance is given that the cooperation between the new parties will indeed take place.[217] The manner in which the law is formulated relies heavily on the instatement of such a protecting power, whereas in practice this concept has not functioned over the past decades.

In circumstances of armed conflict, the Additional Protocols to the Geneva Conventions provided for much needed enhancement of the rights and duties involved in the external provision of humanitarian assistance, but this is not the case concerning occupied territory. Article 69 (2) AP I very summarily declares that those external actions for the provision of humanitarian assistance in occupied territories are governed by the existing Articles of GC IV and Article 71 of AP I.[218] For the potential obligation to provide assistance by third parties therefore, the Additional Protocol does not offer an extra source. Such an approach by the Protocols can indeed be explained by the timeframe of their development, and the period of decolonisation. Over time, circumstances of occupation have decreased, leading to even fewer circumstances of occupation that amount to a humanitarian crisis.

Thus, with regard to the right to provide assistance, recourse must be had to the 1949 Conventions as the Additional Protocols do not provide for new obligations or rights specific to circumstances of occupation. The provisions of the Fourth Geneva Convention are quite explicit concerning the provision of aid by third parties, but solely place an *obligation* upon the *protecting* powers that might be in place. As is apparent from state practice, such protecting powers are no longer common, and as a result, also in times of occupation, the most common form of external provision

[217] Ibid Article 61, 326.

[218] See also Section 7.5.4.

of assistance is that by third states or other third parties such as humanitarian organisations. Whereas their possibilities to provide assistance are indeed incorporated in Article 59 GC IV, these parties do not have a duty as such to provide assistance to an occupied population in the event of a humanitarian crisis, but have a *right to offer* to do so, as may be derived from the wording of Article 59 GC IV.

7.5.4 The Potential Right to Access and the Law of Occupation

As seen in the previous Section, Article 59 GC IV is considered the cardinal provision pertaining to the external provision of humanitarian assistance in times of occupation. Other than in times of armed conflict, the occupying force is obliged to accept such assistance with, according to the *Commentary*, virtually no restrictions.[219] Subsequently, when a potential right to access is considered, Article 59 GC IV equally provides in its final paragraphs that:

> "All Contracting Parties shall permit the free passage of these consignments and shall guarantee their protection. A Power granting free passage to consignments on their way to territory occupied by an adverse Party to the conflict shall, however, have the right to search the consignments, to regulate their passage according to prescribed times and routes, and to be reasonably satisfied through the Protecting Power that these consignments are to be used for the relief of the needy population and are not to be used for the benefit of the Occupying Power".

Pictet has argued in his *Commentary* that these final passages of Article 59 GC IV, articulating the principle of free passage of goods and their protection, are the 'keystone of the whole system' as they contain the obligation for the occupying power to allow the provision of assistance to the population through any barrier the occupier may have set up.[220] The level of consent needed in circumstances such as an international or non-international armed conflict leading to certain control rights, does not translate to circumstances of occupation in the Fourth Convention. The occupying power cannot impose restrictions such as the 'control rights' that exist for the affected parties in times of conflict, as the 'control rights' of the occupier are confined to searching the convoys to determine whether the materials are in fact meant for a needy population, and to regulate their passage accordingly. Yet, the occupier may indeed of course determine for each individual passage of goods and personnel whether the convoy meets such criteria and regulate their passage accordingly.[221]

Access to a territory is, as always, fundamental to the provision of assistance. It is relevant to note in this regard also Article 61(2) GC IV, determining that no charges, taxes or customs may be imposed, to enable the rapid distribution of relief,

---

[219] Pictet, *Commentary on the Geneva Conventions of 12 August 1949* (n 154) Article 59, 320.
[220] Ibid 321-322.
[221] Dinstein, *The International Law of Belligerent Occupation* (n 215) 193.

upon the determination of the occupier that a convoy meets the set criteria. It is the occupier's obligation through its actions to ensure this rapid distribution by facilitating this. The final paragraph of Article 61 GC IV determines:

> "All Contracting Parties shall endeavour to permit the transit and transport, free of charge, of such relief consignments on their way to occupied territories".

Thus, an obligation lies upon *all* parties to the Convention to allow relief consignments designated for occupied territory through their own territory. Although this is certainly not a 'right to access' the occupied territory, the combination of what is prescribed in Article 59 and 61 amounts to a r*ight of third parties to transfer humanitarian assistance* through third territory into the occupied territory for the provision of assistance. Furthermore, also adding to the discussed 'right to access' an occupied territory for the provision of assistance, Article 63 GC IV obliges the occupying power to allow the existing Red Cross Societies and other similar humanitarian organisations in a territory to continue with their activities, with the exception of urgent security-related reasons of the occupier. Such temporary reasons may be the legitimate concerns and interests of the occupier, who might be threatened by imminent danger.[222] The caveat with regard to the framework of humanitarian assistance under the provisions of the Fourth Geneva Convention however remains that such duties only arise upon the establishment of a certain degree of control, and the passing of time, upon which a humanitarian crisis is often not occurring.[223]

The Additional Protocols to the Geneva Convention, which have proven helpful in the determination of more explicit rights and duties in the potential access to a territory in times of armed conflict, do not however expound upon the existing rights and duties enshrined in the Fourth Geneva Convention concerning occupied territory, except for stating the fact that such provision is also governed by Article 71 AP I. As discussed in the above Section pertaining to the right to access and armed conflicts, Article 71 AP I calls upon affected parties to ensure the safety of humanitarian personnel. Although the Article is relevant to the provision of assistance and obtaining access to this end, it does not in itself entail a more elaborate right or duty for third parties in times of occupation than enshrined in the Fourth Geneva Convention. In fact, concerning the participation of relief personnel, Article 71 AP I calls upon the 'approval of the Party in whose territory they will carry out their duties', which makes the application of the Article to occupied territory somewhat problematic. A lack of clarity exists regarding the addressee of the duty, in times of occupation. Thus, applying this Article *mutatis mutandis* to occupied territory, one must conclude that the approval of the occupying power must be sought.[224] As such, where the Fourth Geneva Convention does not

---

[222] Pictet, *Commentary on the Geneva Conventions of 12 August 1949* (n 154) Article 63, 333.
[223] Section 3.2.4 Occupation and the Provision of Humanitarian Assistance.
[224] Dinstein, *The International Law of Belligerent Occupation* (n 215) 194.

expressly stipulate the right of consent for the occupying force, this is now indeed included through the provisions of Article 71 AP I.

As discussed in Section 3.4.2.2, the extraterritorial application of human rights law including the level of 'effective' control or authority needed for its application continues to be a matter of debate and the matter has not crystallised in international law today. Human rights law may be relevant regarding the creation of potential duties to seek international assistance in fulfilling duties regarding the rights to life, food and health for the affected state, in this circumstance the occupying power. Whilst indeed human rights do not cease to exist in times of conflict or occupation, their continued application in occupied territory, in particular relating to the rights to food and health, is more difficult to establish given the positive duties of conduct these place upon the affected state.[225] The ICJ and ECtHR have for example not positively affirmed such extraterritorial obligations for states with regard to economic, social and cultural rights, whilst the provision of humanitarian assistance can be seen as a vehicle in the fulfilment of the rights to life, food and health by a state as duty-bearer.

In the particular case of occupation, the level of control and duration of occupation determine the application of both the provisions in the Geneva Conventions and Protocols, and the potential application of human rights provisions such as Article 11 and 12 ICESCR. Yet, in the longer establishment of occupation, in theory the immediate humanitarian crisis would also subside, no longer warranting the application of human rights law for the provision of emergency aid. Indeed it must be concluded that even upon the recognition that human rights find extraterritorial application in times of occupation, a case-by-case determination of the degree of 'effective control' or authority is needed to assess their factual application. However, the need for their specific application may not be as high as in times of conflict or natural disaster, given the more elaborate provisions of Article 59 GC IV. Indeed, the nature of the circumstance of occupation, also warranting the application of Article 59 GC IV, suggests that the immediate humanitarian crisis has passed.

7.5.5 The Right to Provide Assistance in Times of (Natural) Disaster

As seen in Chapter 6, the provision of humanitarian assistance in times of natural disaster is not guided by a particular legal framework as is the case in times of armed conflict. Certainly, general international law and human rights law find continued applicability, and the General Assembly has increasingly concerned itself with the provision of assistance to disaster victims in the aftermath of such natural disasters. Yet, creating a binding legal framework has proven difficult on numerous occasions, such as in 1927 with the quite extensive, but failed 'Convention establishing an International Relief Union', and subsequently in 1984 with the 'Draft Convention on expediting the delivery of emergency assistance'. To date,

---

[225] See the more elaborate discussion in Section 3.4.2.2 The Potential Extraterritorial Scope of Application of Human Rights Treaties.

only a few legally binding (regional) treaties are in place specifically concerning the rights and duties in the provision of humanitarian assistance in the situation of a natural disaster, such as the 'Inter-American Convention To Facilitate Disaster Assistance' of 1991, which unfortunately could still benefit from the accession of more parties.

This regional treaty interestingly *presupposes* an offer of assistance by third states without specifically addressing this right.[226] Furthermore, humanitarian organisations may, if the affected state consents to this, resort *mutatis mutandis* to the Convention also.[227] However, no specific *duty* to provide humanitarian assistance is incorporated, and the Convention presupposes the right of the affected state to 'accept' the offer, thereby suggesting that a refusal thereof is also a possibility.[228] In short, the Convention places the power of decision resolutely in the hands of the affected state. Another regional initiative is the ASEAN Agreement on Disaster Management and Emergency Response of 2005, which codifies a duty in Article 4(c) for states party to the agreement to 'promptly respond' to a request for assistance by a state affected by disaster, while the 'control' and supervision of coordination and direction remains firmly within the sovereign rights of the affected state as elaborately established in Articles 11 and 12 of the Agreement. Furthermore, according to Article 8 of the Agreement, states have an obligation to coordinate the provision of joint emergency response operations amongst themselves.

With a view to specific types of disasters, the Convention on Assistance in the Case of a Nuclear Accident or Radiological Emergency also sees a responsibility for all parties to it, declaring that they 'shall cooperate between themselves' to 'facilitate prompt assistance'.[229] With such a perspective, the Convention foregoes a 'right to offer' assistance, and rather codifies a *duty* to assist in the specific circumstance of nuclear accidents or radiological emergencies. Yet, such a duty is not unlimited, as Article 2(3) of the Convention provides that the state which is requested by the affected state to assist shall indeed notify this state 'whether it is in a position to render the assistance requested, and the scope and terms of the assistance that might be rendered'. More specifically geared towards *food* assistance is the recent 'UN Food Assistance Convention' which entered into force in January 2013 and proclaims that certain 'eligible countries' are entitled to receive assistance from donors.[230] Signatories to the Convention, amongst which

[226] See in this regard for example the Article I(b), Article II(b) and IV(b) Inter-American Convention To Facilitate Disaster Assistance.
[227] Article XVI(a) Inter-American Convention To Facilitate Disaster Assistance.
[228] Ibid Article II.
[229] Article 1(1) of the Convention on Assistance in the Case of a Nuclear Accident or Radiological Emergency, entered into force on 26 February 1987, 112 state parties to date.
[230] Article 4 Food Assistance Convention. The eligible countries are those placed on the list of 'Official Development Assistance Recipients' by the OECD's Development Assistance Committee. For the recipients of 2012 and 2013 see <www.oecd.org/dac/stats/DAC%20List%20used%20for%202012%20and%202013%20flows.pdf> accessed 23 August 2013.

the EU, must provide a minimum of food assistance annually, although no specificities are provided as to the manner in which such assistance should be legally framed within the discussion of a potential legal duty to provide assistance in a specific circumstance.[231] The legal duty which exists in this particular Convention relates to a quantity or value of aid which must be provided annually, as opposed to the circumstance – such as a humanitarian crisis – which triggers the delivery of aid.

Thus, as the Food Aid Convention does not tailor to the specific *legal aspects* of provision and access for emergency assistance, nor do several of the other international or regional initiatives related to international cooperation in relation to disaster response, only a small regional and topical component is binding upon states.[232] Focarelli has argued along these lines that legal regulation in times of disaster of assistance towards affected persons is 'desperately needed'.[233] Even from the perspective of humanitarian law, support for duties in the provision of humanitarian assistance in the aftermath of disaster is found, as the Commentary to Article 14 AP II declares that starvation of the civilian population 'is nowadays no longer an acceptable phenomenon, irrespective of how it arises (natural disaster or induced by man)' and that such circumstances have 'prompted the international community to organize relief actions'.[234] Such perspectives may be particularly relevant to complex emergencies, where disasters occur in times of conflict. However, human rights law of course remains applicable in disaster situations amounting to a humanitarian crisis. From the perspective of the provision of assistance by third parties, the above Section 7.3.1 has shown that although the primary duty-bearer in the fulfilment of human rights is the affected state, international cooperation is envisaged under Article 2 ICESCR. A right to offer assistance therefore can also flow from such provisions. Soft law initiatives, such as the 'Operational Guidelines on Human Rights and Natural Disasters' similarly adhere to this.[235]

Next to existing human rights law and these few binding regional and topical treaties, developments exist in particular relation to the legal regulation of

---

[231] Article 5 Food Assistance Convention. For the principles by which the food aid must be provided, see Article 2.

[232] See in this regard the Tampere Convention on the Provision of Telecommunication Resources for Disaster Mitigation and Relief Operations (18 June 1998); Framework Convention on Civil Defense Assistance (22 May 2000), although note Article 4(a)(5); European Union Council Decision (2001/792/EC, Euratom) (23 October 2001), establishing a Community mechanism to facilitate reinforced cooperation in civil protection assistance interventions and 'Joint Statement by the Council and the Representatives of the Governments of the Member States meeting within the Council, the European Parliament and the European Commission' (European Consensus on Humanitarian Aid) (30 January 2008) EU Doc 2008/C/25/01.

[233] Focarelli, 'Duty to Protect in Cases of Natural Disasters' (n 2) § 29.

[234] Sandoz, Swinarski & Zimmermann *Commentary to the Additional Protocols* (n 155) Protocol II Article 14, 1458.

[235] 'Operational Guidelines on Human Rights and Natural Disasters' by the Representative on human rights of internally displaced persons UN Doc A/HRC/4/38/Add.1 (26 January 2006) Principle B.1.1 and B1.4.

humanitarian assistance in disaster circumstances in a somewhat more global manner. These include both the IDRL regulations as proposed by the IFRC and the ILC study on 'Protection of persons in the event of disasters' that may provide new perspectives through its Draft Articles. Whilst both initiatives are not *lex lata*, nor do they necessarily aspire to be, as the IDRL Guidelines in particular offer a more practical and domestic approach, these new perspectives may eventually form part of the customary law development. Indeed, from such efforts it becomes evident that the international community as a whole is concerned with strengthening international cooperation in the aftermath of disasters, warranting their discussion in this Section.[236]

7.5.5.1 The Potential Application of the ILC Study: Protection of persons in the event of disaster

Over the past years the ILC has considered through its Draft Articles the possibility of external parties providing assistance in the event of a natural disaster, while their development into codified international law currently remains uncertain. Draft Articles 8 and 9 of the ILC's study stipulate a duty for states to cooperate amongst themselves as well as with humanitarian organisations.[237] Furthermore, a right to offer assistance is explicitly provided in Draft Article 16:

> "In responding to disasters, States, the United Nations, and other competent intergovernmental organizations have the right to offer assistance to the affected State. Relevant non-governmental organizations may also offer assistance to the affected State".[238]

Draft Article 16 thus unambiguously provides for a broad spectrum of third parties to offer their services in the event of a disaster. The Special Rapporteur has argued in favour of such a holistic approach, as he views the protection of persons in the event of a disaster in essence a matter which concerns the international community as a whole.[239] Yet, a duty for the affected state to accept such an offer is clearly missing from the text; a deliberate decision of the ILC to allow the affected state the freedom of choice through the necessity of its consent.[240] Following suit, Draft Article 15 determines that, as is also the case in circumstances of conflict, the affected state may exercise certain 'control rights':

---

[236] See in support of this also 'Promotion And Protection Of All Human Rights, Civil, Political, Economic, Social And Cultural Rights, Including The Right To Development Human Rights And International Solidarity' Note By The United Nations High Commissioner For Human Rights UN Doc A/HRC/12/27 (22 July 2009) § 36.

[237] ILC 'Protection of persons in the event of disasters' Draft Articles UN Doc. A/CN.4/L.831 (15 May 2014) Draft Article 8 and 9.

[238] Ibid UN Doc. A/CN.4/L.831.

[239] UN Doc A/CN.4/643 (n 175) § 78-87.

[240] See in this regard the deliberations of the ILC, 'Provisional summary record of the 3102nd meeting Held at the Palais des Nations, Geneva' UN Doc A/CN.4/SR.3102 (25 January 2012) 8.

> "The affected State may place conditions on the provision of external assistance. Such conditions shall be in accordance with the present draft articles, applicable rules of international law, and the national law of the affected State. Conditions shall take into account the identified needs of the persons affected by disasters and the quality of the assistance. When formulating conditions, the affected State shall indicate the scope and type of assistance sought".[241]

Unlike in the case with the provisions of the Geneva Conventions and their Additional Protocols, the ILC's Draft Articles do not specify which particular rights rest upon the affected state, thereby creating uncertainty for the providing party as to what its rights are in offering assistance.[242] From the Special Rapporteur's discussion of the right of the affected state to place conditions upon the provision of assistance, it can be inferred that states may demand that the assistance provided is in accordance with the national law of the affected state (which may be waived), the affected state should indicate its needs and it may make certain demands regarding the quality of the assistance, but cannot make requests that would deter from the core principles of the provision of assistance.[243] Thus, the ILC Draft Articles currently appear to hold on to the established notion of humanitarian assistance, whilst providing the affected state with ample opportunity to 'mould' the offered assistance into what it needs in a particular circumstance. The duty to cooperate as envisaged by the ILC in its Study however follows the line of existing human rights law, providing for somewhat stronger clauses than for example humanitarian law. However, the notion of state consent is translated from humanitarian law into these Draft Articles.

7.5.5.2 The Potential Application of the IDRL Guidelines and Model Act

As established in Section 6.5.5.2, the IDRL Guidelines are non-binding in their nature and intent, as determined by their method of creation and their role in the IFRC's Disaster Law Programme.[244] Thus, their more practical approach with a domestic perspective foregoes an opportunity to codify in a universal manner the potential legal rights and duties for third states in the provision of humanitarian assistance. Yet, within the context of this research it is relevant to address the possibilities of external parties to provide assistance under the Guidelines. Guideline 3.2 determines that the affected state has a duty to 'seek international and/or regional assistance', and Guideline 10.1 determines more explicitly:

---

[241] ILC 'Protection of persons in the event of disasters' Draft Articles UN Doc. A/CN.4/L.831 (15 May 2014).

[242] ILC 'Fifth report on the protection of persons in the event of disasters by Eduardo Valencia-Ospina, Special Rapporteur' (9 April 2012) UN Doc A/CN.4/652 § 120-130, 146-160.

[243] Ibid § 120-160, 163-169.

[244] IFRC 'Guidelines for the domestic facilitation and regulation of international disaster relief and initial recovery assistance' (IDRL Guidelines) (30 November 2007), adopted at the 30th International Conference of the Movement, Introduction § 1.1.

> "Disaster relief or initial recovery assistance should be initiated only with the consent of the affected State and, in principle, on the basis of an appeal. The affected State should decide in a timely manner whether or not to request disaster relief or initial recovery assistance and communicate its decision promptly [...]".

As can be seen, the Guidelines are restrained in their approach, declaring that humanitarian assistance should only be 'initiated' upon the consent of the affected state *and* on the basis of an 'appeal', thereby falling short of positively declaring a right to offer assistance for third parties. Furthermore, the IFRC Guidelines, as does the ILC in its Study, provide the affected state with 'control rights' based on their state sovereignty. As such, the affected state shall have the right to:

> "coordinate, regulate and monitor disaster relief and recovery assistance provided by assisting actors on their territory, consistent with international law".[245]

Following that approach, the external providers of assistance have the obligation to abide by the national laws of the affected state and coordinate with the local authorities.[246] Given their practical rather than legal applicability, the IDRL Guidelines remain of limited value in their contribution to this analysis of the legal framework pertaining to natural disaster relief.[247] It must be noted however that the UN General Assembly has embraced the Guidelines in its work, thereby adding to the potential formation of some consensus on customary principles concerning disaster relief.[248]

The Guidelines are very restrained and the recently developed 'Model Act for the Facilitation and Regulation of International Disaster Relief and Initial Recovery Assistance' follows this approach.[249] The Model Act, which has yet to be incorporated by states into their domestic disaster response framework, suggests in Article 7(a) and (e) that offers of assistance may be made, but are subject to the acceptance thereof by the affected state. Thus, the Model Act does not venture out into unchartered territory, and merely echoes the IDRL Guidelines in a more legal formulation.

---

[245] Ibid Guideline 3.3.
[246] Ibid Guideline 4.1. According to Guideline 10.3, the affected state should provide such actors with 'adequate information' on domestic law.
[247] See Section 6.5.5.2 The Potential Application of the IDRL Guidelines and Model Act for a more in depth discussion.
[248] Amongst others UNGA Res 63/137 (11 December 2008) UN Doc A/RES/63/137 § 6; UNGA Res 63/139 (5 March 2009) UN Doc A/RES/63/139 'Strengthening of the coordination of humanitarian and disaster relief assistance of the United Nations, including special economic assistance: strengthening of the coordination of emergency humanitarian assistance of the United Nations' § 8; and UNGA Res 63/141 (10 March 2009) UN Doc A/RES/63/141 § 5.
[249] See Section 6.5.5.2 The Potential Application of the IDRL Guidelines and Model Act on the development of this Model Act.

7.5.6 The Potential Right to Access in Times of (Natural) Disaster

The UN Secretary General has argued that whilst security reasons might put some restrictions on humanitarian access, 'it remains that humanitarian considerations should always be given the necessary priority'.[250] The Secretary General suggests creating 'relief corridors' in specific circumstances, to provide access to victims of natural disasters, but reflects that such corridors, functioning as 'life lines' should be instated in coordination with the affected state, in respect of state sovereignty.[251] These arguments, made in 1990, still hold true today, although developments in the law have taken place, not in the least concerning the notion of state sovereignty.[252]

As noted in the previous Section, currently a specific legal framework pertaining to the provision of humanitarian assistance in times of natural disaster is absent, save for the regional provisions of the 'Inter-American Convention To Facilitate Disaster Assistance' of 1991 and the ASEAN Agreement on Disaster Management and Emergency Response.[253] Although according to the Inter-American Convention the assisting states merely have the right to offer assistance and the affected state has a choice to accept such an offer, once accepted, the Convention determines in Article V that access and freedom of movement in the territory, both for humanitarian personnel and convoys, is exempt from all kinds of payments and shall be facilitated fully by the affected state. As seen in times of conflict and occupation, the Convention envisages for the affected state to have certain 'control rights' which include determination of certain routes and acceptance of which personnel enters the territory.[254] Although of only regional consequence, this Convention thus differentiates from humanitarian law, and does not envisage such specific control rights. Similar to the Inter-American Convention, according to the ASEAN 2005 Agreement's Article 3(1) and Article 11(2) the affected state will maintain the right to determine whether or not it consents to the assistance as offered by other state parties. Yet, once a state consents to the provision of assistance, it must according to Article 14 of the Agreement 'exempt' the assisting state from all charges of taxes and facilitate access for both the humanitarian personnel and convoys. Such duties equally rest upon third states, as they must allow and facilitate transit through their territory.[255] Indeed, the ASEAN Agreement provides for many regulations, yet does not assert a right to access a territory in any form. Furthermore, due to its origins, its scope is limited to the practice of the

---

[250] 'New International Humanitarian Order: Humanitarian Assistance to Victims of Natural Disasters and Similar Emergency Situations' Report of the Secretary General (24October 1990) UN Doc A/45/587 §25.

[251] Ibid.

[252] Section 4.2.3.3 Towards a new Definition of Sovereignty.

[253] 'Inter-American Convention To Facilitate Disaster Assistance' (7 June 7 1991, entry into force 16 October 1996). Currently 6 states are party to the treaty. Although the Convention is primarily addressed to states, humanitarian organisations may also have recourse to it; and ASEAN Agreement on Disaster Management and Emergency Response 2005.

[254] Article VI Inter-American Convention To Facilitate Disaster Assistance.

[255] Article 16 ASEAN Agreement on Disaster Management and Emergency Response.

provision of humanitarian assistance amongst South-East Asian states. Limiting control rights of the affected state to the bare necessities remains essential, as the UN Secretary General argued in 1990: 'delayed relief is virtually no relief'.[256]

From the above, it becomes apparent that the two regional binding legal sources do not provide for a right to access, but rather attempt to regulate *the manner in which* such access is given, upon consent of the affected state. Similarly, the Convention on Assistance in the Case of a Nuclear Accident or Radiological Emergency does not codify a right to access for third parties, as assistance is based quite firmly on the request of the affected state. Furthermore, the coordination of the assistance provided remains in the hands of the affected state, thereby granting it a form of 'control' over the external assistance, similar to circumstances of conflict, regulated by humanitarian law.[257] Thus, with no framework specifically in place providing legal solutions, once again resort is had to the framework of human rights law. Whereas this framework also does not formulate a positive right to access for third parties, Section 7.3.2 has addressed that it does in fact, supported by the ICJ and Security Council, at times envisage a duty of the affected state to *allow access* to third parties, as part of its fulfilment of the rights to life, food and health. Human rights law therefore serves as a solid basis, in the absence of more all-encompassing binding provisions specifically tailored to disaster relief.

With a view to the progressive development of the law, the ILC's Draft Articles on the 'Protection of persons in the event of disasters' and the IDRL Guidelines and Model Act must be addressed to assess potential developments in these initiatives. Although this Chapter addresses the current framework and *lex lata*, such developments are indicative of potential developing *opinio juris* and thereby relevant to the potential right to access in times of natural disaster.

7.5.6.1 The Potential Application of the ILC Study: Protection of persons in the event of disaster

The ILC Study has formulated several Draft Articles distinctly positing a right to offer assistance by external parties in the event of a disaster, as well as a duty of states to cooperate amongst themselves and with international organisations. However, as seen in the other circumstances of conflict and occupation, discussed above, often the affected state is granted the opportunity to determine whether or not access to a territory shall be allowed. Indeed, in a similar manner Draft Article 14 denies third parties a 'right' to access as it formulates:

> "1. The provision of external assistance requires the consent of the affected State. 2. Consent to external assistance shall not be withheld arbitrarily. 3. When an offer of

[256] UN Doc A/45/587 (n 250) 3.

[257] Article 3 Convention on Assistance in the Case of a Nuclear Accident or Radiological Emergency.

> assistance is extended in accordance with the present draft articles, the affected State shall, whenever possible, make its decision regarding the offer known".[258]

In this provision, as also formulated in international humanitarian law, *arbitrariness* in a refusal of access shall not be permitted. However, explication of the notion of 'arbitrariness' is not provided for in the text of the Draft Article. The Special Rapporteur in his analysis refers to both humanitarian and human rights law and, despite arguing that such determinations must take place on a 'case-by-case basis' also proffers some suggestions, such as a lack of a 'clear need' for assistance, or not meeting the requirements (such as certain principles for the provision of assistance) and furthermore declares that the affected state must provide reasons for its refusal.[259] The notion continues to be subject of debate in the Commission, also with regard to potential political motivations states might have in the refusal of aid from certain other states.[260] With this formulation, however, the ILC has unequivocally chosen to forego the opportunity to search for new boundaries in this particular aspect of the provision of assistance. Such a perspective appears to be the logical consequence of the ILC's preliminary discussion of the potential 'right to assistance' or 'right to provide assistance', where many members of the Committee proved quite hesitant in their acknowledgment of the existence of such rights.[261] The ILC Draft Articles in their position thus uphold a quite conservative notion of state sovereignty, as the Special Rapporteur argues that although sovereignty does include responsibilities, the affected state may adopt those measures 'it sees fit' in the protection of persons.[262]

On the other hand, Draft Article 17 does explicate in detail in its text the duties of the affected state should it consent to access:

> "1. The affected State shall take the necessary measures, within its national law, to facilitate the prompt and effective provision of external assistance regarding, in particular: (a) civilian and military relief personnel, in fields such as privileges and immunities, visa and entry requirements, work permits, and freedom of movement; and (b) goods and equipment, in fields such as customs requirements and tariffs, taxation,

---

[258] ILC 'Protection of persons in the event of disasters' Draft Articles UN Doc. A/CN.4/L.831 (15 May 2014).

[259] UN Doc A/CN.4/643 (n 175) § 72-74.

[260] ILC 'Fifth report on the protection of persons in the event of disasters by Eduardo Valencia-Ospina, Special Rapporteur' (9 April 2012) UN Doc A/CN.4/652 § 36-40; and ILC 'Sixty-fourth session (second part) Provisional summary record of the 3138th meeting Held at the Palais des Nations, Geneva' (2 August 2012) UN Doc A/CN.4/SR.3138, 13. See in this regard however also the perspective of the ICJ in Military and Paramilitary Activities in and against Nicaragua (Nicaragua v. United States of America), Merits, Judgment 27 June 1986 I.C.J. Reports 1986, p. 14 § 242-243 regarding the fact that strict humanitarian assistance cannot be considered an unlawful intervention, regardless of the political affiliation of the providers.

[261] 'Report of the International Law Commission Sixtieth session (5 May-6 June and 7 July-8 August 2008) General Assembly Official Records Sixty-third session Supplement No. 10' (2008) UN Doc A/63/10 § 241-250 on the deliberations of the members.

[262] Third report on the protection of persons in the event of disasters', ILC Special Rapporteur Eduardo Valencia-Ospina, UN Doc A/CN.4/629 (31 March 2010) § 66-75, in particular 74.

> transport, and disposal thereof. 2. The affected State shall ensure that its relevant legislation and regulations are readily accessible, to facilitate compliance with national law".[263]

If the affected state consents to allow access for third parties providing assistance, it must then also *facilitate the effective provision* of the assistance by taking measures concerning both the personnel providing the assistance as the factual convoys. Herein again a restriction on control rights is seen, compared to the similar provisions in humanitarian law. The experiences from humanitarian practice, where preventing delays in assistance are often crucial to the survival of those in need, have aided the developments in the law from the 1949 Geneva Conventions and their 1977 Protocols, to these more recent initiatives by the ILC.

7.5.6.2 The Potential Application of the IDRL Guidelines and Model Act

As seen above, the IDRL Guidelines follow the line of existing legal provisions with regard to the potential right to access of third parties. As such, the Guidelines do not determine that external parties providing assistance have a right to access. Indeed, the right to *offer* is not even mentioned, as the Guidelines focus on the alternative: a right of the affected state to determine access through 'consent'.[264] Yet, once consent has been provided by the affected states, the IDRL Guidelines envisage the actors involved in the provision of assistance to have certain rights, which must conversely be provided by the affected state as it has the obligation to:

> "Facilitate freedom of access to and freedom of movement in and from the disaster affected area, bearing in mind the safety of disaster relief and initial recovery personnel".[265]

Equally, although the Guidelines do not separately discuss the notion of 'transit states', such states have certain duties, which also apply to the affected state and include the duty to waive or promptly issue visas and exempt assistance from customs or other requirements and restrictions that may delay or impede its provision.[266] The Guidelines indeed are quite detailed, and Guidelines 16 and 17 also set forth specific regulations pertaining to the duties of the affected state to grant telecommunication licenses, access for vehicles and other administrative measures that may speed up and enable the process of the provision of humanitarian assistance in Guidelines 18 and 19. Lastly, although somewhat more common in circumstances of conflict and occupation, the Guidelines also call upon the affected state to take measures in the protection of those actors that they have consented to access their territory:

---

[263] ILC 'Protection of persons in the event of disasters' Draft Articles UN Doc. A/CN.4/L.831 (15 May 2014).
[264] IFRC IDRL Guidelines (2007) (n 244) Guideline 3 and 10.
[265] Ibid Guideline 16.1.d.
[266] Ibid Guideline 16.2 and Guideline 17.

> "Affected States should take appropriate measures to address the safety and security of disaster relief and initial recovery personnel of assisting States and eligible assisting humanitarian organizations and of the premises, facilities, means of transport, equipment and goods used in connection with their disaster relief or initial recovery assistance. Assisting States and assisting humanitarian organizations should also take appropriate steps in their own planning and operations to mitigate security risks".[267]

Although indeed the affected state 'should take appropriate measures' according to Guideline 22, this is not a binding obligation as seen under international humanitarian law or the discussed Security Council appeals.

The Model Act, developed by the IFRC following the Guidelines largely focuses on the practical aspects of access, once consent has been provided. Indeed, like the Guidelines themselves, the Model Act presupposes the acceptance of assistance by the affected state, prior to such actual provision while no direct right to access exists in its provisions.[268] With regard to the practicalities of the provision of assistance by third parties, the Model Act elaborates on the needs regarding aspects such as visas, customs and transportation.[269]

The non-binding nature of the Guidelines has been addressed, but it remains unfortunate that such Guidelines have not attempted to approach the topic of humanitarian access from a more forward, developing perspective, perhaps to incite positive law-making on the topic by states through the development of an international treaty. However, such an approach by the IDRL Guidelines and also by the aforementioned ILC Study aligns with states' perspectives and literature pertaining to the potential development of a legal framework for the provision of humanitarian assistance in the aftermath of a natural disaster. These perspectives commonly assert that a 'right to offer' does not equal a 'right to access'.[270] Indeed, the willingness of third parties to provide assistance does not result in (a right to) access to a territory, nor does it in and of itself indicate the existence of a (human) right for persons to receive humanitarian assistance when in need, as customary law is not created through state practice alone.[271] Yet what can be seen from these Guidelines is a willingness to move away from the exercise of too much 'control' by the affected state, once it has consented to the provision of assistance by third parties, as was also done by the ILC in its Draft Articles. Thus, a somewhat contradictory development appears to be taking place, where on the one hand states are hesitant to relinquish their sovereignty by forfeiting their sovereign right to consent, and on the other hand a recognition exists that placing too many obstacles upon approval of consent continues to delay and obstruct the factual delivery of assistance.

---

[267] Ibid Guideline 22.

[268] See in this regard Articles 7 (a-c) Model Act.

[269] Ibid Chapter VI.

[270] Focarelli, 'Duty to Protect in Cases of Natural Disasters' (n 2) § 15.

[271] Rohan J Hardcastle & Adrian T L Chua, 'Humanitarian Assistance, Towards a Right of access to victims of natural disaster', (1998) 38 *International Review of the Red Cross* 325, 599.

7.5.7 The Right to Provide Assistance under Refugee Law

Chapter 6 has provided the context that although the qualification of 'refugee' or 'IDP' is not a circumstance such as the above discussed circumstances of conflict, occupation or natural disaster, such qualifications do warrant a separate discussion, as a specific (legal) framework is applicable to refugees and IDPs.[272] The specific framework created for the particular protection of refugees and IDPs must be analysed in order to establish the potential obligation to provide assistance to such persons as in circumstances of humanitarian crisis, persons often become refugees and IDPs.

Refugee law becomes applicable in the circumstance that persons are defined as 'refugees' under the 1951 Refugee Convention.[273] Upon such establishment, the Convention itself finds applicability. With regard to the potential duty to provide assistance for third states or other actors such as organisations, the Refugee Convention is silent. Such silence logically follows from the fact that refugee law is applicable with regard to a cross-border situation whereby the 'affected state' is the state receiving the refugees. Thus, the Refugee Convention places certain obligations upon the third state that is the recipient of the refugees, rather than on the state where the refugees originated from.[274]

However, the entirety of the Refugee Convention is based upon equal treatment, and Article 23 of the Convention determines that refugees are entitled to 'public relief' in the same manner as the nationals of said state.[275] By analogy, this would mean that in the event a refugee population is present in a given state and third parties are wishing to provide assistance, such assistance must be given to both the nationals of the state and the refugee population that is present. However, such an obligation is placed by the Refugee Convention upon the affected state that has *received* the refugees. This provision of humanitarian assistance in an equal manner also aligns with the findings of the ICJ in the 2008 case concerning the Application of the International Convention on the Elimination of all Forms of Racial Discrimination (Georgia v. Russian Federation).[276]

7.5.8 The Potential Right to Access under Refugee Law

Given the limited provisions in the Refugee Convention pertaining to a potential obligation to provide aid for third parties or even a right to do so, a potential right to access derived from this is even more difficult to ascertain. In short, the Refugee

[272] Section 2.3.1 Recipients of Humanitarian Assistance.
[273] Ibid.
[274] Section 6.5.7 Duties of the Affected State under Refugee Law. See in this regard also Article 70 GC IV, with regard to the fact that refugees, prior to an outbreak of a conflict, shall be able to continue to be protected in the event the sovereign from which they sought refuge is now an occupying force and Dinstein, *The International Law of Belligerent Occupation* (n 215) 180.
[275] Section 6.5.7 Duties of the Affected State under Refugee Law.
[276] See in more detail Section 5.3 A Human Right to Receive Humanitarian Assistance in International Law?

Convention does not contain provisions from which a potential right to access a territory may be derived. This falls in line with the fact as discussed above that refugee law becomes applicable in situations where persons have moved across borders and 'access' would then occur in the third state. It stands to reason therefore that a potential right to access should have been applied to those circumstances in which the persons in need have not yet crossed the border from their country of origin where the crisis took place. On occasion, in complex situations where natural disasters and conflict coincide, or an unclear situation that enables the addressing of refugees and IDPs together, the General Assembly has called upon states to provide assistance to refugees.[277] Such calls by the General Assembly, although helpful in ascertaining the stance of states in certain specific situations, can however not be considered to indicate an existing international legal principle, nor the (imminent) development of customary international law in this regard, as they are few and far between, as well as focusing on country-specific situations. Recourse must therefore be had to other sources of international law, such as general international law, human rights law, and depending on the circumstances, also humanitarian law.

7.5.9 The Right to Provide Assistance under the (Potential) IDP Framework

As established, although refugees and IDPs are not a 'situation' like conflict or disaster, the qualification of a person as 'refugee' or 'IDP' does trigger the application of a specific set of rules, as in the abovementioned circumstances.

The only binding source of international law tailored to the provision of humanitarian assistance to IDPs is the recent Kampala Convention, applicable regionally in Africa. The Kampala Convention sets out from the perspective of the affected state, as it is the prerogative of this state to seek cooperation from the international community, according to Articles 4(3) and 5(2). Yet more forcefully, and in line with human rights law, Article 5(6) declares a duty for the affected state to reach out to external parties:

> "States Parties shall provide sufficient protection and assistance to internally displaced persons, and where available resources are inadequate to enable them to do so, they shall cooperate in seeking the assistance of international organizations and humanitarian agencies, civil society organizations and other relevant actors. Such organizations may offer their services to all those in need".

Thus, organisations may offer services, but third states are not mentioned here, save perhaps as 'other relevant actors'. In fact, the affected state has a duty to seek out humanitarian organisations, rather than also resorting to assistance from neighbouring states for example. This duty to seek international assistance appears

[277] For example UNGA Res 64/296 (13 October 2010) UN Doc A/RES/64/296 'Status of internally displaced persons and refugees from Abkhazia, Georgia, and the Tskhinvali region/South Ossetia, Georgia' §4: "Underlines the urgent need for unimpeded access for humanitarian activities to all internally displaced persons, refugees and other persons residing in all conflict-affected areas throughout Georgia".

similar to Article 2 ICESCR, calling upon international cooperation when internal resources are lacking.

From a soft law perspective, the Guiding Principles on Internal Displacement offer options with regard to the provision of humanitarian assistance to IDPs by third parties.[278] As such, Guiding Principle 25(2) declares that:

> "International humanitarian organizations and other appropriate actors have the right to offer their services in support of the internally displaced. Such an offer shall not be regarded as an unfriendly act or an interference in a State's internal affairs and shall be considered in good faith. Consent thereto shall not be arbitrarily withheld, particularly when authorities concerned are unable or unwilling to provide the required humanitarian assistance".

No obligation to provide assistance is therefore asserted: the Guiding Principles align with existing international law. The existing law indeed often considers a *right* to offer assistance whilst considering the sovereign rights of the affected state, a notion also expressed in UN context.[279] The more problematic notion of 'arbitrariness' is once again raised, without further indication as to which instances might amount to such arbitrariness. 'Arbitrary' refusal of assistance remains a rather vague notion, as it is unclear at which point a refusal is in fact 'arbitrary', especially when no specifications are provided in law as to the grounds of a potential refusal.

The work of the International Law Association (ILA) is often also considered indicative of *opinio juris*, like the Guiding Principles, despite its composition not being that of states. This status is based on the legal scholarship involved in its research, and regarding the topic at hand the ILA's Committee on Internally Displaced Persons has argued that an 'offer' to provide assistance cannot be construed as a breach of the affected state's sovereignty, as humanitarian assistance to IDPs in itself is 'justified under Articles 1(3), 13(1)(b), 55(c) and 56 of the Charter of the United Nations'.[280] This statement furthermore follows the ICJ *Nicaragua*-judgment, where the Court assessed that strictly humanitarian aid could not be construed as 'an intervention in the internal affairs' of an affected state.[281]

Indeed, from the above it is apparent that next to the duties flowing from human rights law as discussed in Section 7.3.1, the Kampala Convention provides the only binding source for external parties wishing to provide humanitarian assistance to IDPs, as they 'may offer' their assistance. The Guiding Principles remain soft law, and their embracement by many actors has unfortunately not resulted in widespread

---

[278] Section 2.3.1 Recipients of Humanitarian Assistance.

[279] For example 'Human Rights Questions: Human Rights Situations And Reports Of Special Rapporteurs And Representatives: Internally displaced persons' Note by the Secretary-General (24 October 1996) UN Doc A/51/483/Add.1 § 118.

[280] 'Report and Draft Declaration for Consideration at the 2000 Conference', Committee on Internally Displaced Persons, *International Law Association Conference* (2000) 18.

[281] Military and Paramilitary Activities in and against Nicaragua (Nicaragua v. United States of America), Merits, Judgment 27 June 1986 I.C.J. Reports 1986, p. 14 § 243.

state practice of their content in the field, as has been addressed on numerous occasions by the UN Special Rapporteur on IDPs, the Secretary General's Special Representative and the former Commission on Human Rights.[282] The General Assembly has also expressed its particular concern regarding the need for external provision of assistance to IDPs.[283] Indeed, IDPs are a category of persons increasing in number, as humanitarian crises today increasingly occur within the territory of one state; through non-international armed conflicts and (natural) disasters, whereas tailored legal protection remains absent.

7.5.10 The Potential Right to Access under the (Potential) IDP Framework

As noted in the previous Section, the existing legal framework concerning IDPs is somewhat limited, as most of the regulations are contained in soft law instruments. Yet, the regional Kampala Convention of 2009 has addressed the matter of a potential right to access, stating in Article 3(1)(j) that:

> "States Parties undertake to respect and ensure respect for the present Convention. In particular, States Parties shall: [...] ensure assistance to internally displaced persons by meeting their basic needs as well as allowing and facilitating rapid and unimpeded access by humanitarian organizations and personnel".

The Kampala Convention therefore asserts a duty of the affected state to facilitate the 'rapid and unimpeded access' of organizations for the provision of assistance, yet the Convention itself does not refer to a 'right to access'. The obligation is formulated from the perspective of the affected state. The previous Section has shown that no duty to provide assistance exists for third parties, as the affected states are responsible for seeking out assistance. The connected right to obtain access to a territory therefore becomes difficult to establish. Furthermore, the Kampala Convention declares that the principles of state sovereignty and territorial integrity must be upheld.[284] This provision is related to Article 5(7) of the Convention which stipulates in more detail the obligation of the affected state to

---

[282] Amongst others: 'Further Promotion And Encouragement Of Human Rights And Fundamental Freedoms, Including The Question Of The Programme And Methods Of Work Of The Commission on Human Rights, Mass Exoduses And Displaced Persons', Report of the Representative of the Secretary-General (28 November 1994) UN Doc E/CN.4/1995/50/Add.2 § 5; 'Further Promotion And Encouragement Of Human Rights And Fundamental Freedoms, Including The Question Of The Programme And Methods Of Work Of The Commission Human Rights, Mass Exoduses And Displaced Persons Internally displaced persons', Report of the Representative of the Secretary-General (22 February 1996) UN Doc E/CN.4/1996/52 § 415(q); HRC Res 14/6 (23 June 2010) UN Doc A/HRC/RES/14/6 § 5; 'Report of the Representative of the Secretary-General on the human rights of internally displaced persons' (21 January 2010) UN Doc A/HRC/13/21/Add.2 § 61(a); 'Report of the Representative of the Secretary-General on the human rights of internally displaced persons' (23 December 2010) UN Doc A/HRC/16/43/Add.31 § 3.

[283] UNGA Res 49/169 (23 December 1994) UN Doc A/RES/49/169 § 11.

[284] Article 5(12) African Union Kampala Convention.

allow access to those organisations they have sought out to assist in the provision of humanitarian assistance:

> "States Parties shall take necessary steps to effectively organize, relief action that is humanitarian, and impartial in character, and guarantee security. States Parties shall allow rapid and unimpeded passage of all relief consignments, equipment and personnel to internally displaced persons. States Parties shall also enable and facilitate the role of local and international organizations and humanitarian agencies, civil society organizations and other relevant actors, to provide protection and assistance to internally displaced persons. States Parties shall have the right to prescribe the technical arrangements under which such passage is permitted".

From the above, it may be derived that the Kampala Convention does foresee a large role for international humanitarian organisations, but states remain firmly in control of the initial access to a territory. Control rights thus remain a theme throughout the legal framework pertaining to the delivery of humanitarian assistance. Subsequent access however must then be swiftly provided for by states parties. Also, considering times of conflict, the Kampala Convention prescribes similar obligations for armed groups in Article 7(5)(b) and (g):

> "Members of armed groups shall be prohibited from: (b) [...] Hampering the provision of protection and assistance to internally dis- placed persons under any circumstances; (g) [...] Impeding humanitarian assistance and passage of all relief consignments, equipment and personnel to internally displaced persons".

Both in times of conflict and in other times, states parties and armed groups are obliged to refrain from attacking or 'otherwise harming' the humanitarian personnel present in the territory for the purpose of providing assistance.[285] The Kampala Convention is indeed novel in its recognition of the prohibition for armed groups and in doing so adheres to the changes in crises over the past decades.[286] Albeit only of a regional scope, the Convention thereby does address a threatened group of persons; IDPs, and provides legal duties both in times of conflict and disaster, clearly addressing both the state sovereign and armed groups. However, it does not really break new ground with regard to the potential right to access for international parties (in the Convention: organizations) that might wish to provide assistance.[287] Yet all in all, IDPs on the African continent, which is in fact prone to humanitarian crises, have enhanced and tailored protection under the Kampala Convention. This protection, given its formulation from the perspective of the affected state (and armed group) is very similar to the protection afforded by existing human rights

[285] Article 5(10) and Article 7(4)(h) African Union Kampala Convention.

[286] Schwendimann, 'The legal framework of humanitarian access in armed conflict', (n 207) 1001.

[287] See however Chapter 8 on the African Union Kampala Convention and its progressive provisions with regard to regional intervention by the African Union in the event a state does not abide by its obligations in the provision of assistance to IDPs.

law, although of course more elaborate and specific, as the entire convention is tailored towards the protection of IDPs in times of humanitarian crises.

International humanitarian law of course also considers the needs of IDPs in times of conflict besides the Kampala Convention and human rights law. In particular in today's many non-international armed conflicts, the needs of IDPs are manifest. As discussed in Chapter 6, Article 17 of AP II of the Geneva Conventions provides that persons may not be displaced, and that a responsibility lies with the affected state and parties to provide assistance.[288] The ICRC however adds rather progressively to this in its Study on Customary International Humanitarian Law that, given the difficulties many governments face in reaching IDPs for the provision of assistance, such a responsibility also entails the duty to 'permit the free passage of humanitarian assistance' to IDPs.[289] In this regard the Customary IHL Study refers to UN Security Council resolutions, and the non-binding Guiding Principles on Internal Displacement as its legal sources for this assertion.

Indeed, as discussed above in Section 7.4.2, the Security Council resolutions often assert (either under Chapter VII or without such authorisation) an obligation (by 'requesting' or 'urging') for states in specific situations to allow or facilitate the delivery of humanitarian assistance. Whether the practice of the Security Council in this regard amounts to a general norm of customary international law in the absence of other sources declaring the same, is however not as easily ascertained as the ICRC Customary Study would like to do.[290] Arguing an obligation as being part of customary international law due to the Security Council's position in this regard appears somewhat flimsy at best. Indeed, the stance of the Council contributes to, and is indicative of, both state practice and *opinio juris*, but in and of itself cannot be considered to affirmatively reach such a status. This is particularly the case as the Council has mostly asserted such a position in country-specific resolutions rather than thematic resolutions. The ICRC Customary IHL Study proceeds to argue that the Security Council practice also indicates that in the event the displacement of persons was not lawful, the provision of assistance by the international community shall remain lawful.[291] Whilst such an argument may be reasonable, this cannot however be deduced from these Security Council resolutions pertaining to the potential obligation of states (or in some instances other parties to a conflict) to provide access to actors providing assistance. Indeed, an illegality of the provision of assistance in itself would not logically flow from an illegal displacement of persons. More often than not, the actual need for provision of assistance – in a humanitarian crisis – follows an unlawful displacement of

---

[288] 6.5.1.2 Duties of the Affected State and Non-State Actor in Times of a Non-International Armed Conflict and Article 17 AP II.

[289] Henckaerts & Doswald-Beck, ICRC Customary International Humanitarian Law Study (n 149), Rule 131 (Treatment of Displaced Persons).

[290] Ibid. The Customary Study refers in its footnote 27 to Security Council Resolutions 688, 999, 1010, 1019, 1034, 1078 , 1097 and 1120, most of which are discussed in Sections 7.4.1 and 7.4.2 . For the criteria to establish a rule of customary international law, see 1.4.1.

[291] Henckaerts & Doswald-Beck, ICRC Customary International Humanitarian Law Study (n 149), Rule 131 (Treatment of Displaced Persons).

persons, or persons displaced due to circumstances such as natural disasters. As such for example, the Geneva Conventions' Protocols also indicate that offers of assistance shall not be viewed as unlawful interference in a state or an unfriendly act in that regard, echoed by the ICJ in its 1986 *Nicaragua* judgment.[292] This perspective is also reflected in the Guiding Principles on Internal Displacement and supported in literature regarding circumstances of natural disaster.[293]

These Guiding Principles, although non-binding in their nature provide additional guidance to actors in the field.[294] Whereas the previous Section discussed the right to offer assistance as laid down in the Guiding Principles, these Principles also express that although the affected state has the right to 'consent' to the offer of assistance and may therefore determine which assistance enters into the territory, once such consent is provided:

> "All authorities concerned shall grant and facilitate the free passage of humanitarian assistance and grant persons engaged in the provision of such assistance rapid and unimpeded access to the internally displaced".[295]

Thus, the Guiding Principles follow the reasoning which by now has indeed become indicative of the current international legal perspective: although the affected state has the right to determine who enters a certain territory, it must indeed facilitate the rapid and free passage of personnel and convoys for the provision of assistance. The Guiding Principles proceed to express that such personnel and convoys must be respected and protected and may therefore not be attacked.[296] Furthermore, Principle 24(2) declares that the affected state may not divert emergency aid to IDPs, 'in particular for political or military reasons'.

Although the Guiding Principles are embraced by many relevant actors in the field, amongst which many UN organs, the current lack of binding legal obligations resting upon states in the allowance of access for the provision of humanitarian assistance remains problematic. The ILA has in this regard asserted that an obligation rests upon the 'international community to provide humanitarian assistance to IDPs under the Charter of the United Nations'.[297] Such an assertion could indeed find a basis in Articles 55 and 56 of the UN Charter, especially in consideration of Article 2 ICESCR. Yet, state practice continues to be lacking, as

---

[292] Article 70(1) AP I; and Military and Paramilitary Activities in and against Nicaragua (Nicaragua v. United States of America), Merits, Judgment 27 June 1986 I.C.J. Reports 1986, p. 14 § 242-243.
[293] 'Report of the Representative of the Secretary-General, Mr. Francis M. Deng, submitted pursuant to Commission resolution 1997/39', Addendum 'Guiding Principles on Internal Displacement' (Guiding Principles on IDPs) (11 February 1998) UN Doc E/CN.4/1998/53/Add.2 Principle 25(2); and amongst others Plattner, 'ICRC neutrality and neutrality in humanitarian assistance' (n 161) 177 and Vukas, 'Humanitarian Assistance in Cases of Emergency' (n 14) § 22. Also in this regard ILA 'Report and Draft Declaration for Consideration at the 2000 Conference' (n 280) 18.
[294] Section 2.3.1 Recipients of Humanitarian Assistance.
[295] Guiding Principles on Internal Displacement' (11 February 1998) UN Doc E/CN.4/1998/53/Add.2 (n 293) Principle 25(3).
[296] Ibid Principle 26s.
[297] ILA 'Report and Draft Declaration for Consideration at the 2000 Conference' (n 280) 18.

stressed by the UN Secretary General's Special Representative on IDPs in his work in this regard.[298] Within the UN framework, although not addressing the matter as an outright obligation, the General Assembly has further on more than one occasion addressed the need for improved access to IDPs, as has the ILC's Special Rapporteur on the study into the protection of persons in the event of disasters.[299] Such calls for more state practice to allow access for humanitarian purposes have also previously been made by the former Human Rights Commission.[300] Although contributing to the general *opinio juris* on the matter, a distinct right to access cannot be distinguished. Indeed, the fact that such right is lacking, can be related to the general lack of a binding international legal framework tailored to IDPs, with the exception of those falling within the scope of the Kampala Convention. Outside of the African continent, IDPs must continue to resort to other existing legal frameworks, in particular that of human rights law.

7.6 Ascertaining the Legal Framework in a Humanitarian Crisis

The above Sections have established the current legal framework for third parties such as states or international organisations to provide humanitarian assistance and gain access, according to particular fields of law. However, from a more practical perspective, an assessment must take place in which factual circumstances the

[298] Amongst others: UN Doc E/CN.4/1996/52/Add.2 (n 284) § 415(q); 'Report of the Representative of the Secretary-General on internally displaced persons' 'Conference On Internal Displacement In The Inter-Governmental Authority On Development (Igad) Subregion, Experts' Meeting' (17 February 2004) UN Doc E/CN.4/2004/77/Add.4 § 33; 'Report of the Representative of the Secretary-General on the human rights of internally displaced persons' (23 December 2005) UN Doc E/CN.4/2006/71/Add.1 § 45; 'Promotion And Protection Of All Human Rights, Civil, Political, Economic, Social And Cultural, Including The Right To Development: Rights of peoples, and specific groups and individuals', Report of the Representative of the Secretary-General on the human rights of internally displaced persons (24 April 2008) UN Doc A/HRC/8/6 § 83; 'Report Of The Representative Of The Secretary-General On The Human Rights Of Internally Displaced Persons' (21 May 2008) UN Doc A/HRC/8/6/Add.4 § 87; 'Report of the Representative of the Secretary-General on the human rights of internally displaced persons' (21 January 2010) UN Doc A/HRC/13/21/Add.2 § 61(b); 'Report of the Representative of the Secretary-General on the human rights of internally displaced persons' (23 December 2010) UN Doc A/HRC/16/43/Add.3l § 3.

[299] Amongst others in this regard the General Assembly's calls in: UNGA Res 56/164 (19 December 2001) UN Doc A/RES/56/164 'Protection of and assistance to internally displaced persons' § 10; UNGA Res 58/177 (22 December 2003) UN Doc A/RES/58/177 § 11; UNGA Res 62/153 (6 March 2008) UN Doc A/RES/62/153, 'Protection of and assistance to internally displaced persons' § 15; UNGA Res 64/162 (17 March 2010) UN Doc A/RES/64/162 'Protection of and assistance to internally displaced persons' § 16; and UNGA Res 64/296 (13 October 2010) UN Doc A/RES/64/296 § 4. See also the ILC's Special Rapporteur as phrased in ILC 'Preliminary report on the protection of persons in the event of disasters' UN Doc A/CN.4/598 (n 194) § 49.

[300] Commission on Human Rights Res 1999/S-4/1 (27 September 1999) UN Doc. 1999/S-4/1 'Situation of human rights in East Timor' § 1,3,5; Commission on Human Rights Res 2001/54 (24 April 2001) UN Doc E/CN.4/RES/2001/54 § 12; Commission on Human Rights Res 2000/53, (25 April 2000) UN Doc E/CN.4/RES/2000/53 § 11; Commission on Human Rights Res 2003/52 (24 April 2003) UN Doc E/CN.4/RES/2003/52 § 7-8.

provision of humanitarian assistance by parties outside the affected state are most fully developed.

In determining the applicable law in a given instance therefore, it may be relevant to take into account multiple bodies of law that might be applicable simultaneously and may provide different levels of protection dependent on the particular circumstances. In this research into the legal framework in times of humanitarian crises, the perspective is held that the provision of humanitarian assistance warrants an all-encompassing approach. This perspective is based on the position that persons in need of humanitarian aid should be able to receive this aid regardless of the particular circumstance (conflict, occupation or (natural) disaster) that was the origin of their need for assistance. It is in fact the perspective of this research that the determination of a humanitarian crisis itself warrants the provision of emergency aid. A humanitarian crisis is then the determining factor, as opposed to the underlining circumstance, leading to a more equal protection of persons by law. The more harmonious approach taken in this research with regard to the *lex specialis* principle also allows for a focus to lay on gap-filling methods in the applicable *corpora juris*, as well as the prevalence of specific provisions of a certain body of law as opposed to an entire body of law prevailing over another.[301] Thus, the *lex specialis* is the more detailed *provision*, whilst the *lex generalis* remains present as a body of law in the background for application if necessary. In this manner, persons in need of humanitarian assistance can rely on the most protective clause at any given time, resulting in the greatest protection in times of a humanitarian crisis.

In determining the applicable law in a situation of crisis, one can safely establish that general international law remains applicable. Therefore, the obligations or rights which may be derived from the concept of state sovereignty do not alter in times of crisis, but are a constant in international law, as the notion of state sovereignty itself is a continuous factor.[302] Human rights law also retains its applicability throughout circumstances of crisis. Furthermore, the UN the Security Council resolutions are relevant, but confine themselves to circumstances that meet the threshold of a threat to the peace. In a similar fashion international humanitarian law is applicable solely in times of (non-) international armed conflict or occupation, with its particular specificities for each of these (and more) detailed circumstances.[303] It remains relevant therefore to ascertain *all* the provisions of these bodies of law in the establishment of the exact rights and obligations in the external provision of humanitarian assistance in times of conflict, occupation and natural disaster. Through such an establishment, the most protective clauses will become apparent, as will the gaps in protection by the law.

---

[301] 3.4.3 Hierarchy or Convergence of International Legal Norms?.

[302] See in more detail Section 4.2.3.3.

[303] For examples of such circumstances within the various types of conflicts or occupation: Dinstein, 'The Right to Humanitarian Assistance' (n 72) 80.

7.6.1 The Applicable Lex Specialis in Armed Conflict

From the above it has become apparent that in times of armed conflict, the general fields of law remain applicable. Thus, the rights and duties derived from state sovereignty continue to exist, but unfortunately do not provide clear-cut rights or duties for third parties in the provision of assistance. In fact, state sovereignty does not provide indications of potential rights to provide assistance, nor a right to access for the provision of such assistance. Within the UN framework however, the Security Council has over the past decades progressively taken a stronger stance pertaining to situations that amount to 'threats to the peace', culminating in the Council's requirement under Chapter VII of states to assist in the provision of assistance to persons in need in Iraq in 2003.[304] It must be reiterated that these calls are not to be construed as calls for access by means of force. For now, this call appears to be one of the most forward of the Security Council resolutions to date: a culmination of the 'urges' and 'requests' it has made in prior years. Following the situation in Iraq, the Council has not reiterated such language, and 'encouraged' the international community to act. However, with a rather novel approach, the Security Council has called upon third parties to provide assistance in Syria without referencing the consent of the Syrian authorities. Therefore, at this moment it remains to be seen in what way the Council will proceed with future country-situations. Given the political nature of the body, it must be noted that although the Council has found grounds to oblige states to provide humanitarian assistance in the past, such an obligation does not exist in each circumstance for which the Council passes a resolution concerning the provision of assistance. Therefore, as a minimum common standard or threshold in the Council's approach cannot be deduced, it is not possible to determine indisputably that the Council perceives an obligation to provide assistance for third parties. Following on from this, a potential right to access is difficult to ascertain. Yet, conversely, the Council has repeatedly issued resolutions (including resolutions under Chapter VII) calling and urging the affected state to facilitate and allow immediate 'unhindered delivery' of assistance and 'safe access'. In such country-specific situations therefore, it can be concluded that the Council presupposes a willingness of the international community to offer aid and asserts a case-specific right in this regard, when adopting such resolutions under Chapter VII and using the well-known stringent wording such as 'demanding' the 'ensuring' of unimpeded safe access of assistance and personnel.[305]

A similar approach can be seen in the resolutions of the General Assembly, as it indeed views a need for international assistance, but falls short of declaring an existing duty under international law to provide such assistance.[306] Indeed, the General Assembly often surpasses this phase and focuses on the need to allow access but does not particularly address the needs of a conflict situation, although it

---

304 7.4.2 Security Council Resolutions and the Right to Access.

305 Ibid.

306 7.4.3 General Assembly Resolutions and the Right to Offer Assistance.

does address more complex situations than natural disasters alone. From the wording of the General Assembly's resolutions it can be deduced that this principal organ follows a similar approach to the Security Council and often also similar vocabulary, reiterating the importance of access in the provision of assistance, but through its emphasis on the consent of the affected state, the General Assembly falls short of declaring such a right to access to exist, and as such, the Security Council's resolutions may be a more sound basis for such a claim, in a specific instance of armed conflict.

Looking then to international humanitarian law's application to international armed conflicts, Article 10 GC IV formulates a 'right to offer' for international humanitarian organisations, complemented by Article 70(1) AP I that declares assistance 'shall' be provided, in the event the population is inadequately supplied. Such wording notes the obligatory character that AP II ascribes to the provision of assistance, which includes the external provision of such aid. However, control rights continue to exist for the affected state, and uncertainty exists as to the determination of when an affected territory is 'inadequately supplied'. In situations of non-international armed conflicts, Common Article 3 merely provides that international organisations have a subsidiary role as they 'may' offer assistance, thus providing very little solid protection for those persons affected by crises in times of non-international armed conflicts falling outside the scope of AP II and those in which the affected state is not party to the Protocol. Article 18 AP II adds that in the event the local population is suffering 'undue hardship', humanitarian assistance 'shall' be provided. It remains somewhat unclear however who the addressee of this obligation is; either the affected state or the non-state actor exercising control over a particular territory within the state. Whilst according to Article 18 AP II consent of the affected state remains necessary, it does provide a minimum degree of protection as it must be read conjointly with Article 14 AP II concerning the prohibition of starvation as a method of warfare.

As discussed, human rights law contains many specific provisions for the affected state, but this is not the case concerning the provision of assistance by third parties. This circumstance flows from the concept of the law itself, viewing the affected state as primary duty-bearer. From existing human rights law, no duty or potential right to provide assistance is found in relation to the human right to life, food, health (and water). Equally, the potential right to access cannot be discerned in such a way in current existing human rights law. Despite tentative remarks from EU and UN organs, most states and other international actors remain hesitant in acknowledging a right to access based upon human rights law, as in general the state (or actor claiming sovereignty over a territory) is considered the duty-bearer in this field of law.

If then the right to provide assistance (and related right to access) is not viewed from the perspective of the third party, but from the duty of the affected state, possibilities arise. Indeed, the ICJ *did* determine in the case concerning the Application of the International Convention on the Elimination of all Forms of Racial Discrimination (Georgia v. Russian Federation) that both parties had an obligation under the ICERD to allow access for humanitarian aid. Thus, the Court determined such an obligation to exist in times of armed conflict under human rights law, rather than under humanitarian law. Furthermore, such a duty aligns with the structure of the ICESCR as codified in Article 2 ICESCR (as intended in Article 56 UN Charter). Yet such a duty is not definitively asserted within the Convention, and remains the interpretation of the CESCR in particular relating to the right to food in Article 11. Indeed, the Additional Protocol to the ACHR also recognises such obligations resting upon states to cooperate in Article 12. A potential responsibility for third parties may therefore arguably be emerging but, importantly, an existing *duty to allow access and request assistance* can be discerned for the affected state (or acting authority) under current human rights law. This duty flows from its obligations to fulfil the rights to life, food and health as sovereign, for which the provision of humanitarian assistance functions as a vehicle.

It has been concluded that the Kampala Convention also determines that the affected state (in Africa) has the obligation under Article 5(6) to seek the assistance of third parties in the provision of assistance to IDPs, rather than acknowledging an obligation to provide for third parties. The Convention furthermore asserts under Article 3(1)(j) that the affected state has a duty to facilitate access, which is elaborated in Article 5(7), although no direct right to access is mentioned. Specifically geared towards armed groups, the Kampala Convention considers in Article 7(5)(b) and (g) that armed groups are to refrain from attacking or harming humanitarian personnel. Whereas the Kampala Convention follows the approach taken by humanitarian law in the need for consent from the affected sovereign, it does limit the control rights seen in humanitarian law by asserting a need for facilitation of access.

From the above discussion it is apparent that not only international humanitarian law contains certain detailed provisions pertaining to the potential duty to provide or right to access a territory in order to ensure the provision of humanitarian assistance in times of conflict and therefore this body of law as a whole cannot be considered a *lex specialis*. Indeed, the Kampala Convention, Article 2 ICESCR and the Security Council resolutions, when adopted under Chapter VII of the UN Charter and geared towards a country-specific situation also declare obligations under international law. Rather than focusing on the duties of third parties, these treaties focus on the duties of the affected authorities in *allowing access* to those third parties that have proven willing to provide assistance. These obligations must be read jointly with a harmonious approach, in order to establish the greatest protection of persons in the provision of assistance. In practice, at times more security can therefore be found in the provisions outside humanitarian law.

7.6.2 The Applicable Lex Specialis in Occupation

Similar to armed conflict, general international law and its considerations concerning state sovereignty remain applicable in circumstances of occupation, yet they do not contain specific rights or duties pertaining to the provision of aid from external sources. Furthermore as is the case in armed conflict, the Security Council resolutions provide a guideline to possibly consider the provision of assistance by the international community as an obligation, depending on the wording of these resolutions and whether or not such a call for assistance is made under Chapter VII. The General Assembly follows suit, but does not particularly focus on circumstances of occupation, thereby not providing guidelines in this regard.

Specific to circumstances of occupation, whereas human rights law maintains its applicability, the existence of a level of effective 'authority' or 'control' is more difficult to establish extraterritorially in times of occupation and continues to be a debated topic within international law.[307] Such difficulties arise particularly concerning the obligations of conduct as enshrined in the ICESCR. As seen above in the previous Section, international human rights law does not acknowledge a potential right to access a territory based on the existing framework relating to the right to life, food, health or water, which would then be equally lacking for an occupied territory. However Article 2 ICESCR and Article 55 and 56 UN Charter do call upon the international community to cooperate in the fulfilment of human rights. Thus, with regard to circumstances of occupation, a case-specific determination of the level of control is necessary to determine whether or not certain rights can be applied extraterritorially to the occupying force, or whether their fulfilment lies with a different authority.

From a regional perspective, the Kampala Convention may be of relevance. Whilst applying this Convention *mutatis mutandis* to a situation of occupation may appear reasonable given the potential for IDPs in such circumstances, the Convention itself does not mention such possibilities, therefore not providing that the affected state should automatically be assumed to be the occupying power. However, from the formulations of obligations in the Kampala Convention, that uses 'Member State' of the African Union, it follows that a Member State of the African Union that becomes an occupying power, shall continue to be obliged to abide by the provisions of the Convention. Thus, with regard to IDPs it is relevant to note that the Kampala Convention determines that the affected state has the obligation under Article 5(6) to seek the assistance of third parties in the provision of aid. The Convention does not acknowledge an independent obligation to provide assistance for third parties. The Convention furthermore states under Article 3(1)(j) that the affected state has a duty to facilitate access, which is elaborated in Article 5(7) although the Convention does not mention a direct right to access.

Additionally, the Geneva Conventions applicable in times of occupation contain many specific provisions relating to the delivery of aid from external sources, the main provision being Article 59 GC IV stipulating that the occupier must agree to relief schemes, and facilitate them, thereby providing not only a right to provide assistance, but also considering a potential right to access a territory. Although the latter is not affirmatively mentioned, it is one of the most far-reaching provisions in the Convention concerning access. The limitations on the occupier in the

[307] See the more elaborate discussion in 3.4.2.2.

determination of 'control rights' attest to this, while the occupying force maintains the right to ascertain the allowance of passage for each convoy. However, the Additional Protocol refers to the application of Article 71 AP I, applicable in times of armed conflict, which in fact enhances the control rights of the occupying power. The most extensive obligations can be concluded *vis-à-vis* the protecting power in Articles 55 and 61 GC IV, an actor that currently no longer holds much relevance in the field. Also, the occupying power has the obligation under Article 63 GC IV to allow humanitarian organisations already within a territory to continue their activities. This provision today may indeed be useful in practice, as most states have active Red Cross Societies.

7.6.3 The Applicable Lex Specialis in Times of (Natural) Disaster

Lastly, as has been discussed above, no particular legal framework exists pertaining to the delivery of aid in times of natural disaster and recourse must therefore be had to general international law for resources.

Security Council resolutions, which can be of a binding nature as discussed above, have not concerned situations of natural disaster, instead focusing on circumstances that have amounted to a threat to the peace. Although non-binding in character and thereby not amounting to hard law, the General Assembly resolutions do follow the line taken by the Security Council resolutions and *have* considered situations of natural disaster. Falling short of a determination that an external duty to provide assistance exists under international law, the General Assembly does ascertain a *need for external international assistance*, which may be applied to natural disaster circumstances. Through its resolutions, the General Assembly mostly surpasses this initial need for an offer of assistance, focusing on the need for states to allow access to a territory. Yet here too, the Assembly falls short of determining a right to access to exist for third parties, as it emphasises the need for consent of the affected state. In this manner, the approach taken in circumstances of conflict by the Security Council, is echoed.

With no specific body of law in place to regulate circumstances of natural disaster, recourse must be had to another more generally applicable body of law: human rights law. From the above discussions pertaining to human rights law, the determination can be made that the rights to life, food, health (and water) do not provide a basis for a potential external duty to provide assistance or a related right to access. Yet, as in circumstances of conflict and occupation, Articles 2 ICESCR and 56 UN Charter apply and envisage international cooperation in the fulfilment of human rights. Support for this position may also be found regionally through Article 12 of the Additional Protocol to the ACHR. Indeed, this perspective aligns with the duty of the affected state under existing human rights law to provide humanitarian aid as a vehicle in the fulfilment of the rights to life, food and health, which includes requesting international assistance to this end.

Regional and topical developments have taken place specifically concerning disaster situations, culminating amongst others in the provisions of the Inter-

American Convention To Facilitate Disaster Assistance, which presupposes an offer of assistance in Article I(b) and II(b), as well as determining that a right to access cannot be considered as the affected state maintains the right to 'accept' an offer according to Article II, and thereby retains full consent. Furthermore, the regional ASEAN Agreement on Disaster Management and Emergency Response also provides in Articles 11 and 12 that the affected state shall have control with regard to the consent to and provision of assistance. However, Article 4(c) determines a duty to promptly respond to the request by an affected state, upon which according to Article 8 states have the duty to coordinate joint emergency response operations amongst themselves. The Convention on Assistance in the Case of a Nuclear Accident or Radiological Emergency distinctly places the control over access to a territory for the purpose of the provision of aid at the hands of the request for international assistance of the affected state. Pertaining to the right to access, the Inter-American Convention determines in Article 5 that the affected state, once accepting the offer of assistance, shall fully facilitate the access and freedom of movement of the suppliers within its territory, which is equally determined in Articles Article 3(1) and 11(2) of the ASEAN Agreement. Also from a regional perspective, the Kampala Convention stipulates that the affected state is obligated under Article 5(6) to seek the assistance of third parties in the provision of aid to IDPs. The Convention however does not recognise an independent obligation to provide humanitarian aid for external parties, nor does it recognise a right to access. The Kampala Convention conversely determines in Article 3(1)(j) that the affected state has an obligation to facilitate access, which is elaborated in Article 5(7). Thus, the newer, regional developments tailored towards more specific circumstances attempt to limit the control rights of the affected state in order to enhance the facilitation of assistance.

This Section has dealt with the *lex lata* in circumstances of natural disaster, inevitably concluding that not much all-encompassing tailored *lex lata* in this area exists, resulting in dependency on somewhat more general frameworks such as existing human rights law and regional developments. Although the ILC's Draft Articles on 'Protection of persons in the event of disasters' and the IDRL Guidelines are indicative of *opinio juris* as discussed in Section 7.5.6 and thus of the current potential developments in customary international law, they are not hard law, and can therefore not be considered within this Section. The same holds for the Guiding Principles on Internal Displacement, which, although they find great support within the UN system, currently remain soft law.

7.6.4 Determining the Problems and Gaps in the Provision of Humanitarian Assistance

The previous Section concerning the various specific circumstances in which the provision of humanitarian assistance is needed has shown that, although numerous detailed provisions exist in the determination of the rights and duties for third parties involved in the provision of assistance, many gaps, uncertainties and problems also remain in the current legal framework. The various rights and duties for external parties offering assistance vary greatly depending on the circumstances in which these parties find themselves, rather than being dependent on the fact that the constant variable is the need of persons in crisis to receive food, water, shelter and medical aid.

In times of international armed conflict, many *corpora juris* are applicable, including international humanitarian law and human rights law. Furthermore, Security Council resolutions dealing with country-specific situations may result in the application of specific measures over the years. Thus, a level of protection could be obtained in such circumstances, as well as in times of occupation, that may outreach the level of protection for those in need of assistance during a non-international armed conflict; in particular a non-international armed conflict not governed by AP II. The protection offered through Security Council involvement – which can occur in times of non-international armed conflict – also outreaches that of the protection often provided in the aftermath of a natural disaster, as the Council only considers circumstances amounting to a threat to the peace.

The above Sections furthermore display that human rights law does not grant the same amount of possibilities to external parties for the protection of persons, as it does in the relationship between the affected state and the persons in need of assistance. This is explained by the fact that the body of law is tailored to the relationship between citizens and the affected state as duty-bearer, but does have negative practical consequences. Yet, human rights law as a body of law *does* in fact require the affected state to take far-reaching steps in the fulfilment of the rights to life, food and health (through the provision of assistance) which includes seeking international assistance. Conversely, international cooperation is required of states parties to the ICESCR and the UN member states. This body of law maintains applicability in times of a humanitarian crisis, resulting in a base-level of protection for all persons in need of emergency aid regardless of the specific circumstance or continent they find themselves on.

Furthermore, the Kampala Convention, although adding to the enhanced protection of IDPs regionally in Africa, lays bare the fact that the risk of fragmentation of the law is ever-present, as it only grants protection to those IDPs that fall within its scope on the continent of Africa. IDPs as a whole throughout the world, however, are an increasingly larger group in need of assistance, and should not be left behind.

In addition to such results flowing from the previous Sections, several issues in particular remain outstanding. Where the rights-holders and the duty-bearers with regard to the provision of assistance were clear in the previous Chapter, such is not necessarily the case in the event one turns to the provision of aid by third parties. Both third states and international organisations may be involved, and their rights and duties vary greatly depending on the particular legal regime that may be applicable. For example, international humanitarian law often either places emphasis on the role of the ICRC or does not explicate its addressee, while the Security Council mostly demands and urges action from its Member States. Thus, such disparities make it difficult to ascertain a *general* right-holder or duty-bearer, in the provision of assistance from external sources. Such holds true both regarding a potential duty to provide assistance, as regarding a potential right to access for such provision. While indeed the common denominator is that the provision of assistance must remain neutral, impartial and humane, both organisations and states can in essence fulfil these criteria. Arguing that fulfilling these criteria creates an obligation upon states to accept assistance, limiting their use of 'sovereignty' as a shield against such external assistance, or arguing that such neutral offering strengthens a claim by civilians against their sovereign to allow passage has certainly been done.[308] Similarly, the ICJ has argued that such an offer cannot be construed as interference in the domestic affairs of the affected state.[309] Yet, the incorporation of this duty of the affected state to allow access into international *practice* is lacking.

At the same time and very much related to this, the political aspects of the provision of assistance by external parties cannot be neglected, such as the resistance of affected states to accept assistance from countries they may not wish to enter into relations with.[310] Such resistance may result in the stalling of aid by means of the 'control rights' the affected state has in many instances, or putting up other barriers. Such rights are not a (legal) refusal of aid *per se*, but may be setting up practical barriers that constitute an abuse of the sovereigns' legal rights. Examples spring to mind, such as the situations in the Sudan, Zimbabwe, and Ethiopia or Rwanda.

Another unclear aspect of the rights-holder or duty-bearer –ship when considering external duties and rights, is the aspect of 'vicinity', as many provisions discussed in the above Sections recognise a duty of third states to allow the 'transit' of assistance, thereby placing an obligation upon neighbouring countries that do not rest upon other third states. Such responsibilities have also been asserted within UN context in relation to the 'overflow' of internal crises to neighbouring countries and

[308] Amongst others Dinstein, 'The Right to Humanitarian Assistance' (n 72) 79; Hardcastle & Chua, 'Humanitarian Assistance, Towards a Right of access to victims of natural disaster' (n 271) 604.

[309] Military and Paramilitary Activities in and against Nicaragua (Nicaragua v. United States of America), Merits, Judgment 27 June 1986 I.C.J. Reports 1986, p. 14 § 242-243.

[310] For certain examples of North-Korea regarding its famine in the 1990s, the United States with regard to hurricane Katrina in 2005 and Myanmar concerning cyclone Nargis in 2008: Focarelli, 'Duty to Protect in Cases of Natural Disasters' (n 2) § 17. See furthermore ILC 'Sixty-fourth session (second part) Provisional summary record of the 3138th meeting Held at the Palais des Nations, Geneva' (2 August 2012) UN Doc A/CN.4/SR.3138, 13: "During the Commission's deliberations on the topic at its sixty-third session, Mr. Dugard had referred to Myanmar as an example of a State that had withheld consent – arguing in effect for a duty to accept assistance. His own research in international news websites had confirmed that the Myanmar Government had provided reasons for not accepting assistance from United States, French and United Kingdom warships and had insisted on the right to distribute aid itself, as mentioned by Mr. Murase earlier. Could that be considered as arbitrarily withholding consent? The issue was about who provided assistance and under what conditions, and not whether those conditions were accepted. To insist on a duty to provide assistance would require the Commission to address the issue, and he was doubtful that it was in a position to do so. It was certainly not an issue that could be resolved through the commentaries."

the responsibilities that may rest upon such states.[311] Yet, does such a neighbouring location also stretch towards a greater duty to provide assistance, considering the close location to the crisis-area? Or conversely, should a greater obligation rest upon states or organisations with more economic resources or possibilities to act? Alternatively, an argument may be sought to allow access for international organisations at an earlier stage than states, as sovereignty issues may play a lesser role should an organisation wish to provide assistance rather than another sovereign entity. Such lack of clarity in combination with uncertainties in the law address the poignant fact that the legal framework concerning the provision of humanitarian assistance from external sources is in need of greater development, regardless of the factual circumstance of provision amounting to the humanitarian crisis.

Indeed, this is also the case regarding the rights and obligations in the delivery of humanitarian assistance in the event a sovereign may be lacking, such as in 'failed' states. The above Sections have addressed a variety of rights and duties to provide assistance or possibly obtain access to a territory, but the law invariably presupposes the presence of a sovereign in the affected territory (on occasion considering armed groups as the responsible party) as the rights-holder or duty-bearer of the granting of consent to the external party. Yet, what to assert in circumstances such as a failed state? Or circumstances of protracted armed conflict where various parties claim to be the rightful sovereign? Or a potential circumstance that no effective authority exists in the aftermath of a disaster? The potential need for assistance raises the 'critical question' as to whether or not consent is withheld.[312] The current legal framework on the provision of humanitarian assistance does not distinctly provide for the manner in which to proceed with assistance in such circumstances. Merely the Commentary to Article AP II asserts that in the event a lack of clarity exists as to the concerned authorities, consent must be presupposed.[313] This stance, however, is not agreed upon in practice.

Yet another issue that remains to be addressed is the consequence of the disparity between on the one hand the legal and factual practice of 'consent' of the affected state which is necessary to initiate access, and on the other hand the wording of the legal provisions in certain treaties or Security Council resolutions, instructing near obligations to provide assistance to third states by the use of 'shall' or 'demand'.[314] Such disparity results in potential problems with the neutrality and

---

311 'Specific Groups And Individuals: Mass Exoduses And Displaced Persons' Report of the Representative of the Secretary-General UN Doc E/CN.4/2002/95/Add.3 (10 December 2001) § 13: "[...]However, responsibility must also be apportioned to countries of the region affected by the overflow of internal crises and to the international community, which is needed to play a supporting role as the ultimate guarantor of universal human rights and humanitarian standard".

312 Focarelli, 'Duty to Protect in Cases of Natural Disasters' (n 2) §16.

313 Sandoz, Swinarski & Zimmermann *Commentary to the Additional Protocols* (n 155) Protocol II Article 18, 1479.

314 'Further Promotion And Encouragement Of Human Rights And Fundamental Freedoms, Including The Question Of The Programme And Methods Of Work Of The Commission Human Rights, Mass Exoduses And Displaced Persons: Internally displaced persons', Report of the Representative of the Secretary-General (2 February 1995) UN Doc E/CN.4/1995/50 § 112.

impartiality principles to which providers of assistance must adhere. In particular the recent action of the Security Council concerning the provision of assistance in Syria highlights this tension, where the provision of assistance was instructed without the consent of Syrian authorities, but was also not under Chapter VII.[315]

Although an inability might exist to determine whether or not a hard *obligation* exists to provide assistance and a related right to access therefore through external sources, an obligation of the affected state to, upon consent, *allow safe and unimpeded passage without the abuse of control rights* can be discerned. Barber has proffered that the affected state may indeed have the obligation to create an environment in which it is possible to provide assistance 'effectively and safely' to those in need.[316] Such an environment would – upon state consent – allow third states and international organisations to act upon the calls that may be heard in international law to provide assistance. This duty would furthermore also align with the affected states' duties to seek international assistance in their fulfilment of the existing human rights that are relevant to the provision of humanitarian assistance.

Finally, as has been discussed in Chapter 6, the problems arising in the event of a complex emergency have to date not properly been addressed with regard to the legal framework in place for the external provision of assistance. The existing and continued fragmentation of the law, addressing either specific circumstances such as conflict or occupation on the one hand, or a particular region such as the continent of Africa on the other hand, consolidates and amplifies the problems and gaps that exist. Harmonisation will in the very least attempt to ensure an equal and level playing field for those actors willing to provide assistance regardless of the circumstances the persons in need may find themselves in. It is for this precise reason that this research takes an all-encompassing approach to the provision of assistance, to ensure the utmost protection of persons, regardless of their circumstances.

7.7 Conclusion

This Chapter has addressed and discussed two distinct, but interrelated aspects of the provision of humanitarian assistance through third parties: a potential right or duty to provide assistance and a potential right to access, to enable such provision. The current state of the law however is not unambiguous or crystallised. From the above Chapter, it becomes apparent that the legal rights and obligations concerning both the provision of assistance and access to a territory are dependent on a variety of circumstances and a variety of bodies of law. As the above Section pertaining to the current problems and gaps in the legal framework has addressed, it is *not* possible to speak of a 'general' right or duty to provide assistance, *nor* is there a 'general' right to access. Indeed, in certain circumstances third states may be obliged to provide assistance, such as upon a demand from the Security Council

[315] UNSC 2165 (14 July 2014) UN Doc S/RES/2165 § 2.
[316] Barber, 'Facilitating humanitarian assistance in international humanitarian and human rights law', (n 91) 372.

under Chapter VII of the UN Charter, or regionally upon such a demand under the Kampala Convention. Other codifications proclaiming that humanitarian assistance 'shall' be provided, such as the Geneva Conventions, do so without a clear determination of the duty-bearer. Such duties are furthermore restricted through the control rights of the affected authority, existing to various degrees in the most common circumstances amounting to a crisis.

On certain occasions, UN organs might be called upon to comply with a need to provide assistance through resolutions of the General Assembly or Security Council that are lacking binding force. In such instances, the 'duty' to do so is difficult to ascertain. Also in relation to this, state consent and related sovereignty issues continue to play a relevant role and remain unresolved in the current legal framework. Such a need for consent is directly related to the possibility of ascertaining the existence of a right to access; the presence of the latter is in fact impeded by the very existence of the affected states' right to consent. Consent as a threshold for the legality of the provision of assistance is not necessarily problematic *per se*, if such consent is clearly and legally delimited. Such demarcation does however not exist within the legal framework of the provision of humanitarian assistance, as the notion of 'arbitrary refusal' of consent is not clearly delimited, nor has it been established which actor should determine whether or not a certain refusal of consent has been arbitrary.

Yet despite such gaps or lacunae in protection, the current legal framework *does* offer a variety of provisions pertaining to the provision of aid through external sources. General international law, through the notion of state sovereignty, the thematic resolutions of the Security Council and the addressing of the matter in General Assembly resolutions that declare humanitarian assistance a shared responsibility of the international community, all provide an indication that indeed the international community is committed to the provision of humanitarian assistance. As also asserted by the ICJ, indeed the sole provision of aid in itself cannot be a violation of international law. Furthermore, these assessments contribute to the establishment of both state practice and *opinio juris*. However, general international law is not (yet) specifically tailored to the provision of humanitarian assistance, resulting in grey areas as to the practical implementation of this commitment. It is therefore currently not possible to determine a consensus in customary international law with regard to the existence of an *obligation to provide assistance or a right to access*, given the dispersed approach of these issues by various actors and bodies of law.[317] Although perhaps the continued call in various UN resolutions might be construed as constituting *opinio juris*, subsequent state action has been less than consistent, making the second component of customary international law more difficult to establish.[318] The more specific action by the Security Council has, however, amounted to the conclusion that in country-specific circumstances, the Council has shown a willingness to assert a duty of the

[317] Spieker, 'Humanitarian Assistance, Access in Armed Conflict and Occupation' (n 161) § 36.
[318] Barber, 'Facilitating humanitarian assistance in international humanitarian and human rights law', (n 91) 372.

affected state or other relevant parties to *allow access for the provision of humanitarian assistance by third parties, including their subsequent safe and unimpeded passage*.

A distinct international obligation to provide assistance for third parties or a hard right to access cannot be derived from the various specific bodies of law such as international humanitarian law, or from regional law such as the Kampala Convention or the ASEAN Agreement. As seen above however, fragmentation of the law through the haphazard incorporation of rights and duties within a limited regional or topical framework does not necessarily enhance the legal framework concerning the provision of assistance as a whole, nor does it aid persons in need of assistance in general. In fact, fragmentation of the law runs the risk of increasing the existing gaps in protection.

Human rights law as a body however *does* provide recourse both concerning the possibilities of third parties to provide assistance and concerning the duties of the affected state to allow access. Whilst the protection of international human rights law is of international *concern*, the specific *fulfilment* of rights may be placed with the affected state (or non-state actor) as duty-bearer in particular circumstances. Indeed, both Article 56 UN Charter and Article 2 ICESCR establish an obligation of international cooperation. Such formulations oblige international *efforts* in the provision of assistance as a vehicle in the fulfilment of the human rights of persons facing crises by the affected state. In order to reach such fulfilment, access would be necessary to the affected territory. Unlike is the case in humanitarian law, where an emphasis is placed on control rights of the affected state, such control rights are lacking in the more generally formulated codifications of the rights to life, food and health. Naturally, such a lack of specified control rights flows from the origins of the creation of the current existing human rights treaties, not specifically tailored to the provision of assistance as for example the Kampala Convention is, or the Geneva Conventions are, having been created with World War II in mind. However, Chapters 5 and 6 have asserted that the provision of humanitarian assistance functions as the fulfilment of the rights to life, food and health by the affected authority as designated duty-bearer. Therefore, in allowing third parties to obtain access to the affected territory for the provision of humanitarian assistance, the affected state is complying with its own duties to provide assistance (including seeking international help for this purpose) to the affected persons in need of aid, as a vehicle in the fulfilment of the rights to life, food and health. Indeed, such a duty to allow access in human rights law does not exist independently, but is directly related to the affected states' duties to *provide* assistance themselves. This duty, in particular as codified within Article 2 ICESCR, does not merely require the affected state to deplete its own national resources, but to actively seek international assistance.

Furthermore upon access to a territory, following these obligations under human rights law in circumstances that the affected state cannot sufficiently provided assistance itself, third parties should be ensured 'safe and unimpeded passage' as continuously called upon by the Security Council. Such provisions have equally been codified in the Convention on the Security of United Nations and Associated Personnel as well as the ICC Statute (see Chapter 8). Upon consent of the affected state therefore, an *obligation can be determined to exist in current law to allow safe and unimpeded passage, without the abuse of control rights* (existing depending on the circumstances). A distinct duty therefore rests upon the affected state or authority to create an environment in which it becomes safe for the (external) providers of assistance to deliver the aid. Such an obligation is made more specific through the duty, found in many provisions, of the affected state to in fact facilitate such a delivery.[319] Secondly, although an *obligation* for third parties to provide assistance may not be found in existing international law, despite potential developments in this regard through existing *opinio juris*, a distinct *right* to offer assistance can be discerned in the various bodies of law discussed above.[320]

Despite the lack of a right to access, and even a clear general obligation of third parties to provide aid, it has been possible to determine the existing rights and duties pertaining to the delivery of assistance by third parties. The current legal developments, such as the ILC Draft Articles, unfortunately do not attempt to bridge this existing gap in protection, as they equally provide for the affected state's right of consent in the external provision of assistance and do not call for an obligation to provide aid. Rather, these developments add to the disparity and fragmentation in legal protection. The determined obligations of the affected state in Chapter 6 therefore do not have immediate corresponding *obligations to provide* or *rights to access* for third parties under the existing legal framework.

Many existing soft law documents have attempted to bridge the existing gaps and solve the grey areas through their guidelines or resolutions. With regard to the external provision of assistance, the 1991 Guidelines for Humanitarian Assistance, the 1993 San Remo Principles, the 1995 Mohonk Criteria and the Bruges Resolution of 2003 recognise the right of third parties to offer humanitarian assistance to a population in need, similar to many existing legal provisions.[321] Also, the 1991 Guidelines for Humanitarian Assistance, the San Remo Principles and the Bruges Resolution consider an obligation, as asserted above, of the affected state to facilitate the safe passage of assistance and personnel.[322] Furthermore, the duty of neighbouring states to allow the transit of assistance is addressed by the Mohonk Criteria, as well as by the San Remo Principles and the Bruges Resolution,

---

[319] 7.4.2 and 7.5 and further.

[320] Ibid and Military and Paramilitary Activities in and against Nicaragua (Nicaragua v. United States of America), Merits, Judgment 27 June 1986 I.C.J. Reports 1986, p. 14.

[321] See in this regard the 1991 Guidelines for Humanitarian Assistance Guideline 10; 'Guiding Principles on the Right to Humanitarian Assistance' (April 1993) The International Institute of Humanitarian Law in San Remo, Principle 5; 'The Mohonk Criteria for Humanitarian Assistance in Complex Emergencies', (1995) reprinted in 17 *Human Rights Quarterly* 1, 196; Resolution 'Humanitarian Assistance' (2 September 2003) Institute of International Law, Sixteenth Commission, Bruges Session, Principle IV.1.

[322] Ibid the 1991 Guidelines for Humanitarian Assistance Guidelines 2o and 21; 'Guiding Principles on the Right to Humanitarian Assistance' (ibid) Principle 10; Bruges Resolution 'Humanitarian Assistance' (2 September 2003) (ibid) Principle VII; The Mohonk Criteria (ibid) do not assert such a right.

although the latter two do so without specifying a particular duty-bearer.[323] Similarly, both the San Remo Principles and the Bruges Resolution stipulate an obligation of the affected state to not arbitrarily refuse an offer of assistance, where the latter specifies that such an offer must be 'bona fide'.[324] In support of this, Vukas, the original Rapporteur drafting the Bruges Resolution, has argued that as under current international law the protection of human rights of a population no longer exclusively exists within a domestic jurisdiction, third states may therefore, in view of an exacerbated humanitarian catastrophe, call upon the UN to entice the affected state to comply with its obligations.[325]

Proceeding beyond the *status quo* of the law, these soft law documents have attempted to stretch the grounds of the current existing legal framework. Indeed, the Bruges Resolution recognises in this regard an obligation resting upon the affected state to seek assistance from third parties, in a more specified and tailored manner than existing human rights law.[326] Moreover, the Mohonk Criteria have asserted 'the right and obligation to protect and provide relief' of third parties in the event the affected state is unwilling or unable to do so, arguing that the principles of non-interference and sovereignty may not be used by the affected state as an obstacle in the saving of lives.[327]

This brief overview exemplifies that these soft-law documents have attempted to provide greater protection for persons in need of assistance. While these documents indeed arguably contribute to existing *opinio juris* on the matter, such a more far-reaching approach to the external provision of humanitarian assistance is lacking in the existing framework.[328] It must be concluded that current hard law restricts itself to the determination that third parties have a clear *right to offer assistance*, complimented by the *duty of the affected state to seek international assistance for*

[323] Ibid 'The Mohonk Criteria for Humanitarian Assistance in Complex Emergencies', (1995) Criteria II. Responsibility To Provide Assistance During Complex Emergencies 3; 'Guiding Principles on the Right to Humanitarian Assistance' (ibid) Principle 10, and Bruges Resolution 'Humanitarian Assistance' (2 September 2003) (ibid) Principle VII.

[324] 'Guiding Principles on the Right to Humanitarian Assistance' (n 321) Principle 7; and Bruges Resolution 'Humanitarian Assistance' (n 321) Principle VIII. For a further explication of the notion of a 'bona fide' offer and reasons for refusal with regard to the Bruges Resolution: Robert Kolb, 'De l'assistance humanitaire: la résolution sur l'assistance humanitaire adoptée par l'Institut de droit international à sa session de Bruges en 2003', (2004) 86 *International Review of the Red Cross* 856, 868-869.

[325] Vukas, 'Humanitarian Assistance in Cases of Emergency' (n 14) § 24.

[326] Bruges Resolution 'Humanitarian Assistance' (n 321) Principle III.3: "Whenever the affected State is unable to provide sufficient humanitarian assistance to the victims placed under its jurisdiction or *de facto* control, it shall seek assistance from competent international organizations and/or from third States".

[327] 'The Mohonk Criteria for Humanitarian Assistance in Complex Emergencies' (n 321) Criteria II. 4 and 5. The 1991 Guidelines for Humanitarian Assistance, do not provide solace in this particular regard, as they – recognising the sovereignty of the affected state – assert that the external provision of assistance is dependent on the request and consent of the affected state. See in this regard the Guidelines for Humanitarian Assistance, Principle 2(c), 3, 9(a). Yet, conversely, Principle 10 notes that an offer of assistance should not be interpreted as an interference in the domestic affairs of the affected state.

[328] See 1.4.1 on the components of customary international law.

the provision of assistance in the fulfilment of the rights to life, food and health. From this duty flows the *obligation to allow safe and unimpeded access (upon consent) to facilitate the free passage of goods and personnel for the purpose of the delivery of assistance*, in light of the duty to create a safe environment for such provision.

Both in the abovementioned hard law and soft-law documents reference is also made to enforcement mechanisms, should the affected state not allow for access to the affected territory and population. Such matters shall be addressed in the subsequent Chapter, concerning the legal consequences of the denial of humanitarian assistance and the ensuing potential violations of international law.

	Right / Duty to provide by third parties	Right to access by third parties	Source
State Sovereignty	• An offer to provide assistance is lawful, no violation of principle of non-intervention		• Military and Paramilitary Activities in and against Nicaragua (Nicaragua vs. United States), Merits 1986 ICJ REP. 14 (Judgment of 27 June 1986) § 242-243
Security Council Resolutions	• UN and organs have 'humanitarian responsibilities'		• UNSC Res 513 (19 June 1982) UN Doc S/RES/513 'Lebanon' § 3
	• 'Appeals to' / 'welcomes' / 'encourages' / 'urges' Member States or the international community as a whole to provide assistance		• UNSC Res 513 (19 June 1982) UN Doc S/RES/513 'Lebanon' § 2; UNSC Res 688 (5 April 1991) UN Doc S/RES/688 § 6; UNSC Res 733 (23 January 1992) UN Doc S/RES/733 § 2; UNSC Res 775 (28 August 1992) UN Doc S/RES/775 preamble; UNSC Res 1906 (23 December 2009) UN Doc S/RES/1906 preamble; UNSC Res 1701 (11 August 2006) UN Doc S/Res/1701 § 6; UNSC Res 1991 (28 June 2011) UN Doc S/RES/1991 preamble; UNSC Res 2014 (21 October 2011) UN Doc S/RES/2014 § 10; UNSC Res 1970 (26 February 2011) UN Doc S/RES/1970 § 26
	• Chapter VII: calling Member States to 'provide adequate resources for humanitarian assistance in the region and to respond promptly and generously'		• UNSC Res 1199 (23 September 1998) UN Doc S/RES/1199 § 12
	• Chapter VII: 'Calls on the international community also to provide immediate humanitarian		• UNSC Res 1472 (28 March 2003) UN Doc S/RES/1472 § 2

	Right / Duty to provide by third parties	Right to access by third parties	Source
	assistance [...] and in particular to respond immediately to any future humanitarian appeal of the United Nations, and supports the activities of the International Committee of the Red Cross and of other international humanitarian organisations		
		• Calling' / 'insisting' / 'demanding' that Member States allow access / facilitate the delivery of assistance	• UNSC Res 513 (19 June 1982) UN Doc S/RES/513 'Lebanon' § 1; UNSC Res 733 (23 January 1992) UN Doc S/RES/733 § 7; UNSC Res 746 (17 March 1992) UN Doc S/RES/746 § 3; UNSC Res 751 (24 April 1992) UN Doc S/RES/751 § 14; UNSC Res 767 (27 July 1992) UN Doc S/RES/767 § 3; UNSC Res 775 (28 August 1992) UN Doc S/RES/775 § 7; UNSC Res 794 (3 December 1992) UN Doc S/RES/794 §2; UNSC Res 752 (15 May 1992) UN Doc S/RES/752 § 8; UNSC Res 758 (8 June 1992) UN Doc S/RES/758 § 8; UNSC Res 787 (16 November 1992) UN Doc S/RES/787 § 18; UNSC Res 1071 (30 August 1996) UN Doc S/RES/1071 § 10; UNSC Res 1083 (27 November 1996) UN Doc S/RES/1083 § 8; UNSC Res 1258 (6 August 1999) UN Doc S/RES/1258 § 11; UNSC Res 1286 (19 January 2000) UN Doc S/RES/1286 § 9; UNSC Res 1378 (14

	Right / Duty to provide by third parties	Right to access by third parties	Source
			November 2001) UN Doc S/RES/1378 § 2; UNSC Res 1794 (21 December 2007) UN Doc S/RES/1794 § 17; UNSC Res 1868 (23 March 2009) UN Doc S/RES/1868 preamble
		• 'calling' / 'urging' / 'demanding' safe and unhindered passage (also for personnel)	• UNSC Res 733 (23 January 1992) UN Doc S/RES/733 § 8; UNSC Res 746 (17 March 1992) UN Doc S/RES/746 § 8; UNSC Res 751 (24 April 1992) UN Doc S/RES/751 § 14; UNSC Res 767 (27 July 1992) UN Doc S/RES/767 § 3; UNSC Res 775 (28 August 1992) UN Doc S/RES/775 § 7; UNSC Res 794 (3 December 1992) UN Doc S/RES/794 § 3; UNSC Res 758 (8 June 1992) UN Doc S/RES/758 § 8; UNSC Res 787 (16 November 1992) UN Doc S/RES/787 § 18; UNSC Res 813 (26 March 1993) UN Doc S/RES/813 § 15; UNSC Res 1059 (31 May 1996) UN Doc S/RES/1059 § 7; UNSC Res 1071 (30 August 1996) UN Doc S/RES/1071 § 10; UNSC Res 1083 (27 November 1996) UN Doc S/RES/1083 § 8; UNSC Res 1258 (6 August 1999) UN Doc S/RES/1258 § 11; UNSC Res 1286 (19 January 2000) UN Doc S/RES/1286 § 10; UNSC Res 1378 (14 November 2001) UN Doc S/RES/1378 § 2; UNSC Res 1970 (26 February 2011) UN Doc S/RES/1970 § 2; UNSC Res 2014 (21 October 2011) UN Doc S/RES/2014 § 10; UNSC Res 2042 (14 April 2012) UN Doc S/RES/2042

	Right / Duty to provide by third parties	Right to access by third parties	Source
			§ 10; UNSC Res 2043 (21 April 2012) UN Doc S/RES/2043 § 11; UNSC Res 2096 (19 March 2013) UN Doc S/RES/2096 § 29
		• 'Condemning' the denial of full unimpeded access (to personnel)	• UNSC Res 1882 (4 August 2009) UN Doc S/RES1882 § 1
		• Chapter VII: 'demanding' to facilitate and 'ensure' safe and unhindered passage of assistance, as well as to ensure the safety of humanitarian personnel	• UNSC Res 770 (13 August 1992) UN Doc S/RES/770 § 2, 3 and 6; UNSC Res 819 (16 April 1993) UN Doc S/RES/819 § 8 and 10; UNSC Res 824 (6 May 1993) UN Doc S/RES/824 § 4(b); UNSC Res 1004 (12 July 1995) UN Doc S/RES/1004 § 5; UNSC Res 1199 (23 September 1998) UN Doc S/RES/1199 § 4(c) and 10; UNSC Res 1132 (8 October 1997) UN Doc S/RES/1132 § 2; UNSC Res 1270 (22 October 1999) UN Doc S/RES/1270 § 13; UNSC Res 1264 (15 September 1999) UN Doc S/RES/1264 § 2; UNSC Res 1272 (25 October 1999) UN Doc S/RES/1272 § 10 and 11; UNSC Res 1973 (17 March 2011) UN Doc S/RES/1973 'The situation in Libya' § 3; UNSC Res 1975 (30 March 2011) UN Doc S/RES/1975 'The situation in Côte d'Ivoir' preamble and § 10; UNSC Res 1996 (8 July 2011) UN Doc S/RES/1996 § 8; UNSC Res 2046 (2 May 2012) UN Doc S/RES/2046 § 4; UNSC Res 2076 (20 November 2012) UN Doc S/RES/2076 § 11; UNSC Res 2060 (25 July 2012) UN Doc S/RES/2060

	Right / Duty to provide by third parties	Right to access by third parties	Source
			§ 6; UNSC Res 2127 (5 December 2013) UN Doc S/RES/2127 § 51 and 52; UNSC Res 2139 (22 February 2014) UN Doc S/RES/2139 § 5-7
		• Determination that facilitation of assistance is part of a state's responsibility	• UNSC Res 1319 (8 September 2000) UN Doc S/RES/1319 § 1
		• Calling for cross-conflict assistance, without authorisation of (Syrian) authority	• UNSC 2165 (14 July 2014) UN Doc S/RES/2165 para 2.
General Assembly Resolutions	• An offer of assistance from Member States in time of emergency is presupposed		• UNGA Res 2034 (XX) 'Assistance in cases of natural disaster' (7 December 1965) § 2
	• 'Appeal' to states to offer humanitarian assistance		• UNGA Res 2435 (XXIII) (19 December 1968) § 5; UNGA Res 2717 (XXV) 'Assistance in cases of natural disaster' (15 December 1970) § 1; UNGA Res 2816 (XXVI) (14 December 1971) § 9 (a) and (b); UNGA Res 3244 XXIX (29 November 1974) § 2 and 3; UNGA Res 34/127 (14 December 1979) UN Doc A/RES/34/127 'Assistance to the Comoros' § 4; UNGA Res 36/225 (17 December 1981) UN Doc A/RES/36/225 § 12 and 19; UNGA Res 49/139 (20 December 1994) UN Doc A/RES/49/139 § 13. See also the range of General Assembly resolutions pertaining to 'Safety and security of humanitarian personnel and protection of United Nations personnel'
	• Stresses the		• UNGA Res 49/174 (24

	Right / Duty to provide by third parties	Right to access by third parties	Source
	importance of the provision of assistance by the international community; calling upon UN Member States, the organs of the UN as well as humanitarian organisations		February 1995) UN Doc A/RES/49/174 § 6 and 12
	• The provision of humanitarian assistance is a shared international responsibility		• UNGA Res 55/2 (18 September 2000) UN Doc A/RES/55/2 'United Nations Millennium Declaration' § 2 and 26.
	• The provision of assistance is an 'expression of the principle of international solidarity' as enshrined in the UN Charter		• UNGA Res 3244 XXIX (29 November 1974) preamble
	• The international community (in particular the UN system) bears the task of strengthening and improving the humanitarian response in the aftermath of emergencies		• UNGA Res 60/124 (8 March 2006) UN Doc A/RES/60/124 §11; UNGA Res 63/139 (5 March 2009) UN Doc A/RES/63/139 § 3; UNGA Res 64/76 (2 February 2010) UN Doc A/RES/64/76 preamble
	• Member States are 'urged' to assist, a need for cooperation is 'stressed'		• UNGA Res 65/264 (21 June 2011) UN Doc A/RES/65/264 preamble and §8, 12 and 13; UNGA Res 66/119 (7 March 2012) UN Doc A/RES/66/119 preamble, §4 and 10
		• States in need of assistance are invited to facilitate the work of these organisations in implementing	• UNGA Res 43/131 (8 December 1988) UN Doc A/RES/43/131, § 4 and 5; UNGA Res 45/100 (14 December 1990) UN Doc A/RES/45/100 § 4 and 5;

	Right / Duty to provide by third parties	Right to access by third parties	Source
		humanitarian assistance and to give their support to these organisations	UNGA Res 46/182 (19 December 1991) UN Doc A/RES/46/182, Annex, § 6-7; UNGA Res 49/174 (24 February 1995) UN Doc A/RES/49/174 preamble
		• Calls upon' or 'urges' states in the vicinity to facilitate the transit of emergency aid	• UNGA Res 43/131 (8 December 1988) UN Doc A/RES/43/131, § 6; UNGA Res 45/100 (14 December 1990) UN Doc A/RES/45/100 § 7; UNGA Res 59/141 (25 February 2005) UN Doc A/RES/59/141 preamble; UNGA Res 64/251 (30 April 2010) UN Doc A/RES/64/251 § 14; UNGA Res 65/264 (21 June 2011) UN Doc A/RES/65/264 §14; UNGA Res 66/227 (15 March 2012) UN Doc A/RES/66/227 §16; and UNGA Res 67/231 (9 April 2013) UN Doc A/RES/67/231 § 16.
		• 'Calls upon' parties to conflicts or other emergency situations to take all possible necessary measures to ensure impartial, safe and timely humanitarian access to persons in need of assistance, while also calling upon states to ensure 'the safety and security of humanitarian personnel'	• UNGA Res 49/169 (23 December 1994) UN Doc A/RES/49/169 § 12; A/RES/52/167 18 February 1998, § 3; UNGA Res 53/87 (27 January 1999) UN Doc A/RES/53/87 § 11; UNGA Res 54/192 (21 February 2000) UN Doc A/RES/54/192 § 2 and 3; UNGA Res 55/175 (7 March 2001) UN Doc A/RES/55/175 § 3 and 4; UNGA Res 56/217 (19 February 2002) UN Doc A/RES/56/217 § 3, 4 and 12; UNGA Res 58/114 (5 February 2004) UN Doc A/RES/58/114 §8 and 10, UNGA Res 59/141 (25 February 2005) UN Doc

	Right / Duty to provide by third parties	Right to access by third parties	Source
			A/RES/59/141 § 18; UN Doc A/RES/60/1, 16 September 2005 para 169; UNGA Res 60/124 (8 March 2006) UN Doc A/RES/60/124 § 2; UNGA Res 60/123 (24 March 2006) UN Doc A/RES/60/123 § 3 and 4; UNGA Res 61/133 (1 March 2007) UN Doc A/RES/61/133 §3 and 4; UNGA Res 61/134 (1 March 2007) UN Doc A/RES/61/134 § 20; UNGA Res 62/94 (25 January 2008) UN Doc A/RES/62/94 § 24; UNGA Res 62/95 (29 January 2008) UN Doc A/RES/62/95 §3 and 4; UNGA Res 63/138 (5 March 2009) UN Doc A/RES/63/138 §3 and 4; UNGA Res 64/76 (2 February 2010) UN Doc A/RES/64/76 § 26; UNGA Res 64/77 (8 February 2010) UN Doc A/RES/64/77 § 4; UNGA Res 65/132 (1 March 2011) UN Doc A/RES/65/132 §4; UNGA Res 65/133 (3 March 2011) UN Doc A/RES/65/133 § 27; UNGA Res 66/117 (1 March 2012) UN Doc A/RES/66/117 §4; UNGA Res 66/119 (7 March 2012) UN Doc A/RES/66/119 §33; UNGA Res 66/120 (7 March 2012) UN Doc A/RES/66/120 § 12; UNGA Res 67/85 (21 March 2013) UN Doc A/RES/67/85 §4; UNGA Res 67/87 (26 March 2013) UN Doc A/RES/67/87 § 37
		• Asserting the obligations of	• UNGA Res 67/87 (26 March 2013) UN Doc

	Right / Duty to provide by third parties	Right to access by third parties	Source
		parties to humanitarian emergencies *under international law* in ensuring access to providers of aid.	A/RES/67/87 § 37; UNGA Res 68/101 (18 February 2014) UN Doc A/RES/68/101 § 2-4; UNGA Res 68/102 (12 February 2014) UN Doc A/RES/68/102 § 37 and 41
Human Rights Law	• Obligation on UN Member States to ensure universal respect for human rights		• Articles 55 & 56 UN Charter
	• Duty upon those states within the international community that are in a position to assist, to indeed assist in the fulfillment of the right to food		• Article 11 ICESCR (and Article 2 ICESCR)
	• Obligations resting upon states to take measures in cooperating to ensure food security and eradication of malnutrition		• Article 12 of the Additional Protocol to the ACHR in the Area of Economic, Social and Cultural Rights
	• States parties have a joint and individual responsibility to cooperate in providing disaster relief and humanitarian assistance in times of emergency. Moreover, given that some diseases are easily transmissible beyond the frontiers of a State, the international community has a collective		• CESCR interpretation of Article 12 ICESCR (and Article 2 ICESCR)

	Right / Duty to provide by third parties	Right to access by third parties	Source
	responsibility to address this problem		
		• Parties shall facilitate, and refrain from placing any impediments to, humanitarian assistance in support of the rights to which the local population are entitled under the ICERD	• Application of the International Convention on the Elimination of all Forms of Racial Discrimination (Georgia v. Russian Federation), Provisional Measures, Order of 15 October 2008, I.C.J. Reports 2008, p. 353 § 149 B
Law of Armed Conflict	*International Armed Conflict* • Right to offer assistance for international humanitarian organisations	*International Armed Conflict*	*International Armed Conflict* • Article 10 GC IV
	• Relief actions shall be undertaken if the civilian population is inadequately supplied		• Article 70(1) AP I (read in conjuncture with Article 54 AP I)
		• States shall allow the passage of assistance subject to the condition that there are no serious reasons to decide otherwise	• Article 23 GC IV (listing the reasons)
		• States (including third states) shall allow and facilitate rapid and unimpeded passage of all relief consignments, prohibition of delaying humanitarian assistance	• Article 70(2)-(5) AP I
		• States shall provide	• Article 71(2) AP I

	Right / Duty to provide by third parties	Right to access by third parties	Source
		for safety of humanitarian personnel	
	Non-International Armed Conflict • Right to offer assistance by an impartial humanitarian body	*Non-International Armed Conflict*	*Non-International Armed Conflict* • Common Article 3 GC
	• Right to offer relief by local organisation		• Article 18(1) AP II
	• Subject to consent, relief 'shall' be undertaken in the event of undue hardship	• Relief actions shall be undertaken	• Article 18(2) AP II (read in conjuncture with Article 14 AP II)
Law of Occu-pation	• The Occupying Power shall agree to relief schemes on behalf of the population, and shall facilitate them	• The Occupier shall permit the free passage of assistance and shall guarantee their protection, whilst maintaining the right to regulate passage of convoys	• Article 59 GC IV
	• The Protecting Power has the right to check the state of provision of assistance by the occupier		• Article 55 GC IV
	• The Protecting Power shall have the duty to supervise the distribution of assistance (to be facilitated by Occupier)	• Duty of all states to allow assistance designated for occupied territory through their own territory	• Article 61 GC IV
	• Duty of the occupying power to allow the existing Red Cross Societies and other similar humanitarian		• Article 63 GC IV

	Right / Duty to provide by third parties	Right to access by third parties	Source
	organisations in a territory to continue with their activities		
	• The Occupying Power shall have the right to approve participation of personnel	• States shall provide for safety of humanitarian personnel	• Article 71 AP I
Nuclear Accid. or Radio-logical Emer-gency	• Duty to cooperate to provide prompt assistance		• Article 1(1) Convention on Assistance in the Case of a Nuclear Accident or Radiological Emergency
		• Consent and control rights remain with affected state	• Article 3 Convention on Assistance in the Case of a Nuclear Accident or Radiological Emergency
IDRL / ILC Protec-tion of Persons	• Presupposition of an offer of assistance by third states		• Inter-American Convention To Facilitate Disaster Assistance Articles I(b), II(b) and IV(b)
		• Affected state shall, upon consent, facilitate fully the access and freedom of movement in the territory for humanitarian personnel and convoys	• Inter-American Convention To Facilitate Disaster Assistance Articles V and VII
	• Duty for states party to 'promptly respond' to a request for assistance by a state affected by disaster		• ASEAN Agreement on Disaster Management and Emergency Response, Articles 4(c) + 11
	• States have an obligation to coordinate the provision of joint emergency response operations		• ASEAN Agreement on Disaster Management and Emergency Response, Article 8
		• Duty of affected state to 'exempt' the	• ASEAN Agreement on Disaster Management and

	Right / Duty to provide by third parties	**Right to access by third parties**	**Source**
		assisting state from all charges of taxes and facilitate access for both the humanitarian personnel and convoys	Emergency Response, Article 14
		• Duty upon third states to allow and facilitate transit through their territory	• ASEAN Agreement on Disaster Management and Emergency Response, Article 16
	• States, the UN, and other competent intergovernmental organisations and NGOs have the right to offer assistance to the affected State.		• Draft Article 12 ILC (+ control rights in Draft Article 13)
	• Duty for states to cooperate amongst themselves as well as with humanitarian organisations		• Draft Article 5 + 5bis ILC
		• Upon consent, the affected State shall take the necessary measures to facilitate the prompt and effective provision of external assistance	• Draft Article 14 ILC
		• The affected state has a duty to 'seek international and/or regional assistance', but on own initiative	• (IDRL Guideline 3.2 + 10.1)
	• Upon consent, affected state has duty to facilitate freedom of access to and freedom of movement in and from the disaster affected area		• (IDRL Guideline 16.1.d.)

	Right / Duty to provide by third parties	Right to access by third parties	Source
		• Duty of transit states to not create restrictions that may delay or impede provision of assistance, and extra duties of affected state to facilitate	• (IDRL Guideline 16.2 and 17)
		• Call upon the affected state to take measures in the protection of those actors that they have consented to access their territory	• (IDRL Guideline 22)
Refugee Law			
IDP Frame-work	• Duty of affected state to cooperate internationally: where available resources are inadequate, they shall seek the assistance of international organisations and humanitarian agencies, civil society organisations and other relevant actors. Such organisations may offer their services to all those in need		• Article 5(6) Kampala Convention
		• States Parties shall allow rapid and unimpeded passage of all relief consignments, equipment and per-sonnel to IDPs. States Parties shall also enable and facilitate the role of local and	• Article 5(7) Kampala Convention

	Right / Duty to provide by third parties	Right to access by third parties	Source
		international organisations and humanitarian agencies, civil society organisations and other relevant actors, to provide protection and assistance	
		• States Parties shall ensure assistance to IDPs by allowing and facilitating rapid and unimpeded access by humanitarian organisations and personnel	• Article 3(1)(j) Kampala Convention
		• Prohibition for armed groups to impede humanitarian assistance and passage of all relief consignments, equipment and personnel	• Article 7(5)(g) Kampala Convention
	• International humanitarian organisations and other appropriate actors have the right to offer their services in support of the internally displaced		• (Guiding Principles 25(2) IDPs)
		• Authorities concerned shall grant and facilitate the free passage of humanitarian assistance and grant persons engaged in the provision of	• (Guiding Principles 25(3) IDPs)

	Right / Duty to provide by third parties	**Right to access by third parties**	**Source**
		such assistance rapid and unimpeded access to IDPs	
		• Personnel and convoys must be respected and protected and may not be attacked	• (Guiding Principles 26 IDPs)

CHAPTER 8
LEGAL CONSEQUENCES OF THE DENIAL OF HUMANITARIAN ASSISTANCE: METHODS OF ENFORCEMENT

In March 2009, the Sudanese President Omar Al-Bashir reportedly expelled several humanitarian aid organisations from the country, upon his indictment before the International Criminal Court:

"Sudan ordered 10 leading international humanitarian organizations expelled from Darfur on Wednesday after the International Criminal Court issued an arrest warrant for the country's president for alleged atrocities in the conflict-ridden region. United Nations Secretary-General Ban Ki-moon said the action "represents a serious setback to lifesaving operations in Darfur" and urged Sudan to reverse its decision, U.N. deputy spokeswoman Marie Okabe said".

The denial of humanitarian assistance can lead to violations of international law. But in what way can humanitarian assistance be enforced? Through which legal mechanisms can the provision of aid to persons in need be ensured? This Chapter addresses the various methods of enforcement, as part of the larger framework on the provision of humanitarian assistance.[1]

8.1 Introduction

Enforcement as a manner in which a situation violating international law can be brought to an end must be addressed in this research, in the circumstance humanitarian aid cannot be delivered. Part II of this research has dealt with the current rights and obligations in the provision of humanitarian assistance. It has set out the current existing legal framework pertaining to the rights of persons to receive aid in a humanitarian crisis, as well as the duties of the affected state to provide such aid. Part III commenced with the legal framework concerning the delivery of assistance by external parties, in the event the affected state is unable or unwilling to fulfil its duties by itself. In this regard, Chapter 7 set forth the rights of third parties wishing to provide aid to persons in need should the affected state not do so, and the related obligations the affected state may have in allowing such parties access to the affected territories. This access is generally formulated as a duty of the affected state to allow entry to third parties and is important, as the

1 <www.nbcnews.com/id/29492637/ns/world_news-africa/t/sudan-expels-aid-groups-response-warrant/#.VFETffmsWP4> accessed 29 October 2014. See in this regard also <www.theguardian.com/world/2009/mar/05/sudan-aid-agencies-expelled> accessed 29 October 2014.

normative basis for the potential enforcement of such access is found in the protection of the persons in need of assistance.

This Chapter addresses the existing enforcement mechanisms and methods through which the affected state may be held accountable for its potential violations of international law in a step-by-step manner, commencing with a discussion of the law of state responsibility. The substantive enforcement methods operate on a variety of levels and will be addressed subsequently and accordingly. At the interstate level, the *use of force* is relevant in the factual enforcement of access for the delivery of humanitarian assistance, through authorised international operations. Furthermore, *human rights law* and its mechanisms are addressed, reflecting the enforcement method available at a different level, namely that of the individual *vis-à-vis* the state. Lastly, *international criminal law* is relevant in addressing violations of international law by individuals reciprocally in the enforcement of humanitarian assistance. Indeed, the more substantive provisions dealing with enforcement that are found in these bodies of law may well be considered a consequence or result of establishing state responsibility for the denial of humanitarian at various levels. At all levels however, it is important to remain cognisant of the role of state sovereignty. As will be seen, in this Chapter state sovereignty plays a diminished role compared to previous Chapters. Whereas the affected state in certain instances has some discretion in the determination of whether or not humanitarian assistance is needed, the determination that an *unlawful denial of humanitarian aid* has taken place leads to a breach of international law. Such breaches may then be enforced through human rights law, international criminal law or through the use of force, but such enforcement comes through means in which the sovereignty of the affected state tends to be overridden by other aspects of international law. This overriding occurs either based on the character of the UN Security Council and UN member states' obligations under Article 25 of the UN Charter, or for example through the accession to certain human rights treaties or the ICC, resulting in the possibility of holding states or individuals accountable before these bodies. Indeed, the view that access for humanitarian assistance is necessary – a view that has increased in the past years as seen in Chapters 5, 6 and 7 – results in the simultaneous changing of the nature of state sovereignty, to the point where sovereignty must give way to the delivery of food, water, medicine and shelter in times of crisis.

In addressing the legal consequences of the denial of humanitarian assistance by the affected state through the various methods of enforcement existing in international law today, it is crucial to first and foremost establish which acts or omissions amount to an unlawful denial of humanitarian assistance. Chapters 6 and 7 have shown that on occasion, denial of humanitarian assistance may occur, such as for the purpose of military necessity. This Chapter however addresses the legal enforcement mechanisms that can be utilised when considering *unlawful denials* of such aid and to that end firstly addresses the law of state responsibility as related to the provision of humanitarian assistance, in order to establish when a sovereign may be held accountable under international law for such a denial.

8.2 The Law of State Responsibility and Enforcement of Humanitarian Assistance

Violations of substantive international law pertaining to the denial or obstruction of humanitarian assistance may give rise to state responsibility. Indeed, the failure of a state to fulfil its sovereign duties results in the rise of state responsibility. The law of state responsibility connects the violation of a specific duty to provide aid or allow access for third parties to a responsibility under international law.

The recognition of the law of state responsibility as a 'legal category' in which responsibility arises in the event of a breach of an international obligation did not fully develop until well after Grotius' time and into the nineteenth century.[2] When the UN International Law Commission was established in 1947, the law of state responsibility was marked as a field in need of attention, which prompted the development of the Draft Articles on State Responsibility in the ensuing decades, developing gradually into what is known as the law of state responsibility today.[3]

State responsibility is not a field of law containing substantive provisions in and of itself, but rather a field of law which becomes applicable upon the violation of another, primary, norm of international law. Thus by nature, it allows for an overarching, broader, approach to the obligations which may follow from the denial of the provision of humanitarian assistance. Such an overarching approach is in fact seen in the law on state responsibility, as set out today in the ILC's Articles on the Responsibility of States for Internationally Wrongful Acts (ARSIWA), which allow for the determination of a state's responsibility not merely towards another state bilaterally, but also towards other actors in the international field.[4] Although not an independent international treaty, the ARSIWA currently hold international standing as completed work by the ILC and through their status as annexed document to a General Assembly resolution (pending the General Assembly's further action on the topic), as well as having been referred to on countless occasions as (largely) reflecting customary international law.[5] They will therefore be referenced throughout this Section.

As Crawford and Olleson argue, there is no 'uniform code of international law' which reflects the obligations of *all* states operating in the international spectrum.[6] Obligations resting upon states must be determined for each state independently, as these obligations are dependent upon the treaties such states have entered into. Only a limited number of general norms of international law are recognised internationally as universally applicable customary law. Both these norms and the widely accepted treaty provisions codified in humanitarian law and human rights

[2] James Crawford, *State Responsibility: the General Part* (Cambridge University Press 2013) 11-20.
[3] Ibid 35-36.
[4] UNGA Res 56/83 (28 January 2002) UN Doc A/RES/56/83 Annex 'Responsibility of States for internationally wrongful acts' (ARSIWA) (corrected by UN Doc A/56/49 (Vol. I)/Corr.4). The ARSIWA specifically exclude matters pertaining to the responsibility of either international organisations or of other non-state actors.
[5] Crawford, *State Responsibility: the General Part* (n 2) 42-43.
[6] Ibid 446.

laws are addressed in this Chapter. Indeed, as the law of state responsibility is construed upon legal concepts such as a breach, attribution and consequences therefore, it allows for application in a general manner to the variety of obligations resting upon individual states.[7]

Given the fact that the affected state is the primary responsible actor in times of a humanitarian crisis in the provision of humanitarian assistance to persons in need,[8] the notion of state responsibility is of great relevance to this research and must be examined in more depth with a view to states' failures in meeting their obligations regarding the provision of humanitarian assistance.[9] The classical and purely bilateral view of state responsibility has been departed from with the development of the ARSIWA, by incorporating a responsibility *of states* towards not only other states, either individually or together, but also towards individuals, groups or the international community in general.[10] Therefore, the law of state responsibility is of importance to the legal framework regarding the provision of humanitarian assistance, in the event a state does not fulfil its legal obligations under that framework, perhaps raising international responsibility towards the persons in need, or perhaps the international community in general.

8.2.1 State Responsibility, the ARSIWA and Humanitarian Assistance

In order to invoke the international responsibility of a state, the law of state responsibility presupposes in Articles 2 and 3 ARSIWA an *act* or *omission* of that state, in the event such an act or omission is a *breach* of international law and *attributable* to the state. With regard to the provision of humanitarian assistance, in particular this possibility of an attributable 'omission' is of relevance. Specifically the aspects of state responsibility that fall outside the classical *bilateral* view must be considered, given the nature of the responsibility of the affected state in the event of a humanitarian crisis to provide assistance to persons in need of aid. This responsibility includes the duty under the ICESCR to request assistance from abroad and the rights of the international community to offer assistance. At the interstate level, third states may then choose to bring the state that has breached an obligation before the International Court of Justice.

When applying the law of state responsibility to humanitarian assistance, the non-provision of such assistance can be considered a breach of an international obligation. This obligation could according to the ARSIWA be owed to a group of states, should specific treaty provisions be considered, or in general to the international community as a whole, based on the concept of state sovereignty or certain norms of customary international law. The determination of state responsibility for such breaches of obligations held to the international community

---

[7] Ibid.
[8] Chapter 6.
[9] Ibid.
[10] Articles 42 and 48 ARISWA; and 'Report of the International Law Commission Fifty-third session (23 April-1 June and 2 July-10 August 2001)' UN Doc A/56/10 (2001) 62, 66, 293 and 319-320.

as a whole may then be sought before the ICJ. This approach by the ILC in the ARSIWA, diverging from the strict bilateral perspective, follows the ICJ in its judgment in the Barcelona Traction, Light and Power Company Limited (Belgium v. Spain) case (Barcelona Traction case). The ICJ held that:

> "In particular, an essential distinction should be drawn between the obligations of a State towards the international community as a whole, and those arising vis-à-vis another State [...]. By their very nature the former are the concern of all States".[11]

It becomes apparent that a distinction must be made between the bilateral notion of state responsibility, where not all states have a legal interest in the observance of certain duties, and legal obligations which can be considered to affect and interest the international community as a whole; the notion of *erga omnes* obligations, although the ILC does not refer to them as such.[12]

In particular, within the context of the ARSIWA, Articles 42 and 48 both specifically provide for state responsibility in the event a breach of an international obligation occurs that is indeed owed to the international community as a whole. As such, Article 42 stipulates that an injured state may invoke the law of state responsibility if an obligation that is owed to the international community as a whole is breached, and the *injured* state is specifically affected, or the character of the breach changes the position of all other states:

> "A State is entitled as an injured State to invoke the responsibility of another State if the obligation breached is owed to: (a) that State individually; or (b) a group of States including that State, or the international community as a whole, and the breach of the obligation: (i) specially affects that State; or (ii) is of such a character as radically to change the position of all the other States to which the obligation is owed with respect to the further performance of the obligation".

As a humanitarian crisis can affect the larger international community rather than merely one other state, state responsibility might therefore be invoked in the circumstance that a state does not fulfil its sovereign duty to provide assistance to its population, or persons in need within its jurisdiction. Article 42 ARSIWA thus enables an injured state to hold another state in breach of an obligation owed to the international community as a whole if it does not fulfil its responsibilities in the provision of humanitarian assistance, based on its duties under various treaty-law provisions in international humanitarian law and human rights law (as discussed in

---

[11] ICJ *Barcelona Traction, Light and Power Company Limited (Belgium v. Spain)* case *ICJ Reports 1970*, at p.3, p. 32, § 33.

[12] The notion of potential 'erga omnes' obligations shall remain outside the scope of this research, given the current debate still held on the particular content of these obligations. The ILC has for this reason also decided to leave the concept outside of its ARSIWA. See in this regard 'Report of the International Law Commission' UN Doc A/56/10 (n 10) 321-322. For a discussion of the notion of erga omnes, see Maurizio Ragazzi, *The Concept of International Obligations Erga Omnes* (Oxford University Press 1997); Christian J Tams, Enforcing Obligations Erga Omnes in International Law (Cambridge University Press 2010).

Chapters 6 and 7), or other international law prescriptions. An injured state in this circumstance may well be a neighbouring state that is dealing with a large influx of refugees fleeing a state's territory affected by a humanitarian crisis of either man-made or natural origin. Such a state may also be dealing with the environmental consequences of disasters. Articles 28-33 ARSIWA provide for potential legal consequences upon invoking state responsibility, which include cessation, non-repetition and reparation.

Secondly, with a more progressive view, Article 48 ARSIWA provides that not only an *injured* state, but *any* state may invoke the international responsibility of a state should the breached obligation be owed to either a group of states that includes the state invoking the responsibility for the breach, or the international community as a whole:

> "Any State other than an injured State is entitled to invoke the responsibility of another State in accordance with paragraph 2 if: (*a*) the obligation breached is owed to a group of States including that State, and is established for the protection of a collective interest of the group; or (*b*) the obligation breached is owed to the international community as a whole. 2. Any State entitled to invoke responsibility under paragraph 1 may claim from the responsible State: (*a*) cessation of the internationally wrongful act, and assurances and guarantees of non-repetition in accordance with article 30; and (*b*) performance of the obligation of reparation in accordance with the preceding articles, in the interest of the injured State or of the beneficiaries of the obligation breached. 3. The requirements for the invocation of responsibility by an injured State under articles 43, 44 and 45 apply to an invocation of responsibility by a State entitled to do so under paragraph 1".

In stipulating this, Article 48 ARSIWA allows for a non-injured state to invoke state responsibility for the breach of an obligation which is owed to the international community as a whole. Humanitarian assistance in essence is owed to those persons in need of essential food, water, medicine and shelter. Yet, in the absence of the immediate provision of such assistance, humanitarian crises enlarge and spill over into greater areas. Indeed, should a state deny the provision of aid to persons in need, often the circumstances of such persons will escalate and expand the humanitarian crisis at hand. As such, humanitarian assistance is arguably owed to the international community as a whole, as large regions and even the entire world can be affected by the effects of a humanitarian crisis. Article 48 ARSIWA may allow states in the international community to claim that the violations of a state towards its citizens could amount to a breach of an obligation which is owed to the international community as a whole. In the event of non-provision of humanitarian assistance, including the refusal to allow external parties to provide aid and obtain access to a territory, such an argument may very well be made. A deteriorating crisis can amount to several breaches of obligations in international law that are *owed to the international community as a whole*, such as a threat to the peace, large-scale human rights violations, and potentially also one of the four core crimes for which the 'Responsibility to Protect' may be invoked, namely genocide, war crimes, ethnic cleansing and crimes against humanity. As Simma argues, every state may then consider itself legally 'injured', entitling it to resort to certain (non-forceful) countermeasures.[13] As Articles 49 and 50 ARSIWA note, these countermeasures are indeed non-forceful, thus not allowing for the forceful access to a territory. Such a crisis furthermore potentially invokes duties through the provisions of Article 25 UN Charter for the Security Council (as seen in Chapter 7), which as supranational organ of the UN in a way is a reflection of the international community as a whole. In this manner, the ILC has addressed the findings of the ICJ in the Barcelona Traction case above, and incorporated this viewpoint into the ILC's ARSIWA.[14]

In particular concerning humanitarian assistance, such a provision would allow states that are not in the direct vicinity of the affected state to also call upon the affected state to abide by its obligations under international law, in providing humanitarian assistance to its people in a crisis, and even invoke its responsibility therefore under international law. As mentioned above, given the horizontal nature of the law of state responsibility, other states shall have the opportunity to bring the affected state that is in breach of its obligations (potentially Articles 42 and 48 ARSIWA) before the ICJ. It must be noted however that Article 48(2) ARSIWA includes 'progressive development' aspects of international law, which the ILC justifies arguing that the collective interests of the international community may be at stake in certain instances.[15] Such instances may be the case with certain large-scale human rights violations occurring in a humanitarian crisis where the affected state is not fulfilling its duties under the rights to life, food, health (and water), when no other 'injured state' exists due to the particular circumstances at hand.

International responsibility in the absence of another 'injured state' can indeed occur under the law of state responsibility. A state can be held responsible not only for obligations towards another state or the international community; a state may also be held directly responsible under the international law of state responsibility for obligations towards its own citizens. Articles 2 and 3 ARSIWA allow invocation in the event of an attributable breach of international law related to a responsibility of the state towards its citizens.[16] Such possibilities of invoking state responsibility will be of particular relevance in the event of human rights or humanitarian law breaches when humanitarian assistance is denied by the affected state in times of a humanitarian crisis, discussed in Section 8.3. Enforcement will then most likely have to occur through the specific judicial bodies of humanitarian and human rights law, as the individual bearing the consequences of such a breach of international law cannot directly base him/herself on state responsibility: this body of law distinctly operates on the horizontal plane between states, and breaches of the law may only be claimed by other states within the international community;

---

[13] Bruno Simma, 'NATO, the UN and the Use of Force: Legal Aspects', (1999) 10 *European Journal of International Law* 2.

[14] Crawford, *State Responsibility: the General Part* (n 2) 40-41.

[15] 'Report of the International Law Commission' UN Doc A/56/10 (n 10) 323 concerning Article 48(2)(b).

[16] Ibid 62. See also A L Vaurs-Chaumette 'Peoples and Minorities' in J Crawford et al (ed) *The Law of International Responsibility* (Oxford: Oxford University Press, 2010) 994.

see in this regard Articles 42-48 ARSIWA. Whilst the forum for breaches of the law of state responsibility is the ICJ, individuals may turn to human rights bodies or the ICC, to be discussed below.

State responsibility may also be invoked through the attribution of certain acts to a state, when considering a breach of an obligation not directly incurred by the state itself. Articles 4-11 ARSIWA provide the various methods in which acts of individuals or groups might be attributed to the affected state.[17] In the circumstance of the provision of humanitarian assistance, attribution of conduct to the state may play a distinct role, as the provision of humanitarian assistance – or refusal thereof – is sometimes outsourced to various other actors, amongst which international organisations and NGOs, as well as other bodies that may operate within a set structure with the affected state. State responsibility may also incur in circumstances such as described in Articles 9 and 10 ARSIWA, if non-state actors violate human rights law and humanitarian law during a non-international armed conflict, should such non-state actors exercise a degree of control and subsequently gain sovereignty. Problematic for the determination of responsibility under the law of *state* responsibility as also relevant to the provision of humanitarian assistance remains the non-state actor that does not obtain such titles.

With regard to attribution, the ICJ has determined in the *Bosnian Genocide* case that a breach of international law (*in casu* genocide) may be attributable to a State:

> "if and to the extent that the physical acts constitutive of genocide that have been committed by organs or persons other than the State's own agents were carried out, wholly or in part, on the instructions or directions of the State, or under its effective control. This is the state of customary international law, as reflected in the ILC Articles on State Responsibility".[18]

The ICJ therefore determines that 'effective' control is necessary for such attribution. In doing so, it departs from both its own previous 'control' formula in the *Nicaragua* judgment and the ICTY with its *Tadić* 'overall control test', whilst, according to Cassese, failing to constructively reformulate them.[19] Indeed, 'effective' control as proposed by the ICJ differs from the approach taken by the ICTY that differentiated two degrees of control that vary depending on circumstances and subject; such as individuals versus organised groups that as a

---

[17] Article 4 ARSIWA concerns the conduct of organs of a state, Article 5 ARSIWA the conduct of persons or entities exercising elements of governmental authority, Article 6 ARSIWA the conduct of organs placed at the disposal of a State by another State, Article 7 ARSIWA the excess of authority or contravention of instructions, Article 8 ARSIWA relates to the conduct directed or controlled by a state, Article 9 ARSIWA the conduct carried out in the absence or default of the official authorities, Article 10 ARSIWA pertains to the conduct of an insurrectional or other movement and lastly Article 11 ARSIWA concerns conduct acknowledged and adopted by a State as its own.

[18] Application of the Convention on the Prevention and Punishment of the Crime of Genocide (Bosnia and Herzegovina v. Serbia and Montenegro), Judgment, I.C.J. Reports 2007, p. 43 § 401.

[19] Antonio Cassese, 'The Nicaragua and Tadic Tests Revisited in Light of the ICJ Judgment on Genocide in Bosnia', (2007) 18 *European Journal of International Law* 4, 649-668.

whole operate under the control of the state.[20] Without delving too deeply into the matter of types of 'control' in this aspect of attribution as part of the law of state responsibility, it remains therefore that the international tribunals dealing with such matters do as of yet not have one singular approach. From the ICJ's application in the *Bosnian Genocide* case it can be concluded that the Court sees 'effective control' as determinant in the assessment of state responsibility. With regard to the denial of the provision of assistance, such a denial *can* then be attributed to the affected state, should those responsible for the denial have been under the effective control of that state.

8.2.2 The ARSIWA, Peremptory Norms and the Denial of Humanitarian Assistance

With regard to the denial of the provision of humanitarian assistance, the ARSIWA's notion of 'circumstances precluding wrongfulness' as laid down in Articles 20-25 must be considered. These circumstances could function as potential factors in the prevention of the invocation of the law of state responsibility.[21] As argued above, state responsibility for the denial of the provision of humanitarian assistance could arise through violations of substantive provisions and duties found in human rights law or humanitarian law. In this regard, the ILC noted (in relation to Article 21 ARSIWA):

> "As to obligations under international humanitarian law and in relation to non-derogable human rights provisions, self-defence does not preclude the wrongfulness of conduct".[22]

As such, self-defence cannot be invoked by the affected state as a reason to deny humanitarian assistance. Rightfully, Chapter 5 has established that the provision of such assistance is a means of fulfilling non-derogable rights. Indeed, Articles 20-22 and 24-25 ARSIWA relate to matters which the *affected state* in its potential denial of provision of humanitarian assistance cannot call upon, as seen in the following.[23] Specifically with regard to humanitarian assistance and access (with and without force) by third parties, the ARSIWA provision concerning consent in Article 20 is relevant:

> "Valid consent by a State to the commission of a given act by another State precludes the wrongfulness of that act in relation to the former State to the extent that the act remains within the limits of that consent".

[20] *Prosecutor v. Tadić a.k.a "Dule"* (Appeals Chamber Decision on the Defence motion for Interlocutory Appeal on Jurisdiction) IT-94-1-AR72 (2 October 1995) § 120.

[21] Article 20 ARSIWA pertains to consent of a second state, Article 21 ARSIWA concerns matters of self-defence, Article 22 ARSIWA concerns countermeasures in respect of an internationally wrongful act, Article 23 ARSIWA concerns force majeure, Article 24 ARSIWA relates to distress and Article 25 ARSIWA concerns the state of necessity.

[22] 'Report of the International Law Commission' UN Doc A/56/10 (n 10) 178.

[23] For a further discussion 'Report of the International Law Commission' UN Doc A/56/10 (n 10) 173-183 and 189-194. See also Crawford, *State Responsibility: the General Part* (n 2) 283-295 and 301-305.

As discussed above in Chapter 7, in certain instances the provision of external humanitarian assistance is dependent on the consent of the affected state (in particular in times of natural disaster and non-international armed conflict). Despite having established that the *bona fide* offer of assistance; i.e. an offer in accordance with the principles of humanity, neutrality and impartiality, cannot be construed as an interference in the internal affairs of the affected state, it remains relevant to also note that the ARSIWA's provision in Article 20 can also be applied to the circumstance of the provision of assistance. As such, the giving of consent for access by third parties with a view to the provision of assistance would preclude the establishment of an unlawful interference with the affected state's internal affairs.

Furthermore relevant to this discussion is Article 25 ARSIWA concerning necessity which may – and has been – called in as an argument in *favour* of providing humanitarian assistance as opposed to obliging with another duty under international law.[24] International humanitarian law in essence merely allows for very distinct circumstances 'precluding wrongfulness' in consideration of the provision of humanitarian assistance, as Chapters 6 and 7 have addressed, mainly pertaining to the 'control rights' of states and the delaying of assistance for purposes of military necessity, but which specifically *exclude* the potential starvation of civilians.[25] Furthermore, human rights law as specifically related to humanitarian assistance (with regard to the rights to life, food and health) precludes the invocation of a state of emergency, as seen in Chapter 5. Thus, a state cannot circumvent its responsibility for breaches of international obligations under human rights law and humanitarian law in relation to the provision of humanitarian assistance by claiming certain circumstances precluding wrongfulness; specifically necessity, in its conduct based upon *those* fields of law. The ILC notes however that the question concerning the legality of humanitarian interventions (outside the scope of the collective use of force under the UN Charter) is not covered by Article 25 ARSIWA. Thus, the ILC merely considers the past claims towards this concept, whilst not discussing the potential breaches of international law that such claims in itself may amount to, given the fact that the use of force outside the context of Chapter VII or Chapter VIII of the UN Charter in itself is often a violation of a (peremptory) norm of international law. The need to invoke the state of necessity under Article 25 ARSIWA by a *third* state in the external provision of assistance is however somewhat overcome by the ILC's inclusion of Article 41 ARSIWA, which will be discussed in relation to the duty to cooperate.[26]

Potentially Article 23 ARSIWA allows for an invocation by the affected state with regard to a circumstance precluding wrongfulness. Indeed when considering the *denial* of humanitarian assistance 'force majeure' could be considered as a potential excuse by the affected state. Article 23 ARSIWA states:

[24] 'Report of the International Law Commission' UN Doc A/56/10 (n 10) 202,.
[25] Articles 23, 54 and 55 GC IV, as well as 70 and 71 AP I. Furthermore Section 8.3.
[26] Section 8.2.3 State Responsibility and the Potential Duty to Cooperate in the Event of a Breach.

> "1. The wrongfulness of an act of a State not in conformity with an international obligation of that State is precluded if the act is due to force majeure, that is the occurrence of an irresistible force or of an unforeseen event, beyond the control of the State, making it materially impossible in the circumstances to perform the obligation. 2. Paragraph 1 does not apply if: (a) The situation of force majeure is due, either alone or in combination with other factors, to the conduct of the State invoking it; or (b) The State has assumed the risk of that situation occurring".

Wrongfulness is precluded in the event of *force majeure* when three elements are cumulatively met: (1) an unforeseen event or irresistible force, (2) beyond control of the affected state, (3) making performance of the obligation materially impossible. Considering Article 23 ARSIWA relating to 'force majeure', the ILC has held in its *Commentary* that a state cannot claim 'force majeure' in the event it has itself 'caused or induced the situation in question'.[27] Thus, invoking 'force majeure' as a reason for the non-provision of humanitarian aid in times of conflict or occupation amounting to a humanitarian crisis that the affected state is to any extent partially responsible for, shall be quite difficult. The ILC has indeed focused rather on natural disasters, clarifying instances in which a state may appeal *force majeure* for its actions through circumstances such as 'earthquakes, floods or drought', but also in the event the affected state's territory should be lost due to an insurrection or military operations carried out by a third state.[28] While Crawford argues that a 'material impossibility' leading to a claim of *force majeure* might also arise in the event of a combination of factors such as the impossibility of a state to assist foreigners affected by a natural disaster because a particular area of a territory is under rebel control, responsibility does not necessarily disappear, as it shifts from one actor to another.[29] In the latter events, the responsibility to provide humanitarian assistance is transferred to either the armed groups,[30] or at a later stage to the newly occupying force; as the provisions pertaining to the delivery of humanitarian assistance may be invoked at a certain stage of occupation.[31] Also, the ILC *Commentary* argues that Article 23 ARSIWA may not be invoked as a circumstance precluding wrongfulness for situations in which the fulfilment of the obligation has merely become 'more difficult' rather than *impossible*, such as in the event of a political or economic crisis, nor may it be invoked should the situation be the result of neglect of the affected state.[32] Crawford also argues that *force majeure* differs from the circumstances precluding wrongfulness such as distress and

[27] 'Report of the International Law Commission' UN Doc A/56/10 (n 10) 188. See in support of this also the Arbitral Tribunal *Libyan Arab Foreign Investment Company v. Republic of Burundi,* I.L.R., vol. 96 (1994), p. 279 and 318 § 55. The ILC argues that Article 23 follows by analogy Article 61 of the Vienna Convention on the Law of Treaties.
[28] 'Report of the International Law Commission' UN Doc A/56/10 (n 10) 184.
[29] Crawford, *State Responsibility: the General Part* (n 2) 298.
[30] Section 6.5.1.2 regarding the obligations of armed groups in the provision of humanitarian assistance as argued amongst others by the Security Council and AP II.
[31] Section 6.5.3 on the invocation of provisions pertaining to the delivery of aid at various stages of occupation.
[32] 'Report of the International Law Commission' UN Doc A/56/10 (n 10) 184.

necessity in the sense that it implies an essentially involuntary act.[33] Natural disasters such as cyclones, tornadoes, droughts and tsunamis are clearly not voluntary acts by the affected state. Claiming *force majeure* as a circumstance precluding wrongfulness specifically *for the non-provision of humanitarian assistance* in the aftermath of a natural disaster shall however remain difficult due to a state's obligations under human rights law and in particular with a view to Article 2 ICESCR which provides for international assistance. As such, the ILC's *Commentary* in this respect does not provide a satisfactory explanation, as it alludes to the possibility of invoking Article 23 ARSIWA in circumstances of natural disaster, whilst the ICCPR does not allow for derogation of the right to life in times of emergency and the ICESCR in its entirety does not contain a derogation clause. If and when the affected state is not capable itself of performing this duty to provide assistance under human rights law, it continues to have obligations under said law to ensure the rights to life, food and health of persons within its jurisdiction, upon which according to Article 2 ICESCR it must resort to external parties that are offering their assistance. The state of emergency clauses in the various relevant treaties particular to the rights with regard to the provision of assistance cannot be invoked, as discussed in Chapter 5. Not requesting such assistance or not allowing external assistance by third parties into the affected territory shall not be considered *force majeure* and thereby an acceptable circumstance precluding the wrongfulness of the non-provision of assistance to persons in need. Whereas the natural disaster itself may be considered *force majeure*, the non-provision of assistance shall not be considered as such. State responsibility for the denial of humanitarian assistance may very well ensue. Indeed, as the ILC itself has argued, in practice many of the appeals to *force majeure* have failed, as the circumstance was not 'impossible' itself, but rather increasingly difficult to perform.[34] Allowing external help into a territory moreover is not difficult *per se*.

Furthermore Article 26 ARSIWA must be taken into account regardless of the specific circumstance precluding wrongfulness an affected state may attempt to claim as potential justification for its denial of humanitarian assistance. Article 26 ARSIWA stipulates with regard to the chapter in ARSIWA pertaining to circumstances precluding wrongfulness:

> "Nothing in this chapter precludes the wrongfulness of any act of a State which is not in conformity with an obligation arising under a peremptory norm of general international law".

Thus, conduct in breach of a peremptory norm is excluded from the scope of circumstances the ARSIWA recognises as precluding the wrongfulness of an act under international law. A 'circumstance precluding wrongfulness' as meant in Articles 20-25 ARSIWA may not be claimed as a waiver of responsibility for the violation of a norm of *jus cogens*. Although a discussion continues to exist as to

---

[33] Crawford, *State Responsibility: the General Part* (n 2) 295.
[34] 'Report of the International Law Commission' UN Doc A/56/10 (n 10) 185.

those norms which are currently accepted in international law as *jus cogens*,[35] the ICJ has determined that peremptory norms certainly include the prohibition of aggression, genocide, torture, slavery and racial discrimination.[36] In the above Chapters it has been discussed on numerous occasions that humanitarian assistance cannot be based upon racial discrimination, and moreover the non-provision of assistance may not lead to genocide. Through various cases before the ICTY, war crimes and crimes against humanity have also been recognised by this tribunal as peremptory norms of international law.[37] As will be discussed in more depth in further Sections, the denial of assistance may amount to such crimes. Furthermore, the ICJ has noted in its 1996 Advisory Opinion on the *Legality of the Threat or Use of Nuclear Weapons* that certain principles of international humanitarian law constitute 'intransgressible principles of international customary law'.[38] In its 2006 Fragmentation of International Law Study, the ILC has reiterated these 'candidates' for the status *of jus cogens*.[39]

The ICJ places the well-known Martens Clause amongst such principles, and declares it to have found a modern codification in Article 1(2) AP I of the Geneva Conventions. This Article distinctly refers to the principle of humanity and thus the notion of peremptory norms becomes even more relevant to the discussion

[35] See for a discussion on the norms which amount to *jus cogens* amongst others: Rafael Nieto Navia, 'International Peremptory Norms (Jus Cogens) And International Humanitarian Law' in LC Vohrah, F Pocar et al, (eds) *Man's Inhumanity to Man: Essays in Honour of Antonio Cassese* (Kluwer Law International 2003); Alexander Orakhelashvili, *Peremptory Norms in International Law* (Oxford University Press 2006); and Malcolm Shaw, *International Law* (Cambridge University Press 2008) 303, 720-721.

[36] *Armed Activities on the Territory of the Congo* (New Application : 2002) (Democratic Republic of the Congo v. Rwanda), Jurisdiction and Admissibility, Judgment, I.C.J. Reports 2006, p. 6, § 64 concerning the prohibition of genocide; Questions relating to the Obligation to Prosecute or Extradite (Belgium v. Senegal), Judgment, I.C.J. Reports 2012, p. 422 § 99 concerning the prohibition of torture; somewhat more generally concerning *erga omnes* obligations the ICJ Barcelona Traction, Light and Power Company Limited (Belgium v. Spain) case ICJ Reports 1970, § 33-34 regarding the prohibition of aggression and genocide, as well as 'basic human rights' such as the protection from slavery and racial discrimination.

[37] *Prosecutor v. Kupreškić et al. (IT-95-16) "Lašva Valley"*(Judgment Trial Chamber) IT-95-16-T (14 January 2000 § 520; *Prosecutor v. Furundzija* (Trial Judgment) IT-95-17/1-T (ICTY 10 December 1998) § 151-157; *Prosecutor v. Zejnil Delalic, Zdravko Mucic (aka "Pavo"), Hazim Delic and Esad Landžo (aka "Zenga") (Celebici - Case)* (Appeals Chamber) IT-96-21-A (20 February 2001) § 172; *Prosecutor v. Krstic* (Trial Judgment) IT-98-33-T (2 August 2001) § 541.

[38] Legality of the Threat or Use of Nuclear Weapons, Advisory Opinion, I.C.J. Reports 1996, p. 226, § 78-79.

[39] 'Fragmentation Of International Law: Difficulties Arising From The Diversification And Expansion Of International Law', Report of the Study Group of the International Law Commission (13 April 2006) UN Doc A/CN.4/L.682 § 374: "Overall, the most frequently cited candidates for the status of jus cogens include: (a) the prohibition of aggressive use of force; (b) the right to self-defence; (c) the prohibition of genocide; (d) the prohibition of torture; (e) crimes against humanity; (f) the prohibition of slavery and slave trade; (g) the prohibition of piracy; (h) the prohibition of racial discrimination and apartheid, and (i) the prohibition of hostilities directed at civilian population ("basic rules of international humanitarian law")".

concerning responsibilities in the provision of humanitarian assistance.[40] By considering the Martens Clause as part of these 'intransgressible principles of international customary law', the ICJ thus places Article 1(2) AP I and thereby the principle of humanity, one of the core foundations and cornerstones upon which the legal framework concerning the provision of humanitarian assistance is set, within this context also. It stands to reason that if the text of Article 1(2) AP I which states that civilians remain 'under the protection and authority of the principles of international law derived from [...] the principle of humanity' is considered by the ICJ to be the modern translation of the Martens Clause, which itself is an 'intransgressible principle' of customary international law, then the protection of civilians by the principle of humanity *itself* must also be considered as such. Indeed, the principle of humanity has in Chapter 2 been explicated as one of the guiding principles along which assistance is provided. Therefore, abiding by the principle of humanity – by way of the Martens Clause – is a manner of keeping in line with peremptory norms of international law.[41]

In relation to the provision of humanitarian assistance given the nature of the topic, namely the delivery of emergency aid in times of a humanitarian crisis, potential violations of *jus cogens* will most likely be related to the prohibition of war crimes, crimes against humanity and racial discrimination.[42] Violating the protection of persons in times of crisis by violating the principle of humanity would then potentially be considered as such also by the ICJ. The deprivation by the affected state of humanitarian assistance to persons in need may very well turn the 'affected' state into the 'inflicting' state, leading to state responsibility for the non-provision of humanitarian assistance. Such responsibility is specific to the circumstance and the related breach of international law. In times of conflict or occupation, depriving a population of food, water, shelter and medicine could lead to war crimes. At all times, and therefore also in times of conflict, occupation or a (natural) disaster, racial discrimination is prohibited and the (non)-provision of humanitarian assistance may not be based upon this.[43] It has furthermore been established by the ICJ, in referral to the ICERD, that access to humanitarian assistance is a right of persons under the ICERD and human rights law.[44] Crimes against humanity may also occur in either conflict, occupation or (natural) disaster as it has been established in international law that the nexus to an armed conflict is

---

[40] Article 1(2) AP I states: "In cases not covered by this Protocol or by other international agreements, civilians and combatants remain under the protection and authority of the principles of international law derived from established custom, from the principles of humanity and from the dictates of public conscience".

[41] 2.2.3 The Principles for the Delivery of Assistance.

[42] 8.6.2 Enforcement through International Criminal Law.

[43] See in this regard Georgia's attempt to claim 'obstruction of access to humanitarian assistance' as potential racial discrimination in Application of the International Convention on the Elimination of All Forms of Racial Discrimination (Georgia v. Russian Federation), Preliminary Objections, Judgment, I.C.J. Reports 2011, p. 70 § 17.

[44] Application of the International Convention on the Elimination of all Forms of Racial Discrimination (Georgia v. Russian Federation), Provisional Measures, Order of 15 October 2008, I.C.J. Reports 2008, p. 353 § 149 B.

no longer required for crimes against humanity and that such crimes may therefore occur also in circumstances which are not related to an armed conflict.[45] Meron notes that 'systematic gross violations of human rights directed at civilians' are also considered as crimes against humanity.[46] This above determination regarding war crimes, crimes against humanity and the prohibition of racial discrimination (the latter in particular respect to various human rights) provides for a broad range of potential violations of peremptory norms of international law that are related to the framework of the provision of humanitarian assistance and that may lead to incurring state responsibility. In particular, given their broad applicability, crimes against humanity or racial discrimination could be the peremptory norms through which state responsibility will most likely be claimed with regard to the denial of humanitarian assistance, in particular if the circumstance is lacking an armed conflict, but might be related to a (natural) disaster.

Article 23 ARSIWA concerning *force majeure*, which is the only Article in the ARSIWA's circumstances precluding wrongfulness that may potentially be invoked by the affected state as a reason it has denied humanitarian assistance, may therefore not be invoked in the event such a denial leads to a breach of the prohibition of genocide, crimes against humanity, war crimes, or racial discrimination. Thus, justifiably invoking Article 23 ARSIWA has another added threshold for the affected state: it may not include a breach of a norm of *jus cogens*, alongside the difficulties of arguing *force majeure* if it has not requested assistance from third parties to provide external emergency aid following Article 2 ICESCR and 55 and 56 UN Charter. Furthermore, although not immediately recognised as 'jus cogens', states must also ensure they do not violate the principle of humanity, as determined by the ICJ. By way of the Martens Clause, which the ICJ has argued forms part of what it coined 'intransgressible principles of international customary law', this principle is arguably part of the body of *jus cogens* norms. This is a new concept as such, given that this phrasing of 'intrangressible norms' was not previously part of international legal lingo. It appears, as argued by Vincent Chetail, that the Court has wanted to emphasise that such norms, within international humanitarian law as a legal field, hold particular importance compared to other norms of customary international legal nature.[47]

It must be noted that, given the fact that the ARSIWA have only recently been codified, they have to date not been used in the enforcement of a state's obligation in the provision of humanitarian assistance, nor have those pre-existing elements of customary status been invoked in this regard. Therefore, it may be too soon to tell whether in fact states will resort to the use of Articles 42 and 48 ARSIWA in their

---

[45] *Prosecutor v. Tadić a.k.a "Dule"* (Appeals Chamber Decision on the Defence motion for Interlocutory Appeal on Jurisdiction) IT-94-1-AR72 (2 October 1995) § 141; UN CHR Report of the Secretary General 'Promotion and Protection of Human Rights: Fundamental Standards of Humanity' (18 December 1998) UN Doc E/CN.4/1999/92 § 12; and ICC Statute Article 7. See also 8.6.2.

[46] Theodor Meron, 'The Humanization of Humanitarian Law', (2000) 94 *American Journal of International Law* 2, 265.

[47] Vincent Chetail, 'The contribution of the International Court of Justice to international humanitarian law', (2003) 85 *International Review of the Red Cross* 850, 250-251.

attempt to hold a state affected by a humanitarian crisis responsible for the denial of humanitarian assistance, or whether such a state will indeed claim a circumstance precluding the wrongfulness of its actions, such as that of Article 23 ARSIWA, despite difficulties concerning norms of *jus cogens* and obligations under existing human rights law.[48]

8.2.3 State Responsibility and the Potential Duty to Cooperate in the Event of a Breach

The law concerning the international responsibility of states lastly not only places responsibilities on the affected state, but also places a responsibility upon third states *to cooperate* to bring violations of international law to an end. Thus, not only the *affected* state could have a duty under the law of state responsibility to provide assistance to persons in need, but *third* states may have also certain responsibilities.[49] These responsibilities must be distinguished from the rights and duties discussed in Chapter 7 regarding the provision of assistance by third parties. Such rights of third parties are related *directly* to the provision of assistance under substantive bodies of law such as human rights or humanitarian law. Subsequently, the denial of this provision of assistance through external sources could indeed result in circumstances which might be construed as violations of international law that must be brought to an end. This is the subject-matter at hand: the duty to cooperate for third states under the law of state responsibility as an enforcement mechanism to bring violations of international law to an end. Such a duty is derived and results from the duties of the affected state not to violate international law through the unlawful denial of humanitarian assistance.

Article 1(3) of the UN Charter states that it is a purpose of the Organization to 'achieve international cooperation in promoting and encouraging respect for human rights and fundamental freedoms for all'. In relation to the provision of humanitarian assistance, this principle is brought into practice through calls upon the international community by the General Assembly and especially the Security Council as discussed in Chapter 7 with regard to assisting in the provision emergency aid, to put an end to certain serious on-going crises.[50] The UN therefore recognises a responsibility of the international community at large to act in the face of large-scale crises and human rights violations. This responsibility was asserted very early on in the work of the UN in the well-known General Assembly's 'Declaration on Principles of International Law concerning Friendly Relations and Co-operation among States in accordance with the Charter of the United Nations'

[48] The consequences of invoking a circumstance precluding the wrongfulness of an act under international law remain beyond the scope of this research. In that regard, see Article 27 ARSIWA and further.

[49] This research will not address the various rights and duties states may have under their national legislation, but will rather focus on the international legal aspects.

[50] Sections 7.4.2 Security Council Resolutions and the Right to Access and 7.4.4 General Assembly Resolutions and the Right to Access.

of 1970, that formulated the 'duty of States to co-operate with one another in accordance with the Charter'.[51]

Today, the ILC has codified more extensively the duties and responsibilities of the international community with regard to breaches of peremptory and other norms of international law. Article 41(1) ARSIWA distinctly calls upon third states to cooperate in bringing to an end any breach of peremptory norms that 'involves a gross or systematic failure by the responsible State'.[52] The obligation therefore only arises should there be a breach of a peremptory norm, *and* if the affected state was involved through a gross or systematic failure. This provision envisages a *positive* obligation, that may be executed either through an institution such as the UN, or in a non-institutionalised manner.[53] Thus, if the lack of provision of humanitarian assistance by the affected state results in the gross or systematic breach of a peremptory norm of international law, third states may have a responsibility to bring this breach to a halt. Given the current restricted number of norms that are recognised in the international community as *jus cogens*, such a situation may only in reality apply to the legal framework of humanitarian assistance in the event the deprivation of receipt of humanitarian assistance by a population amounts to crimes against humanity, war crimes, genocide or racial discrimination. Benvenisti concurs, arguing that indeed circumstances such as crimes against humanity and grave breaches of humanitarian law are 'recognized instances where sovereigns are required to invest resources in the effort to protect humanity's concerns'.[54] While Article 41(1) calls for 'lawful' measures, difficulties might arise when these serious breaches remain within the territorial jurisdiction of the affected state, and no particular third state may be inclined to initiate the ending of the breach.[55] Often resort shall be had to the UN Security Council and the collective use of force, whereas another international legal discussion might arise as to the lawfulness of the use of force in ending the breach according to Article 41(1) ARSIWA.[56]

Arguably the vicinity of a state to the crisis can be relevant in the provision of assistance and the related legal rights or duties. Naturally, such states may have a greater motivation concerning the upholding of political, economic and social stability in their particular area of the world. Legally however, if a state may have a responsibility in the creation of a crisis, such as can be the case with trans-boundary natural or man-made disasters, should such a state also bear active responsibility for the delivery of aid to its neighbouring state? According to Vukas, principal drafter of the Bruges Resolution of 2003, the state which 'bears some

---

[51] UNGA Res 2625 (XXV) (24 October 1970) 'Declaration on Principles of International Law Concerning Friendly Relations and Cooperation among States in Accordance with the Charter of the United Nations', Annex.
[52] Article 40 and 41 ARSIWA.
[53] 'Report of the International Law Commission' UN Doc A/56/10 (n 10) 286-287.
[54] Eyal Benvenisti 'Sovereigns as Trustees of humanity: The Concept and its Normative Implications', (2012) *SSRN* accessed 24 January 2012, 27.
[55] Crawford, *State Responsibility: the General Part* (n 2) 386-387.
[56] Ibid 386-387; see also 8.4 on the use of force.

responsibility for a disaster' that then affects another state, will also be obliged to provide assistance.[57] Furthermore, Vukas argues that in particular those states in the vicinity of the humanitarian crisis should offer aid to the victims to 'the maximum extent possible'.[58] A somewhat vague conclusion therefore remains concerning neighbouring states. Indeed, as assessed in Chapter 6, bearing responsibility as 'affected state' leads to the duty to provide assistance. The ARSIWA also address the issue of vicinity with regard to the duties of the international community according to Article 41 ARSIWA. The Article stipulates that the duty to cooperate for third states is applicable regardless of whether or not such states were affected by the serious breach themselves.[59] The ILC Commentary to the ARSIWA argues that while Article 41(1) might according to some be a reflection of 'progressive development', such cooperation, in particularly in an institutionalised manner, is in practice already being carried out in response to the gravest violations of international law.[60] Such arguments are supported by the UN Charter and practice, as seen above. As such, the ILC argues that Article 41(1) is an attempt to:

> "strengthen the existing mechanisms of cooperation, on the basis that all States are called upon to make an appropriate response to the serious breaches referred to in article 40".[61]

Indeed, often such responses occur through the UN framework by means of the Security Council and the use of force, which is addressed in following Sections. Furthermore, Article 41(2) ARSIWA distinctly provides that states are prohibited from maintaining a circumstance which is 'opposable to all States in the sense of barring *erga omnes* the legality of a situation which is maintained in violation of international law'.[62] Thus, not only do states have a positive duty to cooperate in ending a serious breach of a peremptory norm, the law of state responsibility will hold *third states* responsible should they assist in maintaining such breaches after the fact.[63] In line with this perspective, the General Assembly has held the viewpoint pertaining to the provision of humanitarian assistance that it is in fact also a 'collective responsibility' to uphold principles such as human dignity, and to ensure that the victims of humanitarian emergencies are given 'every assistance' possible.[64]

---

57 Budislav Vukas, 'Humanitarian Assistance in Cases of Emergency', (2007) *Max Planck Encyclopedia of Public International Law* § 22.
58 Ibid.
59 'Report of the International Law Commission' UN Doc A/56/10 (n 10) 287.
60 'Report of the International Law Commission' UN Doc A/56/10 (n 10) 287.
61 Ibid.
62 Legal Consequences for States of the Continued Presence of South Africa in Namibia (South West Africa) notwithstanding Security Council Resolution 276 (1970), Advisory Opinion, ICJ Reports (1971) p. 16, § 126.
63 'Report of the International Law Commission' UN Doc A/56/10 (n 10) 290.
64 UNGA Res 55/2 (18 September 2000) UN Doc A/RES/55/2 'United Nations Millennium Declaration' § 2, 26.

Moreover, this perspective of cooperation has also been asserted by the ICJ in its 2007 *Bosnia v Serbia* judgment, where the Court argued that 'an obligation of conduct' exists for state parties to the Genocide Convention to prevent the occurrence of genocide. Although the ICJ expressly asserts that it is merely reflecting the Genocide Convention's scope of the 'duty to prevent' and is not attempting a general jurisprudence on the matter, it *does* acknowledge that the Genocide Convention is certainly not the only international legal instrument that provides for a duty of states parties to take steps in the prevention of acts the instrument attempts to prohibit.[65] In its assessment of such an obligation under the Genocide Convention, the Court determines:

> "It is clear that the obligation in question is one of conduct and not one of result, in the sense that a State cannot be under an obligation to succeed, whatever the circumstances, in preventing the commission of genocide: the obligation of States parties is rather to employ all means reasonably available to them, so as to prevent genocide so far as possible. A State does not incur responsibility simply because the desired result is not achieved; responsibility is however incurred if the State manifestly failed to take all measures to prevent genocide which were within its power, and which might have contributed to preventing the genocide. In this area the notion of "due diligence", which calls for an assessment *in concreto*, is of critical importance. Various parameters operate when assessing whether a State has duly discharged the obligation concerned. The first, which varies greatly from one State to another, is clearly the capacity to influence effectively the action of persons likely to commit, or already committing, genocide. This capacity itself depends, among other things, on the geographical distance of the State concerned from the scene of the events, and on the strength of the political links, as well as links of all other kinds, between the authorities of that State and the main actors in the events. The State's capacity to influence must also be assessed by legal criteria, since it is clear that every State may only act within the limits permitted by international law; seen thus, a State's capacity to influence may vary depending on its particular legal position vis-à-vis the situations and persons facing the danger, or the reality, of genocide. On the other hand, it is irrelevant whether the State whose responsibility is in issue claims, or even proves, that even if it had employed all means reasonably at its disposal, they would not have sufficed to prevent the commission of genocide. As well as being generally difficult to prove, this is irrelevant to the breach of the obligation of conduct in question, the more so since the possibility remains that the combined efforts of several States, each complying with its obligation to prevent, might have achieved the result — averting the commission of genocide — which the efforts of only one State were insufficient to produce".[66]

The Court determines in the above that a 'manifest failing to take all measures' in the prevention of genocide might lead to the determination of state responsibility for third states, whilst it recognises several criteria that may influence whether indeed such a duty is fulfilled. The Court notes in this regard a capacity of third

---

[65] Application of the Convention on the Prevention and Punishment of the Crime of Genocide (Bosnia and Herzegovina v. Serbia and Montenegro), Judgment, I.C.J. Reports 2007, p. 43 § 429.
[66] Ibid § 430.

states to influence those committing genocide, which may depend on geographical distance, the strength of political or other ties and other factors. Interestingly, and in line with the ARSIWA's approach on the duty to cooperate, the ICJ notes the obligation of conduct is not waived in the event a state's efforts 'would not have sufficed', given the fact that the combined efforts of several states *could* have achieved the desired result. Thus, an obligation continues to lie on each individual state, whilst taking into account the criteria recognised by the Court. Drawing a parallel between the crime of genocide and the duty of the affected and third state to provide humanitarian assistance, in the latter instance an obligation of conduct can be discerned also, in particular when considering the provisions in human rights law and international humanitarian law. Both fields of law ascertain various duties of the affected state to provide humanitarian aid in times of crisis, varying from specific duties to *not obstruct* the assistance being provided to the duty in human rights law to *actively seek* assistance from third parties in the fulfilment of the rights as enshrined in the ICESCR.[67] The international community is called upon in both *corpora juris* to assist in the provision of aid or the fulfilment of certain rights, from which a duty can be deduced to refrain from performing an opposite act, namely reinforcing the crisis.[68]

Regarding the matter of vicinity, the joint findings of the ARSIWA Commentary and the ICJ conclude that indeed, while it may not be relevant that third states are individually affected by the breach in question, the duty of conduct (as formulated by the ICJ) and duty to cooperate (as formulated in Article 41 ARSIWA) might be found more easily and at a lower threshold for a neighbouring country. In particular in relation to a humanitarian crisis, with its risks of spilling over into neighbouring countries and thereby enhancing the instability in a particular region, proximity is a factor, albeit difficult to definitively ascertain legally. Such difficulties arise from the fact that the duty to prevent large-scale violations of human rights as currently laid down in international law rests upon the international community as a whole. Yet, the notion of proximity and geography cannot be swept aside. In particular, this is supported by the large amount of regional organisations taking responsibilities upon themselves in the face of crises.[69] This duty for third states to prevent the exacerbation of the crisis, as seen in the Court's analysis of the duty in the context of the Genocide Convention, must therefore not be seen in a vacuum, but in combination of this same duty of other states parties to the treaty at hand. An example is the regional Kampala Convention pertaining to the protection and assistance of IDPs, where

[67] Annex to Chapter 6.
[68] Annex to Chapter 7.
[69] Amongst others ASEAN's initiative to launch a Humanitarian Assistance Centre for the purpose of collective responses to disasters and the African Union's Stand-by Force as created in Article 4(h) of its Constitutive Act in order to intervene in member states should war crimes, genocide or crimes against humanity take place. The tasks and mandate of the Stand-by Force are elaborated upon in the Protocol Relating To The Establishment Of The Peace And Security Council Of The African Union Adopted by the 1st Ordinary Session of the Assembly of the African Union Durban (9 July 2002) Article 3(f) and Article 15.

this perspective is translated into a right of the African Union to intervene in the event of war crimes, crimes against humanity and genocide.[70] Together, a combined 'duty to prevent' of both neighbouring states and those further away but with potentially more financial means or resources at their disposal, might be positively formulated as a duty to cooperate; as done by Article 41(1) ARSIWA. However, a duty may not be imposed upon assisting states according to the ARSIWA unless non-provision results in the violation of peremptory norms, or such norms are violated and the affected state was involved through a gross or systematic failure.[71] Therefore, from the above it can be determined that states may have an obligation of conduct individually in the prevention of certain breaches of international law, which may amount to a combined duty of the larger international community to cooperate in such prevention or bringing to a halt of breaches of peremptory norms as determined by the ARSIWA. In particular in relation to humanitarian assistance, such duties would rest upon states in relation to crimes against humanity, war crimes and/or racial discrimination, and potentially genocide.

The ARSIWA's approach with regard to the duty to cooperate is echoed *verbatim* in Article 42 of the ILC Draft Articles on the responsibility of international organisations.[72] Thus, international organisations such as the UN, or other regional institutions would, under these Draft Articles, have a similar duty to that of states in the cooperation to end serious breaches of international law *by an international organisation.*[73] Interestingly therefore, international organisations according to these Draft Articles could be held responsible for failing to cooperate with states in ending such serious breaches. Considering the nature of the norms, the 'jurisdiction' of the UN Security Council would in particular be affected. Under Article 43 of the Draft Articles on the responsibility of international organisations, responsibility for breaches may be invoked by other international organisations or states, not individuals or other actors. For the purpose of this research however, it must be noted that the role of international organisations is considered that of *provider* of humanitarian assistance, rather than that of *denier*, which is also reflected in practice, where international organisations assume the role of provider in the event the affected state does not provide assistance. Should, however, an international organisation violate a peremptory norm of international law, Draft Article 42 might provide relief. But currently it remains to be seen whether the General Assembly will adopt the Articles as developed by the ILC.

A well-known manner in which international organisations have taken a duty to cooperate in the event of a breach (by a state) upon themselves in cooperation with states is the *collective use of force* to end certain violations of peremptory norms

---

70 Articles 8(1) and 9 African Union Convention for the Protection and Assistance of Internally Displaced Persons in Africa (Kampala 22 October 2009).

71 Articles 40 and 41 ARSIWA.

72 Article 42 of the 'Draft articles on the responsibility of international organizations' of 2011.

73 'Draft articles on the responsibility of international organizations, with commentaries' adopted by the ILC at its sixty-third session UN Doc A/66/10 (2011) 66.

that have been addressed: violations of the prohibition of the use of force, genocide, crimes against humanity or war crimes. Often, serious breaches of international humanitarian law or human rights law also lead to the establishment of a need for the collective use of force. This has been distinctly reflected in Article 89 AP I of the Geneva Conventions, which declares:

> "In situations of serious violations of the Conventions or of this Protocol, the High Contracting Parties undertake to act, jointly or individually, in co-operation with the United Nations and in conformity with the United Nations Charter".

The Additional Protocol thereby clearly recognises a duty to cooperate through the call 'to act' in conformity with the UN Charter should 'serious violations' of international humanitarian law take place in times of an international armed conflict. AP I itself does not provide for the specific measures which are to be taken in such cooperation to bring the violations of the law to an end, but rather leaves these open according to the practices of the UN Charter. The Commentary, however, does explicate that such serious violations are not confined to the 'grave breaches' regime of the Conventions, and may therefore cover a wider scope.[74] As such, they may include amongst others violations pertaining to the duties concerning the provision of humanitarian assistance. In this sense, in particular the violation of the protection of civilians in accordance with the principle of humanity as codified in Article 1(2) AP I is of relevance. The circumstances in international law relating to (the denial of) the provision of assistance which may amount to the enforcement through the use of force is addressed in the following Sections. The wording of Article 89 AP I itself follows that of Article 56 UN Charter, calling upon member states to 'pledge themselves to take joint and separate action in co-operation with the Organization for the achievement of the purposes set forth in Article 55', which in turn reflects the duty of states to promote human rights (development). These two Articles are a further explication of Article 1(3) UN Charter that was discussed at the beginning of this Section. Such a view is also held by Article 1 common to the four Geneva Conventions, declaring that all states have a duty to ensure respect for the Convention in all circumstances, implying a duty to ensure compliance even when that state party is not involved in a particular conflict.[75] Thus, when third states must uphold the provisions of this Convention, this naturally includes those provisions pertaining to the provision of humanitarian assistance.

It must therefore be noted that throughout various sources of international law; including the UN Charter, the ARSIWA, the Geneva Conventions and the jurisprudence of the ICJ, a duty to cooperate exists for the international community

[74] Yves Sandoz, Christophe Swinarski & Bruno Zimmermann (eds) *Commentary on the Additional Protocols of 8 June 1977 to the Geneva Conventions of 12 August 1949, Protocol I and II (*International Committee of the Red Cross 1987*)* Protocol I Article 89, 1033-1034. See also Section 8.6 Methods of Enforcement through Individual (Criminal) Responsibility.

[75] This has also been reiterated by the ICJ in its Legal Consequences of the Construction of a Wall in the Occupied Palestinian Territory, Advisory Opinion, I.C.J. Reports 2004, p. 136, § 158.

to bring serious breaches of international law that can be related to the denial of humanitarian assistance, to an end.

8.2.4 State Responsibility, Humanitarian Assistance and Legal Developments

Another legal development by the ILC – although not (yet) codified like the ARSIWA – is the work on the 'Protection of persons in the event of disasters'. These Draft Articles are currently being developed and thereby do not amount to *lex lata*, compared to large parts of the ARSIWA, yet are relevant to consider as potential state responsibility may be invoked should they be developed into law. Thus, although they do not form part of the body of hard law, they *are* more specifically tailored towards the provision of assistance. Whereas the purpose of these Draft Articles is not to attempt the drafting of a new human rights convention, the Articles do incorporate a responsibility of the affected state to provide in humanitarian assistance and seek international assistance should the national capacities be overwhelmed, in a similar manner to Article 2 ICESCR.[76] Interestingly, Draft Article 12 notes a 'primary *role'* of the affected state in the coordination and direction of aid although not strongly formulating a 'responsibility', which leads to the inference of a 'secondary *role*' for potential third parties, for the provision of humanitarian assistance. In the absence of an actual legal 'responsibility', it would then also not be possible to assert state *responsibility* for such third parties in the event *they* fail to comply with such coordination or direction. Enforcement of such an Article, should it be codified, shall therefore remain difficult.

Currently, the Draft Articles are formulated generally from the perspective of the affected state, as opposed to drafting a potential (joint) responsibility for third parties in cooperation or assistance in the aftermath of a disaster. Draft Article 12 decisively states that the affected state has the 'duty to ensure the protection of persons and provision of disaster relief and assistance on its territory'. This formulation of a responsibility of 'result' shall thus allow the invocation of state responsibility in the event these Draft Articles are codified and in the event an affected state does not comply with said duty. Although the Draft Articles' outlook is that of the affected state, Draft Article 8 has a more encompassing view and clearly formulates that:

> "In accordance with the present draft articles, States shall, as appropriate, cooperate among themselves, and with the United Nations and other competent intergovernmental organizations, the International Federation of Red Cross and Red Crescent Societies and the International Committee of the Red Cross, and with relevant non-governmental organizations".

Thus, through the wording 'shall', the ILC envisages a duty of states to 'cooperate', which has been elaborated upon in Draft Article 9 to include humanitarian

[76] See Draft Articles 8, 12 and 13 as well as Sections 6.5.9, 6.5.10, 7.5.9 and 7.5.10.

assistance.[77] Such a duty can be read as a duty of conduct, as opposed to a duty of result such as enshrined in Article 41 ARSIWA (dealing with breaches of peremptory norms). In the absence of a duty of result with regard to international cooperation, arguing state responsibility for the violation of such a duty remains difficult, whilst potentially the failure to 'try' may be argued. The ILC Draft Articles, with a view to enforcement, appear to be taking the route therefore of creating international responsibility for the affected state, but such responsibility remains lacking for third states or other parties, should they fail to comply with the duty to cooperate in the provision of assistance. However, that being said, should such a failure to provide aid result in a breach of Articles 40 and 41 ARSIWA, the international community may still be held responsible. Naturally, the affected state shall also continue to be held responsible under the current regime of Articles 2, 3, 42 and, progressively, 48 ARSIWA.

8.3 Acts Constituting Denial or Obstruction of Humanitarian Assistance

Denial or obstruction of humanitarian assistance by the affected state can be twofold, as the affected state *itself* may deny the affected population the provision of aid, and/or alternatively the state may deny *third parties* access for the provision of assistance to the affected population. Given the potential dual nature of the denial of assistance, a state may indeed be in violation of international law on multiple accounts. Only upon the establishment of a violation of a norm of international law, is enforcement a possibility. Reality on the ground in times of a humanitarian crisis indeed often does not mirror the rights and duties reflected in the legal provisions at hand. This discrepancy results in both a need and a calling for enforcement methods in the event the affected state does not abide by the duties resting upon it according to international law, and does not allow persons in need or third parties to exercise their rights according to that same law in the provision of international humanitarian assistance. In certain instances, the 'affected' state may even become the 'inflicting' state. A well-known recent example in the field of natural disasters includes that of cyclone Nargis hitting Myanmar in 2008, upon which the government was not willing to allow certain rescue teams into the country.[78] In the context of armed conflict, the dire situation in Syria also comes to mind, as the Syrian government has repeatedly refused international aid to be allowed into the country, as well as refusing international providers of such aid.[79]

---

[77] Draft Article 9 ILC protection of persons in the event of disasters declares: "For the purposes of the present draft articles, cooperation includes humanitarian assistance, coordination of international relief actions and communications, and making available relief personnel, equipment and goods, and scientific, medical and technical resources".

[78] Reports of the Myanmar government refusing external delivery of aid can be found at <www.hrw.org/news/2010/04/29/burma-after-cyclone-repression-impedes-civil-society-and-aid-0> accessed 2 October 2013; and <http://reliefweb.int/report/myanmar/myanmar-cyclone-nargis-ocha-situation-report-no-6> accessed 2 October 2013.

[79] Reports of the denial by Syria of access by the UN Emergency Relief Coordinator Valerie Amos can be found at <www.reuters.com/article/2012/02/29/us-syria-un-idUSTRE81S20Z20120229> accessed 2

In such instances, the affected state may be violating international law, as it denies the provision of humanitarian assistance to its population, leading to a need for enforcement. Having asserted that persons in need of food, water, medical supplies and shelter should be enabled to receive such assistance, the legal consequences of the denial of there become relevant, with a view to potential enforcement methods. Legal consequences must specifically be addressed, as they enable persons in need of assistance to obtain such assistance through legal methods and mechanisms. Such legal, and in particular forceful, consequences as discussed in this Chapter must however be seen as a last resort. All other options, via diplomatic and humanitarian channels, must be sought after first.[80] The legal approach of enforcement is not necessarily the quickest or most viable solution in all situations, but it is important to establish which manners of redress are possible in the event of such flagrant violations of international law that amount to the denial of assistance, when other attempts (such as diplomatic methods) have failed.

8.3.1 Circumstances of Denial or Obstruction: Determining a Humanitarian Crisis

In the law pertaining to the provision of humanitarian assistance, one of the greatest problems is the determination of *what specifically* constitutes an act of 'denial of humanitarian assistance', or obstruction thereof. Indeed, as discussed in Chapters 6 and 7, in certain instances it is up to the discretion of the affected state and its sovereignty to determine whether or not it shall allow the external provision of humanitarian assistance. This discretion is, however, limited by the boundaries in international law that might lead to state responsibility or even individual responsibility. Chapters 5, 6 and 7 have indeed asserted that the current legal framework on the provision of humanitarian assistance demands far-reaching efforts from the affected state. In fact, it is not only the concept of state sovereignty as a 'responsibility' towards citizens that enforces this viewpoint, but also *vice versa*: the currently held perspective that the needs of those in times of a crisis must be met, through access for humanitarian assistance, is changing the nature of sovereignty. As Spieker has argued, although a right to offer or provide external assistance can be established, the problem lies in the enforceability of that title.[81] Several distinct and tiered questions are indeed crucial in this assertion and determination.

Firstly, the question whether a territory and population are in fact *dealing with a humanitarian crisis* needs to be addressed. In Section 3.3.3 it has been proposed

---

October 2013; and by Ban Ki Moon at <http://in.reuters.com/article/2014/07/24/syria-crisis-un-aid-idINKBN0FT28A20140724> accessed 22 May 2015.

[80] 'Further Promotion And Encouragement Of Human Rights And Fundamental Freedoms, Including The Question Of The Programme And Methods Of Work Of The Commission Alternative Approaches And Ways And Means Within The United Nations System For Improving The Effective Enjoyment Of Human Rights And Fundamental Freedoms' Note by the Secretary-General UN Doc E/CN.4/1993/35 (21 January 1993) § 267.

[81] Heike Spieker, 'Humanitarian Assistance, Access in Armed Conflict and Occupation' (2013) *Max Planck Encyclopedia of Public International Law* § 38.

that a humanitarian crisis is 'a situation deriving from a variety of origins, including natural or man-made disaster, armed conflict and occupation; causing grave damages of a personal or material nature to persons, where (national/external) assistance is needed as the local capacity is either overwhelmed, unable or sometimes unwilling to manage the circumstances'. Thus, a situation must exist in which a *need or necessity* for humanitarian assistance exists, either from within the state or from external sources.

Important in answering this initial question is a second related question: *Who* determines whether or not a local capacity is overwhelmed, unable or unwilling to provide assistance; leading to the term used in international humanitarian law of an 'inadequately supplied' territory? Based on the cornerstone notion in international law of state sovereignty, a certain margin of appreciation is left to the affected state. Examples of this can be found in the law pertaining to non-international armed conflicts and which are based on the incorporation of *consent* of the affected state.[82] But today as established, state sovereignty entails not only an external shield but also an internal responsibility, and consent to offers by third parties may not always be withheld, which is directly related to this notion of 'adequacy of supply'.[83] Leaving the determination of the 'inadequacy of supply' solely in the hands of the affected state, would result in this state determining *itself* whether or not it is violating international law. As such, the determination in international law regarding the question of whether or not humanitarian assistance is *needed* in certain instances should by default be handed over to an authoritative body.[84] If the denial of (internal or external) humanitarian assistance is a violation of international law; namely when the denial cannot be justified according to the provisions discussed in Chapters 6 and 7, then the determination of what *constitutes* denial of the provision should not be left to the affected state. As will be seen in this Chapter, such a body can be a judiciary body like the ICJ, ICC and various human rights courts, or a supranational body such as the Security Council. Not one single body is, or can be authoritative, as the nature of the crisis may determine which body shall be the recipient of the question to answer. Also, whilst such bodies cannot be presumed infallible, in the absence of one single judiciary, this is the current system in international law which can be utilised and will be explored in this Chapter.

Based on the above, it is thus possible to establish that the initial assessment for enforcement options lies in the determination of whether or not a territory is suffering from a humanitarian crisis, and whether the affected territory is adequately supplied by the affected state. The determination of this lies initially with the affected state, given its sovereign duties, but may – considering potential violation of international norms – be extrapolated to the judgment of an international authoritative body.

---

[82] Amongst others Article 18 AP II.

[83] 4.2.3 and 4.3 on the notion of state sovereignty today.

[84] UNGA Res 60/1 (24 October 2005) UN Doc A/RES/60/1 'World Summit Outcome Document' § 118, 138 and 139.

8.3.2 The Refusal of Consent: Arbitrariness and Enforcement

Enforcement becomes relevant when the affected state is not fulfilling its duties under international law. This relevancy has a 'tiered' approach. Only upon establishing the first tier or criterion, namely that assistance is needed in a specific territory and that the affected state is not fulfilling its own duties under international law (Chapter 6), does the second tier become relevant, which is related to international assistance. In this subsequent tier the question is raised whether or not an offer of humanitarian assistance from external parties may be refused; in other words: whether or not the *consent* of the affected state may be withheld (Chapter 7) and when such withholding is in line with international law.

Again, a certain degree of autonomy in answering this question may be assumed from the notion of state sovereignty.[85] However, international law has developed certain criteria that can be applied to this question, to create narrower margin of appreciation for the affected state: withholding consent is limited to specific reasons in international law. Put differently, the discretion of the affected state for refusing consent is limited by norms in international law, which are explored below.[86]

At an early stage, the ICJ has asserted in its *Nicaragua* judgment that it is not 'an intervention in the internal affairs' of the affected state to provide indiscriminate assistance for the purpose of prevention and alleviation of human suffering, as well as to 'protect life and health and to ensure respect for the human being'.[87] This assertion has also been held by Vukas, arguing that an international offer of assistance cannot be construed as an unlawful interference in the 'domaine reservé', thereby reserving the protection of human rights exclusively to domestic jurisdiction.[88]

As such, 'humanitarian assistance' as defined in this research as 'consisting of food, medicine, shelter and logistics for its provision; for urgent purposes and which is indispensable to the survival of the people at whom it is aimed', which abides by the principles of humanity, neutrality and impartiality, must be seen as a rightful offer in times of crisis.[89] Indeed, soft law documents such as the Bruges Resolution and the San Remo Principles have also elaborated on this notion of an 'offer' and reasoned that it should be 'bona fide' and not be regarded by the

[85] This has been argued also by Walter Kälin, Representative of the Secretary-General on the Human Rights of Internally Displaced Persons in 'Promotion And Protection Of All Human Rights, Civil, Political, Economic, Social And Cultural Rights, Including The Right To Development' Report Of The Representative Of The Secretary-General On The Human Rights Of Internally Displaced Persons UN Doc A/HRC/10/13/Add.1 (5 March 2009) § 38; and Chapter 7.

[86] FAO Legislative Study 'Right to Adequate Food in Emergencies' (2002) 79; and Chapter 7.

[87] Military and Paramilitary Activities in and against Nicaragua (Nicaragua v. United States of America), Merits, Judgment 27 June 1986 I.C.J. Reports 1986, p. 14 § 243.

[88] Vukas, 'Humanitarian Assistance in Cases of Emergency' (n 57) 5.

[89] 2.2.2 Defining Humanitarian Assistance and further.

affected state as an interference in its internal affairs.[90] This notion can be as basic as a choice to deliver aid in non-military ships, to avoid doubt as to the intent of the external party. The notion of a *bona fide* offer can also be considered to be fulfilled when in accordance with the principles of humanity, neutrality and impartiality.[91] The Bruges Resolution furthermore elaborates that such an offer may not be 'arbitrarily and unjustifiably' rejected, and that the offering states should call upon the UN Security Council should they fear a 'humanitarian catastrophe'.[92] A similar approach can be seen in the ILC's Draft Articles on Protection of persons in the event of disasters that currently state a duty of the affected state to seek international assistance should local capacity be exceeded (Draft Article 13), a requirement of consent from the affected state which may not be withheld 'arbitrarily' (Draft Article 14) and a duty for the affected state to facilitate external assistance (Draft Article 17).[93] Arguably, the wording of Draft Article 14 which uses 'shall' as opposed to 'should' in formulating the magnitude of the duty of the affected state to consent to external assistance goes beyond common practice today. However, the using of 'shall' is limited to the arbitrariness of a refusal (generally accepted in international law) as well as with regard to the communication of a decision concerning offers of aid. The wording is *not* specifically geared towards the content of that communication, and the affected state continues to have the opportunity to decide against accepting assistance, provided that it can prove such a denial of aid is not arbitrary.

Thus, in these legal development processes, the nature of the offer is related to the extent to which the affected state can refuse consent. Should a humanitarian crisis be in place and an offer be 'bona fide' and in line with the ICJ's assertions of non-discrimination, it shall be difficult for the affected state to argue reasons for withholding consent that shall not be construed as '*arbitrary*'. In this way, it becomes apparent that the sovereignty of the affected state is curbed by this notion of '*arbitrariness*'. Whereas no legal definition of the concept exists in relation to the provision of humanitarian assistance, it remains the concept utilised in the law today, and is commonly defined as random, lacking a specific reason, or without concern for what is fair.[94].

This assessment regarding arbitrariness and the need for consent furthermore aligns with existing international law. Firstly, it finds ground in the duties of the affected state to seek international assistance in the fulfilments of the rights to food and health as codified in Article 2 ICESCR.[95] It has been concluded that the

---

[90] 'Guiding Principles on the Right to Humanitarian Assistance' (April 1993) The International Institute of Humanitarian Law in San Remo, Principle 5.

[91] 2.2.3 The Principles for the Delivery of Assistance.

[92] Resolution 'Humanitarian Assistance' (2 September 2003) Institute of International Law, Sixteenth Commission, Bruges Session § VIII.

[93] ILC 'Protection of persons in the event of disasters' Draft Articles UN Doc A/CN.4/L.831 (15 May 2014).

[94] See in this regard the definitions as provided by Merriam-Webster and Oxford.

[95] 7.3 The Provision of Humanitarian Assistance by Third Parties Under Human Rights Law; Article 2 ICESCR and CESCR General Comment 12 (Article 11 ICESCR) UN Doc E/C.12/1999/5 'The right to

provision of humanitarian assistance can be a vehicle in the fulfilment of these rights.[96] Thus, should assistance be denied or obstructed, a state may be in violation of its duties under these (and other) international conventions. It is not only at the level of complete 'inaction' that a violation of human rights law is incurred; indeed these rights entail *positive* duties from the affected state as the CESCR has argued that a violation of the right to food can occur through actions including the 'prevention of access to humanitarian food aid in internal conflicts or other emergency situations'.[97] As such Barber has argued that a state party to the ICESCR will be considered to be in violation of its obligations under the Convention when it fails to provide essential food and healthcare, 'unless it can demonstrate that it has made every effort to use all resources at its disposal – including international assistance – in an effort to satisfy its obligations'.[98] Minimum core obligations remain to be fulfilled within the scope of the ICESCR. Similarly, the fulfilment of the right to life entails to not 'arbitrarily deprive' persons of that right and their life.[99] Such provisions therefore place an active obligation upon the affected state to seek assistance in the fulfilment of these rights by indeed allowing access to its territory for the provision of emergency aid by third parties.

At the same time, a duty to seek or request assistance under human rights law does not imply an immediate related duty to accept or consent to the help offered: Such help must remain in line with the principles of international law related to the provision of humanitarian assistance: humanity, neutrality and impartiality. It is along these lines that for example the US and Cuba refused each other's assistance following natural disasters in the past decade for political reasons.[100] Similarly, although not humanitarian assistance *per se*, in the situation of the Former Yugoslavia, concerns were raised regarding the impartiality of certain (neighbouring) countries offering assistance to UNPROFOR.[101] Only when aid offered is categorised as 'humanitarian assistance' can it not be arbitrarily refused.

The notion of arbitrariness is furthermore widely incorporated in international humanitarian law. Although acquiescing in particular in circumstances of non-

---

adequate food' (12 May 1999) § 17 and § 19. See also 'The right to food', Report of the Special Rapporteur, Note by the Secretary General UN Doc A/63/278 (21 October 2008) § 12.

[96] Section 5.4 Humanitarian Assistance Within the Context of Existing Human Rights.

[97] See Articles 2 and 11 ICESCR amongst others; see also CESCR General Comment 12 (n 95) § 19.

[98] Rebecca Barber, 'Facilitating humanitarian assistance in international humanitarian and human rights law', (2009) 91 *International Review of the Red Cross* 874, 393.

[99] Amongst others Articles 6 UDHR, 6 ICCPR and 4 ACHR.

[100] Amongst others the US refusal of Cuban aid in the wake of hurricane Katrina <http://edition.cnn.com/2005/WORLD/americas/09/05/katrina.cuba/> accessed 6 July 2014 and the Cuban refusal following a hurricane in 2008 <http://edition.cnn.com/2008/WORLD/americas/09/15/cuba.us/> accessed 6 July 2014 as well as <www.reuters.com/article/2008/09/17/us-cuba-castro-usa-idUSN1740403120080917> accessed 6 July 2014. See also Carlo Focarelli, 'Duty to Protect in Cases of Natural Disasters', (2010) *Max Planck Encyclopedia of International Law* § 17.

[101] Christine Grey, 'Host-State Consent And United Nations Peacekeeping In Yugoslavia', (1996) 7 *Duke Journal of Comparative & International Law* 250-251.

international conflict that access for third parties is subject to the consent of the affected state, international humanitarian law furthermore states that assistance may not be 'arbitrarily denied' nor that it may be viewed as 'interference in the armed conflict or as unfriendly acts', as codified in Articles 23 and 59 GC IV and 70 AP I. Such more explicit references to the need for consent from the affected state in humanitarian law also flow from the assumption often taken that a greater willingness will exist for the affected state to accept external assistance in the aftermath of a disaster as opposed to conflict. A recent example that however proves the contrary, remains the attitude of Myanmar in the aftermath of cyclone Nargis. The Security Council has held on various occasions that the 'intentional denial', 'impeding' or 'obstruction' of humanitarian assistance constitute violations of international law and state obligations under said law, for which consequences must be had.[102] Another norm in times of (non-) international armed conflict is the boundary formed by the prohibition of starvation in Articles 54 AP I and 14 AP II.

Thus, support can be found in international law at various levels and in various *corpora juris* to argue that a state must have legitimate reasons not to accept offers of assistance when facing a humanitarian crisis. Such legitimate reasons are, however, only elaborated upon in international humanitarian law, which explains examples like sieges and blockades as pertaining to 'military necessity', where a side-effect may be the refusal (or delaying) of external assistance.[103] Military necessity may be supplemented by certain 'control rights' of the affected state to check the content of the assistance, or determine the route it takes to the desired location as discussed in Chapter 7.[104] Such an argument for military necessity may not, however, lead to a complete denial of assistance for a prolonged period of time. In the absence of legitimate reasons to refuse an offer of assistance, international humanitarian law reflects that such a refusal amounts to an 'arbitrary denial' of assistance, which is a violation of humanitarian law. Furthermore, also relevant to circumstances of non-international armed conflict, the Guiding Principles on Internal Displacement also argue that consent shall not be 'arbitrarily withheld' by the affected state.[105] It has been suggested that in particular in times of conflict, weighing military necessity against humanitarian needs, in order to determine whether or not consent is required, is akin to the 'proportionality test'

[102] Amongst others UNSC Res 1674 (28 April 2006) UN Doc S/RES/1674 § 5; UNSC Res 1894 (11 November 2009) UN Doc S/RES/1894 § 4; and UNSC Res 2093 (6 March 2013) UN Doc S/RES/2093 § 43. See in this regard also S Talmon, 'The Statements of the President of the Security Council', (2003) 2 *Chinese Journal of International Law*, 441.

[103] Articles 55 GC IV, 54, 70(3) and 71 AP I; Jean-Marie Henckaerts & Louise Doswald-Beck (eds), *Customary International Humanitarian Law (ICRC Study)* (Cambridge University Press 2006), Rules 53 (Starvation as a Method of Warfare) and 54 (Attacks against Objects Indispensable to the Survival of the Civilian Population).

[104] Section 7.5.2 and Articles 23 and 59(3) GC IV and 70 AP I.

[105] 'Report of the Representative of the Secretary-General, Mr. Francis M. Deng, submitted pursuant to Commission resolution 1997/39', Addendum 'Guiding Principles on Internal Displacement' (Guiding Principles on IDPs) (11 February 1998) UN Doc E/CN.4/1998/53/Add.2 Principle 25.

frequently applied in humanitarian law.[106] Such an analogy however should be considered with care, as the principle of proportionality in humanitarian law has a specific character of its own. The question is thus raised how *long* a sovereign might take to assess whether or not an offer of assistance is accepted. It is not possible to ascertain a specific timeframe as such issues will have to be addressed on a case-by-case basis. Yet, considering the intensity of the need of persons in a crisis to receive humanitarian assistance, such contemplation should not take a prolonged period of time.

It remains vital therefore to assess factual circumstances on the ground through these questions pertaining to the legal framework on the delivery of humanitarian assistance. Resulting from this assessment, it can be concluded that certain acts or omissions of the affected state or sovereign are obstructions or denials of humanitarian assistance. These have been dealt with in Chapters 6 and 7, as potential violations of the right to life, food, health (and water), or violations of specific provisions of international humanitarian law. These acts or omissions of 'obstruction or denial' of assistance are the *causal link* between the violations of certain rights and duties as discussed in Chapters 6 and 7, and the consequences of these under international law, through the enforcement mechanisms that are discussed in the present Chapter.

When addressing the tiered approach in the determination of whether or not an act or omission amounts to a violation of international law, another 'tier' can be added to the existing questions pertaining to (1) the existence of a humanitarian crisis and (2 and 3) whether or not the affected state is complying with its own (twofold) duties under international law to provide aid or allow access for this. The fourth question then becomes whether or not the refusal of assistance is 'arbitrary'.

Several elements can be discerned concerning the notion of 'arbitrariness'. Refusal of a *bona fide* offer, in accordance with the principles of humanity, impartiality and neutrality could lead to the conclusion that such a decision is 'arbitrary'. Furthermore, a refusal resulting in circumstances that would amount to violations of the minimum core obligations of human rights law, and in times of conflict, also violations of those provisions of humanitarian law such as Articles 23 and 59 GC IV, 70 AP I and 18 AP II that oblige access (with due regard to control rights) could be considered arbitrary.

8.3.3 The Denial or Obstruction of Assistance: a Violation of International Law

The determination of which acts or omissions precisely amount to violations of international law pertaining to the denial or obstruction of humanitarian assistance can and must only be done on a case-by-case basis. In every situation, an assessment must be made firstly whether a humanitarian crisis exists, secondly whether an offer of assistance is subject to consent, and whether such consent is arbitrarily denied. Related to this, the facilitation of access must be assessed. It is

[106] Emanuela-Chiara Gilliard, 'The law regulating cross-border relief operations', (2013) 95 *International Review of the Red Cross* 890, 362.

not possible to create an exhaustive list of those acts or omissions, although various suggestions have been proffered; a few of which will be named and elaborated upon in the following Sections. As in many instances pertaining to the legal framework on the delivery of humanitarian assistance, international humanitarian law is quite elaborate, suggesting amongst others as being potential acts constituting denial or obstruction of aid the destroying of foodstuffs or agricultural areas, drinking installations, denying access which might result in starvation, and attacking convoys or personnel involved in the delivery of aid.[107] Along these lines the duty to allow 'rapid and unimpeded' passage of goods as reflected in international humanitarian law and consistently reiterated by the Security Council may consist of avoiding putting up barriers such as customs, visa requirements and taxes for the aid shipments and providers.[108] Other examples proffered include the diversion of aid from civilians to the military, excessive searching of convoys, creating roadblocks, holding blockades or sieges with the purpose of starvation, expelling aid providers from the country, requesting travel permits, or even claiming that the security of those providing aid cannot be guaranteed.[109]

From the above Sections, however, general questions that must be addressed in each case have been derived, whilst the assessment is case-specific. A primary assessment must be made whether or not a humanitarian crisis exists. Secondly, an assessment must be made whether or not the affected state is capable of adequately supplying the affected territory itself and is in fact doing so. Should the latter question not be answered affirmatively, an assessment shall have to take place whether an offer to provide humanitarian assistance, abiding by the proper principles, was done, and whether or not consent was refused in an arbitrary manner. Denial of assistance and denial of access both lead to violations of international law, as both constitute norms that the affected state must abide by. This assessment leads to distinct questions to determine whether or not a violation of international law has occurred for which enforcement options are available:

1. *Is a population within a territory facing a humanitarian crisis?*
2. *Is the affected state fulfilling its own sovereign duties and providing an adequate supply of aid?*

---

[107] Articles 71AP I 14 and 18 AP II, and Articles 7 and 8 ICC Statute for corresponding crimes.

[108] Article 70 AP I and Section 7.4.2; and Henckaerts & Doswald-Beck, ICRC Customary International Humanitarian Law Study (n 103), Rule 55 (Access for Humanitarian Relief to Civilians in Need).

[109] Amongst others Henckaerts & Doswald-Beck, ibid Rule 53 (Starvation as a Method of Warfare); Stuart Ford, 'Is The Failure To Respond Appropriately To A Natural Disaster A Crime Against Humanity? The Responsibility To Protect And Individual Criminal Responsibility In The Aftermath Of Cyclone Nargis', (2009) 38 *Denver Journal of International Law & Policy* 2, 26; Christa Rottensteiner, 'The denial of humanitarian assistance as a crime under international law', (1999) 81 *International Review of the Red Cross* 835, 560; Barber, 'Facilitating humanitarian assistance in international humanitarian and human rights law' (n 98) 377-378. Specifically concerning the blocking of aid convoys *Prosecutor v. Krstic* (Appeal Judgment) IT-98-33-A (19 April 2004) § 89.

3. *If this is not the case, is the affected state withholding consent to third parties offering assistance?*
4. *Is the refusal of consent legitimate or arbitrary under international law?*

In the assessment of these questions, the international legal world lacks one central authoritative body. As Ryngaert argues, one of the essential problems lies in the fact that 'no independent mechanism that weighs the evidence and checks whether the reasons invoked by states to deny assistance correspond to reality' and thus, a state may for example argue lack of impartiality when withholding access to providers of assistance whilst in reality punishing civilians it fears may sympathise with rebels within its territory.[110] The assessment of which acts or omissions amount to a violation of international law takes place by various bodies at various times. During or in the immediate aftermath of a humanitarian crisis, such an assessment may occur by the Security Council that determines whether or not to take action (enforcement through the use of force and targeted sanctions). A longer time after the crisis, the assessment may take place by the ICJ in its judgments (enforcement through potential state responsibility), by the international human rights courts and committees (enforcement through human rights law) and the ICC or potential *ad hoc* tribunals (enforcement through international criminal law). These bodies have been given the authority in international law through state parties to treaties and member states of their organisations to (judicially) assess whether or not a violation of international law has taken place, and must therefore be considered as the authoritative institutions available for international legal enforcement, despite the lack of a central body.

As determined above, such a violation of international law can be of two distinct norms and duties: firstly, the unlawful denial of assistance by the affected state *itself* (as discussed in Chapter 6), and secondly, the unlawful denial of an offer of *external aid* from third parties and a related right to access, by the affected state (as discussed in Chapter 7). Yet, as the ICJ put forward in its Advisory Opinion on the 'Legal Consequences for States of the Continued Presence of South Africa in Namibia (South West Africa) notwithstanding Security Council Resolution 276 (1970)', qualifying a situation as illegal does not in itself end the situation; it is but the first step in an effort to put an end to such a situation.[111] *Enforcement* is indeed a manner in which a situation violating international law can be brought to an end. Enforcement of humanitarian assistance through international law can take place at various levels, and the following Sections in this Chapter address them at an interstate level through a discussion of the use of force by the Security Council, followed by the more vertical level as discussed through

[110] Cedric Ryngaert, 'Humanitarian Assistance and the Conundrum of Consent: A Legal Perspective', (2013) 5 *Amsterdam Law Forum* 2, 10. Ryngaert suggests revisiting the International Fact-Finding Commission as created pursuant to Article 90 AP I, although noting the lack of viability in this idea, as the Commission's jurisdiction is dependent on the consent of the affected state.

[111] 'Legal Consequences for States of the Continued Presence of South Africa in Namibia' ICJ Advisory Opinion (n 62) § 111.

enforcement by various human rights bodies. Such bodies, however, also have the opportunity of a horizontal approach through the interstate complaint mechanism.[112] Lastly, this Chapter addresses enforcement through individual responsibility, either through targeted sanctions as imposed by the Security Council and through individual criminal responsibility; in particular for war crimes and crimes against humanity.

8.4 Enforcement through the Use of Force

The use of force is a consequence or aftereffect of the determination that a state is in violation of a breach of international law, and as a result may be held responsible under international law. It must be clear that the use of force shall always be an ultimate resort, in the event other methods of enforcing the provision of aid, such as through diplomatic means and non-military measures, are not successful.[113] The Mohonk Criteria for example refer to a variety of options besides diplomatic initiatives, such as the threat of economic sanctions under Article 41 UN Charter, or cross-border assistance operations initiated from the territory of a neighbouring state.[114] Such an approach is also addressed by Ryngaert who has argued that whilst the crossing of borders by NGOs to gain access may be clandestine, their contested status under international law may provide practical solutions.[115]

In this particular research, the use of force, authorised by the Security Council under Chapter VII, may be a consequence of the denial of humanitarian assistance when such denial leads to a breach of international law for which the affected state may be held responsible. The use of force in international law can be resorted to by way of self-defence and also by the Security Council under Chapter VII of the UN Charter.[116] Given the large number of member states in the UN, the provisions of Article 25 UN Charter obliging them to adhere to the Council's decisions and the otherwise strict prohibition of the use of force in Article 2(4) UN Charter outside of self-defence, the Security Council is the organ under current international law with the most means of enforcing aid through the use of force. It must be reiterated that a clear distinction must be upheld between those *providing* aid and abiding by the principles of humanity, neutrality and impartiality and those using force to *enable* the provision of such aid.

[112] 8.5.1 Enforcement through Human Rights Treaty Mechanisms .

[113] Such a perspective is also reflected in the doctrine of the Responsibility to Protect as embraced by the United Nations.

[114] 'The Mohonk Criteria for Humanitarian Assistance in Complex Emergencies', (1995) reprinted in 17 *Human Rights Quarterly* 1, Criteria VII.1.

[115] Ryngaert, 'Humanitarian Assistance and the Conundrum of Consent: A Legal Perspective' (n 110) 13.

[116] Both the delivery of humanitarian assistance and the use of force as an enforcement mechanism by peacekeeping operations under the auspices of the UN will not be addressed in detail within this research. Solely the Security Council as a primary actor in such decision-making will be considered.

Furthermore, the use of force may *also* be considered as a manner to give effect to the determination in Article 41(1) ARSIWA that states have a duty to cooperate in bringing a breach of international law to an end.[117] In practice, ending such a breach may result in the access of a territory. However, the legal framework on the international responsibility of states does not explicitly provide for the right to access a territory for such purposes. As a result, the ARSIWA also does not indicate the manner in which such access could be obtained for the purposes of Article 41(1). Article 20 ARSIWA provides that if 'valid consent' is given by a state, the wrongfulness of an act is precluded. Thus, the consent must be given in accordance with proper authorisation and authority, but may occur at any time prior or even during the act.[118] As the *Commentary* explicates:

> "Consent must be freely given and clearly established. It must be actually expressed by the State rather than merely presumed on the basis that the State would have consented if it had been asked".[119]

The *Commentary* has also provided for several examples of consent given by states, including 'humanitarian relief and rescue operations' within the list of possible actions that may fall within the scope of Article 20.[120] Should consent not have been given, the state(s) gaining access to the territory of the affected state may in turn be in breach of the principle of non-intervention. Therefore, in the absence of consent, the state(s) obtaining access to the territory on which the humanitarian crisis is taking place must ensure that their action is not in violation of international law, as envisaged by Articles 2(4) and 2(7) UN Charter. The use of force authorised by the Security Council would indeed not amount to such a violation. In relation to this, Article 25 ARSIWA regarding 'necessity' has been claimed as a reason to breach a rule of international law (the principle of non-intervention), in favour of the enforcement of providing humanitarian assistance.[121] As seen above, the ILC does not address the matter concerning the *legality* of an intervention outside the umbrella of the UN Charter's collective use of force, stating:

> "The question whether measures of forcible humanitarian intervention, not sanctioned pursuant to Chapters VII or VIII of the Charter of the United Nations, may be lawful under modern international law is not covered by article 25 *[ARSIWA]*".[122]

It stands to reason that the ILC does not deal with this legal issue in its *Commentary* on the ARSIWA, as it falls outside the scope of the matter at hand. Yet, should a state forego its primary obligation to protect its citizens and provide

[117] Section 8.2.3 State Responsibility and the Potential Duty to Cooperate in the Event of a Breach.
[118] 'Report of the International Law Commission' UN Doc A/56/10 (n 10) 174.
[119] Ibid 175.
[120] Ibid 176.
[121] Ibid 202.
[122] 'Report of the International Law Commission' UN Doc A/56/10 (n 10) 205.

humanitarian assistance, a secondary duty under the law of state responsibility may be placed upon international actors to ensure that such assistance is provided.[123] Ensuring such provision can then be done through the use of force, provided that this use of force is in accordance with international law.

The use of force, authorised by the Security Council under Chapter VII of the UN Charter as an enforcement mechanism, is legitimised rather by the (potential) violation of peremptory norms such as genocide, racial discrimination, crimes against humanity and war crimes in the event a state denies humanitarian assistance, as opposed to by the independent violation of a right to receive humanitarian assistance from the international community. Such a latter right indeed cannot be definitively ascertained in positive international law.[124] Also, this approach can be seen in the perspective of the ARSIWA that addresses the duty of third states to cooperate in bringing to an end the violation of a peremptory norm of international law.[125] The use of force must furthermore be resorted to *in lieu* of political or economic enforcement measures should these not suffice, given the impact of the use of force on the international community, as well as primarily on the affected state. In the event 'inducing' the affected state to discontinue its denial of access or provision of assistance through softer mechanisms is ineffective, resort may in certain instances be had to the use of force.[126] Using force is never the 'quick' or 'easy' solution in international law, as evidenced amongst others by the recent international actions in Afghanistan and Iraq. Once force is used, an international coalition of states or individual states must be willing to commit themselves to the *potential* that their involvement shall go beyond the factual delivery of humanitarian assistance, which was the initial occasion or reason for the use of force. The absence of a distinct and legally delimited right to assistance furthermore makes enforceability difficult: the choice to resort to the use of force must be based not on the violation of *actions*, but rather on an assessment of what has 'not' been done, or not been done *sufficiently*: the provision of assistance.

8.4.1 Security Council Action: Enforcement through the UN system and the Responsibility to Protect

The role of the Security Council in this setting concerning the use of force is that of an enforcer, as opposed to its role in the previous Chapters, where its role has been discussed as related to distilling standard-setting and normative developments. Yet, this research specifically views the role of the Security Council within the UN framework as that of an authoritative body, given the powers bestowed upon it, with regard to the establishment of a threat to the international peace pursuant to Article 39 UN Charter. It is clear from the UN Charter that not just *any* breach of an international legal norm legitimises the use of force: only if and when such a

[123] Focarelli, 'Duty to Protect in Cases of Natural Disasters' (n 100) § 27.
[124] 8.2.2 The ARSIWA, Peremptory Norms and the Denial of Humanitarian Assistance.
[125] Article 40 and 41 ARSIWA.
[126] Vukas, 'Humanitarian Assistance in Cases of Emergency' (n 57) 5.

breach of international law results in a 'threat to the international peace', does the use of force become an accepted option under Article 39 UN Charter. Such an approach falls in line with the perspective that the use of force is legitimised by a serious breach of a peremptory norm of international law. The circumstances that hence will be examined pertaining to the use of force shall therefore remain within the scope of the UN Charter and thus clearly within the scope of existing international law. This Charter will be the basis of their legality in international law. Furthermore, it must be noted that the UN Charter declares in Article 103 that precedence must be given to the Charter and consequentially the Security Council's decision to use force over conflicting obligations Member States may have. This supports furthermore the choice within this research to only consider the use of force within the context of the UN Charter and the authority of the Security Council as decision-making organ, considering that in the absence of the decision to use force by the Council, Article 2(4) of the UN Charter prohibiting the use of force must be given precedence over conflicting obligations. As Simma has argued, even 'the purest of humanitarian motives' might not be able to overcome the legal obstacles of straying outside of the Charter with the use of force.[127] For these reasons, an assessment must be made by an authoritative body in international law as to whether or not a humanitarian crisis exists, before proceeding to enforcement options through the use of force.

Chapter 7 of this research has addressed the Security Council's current perspective on the duty of the affected state to allow and ensure access to third parties in the provision of assistance.[128] However, the Council has not asserted that a failure of the affected state to comply with such duties automatically translates into a right to access. As said before, a situation falling within the scope of Article 39 of the Charter must furthermore arise. This would correspond with the breach of law occurring through the non-provision of humanitarian assistance by the affected state, which would then result in a denial of aid that may amount to serious crimes. Such crimes include war crimes, crimes against humanity or racial discrimination (and potentially genocide), as peremptory norms of international law, or include the four core crimes as defined by the notion of the Responsibility to Protect in the World Summit Outcome Document of 2005. Such circumstances then warrant Security Council action. Furthermore, such a use of force may also, as seen above, be implemented in light of the duty to cooperate under Article 41(1) ARSIWA. This duty also acknowledges a potential need to use force to end the violation of a peremptory norm of international law. The ARSIWA asserts such a duty, but the Security Council, by way of Chapter VII, has the potential to *execute* it. Thus, the use of force may be resorted to in the insurance of the delivery of assistance based on both Article 39 of the UN Charter in connection to the threat to the peace, as well as Article 41(1) ARSIWA. In both instances however, although the ARSIWA itself does not mention the Security Council, the monopoly in the determination to in fact resort to force remains with one central body, namely the Security Council,

---

[127] Simma, 'NATO, the UN and the Use of Force: Legal Aspects' (n 13) 5-6.

[128] Sections 7.4.1 and 7.4.2.

given the abovementioned provisions of 2(4) UN Charter and the fact that members of regional organisations also form part of the UN.[129]

In one of its first thematic resolutions on the protection of civilians (Resolution 1265), the Council has formulated its perspective and role regarding the delivery of humanitarian aid, potentially alluding to the use of force, as the Council declared that it:

> "Expresses its willingness to respond to situations of armed conflict where civilians are being targeted or humanitarian assistance to civilians is being deliberately obstructed, including through the consideration of appropriate measures at the Council's disposal in accordance with the Charter of the United Nations".[130]

Indeed, the Council does not use its common phrasing of 'all necessary means' and asserted the use of force outright. However, the Council speaks of 'appropriate measures' at the *Council's* disposal. As the primary task of the Security Council is the maintenance of peace, the allusion to the use of force is arguably implied. The Security Council has addressed that it shall seemingly not condone the 'deliberate' obstruction of humanitarian assistance in the event of an armed conflict. This statement falls in line with the earlier discussed perspective of the Council that indeed impeding the provision of humanitarian aid constitutes a violation of international humanitarian law.[131] Indeed, this approach also corresponds with the Council's take, as discussed in Chapter 7 of this research, of the role of third parties in the provision of aid. Although the Council does not affirmatively assert a right to access or an external duty to provide *per se*, it often presupposes an offer of assistance and cooperation of its member states in the provision of emergency assistance.[132] The manner in which the Council came to this formulation will be subsequently addressed.

From the start, once again a very clear distinction must be made between those actors *providing aid*, and those *using force* for the purpose of the enforcement of aid delivery. The provision of assistance must be done according to the principles of humanity, neutrality and impartiality, in order to qualify as provision of *humanitarian assistance*.[133] To distinguish between those providing such assistance and those using force in order to ensure that the assistance reaches the affected persons, is of paramount importance given the circumstances in which such enforcers operate. The use of force to *enforce aid* is only necessary if and when the authorities in the affected territory do not look favourably upon the external

[129] 4.2.2.2 Humanitarian Interventions and Humanitarian Assistance. Theoretically, the UN General Assembly may also resort to the use of force under the 1950 'Uniting for Peace' Resolution. The General Assembly has however never invoked this rather controversial aspect of the Resolution.

[130] UNSC Res 1265 (17 September 1999) UN Doc S/RES/1265 § 10.

[131] UNSC Res 771 (13 August 1992) S/RES/771 preamble; UNSC Res 819 (16 April 1993) UN Doc S/RES/819 § 8; UNSC Res 824 (6 May 1993) UN Doc S/RES/824 preamble. For a more in depth discussion see Section 7.4.2.

[132] Ibid 7.4.2.

[133] See for a discussion of these principles Sections 2.2.3 and further.

provision of aid, and deny consent arbitrarily. Should the affected state or others exercising authority in the affected territory be advocates or proponents of the provision of assistance, the use of force would not be necessary as such. Thus, those using force shall likely be met with opposition. Such opposition will raise issues concerning the upholding of the principle of neutrality or potentially even the principle of impartiality. As Dungel argued, these problems arise when the actors enforcing assistance have to take action *against* those opposing the provision of aid; at this point the enforcement mission is 'flawed with an inherent lack of neutrality' as the involved parties have engaged with each other.[134] Maintaining a clear distinction between those exercising force and those actors providing the actual assistance is therefore paramount, as even the slightest appearance of bias may influence the acceptance of humanitarian initiatives and diminishes its legitimacy. It is along these lines that the ICRC has suggested that military forces should themselves not be directly involved in the provision of aid, especially during an on-going conflict.[135] Equally, the EU has argued that circumstances in which the military 'supports' humanitarian aid workers – such as in complex emergencies – must be seen as a last resort, so as to not result in a blurring of the lines between the two.[136] An ensuing risk of such a blurring of the lines would be a situation in which the *providers* of aid will be targeted themselves, as part of the conflict. Whereas the safety and security of humanitarian personnel is essential for the provision of humanitarian assistance, this aspect of the delivery of assistance shall remain largely outside the scope of this research (with the exception of their discussion as part of facilitating access), as such issues become relevant *upon* providing aid.[137]

The use of force by definition presupposes choosing 'sides' – be it the side of the affected persons in need of assistance which is denied by the authorities in place, or a side to a conflict in itself; a challenge in particular in the case of a non-international armed conflict. Therefore, the 'enforcers' run the risk of being (or being perceived) as either a party to the conflict at hand, or, should this be a situation of a natural or man-made disaster, the creator of a 'conflictual'

[134] Joakim Dungel, 'A Right to Humanitarian Assistance in Internal Armed Conflicts Respecting Sovereignty, Neutrality and Legitimacy: Practical Proposals to Practical Problems', (2004) *Journal of Humanitarian Assistance*, 4 <http://sites.tufts.edu/jha/archives/838> accessed 24 November 2014.

[135] Jean-Daniel Tauxe (Director of Operations, ICRC Geneva) stated at the 45th Rose-Ross Seminar (Montreux, Switzerland 2 March 2000): "Military operations should be clearly distinct from humanitarian activities. Particularly at the height of hostilities, military forces should not be directly involved in humanitarian action, as this would or could, in the minds of the authorities and the population, associate humanitarian organizations with political or military objectives that go beyond humanitarian concerns".

[136] 'Joint Statement by the Council and the Representatives of the Governments of the Member States meeting within the Council, the European Parliament and the European Commission' (European Consensus on Humanitarian Aid) (30 January 2008) EU Doc 2008/C/25/01 § 60-63.

[137] Amongst others various UN thematic resolutions, such as UNGA Res 56/217 (19 February 2002) UN Doc A/RES/56/217; UNGA res 61/133 (1 March 2007) UN Doc A/RES/61/133 'Safety and security of humanitarian personnel and protection of United Nations personnel' § 3 and 4; UNGA Res 65/132 (1 March 2011) UN Doc A/RES/65/132 §3; UNGA Res 62/95 (29 January 2008) UN Doc A/RES/62/95 § 9.

situation.[138] Ensuring the separation of the providers of aid from its enforcers, to maintain the principles of humanity, neutrality and impartiality in the provision of assistance is therefore required, as well as the realisation that the use of force must also adhere to the standards laid down in international law. For this reason, the use of force, as an ultimate and last resort in the enforcement of humanitarian aid, is still considered solely within the context of the Security Council.

In the previous Chapters, the dilemma concerning the 'adequate supply' of a territory has been addressed on several occasions.[139] One of the greatest challenges of the provision of assistance is the determination of whether assistance is in fact needed. Upon this assertion, the particular responsibilities of the affected state in relation to the provision of aid are 'activated', as well as potential roles of the international community. In the previous Chapters, it has been discussed that a margin of appreciation in the determination of the adequacy of supply remained with the affected state. However, a determination by the Security Council that the use of force is warranted to ensure the provision of assistance to persons in the event of a crisis, is *simultaneously* also a determination that indeed a territory is *inadequately* supplied and that the affected state is not properly attending to its citizens: *that in fact a humanitarian crisis is taking place*. In doing so, the Council in essence determines that the affected state is not providing for persons in need within its jurisdiction. Thus, answering the question of whether a territory is indeed 'adequately supplied' becomes a matter for the Security Council to determine when it is contemplating the use of force, as argued above in Section 8.3.3. This body may decide whether or not the situation at hand is becoming so topical and severe – a *humanitarian crisis* – that it must interfere to 'enforce' the provision of assistance. Within the current legal framework pertaining to the provision of assistance therefore, the Security Council is the one actor, besides the affected state, that has the opportunity in a circumstance it deems a threat to the peace, to determine whether or not a humanitarian crisis is taking place and the (external) provision of humanitarian assistance is warranted.

8.4.2 The Beginning of Security Council Action

The analysis of Security Council action over the past decades has played a role in the establishment in Chapters 6 and 7 of this research that a legal obligation may exist for states to allow access for the provision of assistance if and when the Council adopts a resolution under Chapter VII using specific wording in that regard. Equally, third states and/or regional organisations are called upon to resort to the use of force in specific instances through the wording of the Council. Determined by Article 25 UN Charter stating that 'the Members of the United Nations agree to accept and carry out the decisions of the Security Council in

[138] Dungel, 'A Right to Humanitarian Assistance in Internal Armed Conflicts Respecting Sovereignty, Neutrality and Legitimacy: Practical Proposals to Practical Problems' (n 134), 17.
[139] Chapters 6 and 7 and Section 8.3.

accordance with the present Charter', third parties are then obliged to assist in achieving this.

The Security Council's mechanism for the use of force, the system of collective security on the basis of Articles 39 and 41/42 UN Charter, has only been implemented for the enforcement of the provision of humanitarian assistance in recent decades, following certain enforcement issues relating to peacekeeping missions upon the end of the Cold War. In the early decades of the Security Council's action, in part due to the Cold War, the authorisation of the use of force was an exception rather than the rule.[140] The Security Council's and the UN's general inaction in the face of the Biafran crisis in the late 1960s today still stands as an example held by many of a failure to 'enforce' humanitarian assistance. The Biafran airlift was instigated and operated by humanitarian organisations, without the use of force, and is reported to have saved the lives of approximately one million civilians. It was argued by some states, such as England, that the role of the Security Council was to be concerned with 'the maintenance of international peace and security, not with the relief of suffering'.[141] Subsequently in the late 1980s to early 1990s, the Security Council remained motionless in another well-known situation: the dire famine during the protracted civil war in the Sudan.

However, despite the immovability of the Security Council, the UN as an organisation *did* come into action, creating 'Operation Lifeline', an airlift into the Sudan following a General Assembly resolution.[142] This airlift was developed and carried out by humanitarian agencies in cooperation with the UN, through agencies such as the World Food Programme and UNICEF, supported by the UN General Assembly, as well as in cooperation with the authorities in Sudan itself.[143] As such, it was the first humanitarian operation, lasting from 1989-2005, in which civilians were assisted within a sovereign country during an on-going conflict. The division of tasks within the UN follows the development of the UN Security Council's stance on the concept of 'humanitarian assistance' and its own role as an organ of the UN therein. As discussed in Section 7.4.1, the UN Security Council did not commence addressing a potential role for external parties in the provision of assistance until well into the 1980s. In doing so, the Council adopted resolutions calling for the UN and its agencies to provide aid, but does not mention the use of force, nor is Chapter VII of the UN Charter involved.[144]

---

[140] Niels Blokker, 'The Security Council and the Use of Force: On Recent Practice', in Niels Blokker & Nico Schrijver (eds) *The Security Council and the Use of Force: Theory and Reality – A Need for Change?* (Martinus Nijhoff Publishers 2005) 12.

[141] This was the position voiced by the then British minister of foreign affairs, Lord Chalfont. Transcripts of the meeting in the House of Lords (15 July 1968): <http://hansard.millbanksystems.com/lords/1968/jul/15/biafra-united-nations-and-international> accessed 13 November 2013.

[142] UNGA Res 44/12 (24 October 1989) UN Doc A/RES/44/12, 'Operation Lifeline Sudan'.

[143] UNGA Res 43/8 (18 October 1988) UN Doc A/RES/43/8; UNGA Res 43/52 (6 December 1988) UN Doc A/RES/43/52; UNGA Res 45/226 (21 December 1990) UN Doc A/RES/45/226; UNGA Res 46/178 (9 December 1991) UN Doc A/RES/46/178.

[144] UNSC Res 513 (19 June 1982) UN Doc S/RES/513 'Lebanon'.

Human rights law, in particular Article 2 ICESCR, together with Articles 55 and 56 of the UN Charter, also envisages a duty to cooperate in the fulfilment of various human rights. It has been discussed that both the ARSIWA (in Article 41) and international humanitarian law (in the form of Article 89 AP I) recognise a duty to cooperate in the event of breaches of peremptory norms or of serious violations of humanitarian law respectively. The manner in which such cooperation, when amounting to force, takes place has with time been set within the Security Council's framework of action, as this action falls within the UN Charter and international law's general perspective on the non-prohibited use of force.

Prior to the thematic Resolution 1265 of 1999, which was addressed in the previous Section, the Security Council had the opportunity to consider its stance with regard to the internal conflict in Somalia and with regard to the conflict in the Former Yugoslavia, both in the early 1990s, followed by the well-known dramatic turn of events in Rwanda in the mid-1990s. Somalia requested such a consideration from the Council itself on several occasions, whereas also the then Republic of Yugoslavia 'welcomed' the Security Council's consideration of the situation.[145] Both country situations unfolded somewhat simultaneously, and the Council addressed the use of force in both situations, through the implementation in first instance of peacekeeping missions. These missions were based upon the consent of the affected states and parties involved.[146] Therefore, they functioned on the basis of certain agreed principles, such as impartiality, the non-use of force unless in self-defence and the absence of participation of forces of the permanent members of the Security Council.[147] However, as Grey rightly notes, once the Security Council operates under Chapter VII of the UN Charter and the original peacekeeping missions are altered, the matter of the necessity of consent of the affected state alters also.[148]

The changing nature of conflicts in the 1990's has increasingly impacted the Security Council's approach to the mandate of peacekeeping missions, as well as the particular UN Charter basis upon which it operates and also its perspective on the enforcement of humanitarian assistance. Indeed, it is then the role of the Security Council as enforcer rather than in a more regulatory or normative capacity as was discussed in Chapter 6 and 7 of this research, that comes to the forefront. The Security Council noted concerning Somalia that the delivery of humanitarian assistance was an 'important element in the effort of the Council to restore

---

145 Amongst others with regard to Somalia: UNSC Res 733 (23 January 1992) UN Doc S/RES/733 preamble; UNSC Res 764 (17 March 1992) UN Doc S/RES/764; UNSC Res 751 (24 April 1992) UN Doc S/RES/751; and with regard to Yugoslavia: UNSC Res 713 (25 September 1991) UN Doc S/RES/713 preamble.

146 See with regard to the intricacies Grey, 'Host-State Consent And United Nations Peacekeeping In Yugoslavia' (n 101).

147 Ibid 282.

148 Ibid 255. Discussing the development of peacekeeping missions falls beyond the scope of this research. This research will restrict itself to a brief discussion in light of the current trends in the use of force for the purpose of delivering humanitarian assistance.

international peace and security in the area' and as such, authorised an 'urgent airlift operation' to indeed deliver such aid.[149] The Security Council then, in calling upon the parties to the conflict to cooperate with the UN and its security personnel and assist in the stabilisation of the situation, asserted that:

> "In the absence of such cooperation, the Security Council does not exclude other measures to deliver humanitarian assistance to Somalia".[150]

The Council thus appears to indirectly open the door to the potential future *use of force for the provision of assistance* but does not actually formulate it as such. As seen above, this formulation by the Council is echoed in its subsequent thematic Resolution 1265 'Protection of Civilians in Armed Conflict' of 1999, but can be seen also as merely referring to non-forceful measures. In this present Resolution, the Council more distinctly interlinks the 'other measures' to the delivery of emergency aid. Although the Council does not reiterate this stance in its subsequent dealing with the situation in Somalia, it does reaffirm its approval of the initiatives that have been undertaken through the airlift operations.[151] It must be noted that the Somalian government itself *requested* the UN's involvement in the delivery of aid, as continuously stressed by the Security Council.[152] As months progressed and the humanitarian situation deteriorated, not in the least due to the continued impediment of the delivery of aid, UN member states offered to assist in the establishment of a safe environment in which to provide humanitarian assistance, upon which the Security Council determined that, acting under Chapter VII of the UN Charter, it:

> "authorizes the Secretary General and Member States cooperating to implement the offer referred to in paragraph 8 above to use all necessary means to establish as soon as possible a secure environment for humanitarian relief operations in Somalia".[153]

Thus, the Council called upon the use of force by member states, through its well-known phrase to 'use all necessary means', unequivocally *for the purpose of the delivery of humanitarian assistance*. This was in fact the first time the Council authorised the use of force for the purpose of the delivery of emergency assistance in a humanitarian crisis.[154] As such, it has opened the door to a major change in the enforcement of the provision of humanitarian assistance: Over the past decades Security Council action has consistently been a contributing factor in the enforcement of aid provision. In general, the intervention in Somalia is considered a success, as the international force UNITAF was able to create safer areas on the

149 UNSC Res 767 (27 July 1992) UN Doc S/RES/767 preamble and § 2. See also UNSC Res 775 (28 August 1992) UN Doc S/RES/775 preamble.
150 Ibid S/RES/767 § 4.
151 UNSC Res 775 (28 August 1992) UN Doc S/RES/775 preamble and § 4.
152 UNSC Res 794 (3 December 1992) UN Doc S/RES/794 preamble.
153 Ibid § 8 and 10.
154 The subsequent use of force was then carried out by the Unified Task Force (UNITAF).

ground, and enabled the provision of assistance to the Somalians in need.[155] This mission was succeeded by UNOSOM II, one of the most ambitious peace operations of the UN at that time, as the use of force beyond self-defence was mandated, amongst other matters for the delivery of humanitarian assistance.[156]

Yet, a clear line was not to be distinguished in the work of the Council at this stage. As mentioned, the conflict in the Former Yugoslavia unfolded at approximately the same time as the conflict in Somalia which led to the determination of the use of force by the Security Council. Although both situations are clearly distinct, given that the assertion to use force was not done in the case of the Former Yugoslavia, the common denominator is that the provision of humanitarian assistance played an important role in the Council's decision-making. The Council asserted in a similar fashion to it resolutions concerning Somalia the importance of the provision of emergency aid in the restoration of international peace and security and acknowledged the rapid deterioration of the situation on the ground, as well as the need for delivery of assistance.[157] The Security Council commenced by instating an arms embargo, prior to asserting the need for a peacekeeping operation, followed by a Chapter VII decision for all parties to create conditions for the unimpeded passage of humanitarian assistance, including the 'establishment of a security zone encompassing Sarajevo and its airport'.[158] In the subsequent resolution, the reopening of the airport was acknowledged as a first step in the establishment of such a security zone.[159] Whilst the Council addressed the provision of humanitarian assistance through the established peacekeeping operation, it appeared to lean towards the use of force by member states as an enforcement mechanism similarly to the circumstances in Somalia, given that the Council considered 'other measures' to deliver humanitarian aid as it had done in Somalia in July of 1992.[160] The Council called upon its member states in August of that year:

> "to take nationally or through regional agencies or arrangements all measures necessary to facilitate in coordination with the United Nations the delivery by relevant United

[155] Trevor Findlay, *The Use of Force in UN Peace Operations* (SIPRI/Oxford University Press 2002) 181.
[156] UNSC Res 814 (26 March 1993) UN Doc S/RES/814 and UNSC Res 837 (6 June 1993) UN Doc S/RES/837.
[157] UNSC Res 770 (13 August 1992) UN Doc S/RES/770 preamble; UNSC Res 752 (15 May 1992) UN Doc S/RES/752 preamble.
[158] Concerning the arms embargo: UNSC Res 713 (25 September 1991) UN Doc S/RES/713; UNSC Res 721 (27 November 1991) UN Doc S/RES/721; UNSC Res 724 (15 December 1991) UN Doc S/RES/724; UNSC Res 727 (8 January 1992) UN Doc S/RES/727; UNSC Res 740 (8 February 1992) UN Doc S/RES/740; and with regard to the peacekeeping mission UNSC Res 743 (21 February 1992) UN Doc S/RES/743; UNSC Res 749 (7 April 1992) UN Doc S/RES/749; UNSC Res 752 (15 May 1992) UN Doc S/RES/752. With regard to the Chapter VII decision of the Council, see UNSC Res 757 (30 May 1992) UN Doc S/RES/757 § 17.
[159] UNSC Res 758 (8 June 1992) UN Doc S/RES/758 § preamble.
[160] UNSC Res 761 (29 June 1992) UN Doc S/RES/761 § 1 and 4.

Nations humanitarian organizations and others of humanitarian assistance to Sarajevo and wherever needed in other parts of Bosnia and Herzegovina".[161]

Explicitly in this Resolution however, the Council takes note of the sovereignty of Bosnia and Herzegovina.[162] Also, the politics of the permanent five members of the Council must be taken into consideration, as not all members were in favour of intervention. Furthermore, in the case of the Former Yugoslavia as compared to Somalia, this *potential* use of force is specifically related to the provision of aid *by the UN itself.* Grey has argued that this phrasing is an appeal to 'use force for humanitarian purposes', but falling under Article 53 of the UN Charter for the purposes of regional organisations.[163] Findlay has argued it to be a 'threat' by the Council of the use of force by member states or the North Atlantic Treaty Organization (NATO).[164] Whether or not this call may indeed, or could have been construed as an authorisation to use force by member states is however a question the Council took care of. In a subsequent resolution, the Council, while thanking member states for offering military personnel, decided to enlarge the mandate of UNPROFOR, the peacekeeping mission on the ground.[165] Although this Resolution 776 itself was not taken under Chapter VII, it referred back to Resolution 770, thereby allowing the UNPROFOR peacekeeping mission to use force in self-defence as meant under Chapter VII *for the purpose of delivering humanitarian aid*, although this was not the mission's original mandate to which the parties involved had consented.[166] As such, the facilitation and protection of the delivery of humanitarian assistance by UNPROFOR was enforced upon the parties by the Security Council. Despite having acted under Chapter VII, the Council determined that consent of the host state remained a necessary component for the peacekeeping mission to operate, and replaced UNPROFOR by UNCRO.[167]

Thus, in such early instances of peacekeeping missions, even where the potential use of force was mandated, the mandate of the Council relating to the peacekeeping mission did not necessarily supersede the need to obtain *and hold* the consent of the affected state. Interestingly however, in Resolution 781 pertaining to the situation in Bosnia and Herzegovina, the Security Council installed a flight ban on military flights over the airspace of Bosnia and Herzegovina, *for the purpose of securing the safety of the delivery of humanitarian assistance*.[168] Reaffirming this ban in a following resolution, the Council did not reiterate its earlier statements pertaining to the sovereignty of Bosnia and Herzegovina, and thereby appeared to be

[161] UNSC Res 770 (13 August 1992) UN Doc S/RES/770 § 2.
[162] Ibid preamble.
[163] Christine Grey, *International Law and the Use of Force* (Oxford University Press 2008) 424.
[164] Findlay, *The Use of Force in UN Peace Operations* (n 155) 137.
[165] UNSC Res 776 (14 September 1992) UN Doc S/RES/776 preamble and § 2.
[166] Grey, 'Host-State Consent And United Nations Peacekeeping In Yugoslavia' (n 101) 259.
[167] UNSC Res 947 (30 September 1994) UN Doc S/RES/947 and UNSC Res 981 (, 31 March 1995) UN Doc S/RES/981 preamble and § 2. See also ibid Grey 266-267 and H J Langholtz and C E Stout (eds) *The Psychology of Diplomacy* (Praeger Publishers 2004) 56-57.
[168] UNSC Res 781 (9 October 1992) UN Doc S/RES/781 § 1.

distinguishing such actions of a more autonomous character from the peacekeeping mandate where the use of force was intrinsically linked to self-defence.[169] Imposing a flight ban for the purpose of the delivery of assistance, whilst acting under Chapter VII and with a peacekeeping mission on the ground that is authorised to use (a limited amount) of force, certainly gives an outward impression that, whether or not this was intentional, the sovereignty of Bosnia and Herzegovina was compromised through such acting on the part of the Security Council. Yet, in ensuing resolutions, the Council does revert back to reiterating the sovereignty of Bosnia and Herzegovina.[170] From these examples of Somalia and the Former Yugoslavia, it becomes apparent that the Council is open to the use of force *for the purpose of the delivery of aid*, as well as exploring the boundaries of the affected states' sovereignty.

With much of the focus on the conflict, it appears almost as if the Council's initial consideration of the use of force by member states to 'enforce' the delivery of aid goes by unnoticed, as the body continued to grapple with the mandate of the peacekeeping mission and with the protracted conflict over the next few years.[171] The mission appears to remain within the realm of Article 40 UN Charter, also designated by the UN itself as a means to ensure the creation of a situation that allows for unimpeded delivery of humanitarian assistance.[172]

In relation to the provision of humanitarian assistance, the Security Council however asserted a need for 'safe areas' in Bosnia and Herzegovina (such as the well-known enclave pertaining to Srebrenica) to which humanitarian aid providers would have full access.[173] Yet, the extent to which UNPROFOR was allowed to use force, also in particular concerning the facilitation of the delivery of humanitarian assistance, cannot be considered of the same magnitude and depth as the call by the Security Council to its *member states* to use force for the purpose of aid delivery in Somalia, which had subsequently been strengthened by Resolutions 814 and 837, also allowing the ensuing peacekeeping mission UNOSOM II to use force to ensure the delivery of aid to civilians.[174] The latter appeal was indeed the authorisation of the use of force, *for the purpose of the delivery of humanitarian assistance*. With the benefit of hindsight, knowing the circumstances as occurred in Srebrenica, it is

---

[169] UNSC Res 786 (10 November 1992) UN Doc S/RES/786 § 2.

[170] For example UNSC Res 819 (16 April 1993) UN Doc S/RES/819 preamble.

[171] Amongst others subsequent resolutions: UNSC Res 787 (16 November 1992) UN Doc S/RES/787; UNSC Res 807 (19 February 1993) UN Doc S/RES/807; UNSC Res 816 (31 March 1993) UN Doc S/RES/816; UNSC Res 819 (16 April 1993) UN Doc S/RES/819; UNSC Res 824 (6 May 1993) UN Doc S/RES/824; UNSC Res 836 (4 June 1993) UN Doc S/RES 836; UNSC Res 908 (31 March 1994) UN Doc S/RES/908; UNSC res 958 (19 November 1994) UN Doc S/RES/958.

[172] Article 40 UN Charter. See also H Nasu, *International Law on Peacekeeping: A Study of Article 40 of the UN Charter* (Brill Martinus Nijhoff 2009) 189-192; and Repertoire of the Practice of the Security Council (1996-1999), Chapter XI 'Consideration of the provisions of Chapter VII of the Charter', Part II Provisional measures to prevent the aggravation of a situation under Article 40 of the Charter 1127.

[173] Amongst others UNSC Res 819 (16 April 1993) UN Doc S/RES/819 § 1; UNSC Res 824 (6 May 1993) UN Doc S/RES/824 § 4.

[174] UNSC Res 814 (26 March 1993) UN Doc S/RES/814 § 5 and 6; UNSC Res 837 (6 June 1993) UN Doc S/RES/837 § 7 and 8.

of course regrettable that the Council did not apply the Somalian model as a viable option in the Former Yugoslavia. As discussed however, other factors aside from the delivery of humanitarian assistance played a role in that particular conflict.[175] Nonetheless, despite the differences in both situations, the Council asserted the powers of UNPROFOR to use force, albeit on a somewhat flimsy legal basis. As such, from the above, it is possible to derive that in the early stages of the enforcement of the delivery of humanitarian assistance through the use of force, the Security Council was at least willing and able to acknowledge and call upon the need for the *use of force in the provision of humanitarian assistance* upon the request or acknowledgment of the affected state, whilst considering this states' sovereignty. Such a possibility of the use of force was recognised strongly in the case of Somalia through an appeal to member states. In the case of the Former Yugoslavia, it came into being through an enlargement of the mandate of the peacekeepers on the ground.

The above situations illustrate the difficulties the Council faced in adapting the traditional peacekeeping missions to the situations developing in the 1990's where the use of force could have been necessary, and the ensuing blurring of the lines of the mandates. Assessing the technicalities in these mandates is relevant to the determination of *to what extent the Council envisages the potential to use force for the provision of humanitarian assistance*. While it is not possible to examine all peacekeeping operations or subsequent situations in which the Security Council authorised the use of force in relation to the provision of humanitarian assistance, several instances may be highlighted. Through these brief highlights, a line in the practice of the Council can be discerned.

The struggles the Council faced in the Former Yugoslavia were magnified in Rwanda, as the UN's mission UNAMIR had similar problems with its mandate, which did not allow for the use of force, but was a traditional Chapter VI peacekeeping operation and could therefore not 'enforce' humanitarian assistance.[176] As Findlay put it, UNAMIR had the 'misfortune to be established in the wake of the Somalia debacle and during the continuing traumas of Bosnia'.[177] The mission is notoriously known as a failure in the protection of the people in Rwanda, as it lacked the proper backing of the UN and the international community. Finally, after continuous resolutions not allowing for the use of force,[178] an international mission was mandated under Chapter VII 'for humanitarian purposes'.[179] The devastating tragedy in Rwanda, which followed the already tragic events that occurred in Bosnia, lay bare the difficulties the UN faced

[175] The detailed particularities of the conflict in the Former Yugoslavia, as well as the detailed mandate of UNPROFOR and subsequent missions remain beyond the scope of this research. For a discussion of the Rules of Engagement and mandate (under Article 40 of the UN Charter) see amongst others Nasu, *International Law on Peacekeeping: A Study of Article 40 of the UN Charter* (n 172) 189-192.
[176] UNSC Res 872 (5 October 1993) UN Doc S/RES/872.
[177] Findlay, *The Use of Force in UN Peace Operations* (n 155) 277.
[178] UNSC Res 918 (17 May 1994) UN Doc S/RES/918.
[179] UNSC Res 929 (22 June 1994) UN Doc S/RES/929.

in the 'enforcement' of humanitarian assistance or otherwise using force in missions that originally set out as peacekeeping operations.

Following these three missions, which are often considered as the early source of more robust operations, the Council asserted on several occasions the possibility of the enforcement of the delivery of humanitarian assistance by both peacekeeping forces and UN member states in the late 1990's. Whilst UNPROFOR and UNOSOM II in the Former Yugoslavia and Somalia respectively were potentially operating beyond a traditional peacekeeping mandate and actually providing peace-enforcement without a proper corresponding mandate, the Council had the opportunity to provide different tools to ensuing operations, in particular *relevant to the enforcement of humanitarian assistance.*[180] As such, these later assertions by the Security Council were often under the umbrella of Chapter VII of the UN Charter and on occasion allowed for a more robust use of force with a view to the delivery of assistance. An example includes the multinational force INTERFET that supported the UN's mission UNAMET in East-Timor with a Chapter VII mandate to 'use all necessary force', with the purpose of facilitating the humanitarian assistance operations.[181] Also in 1999, the UN mission in Sierra Leone UNAMSIL was deployed which, although not given the permission to use all necessary force, was mandated under Chapter VII with amongst others the purpose of facilitating humanitarian assistance.[182] Similarly, the UN mission in the Congo, MONUC, was mandated under Chapter VII to use force to 'protect civilians under imminent threat of physical violence'. Whereas the protection of civilians in immediate physical danger is not equal to the protection of civilians through the provision of humanitarian assistance, it is exemplary of the Council's inclination to expand peacekeeping mandates and use Chapter VII as the authorisation of the use of force for broader purposes. Over the years however, as the Council saw more and more reason to authorise the use of force; it called upon military coalitions of the 'able and willing' to use 'all necessary measures', rather than expanding the traditional peacekeeping mandates of existing UN missions.[183] Indeed, it is in this sense important to distinguish between traditional peacekeeping, peace-enforcement and such coalitions that use force to establish peace.[184] Ascertaining the proper (legal)

---

[180] For the mandate of UNPROFOR: UNSC Res 770 (13 August 1992) UN Doc S/RES/770 and onwards; for the mandate of UNOSOM II: UNSC Res 814 (26 March 1993) UN Doc S/RES/814 and UNSC Res 837 (6 June 1993) UN Doc S/RES/837 onwards.

[181] UNSC Res 1264 (15 September 1999) UN Doc S/RES/1264 § 3.

[182] UNSC Res 1270 (22 October 1999) UN Doc S/RES/1270 § 13-14, expansion of the mandate to also protect civilians; UNSC Res 1289 (7 February 2000) UN Doc S/RES/1289.

[183] Blokker, 'The Security Council and the Use of Force: On Recent Practice' (n 140) 14. See in this regard for example the situation in Cote d'Ivoire where the Council provided, acting under Chapter VII, the French troops with the mandate 'to use all necessary means' to support the UNOCI mission that was in place: UNSC Res 1528 (27 February 2004) UN Doc S/RES/1528 and reiterated in UN Doc S/RES/1975. Also Niels Blokker, 'Is the Authorization Authorized? Practice of the UN Security Council to Authorize the Use of Force by 'Coalitions of the Able and Willing', (2000) 11 *European Journal of International Law* 3, 541-568.

[184] A discussion of these notions falls beyond the scope of this research as a focus is maintained on the delivery of humanitarian assistance.

foundations in the Charter, such as Chapter VII, and in the Security Council action, is relevant to distilling the approach of the Security Council regarding the use of force for the purpose of the delivery of humanitarian aid. The Security Council's practice itself however is somewhat blurred in these early stages, as the above discussion has shown. As argued by Blokker, over the years, although the 'peacekeeping operations' and the 'authorization operations' are fundamentally different, they have increasingly come to resemble each other.[185]

The Security Council commenced adding humanitarian issues as thematic topics to its agenda due to the country-situations that came before it, providing more clarity to the determination of the use of force for the provision of assistance. As of May 1997, the Council added the topic 'Protection for humanitarian assistance to refugees and others in conflict situations' to its agenda, upon which many member states addressed the fact that when necessary, peacekeeping missions needed a clear mandate under Chapter VII, in order to protect and enable the provision of humanitarian assistance.[186] The Deputy Secretary General argued that it was indeed the responsibility of the Council to be 'bold committed and determined' in confronting today's crises and in ending conflicts and securing peace, as such actions would support humanitarian actors in their delivery of aid.[187] More generally furthermore, starting in January 1999, the Council included the item of 'Promoting peace and security: humanitarian activities relevant to the Security Council' in its agenda, upon which the Under-Secretary-General for Humanitarian Affairs and Emergency Relief Coordinator suggested that the Security Council should consider specific action that might aid humanitarian actors, including 'ensuring access to populations in need'.[188] The Under-Secretary-General asserted that both peacekeeping operations and political actions, as well as well-targeted sanctions may assist in averting and reducing humanitarian crises.[189] Most Council members concurred the following year, as they highlighted the importance the Council may have in ensuring access of humanitarian assistance to civilians in need. However, discrepancies existed among the members as to whether or not the determination of massive human rights violations or humanitarian difficulties – although a threat to the peace – would warrant the use of force.[190]

[185] Blokker, 'The Security Council and the Use of Force: On Recent Practice' (n 140) 28.

[186] Repertoire of the Practice of the Security Council (1996-1999), Chapter VIII, 'Consideration of questions under the responsibility of the Security Council for the maintenance of international peace and security', Section 37 Protection for humanitarian assistance to refugees and others in conflict situations, Initial proceedings Deliberations of 21 May 1997 (3778th meeting) 1023-1024.

[187] Ibid 1026.

[188] Repertoire of the Practice of the Security Council (1996-1999), Chapter VIII, 'Consideration of questions under the responsibility of the Security Council for the maintenance of international peace and security', Section 42 Items relating to promoting peace and security; A. Promoting peace and security: humanitarian activities relevant to the Security Council, Initial proceedings Deliberations of 21 January 1999 (3968th meeting) 1047.

[189] Ibid.

[190] Repertoire of the Practice of the Security Council (1996-1999), Chapter VIII, 'Consideration of questions under the responsibility of the Security Council for the maintenance of international peace and security' Section 42 Items relating to promoting peace and security; C. Maintaining peace and

Somewhat simultaneously, the Council addressed the potential capacity to use force in its thematic resolutions pertaining to the protection of civilians in times of armed conflict. The use of force in the protection of civilians – amongst others including for the provision of aid – can therefore be seen as an expanding thread in the work of the Council. In a primary statement, the Council 'expressed its willingness to respond' to such situations in which 'humanitarian assistance to civilians has been deliberately obstructed'.[191] The Secretary General then recommended that the Council stress the need for civilian populations 'to have unimpeded access to humanitarian assistance' in its resolutions.[192] From the above deliberations ensued thematic resolutions such as Resolution 1296, pertaining to the Protection of Civilians in Armed Conflict that has been discussed several times in this research. Most relevant to the aspect of enforcement by the Security Council is the paragraph cited above in which the Council expressed its willingness to address those situations in which 'humanitarian assistance to civilians is being deliberately obstructed, including through the consideration of appropriate measures at the disposal of the Council'.[193] The Secretary General has continued to emphasise the pressing need of the Council to deliberate this issue, given the millions of people that continue to be denied assistance.[194] The deliberations of the Council led to the adoption of a subsequent thematic resolution, also pertaining to the protection of civilians in armed conflict in which the Council addressed that the *deliberate denial* of access for humanitarian personnel to civilians:

> "may constitute a threat to international peace and security, and, in this regard, expresses its willingness to consider such information and, when necessary, to adopt appropriate steps".[195]

In this regard the Council also addressed its willingness to:

> "consider the appropriateness and feasibility of temporary security zones and safe corridors for the protection of civilians and the delivery of assistance in situations

---

security: humanitarian aspects of issues before the Security Council, Initial proceedings, Decision of 9 March 2000 (4110th meeting) 712-713.

191 Statement by the President of the Security Council (12 February 1999) UN Doc S/PRST/1999/6.

192 'Protection of civilians in armed conflicts' Report of the Secretary General (8 September 1999) UN Doc S/1999/957; also found in Repertoire of the Practice of the Security Council (1996-1999), Chapter VIII, 'Consideration of questions under the responsibility of the Security Council for the maintenance of international peace and security' Section 43, Protection of civilians in armed conflict, Initial proceedings 1054.

193 UNSC Res 1265 (17 September 1999) UN Doc S/RES/1265 § 10.

194 'Protection of civilians in armed conflicts' Report of the Secretary General (26 November 2002) UN Doc S/2002/1300; also in Repertoire of the Practice of the Security Council (2000-2003), Chapter VIII, 'Consideration of questions under the responsibility of the Security Council for the maintenance of international peace and security', Section 41 Protection of civilians in armed conflict, Decision of 20 December 2002 (4679th meeting): statement by the President 776.

195 UNSC Res 1296 (19 April 2000) UN Doc S/RES/1296 § 8.

> characterized by the threat of genocide, crimes against humanity and war crimes against the civilian population".[196]

As such, the Council addressed the potential consequences it attaches to the denial of assistance, and to the protection of those civilians facing serious violations and crimes. To that end, the Council would take 'appropriate steps' and consider creating security zones. Although the Council does not reference the use of force, in reality in such circumstances safe zones may only be feasible if indeed protected by those mandated to use force (at least in self-defence). Indeed, ascertaining that a situation is a threat to the peace allows the Council to invoke action under Articles 41 and 42 of the Charter. Thus, the Council asserts that a deliberate denial of assistance, which as seen above in Section 8.3.2 violates international law if done arbitrarily, opens the door to the use of force with a view of *enforcing the provision of aid.*

For the purpose of this research, it is relevant to be able to establish from the above that the Council is comfortable asserting a need to act under Chapter VII to ensure the provision of humanitarian assistance. Yet as the Security Council itself puts it in its *Repertoire*, creating 'conditions necessary for unimpeded delivery of humanitarian assistance' would rather fall under the scope of Article 40 of the UN Charter, pertaining to provisional measures under Chapter VII to prevent the aggravation of a situation, as opposed to Article 42.[197] The Council also on occasion names concrete examples of how this should be done, such as through safe corridors or security zones.[198] Although the mandates may vary, from the early 1990's onwards, the *option* to use force has been viable according to the practice of the Council. However, the manner of operating of the Council is case-specific and *ad hoc*; one cannot easily discern a line of precedence in its work. Whether the Council remains with a mandate under Article 40 of the UN Charter or proceeds to use force as directed by Article 42 is not clear from the outset. Furthermore, as O'Connell rightly notes, in its authorisation of the use of force, the Council itself remains bound by international law, specifically the UN Charter and customary international law such as the principles of necessity and proportionality.[199] As such, international law mandates that the Council take other options into consideration *prior* to the actual use of force. With regard to the provision of humanitarian assistance, such options would potentially include the delivery of emergency aid with 'heightened security'.[200]

---

[196] Ibid § 15.
[197] Article 40 UN Charter. See also Repertoire of the Practice of the Security Council (1996-1999), Chapter XI 'Consideration of the provisions of Chapter VII of the Charter, Part II Provisional measures to prevent the aggravation of a situation under Article 40 of the Charter' 1127.
[198] For example UNSC Res 1078 (9 November 1996) UN Doc S/RES/1078 pertaining to the situation in the Great Lakes Region §10.
[199] Mary Ellen O'Connell, 'The United Nations Security Council and the Authorization of Force: Renewing the Council Through Law Reform', in Niels Blokker & Nico Schrijver (eds) *The Security Council and the Use of Force: Theory and Reality – A Need for Change?* (Martinus Nijhoff Publishers 2005) 58.
[200] Ibid 62.

Indeed, the practice of the Security Council is growing, and as such would benefit from a more streamlined approach. Today, the doctrine of the 'responsibility to protect' has permeated the peacekeeping, peace-enforcement and other 'use of force' mandates. The UN General Assembly has adopted this concept as a notion through which the use force in the protection of civilians in need may be called for.[201] This concept, embedded with a clear humanitarian perspective, is able to provide more guidance as to the manner in which the use of force is authorised for the purpose of the delivery of humanitarian assistance. In the face of war crimes and crimes against humanity, both potential results from the non-provision of assistance, the doctrine can be put into practice.

8.4.3 Security Council Action since the UN embracement of the Responsibility to Protect

Should the Security Council decide to use force in a specific circumstance, the doctrine of Responsibility to Protect is of relevance. Although RtoP is not a legal doctrine, nor does the notion hold specific legal standing in and of itself, it may have the potential to add to the manner in which the Security Council approaches the use of force. Despite the embracement of the notion of RtoP, seen by many as the more viable alternative to the contested concept of a 'humanitarian intervention' the Security Council did not immediately implement it into its resolutions.[202] Furthermore, despite the UN-wide embracement of the doctrine in 2005, as well as subsequent implementation by the Security Council, the following Section will show that certainly not every call for the use of force (in relation to the provision of humanitarian assistance) can be qualified or classified as an implementation of the doctrine.

In its thematic resolution pertaining to the protection of civilians in armed conflict, the Council addressed in further detail the circumstances in which it would consider its readiness 'to adopt appropriate steps' as:

> "the deliberate targeting of civilians and other protected persons, and the commission of systematic, flagrant and widespread violations of international humanitarian and human rights law in situations of armed conflict, may constitute a threat to international peace and security".[203]

It has already been established that the (arbitrary) denial of humanitarian assistance constitutes a violation of both international human rights law and humanitarian law, as well as potentially certain norms of *jus cogens*, should the denial of assistance amount to for example war crimes, crimes against humanity, racial discrimination or genocide.[204] With the formulation in the above Resolution, the Council

[201] Section 4.2.3 and UNGA Res 60/1 (24 October 2005) UN Doc A/RES/60/1 'World Summit Outcome Document'.
[202] Section 4.2.2 Reconceptualising Sovereignty?. As noted above, this research shall be restricted to forceful action within the context of the UN Security Council.
[203] UNSC Res 1674 (28 April 2006) UN Doc S/RES/1674 § 26.
[204] Chapters 6 and 7 and Section 8.3.3.

recognises therefore that it will indeed consider taking action in the face of such violations of the law. In a subsequent resolution in 2006 the Council reiterated its stance, declaring once more the readiness to take action in the face of flagrant violations of humanitarian law and human rights law.[205] Throughout the following years, the Council continued to embrace the theme of humanitarian assistance in its work, as well as discussing the need for methods to strengthen humanitarian access to civilians.[206]

On various occasions the Council continued to envisage *enforcement of humanitarian assistance* through enhancement of the mandates of UN missions in countries. The Council did so both referring to the use of force *and* under Chapter VII. As such, it has called upon UN missions such as UNOCI, deployed in Côte d'Ivoire upon the conclusion of the 2003 peace agreement, to help 'establishing the necessary security conditions' for the 'free flow' and provision of assistance.[207] Similarly, MINURCAT which was established in 2009 in consultation with the government of Chad, was authorised to use all necessary measures 'to facilitate the delivery of humanitarian assistance'.[208] These examples illustrate the fact that through such wording the Council positively affirms the possibility to use force *for the sole purpose* of ensuring the delivery of humanitarian assistance. Yet, the wording itself falls short of actually calling upon either a mission or member states to indeed *use* force, although Resolution 1975 allows UNOCI this possibility in the protection of civilians. This indeed relates back to the earlier discussion pertaining to Article 40 of the UN Charter as opposed to the use of force under Article 42. As can be seen, the Council furthermore adopts these resolutions outside the framework of RtoP.

The Council has also authorised regional missions, such as the hybrid mission 'UNAMID' of the African Union and the UN in Darfur, to 'ensure the freedom of movement of humanitarian workers' and 'ensuring humanitarian access'.[209] The African Union in particular as a regional organisation has embraced the Security Council's tendency to exercise its collective use of force through its member states and has established a 'Peace and Security Council' in 2002 that is mandated, *inter alia*, to provide humanitarian assistance.[210] Such a development further extends the Security Council's approach to the enforcement of the provision of aid, as it actively pursues the security of those actors providing aid.

---

[205] UNSC Res 1738 (23 December 2006) UN Doc S/RES/1738 § 9.

[206] Repertoire of the Practice of the Security Council (2004-2007), Chapter VIII, 'Protection of Civilians in armed conflict', 15; Repertoire of the Practice of the Security Council 16th Supplement (2008 – 2009) 'Protection of Civilians in armed conflict'. See also UNSC Res 1674 (28 April 2006) UN Doc S/RES/1674 'Protection of civilians in armed conflict'; UNSC Res 1738 (23 December 2006) UN Doc S/RES/1738.

[207] UNSC Res 1739 (10 January 2007) UN Doc S/RES/1739 § 2 (h).

[208] UNSC Res 1861 (14 January 2009) UN Doc S/RES/1861 § 7.

[209] UNSC Res 1769 (31 July 2007 UN) Doc S/RES/1769 § 15; UNSC Res 1828 (31 July 2008) UN Doc S/RES/1828 § 7.

[210] See in this regard the Protocol Relating To The Establishment Of The Peace And Security Council Of The African Union Adopted by the 1st Ordinary Session of the Assembly of the African Union Durban (9 July 2002) Mandate § 3(f); and Article 15.

In affirmation of the UNAMID mission in Darfur the Council also asserted that it would be ready to take action against any party *impeding* humanitarian assistance in Darfur.[211] This approach aligns with the above establishment in Section 8.3 that *impeding* humanitarian assistance amounts to a violation of international law, warranting enforcement of such assistance. In the protracted situation of Somalia for example, the Council has again authorised the African Union to act, although rather than the hybrid form of UNAMID, as a singular mission. With regard to the provision of aid, the Council declared under Chapter VII that the member states of the African Union would be authorised, taking all necessary measures, to contribute 'to the creation of the necessary security conditions for the provision of humanitarian assistance'.[212] The Council also encouraged such member states participating in the AMISOM mission to 'take appropriate action to protect merchant shipping, in particular the transportation of humanitarian aid' against acts of piracy.[213] This cannot be but seen as an unambiguous call of the Council to enforce and ensure the provision of aid through the use of force.

Thus, not only in peacekeeping missions does the Council note the possibility to use force explicitly *for the purpose of* the enforcement of humanitarian assistance, such options even more so become available for *hybrid constructions and regional organisations* fulfilling the mandate of the Security Council. Whilst acting under Chapter VII of the UN Charter, most of these missions were, however, in cooperation with the affected state and government. As such, although the use of force was mandated, the sovereignty of the affected state was not seriously impaired, and international legal standards not overly stretched.

Sovereignty continues to remain one of the paramount considerations in the provision of humanitarian aid. In particular due to the explicit responsibilities of the affected states to provide in humanitarian aid themselves, risks of violations of sovereign duties and a larger permeability of the shield of sovereignty ensues should they not do so.[214] Yet the Security Council did become more explicit concerning the enforcement of the delivery of aid, as it expressed in reiteration of its earlier thematic resolution on the protection of civilians in 2009, its willingness to *also* respond to those circumstances of armed conflict in which:

> "civilians are being targeted or humanitarian assistance to civilians is being deliberately obstructed, including through the consideration of appropriate measures at the Security Council's disposal in accordance with the Charter of the United Nations".[215]

---

211 UNSC Res 1828 (31 July 2008) UN Doc S/RES/1828 § 18: "Reiterates its readiness to take action against any party that impedes the peace process, humanitarian assistance or the deployment of UNAMID; and recognizes that due process must take its course".

212 UNSC Res 1744 (21 February 2007) UN Doc S/RES/1744 § 4 (d); UNSC Res 1772 (20 August 2007) UN Doc S/RES/1772 § 9(d); UNSC Res 1801 (20 February 2008) UN Doc S/RES/1801 § 1; UNSC Res 1863 (9 July 2009) UN Doc S/RES/1863 § 2.

213 UNSC Res 1801 (20 February 2008) UN Doc S/RES/1801 § 12.

214 Chapter 6.

215 UNSC Res 1894 (11 November 2009) UN Doc S/RES/1894 § 4. § 3 reiterates the wording of the Council's resolution on the matter in 2006: "Notes that the deliberate targeting of civilians as such and other protected persons, and the commission of systematic, flagrant and widespread violations of

Hence, not only in country-specific circumstances does the Security Council address the potential to use force for the enforcement of the provision of humanitarian assistance: through its thematic resolution, the Council opens the door to the use of force as a mechanism to ensure the provision of humanitarian assistance in instances where its provision is 'deliberately obstructed'. Such phrasing is in fact in line with the discussed arbitrary refusal of a bona fide offer, as noted in Section 8.3.2, and forms part of the developments in international law. For example, should a country specifically use starvation as a method of warfare, the Security Council can assert the need to use force in the enforcement of humanitarian assistance.[216] This line of action by the Council also aligns with the crimes as codified in the Rome Statute of the International Criminal Court, which entered into force in 2002, and that are addressed in more detail in Section 8.6.2.[217] In more recent years, the Council has furthermore considered such an approach in practice, whilst embracing the notion of the Responsibility to Protect.

In due course, RtoP *in relation to the enforcement* of the provision of humanitarian assistance has seeped into the wording of the Council in its resolutions. The Council has in fact on various occasions called upon member states to use force with a view to the protection of civilians and the provision of humanitarian assistance. In the situation concerning Libya in 2011, the Council, through the by now familiar phrase, first asserted its 'readiness to consider taking additional appropriate measures' to achieve the provision of humanitarian assistance.[218] Subsequently, in its well-known Resolution 1973 of 2011, the Council acted upon this 'readiness' through the use of force, recalling this specific paragraph of resolution 1970. The Council considered that a flight ban would constitute an important element in this regard (with the exception of flights for humanitarian purposes), as well as authorising member states to take all necessary measures 'to protect civilians'.[219] This well-known Resolution has been credited with being the first practical application of the use of force within the framework of the Responsibility to Protect. It is therefore striking that such a call has been made *in connection to the enforcement of the provision of humanitarian assistance*. Such an outspoken call by the Security Council has, however, subsequently not been seen.

The Council has amongst others successively acted under Chapter VII with regard to the on-going situation in Somalia and also concerning South Sudan, but has failed to do so with regard to Syria, as well as for example in Mali in 2013. The

---

applicable international humanitarian and human rights law in situations of armed conflict may constitute a threat to international peace and security, and reaffirms in this regard its readiness to consider such situations and, where necessary, to adopt appropriate steps".

216 See more explicitly Articles 70 AP I and 14 AP II.

217 See Article 8 ICC: Rome Statute of the International Criminal Court, A/CONF.183/9 of 17 July 1998 and corrected by process-verbaux of 10 November 1998, 12 July 1999, 30 November 1999, 8 May 2000, 17 January 2001 and 16 January 2002. The Statute entered into force on 1 July 2002.

218 UNSC Res 1970 (26 February 2011) UN Doc S/RES/1970 § 26.

219 UNSC Res 1973 (17 March 2011) UN Doc S/RES/1973 'The situation in Libya' preamble and § 4 and 7.

conflict in Somalia has been on-going for decades, as has the Security Council's involvement in this situation. Its particular circumstance, being often classified as a 'failed state', has added to the difficulties of the Council in finding a solution.[220] Concerning the South Sudan, the Council authorised its mission UNMISS to contribute to 'the creation of security conditions conducive to safe, timely, and unimpeded humanitarian assistance'.[221] Such phrasing is recognised from the above peacekeeping missions that have been discussed, in which the Council acts under Chapter VII but maintains cooperation with the affected governments, and therefore does not assert the use of force as such, rather phrasing it in a somewhat 'softer' manner, most likely remaining within the scope of Article 40.

Equally, the approach taken through RtoP in the situation in Libya is not echoed unambiguously by the Council in its resolutions concerning Syria, but a novel approach is taken. The Council did not commence with a forward approach, merely calling upon parties to implement the 'Six-Point Proposal of the Joint Special Envoy of the United Nations and the League of Arab States' that in relation to the provision of humanitarian assistance calls for the implementation of a 'daily two hour humanitarian pause to ensure the timely provision of humanitarian aid'.[222] In 2014, the Council arguably somewhat referenced to the Responsibility to Protect, mentioning in Resolutions 2139 and 2165 that Syria holds the primary responsibility to protect its population, and 'demanding' that all parties allow access for assistance.[223] Also in Resolution 2165 the Council, although not referring to Chapter VII, but instead 'underscoring that Member States are obligated under Article 25 of the Charter of the United Nations to accept and carry out the Council's decisions' decides:

> "[...] that the United Nations humanitarian agencies and their implementing partners are authorized to use routes across conflict lines and the border crossings of Bab al-Salam, Bab al-Hawa, Al Yarubiyah and Al-Ramtha, in addition to those already in use, in order to ensure that humanitarian assistance, including medical and surgical supplies, reaches people in need throughout Syria through the most direct routes, with notification to the Syrian authorities, and to this end stresses the need for all border crossings to be used efficiently for United Nations humanitarian operations, [...] that all Syrian parties to the conflict shall enable the immediate and unhindered delivery of humanitarian assistance directly to people throughout Syria, by the United Nations humanitarian agencies and their implementing partners, on the basis of United Nations assessments of need and devoid of any political prejudices and aims, including by immediately removing all

[220] Issues concerning the absence of a sovereign are addressed in more detail in Section 8.7.
[221] UNSC Res 1996 (8 July 2011) UN Doc S/RES/1996 § 3(b)(vi).
[222] UNSC Res 2042 (14 April 2012) UN Doc S/RES/2042 'The situation in the Middle East' § 1 and similarly UNSC Res 2043 (21 April 2012) UN Doc S/RES/2043 § 1. The 'Six-Point Proposal of the Joint Special Envoy of the United Nations and the League of Arab States' calls under point 3 to: "ensure timely provision of humanitarian assistance to all areas affected by the fighting, and to this end, as immediate steps, to accept and implement a daily two hour humanitarian pause and to coordinate exact time and modalities of the daily pause through an efficient mechanism, including at local level".
[223] UNSC Res 2139 (22 February 2014) UN Doc S/RES/2139 § 5 and 12; see also UNSC 2165 (14 July 2014) UN Doc S/RES/2165, preamble.

> impediments to the provision of humanitarian assistance; [...] notes in this regard the role that ceasefire agreements that are consistent with humanitarian principles and international humanitarian law could play to facilitate the delivery of humanitarian assistance in order to help save civilian lives, and further underscores the need for the parties to agree on humanitarian pauses, days of tranquility, localized ceasefires and truces to allow humanitarian agencies safe and unhindered access to all affected areas in Syria in accordance with international humanitarian law".[224]

Whilst the Security Council here certainly does not assert a right to use force by member states, it does address the option of *entering* into a territory without the sovereigns' specific consent, and very distinctly addresses the actions that should be taken by parties to the conflict, to enable the provision of humanitarian assistance. It has been the first time that the Council refers to such assistance 'across conflict lines'. As such, a novel approach is taken, although it currently remains to be seen how the Council will proceed.

Furthermore in the situation in Mali, the Council acted under Chapter VII, yet refrained from the active use of force by member states, merely providing through familiar wording the 'African-led International Support Mission in Mali (AFISMA)' with the mandate to:

> "support the Malian authorities to create a secure environment for the civilian-led delivery of humanitarian assistance and the voluntary return of internally displaced persons and refugees, as requested, within its capabilities and in close coordination with humanitarian actors".[225]

Interestingly, the Council specifically refers to the *civilian-led* provision of aid. In such a manner, the Council appears to attempt to distinguish clearly between those *providing* aid, and those *enforcing* the provision. Such a distinction is also often seen in the General Assembly's resolutions pertaining to the delivery of humanitarian assistance, as that body often 'emphasizes the fundamentally civilian character of humanitarian assistance', whilst affirming the potential for military support in the implementation of such aid. [226] This has also been asserted by the ICRC in its proclamation that neutrality in the provision of aid is paramount, as a result of which military forces should according to the ICRC not directly be

---

[224] UNSC 2165 (14 July 2014) UN Doc S/RES/2165, § 2, 6 and 7.

[225] UNSC Res 2085 (20 December 2012) UN Doc S/RES/2085 § 9(e).

[226] See amongst others for example UNGA Res 60/124 (8 March 2006) UN Doc A/RES/60/124 'Strengthening the coordination of humanitarian emergency assistance of the United Nations' § 7; UNGA Res 61/134 (1 March 2007) UN Doc A/RES/61/134 § 5; UNGA Res 65/133 (3 March 2011) UN Doc A/RES/65/133 preamble. See also other affirmations hereof, such as for example 'Report of the Representative of the Secretary-General on the human rights of internally displaced persons', UN Doc A/HRC/13/21 (5 January 2010) § 64: "Where both humanitarian and military efforts to broaden protection of civilians coincide, the Representative has emphasized that the fundamental distinction between humanitarian action and military action be upheld at all times so as not to call into question the impartiality of humanitarian activities. Fostering a mutual understanding of each other's role will certainly contribute to better coordination. The political and military arms of an integrated mission should reach out to non-United Nations humanitarian actors to promote this understanding".

providing aid in an ongoing conflict.[227] Yet, the General Assembly has also maintained as recently as 2013 that the use of the military for the purpose of the provision of assistance should be 'with the consent of the affected State', thereby taking a different stance than the way the practice of the Security Council has developed.[228] It is of course possible for the General Assembly to take a different path than the Security Council, although in situations involving the use of force, the Security Council has the leading role. As such, and also given the fact that the resolutions of the latter are of binding legal value when taken under Chapter VII, they shall have more impact on the developments in the field.

Some examples from the Council's practice illustrate the gradual specificity the Security Council has reached over the past years, in particular in relation to the use of force for the purpose of enforcing the delivery of assistance. Increasingly, the Council has asserted the potential to use force in order to specifically carry out the task of securing the provision of aid. As such, in its discussion of the transition from AFISMA to the peacekeeping mission MINUSMA following the French intervention in support of the government in Mali in January of 2013, similar to earlier resolutions the Council has asserted under Chapter VII that this missions mandate shall include the support for humanitarian assistance and as such shall 'contribute to the creation of a secure environment for the safe, civilian-led delivery of humanitarian assistance', thereby echoing its earlier phrasing.[229] Subsequently, in March of 2013, the African Union's Member States were authorised by the Council to:

> "take all necessary measures, in full compliance with its obligations under international humanitarian law and human rights law, and in full respect of the sovereignty, territorial integrity, political independence and unity of Somalia, to carry out the following tasks: [...] To contribute, as may be requested and within capabilities, to the creation of the necessary security conditions for the provision of humanitarian assistance".[230]

Thus, the Council envisioned AMISOM to *create* the secure environment which would enable the provision of aid. Similarly, with regard to the situation in the Cote d'Ivoire, the Council has noted in July of 2013 that, in extending the mission of UNOCI under Chapter VII the mission shall:

> "facilitate, as necessary, unhindered humanitarian access and to help strengthen the delivery of humanitarian assistance to conflict-affected and vulnerable populations, notably by contributing to enhancing security for its delivery".[231]

---

227 Statement by Tauxe (n 135).

228 UNGA Res 65/133 (3 March 2011) UN Doc A/RES/65/133 preamble; UNGA Res 66/119 (7 March 2012) UN Doc A/RES/66/119 preamble; and UNGA Res 67/87 (26 March 2013) UN Doc A/RES/67/87 preamble.

229 UNSC Res 2100 (25 April 2013) UN Doc S/RES/2100 § 16(e).

230 UNSC Res 2093 (6 March 2013) UN Doc S/RES/2093 § 1(e).

231 UNSC Res 2112 (30 July 2013) UN Doc S/RES/2112 § 1 and 6(g).

This phrasing by the Security Council focuses on certain *specific elements in the delivery of assistance*. The Council in fact integrates its earlier lingo from previous resolutions into one singular phrasing. A similar tendency towards such specificities can be seen in the Council's resolution pertaining to MISCA, the mission to the Central African Republic where the Council adopted a lengthy resolution containing many new considerations (amongst others also pertaining to the exploitation of natural resources in times of conflict). It has been argued that such a breakdown of the concepts through emphasis on the various issues relevant to the provision of assistance would indeed be beneficial.[232] Such an argument certainly is valid, as emphasis is placed on a variety of relevant issues within the specific situation under the Council's attention. With regard to the provision of humanitarian assistance the Council echoed its approach used concerning UNMISS in the South Sudan, where it had called upon the mission to contribute to 'the creation of security conditions conducive to safe, timely, and unimpeded humanitarian assistance'. Yet MISCA is authorised to 'take all necessary measures', wording of the Council which often implies a more forceful approach under Article 42 of the UN Charter.[233] In 2014, MISCA transitioned into the UN peacekeeping force MINUSCA, with a mandate under Chapter VII to 'facilitate the immediate, full, safe and unhindered delivery of humanitarian assistance'.[234]

Whilst the use of force by peacekeeping missions is not explicitly mentioned by the Council, it has mentioned this with regard to hybrid missions, those undertaken by regional operations or coalitions of member states, such as for example the missions discussed above in East Timor (INTERFET) and AMISOM.[235] In a new initiative, the Security Council has in 2013 created an 'Intervention Brigade' as part of its MONUSCO mission in the DRC.[236] Although it is the first time a UN peacekeeping mission is enhanced with the task to in fact 'carry out targeted offensive operations' to neutralise armed groups in the protection of civilians, as well as ensure the protection of civilians and humanitarian personnel, this Resolution can be placed in the context of the evolving Security Council action.[237]

Indeed, in many circumstances over the past years where a threat to the peace has existed and a strong authority was absent, such as the circumstances discussed in Somalia, Mali and the Sudan, the Security Council has opted to be increasingly specific in ensuring that the mandate of its peacekeeping missions or that the assisting member states are functioning under Chapter VII, with the potential to stabilise the territory for the purpose of protecting civilians and enforcing the

---

232 'Security Council, Internal Displacement And Protection: Recommendations For Strengthening Action Through Resolutions', *Brookings Institute* (September 2011) 21.
233 UNSC Res 2127 (5 December 2013) UN Doc S/RES/2127 § 28 and 51-52.
234 UNSC Res 2149 (10 April 2014) UN Doc S/RES/2149 § 30(c).
235 See for a discussion also Repertoire of the Practice of the Security Council (1996-1999), Chapter XI 'Consideration of the provisions of Chapter VII of the Charter, Part IV Other measures to maintain or restore international peace and security in accordance with Article 42 of the Charter' 1147.
236 UNSC Res 2098 (28 March 2013) UN Doc S/RES/2098 § 9.
237 Ibid § 12.

provision of humanitarian assistance.[238] The door to the use of force for the purpose of the enforcement of the provision of humanitarian assistance has therefore indeed been opened by the Council. The Council, through using the well-known phrasing related to the use of force, as well as increased specificities in its resolutions, thereby clearly considering the provision of humanitarian assistance as an object of the use of force, is identifying the importance of the enforcement of the provision of emergency aid.

Yet, the *willingness* to act on the one hand, and the *existing legal rights or duties* on the other hand relating to state sovereignty do not always coincide. The sovereignty of the affected state in the provision of assistance, in practice, continues to be an obstacle that the Security Council faces, although Chapters 5, 6 and 7 have addressed the fact that indeed the viewpoint that access for humanitarian aid is needed, has resulted in more permeability of the notion of sovereignty today, next to the independent evolution of this concept within the 21st century. Equally, the political composition of the Council is a determining factor in its possibility to act. This is also apparent from the singularity of the Libyan action by the Security Council. Only a few times previously has the Council authorised the use of force specifically for the purpose of the provision of humanitarian assistance and the protection of civilians, *against the wishes of the sovereign*. Such was the case in the discussed Resolution 794 pertaining to the situation in Somalia in 1992 where the humanitarian crisis existed in the absence of a central government. Specific to the situation in Libya, however, was that the use of force in Libya was directly *against* the wishes of the government.[239] The operation has to a certain extent reopened the debate on the notion of the use of force for 'humanitarian purposes' under the auspices of the Council, following the humanitarian 'intervention' in Kosovo by NATO in 1999, outside the scope of the Council.[240] Some members of the Security Council have expressed negative responses to the use of force for humanitarian purposes, also in the context of the notion of the responsibility to protect, with a view to the political consequences of the use of force in Libya.[241] Such responses may explain the reason for the lack of political will in the Council to respond through the use of force to ensuing circumstances that may otherwise have warranted a forceful action to aid persons in need of emergency assistance, such as in Syria.

---

[238] Aurelie Ponthieu, Christoph Vogel, Katharine Derderian, 'Without Precedent or Prejudice? UNSC Resolution 2098 and its potential implications for humanitarian space in Eastern Congo and beyond', (2014) *The Journal of Humanitarian Assistance* <http://sites.tufts.edu/jha/archives/2032> accessed 3 March 2015 (online publication).

[239] A J Bellamy & P D Williams, 'The new politics of protection? Côte d'Ivoire, Libya and the responsibility to protect', (2011) 87 *International Affairs* 4, 825–850.

[240] 4.2.2 Reconceptualising Sovereignty?.

[241] Bruno Pommier, 'The use of force to protect civilians and humanitarian action: the case of Libya and beyond', (2011) 93 *International Review of the Red Cross* 884, 1081-1082; Carsten Stahn, 'Syria and the Semantics of Intervention, Aggression and Punishment On 'Red Lines' and 'Blurred Lines', (2013) 11 *Journal of International Criminal Justice* 961.

Certainly, if one attempts to use force in the protection of civilians and the provision of humanitarian assistance to that end against the will of the sovereign state, an outcome most often will be the use of force *against* that sovereign. Yet, distinguishing between the enforcement of humanitarian assistance and a 'humanitarian intervention' which by definition touches upon the sphere of state sovereignty, remains necessary. The use of force as authorised by the Security Council is furthermore not in violation as such of international law. Hence, this research has focused on the use of force within the context of the Council. The use of force outside the Security Council, even for the strict purpose of (the enforcement of) the provision of humanitarian assistance, risks lacking the legality and legitimacy of that use by the Council and would therefore be open to a debate.[242] Such a debate must remain outside the scope of this research, as the focus lies on the enforcement options that are *currently* legally viable *and recognised as such* for the provision of humanitarian assistance.

The Security Council has to date only decided to resort to the use of force with regard to circumstances that may prove to be a threat to the peace, whereas it does not touch upon instances following natural disasters or other crises that may not amount to a threat to the peace. Indeed, within international law, no consensus exists regarding the establishment of such a 'right to use force' in situations that do not amount to a threat to the peace.[243] The IDRL Guidelines for relief in the aftermath of a natural disaster do open the door to potential 'military assets' to be deployed, but envision such relief to be 'only at the request or with the express consent of the affected State', and only upon exhaustion of civilian alternatives.[244] As such, the Guidelines do not attempt to open the door to a potential enforcement of assistance. Similarly, the 'Guidelines on the Use of Foreign Military and Civil Defence Assets in Disaster Relief' (Oslo Guidelines) used by OCHA and the IASC do not break new ground.[245] Vukas (drafter of the Bruges Resolution) argues that despite the *lex lata* not having developed in this direction, the use of force under the auspices of the Security Council should be considered also in cases of 'extreme danger for the survival of the victims' of disasters whilst there should be no risk that the resistance of the affected state to the 'imposed humanitarian assistance' would cause more harm and suffering than its *sec* denial.[246] Vukas has argued that such a perspective would not be contrary to the terms of the UN Charter, as the Council would be asserting its duty to protect persons from gross human rights

[242] See amongst others Yoram Dinstein, 'The Right to Humanitarian Assistance' (2000) LIII *Naval War College Review* 4, 87-89; Dungel, 'A Right to Humanitarian Assistance in Internal Armed Conflicts Respecting Sovereignty, Neutrality and Legitimacy: Practical Proposals to Practical Problems' (n 134), 9; Stahn ibid 962.

[243] UN Charter Article 2(4) and 39. See also Vukas, 'Humanitarian Assistance in Cases of Emergency' (n 57) 6.

[244] IFRC 'Guidelines for the domestic facilitation and regulation of international disaster relief and initial recovery assistance' (IDRL Guidelines) (30 November 2007), adopted at the 30th International Conference of the Movement, Guideline 11.

[245] <https://docs.unocha.org/sites/dms/Documents/ENGLISH%20VERSION%20Guidelines%20for%20Complex%20Emergencies.pdf> accessed 1 November 2014.

[246] Vukas, 'Humanitarian Assistance in Cases of Emergency' (n 57) 6.

violations.[247] Equally, the Bruges Resolution itself concurs with such action by the Security Council, although declaring more conservatively in line with current international law in Principle VII(3) that when the refusal of a *bona fide* offer of assistance leads to a 'threat to international peace and security', the Council indeed should be able to take Chapter VII measures.[248] The Bruges Resolution thereby remains in line with international law when it comes to the consideration of the use of force for the purposes of the provision of assistance. At an earlier stage in the 1990's, when the Council itself was even so more than today still struggling to determine the extent of the potential use of force in the averting of a humanitarian crisis, the San Remo Principles of 1993 stated that *should a state already have agreed upon assistance*, yet regress into refusal, 'all necessary steps to ensure such access' would be warranted, in conformity with international law.[249] The San Remo Principles went on to formulate that the UN would be competent to undertake 'coercion measures' in the event of prolonged and severe suffering of a population, should an offer of assistance be refused or encounter serious difficulties.[250]

Indeed, finding a formulation that would entice the Council to take more firm action does appear necessary, as consistency continues to remain lacking in the Council's approach to dealing with situations that *are* a threat to the international peace and security. This can be seen through its *in*action concerning the situation in Syria after having taken action through the authorisation of the use of force in Libya, as well as for example expanding UNOCI's mandate in Cote d'Ivoire. In practice however, such a 'standard' formulation does not appear viable, also considering the political composition of the Council. Although consistency in the Council's work is lacking, the determination that the use of force is not *viable* in *all* circumstances has not become an argument that its use should be *prohibited* everywhere. The above discussion has demonstrated that *the Council is in fact ready to assert the need to use force for the purpose of the delivery of humanitarian assistance when facing a humanitarian crisis*. The willingness of the Council has been brought into practice both in circumstances in which the affected state has cooperated (somewhat) and in circumstances in which the sovereign has not been willing to cooperate. Such forceful action through the Chapter VII framework of Security Council resolutions and action furthermore contributes to lessening the international legal debate with regard to issues pertaining to state sovereignty when considering a potential forceful intervention. Arguments in favour of such developments in the Council's action have been made, on the one hand, towards an already existing erosion of state sovereignty due to the changing nature of conflicts today and the contribution of viewpoints concerning the provision of humanitarian assistance to this erosion, as well as with regard to the use of force as a means to prevent a worsening crisis that may destabilise an entire

[247] Ibid.
[248] Bruges Resolution 'Humanitarian Assistance' (2 September 2003) (n 92) Principle VII(3).
[249] 'Guiding Principles on the Right to Humanitarian Assistance' (n 90) Principle 6(2).
[250] Ibid Principle 7(1).

region as opposed to one country.[251] Tomuschat has along this line argued that sovereignty is a 'distinction' conferred upon an entity 'as a recognition of its ability and willingness to take care of law and order and to administer justice' as opposed to an 'inherent quality' of that entity, and thus when a sovereign commits gross violations of international law such as genocide, it must be recognised as an abuse of that state's sovereign rights and as a forfeit of the protection that sovereignty grants under international law, leading to certain consequences.[252] On the other hand the more conservative argument has been made that RtoP has not yet developed fully enough as a concept to be used in foregoing consent in the delivery of assistance in and of itself.[253] Indeed, the International Commission on Intervention and State Sovereignty (ICISS) , as developer of what has been embraced as the notion of RtoP, has argued that whilst sovereignty issues 'necessarily arise' when discussing a forcible intervention, such a potential suspension of sovereignty must be *de facto* rather than *de jure*, as the objective is not to undermine sovereignty but to rather sustain and protect the constitutional arrangements in a country that protect the population in need of assistance.[254] Even so, this argument would still allow for a forceful intervention that would be determined on a case-by-case basis. Whilst the Security Council has embraced the notion of RtoP, it has obviously chosen not to implement it in certain resolutions following the action taken in Libya. Whether or not it shall continue to do so it not yet clear at this time, and remains to be seen. What can however be distilled from the above, is the fact that where the Security Council has the legal means to use force, it has also shown the willingness to assert these means *for the enforcement purpose of the delivery of aid (against the will of a sovereign)*. When and how the Council will choose to do so next shall, in the absence of a clear line in the work of the Council, remain to be determined on an *ad hoc* basis.

8.5 Enforcement through Human Rights Law

The enforcement of human rights law, in the face of gross violations, may not only occur through the use of force on a state *vis-à-vis* state level as discussed above. Such enforcement may also occur at the interstate level without the use of force and alternatively, human rights enforcement mechanisms exist where human rights violations can be claimed directly by individuals. These mechanisms are open to the enforcement of the provision of humanitarian assistance, as its provision functions as a vehicle in the fulfilment of existing human rights. Two distinct sets of

---

[251] See respectively J Maogoto & K Kindiki, 'A People Betrayed – the Darfur Crisis and International Law: Rethinking Westphalian Sovereignty in the 21st Century', (2007) 19 *Bond Law Review* 2, 114; Roberta Cohen, 'Humanitarian Imperatives are Transforming Sovereignty', (2008) 9 *Northwestern Journal of International Affairs* 1, 5.

[252] Christian Tomuschat, *Human Rights: Between Idealism and Realism* (Oxford University Press 2008) 277.

[253] Spieker, 'Humanitarian Assistance, Access in Armed Conflict and Occupation' (n 81) § 36.

[254] 'The Responsibility to Protect', Report of the International Commission on Intervention and State Sovereignty (ICISS 2001) 44.

enforcement mechanisms exist: through the UN Charter-based system with public 'naming and shaming' functions as well as through UN treaty body mechanisms such as courts and supervisory expert committees. The treaty bodies and courts would be requested to determine whether or not the non-provision of humanitarian assistance would be a violation of *human rights law*. In this regard, Section 7.3.2 has addressed the fact that the ICJ has determined that an obligation to allow access can exist on the basis of the ICERD and other human rights obligations, also in times of conflict. Thus, whilst many human rights treaty bodies refrain from referring to international humanitarian law, considering whether the affected state has fulfilled its duties in the provision of humanitarian assistance would not be a reference to humanitarian law, despite potentially judging violations occurring in times of conflict.

Traditionally, human rights law operates at the level between the affected state and an individual.[255] Prior discussion in Chapter 5 has ascertained a lack of an existing independent human right to humanitarian assistance and determined that its *provision* marks a state's fulfilment of duties that exist under the established rights to life, food, health (and water). Therefore, what remains is the determination in which manners individuals or other states may hold the affected state accountable for violations of *these* existing human rights, in order to enforce the provision of the delivery of humanitarian assistance, in the fulfilment of the rights to life, food, health (and water). This Section addresses enforcement through treaty body mechanisms first, as such mechanisms amount to more legal enforcement mechanisms, compared to the political regime of the UN system. The UN system, however, has the potential of ensuring the enforcement of the delivery of humanitarian assistance whilst a crisis may still be on-going. Given the amount of time that passes in the assessment of a potential human rights violation, as well as the fact that such claims are brought well *after* an occurrence, the human rights treaty bodies and courts shall be the institutions determining *ex post facto* whether or not such delivery of humanitarian assistance should in fact have taken place and whether or not the affected state is or was in violation of its duties under the rights to life, food, health (and water).

8.5.1 Enforcement through Human Rights Treaty Mechanisms

Chapter 6 has determined that the major treaties dealing with the rights to life, food and health as related to the provision of assistance are the ICCPR, the ICESCR and the ICERD, as well as regional treaties such as the ECHR, the European Social Charter, the ACHR and its Additional Protocol in the Area of Economic, Social and Cultural Rights, the ACHPR and its Additional Protocol on the Rights of Women in Africa, the African Charter on the Rights and Welfare of the Child. Also, more specific treaties such as the CRC, the CEDAW and the CRPD, as well as the Kampala Convention which is both regional and specific to IDPs deal with the

[255] Section 5.2.

subject matter in relation to the rights incorporated in their conventions. Focarelli has asserted that states parties to human rights treaties that do not (sufficiently) provide humanitarian assistance may indeed incur responsibility for the violation of certain rights.[256] This has also been concluded in Chapters 5 and 6, based on the various provisions in these treaties. Such treaties provide for monitoring bodies that allow for various complaint mechanisms, varying from procedures in which those that did not receive humanitarian assistance may appeal that the contracting affected state has not provided (sufficient) humanitarian assistance in the face of a humanitarian crisis, to appeals from other contracting states.[257]

Several courts today have a very broad jurisdiction *ratione materiae*, such as the ICJ, the International Tribunal for the Law of the Sea and the International Criminal Court, the latter of which shall be dealt with further on. Human rights treaty bodies are limited to the scope allotted to them by their respective treaties, thereby focusing on the rights within their scope that might relate to states parties and the provision of assistance. As most of the current relevant human rights treaties do not contain references to international humanitarian law, with the exception of for example the CRC (in Article 38(1)) and the Protocol to the ACHPR (in Article 11), their enforcement bodies have been hesitant to incorporate it in their decision-making process. As discussed in Section 3.4.2.1, various treaty bodies and the ICJ have asserted the continued applicability of human rights treaties in times where international humanitarian law is also applicable.[258] Explicit references to or application of humanitarian law can indeed be found in certain decisions, although they are not distinctly necessary for the enforcement of the provision of humanitarian assistance, which may also be reached through human rights law enforcement. Indeed, the judgment of these bodies may be based on the determination of a possible violation of the rights to life, food, health (and water), should humanitarian assistance not be provided in the event of a humanitarian crisis – be it a natural disaster, or a circumstance in which humanitarian law is applicable.

The ICCPR, with its wide status of ratification, can provide various methods through which the right to life might be enforced for the purpose of enforcement of humanitarian assistance, although the findings of the Human Rights Committee are not binding in themselves. The HRC has however assessed that the non-compliance with its interim measures is 'incompatible with the obligation to respect in good

---

256 Focarelli, 'Duty to Protect in Cases of Natural Disasters' (n 100) § 18.

257 This research will focus on international complaint mechanisms, as opposed to national enforceability. It is however recognised that the enforcement of rights such as in the ICESCR face more challenges in national courts; often such economic, social and cultural rights are not self-executing and face the additional hurdle of a requirement of national implementation legislation for insurance of domestic legal effects. The enforceability issues however remain separate from the assessment that such rights exist, and as such individuals claiming fulfilment of their (economic social and cultural) rights through the provision of humanitarian assistance must find a platform.

258 Section 3.4.2; *Isayeva, Yusupova and Bazayeva v.* Russia (App nos 57947/00, 57948/00 and 57949/00) ECHR 24 February 2005; Inter-American Court on Human Rights, *Case of Bámaca-Velasquez v. Guatemala* (November 25 2000) (Merits), Series C No. 70 § 207; and *Armed Activities on the Territory of the Congo* (Democratic Republic of the Congo v. Uganda), Judgment, I.C.J. Reports 2005, p. 168, § 216.

faith the procedure of individual communication', thereby alluding to the duty of states parties to the ICCPR to abide by the findings of the Committee on the principle of good faith.[259] States parties have the opportunity to address potential human rights violations of other states parties through the complaint procedure of Article 41 ICCPR. To date, such allegations have not been made with regard to the provision of humanitarian assistance, nor can they be expected anytime soon, given the diplomatic and political implications of the state complaint procedure. The HRC however also investigates the human rights situations of its state parties on its own merits.[260] An example includes the recent request of the HRC to Sudan, asking in relation to Article 6 ICCPR to:

> "Please comment on allegations indicating that the State party has restricted or denied the delivery of humanitarian assistance to conflict-affected areas, especially those controlled by rebel groups. Please also provide information on the measures taken to ensure that people affected by the conflicts in Darfur, South Kordofan and Blue Nile states, even if living in rebel controlled areas, receive humanitarian assistance".[261]

Thus, the HRC indeed *in practice* addresses the potential violation of the right to life through the denial or obstruction of the provision of humanitarian assistance. The outcome of such reports is however also not binding, and clearly such addresses take place *after* the immediate need for assistance is recognised. Such public addresses however do contribute to the pressure upon a state to comply with the human rights regime of the treaty it is a state party to. More specific and potentially more intrusive for the state furthermore is the individual complaint procedure open to individuals of states parties to the Additional Protocol of the ICCPR.[262] Equally, such procedures are limited in the enforcement of actual provision of assistance as the path an individual must travel to reach the HRC is long, and should be considered an enforcement of a right by means of *reparation*, rather than the actual provision of food or medicine. A finding by the Committee of a violation of Article 6 can also be considered an international (political) 'slap on the wrist', even though the ruling is not legally binding.

Since 2013, the CESCR, pursuant to the ICESCR, also considers individual complaints through its Optional Protocol.[263] Given the short timespan since this development, only few individual complaints have been brought to the CESCR to date. The CESCR can however bring forward issues regarding Articles 11, pertaining to an adequate standard of living, and 12 concerning the highest attainable standard of health, should it consider these rights to be infringed when

[259] HRC General Comment 33 (5 November 2008) UN Doc CCPR/C/GC/33 § 19.
[260] Article 40 ICCPR.
[261] Human Rights Committee 'List of issues in relation to the fourth periodic report of the Sudan' (22 November 2013) UN Doc CCPR/C/SDN/Q/4 § 14.
[262] Article 1 Additional Protocol ICCPR. For the specificities of this complaint mechanism, see Articles 2-5 Additional Protocol.
[263] Articles 1-4 Optional Protocol to the International Covenant on Economic, Social and Cultural Rights (10 December 2008, entry into force 5 May 2013).

humanitarian assistance is not provided in certain circumstances. Similar to enforcement via the ICCPR, the CESCR has noted in a General Comment that reparation may be sought, taking the form of 'restitution, compensation, satisfaction or guarantees of non-repetition'.[264] It has been addressed previously in Chapter 7 that the CESCR indeed considers the possibility of a violation of these Articles when food is not provided or access for this is denied in emergencies, or if the affected state does not seek international assistance.[265] According to the CESCR, non-compliance with the duty to provide access to basic shelter, water and sanitation furthermore results in a violation or Article 12 ICESCR.[266] Such findings however are published in the CESCR's General Comments, which – although of relevance – are not binding in nature, nor do they hold a particular state responsible for its actions. It has been argued by Dennis that due to the 'obligation of conduct'-nature of the rights enshrined in the convention, the ICESCR is lacking 'sufficiently clear and precise substantive legal standards' to allow for an adjudicative individual complaints procedure.[267] Indeed the nature of most (albeit not all) of these rights can be seen as an impediment to enforcement procedures, as opposed to the more result-oriented nature of civil and political rights. The fact that such rights are often not self-executing furthermore warrants national implementation for domestic legal effect, in the event an individual wants to lodge a complaint against its sovereign to ensure enforcement. This may in practice make the enforcement of humanitarian assistance through human rights law somewhat more challenging.

Although Article 2 ICESCR incorporates 'progressive development', certain minimum core obligations remain relevant at all times, amongst which those concerning the provision of humanitarian assistance. Furthermore, examples exist of accountability with regard to progressive development also, as the European Committee of Social Rights for example held Greece in violation of Article 11 ESC concerning the right to health, considering it had not demonstrated to have implemented enough measures to improve the right to health in a particular area.[268] Indeed, both the treaty bodies of the ICCPR and ICESCR are also capable of 'naming and shaming' and formulating general concerns for the violation of certain human rights within their respective treaties, but they are both not able to *enforce* the provision of humanitarian assistance through their decisions. Despite the non-binding nature of the mechanisms, both bodies clearly view the non-provision of humanitarian assistance as a potential violation of the rights within their treaties, and as such speak out on the need for non-violation of these rights through the provision of humanitarian aid.

---

[264] CESCR General Comment 12 (n 101) § 32.

[265] Ibid § 17 and § 19.

[266] CESCR General Comment 14 (11 August 2000) UN Doc E/C.12/2000/4 'The right to the highest attainable standard of health', § 43.

[267] Michael J Dennis, 'Application of Human Rights Treaties Extraterritorially in Times of Armed Conflict and Military Occupation', (2005) 99 *American Journal of International Law* 1, 139.

[268] European Committee of Social Rights 'Conclusions 2009' Greece: 2009/def/GRC/ (1 December 2010).

Although it is beyond the scope of this research to address all regional and specialised bodies, several well-known bodies that *do* take legally binding decisions concerning human rights law violations can be highlighted. Arguably, the European Court of Human Rights is the most important of the regional specialised courts due to its extensive case law and effective implementation mechanism throughout its large membership, as well as its age.[269] Article 34 ECHR provides for an individual complaint procedure, whilst Article 33 ECHR provides for an interstate complaint mechanism as also seen in the ICCPR, although binding in nature on both accounts.[270] Similarly to the previously discussed treaty bodies, the ECtHR procedures are lengthy, and the Court is known to be reactive rather than proactive.[271] The ECtHR however does indeed consider the need for humanitarian assistance, for example in *Benzer And Others V. Turkey*, where it states:

> "The Court is further struck by the national authorities' failure to offer even the minimum humanitarian assistance to the applicants in the aftermath of the bombing".[272]

However, the Court has of yet not established a clear direct or causal link between the denial or non-provision of assistance and the violation of a particular human right in its Convention. In its mentioning of humanitarian assistance, to date the Court has done so in relation to potential violations of Article 3 ECHR, pertaining to cruel or inhuman treatment, rather than the right to life (the ECHR does not contain other provisions relating to humanitarian assistance such as the right to food or water).[273] The Court furthermore however cites 'the obstruction of humanitarian assistance' as a 'serious abuse' in its jurisprudence, rather than as a human rights abuse.[274] Such a distinction by the Court is unfortunate for the enforcement of humanitarian assistance through human rights law as in doing so, the Court foregoes the opportunity to make the potential claim immediately viable that obstructing humanitarian assistance might result in a Court decision that a *human rights violation* has taken place. It therefore remains to be seen which potential route the ECtHR shall take with regard to the enforcement of humanitarian assistance within the context of the ECHR, but such an approach via direct assertion of human rights violations currently does not appear imminent.

The Inter-American Court of Human Rights, like the previously discussed bodies, recognises the individual complaint procedure in Article 44 ACHR, which includes the possibility of complaints by groups of persons or NGOs and also

---

[269] Tomuschat, *Human Rights: Between Idealism and Realism* (n 252) 239.

[270] Admissibility criteria can be found in Article 35 ECHR.

[271] Ruth Abril Stoffels, 'Legal Regulation of Humanitarian Assistance in Armed Conflict: Achievements and Gaps', (2004) 86 *International Review of the Red Cross* 855, 526.

[272] *Benzer And Others v. Turkey* (App No 23502/06) ECHR 12 November 2013, Final 24 March 2014, § 211.

[273] Ibid; *Sufi And Elmi v. The United Kingdom* (App nos 8319/07 and 11449/07) ECHR 28 June 2011, Final 28 November 2011, § 292; *Popov v. France* (App nos 39472/07 and 39474/07) ECHR 19 January 2012 § 91.

[274] *Mohammed v. Austria* (App no 2283/12) ECHR 6 June 2013, Final 6 September 2013 § 52.

recognises an interstate communication in Article 45 ACHR. Moreover, individuals and NGOs may also bring a complaint before the African Court on Human and Peoples' Rights under Article 34(6) of the Protocol to the African Charter on Human and Peoples' Rights on the Establishment of the African Court on Human and Peoples' Rights *if* the ratifying state has so declared.[275] As with the other regional courts and the international complaint mechanisms, the Protocol to the African Charter also provides for the possibility of a state complaint to the African Court.[276] Although the interstate complaint mechanism that exists throughout these enforcement bodies has been used concerning the situation in Libya in March 2011, it is not often used in practice but as a mechanism reflects a broader principle in international law, clarifying that human rights violations within the treaty regime are not solely between the state and its population. The interstate mechanism reflects a shared responsibility of all states parties for the common goal they have chosen to pursue through the creation of the human rights convention.[277] Indeed, whilst within the human rights regime this role for third states is formulated as a 'right', such a perspective falls in line with the route taken by the ICJ in its Barcelona Traction case as discussed above.[278] The approach is somewhat similar, as a possibility is left open for third states to assert the responsibility of the affected state for certain violations of international law, whilst these third states are not directly affected themselves. Indeed this notion, as incorporated by various human rights treaties has been subsequently embraced by the ARSIWA in its Article 48. The ILC has argued, referencing such human rights mechanisms, that a justification for such progressive development in the Articles lies in the protection of the international community as a whole.[279] Similarly, the provision of humanitarian assistance contributes to preventing exacerbations of humanitarian crises and their effect on the international community.

With regard to the potential of enforcement of the provision of humanitarian assistance, the treaty bodies and courts will face the difficult task, as does the Security Council when contemplating the use of force, of ascertaining whether indeed *enough* has been done by the affected state to *fulfil* the basic requirements of the right to life, the right to food, the right to health (and the right to water) so as to not violate these rights. Questions such as whether or not blankets were provided, safe drinking water and food rations sent out, all in an indiscriminate manner, will have to be addressed by these institutions when considering whether a right has been potentially violated. Whilst the Security Council considers a potential threat to the international peace and observes from a more overall approach whether a humanitarian crisis takes place, treaty-based monitoring bodies have the

---

[275] As of October 2012, only 5 states had provided such a declaration: Tanzania, kina Faso, Ghana, Mali and Malawi.

[276] Article 5 of the Protocol to the African Charter on Human and Peoples' Rights on the Establishment of the African Court on Human and Peoples' Rights.

[277] Tomuschat, *Human Rights: Between Idealism and Realism* (n 252) 272. See also ECtHr Ireland v UK 18 January 1978 (A 25) para 239.

[278] Section 8.2.3.

[279] 'Report of the International Law Commission' UN Doc A/56/10 (n 10) 323.

opportunity to rather assess individual violations. Also of course, a different approach is possible as they are operating in the aftermath of the crisis rather than at its peak, although most mechanisms can apply 'interim measures' should there be some urgency still remaining.[280] To date, the main treaty enforcement bodies have shied away from such a formal assessment; not using human rights standards to measure indeed whether enough food and water has been provided in certain specific instances, or whether it has been provided fast enough. In theory however, the existing human rights courts and treaty bodies can be an enforcement mechanism for the provision and delivery of aid, should they choose to determine in cases before them that the non-provision of aid has resulted in a violation of the right to life, food, health (or water). To date however, such an establishment has not taken place although the possibility continues to be available to them. As established in Chapter 5, the provision of humanitarian assistance at a time of crisis can function as the fulfilment of the affected state's obligations under the right to life, food, health (and water). With wording such as 'arbitrary refusal' that has been developed in humanitarian law in relation to the denial of humanitarian assistance, as well as notions pertaining to state responsibility, human rights mechanisms should be able to assess the human rights in their respective treaties fully when it comes to the matter of providing humanitarian assistance. In fact these rights to life, food, health (and water) are not so vaguely formulated that the enforcement bodies should not be able to assess in a particular circumstance whether or not a violation took place because humanitarian assistance was not provided sufficiently, or lacking entirely. The willingness of various bodies to indeed address humanitarian assistance within their case law or comments is proof that such assistance is well placed within the realm of existing human rights law. As a manner of enforcement however, given the duration of procedures, these bodies are often not tailored to ensure the timely provision of assistance when a crisis is still on-going. As such, these bodies provide a different enforcement perspective than of course the Security Council may provide.

8.5.2 Human Rights Enforcement through the UN Charter System

Whilst treaty bodies exist for the monitoring, supervision and control of the various human rights conventions, states parties to such treaties have been quite reluctant to enter into institutionalised forms of human rights enforcement.[281] Indeed, within the UN Charter system, human rights enforcement initially remained outside of the realm of the Security Council, as the task was originally left to the General Assembly, based on Articles 13(1)(b) and 68 of the Charter. In the above Sections, the potential use of force by the Security Council has been addressed, in times when flagrant human rights violations or serious humanitarian crises become a threat to

[280] Rules of Procedure of the African Court of Human and Peoples' Rights, Rule 51; Inter-American Court of Human Rights, rule 25; ECtHR, Rule 39. See also Rules of Procedure of the Human Rights Committee, Rule 86 and OP-ICESCR, Article 5.
[281] Tomuschat, *Human Rights: Between Idealism and Realism* (n 263) 265.

the international peace and security. Yet, what recourse can be sought outside the realm of the Security Council, within the UN system, for the 'enforcement' of humanitarian assistance through human rights law should states be in violation of their duties to fulfil the right to life, food, health (and water)? After all, Article 1(3) of the UN Charter proclaims that one of the purposes of the UN is to promote and encourage 'respect for human rights and for fundamental freedoms for all without distinction as to race, sex, language, or religion'. Furthermore, articles 55 and 56 of the UN Charter lay an obligation upon all UN member states to ensure the universal respect for human rights. As such, states have instated human rights enforcement mechanisms via the UN Human Rights Council, operating directly under the UN General Assembly. The Charter-based organs and bodies of the UN are not restricted by the provisions in various conventions like the treaty-based bodies discussed above are. These bodies have a broader, political mandate and derive their mandates from the human rights provisions in the UN Charter.[282]

The UN Human Rights Council, established in 2006, operates with the older and well-known mechanism of Special Rapporteurs, as well as the new concept of Universal Periodic Review in order to determine the *status quo* of various human rights situations in member states.[283] Much like the Human Rights Committee of the ICCPR and the Committee for Economic Social and Cultural Rights, the UN Special Rapporteurs, Universal Periodic Review (UPR) documentation and Human Rights Council resolutions are not binding by nature.

Several UN Special Rapporteurs have been quite vocal in their assertion that the lack of provision of humanitarian assistance results in human rights violations.[284] Yet, they have also on occasion gone so far as to condemn certain states specifically for their (in)actions. Whilst the Special Rapporteur on the right to life mostly calls for the allowance of humanitarian assistance and an ending to human rights violations in broader terms,[285] the Rapporteur has, for example, also more explicitly announced:

> "According to reports forwarded by non-governmental sources, the government forces and rival factions of the SPLA had created a humanitarian disaster by waging war on villagers and herders. The displacement of millions of people and the killing of thousands of civilians have not been by-products of the conflict but a tactic integral to it. The flagrant violations of human rights standards and of the principles protecting civilians in times of conflict have created famine and dependency on food relief in many areas affected by war. Hundreds of thousands of people have lost their lives through illness, food shortage or deliberate assault (...) The Special Rapporteur calls on all parties to conflicts, international or internal, to respect the norms and standards of

---

[282] H Steiner, P Alston & R Goodman, *International Human Rights in Context: Law, Politics, Morals* (Oxford University Press 2007) 74-741.

[283] For more information on the UPR system <www.ohchr.org/en/hrbodies/upr/pages/BasicFacts.aspx> accessed 2 November 2014.

[284] Section 5.3.2.

[285] Report of the Special Rapporteur on the Right to Life (23 December 1996) UN Doc E/CN.4/1997/60/Add.1 § 303 regarding Liberia; § 403 concerning Russia and §466 concerning Tajikistan.

> international human rights and humanitarian law which protect the lives of the civilian population and those combatants who are captured or lay down their arms. He also appeals to all those involved in armed conflicts to allow convoys of humanitarian aid to reach their destinations as well as to allow the evacuation of the wounded, elderly persons and children. All those responsible for violations of the right to life in situations of armed conflicts must be held accountable".[286]

Indeed while the Special Rapporteur himself cannot enforce human rights law, the mechanism and reports do function as public awareness and an incentive to alter a state's behaviour. In other instances, the Rapporteur has linked the 'deprivation of food' to 'large-scale and widespread violations of human rights' which have resulted in the death of many civilians.[287] More explicitly, the Rapporteur has held concerning the conflict in the Former Yugoslavia that:

> "the policy of deliberately depriving the population of the food, heating, shelter and other essentials necessary for survival, practised by Bosnian Serbs against the population of besieged cities and areas, should also be viewed as extrajudicial, summary or arbitrary execution (...) These deaths are not unavoidable collateral consequences of the conflict but are due to the deliberate refusal to allow delivery of sufficient humanitarian relief".[288]

In doing so, the Rapporteur clearly attempts to phrase the denial of humanitarian assistance in the context of a violation of the right to life. Equally, the Special Rapporteur on the right to the highest attainable standard of health has been known to make recommendations to the Administrator of the Coalition Provisional Authority in Iraq as occupying power, that it establish an inquiry into the health situation of Falluja's civilian population following allegations including:

> "the use of indiscriminate force resulting in civilian deaths and casualties; blocking civilians from entering Falluja's main hospital; preventing medical staff from either working at the hospital or redeploying medical supplies to an improvised health facility; occupying the hospital; and firing upon ambulances. According to reports, Falluja was experiencing a severe shortage of medicines and other essential supplies".[289]

The Special Rapporteur recommended looking into the role of both state and non-state actors, thereby indicating the possibility of multiple parties violating certain provisions of international law.[290] Unfortunately, like the Human Rights Council itself, Special Rapporteurs themselves have on occasion been criticised for having

---

[286] Report of the Special Rapporteur on the Right to Life (7 December 1993) UN Doc E/CN.4/1994/7 § 560 and 707.

[287] Report of the Special Rapporteur on the Right to Life (14 December 1994) UN Doc E/CN.4/1995/61 § 53.

[288] Report of the Special Rapporteur on the Right to Life (23 December 1992) UN Doc E/CN.4/1993/46 § 666.

[289] Report of the Special Rapporteur on the right of everyone to the enjoyment of the highest attainable standard of physical and mental health 'Addendum: Summary of cases transmitted to Governments and replies received' (2 February 2005) UN Doc E/CN.4/2005/51/Add.1 § 73.

[290] Ibid.

political inclinations and motivations, which of course places their respective resolutions and statements within a certain political context and lessens their value.[291]

Secondly, the UPR system as a public 'naming and shaming' mechanism of the UN Human Rights Council has also functioned as a platform in bringing the provision of humanitarian assistance to the human rights arena. Although the system is not binding, on approximately a dozen occasions states have been recommended in various wordings to 'allow for humanitarian access' to a certain region or to IDPs within their borders,[292] or to allow the ICRC or other organisations to provide humanitarian assistance,[293] as well as to enhance or continue existing mechanisms for the provision[294] and to 'facilitate humanitarian assistance'.[295] It must be noted that all such recommendations have come from other states or regional organisations participating within the UPR. Thus, the system *can*, and in fact *is* being used for certain inter-state 'condemnations', although they are framed and formulated as *recommendations*.

Unlike the interstate complaint mechanisms of human rights treaty bodies which have remained virtually unused, the UPR thus does appear to bring some third states to recommend issues pertaining to humanitarian assistance in other countries. Given the phrasing as recommendations, such calls in the UPR system have only on a few occasions been outright rejected by the affected state.[296] Indeed, framing such

291 In particular the former Special Rapporteur on the right to food, Jean Ziegler, has been subject of such criticism. The Human Rights Council has, amongst other instances, received criticism for example in the context of the Libyan conflict.

292 With regard to Syria 'Report of the Working Group on the UPR' (24 January 2012) UN Doc A/HRC/19/11 § 100 recommendation 26 and 27 by Malaysia and Thailand, § 101 recommendation 5 by Poland, § 104 recommendations 26-28 by Norway, the United States and Australia which were rejected by Syria; concerning the Sudan 'Report of the Working Group on the UPR' (11 July 2011) UN Doc A/HRC/18/16 § 83 recommendation 57, 131 and 160 by Canada, Ireland and Thailand; concerning Sri Lanka 'Report of the Working Group on the UPR' (5 June 2008) UN Doc A/HRC/8/46 § 82 recommendation 14 by Canada and Ireland; concerning Somalia 'Report of the Working Group on the UPR' (11 July 2011) UN Doc A/HRC/18/6 § 98 recommendations 96, 97 and 141 by Sweden, Australia and Slovakia; regarding Israel 'Report of the Working Group on the UPR' (8 January 2009) UN Doc A/HRC/10/76 § 100 recommendation 38 by Jordan; regarding Myanmar 'Report of the Working Group on the UPR' (24 March 2011) UN Doc A/HRC/17/9 § 107 recommendation 15 and 28 by the Republic of Korea and France and rejected by Myanmar; and concerning Ethiopia 'Report of the Working Group on the UPR' (4 January 2010) UN Doc A/HRC/13/17 § 99, recommendation 13 by the United States and rejected by Ethiopia.

293 Ibid A/HRC/17/9 § 107 recommendation 16 and 34 by New Zealand and Uruguay and rejected by Myanmar; concerning Bangladesh: 'Report of the Working Group on the UPR' (8 July 2013) UN Doc A/HRC/24/12 § 129 recommendation 157 by Canada and para 130 recommendation 26 by the United States; regarding DPR Korea: 'Report of the Working Group on the UPR' (4 January 2010) UN Doc A/HRC/13/13 § 90 recommendation 97, 104, 107 and 108 by Switzerland, the Netherlands, Belgium and Canada.

294 Iraq: 'Report of the Working Group on the UPR' (15 March 2010) UN Doc A/HRC/14/14 § 81 recommendation 128 by Bosnia and Herzegovina; Libya: 'Report of the Working Group on the UPR' (4 January 2011) UN Doc A/HRC/16/15 § 93 recommendation 56 by Vietnam.

295 Georgia: 'Report of the Working Group on the UPR' (16 March 2011) UN Doc A/HRC/17/11 § 106 recommendation 13 by Venezuela.

296 See above in the case of Syria, Myanmar and Ethiopia.

calls as recommendations allows the affected state to be more receptive, as well as allowing a more active role of third states. Human rights enforcement in practice has, however, shown a rather politicised perspective on the part of states, as research has shown states to often act in condemnation of political adversaries, whilst protecting allies and befriended states.[297] This indeed can be seen to be true also in the relation between those states making recommendations in the UPR framework and the particular state under review.

A challenge today, however, continues to be the lack of political will amongst states to hold each other responsible and accountable under the existing frameworks and mechanisms. In that regard, taking the more judicially institutionalised approach to the enforcement of humanitarian assistance through the enforcement of human rights law by the judiciary (or treaty bodies) ensures a more balanced and fair legal evaluation, albeit non-binding in the case of the HRC and CESCR. Indeed, considering the fact that the Security Council has the duty to weigh the facts of a specific situation *whilst it is taking place*, the role of the judiciary continues to remain relevant in the aftermath of a crisis, and as such holds a relevant place within the existing enforcement mechanisms relating to the provision of humanitarian assistance.

8.6 Methods of Enforcement through Individual (Criminal) Responsibility

Individual responsibility in international law has become increasingly relevant in the past decades, through the application of international criminal law by international courts and tribunals, and through the use of certain 'targeted sanctions' by international organisations. Both methods could potentially enforce the delivery of humanitarian assistance. Prior to these developments, the Geneva Conventions had also attempted to regulate the respect for international humanitarian law itself through the creation of the International Fact Finding Commission.[298] Although created in the 1977 Additional Protocol I, the Commission was not officially constituted until 1991. The Commission has expressed its willingness to address issues pertaining to non-international conflicts also, upon the approval of the parties involved, but to date, no appeal has been made to it, both in times of international and in non-international armed conflict.[299]

Whereas a large part of this research has dealt with 'state sovereignty' as a crucial factor in the provision of humanitarian assistance, individuals form part of the authority acting as sovereign. Indeed, the provision, denial and obstruction of emergency aid all takes place at the hands of human beings. In the circumstance that these persons act with the control to indeed *deny* humanitarian assistance to persons in need of such aid, international law has the opportunity to hold them responsible for such acts or omissions. Individual (criminal) responsibility for the

[297] Tomuschat, *Human Rights: Between Idealism and Realism* (n 263) 280.
[298] Article 90 AP I.
[299] With regard to non-international armed conflicts <www.ihffc.org/index.asp?page=recognition_general> accessed 2 November 2014.

denial or obstruction of humanitarian assistance serves the point, similar to the manner in which human rights mechanisms operate, of holding individuals responsible even though such enforcement does not take place at the time a humanitarian crisis is on-going. Targeted sanctions, on the other hand, allow for immediate action in the midst of a crisis in order to persuade individuals or leaders of regimes to alter their course.

8.6.1 Enforcement through Targeted Sanctions

Sanctions have been an enforcement mechanism of the Security Council for many years since the early 1990's and the end of the Cold war, as a response to internationally wrongful acts.[300] These sanctions focus on individuals and their assets, as opposed to the state or sovereign authority in general and take place under Article 41 of Chapter VII of the UN Charter. 'Targeted' or 'smart' sanctions have been introduced, to ensure minimal humanitarian damage or consequences whilst maintaining the possibility of individual responsibility.[301] The CESCR, out of care for economic, social and cultural rights, in the 1990's even dedicated a General Comment to voice its concern that sanctions should remain in careful consideration of the rights within the ICESCR.[302] In particular, the well-known problems with the 'Oil for Food Programme' in Iraq following Resolution 661 instigated such comments and the need for further development of the concept of sanctions.[303] Targeted or smart sanctions thereby provide a solution to both the more invasive use of force and the targeting of large groups, directing themselves at specific individuals or entities, whilst attempting to avoid massive impact on a population. At the same time, these sanctions do take place whilst a 'threat to the peace' is still present, as the Security Council takes its action upon such an establishment. These sanctions therefore must be differentiated from the potential enforcement mechanisms that are open to human rights bodies. They are furthermore different as they target *individuals*, as opposed to the responsible state or sovereign.

In more recent years, the Security Council has initiated the use of targeted or smart sanctions for those responsible for human rights law and humanitarian law

[300] August Reinisch, 'Developing Human Rights and Humanitarian Law Accountability of the Security Council for the Imposition of Economic Sanctions', (2001) 95 *American Journal of International Law* 4, 851; Andrés Franco, 'Armed Non-State Actors', in David Malone (ed) *The UN Security Council: From the Cold War to the 21st Century* (Lynne Rienner Publications 2004) 119.

[301] David Cortright & George A Lopez, 'Reforming Sanctions' in Malone *The UN Security Council: From the Cold War to the 21st Century* (ibid) 170.

[302] CESCR General Comment 8 (12 December 1997) UN Doc E/C.12/1997/8 'The relationship between economic sanctions and respect for economic, social and cultural rights'.

[303] The legality of these sanctions will not be discussed. See in this regard amongst others: Reinisch, 'Developing Human Rights and Humanitarian Law Accountability of the Security Council for the Imposition of Economic Sanctions' (n 300) 851-872 and Bardo Fassbender, 'Targeted Sanctions Imposed By The UN Security Council And Due Process Rights: A Study Commissioned By The UN Office Of Legal Affairs And Follow-Up Action By The United Nations', (2006) 3 *International Organizations Law Review* 437–485.

violations *that can be related to the provision of humanitarian assistance*. As such, the Council has upon expressing more generally its willingness to take 'appropriate measures' in circumstances where humanitarian assistance is obstructed,[304] also asserted with regard to for example the Cote d'Ivoire over the course of the past decade that it is 'fully prepared to impose targeted measures' against those who are 'responsible for serious violations of human rights and international humanitarian law'.[305] Furthermore, the Council has requested to be informed of those instances in which humanitarian assistance is 'denied as a consequence of violence directed against humanitarian personnel and United Nations and its associated personnel'.[306] More specifically however, the Security Council has determined concerning Somalia that targeted sanctions, such as the prevention of entry or transit through UN member states, financial asset freezing and the prevention of supply and sale of weapons or military equipment or training should be imposed against those individuals and entities:

> "as obstructing the delivery of humanitarian assistance to Somalia, or access to, or distribution of, humanitarian assistance in Somalia".[307]

Thus, the Council clearly determines that targeted sanctions can be imposed against individuals or entities that obstruct the delivery, access and distribution of humanitarian assistance.

Following the situations in Cote d'Ivoire and Somalia, the Security Council has reiterated its willingness to consider measures in situations where humanitarian assistance 'is being deliberately obstructed' or where constraints exist on humanitarian access, such as in the Democratic Republic of the Congo.[308] Very specifically, the Council has chosen to impose 'financial and travel measures' against various categories of persons, amongst which 'individuals or entities obstructing the access to or the distribution of humanitarian assistance in the eastern part of the Democratic Republic of the Congo'.[309] On occasion the Security Council has also made a point of *excluding* equipment for humanitarian use and purposes from the targeted sanctions placed upon entities and persons, as done amongst others in Libya and the CAR.[310] Most recently in January 2015 regarding the situation in the CAR, the Council determined an asset freeze and a travel ban

---

[304] UNSC Res 1265 (17 September 1999) UN Doc S/RES/1265 § 10; UNSC Res 1296 (19 April 2000) UN Doc S/RES/1296 § 5.
[305] UNSC Res 1727 (15 December 2006) UN Doc S/RES/1727 § 12(d); UNSC Res 1842 (29 October 2008) UN Doc S/RES/1842 § 16(e); UNSC Res 1893 (29 October 2009) UN Doc S/RES/1893 § 20(d); UNSC Res 1946 (15 October 2010) UN Doc S/RES/1946 § 6(d); UNSC Res 1980 (28 April 2011) UN Doc S/RES/1980 § 10(d); UNSC Res 1975 (30 March 2011) UN Doc S/RES/1975 'The situation in Côte d'Ivoir' § 12.
[306] UNSC Res 1844 (20 November 2008) UN Doc S/RES/1844 § 8(b).
[307] Ibid § 1,3,7, and specifically 8(c).
[308] UNSC Res 1894 (11 November 2009) UN Doc S/RES/1894 § 4 and 17.
[309] UNSC Res 2078 (28 November 2012) UN Doc S/RES/2078 § 4 (f).
[310] UNSC Res 1970 (26 February 2011) UN Doc S/RES/1970, § 9(a)(b); UNSC Res 2127 (5 December 2013) UN Doc S/RES/2127 § 54(b).

for those persons 'obstructing the delivery of humanitarian assistance to CAR, or access to, or distribution of, humanitarian assistance in CAR'.[311]

With time, as has been seen in the previous analysis of the Security Council's resolutions, the Council has thus become increasingly specific in its wording, allowing the use of targeted sanctions against those who obstruct the delivery of humanitarian aid in the widest possible sense. This manner of enforcement, depending of course on the level of implementation by the UN member states, has the opportunity to provide a very effective alternative to the invasiveness of the use of force.[312] Furthermore, *without* the use of force and *if* the sanctions target a cross-range of persons involved in the obstruction of assistance, concerns for a loss of neutrality, one of the core principles, in the provision of humanitarian assistance would also be minimalised.[313]

8.6.2 Enforcement through International Criminal Law

As opposed to the targeted or smart sanctions that may be instated by the Security Council, the enforcement of the provision of humanitarian assistance through international criminal law occurs in the same manner as enforcement through human rights law: by judiciary bodies and after the humanitarian crisis has taken place. Unlike enforcement through human rights law, and congruent to smart sanctions, international criminal law aims to bring individuals to justice, focusing on a criminalisation of violations of humanitarian law. Within the Geneva Conventions, this was envisaged through the 'grave breaches' regime which obliged states parties to enact 'legislation necessary to provide effective penal sanctions' for certain severe violations of humanitarian law.[314] However, this legislation would operate at the national, as opposed to the international level. Attempts of the ILC to create a 'state criminal responsibility' have failed in the past, resulting in a renewed focus on the individual that may have committed violations of international humanitarian law.[315] Following an unsuccessful proposal by the UN Secretary General in 1969 for an independent institution that would supervise adherence to international humanitarian law, it took a while for new suggestions to be put forward.[316] Although individual criminal responsibility existed through customary humanitarian law as well as a duty to prosecute violations of that law, the recognition that all states should have the jurisdiction to

---

[311] UNSC Res 2196 (22 January 2015) UN Doc S/RES/2196 § 4,7 and 12(e).
[312] Dungel, 'A Right to Humanitarian Assistance in Internal Armed Conflicts Respecting Sovereignty, Neutrality and Legitimacy: Practical Proposals to Practical Problems' (n 134) § 5.1.
[313] Ibid § 6.1.2.
[314] Article 146 GC IV. The content of the breaches are explained in Article 147 GC IV.
[315] Recently reaffirmed in Application of the Convention on the Prevention and Punishment of the Crime of Genocide (Bosnia and Herzegovina v. Serbia and Montenegro), Judgment, I.C.J. Reports 2007, p. 43 § 170. See in this regard also Stahn, 'Syria and the Semantics of Intervention, Aggression and Punishment On 'Red Lines' and 'Blurred Lines' (n 241) 970.
[316] UN Secretary General Report 'Respect for Human Rights in Armed Conflict' (20 November 1969) UN Doc A/7720.

prosecute certain crimes has enhanced the enforcement of international humanitarian law, which is relevant to the enforcement of the provision of humanitarian assistance.[317] As seen in previous situations concerning the interstate complaint mechanism in human rights law, whilst a *belief* might exist amongst states that prosecution may be in order, in practice states remained reluctant, as a result of which the development of the International Criminal Tribunal for the former Yugoslavia and the International Criminal Tribunal for Rwanda (ICTR) was considered a welcome solution by many.[318] It was only a few months prior to the establishment of the ICTY that the Security Council had condemned:

> "the deliberate impeding of the delivery of food and medical supplies to the civilian population of the Republic of Bosnia and Herzegovina, and reaffirms that those that commit or order the commission of such acts will be held individually responsible in respect of such acts".[319]

The Security Council thereby explicitly underscores the individual responsibility for acts such as impeding food and medical aid. Shortly thereafter, the Security Council reaffirmed this stance with regard to individual responsibility for such acts in Somalia.[320] With the establishment of the ICTY, the Security Council has certainly provided the opportunity to indeed bring those responsible before a judiciary.[321] Cassese has also argued that an increase of national prosecutions of violations of humanitarian law has taken place following the development of the two *ad-hoc* tribunals.[322] For its part, the Security Council has continued to stress the importance of national prosecutions of those 'responsible for war crimes, genocide, crimes against humanity and serious violations of international humanitarian law'.[323] Following the successes of these two tribunals, in 1998 the Rome Statute of

---

[317] Article 49 of Convention I, Article 50 of Convention II, Article 129 of Convention III, or Article 146 of Convention IV. Regarding prosecution for grave breaches, see Articles 50/51/130/147 respectively. However, the first time common article 3 of the 1949 Geneva Conventions was criminalised, was with the creation of the ICTR Statute: 'Report of the Secretary General Pursuant to Paragraph 5 of the Security Council Resolution 955' (13 February 1995) UN Doc S/1995/134 § 12; see also Jean-Marie Henckaerts, 'Assessing the Laws and Customs of War: The Publication of 'Customary International Humanitarian Law', (2005) 13 *Human Rights Brief* 2, 11; René Provost, International Human Rights and Humanitarian Law (Cambridge University Press 2002) 110; Meron, 'The Humanization of Humanitarian Law' (n 46) 253; and A. Cassese, Human Rights in a Changing World 178 (1990).

[318] Antonio Cassese, 'On the Current Trend towards Criminal Prosecution and Punishment of breaches of International Humanitarian Law', (1998) 9 *European Journal of International Law* 1, 17.

[319] UNSC Res 787 (16 November 1992) UN Doc S/RES/787 § 7.

[320] UNSC Res 794 (3 December 1992) UN Doc S/RES/794 § 5.

[321] See in this regard amongst others *Prosecutor v. Krstic* (Appeal Judgment) IT-98-33-A (19 April 2004) § 89 in which the blocking of aid convoys – denying humanitarian assistance – formed a part of the finding by the ICTY that crimes were committed.

[322] Cassese, 'On the Current Trend towards Criminal Prosecution and Punishment of breaches of International Humanitarian Law' (n 318) 6. Evidence hereof is a first example such as the Danish case concerning the conflict in the Former Yugoslavia '*The Prosecution v. Saric*', Eastern Division of High Court (Third Chamber) (25 November 1994).

[323] UNSC Res 1674 (28 April 2006) UN Doc S/RES/1674 § 8.

the International Criminal Court was developed to ensure permanent possibilities for prosecution and individual criminal responsibility, as set out in Article 25 of the Rome Statute.[324] With the creation of this Court, problems faced with regard to potential immunities of heads of states and state sovereignty were also set aside in a novel manner by those states that have ratified the Statute.[325] The Security Council furthermore maintains the possibility of referring situations to the ICC (given its role in the creation of the ICTY and ICTR), and has on occasion already done so.[326]

As such, the potential legal enforcement following the denial of humanitarian assistance through international criminal law provides for distinct manners in which to forego issues relating to state sovereignty that prove to be a recurring problematic theme within the legal framework concerning the provision of humanitarian assistance. Indeed, whilst states remain largely capable of determining whether or not humanitarian assistance should be provided within their sovereign rights (and duties), international criminal law provides for a method of enforcement upon determination that indeed humanitarian assistance was denied or obstructed contrary to international law. Of course, considering and recognising that *individual* criminal responsibility is at hand, it remains relevant to address the potential responsibility of the sovereign authorities for the denial of assistance. But, such individual responsibility – in particular through Security Council referrals – furthermore counts on situations in which the affected state cannot shirk away from its responsibility to 'hand over' those indicted by the ICC.

With regard to the denial or obstruction of the delivery of humanitarian assistance, certain crimes under international law and as incorporated in the ICC Statute are of particular relevance. The General Assembly for its part has welcomed the inclusion of certain provisions in the Statute that are particularly related to the provision of assistance and the safety of those delivering aid.[327] Indeed, the ICC Statute provides for the criminalisation of several acts in international humanitarian law that are specifically relevant to the delivery of humanitarian assistance. Chapters 6 and 7 have shown that a multitude of provisions exist in the Geneva Conventions and their Protocols concerning the duties and rights in relation to the provision of humanitarian assistance.[328] To briefly recapture these it is relevant to note that with regard to an international armed conflict, states are obliged to allow the passage of assistance subject to the condition that there are no serious reasons to decide otherwise (Article 23 GC IV), and are prohibited to destroy objects that are 'indispensable to the survival of the civilian population' (Article 54 AP I). In conjunction with Article 54 AP I, relief actions 'shall be undertaken' if the civilian population is inadequately supplied (Article 70 AP I). States must furthermore

[324] Rome Statute of the International Criminal Court (n 217).
[325] Article 27 and Article 98 ICC Statute.
[326] For example the referral of the situation in Darfur: UNSC Res 1593 (31 March 2005) UN Doc S/RES/1593 § 1-3.
[327] Amongst others UNGA Res 54/192 (21 February 2000) UN Doc A/RES/54/192 preamble and § 4; UNGA Res 56/217 (19 February 2002) UN Doc A/RES/56/217 preamble. More recently see UNGA Res 65/132 (1 March 2011) UN Doc A/RES/65/132 preamble.
[328] See in particular the Annexes to Chapter 6 and Chapter 7 for an overview.

allow and facilitate the rapid and unimpeded passage of all relief consignments, prohibition of delaying humanitarian assistance (Article 70 AP I) and provide for the safety of humanitarian personnel (Article 71 AP I). Concerning non-international armed conflicts, a prohibition of starvation of civilians 'as a method of combat' exists (Article 14 AP II) and as a corollary, subject to the consent of the state, relief 'shall' be undertaken in the event of undue hardship (Article 18 AP II). Lastly, regarding a situation of occupation, the Geneva Convention provides that the duties of the occupier include to 'ensure to the fullest extent of the means available' that the population is provided with food and medical supplies (Article 55 GC IV). The occupier shall furthermore agree to relief schemes on behalf of the population, and shall facilitate them, as well as permitting the free passage of assistance and guaranteeing the protection of those providing assistance, whilst maintaining the right to regulate passage of convoys (Article 59 GC IV). Furthermore, the occupying power has a duty to allow existing Red Cross societies and other similar humanitarian organisations in a territory to continue with their activities (Article 63 GC IV) and must 'to the fullest extent of the means available to it', also ensure clothing, shelter and other supplies that may be 'essential to the survival of the civilian population' (Article 69 AP I). Under human rights law, the rights to life, food and health remain relevant. The ICC Statute, as discussed below, allows for potential individual criminal responsibility for violations of certain of these acts, rights and duties.

This brief revisit will allow a discussion of the provisions in the Rome Statute that provide for the criminalisation of certain acts related to the Geneva Conventions and their Protocols. The ICC has jurisdiction over the crimes of genocide, aggression, crimes against humanity and war crimes.[329] In particular the latter two, as opposed to genocide and aggression, are of relevance in the enforcement of the provision of humanitarian assistance as their specific provisions are most tailored to circumstances of denial of humanitarian assistance. For both crimes, a level of 'intent and knowledge' is required as determined by Article 30 of the ICC Statute.

Aside from the ICC Statute, certain acts have also been criminalised in regional international law, but cannot be focused on specifically in this Section. A primary example however includes Article 7(4) and (5)(g-i) of the Kampala Convention, asserting criminal responsibility for members of armed groups that obstruct the safe passage and access of humanitarian assistance and personnel. Given the role played by the ICC in international criminal law today, a focus will be had on this institution, supported by the case law of other (regional) tribunals and customary international law.

[329] Article 5.1 ICC Statute.

8.6.2.1 War Crimes and Humanitarian Assistance

A connection between a crime and an armed conflict must be established, in order for the crime to be considered constituting a 'war crime'.[330]

Specifically, Article 8 ICC Statute regarding war crimes holds several elements that can be applied to circumstances pertaining to the delivery of humanitarian assistance. As such, with regard to an international armed conflict and relevant to the criminalisation of the denial of humanitarian assistance, Article 8(2) ICC Statute declares:

> "For the purpose of this Statute, 'war crimes' means: (a) Grave breaches of the Geneva Conventions of 12 August 1949, namely, any of the following acts against persons or property protected under the provisions of the relevant Geneva Convention: [...] (ii) [...] inhuman treatment [...] (iii) Wilfully causing great suffering, or serious injury to body or health; [...] (b) Other serious violations of the laws and customs applicable in international armed conflict, within the established framework of international law, namely, any of the following acts: [...] (iii) Intentionally directing attacks against personnel, installations, material, units or vehicles involved in a humanitarian assistance or peacekeeping mission in accordance with the Charter of the United Nations, as long as they are entitled to the protection given to civilians or civilian objects under the international law of armed conflict; (iv) Intentionally launching an attack in the knowledge that such attack will cause incidental loss of life or injury to civilians or damage to civilian objects or widespread, long-term and severe damage to the natural environment which would be clearly excessive in relation to the concrete and direct overall military advantage anticipated; [...] (xxi) Committing outrages upon personal dignity, in particular humiliating and degrading treatment; [...] (xxiv) Intentionally directing attacks against buildings, material, medical units and transport, and personnel using the distinctive emblems of the Geneva Conventions in conformity with international law; (xxv) Intentionally using starvation of civilians as a method of warfare by depriving them of objects indispensable to their survival, including wilfully impeding relief supplies as provided for under the Geneva Conventions".[331]

Thus, the ICC Statute considers a large range of actions that may be related to the denial or obstruction of the provision of assistance as potential war crimes in an *international* armed conflict (see supra Sections 6.5.1.1 and 7.5.2.1). These include wilfully causing great suffering or injury to persons health, intentional attacks against civilians or personnel involved in humanitarian assistance, launching an attack which might severely damage the environment (the principle of

---

[330] *Prosecutor v. Tadić a.k.a "Dule"* IT-94-1-AR72 (n 45) § 70; *Prosecutor v. Zejnil Delalic, Zdravko Mucic (aka "Pavo"), Hazim Delic and Esad Landžo (aka "Zenga") (Celebici - Case)* (Trial Chamber) IT-96-21-T (16 November 1998) § 193.

[331] Article 8(1) furthermore provides that: "1. The Court shall have jurisdiction in respect of war crimes in particular when committed as part of a plan or policy or as part of a large-scale commission of such crimes". It must however be noted that this is not an element of the crime; even one isolated act can be considered a war crime. See in this regard Robert Cryer, Hakan Friman, Darryl Robinson and Elisabeth Wilmshurst, *An Introduction to International Criminal Law and Procedure* (Cambridge University Press 2010) 288.

proportionality), outrages upon personal dignity, directly attacking personnel displaying the emblems of the Geneva Convention (the principle of distinction) and using starvation as a method of warfare. From the above, it becomes apparent that in particular Article 8(2)(b)(iii) and (xxv) concerning the attacks on those providing humanitarian assistance and the use of starvation by depriving civilians of means for survival respectively, are most specifically tailored towards the enforcement of the provisions in the Geneva Conventions and their Protocols concerning the delivery of emergency aid to persons in need. The ICRC Customary International Humanitarian Law Study argues that its rule 'Objects used for humanitarian relief operations must be respected and protected' functions as a corollary to the prohibition of starvation.[332] Furthermore, human rights law continues to be applicable, and as such these crimes may also be violations in more general terms of the rights to life and food. Other than the ICRC Study, the ICC Statute and the Geneva Conventions maintain distinct provisions for the prohibition of starvation and the protection of those providing assistance. Article 8(2)(b)(iii) ICC Statute indeed quite succinctly reflects the wording of Article 71 AP I. It also formulates the international criminalisation of Article 9 of the Convention 'On The Safety Of United Nations And Associated Personnel', which entered into force in 1999.[333] Furthermore, the ICC 'Elements of the Crime' reflect that the attack – within the context of an armed conflict – must have been intentionally directed towards those persons or materials involved in the provision of aid whilst they were entitled to protection, and the perpetrator must have been aware of these circumstances.[334] A certain degree of *wilfulness and knowledge* of the circumstances are therefore presupposed, for an attack against humanitarian personnel or materials to amount to a war crime in an international armed conflict.

Closely related to Article 8(2)(b)(iii) is Article 8(2)(b)(xxiv). It has been argued that Article 8(2)(b)(xxv) then reflects the obligations as set out in Article 23 GC IV and Articles 54 and 70 AP I and thus the *deliberate obstruction* of relief supplies can be distinguished as a war crime.[335] Indeed, Article 8(2)(b)(xxv) states that only the 'wilful' impediment of humanitarian assistance shall amount to a crime. In this manner Article 8(2)(b)(xxv) continues to 'leave the door ajar' to the potential refusal by the affected state of consent to allow assistance from outside a territory.[336] The ICC Elements of the Crime explain that here too a nexus to an international armed conflict is required, with an awareness thereof by the

[332] Henckaerts & Doswald-Beck, ICRC Customary International Humanitarian Law Study (n 103) Rule 32 'Objects used for humanitarian relief operations must be respected and protected'. The ICRC argues this rule to be a corollary of Rule 53 regarding the prohibition of starvation.

[333] Article 9 of the Convention 'On The Safety Of United Nations And Associated Personnel', United Nations, Treaty Series , vol. 2051, p. 363, New York, 9 December 1994 (entered into force 15 January 1999) pertains to the attacking of such personnel.

[334] ICC Elements of the Crime concerning Article 8(2)(b)(iii) ICC Statute.

[335] Dinstein, 'The Right to Humanitarian Assistance' (n 242) 82; Rottensteiner, 'The denial of humanitarian assistance as a crime under international law' (n 109) 565.

[336] Ryngaert, 'Humanitarian Assistance and the Conundrum of Consent: A Legal Perspective' (n 110) 7.

perpetrator, who must have 'intended to starve civilians as a method of warfare' by depriving them of objects which would be 'indispensible' to their survival.[337] As such, the current provisions in Article 8 of the Statute criminalise the existing legal framework in terms of reflecting both the provisions of the Geneva Conventions and their Protocols as well as the human rights to life, food and health.[338]

The discussed crimes, however, are not listed as the 'grave breaches' of international humanitarian law in Article 147 GC IV. Yet, besides the provisions of Article 8(2)(b)(iii) and (xxv) that are not considered grave breaches of humanitarian law as their origins lie with the Hague Conventions, other instances *are* listed as grave breaches and may also reflect certain actions *related* to the provision of humanitarian assistance. As such, Article 8(2)(a)(iii) concerning the wilful causing of 'great suffering, or serious injury to body or health' falls within that category, and it can be argued that withholding water, food, medical and other supplies necessary for the immediate survival of persons can be considered at least the causing of serious injury to the health of a person; and thereby a violation of their right to health. Relevant in this situation is in particular that the suffering should amount to the causing of 'great physical or mental pain or suffering to, or serious injury to body or health of, one or more persons'.[339] A level of intentionality is required, which is however not required for Article 8(2)(a)(ii) concerning 'inhuman treatment' and might therefore be argued more easily concerning the withholding of humanitarian aid. As opposed to Article 8(2)(a)(iii) for which the Elements of the Crime explain that the perpetrator must 'cause' the suffering; the Elements of the Crime explain concerning Article 8(2)(a)(ii) that the perpetrator must merely 'inflict' such pain or suffering.[340] Considering the denial of humanitarian assistance either wilful killing or torture as a war crime however may be one bridge too far, given the elements of these crimes.[341]

Other potential provisions exist in the ICC Statute that – although not particularly tailored to size – may be related to the denial of humanitarian assistance. Such clauses fall outside the 'grave breaches' regime, as does the above discussed Article 8(2)(b)(iii) and (xxv). In particular Article 8(2)(b)(iv) concerning attacks that lead to damages to the environment or Article 8(2)(b)(xxi) concerning acts that result in outrages upon personal dignity, may be related to the denial or obstruction of humanitarian assistance. With regard to Article 8(2)(b)(iv), a presupposition of knowledge of the extent of the damages is assumed, as well as the fact that the attack must be 'clearly excessive in relation to' the military advantages.[342] This reflects the proportionality principle as enshrined in international humanitarian law. Article 54(2) AP I declares a prohibition to 'destroy objects indispensable to the survival of the civilian population', as an explanation of

[337] ICC Elements of the Crime concerning Article 8(2)(b)(xxv) ICC Statute.
[338] 'The Right to Food – Note by the Secretary-General' (23 July 2001) UN Doc A/56/210 § 45 and 28.
[339] ICC Elements of the Crime concerning Article 8(2)(a)(iii) ICC Statute.
[340] ICC Elements of the Crime concerning Article 8(2)(a)(ii)-2 ICC Statute.
[341] See ICC Elements of the Crimes. For an alternative perspective Rottensteiner, 'The denial of humanitarian assistance as a crime under international law' (n 109) 565-566.
[342] ICC Elements of the Crime concerning Article 8(2)(b)(iv) ICC Statute.

the most common ways in which the starvation of a population is obtained. The *Commentary* to the Protocol asserts that this includes agricultural areas in 'the widest sense' and acknowledges that this excludes circumstances of military necessity.[343] As such, whilst it perhaps does not specifically tailor to the obstruction of aid, Article 8(2)(b)(iv) ICC Statute concerning damages to the environment may indeed reflect the provisions of Article 54(2) AP I when it comes to deliberately obstructing a population from sustaining themselves and thereby exacerbating a humanitarian crisis and violating the right to food of these persons. Article 8(2)(b)(xxi) ICC Statute concerning acts that result in outrages upon personal dignity may also be placed within a human rights discourse, as reflecting a violation of a person's right to life or health. The Elements of the Crime explain that in order for acts to amount to such a crime, one or more persons must be humiliated, degraded or 'otherwise violated' in their dignity to the extent that it is 'generally recognized as an outrage upon personal dignity'.[344] It follows from this explanation that potentially this provision in the ICC Statute might serve as a subsidiary provision when prosecuting persons for the denial or obstruction of humanitarian assistance.

It remains important to be cognisant that whereas certain circumstances may *appear* to be a denial of humanitarian assistance, military necessity may be grounds for justification of certain acts.[345] Certainly, the element of 'intentionality' will in such circumstances be difficult to prove, if and when the specific intent to harm a group of people was absent from the outset. However, such military necessity at least in an international armed conflict may never amount to the situation in which it 'leaves the civilian population with such inadequate food or water as to cause its starvation'.[346] As a result, the actual *denial* of emergency aid is not to be justified with an argument towards military necessity.

Furthermore, Articles 59 GC IV and 69 AP I pertaining to humanitarian assistance in times of occupation are not reflected in the 'grave breaches' regime of the Geneva Conventions, nor are they reflected as such in the ICC Statute.[347] The ICC distinctly only differentiates between international and non-international armed conflicts, as is also reflected in the need for a nexus to an armed conflict. Establishing individual criminal responsibility *specifically* for the obstruction of emergency aid as a war crime appears therefore to be restricted to circumstances of either international or non-international armed conflict.

Similar to circumstances of international armed conflict, the ICC Statute provides for the potential of individual criminal responsibility for war crimes in a *non-international* armed conflict for actions related to the denial or obstruction of

---

343 Sandoz, Swinarski & Zimmermann *Commentary to the Additional Protocols* (n 74) Protocol I Article 54, 655-656.

344 ICC Elements of the Crime concerning Article 8(2)(b)(xxi) ICC Statute.

345 Eyal Benvenisti, 'International Protection of the Right to Water', (October 2010) *Max Planck Encyclopedia of Public International Law* § 20.

346 Article 54(3)(b) Additional Protocol I.

347 Yoram Dinstein, *The International Law of Belligerent Occupation* (Cambridge University Press 2009) 192.

the provision of humanitarian assistance. Article 8(2) ICC Statute notes that serious violations of Common Article 3 of the Geneva Conventions shall be considered war crimes, namely:

> "(c) [...] any of the following acts committed against persons taking no active part in the hostilities, including members of armed forces who have laid down their arms and those placed hors de combat by sickness, wounds, detention or any other cause: [...] (ii) Committing outrages upon personal dignity, in particular humiliating and degrading treatment; [...]
> (e) Other serious violations of the laws and customs applicable in armed conflicts not of an international character, within the established framework of international law, namely, any of the following acts: [...] (ii) Intentionally directing attacks against buildings, material, medical units and transport, and personnel using the distinctive emblems of the Geneva Conventions in conformity with international law; (iii) Intentionally directing attacks against personnel, installations, material, units or vehicles involved in a humanitarian assistance or peacekeeping mission in accordance with the Charter of the United Nations, as long as they are entitled to the protection given to civilians or civilian objects under the international law of armed conflict".

Thus, the ICC Statute declares that in a non-international armed conflict, similar to in an international armed conflict, attacking those persons or objects involved in the provision of humanitarian assistance shall amount to war crimes (Article 8(2)(e)(ii) and (iii)). These provisions do not find their equivalent specifically in the Geneva Conventions or the Additional Protocol pertaining to non-international armed conflicts, but are a reflection of those provisions pertaining to international armed conflicts with customary law status. Furthermore, the provisions of 8(2)(e) exclude circumstances of 'internal disturbances and tensions, such as riots, isolated and sporadic acts of violence or other acts of a similar nature' that do not meet the threshold of a 'protracted armed conflict'.[348] Articles 8(2)(b)(iii) and (2)(e)(iii) of ICC Statute therefore define both in international and non-international armed conflict the intentionally attacking of humanitarian personnel and materials as a war crime. Although this has been established as reflecting pre-existing international law, it does indeed also reflect the international community's continued dedication to the provision of humanitarian assistance in times of a humanitarian crisis.

The Security Council has repeatedly also condemned such violence against humanitarian personnel and called upon states to abide by their obligations under international law with regard to such personnel.[349] The Special Court for Sierra Leone was in 2009 the first international tribunal to indeed *convict* persons for attacking humanitarian personnel under Article 4(b) of its Statute concerning 'Other Serious Violations of International Humanitarian Law':

---

[348] Article 8(2)(f) ICC Statute.

[349] UNSC Res 1502 (26 August 2003) UN Doc S/RES/1502 'Protection of Personnel in Conflict zones' § 1 &3; in this regard also concerning the DRC: UNSC Res 1794 (21 December 2007) UN Doc S/RES/1794 § 17; UNSC Res 1991 (28 June 2011) UN Doc S/RES/1991 preamble; as well as in Afghanistan UNSC Res 1868 (23 March 2009) UN Doc S/RES/1868 preamble; and UNSC Res 1894 (11 November 2009) UN Doc S/RES/1894 § 16.

> "The Chamber holds that the elements of the offence of intentionally directing attacks against personnel, installations, material, units or vehicles involved in a humanitarian assistance or peacekeeping mission in accordance with the Charter of the United Nations are as follows: (i) The Accused directed an attack against personnel, installations, material, units or vehicles involved in a humanitarian assistance or peacekeeping mission in accordance with the Charter of the United Nations; (ii) The Accused intended such personnel, installations, material, units or vehicles to be the object of the attack; (iii) Such personnel, installations, material, units or vehicles were entitled to that protection given to civilians or civilian objects under the international law of armed conflict; and (iv) The Accused knew or had reason to know that the personnel, installations, material, units or vehicles were protected. In the view of the Chamber, the primary object of the attack must be the personnel, installations, material, units or vehicles involved in a humanitarian assistance or peacekeeping mission. There exists no requirement that there be actual damage to the personnel or objects as a result of the attack and this Chamber opines that the mere attack is the gravamen of the crime [...]".[350]

In doing so, the Special Court elaborated on the scope of the crime to include an intentional attack, whilst the perpetrator was knowledgeable of the fact that it was directed at persons who were entitled to protection. Subsequently in 2010, the ICC Prosecutor also argued a potential violation of Article 8(2)(e)(iii) ICC Statute.[351] The elaboration of the Special Court for Sierra Leone is indeed also reflected in the ICC's Elements of the Crime concerning both Article 8(2)(e)(ii) and (iii), which states a need for intentionality and awareness that the objects of the attack were under protection of the Geneva Conventions.[352]

Conversely, unlike the case concerning international armed conflicts, Article 8 ICC Statute does *not* criminalise starvation as a method of warfare in non-international armed conflicts, which *has* been recognised by Article 14 AP II, followed by the provision of Article 18 AP II that relief shall be undertaken 'in the event of undue hardship'. Thus, the ICC Statute undeniably differentiates between international and non-international armed conflicts and does not follow the line of AP II. The explanation can be sought in the fact that at the time of the drafting, consensus could not be reached on these potential acts amounting to war crimes in international customary law, although they had been criminalised in the national legislation of multiple states.[353] Given the rise in non-international armed conflicts around the globe over the past years, this lacuna in Article 8 results in the situation that the denial of humanitarian assistance in a non-international armed conflict *per*

---

[350] *Prosecutor v. Issa Hassan Sesay, Morris Kallon and Augustine Gbao (the RUF accused) (Trial judgment)*, Case No. SCSL-04-15-T, Special Court for Sierra Leone, 2 March 2009 § 214 and more specifically 219-220.

[351] *The Prosecutor v. Abu Garda*, Case No ICC-02/05-02/09 Decision on Confirmation of Charges (8 February 2010) § 21(ii).

[352] ICC Elements of the Crime concerning Article 8(2)(e)(ii) ICC Statute and ICC Elements of the Crime concerning Article 8(2)(e)(iii) ICC Statute.

[353] Cryer, Friman, Robinson and Wilmshurst, *An Introduction to International Criminal Law and Procedure* (n 331) 278; Felix Schwendimann, 'The legal framework of humanitarian access in armed conflict', (2011) *93 International Review of the Red Cross* 884, 1005.

se would not be punishable under the current provisions of the Statute. Only an *attack* on those providing assistance or their resources would be considered a war crime in a non-international armed conflict under the ICC Statute. The provisions of the Statute, however, do not entirely preclude the consideration that 'starvation as a method of warfare' is considered prohibited in international humanitarian law, potentially as customary international law as embraced by the ICC Statute.[354] Indeed, in certain instances prior to the establishment of the Rome Statute, the Security Council already asserted that those whom 'deliberately *impede'* (not 'attack') the provision of assistance in non-international armed conflicts shall be held individually responsible for such acts.[355] Therefore, despite the non-inclusion of such acts in the Rome Statute, the Security Council and AP II recognise the prohibition of the deliberate impediment of aid in non-international armed conflicts, leading to the possibility of individual states prosecuting persons within their jurisdiction for such acts. Alternatively, state responsibility might be asserted for such deliberate impediments, should the impediments occur by way of the sovereign, as opposed to armed groups without such a title. Given the Security Council's assertions, as well as the incorporation of such acts in the national penal codes of several countries, a case might be made as to the customary international legal status of the prohibition of starvation in non-international armed conflicts. Indeed, the ICRC has argued the existence of such a rule in customary international humanitarian law.[356] Adding hereto, such arguments may also be made with regard to violations of the right to life and food, in instances of starvation through the denial of humanitarian assistance in times of non-international armed conflict, as human rights law does not cease to be applicable. This would indeed allow for criminalisation on a different international legal basis. Furthermore, it has been asserted by the ICTY that in the absence of the codification of a specific provision of prohibition of an act in the Geneva Conventions, criminal responsibility for the act may still be established.[357] However, consensus could not be reached in the ICC Statute regarding this provision, which opposes the argument held in the ICRC's customary law study. Given the surge of non-international armed conflicts over the past decades, it is evidenced that the denial of humanitarian assistance continues to

[354] See in this regard Article 10 ICC Statute: "Nothing in this Part shall be interpreted as limiting or prejudicing in any way existing or developing rules of international law for purposes other than this Statute".

[355] For example the Security Council with regard to the situation in the Former Yugoslavia, UNSC Res 787 (16 November 1992) UN Doc S/RES/787 § 7 (cited above); UNSC Res 794 (3 December 1992) UN Doc S/RES/794 § 5 concerning Somalia: "Stronglv condemns all violations of international humanitarian law occurring in Somalia, including in particular the deliberate impeding of the delivery of food and medical supplies essential for the survival of the civilian population, and affirms that those who commit or order the commission of such acts will be held individually responsible in respect of such acts".

[356] Henckaerts & Doswald-Beck, ICRC Customary International Humanitarian Law Study (n 103) Rule 53 Starvation as a Method of Warfare.

[357] *Prosecutor v. Tadić a.k.a "Dule"* IT-94-1-AR72 (n 45) § 128 where the ICTY follows the line of reasoning of the Nuremburg Tribunal. See also Rottensteiner, 'The denial of humanitarian assistance as a crime under international law' (n 109) 565.

play a role and that it remains relevant therefore to determine to what extent starvation may be considered a war crime in a non-international conflict, and under which circumstances. In this regard, should the notion continue to develop and be established as a customary international legal norm, it can be implemented through Articles 21(1)(b) and (c) and 21(2) of the ICC Statute, allowing the applicability of the law of armed conflict, general principles of law and previous findings in case law of the Court.[358] Through this consideration, the provisions of AP II can indeed also be embraced at this time.

Another provision which is criminalised in both international and non-international armed conflicts according to Article 8(2)(c)(ii) ICC Statute is the concept of 'outrages upon personal dignity'. Under the ICC Statute such acts are punishable as a war crime also in regard to non-international armed conflicts, since it draws from Common Article 3 of the Geneva Conventions.[359] Whilst not distinctly framed with a view to the provision of humanitarian assistance, it may certainly be argued that the non-provision of humanitarian aid results in an outrage on a person's dignity, in view of the Elements of the Crime that are similar to those of the crime in an international armed conflict.[360] Lastly, it must be noted that Article 8(2)(b)(iv) concerning damages to the environment is absent from the provisions of Article 8 ICC Statute with regard to non-international armed conflicts, as is Article 8(2)(a)(iii) regarding the 'grave breach' of doing wilful damage to a person's health. Whilst both provisions are not specifically tailored to the denial of the provision of humanitarian assistance, in fact the obstruction of a person's ability to sustain themselves through damages to the environment may well result in an outrage on a person's dignity; both in an international and in a non-international armed conflict.

Despite the intentional stripping down of individual criminal responsibility for acts during non-international armed conflicts in the ICC Statute compared to acts which may be equivalent during international armed conflicts, ample opportunity remains to prosecute individuals for war crimes that have denied or obstructed the provision of humanitarian assistance. Indeed, the ICC Statute provides for opportunities to prosecute individuals for war crimes related to the obstruction of the provision of assistance in both international and non-international armed conflicts. The breadth of the opportunity however does differ. Codification of individual criminal responsibility for attacking those involved in the provision of assistance or their resources has been criminalised by the ICC Statute with regard to both types of conflicts, as well as criminalising outrages upon personal dignity. However, the Statute only recognises the possibility of prosecution for starvation as a method of warfare and for damages to the environment as well as the 'grave breach' of inhuman treatment and wilfully causing great suffering to a person's

[358] In these circumstances Article 22 ICC Statute regarding the principle of 'nullum crimen sine lege' remains relevant of course.

[359] Cryer, Friman, Robinson and Wilmshurst, *An Introduction to International Criminal Law and Procedure* (n 331) 291.

[360] ICC Elements of the Crime concerning Article 8(2)(c)(ii) ICC Statute.

health, in the situation of an international armed conflict and it is regrettable that the criminalisation of such acts has not been more equal.

8.6.2.2 Crimes Against Humanity and Humanitarian Assistance

Secondly, relevant to the obstruction of the delivery of assistance, the ICC Statute provides for the individual criminal responsibility for crimes against humanity in Article 7. With regard to the enforcement of humanitarian assistance, specifically relevant are the provisions of Article 7 stating:

> "1. For the purpose of this Statute, 'crime against humanity' means any of the following acts when committed as part of a widespread or systematic attack directed against any civilian population, with knowledge of the attack: [...] (b) Extermination; [...] (k) Other inhumane acts of a similar character intentionally causing great suffering, or serious injury to body or to mental or physical health.
> 2. For the purpose of paragraph 1: [...] (b) 'Extermination' includes the intentional infliction of conditions of life, inter alia the deprivation of access to food and medicine, calculated to bring about the destruction of part of a population".

With regard to the denial of the provision of assistance, several aspects are key in Article 7 of the Rome Statute. Firstly, no distinction can be found between an international or non-international armed conflict; in fact, the nexus to an armed conflict has been completely removed from the notion of a 'crime against humanity' in the ICC Statute; it is not even mentioned in the provision. Today such a nexus is no longer necessary and such crimes may also take place outside the context of a conflict altogether.[361] This also results in the opportunity to somewhat forego the debate regarding the *lex specialis* relationship between humanitarian law and human rights law in the consideration of which provisions underlie the crime as phrased in Article 7 ICC Statute.[362] Indeed, a state's duties pertaining to its obligations in upholding the right to life, food, health (and water) remain at the forefront also in particular concerning Article 7(2) ICC Statute, which explains the notion of 'extermination'. Thus 'most tailored' or most specific clause can be considered as the *lex specialis*, regardless of whether it may be a provision of humanitarian law or human rights law.[363]

---

[361] Note the development in this regard from Article 5 ICTY Statute that does require a nexus ("The International Tribunal shall have the power to prosecute persons responsible for the following crimes when committed in armed conflict, whether international or internal in character, and directed against any civilian population [...]"), to Article 3 ICTR where this is no longer needed ("The International Tribunal for Rwanda shall have the power to prosecute persons responsible for the following crimes when committed as part of a widespread or systematic attack against any civilian population on national, political, ethnic. racial of religious grounds [...]"). See in this regard also *Prosecutor v. Tadić a.k.a "Dule"* IT-94-1-AR72 (n 45) § 141 on the development thereto in customary law. Concurring furthermore the UN CHR Report of the Secretary General 'Promotion and Protection of Human Rights: Fundamental Standards of Humanity' (18 December 1998) UN Doc E/CN.4/1999/92 § 12.
[362] See also Article 21(3) ICC Statute.
[363] Section 3.4.3

Today, ascertaining that a situation (outside of armed conflict) amounts to a crime against humanity also gives rise to the responsibilities of states and the UN Security Council for the potential use of force under the Responsibility to Protect doctrine, given the incorporation of crimes against humanity as one of the 'core crimes'.[364] Such use of force is traditionally reserved for situations threatening the international peace and security through armed conflict, but has been accepted to include 'crimes against humanity' which do not require such a nexus, although they do in and of themselves quite logically through their nature affect the international peace and security. These arguments were also raised in the aftermath of cyclone Nargis in 2008 as manner to convince the taking of international action by the Council (which did not occur). As such, the Security Council may be inclined to act upon the establishment that a crime against humanity has taken place despite the lack of an armed conflict. In practice, however, criminal enforcement takes place at a later stage than when forceful action of the Security Council might be necessary, resulting in a potential action of the Security Council prior to a definitive judicial finding regarding the crime.[365]

Furthermore, whereas one single act may amount to a war crime, for an act to be considered a crime against humanity, it must occur 'as part of a widespread or systematic attack'. As such, with regard to the denial or obstruction of humanitarian assistance, for such an act to be considered the 'deprivation of access to food and medicine' and thereby amount to extermination of civilians (or other inhumane acts) as described by Article 7(1)(b) (k) and 7(2) ICC Statute, some form of systematic or widespread targeting of a particular group must be involved, or alternatively, a single strategic action with the *intent* of impacting a large group of people.[366] This shall to a certain extent have an effect on the applicability of the crime in times of a non-international armed conflict, as the level of organisation needed for such a crime might not be present or possible to prove for certain armed groups or non-state actors. Yet, intent towards the causation of the *attack* itself (as opposed to the targeting of a group of people) needs not to be proved; suffice that the accused be aware of the fact that the attack took place.[367] Such consideration has also been given by the ICTY in several instances, where the Tribunal has noted the option that *one* act may amount to a crime against humanity should there be a connection to being a widespread or systematic attack, or knowledge of the broader context in which the act is committed.[368]

---

[364] UNGA Res 60/1 (24 October 2005) UN Doc A/RES/60/1 'World Summit Outcome Document' regarding the crimes giving rise to the Responsibility to Protect doctrine within the United Nations.
[365] Ford, 'Is The Failure To Respond Appropriately To A Natural Disaster A Crime Against Humanity? The Responsibility To Protect And Individual Criminal Responsibility In The Aftermath Of Cyclone Nargis', (n 109) 238-240.
[366] Dungel, 'A Right to Humanitarian Assistance in Internal Armed Conflicts Respecting Sovereignty, Neutrality and Legitimacy: Practical Proposals to Practical Problems' (n 134) 8; and Rottensteiner, 'The denial of humanitarian assistance as a crime under international law' (n 109) 568.
[367] Ford, 'Is The Failure To Respond Appropriately To A Natural Disaster A Crime Against Humanity? The Responsibility To Protect And Individual Criminal Responsibility In The Aftermath Of Cyclone Nargis', (n 109) 256.
[368] *Prosecutor v. Tadić a.k.a "Dule"* (Judgment Trial Chamber) IT-94-1-T (7 May 1997) § 649.

The ICC Elements of the Crime do not elaborate on the inclusion of 'deprivation of access to food and medicine' as part of the crime of extermination in Article 7(1)(b) and 7(2) ICC Statute, but do indeed reiterate the need for intent to 'bring about the destruction of part of a population' as well as an awareness on the part of the perpetrator that the act was part of such a widespread or systematic attack against a civilian population.[369] Furthermore, concerning Article 7(1)(k) ICC Statute, the Elements of the Crime note that 'serious injury to body or to mental or physical health, by means of an inhumane act' must have been inflicted, again as part of a widespread or systematic attack, including an awareness on the part of the perpetrator.[370] The ICTY has noted similar elements with regard to 'inhumane acts' (as codified in the ICC Statute in Article 7(1)(k)), whilst including that such acts might also amount to a crime against humanity in the case of an 'omission' and that while lasting effects of the act are not necessary to amount to 'inhumane acts', they can be evidence of the seriousness of the act.[371] It follows reason that indeed also an 'omission' as opposed to an 'act' can result in a crime against humanity, should the element of intent be present.[372]

Interestingly, the fact that the choice was made to elaborate on the notion of 'extermination' in the ICC Statute itself – as opposed to incorporation in the Elements of the Crime – specifically including the deprivation of access to food and medicine, can be seen as evidence of the willingness to consider the seriousness of the obstruction or denial of humanitarian assistance as a crime against humanity. In particular concerning the obstruction of humanitarian assistance, the ICTY has found that the blocking of access to aid as envisaged by the Serbian Republic in its 'Directive 7' with regard to Muslim enclaves was with 'catastrophic' results that functioned as a prelude and amongst other factors lead to individual responsibility for both inhumane acts and persecution; therefore as crimes against humanity.[373] With regard to extermination as potential crime against humanity, it goes to reason that a certain 'number' or 'amount' of persons must be affected. The ICTY has argued that less than 1700 people or, in referral to the Nuremberg Tribunal, even less than 800 people may be sufficient to amount to 'extermination'; declaring itself unwilling to suggest a threshold, although a 'collective' element should be present rather than singling out individuals.[374]

---

369 ICC Elements of the Crime concerning Article 7(1)(b) ICC Statute.

370 ICC Elements of the Crime concerning Article 7(1)(k) ICC Statute.

371 *Prosecutor v. Dario Kordić and Mario Čerkez* (Appeal Judgment) IT-95-14/2-A (17 December 2004) § 117; *Prosecutor v. Vasiljevid* (Appeal Judgment) IT-98- 32-A (25 February 2004) § 16; *Prosecutor v. Galić* (Trial Judgment) IT-98-29-T (5 December 2003) § 152-154; *Prosecutor v. Blagojević & Jokić* (Trial Judgment) IT-02-60-T (17 January 2005) § 626-627.

372 Ford, 'Is The Failure To Respond Appropriately To A Natural Disaster A Crime Against Humanity? The Responsibility To Protect And Individual Criminal Responsibility In The Aftermath Of Cyclone Nargis', (n 109) 243.

373 *Prosecutor v. Krstic* (Trial Judgment) IT-98-33-T (2 August 2001) § 28, 615 and 653. See also *Prosecutor v. Krstic* (Appeal Judgment) IT-98-33-A (19 April 2004) § 89.

374 *Prosecutor v. Radoslav Brdanin* (Trial Judgment) Case No IT-99-36-T (1 September 2004) § 465. In the *Prosecutor v. Mitar Vasiljevic* (Trial Judgment) Case No IT-98-32-T (29 November 2002) the ICTY notes regarding the concept of 'extermination' in *footnote* 587: "in one case, the court used the

Some have argued that individual responsibility for torture (7(1)(f)), persecution (7(1)(h)) and murder (7(1)(a)) as crimes against humanity may also be incurred when humanitarian aid is obstructed.[375] Yet, Articles 7 and 8 ICC Statute contain specific clauses related directly to the provision of aid and the obstruction thereof, as well as related to the denial of access or targeting of those providing humanitarian aid, allowing for a more tailored prosecution by way of these provisions. Furthermore, whilst the proper incurrence of individual criminal responsibility for the denial or obstruction of humanitarian assistance is of the utmost importance as the insurance of the provision of aid to those in need is fundamental, it remains important to not attempt to 'adjust' the criteria or elements of certain crimes in international law to fit the 'mould' of humanitarian assistance. For instance, a too frequent coining of a situation as 'genocide' may water down this specific crime. In order for the denial of humanitarian aid to be considered as genocide, a specific kind of intent to destroy a particular group of people must be present; an intent that may be difficult to prove in the case of the denial of aid.[376] In fact, the *allowance* of the provision of humanitarian assistance has been used to argue the *lack* of genocidal intent in the case of Darfur.[377] Conversely, despite not (yet) resulting in specific convictions for this fact, the Prosecutor of the ICC has argued that the denial of humanitarian assistance has formed part of genocidal intent.[378] The Prosecutor has specifically stated that 'denial and hindrance of medical and other humanitarian assistance needed to sustain life in IDP camps' formed a method of destruction as part of the Sudanese President Al Bashir's genocidal plan, as well as arguing that the 'obstruction of humanitarian aid' amounted to the crime of extermination.[379] Such allegations from the Prosecutor – as well as the Prosecutor's willingness to assert that the denial of assistance leads to other crimes under international law – prove that at least the Office is willing to assert that the denial of humanitarian assistance leads to individual criminal responsibility in practice, and that such actions must lead to consequences.

Intentionality with regard to the denial or obstruction of humanitarian assistance shall also continue to be a difficult aspect of arguing that a certain act amounts to a

---

expression "extermination" when referring to the killing of 733 civilians (United States v Ohlendorf and others ("Einsatzgruppen case"), IV Trials of War Criminals before the Nuremberg Military Tribunal under Control Council Law No 10, 421). The Trial Chamber is not aware of cases which, prior to 1992, used the phrase "extermination" to describe the killing of less than 733 persons. The Trial Chamber does not suggest, however, that a lower number of victims would disqualify that act as "extermination" as a crime against humanity, nor does it suggest that such a threshold must necessarily be met".

[375] Rottensteiner, 'The denial of humanitarian assistance as a crime under international law' (n 109) 568-570; Dungel, 'A Right to Humanitarian Assistance in Internal Armed Conflicts Respecting Sovereignty, Neutrality and Legitimacy: Practical Proposals to Practical Problems' (n 134), 8; Schwendimann, 'The legal framework of humanitarian access in armed conflict', (n 355) 1006.

[376] Ibid Rottensteiner 571.

[377] 'Report of the International Commission of Inquiry on Darfur to the United Nations Secretary-General' (25 January 2005) § 515.

[378] *The Prosecutor v. Al Bashir*, Case No ICC-02/05-01/09 Second Decision on the Prosecution's Application for a Warrant of Arrest (12 July 2010) § 34 and 35.

[379] Ibid.

crime against humanity. Denying humanitarian assistance in and of itself amounts to certain specific crimes. Should a circumstance match the framework of another crime, it may be tried before the ICC as such, on its own merits. Thus, a more specific framework for the denial of assistance within international criminal law already exists, and there is no immediate need to have recourse to a series of particular crimes that have specificities that will be difficult to fulfil when considering the obstruction of the delivery of aid, such as torture, persecution and murder. The above examined crimes of extermination and 'other inhumane acts' are at this stage best designed for this purpose within the spectrum of crimes against humanity as laid down in Article 7 ICC. That being said, of course this does not preclude the potential determination that for example the denial of humanitarian aid in a particular circumstance amounts to persecution (as formulated in Article 7(1)(h) ICC Statute) should the criteria be fulfilled. Also, given that the ICC applies – next to the explicit provisions of its own Statute – the 'principles and rules of international law' as well as 'general principles of law', it has the opportunity to embrace those developments in humanitarian law or human rights law as related to humanitarian assistance that may take place in the future.[380] Furthermore, individual criminal responsibility for certain crimes under international law does not preclude the possibility discussed above of holding a *state* responsible under the law of state responsibility for certain situations in which the denial of humanitarian assistance amounts to a violation of international law that may be attributable to it.

8.7 The Enforcement of Humanitarian Assistance and the Absence of a Sovereign

This Chapter has touched upon the legal enforcement mechanisms of the international community in relation to the provision of humanitarian assistance, and the present Section lastly addresses the more problematic circumstance of dealing with the delivery and enforcement of humanitarian assistance in the absence of a sovereign. The absence of a sovereign may occur in a variety of circumstances, such as in 'failed' or 'failing' states, times of non-international armed conflict with a loss of control by the affected state and no clear entity to fill the void, or disasters in fragile states, also resulting in a lack of control. In the absence of a true sovereign entity in the territory of the 'affected state', an alternative method of enforcement of the duties to provide assistance must be sought, similar to the circumstance that the 'affected' state becomes the 'inflicting' state. Yet, these circumstances cannot be compared entirely, as the 'inflicting' state shall actively oppose the provision of assistance (leading to circumstances in which the Security Council might enforce the provision of aid through the use of force), whereas the absence of a sovereign leaves a vacuum as to the determination of a responsible actor in the provision of assistance and thereby also in its enforcement. In reality of

[380] Article 21(1)(b) and (c) ICC Statute.

course, such circumstances might also lead to a threat to the peace, warranting Security Council action.

What *can* be assessed, however, is that if no entity is in place to fulfil the role of sovereign, no duties of the 'affected state' can be imposed. Given the fact that Chapters 6 and 7 have shown that the primary duties and responsibilities for the provision of aid and access therefore lie with the 'affected state', an absence of such an entity brings a problem of enforcement to the forefront. Such circumstances where no sovereign exists may be armed conflict, natural disaster or other crises in which a collapse of state authority takes place such as just mentioned above. These may be natural disasters in failed or fragile states, where it is simply unclear which entity assumes responsibility over the territory like for example in Somalia. One can also consider disasters in areas where insurrectional movements are active that make the sovereign hesitant to allow access to those particular regions of a state where a loss of control exists when disaster strikes, such as was the case in Sri Lanka. Furthermore, considering non-international armed conflicts, the circumstance in which the affected state may not be in the position to provide assistance due to the fact that access to the specific territory may be impeded by the presence of armed groups is relevant, as the past years in Syria have evidenced. Alternatively however, in a circumstance of occupation, the void of the original sovereign of a territory is filled with an occupier that shall take on the responsibilities of a sovereign.[381]

In the absence of an entity fulfilling the 'primary' responsibility of the affected state, the void must be filled by other actors in the international community, for the simple reason that the affected persons are in a humanitarian crisis and are in need of assistance. The absence of a sovereign with certain responsibilities does not change the circumstances of those in need of assistance. Whilst no hard 'human right to receive' aid can be claimed, it is a vehicle in the fulfilment of many human rights, which are held by persons against their sovereign, as addressed in Chapter 5. Should any of the above circumstances arise in which a territory may be *lacking* a sovereign, enforcement of the provision of humanitarian assistance must be transferred to the international community.[382] It goes without saying that the provision of humanitarian assistance in failed states should be for the purposes of remedying the crisis in which persons find themselves. The international community, when providing such aid, should be well aware of the risks of exacerbating a crisis in the event that assistance is provided without proper distribution channels due to a lack of authorities in a territory.[383] In that sense, to avoid prolonging a crisis more action than the *sec* provision of assistance may be necessary. Thus, the law must be examined to determine on which basis the

---

[381] Sections 6.5.3 and 3.2.2.1.

[382] Determining exactly when 'a sovereign is lacking' or 'absent' remains outside the scope of this research. For the purpose of this research, it will be assumed that such an assessment will have taken place by an authoritative body in international law, such as relevant UN organs or international courts or tribunals, as part of their assessment whether or not humanitarian aid needs to be delivered.

[383] The Netherlands Advisory Council on International Affairs (AIV), Report 'Failing States A Global Responsibility' No. 35 (May 2004) 51.

international community, in the absence of a primary duty-bearer (under human rights law, humanitarian law or other principles of law) in the form of a sovereign entity, has the right or duty to enforce the provision of assistance. The current conflict in Syria with continued clashes between governmental forces and the Islamic State, increasingly obtaining control, is a prime example of these difficulties.

Firstly, a distinction must be made between a 'de facto' government or authority and a failed state in which no sovereign entity exists altogether. The ARSIWA note that the conduct of an insurrectional movement which becomes 'the new government' of that particular state or which creates a new state in that same territory, shall be considered as the conduct of that state for means of state responsibility.[384] Furthermore, the ARSIWA declares in Article 9 that state responsibility can also be applied to 'de facto' regimes:

> "The conduct of a person or group of persons shall be considered an act of a State under international law if the person or group of persons is in fact exercising elements of the governmental authority in the absence or default of the official authorities and in circumstances such as to call for the exercise of those elements of authority".

The exercise of governmental authority thereby provides the means for state responsibility to be applied to certain groups or movements that exercise a sufficient level of control, yet the ARSIWA distinctly do not apply to non-state actors.[385] A somewhat more broad and pragmatic view was held by the ICJ in its Advisory Opinion on Namibia, arguing that the exercise of physical control over a territory 'and not sovereignty or legitimacy of title' serves as the basis for liability.[386] Should therefore forms of control be exercised by authorities with some form of organisation, a claim can be made as to their responsibility in providing aid or consenting to its provision subject to international legal regulations. Alternatively, such regimes may themselves address the international community in an attempt to receive external assistance in the provision of aid when facing a humanitarian crisis. Evidence of this can be seen amongst others in Somalia, where Farole, leader of Puntland, called upon the UN to assist in the delivery of humanitarian assistance following a tropical storm in 2013, which was indeed delivered.[387]

Yet, in the absence of any proper and sufficient governmental authority, direct recourse must be had to provisions in human rights law and international

---

[384] Article 10 ARSIWA.

[385] 'Report of the International Law Commission' UN Doc A/56/10 (n 10) 62.

[386] 'Legal Consequences for States of the Continued Presence of South Africa in Namibia' ICJ Advisory Opinion (n 62) § 118.

[387] <http://m.nos.nl/artikel/573773-somali-vraagt-hulp-vn-na-storm.html> News of 11 November 2013, accessed 8 July 2014 and <http://reliefweb.int/report/somalia/un-envoy-somalia-puntland-discuss-tropical-cyclone-response-and-forthcoming-elections> news of 20 November 2013, accessed 8 July 2014. In particular with a view to the provision of aid, the UN Security Council had earlier lifted the embargo on Member States related to the situation in the country, for the purpose of delivering humanitarian assistance to Somalia: UNSC Res 2060 (25 July 2012) UN Doc S/RES/2060 § 7.

humanitarian law. In principle, human rights conventions lay obligations upon states parties, through which responsibilities exist to provide – and thereby as a derivative also to enforce – humanitarian assistance. Yet, Chapter 6 has addressed the status of responsibility for non-state actors in the provision of humanitarian assistance under human rights law, noting that it has become generally accepted in international law today that non-state actors or those exercising *de facto* control over a territory must abide by human rights obligations.[388] Therefore, a prohibition rests upon those exercising control over a territory to violate the human rights of persons under their control. However, enforcement through human rights mechanisms, as seen above, shall remain challenging, considering that this route is merely open to those wishing to hold a state party to a treaty accountable, or a state in a UN context, as opposed to non-state actors.[389] Thus, whilst non-state actors must abide by international human rights law, enforcement of breaches by the judiciary remains lacking.

In the event such breaches become threats to the international peace and security, the UN Security Council does have the opportunity based on Article 39 UN Charter to take enforcement measures, similar to circumstances in which a state would have been responsible for such breaches. This can indeed also be deduced from the fact that the Security Council has for many years assumed such responsibilities for non-state actors, calling in its resolutions upon 'all parties' (to a conflict) to abide by human rights law, humanitarian law and other bodies of law relevant to the provision of humanitarian assistance.[390] Through the reiteration of such wording, the addressing of non-state actors by the Council is reflected. Furthermore, such action towards enforcement is also supported by the doctrine of the Responsibility to Protect that has been embraced by the Security Council, which argues a responsibility for the international community in the event the affected state does not take up responsibility itself.[391] Thus, the Security Council sees opportunities for the international community to take action, should non-state actors or armed groups not abide by their duties under human rights law (such as the duty to provide aid in the fulfilment of the rights to life, food, health (and water)) which amount to a threat to international peace and security. The above Section 8.4 must therefore be seen in this light.

Given the fact that threats to international peace and security often amount to armed conflicts, humanitarian law remains relevant too. The stance of the Security Council is indeed also in line with international humanitarian law as discussed in Chapter 6, which notes that the responsibility to provide assistance is transferred to the entity *acting as sovereign* when a conflict exists in a certain territory that does not fall under the control of the sovereign, which in such a circumstance will be the

---

[388] Section 6.3.1.

[389] Section 8.5.

[390] Amongst others UNSC Res 1265 (17 September 1999) UN Doc S/RES/1265 § 4; UNSC Res 1863 (9 July 2009) UN Doc S/RES/1863 § 19 and UNSC Res 2036 (22 February 2012) UN Doc S/RES/2036 § 16.

[391] Section 4.2.3.1.

armed group.[392] Of particular relevance in the case of the *absence* of a sovereign, however, is the matter of enforcement in times of a non-international conflict, where such an absence is most likely to occur in practice. During such conflicts, armed groups or other non-state actors may not have acquired the level of organisation necessary to consider them as 'de facto' regimes, and the result may be a more general lack of control and sovereign power. In this regard, the Commentary to Article 18 AP II pertaining to the delivery of aid, notes that:

> "In exceptional cases when it is not possible to determine which are the authorities concerned, consent is to be presumed in view of the fact that assistance for the victims is of paramount importance and should not suffer delay".[393]

The Additional Protocol therefore operates under the *assumption* that in the absence of a sovereign, or in the event of difficulty establishing which actor is the authority, the consent to gain access to a territory may be assumed. Whilst such an assertion may seem forward and bold, in reality it matches the manner in which the Geneva Conventions and Protocols deal with the matter of consent when a sovereign *does* exist: such a sovereign may not 'arbitrarily' refuse access to a bona fide offer of assistance.[394] In the absence of a sovereign to make such judgment calls, the assumption is held that no reasons exist to refuse consent and therefore the international community shall have the opportunity to gain access to enforce the provision of assistance.

From the above, it becomes apparent that the absence of a sovereign also leads to the absence of 'holding a sovereign accountable' under international law. State responsibility and human rights law do not offer solutions for such accountability in the absence of a sovereign, and the Security Council's manner of enforcement often entails the use of force. International criminal law however is tailored towards the responsibility of individuals in international law, and as such can be a mechanism in holding those responsible that have violated amongst others Article 7 or 8 of the ICC Statute.[395] Yet here too, an assumption is made that 'a responsibility' exists, either through the existence of persons exercising governmental authority or through *de facto* regimes and armed groups, rather than providing solutions for the actual absence of an authority. This remains logical, as in the absence of a *factually* responsible person or party, holding a person or party *legally* responsible shall be difficult to prove in a court of law. Indeed, in the total absence of a responsible actor, the obstruction or impediment of humanitarian assistance is often not the largest problem, rather the factual provision of assistance to those persons in crisis with no authority to turn to.

---

[392] Section 6.4.1 and 6.5.1.2 regarding the obligations of armed groups in the provision of humanitarian assistance.

[393] Sandoz, Swinarski & Zimmermann *Commentary to the Additional Protocols* (n 74) Protocol II Article 18, 1479.

[394] Section 8.3.

[395] Section 8.6.2.1 and 8.6.2.2.

The Security Council, as a body dealing with impending crises as opposed to judicial responsibilities after the fact, is therefore in the current international legal order the most appropriate enforcer of humanitarian assistance in circumstances where a humanitarian crisis takes place in the absence of a sovereign. The Council, in particular, will be most suitable for responses to natural disasters in areas where a sovereign is absent, as such disasters are often sudden, and require quick and decisive action. Equally, such action is suitable to circumstances of non-international armed conflicts where often a lack of control or absence of a sovereign over parts of a territory exists. In such circumstances where massive humanitarian crises arise without a sovereign to take charge and provide assistance, it may be argued that a threat to the peace exists, warranting Security Council action. Furthermore, it remains relevant that after the fact, armed groups, or other non-state actors might be held responsible in national judicial proceedings.

It must be noted that much of the law pertaining to the absence of a sovereign is through inference; deducing the law, based upon other existing obligations. The ILC has sought to prevent such analogies by incorporating an option for enforcement in its Draft Articles on the Protection of Persons in the Event of Disasters in the absence of a sovereign. Draft Article 14(3) notes that pursuant to an external offer of humanitarian assistance, the affected state shall 'whenever possible, make its decision regarding the offer known'.[396] This ambiguous wording has been explained by the ILC's Drafting Committee as to acknowledge the possibility that a functioning sovereign may be absent, upon which consent must be considered implied.[397] Such wording follows the line of reasoning of AP II concerning matters in a non-international armed conflict as discussed above. Although the Draft Articles are not hard law (yet), Draft Article 14(3) follows the current state of the law, where the Security Council – as authoritative body – shall have the opportunity to assess whether or not a threat to the peace exists upon which assistance is needed, and whether or not consent must be implied. Whilst the current law on enforcement in the absence of a sovereign is vague, and provisions are few and far between, in practice, the absence of a sovereign in (parts of) a territory upon which a non-international armed conflict exists or natural disaster takes place is the reality on the ground. Often non-governmental actors providing aid will continue to attempt to reach such territories, in order to supply persons in need with humanitarian assistance. These circumstances in particular point out the need for clarity of the law, to enable providers of aid guidance in their work.

---

[396] ILC 'Protection of persons in the event of disasters' Draft Articles UN Doc A/CN.4/L.831 (15 May 2014).

[397] 'Statement of the Chairman of the Drafting Committee pertaining to Article 14 [11] Protection of Persons in the Event of Disasters' (2 August 2011) 5.

8.8 Conclusion

This Chapter has taken the research into the legal framework on the provision of humanitarian assistance to the level of enforcement. In the event of a sovereign not fulfilling its duties and providing assistance (duties such as discussed in Chapter 6) or allowing assistance by third parties (discussed in Chapter 7), this Chapter has addressed the potential methods of enforcement of humanitarian assistance through international law. These methods consist of applying the law at an interstate level through state responsibility, the use of force by way of the Security Council and enforcement through human rights mechanisms, as well as individual responsibility through targeted sanctions or individual criminal responsibility.

State sovereignty continues to play an important role in this aspect of the legal framework. In particular, with regard to the assessment of which acts or omissions may lead to an obstruction or denial of humanitarian assistance, the affected state has the primary responsibility. The enforcement of humanitarian assistance through state responsibility remains the primary approach, given the fact that the affected state's sovereignty entails the responsibility to provide assistance in times of a crisis. As the ICJ in its Barcelona Traction judgment and the ARSIWA have both left the purely bilateral view to state responsibility behind, the international community can now be seen to be vested with joint responsibility.[398] Whereas state responsibility presupposes an act or omission of a state which amounts to a breach of international law that is attributable to that state (Articles 2 and 3 ARSIWA), state responsibility is also possible for those acts attributable to a state through various other means (Articles 4-11 ARSIWA).[399] The ARSIWA provide in circumstances precluding wrongfulness in its Articles 20-25, whereas most relevant regarding the provision of assistance is Article 23 concerning *force majeure*. In practice it might be potentially invoked by an affected state as a reason for denial of humanitarian assistance, although such a denial may not lead to breaches of peremptory norms. In particular concerning the delivery of humanitarian assistance, such norms include the prohibition of genocide, racial discrimination, war crimes and crimes against humanity.[400] Interestingly, with a more communal approach, the ARSIWA envisages through Articles 42 and 48 the possibility for third states to

---

398 8.2.1 State Responsibility, the ARSIWA and Humanitarian Assistance

399 8.2.2 The ARSIWA, Peremptory Norms and the Denial of Humanitarian Assistance.

400 See amongst others *Armed Activities on the Territory of the Congo* (New Application: 2002) (Democratic Republic of the Congo v. Rwanda), Jurisdiction and Admissibility, Judgment, I.C.J. Reports 2006, p. 6, § 64 concerning the prohibition of genocide; Questions relating to the Obligation to Prosecute or Extradite (Belgium v. Senegal), Judgment, I.C.J. Reports 2012, p. 422 § 99 concerning the prohibition of torture; Barcelona Traction, Light and Power Company Limited (Belgium v. Spain) case ICJ Reports 1970, § 33-34 regarding the prohibition of aggression and genocide, as well as 'basic human rights' such as the protection from slavery and racial discrimination; and *Prosecutor v. Kupreškić et al. (IT-95-16) "Lašva Valley"*(Judgment Trial Chamber) IT-95-16-T (14 January 2000 § 520; *Prosecutor v. Furundzija* (Trial Judgment) IT-95-17/1-T (ICTY 10 December 1998) § 151-157; *Prosecutor v. Zejnil Delalic, Zdravko Mucic (aka "Pavo"), Hazim Delic and Esad Landžo (aka "Zenga") (Celebici - Case)* (Appeals Chamber) IT-96-21-A (20 February 2001) § 172; *Prosecutor v. Krstic* (Trial Judgment) IT-98-33-T (2 August 2001) § 541.

hold the affected state accountable for a breach of an obligation owed to the international community in general; an aspect of particular relevance in the provision of assistance. This non-provision may either affect a larger territory and thus amount for example to a threat to the international peace, or such non-provision may be a breach of a peremptory norm which shall according to the ARSIWA induce the international community to act.

As such, Articles 40 and 41 ARSIWA specifically call upon third states to take responsibility through a *positive* obligation, and cooperate in bringing breaches of peremptory norms that are gross failures of the affected, responsible state to an *end*: envisioning an obligation of result.[401] The ICJ has also seconded this view, although arguing an 'obligation of conduct' for state parties to the Genocide Convention, which, when such an obligation of conduct for third parties is applied to the provision of humanitarian assistance, can found also in both human rights law and humanitarian law.[402] In these bodies of law the affected states can be held accountable, whilst the international community (mostly under the ICESCR and the Geneva Conventions) can be seen to be called upon in assistance. The ARSIWA's 'duty to cooperate' for the international community under Articles 40 and 41 to bring such violations to an end can also be found in Article 42 of the ILC Draft Articles on the responsibility of international organisations as well as in Article 89 AP I. Although none of these provisions argue that states in the direct vicinity have a higher duty, their possibilities are often greater due to their location close to the affected territory. Lastly with regard to state responsibility, this Chapter has considered the role of the ILC Draft Articles on the protection of persons in the event of disasters, and concluded that these Articles too express a potential (although softer) obligation for third states to cooperate in the face of disaster under Draft Article 8 (and a role under Draft Article 12).[403] Given the formulations, these Draft Articles must also be read as duties of conduct, should they be codified in the future.

Upon a lack of provision of aid by the affected sovereign, a body such as the Security Council or an international court upon which authority has been bestowed shall have to determine whether or not enforcement is or was indeed necessary.[404] Of course, the current existing international bodies are not infallible, nor can each decision be presumed just, in particular due to the political realities with which the world deals, but in the current state of the law these bodies are those that have been given jurisdiction or power by sovereign states to act. The exact determination of which acts or omissions amount to violations of international law – through specific duties in human rights law and humanitarian law – can only be made on a case-by-case basis, through the assessment of several key factors.

[401] 8.2.3 State Responsibility and the Potential Duty to Cooperate in the Event of a Breach.
[402] Application of the Convention on the Prevention and Punishment of the Crime of Genocide (Bosnia and Herzegovina v. Serbia and Montenegro), Judgment, I.C.J. Reports 2007, p. 43 § 430.
[403] 8.2.4 State Responsibility, Humanitarian Assistance and Legal Developments.
[404] 8.3 Acts Constituting Denial or Obstruction of Humanitarian Assistance.

The authoritative body in a particular circumstance shall determine (1) whether or not a humanitarian crisis exists in which the population is inadequately supplied, thereby warranting assistance, (2) subsequently whether or not the affected state is fulfilling its sovereign duties in the provision of aid, (3) in the event it is not capable of doing so, whether it has requested help or refused consent to an offer of assistance (sovereignty considerations are granted the most leeway in circumstances of natural disaster and non-international armed conflict) and (4) lastly, whether or not such consent was arbitrarily denied.

Upon establishment of the above, the facilitation of access by the Security Council's resort to the use of force, or determination of legal responsibility through an international legal body, can be done. Both types of bodies have been donned with the appropriate authority to consider such assessments. The assessments regarding potential violations of international law remain twofold: firstly, the assessment whether or not the affected state itself has unlawfully denied humanitarian assistance (according to the duties discussed Chapter 6) and secondly, whether the affected state unlawfully denied the external offer of assistance and the related right of third parties to access the affected territory (as discussed in Chapter 7).

When the affected state violates its duties, it is seen above that a secondary responsibility is put to third states. Third states may ensure the enforcement of the provision of assistance following violations of peremptory norms of international law, through the use of force by way of the Security Council. The Council is the current appropriate body to this end as it has been provided with authority through Articles 25, 39 and 103 of the UN Charter. In this manner of enforcement, it remains crucial to continue to distinguish between those *providing* aid and those enforcers taking action to *enable the providers* of assistance. In the current legal framework regarding the provision of humanitarian assistance and the use of force, the Security Council is the sole body with the opportunity to determine in a situation that amounts to a threat to the peace, whether or not a humanitarian crisis is taking place, and whether or not external assistance is needed; upon which it may decide to 'enforce' such assistance.[405] Such a determination is simultaneously also the determination that the affected territory is inadequately supplied and the affected state is not fulfilling its sovereign obligations to take care of those under its jurisdiction. Whilst the influence of the veto powers of the 'permanent five' indeed cannot be neglected, it does not appear likely that the current composition and *modus operandi* of the Council will change in the foreseeable future.

As discussed in Section 8.4.2, the Council commenced with enforcement actions in the early 1990's, in Somalia, followed by a more troubled approach in the Former Yugoslavia, upon which the theme of 'humanitarian assistance' was brought to the table in a more consistent manner. This was done through adding the topic 'Protection for humanitarian assistance to refugees and others in conflict situations' in 1997 and in 1999 the item of 'Promoting peace and security:

[405] 8.4.1 Security Council Action: Enforcement through the UN system and the Responsibility to Protect.

humanitarian activities relevant to the Security Council' to the Council's agenda, as well as the thematic resolutions on the protection of civilians in armed conflict (most notably Resolution 1265). Whilst the Security Council faced certain difficulties in this initial period, pertaining amongst other problems to the adaptation of traditional peacekeeping missions to circumstances warranting more explicit use of force, ascertaining whether or not the Council authorises the use of force under Chapter VII continues to be of importance to distilling the approach taken by the body in the enforcement of the provision of aid. It becomes apparent in the above that in fact the Council today is quite comfortable asserting the use of Chapter VII, to ensure the provision of humanitarian assistance, whilst in its initial period in the 1990's the Council was reserved in the use of force pursuant to Article 42 UN Charter and did not set out a clear line of action though the *option* of the use of force was on the table.[406]

Following the UN embracement of the Responsibility to Protect in 2005, the Security Council did not classify each act under Chapter VII as such, but does continue to express its readiness to take action in the face of flagrant and widespread violations of human rights or humanitarian law and continues to address the need for methods to strengthen humanitarian access.[407] Whilst most peacekeeping missions and hybrid missions were in cooperation with the affected state, whose sovereignty therefore was not too tainted or affected, the Council does increasingly note the possibility to use force explicitly *for the purpose of the enforcement of humanitarian assistance* as well as opening the door to the use of force where humanitarian assistance is 'deliberately obstructed' as noted in its thematic resolutions. The circumstances in Libya in 2011 have shown the Security Council's willingness to use both force and to apply the RtoP doctrine, strikingly in direct connection to the enforcement of humanitarian assistance.[408] Despite subsequent Chapter VII action in Somalia and the South Sudan, the Council fails in consistency as it did not embrace RtoP in these circumstances, nor did it refer to Chapter VII in the case of Mali and Syria to date, although it alluded to Syria's responsibility to protect its citizens. Indeed, in a novel approach the Council has called upon the provision of humanitarian assistance in Syria 'across conflict lines'.

Increasingly the Council has also become more specific with the language in its resolutions, focusing with greater detail on the use of force for *the purpose of enforcement* of aid delivery, such as in Somalia and Mali, yet continues to grapple with the difficulties of state sovereignty. Thus, as concluded above, it may be useful to find a formulation for the Council to take more consistent and firm action, although this may not be realistic and viable in practice, given the *ad hoc* basis upon which the Council operates.[409] Despite lacking consistency in action, this must not be read as a determination that the use of force is *prohibited*, as the Council has clearly demonstrated its willingness and readiness to use force either through

[406] Section 8.4.2 The Beginning of Security Council Action.
[407] 8.4.3 Security Council Action since the UN embracement of the Responsibility to Protect.
[408] Ibid.
[409] Ibid.

strengthening existing missions, or through calling upon its member states, both in circumstances where the sovereign has cooperated and in circumstances against the direct wishes of such a sovereign. The Council's actions hereby follow the line of the on-going debate pertaining to issues with the permeability of state sovereignty in the event a sovereign does not protect those under its jurisdiction. With the on-going developments surrounding RtoP, a case-by-case analysis will continue to be the manner in which to follow the Council's actions in order to distil more clarity.

Besides the ad-hoc action by the Security Council, enforcement options are also available through human rights law, either by way of (semi-) judicial treaty-bodies or through the UN Charter system, in which both individuals and states may hold the affected state accountable for violations of the rights to life, food, health (and water) that may incur should humanitarian assistance not be provided.[410] This Chapter has addressed the position of four main treaty body mechanisms concerning the enforcement of humanitarian assistance, which are all limited in their scope of application to the content of their respective treaties. Both the ICCPR and ICESCR have treaty bodies: their findings are not binding and cannot hold states legally accountable for potential violations of human rights.[411] Their interstate complaint mechanism has furthermore not been used, nor is it expected to be used, given the political implications. Independently, the HRC has recognised on occasion that the non-provision of humanitarian assistance may amount to a violation of the right to life under the ICCPR, thereby opening the door to subsequent findings. Problematic to the CESCR is that the rights in the ICESCR are obligations of conduct rather than hard result (with the exception of the minimum core obligations) and as such may be more difficult to argue as having been violated. For the purpose of the delivery of humanitarian assistance however, the minimum core obligations are of particular relevance, as addressed in Chapter 5. Furthermore, the CESCR individual complaint procedure has not existed long enough to have allowed for any findings related to the delivery of humanitarian assistance, leaving only the General Comments procedure through which the Committee has indeed argued potential violations of Articles 11 and 12 should humanitarian assistance not be provided.

It is particularly regrettable that the ECtHR, although having had ample opportunity, has neglected to connect the non-provision of humanitarian assistance consistently to the violation of human rights under its Convention. The Court has done so only in relation to potential violation of Article 3 (cruel or inhuman treatment), and noting the obstruction of aid as a serious 'abuse' rather than as a human rights abuse, thereby foregoing the opportunity to classify the denial of aid as a violation of a human right, more specifically as a violation of the right to life.[412] The IACtHR lastly also recognises both the individual and state complaint procedure, but no jurisprudence to date is specifically relevant to this research into the enforcement of humanitarian assistance.

[410] 8.5 Enforcement through Human Rights Law.
[411] 8.5.1 Enforcement through Human Rights Treaty Mechanisms.
[412] *Mohammed v. Austria* (App no 2283/12) ECHR 6 June 2013, Final 6 September 2013 § 52.

The latter notion of 'state complaints' reflects a shared responsibility of all states parties to the respective Conventions, such as also can be seen in the ARSIWA and the ICJ's perspective in the *Barcelona Traction* case. Difficult for the treaty bodies however remains, in particular concerning obligations of conduct, the ascertaining of whether or not *enough* has been done by the affected state to fulfil the basic requirements of the right to food, health (and water), as well as ensuring the right to life; through the indiscriminate provision of emergency assistance. Given the attempts, slowly, to also apply humanitarian law where necessary, these bodies may well use the wording of that law such as 'arbitrary refusal' or 'adequate supply' to add more specificity to their findings. However, even outside of armed conflict, the formulations of the rights to life, food and health are not so vague as to not allow the enforcement bodies to assess whether or not the non-provision of assistance entailed a violation of a right.[413]

Operating next to the treaty bodies are the Charter-based organs and bodies of the UN, with a more broad and political mandate, such as the Human Rights Council with its UPR system and the Special Rapporteurs.[414] Both in the UPR system as well as through the Special Rapporteurs, the UN member states have been called on to allow for humanitarian access and assistance, and such bodies have placed the denial of assistance clearly within a human rights context, condemning states for inaction. Such recommendations (some coming from third states) contribute to the general consensus that the enforcement of humanitarian assistance can be viewed from a human rights perspective, although they remain non-binding. In particular, the politics of the Human Rights Council mechanisms must be recognised and taken into consideration, when addressing their value.

Lastly, individual responsibility is addressed in this Chapter through targeted sanctions and criminal responsibility. Individual responsibility can be asserted by the Security Council, in its appliance of sanctions as an enforcement mechanism 'targeted' towards individuals, a mechanism it has used since the 1990's and which has become more and more specific over recent years, also with regard to those responsible for human rights- and humanitarian law violations related to the non-provision of humanitarian assistance.[415] In instances such as in Cote d'Ivoire, Somalia, the DRC and the CAR, the Security Council has expressed its willingness to take action against those that have denied or obstructed humanitarian assistance or directed violence towards humanitarian personnel, through asset freezing, travel bans and similar sanctions. This enforcement mechanism of the Council has proven an increasingly useful tool, as it avoids the impact on the civilian population in general that may be had by the use of force. As it is subject to the implementation of member states, its impact may however not be great enough to pressure authorities into allowing aid into a territory.

Unlike targeted sanctions, individual criminal responsibility is allocated often after the crisis has taken place, similar to the work of human rights enforcement

413 8.5.1 Enforcement through Human Rights Treaty Mechanisms.
414 8.5.2 Human Rights Enforcement through the UN Charter System.
415 8.6.1 Enforcement through Targeted Sanctions.

mechanisms. With the creation of the ICC a permanent court has jurisdiction over the crimes of aggression, genocide, war crimes and crimes against humanity, the latter two of which are of particular relevance to the enforcement of the provision of humanitarian assistance.[416] The ICC has also the crucial novel capacity to forego many obstacles pertaining to the immunities of sovereigns and other authorities. Article 8 ICC Statute pertaining to war crimes recognises a wide variety of actions that may be related to the denial or obstruction of humanitarian aid, separately in an international armed conflict and in a non-international armed conflict.[417] In an international armed conflict, such actions include wilfully causing great suffering or injury to a person's health, intentional attacks on civilians or personnel involved in humanitarian assistance, launching attacks which might severely damage the environment (a violation of the principle of proportionality), outrages upon personal dignity, directly attacking personnel displaying the emblems of the Geneva Convention (a violation of the principle of distinction) and using starvation as a method of warfare. The provisions of the ICC reflect the criminalisation of provisions in the Geneva Conventions and their Protocols, such as Articles 23 GC IV, and 54 and 71 AP I as well as the human rights to life and food. The ICC does leave room for the consent of the affected state, as it criminalises the 'wilful impediment' of aid in Article 8(2)(b)(xxv). However, such intentionality is not necessary with regard to the crime of inhuman treatment: Article 8(2)(a)(ii) clarifies that merely 'inflicting' pain or suffering suffices for criminalisation.

In particular it must be noted that military necessity may be argued as a justification for certain acts of non-provision of humanitarian assistance as long as these do not amount to starvation.[418] In non-international armed conflicts, the ICC Statute has criminalised serious violations of common Article 3 of the Geneva Conventions, detailing these as intentionally attacking those persons or objects involved in the provision of humanitarian assistance (Article 8(2)(e)(ii) and (iii)). However, starvation as a method of warfare is not criminalised, despite the recognition of its unlawfulness both by AP II and the Security Council. Alternative methods of prosecution would be possible through the argument that this norm is part of customary international law. Another distinction between international and non-international armed conflicts – although 'outrages upon personal dignity' are criminalised for both, is that the ICC Statute furthermore only criminalises damages to the environment as well as the 'grave breach' of inhuman treatment and wilfully causing great suffering to a person's health in the situation of an international armed conflict.

Secondly, individual criminal responsibility for the obstruction or denial of humanitarian assistance is possible through Article 7 ICC Statute pertaining to crimes against humanity. Unlike war crimes, crimes against humanity no longer warrant a nexus to an armed conflict, thereby also putting the debate concerning the concept of the 'lex specialis' relationship between human rights law and

[416] 8.6.2 Enforcement through International Criminal Law.
[417] 8.6.2.1 War Crimes and Humanitarian Assistance.
[418] Ibid.

humanitarian law somewhat more aside.[419] In particular in relation to the non-provision of assistance, Article 7(2) ICC Statute criminalises 'extermination', which includes the 'deprivation of access to food and medicine'. A crime against humanity however must be a widespread or systematic attack, or, in the event of a single strategic act, it must have occurred with the intent of impacting a larger group, bringing about the destruction of part of a population.[420] Intentionality remains a difficult aspect of this crime in relation to humanitarian assistance, but the willingness of states to put the delivery of humanitarian assistance at the forefront of criminalisation can be seen in their inclusion of such obstruction as an act of 'extermination' *within the text* of Article 7 of the ICC Statute. 'Other inhumane acts' as mentioned in Article 7 ICC Statute shall then provide for alternative means of prosecution in the denial or obstruction of assistance by certain individuals.

Finally, this Chapter has also ascertained in what manner enforcement options are available in those circumstances in which a sovereign is absent partly or entirely. Given that the sovereign is the primary responsible party for the provision of assistance, state responsibility shall not be able to be asserted, save for in the circumstance of a de facto regime as meant in Article 9 ARSIWA.[421] The ICJ has declared more broadly that the 'exercise of physical control over a territory 'and not sovereignty or legitimacy of title' serves as the basis for liability.[422] Indeed, the absence of a sovereign does not change the fact that a crisis may take place, and that persons may be in dire need of humanitarian assistance. The provision of assistance continues to be a fulfilment of the human rights of such persons as well as a fulfilment of certain provisions in humanitarian law (should an armed conflict take place). The international community shall therefore have the opportunity to enforce the provision of humanitarian assistance directly on the basis of these bodies of law, as both bodies recognise the responsibility of non-state actors to abide by international law.[423] In particular Article 18 AP II presupposes the consent to access a territory in the event of difficulty establishing which actor is the authority.

Naturally international criminal law is also tailored to individual responsibility, and as such can also hold those non-state actors responsible that have committed violations of Articles 7 or 8 of the ICC Statute, although difficulties will continue to exist in an absolute void of authority. Such a void shall however potentially enhance the opportunity of the Security Council to take immediate action to provide aid, without struggling with the difficulties of crossing sovereignty

[419] 8.6.2.2 Crimes Against Humanity and Humanitarian Assistance.
[420] Ibid.
[421] 8.7 The Enforcement of Humanitarian Assistance and the Absence of a Sovereign.
[422] 'Legal Consequences for States of the Continued Presence of South Africa in Namibia' ICJ Advisory Opinion (n 62) § 118.
[423] 6.3.1 Duties of the Affected State and Non-State Actor under Human Rights Law and AP II. See amongst others also for the position of the Security Council UNSC Res 1265 (17 September 1999) UN Doc S/RES/1265 § 4; UNSC Res 1863 (9 July 2009) UN Doc S/RES/1863 § 19 and UNSC Res 2036 (22 February 2012) UN Doc S/RES/2036 § 16.

barriers. In particular for circumstances of natural disaster, the ILC Draft Articles attempt to fill the gap through Draft Article 14(3) allowing for an implied consent in the absence of a sovereign.[424] Problematic to the complete absence of a sovereign, however, is the need to *infer* many of the enforcement options throughout the bodies of law. As seen throughout this Chapter, many of the circumstances bound to occur in practice do not have explicit legal equivalent solutions. As such, in international law enforcement currently continues to be a case-by-case assessment.

[424] 8.7 The Enforcement of Humanitarian Assistance and the Absence of a Sovereign.

CHAPTER 9
CONCLUSIONS AND RECOMMENDATIONS

The tragedies of World War II, in particular the persecutions and horrendous death camps, were the epitome of a humanitarian crisis and caused the international community to cry out 'never again!'. Yet within a single century, the world has been witness to numerous disasters, emergencies and conflicts, resulting in millions of people in dire need of aid, but not receiving it. The provision of aid to persons in need, a concept founded on basic human dignity and the principle of humanity, turned out not to be as self-evident as perceived. The provision of humanitarian assistance continues to raise legal questions and faces legal barriers to this day. These struggles have triggered the present research into the legal framework on the provision of humanitarian assistance.

9.1 Conclusions Pertaining to the Existing Legal Framework

This research has proposed addressing the provision of humanitarian assistance from an all-encompassing and integral 'umbrella' perspective, to ensure a common denominator for all persons who may find themselves in need of humanitarian assistance. Although recognising the historical context through which the delivery of humanitarian assistance – as a concept – has developed in times of war, separately from in times of peace, it must be concluded that the *persons* in need of assistance remain a constant factor, as do their needs: regardless of facing a conflict or hurricane, basic human *needs* remain constant. Indeed, the *purpose* of humanitarian assistance: protecting victims of crises, should allow their equal protection. In international law, a clear-cut definition of the concept of humanitarian assistance remains lacking. Therefore, based upon the various definitions suggested in soft law, it has been proffered in Chapter 2 that for the purpose of this research,

> *humanitarian assistance shall be considered assistance consisting of food, medicine, shelter and logistics for its provision, for urgent purposes and which is indispensable to the survival of the people at whom it is aimed.*[1]

This succinct definition restricts humanitarian assistance to emergency aid for the immediate survival of persons in need. Similar to the fact that a plethora of potential definitions of assistance exist, so do various actors involved with its provision hold different viewpoints on the manner in which it should be provided, amongst which the ICRC/IFRC and the UN. Again, in searching for a common denominator, this research has confirmed three principles that find common ground

[1] 2.2 The Concept of Humanitarian Assistance.

amongst the main providers of aid. These principles are the principles of humanity, impartiality and neutrality. Human dignity plays a central role, as well as non-discrimination and refraining from involvement in the crisis on the territory in which assistance takes place. From the principles through which assistance is provided, the recipients and providers of said assistance can be distilled.[2] Chapter 2 addresses that these recipients shall be civilians, regardless of the specific circumstances in which aid is provided, and may include refugees or IDPs. With the principles of assistance in mind, this 'civilian' requirement is indeed necessary for aid to be considered humanitarian assistance, and similarly requirements exist for those providing aid. First and foremost, the affected state has a primary role, as it is the authority in the territory in which the crisis takes place. Secondly, when abiding by the principles of humanity, neutrality and impartiality, international organisations and third states may also provide assistance.

Establishing the boundaries of this research thus immediately brings several initial gaps in the legal framework pertaining to the delivery of humanitarian assistance to the forefront. Whilst 'humanitarian assistance' is a common term involving legal rights and duties, the concept itself has not been defined definitively or conclusively, thereby warranting a definition in this research. Furthermore, several of the providers of assistance hold differentiating views on the manner in which assistance should be provided, leading to the need to distil common denominators that are accepted by all those who provide aid.

The need for humanitarian assistance, as argued in this research, arises in times of a humanitarian crisis. A crisis in reality can be any factual circumstance, provided that it meets a certain threshold of severity and as such aligns with the overarching approach to the provision of assistance taken in this research. To this end, the definition for such a crisis is stipulated in Chapter 3:

> *A humanitarian crisis is a situation deriving from a variety of origins, including natural or man-made disaster, armed conflict and occupation; causing grave damages of a personal or material nature to persons, where (external) assistance is needed as the local capacity is either overwhelmed, unable or sometimes unwilling to manage the circumstances.*[3]

This definition of a humanitarian crisis allows for a multitude of factual circumstances to 'amount' to a crisis, as long as a basic threshold is met, regardless of the legal qualification of such circumstances. As is well-known, the law follows the facts, not the other way around. When considering these circumstances, it becomes apparent that the law pertaining to the provision of aid differentiates between assistance in times of natural disasters, (non-) international armed conflicts and occupation. A variety of rights and duties exists regarding the provision of assistance that are dependent on the specific legal qualification, which is not conducive to the comprehensive assertion that a person in need of aid should

[2] 2.2.3 The Principles for the Delivery of Assistance.
[3] 3.3.3. Defining a Humanitarian Crisis.

receive such aid, as human dignity proscribes. In practice therefore, 'classifying' a crisis results in a disparity in the level of protection of persons in need of aid, warranting this research. The law is most explicit concerning relief provided in circumstances of occupation, a logic that originates from the law being created in the aftermath of Nazi occupation throughout Europe. Yet today, a trend developing since the early 1990s, non-international armed conflicts and natural disasters claim most casualties, as victims of these circumstances often desperately need emergency aid but remain without receiving it.

For these purposes, this research has assessed in Chapter 3 the definitions of these legal denominations, as well as their thresholds. Circumstances of natural disaster are not clearly delimited, as the notion of a natural disaster itself is not properly defined in international law. Therefore, this research has suggested upon distilling from various offered soft law definitions that:

> *A natural disaster is a sudden or slow-onset natural occurrence or course of events that may include a variety of environmental origins (including biological, climatological, geophysical, hydrological, etc.), resulting in an overwhelming of the local or national capacity and an immediate need for assistance to a civilian population.*[4]

Such a wide scope allows for a broad range of circumstances that may create a need for persons to receive aid. Perhaps consequential to a lacking definition to apply to legal rights and duties, so is a specific legal framework lacking for the provision of assistance in times of disaster. For the applicable rights and duties in times of natural disaster, resort must therefore be had to general international law and human rights law. For armed conflicts, the determination that such a circumstance is occurring, remains factual and is done case-by-case, most often through the judiciary's application of the well-known *Tadić*-definition. Upon determination of this and thereby application of international humanitarian law, the duties pertaining to the delivery of aid specific to this field of law immediately apply, simultaneous to general international law and human rights law.[5] Establishing a circumstance such as occupation is also a factual assessment and requires the ascertainment that a form of authority is established in a territory, which is also exercised and covers parts of or the whole territory. However, the legal rights and obligations pertaining to the provision of assistance, unlike in times of armed conflict, do not *immediately* apply to the occupier due to this abovementioned 'exercise of control' criterion. It must be reiterated that the threshold of a *humanitarian crisis* must be applied to each of these circumstances: not every conflict, disaster and particularly not every circumstance of occupation warrants the delivery of aid. Such aid should be provided if and when the situation amounts to a humanitarian *crisis*. In the 21st century, the first decade has shown

[4] 3.2.5 Defining a (Natural) Disaster.
[5] 3.2.2 Armed Conflicts and the Provision of Humanitarian Assistance.

that such circumstances amounting to a crisis more often than not are natural disasters and non-international armed conflicts.

Chapter 3 has also addressed the particular relationship between human rights law and humanitarian law, given their simultaneous applicability to certain instances that may amount to humanitarian crises. Acknowledging the various perspectives on the *lex specialis*-doctrine in international law, as well as the debate on the extra-territorial applicability of human rights law, it can be firmly established that both human rights law and humanitarian law share the common goals of serving the protection of persons and humanity. As a result, this research submits that the *lex specialis*-principle must be read as a manner in which to apply the most specific provision in a specific circumstance; resulting in the application of a human rights provision in some instances, and a provision deriving from humanitarian law in others. Given the topic of the research, this will result in the application of the most *protective* clause in all circumstances. This converging approach of the *lex specialis*-doctrine again aligns with the overarching approach taken by this research that persons in need of assistance should be able to receive such assistance, equally protected by the law, regardless of which factual circumstance has amounted to the humanitarian crisis in which they find themselves.[6]

Determining the circumstances in which aid is needed, as well as the applicable law, has raised more issues pertaining to the existing legal framework. The above portrays the difficulties arising in the assessment of what in fact amounts to a circumstance in which assistance is necessary, which has prompted this research to provide not only a definition of a natural disaster, but more importantly, a definition of a 'humanitarian crisis'. Likewise, offering a perspective on the *lex specialis*-doctrine is done for the purpose of establishing which provisions must be adhered to, in the event of a lack of clarity in the law *that has the purpose of protecting individuals*. It is for this reason that it is suggested that the most specific and protective *clause* must be adhered to in various circumstances, as opposed to an *entire* body of law, which has more and less specific provisions. More support and clarification of this position in international law would benefit the persons the law is attempting to protect.

Critical to the provision of humanitarian assistance is furthermore the concept of 'state sovereignty', addressed in Chapter 4. The Westphalian notion of state sovereignty today is somewhat outdated, as well as the *Lotus*-perspective of the PCIJ. The erosion of the notion of sovereignty as a 'shield' over the course of the 21st century followed various developments, such as greater international interdependence, the embracement of the UDHR and various human rights treaties allowing for a larger role of individuals on the international plane and the subsequent creation of multiple international tribunals and courts. With the embracement of the 'Responsibility to Protect'-doctrine in the UN, another effort has been taken to pierce the sovereign veil. Indeed, in the 21st century, sovereignty must be seen as a reciprocal relationship between rights and duties *of the sovereign*

[6] 3.4.3 Hierarchy or Convergence of International Legal Norms?.

authority. Whilst the principles relevant to the provision of humanitarian assistance, such as those of non-intervention, respect for the domestic jurisdiction of a state and consent continue to be upheld, not only do such *rights* exist for the sovereign, duties exist also. In other words, these principles are not void of boundaries: a responsibility rests upon the sovereign to take care of those under its jurisdiction. Consequently, when the sovereign fails to fulfil its obligations in this regard, the obligation to protect civilians falls to the international community. In particular, this obligation arises under RtoP for crimes such as genocide, war crimes, crimes against humanity and ethnic cleansing. RtoP may not be fully developed yet nor put into much practice, but it does represent a tendency in the international community to view sovereignty increasingly as a notion that includes a responsibility towards those under the sovereign's authority, as well as a secondary responsibility for the international community itself.[7] Furthermore, as international law recognises individuals as legal subjects, it allows such individuals to reach out to the international community through a request to fulfil their human rights through the provision of humanitarian assistance. The provision of humanitarian assistance in this sense is a key example of the manner in which sovereignty is exercised. It is a method for sovereign authorities to fulfil their responsibilities, but upon failing to do so, it becomes a vehicle through which the international community can fill the sovereign's void. Sovereign responsibilities then become translated from internal, belonging to the sovereign, to external; for the international community to provide. Such duties are discussed in Chapters 6, 7 and 8, in consideration of responsible state sovereignty.

From the perspective of the individuals receiving humanitarian assistance, Chapter 5 addresses the matter of a potential human right to receive aid. At this time, no such individual, independent human right exists. However in treaty law, the CRC, CRPD and African Charter on the Rights and Welfare of the Child recognise a right to receive aid *in connection to* the fulfilment of other rights within the respective treaties. Equally, in customary international law no such right can be distilled, despite various soft law initiatives that refer to the potential existing of *opinio juris* on the matter. A problematic aspect of the determination of an independent human right is the assessment of the content and scope of the right, with a view to assessing rights-holders and duty-bearers in the particular provision of humanitarian assistance.[8] Chapter 5 has addressed that a right to humanitarian assistance would potentially fall in the category of 'third generation', or 'solidarity' rights, which often have very broad scopes. Whilst this would not be the case for humanitarian assistance given the quite narrow definition of the concept provided above in relation to its provision in times of emergencies only, it remains that the entire collective of individuals needing assistance would be considered rights-holders. Furthermore, whilst the state would be the first and foremost duty-bearer, a responsibility to provide aid may rest upon the international community as a whole. As such, the development of a human right to receive humanitarian

[7] 4.2.3.3 Towards a new Definition of Sovereignty.

[8] 5.3 A Human Right to Receive Humanitarian Assistance in International Law?.

assistance would place such a right in the problematic category of 'collective rights'. From this perspective, as well as taking into consideration the lack of development in treaty incorporation, it is more pragmatic to consider the provision of humanitarian assistance within the context of existing human rights.

Indeed, when assessing the existing body of human rights from the perspective of the provision of humanitarian assistance, it becomes clear that the need for the development of an individual right is not necessarily acute in international law today. Humanitarian assistance can – and does – function as a vehicle in the fulfilment of existing human rights. A strong basis is found in Articles 55 and 56 of the UN Charter and in particular, given the content of emergency aid, in the rights to life, food, health (and water). Chapter 5 has discussed these existing rights as incorporated in the UDHR, ICESCR, ICCPR, ECHR, ACPHR, ACHR, ICERD, CRC, CRPD, CEDAW and various other human rights treaties.[9] The formulations of these rights, the lack of restrictions by states in their reservations to the various treaties and moreover the interpretations of the treaty bodies accumulatively allow for the assessment that the delivery of humanitarian assistance is a manner in which to fulfil the rights to life, food, health (and water). This assessment is supported by the fact that those treaties which include a 'state of emergency'-clause, exclude the right to life from such derogation, as well as the fact that, whilst the ICESCR does not contain such a clause and is considered generally to entail mostly obligations of conduct, the treaty does recognise certain 'minimum core obligations'. Adding to this, the ICJ has declared in its *Nicaragua*-case that humanitarian assistance serves for the protection of 'life and health', providing additional arguments for the framing of humanitarian assistance in such a human rights context.

Therefore it can be concluded that the absence of a specific individual *human right* to humanitarian assistance is not necessarily an absence of a right to receive humanitarian assistance in itself. The right to receive assistance forms part of the entire body of human rights, most specifically the rights to life, food, health (and water) as enshrined in existing international law. Whereas the development of an individual human right might facilitate claiming such receipt, it may also attribute to the proliferation of human rights. Strengthening the current body of rights and simultaneously strengthening the function of humanitarian assistance as a vehicle in the fulfilment of such rights is more pragmatic and realistic, when considering the lack of developments of such a potential individual right. Furthermore, such a development should also not be considered *necessary* for individuals in their receipt of assistance, as they are currently able to receive assistance through claiming such a need based on the existing rights to life, food, health (and water).[10]

A core part of this research (in Chapters 6, 7 and 8) has focused on the specific legal rights and duties of the potential providers and recipients of humanitarian assistance according to the various legal sources that are of relevance to its provision. Legal sources such as human rights law, international humanitarian law

[9] 5.4 Humanitarian Assistance Within the Context of Existing Human Rights and further.
[10] 5.5.2 Humanitarian Assistance as a Vehicle in the Fulfilment of Existing Human Rights.

and refugee law have been examined as well as Security Council resolutions. The primary responsibility for the provision of humanitarian assistance lies first and foremost with the authority of the territory on which the crisis takes place. In essence, this is a reflection of the newer interpretation of state sovereignty, and is recognised also by the Security Council in resolutions dating from 2006, as well as General Assembly resolutions concerning natural disaster situations, the first dating back to 1991 and which later also embraced duties under international humanitarian law. Both *corpora juris* do not recognise an explicit 'right' of persons to receive aid, but do assert that the duties to provide assistance are not limited to the state, and can include other 'parties' such as non-state actors. In particular concerning the provision of aid in non-international armed conflicts, this is of relevance. That such actors – exercising a certain level of control – hold responsibilities under international law has also been asserted by the ICJ in its *Namibia*-opinion.[11]

In human rights law as seen in Chapter 5, rights and duties concerning the provision of humanitarian assistance can also be found, at a greater level of specificity than through the UN bodies' resolutions. With a strong foundation in Articles 55 and 56 of the UN Charter, UN member states are obliged to promote observance of human rights; which can today also be applied to non-state actors acting as (local) sovereigns. More specifically concerning the right to life, states have a positive obligation to not arbitrarily deprive persons of the right to life under Article 3 UDHR, Article 6 ICCPR, Article 2 ECHR, Article 4 ACHR and Article 4 ACHPR. This includes an individual's right to protection in this regard from the state, and as interpreted by the HRC an obligation of the sovereign to reduce 'malnutrition', which is of relevance in the provision of assistance. Specifically Articles 6 and 22 CRC recognise the duty to provide assistance in the fulfilment of the non-deprivation of life for children. The right to adequate food has been codified mostly as a state duty in Article 11 ICESCR, where the sovereign needs to demonstrate, in order to fulfil its minimum core obligations under the convention, having utilised all possible resources; including seeking international cooperation under Article 2 ICESCR. The CESCR has interpreted the non-provision of humanitarian assistance as a violation of this duty. The obligation to provide food – rather formulated as such than as a right to receive – can also be found in Article 24(2)(c) CRC, Article 12(2) CEDAW, Article 28 CRPD, Article 12 Additional Protocol to the ACHR in the area of Economic, Social and Cultural Rights, as well as Article 15 of the Additional Protocol to the ACHPR on the Rights of Women in Africa. The right to health finds a main provision in Article 12(2)(c) ICESCR, specifically calling upon the 'prevention, treatment and control of epidemic, endemic, occupational and other diseases', where international cooperation continues to be a fulfilment of the minimum core obligations. The right to health is furthermore codified in Articles 25 UDHR, 5(e)(iv) ICERD, 24 CRC, 11 European Social Charter, 10 Additional Protocol to the ACHR in the area of Economic, Social and Cultural Rights, 16 ACHPR, 14 African Charter on the

[11] 6.4 Duties and Rights under the UN Framework: the Security Council and General Assembly.

Rights and Welfare of the Child and 14 of the Additional Protocol to the ACHPR on the Rights of Women in Africa. There are some differentiations amongst the provisions, and as a result, difficulties ensue in formulating this as a clear-cut 'right' to receive for individuals. Concerning humanitarian assistance specifically, a consensus can be found in the obligation of the sovereign to prevent diseases and in the provision of aid, to prioritise a vulnerable population. Although water is of essential value to human beings, no distinct international right to water has been codified. With a more haphazard incorporation, provisions can be found in Articles 24(1)(c) CRC, 14(2)(h) CEDAW, 28 CRPD, 15(a) Additional Protocol to the ACHPR on the Rights of Women in Africa and 14(2) African Charter on the Rights and Welfare of the Child. These treaties recognise a duty of the sovereign to provide access to safe drinking water, and the CESCR has also 'read' this right in Articles 11 and 12 ICESCR. From a more general perspective, the CRPD quite uniquely has also asserted in Article 11 that states parties have the obligation to take 'all necessary measures' to ensure the protection of those with disabilities in humanitarian emergencies. Turning to soft law instruments, equally the well-known Vienna Declaration has asserted the importance of the provision of humanitarian assistance in the context of human rights. The provision of humanitarian assistance therefore functions as a method through which states can fulfil their duties under human rights law.[12]

International humanitarian law contains a variety of provisions specifically tailored to the delivery of assistance, formulated as *duties* of the sovereign rather than as rights of individuals to receive assistance. The law however differentiates the duties of the authorities (or non-state actors, depending on the circumstances) according to the situation in which the need for assistance arises. Should a humanitarian crisis arise in times of international armed conflict, non-international armed conflict or occupation, the duties are diverse. Whilst the latter is rarely topical in international law today, the opposite can be said for non-international armed conflicts. Upon examining the law, it becomes apparent that in an international armed conflict, Article 54 AP I contains the obligation to refrain from causing starvation amongst civilians, but the Geneva Conventions and Protocols do not contain a strong positive obligation to provide aid. From Article 70 AP I, referring to the fact that relief schemes 'shall be undertaken' when a civilian population is in need, a right to receive aid might be *inferred* at best, but is not explicitly mentioned.[13] Furthermore, 'military necessity' may be a reason for a state to temporarily delay or not be capable of providing aid, although it may not be utilised as an argument to withhold assistance entirely. In times of occupation, no explicit rights are mentioned, but duties rest upon the occupying force under Article 55 GC IV to ensure food and medical supplies in the territory if it should be inadequately supplied, under Article 56 to maintain hospitals, public health and prevention of epidemics (but all in cooperation with the local authorities) and under Article 69 AP I also to ensure clothing, shelter and other essential items for

[12] 6.3 Duties and Rights under Human Rights Law.

[13] 6.5.1.1 Duties of the Affected State in Times of an International Armed Conflict.

the civilian population.[14] Conversely, in times of non-international armed conflict, no specific rights to receive and no positive obligations to provide aid are codified. The provision of humanitarian assistance in times of a non-international armed conflict is based upon the duty to provide humane treatment as codified in common Article 3 of the Geneva Conventions, and the prohibition of starvation as incorporated in Article 14 AP II. Whereas 'military necessity' is not a grounds for exception in non-international armed conflicts, the Geneva Conventions and Protocols unfortunately are based upon the somewhat rosy perspective – reflecting the timeframe of their codification – that in a non-international armed conflict, the sovereign is inclined to provide for those in need upon its territory. Today, where civilian suffering is a constant integral *part* of warfare in non-international armed conflict, it is apparent that this view is no longer tenable.[15]

Chapter 6 has also addressed the rights and duties as available to those in times of natural disasters amounting to humanitarian crises. Human rights law remains applicable, and the General Assembly has – as noted above – asserted as early as 1991 a primary duty of the affected state in the provision of aid. A body of law tailored to the protection of persons in such times is currently under development with the ILC, and its Draft Articles call for a respect for human rights (Draft Article 6) and also such a primary duty for the state to ensure protection of persons through the provision of assistance on its territory (Draft Article 12). The likelihood of this codification initiative materialising into treaty law however remains to be seen. In current law, this duty has been codified regionally through Article IV(a) of the Inter-American Convention to Facilitate Disaster Assistance and Article 3 of ASEAN Disaster Management Agreement. Again, the absence of law indicates a presumption by the international community that the affected sovereign shall be keen to provide aid to its civilians, a presumption not always reflected in reality.[16]

Should emergencies cause the creation of groups of IDPs or refugees, several distinct duties pertaining to the provision of assistance can be found and the Security Council has asserted that such persons are entitled to protection.[17] Article 23 of the Refugee Convention notes that a state has the duty to treat refugees as its own nationals in the provision of public relief. Furthermore, Articles 22 CRC and 23 African Charter on the Rights and Welfare of the Child note a right to receive assistance as within the context of the enjoyment of the human rights in both conventions. The latter Charter also reflects the protection of IDPs. IDPs on the African continent are furthermore protected in the new Kampala Convention, which codifies a duty to ensure assistance to IDPs, in combination with the participation of IDPs in this process under Article 9. The same views are reflected in the non-binding, but well-known, Guiding Principles on Internal Displacement.

[14] 6.5.3 Duties of the Affected State (Occupying Power) in Times of Occupation.
[15] 6.5.1.2 Duties of the Affected State and Non-State Actor in Times of a Non-International Armed Conflict.
[16] 6.5.5 Duties of the Affected State in Times of (Natural) Disaster.
[17] 6.5.9 Duties of the Affected State under the (Potential) IDP Framework.

A limited protection can finally also be found in Article 17 AP II, prohibiting the forced movement of populations.

From the above reflection of the law as discussed in Chapter 6, it can be concluded that the current law is by no means all-encompassing. The applicable law is dependent on the specific circumstance amounting to a humanitarian crisis. Whilst a primary duty for the affected state or authority can be discerned, a need exists for harmonisation and a common minimum standard. Currently, a rather 'sectoral' protection exists, risking fragmentation in the law and in the level of protection for those in need. Although the international community is hesitant to recognise a right to receive aid, a duty to provide such assistance can be derived from the above. International humanitarian law contains several detailed provisions, but lacks general duties, in particular concerning non-international armed conflicts, often resulting in acute problems such as the issues seen in the protracted conflict in Syria. Conversely, human rights contain more general provisions, yet it can be argued that the law is specific enough to be considered the *lex specialis* on various occasions when international humanitarian law is lacking such duties. In particular, the human rights provisions regionally on the African continent and topically for children and IDPs are very suitable for the adequate fulfilment of such a role. In an attempt to fill certain gaps, soft law documents such as the San Remo Principles, the Bruges Resolution and the Mohonk Criteria all recognise a duty of the sovereign to provide aid, as well as a right to request the receipt of such assistance from the sovereign. Again, such recognition goes to the argument of existence of *opinio juris* on the matter, but does not fill the gaps in the *lex lata*.

Following an ascertainment of the legal rights and duties of the civilian population and the affected state, Chapter 7 expands upon this with the assessment of the legal framework concerning assistance from outside the affected territory; the examination of a potential right to offer and provide assistance, and a related right to access therefore. State sovereignty continues to function as a constant and consistent thread throughout international law and therefore also in this aspect of the research. In relation to external humanitarian assistance, sovereignty plays a continuing crucial role, as the state is the primary responsible actor for the provision of assistance.

In human rights law, a distinction can be made between the civil right to life, and the economic and social rights to food, health and water when considering the manner in which duties manifest themselves. As the right to life can be considered a right to be 'free from arbitrary deprivation' thereof, human rights law does not proscribe a specific duty of the affected state or right of third parties in human rights conventions to positively ensure such a right. Conversely, the rights to food and health in the ICESCR acknowledge an obligation of conduct of the affected state as well as in particular in Article 2 ICESCR, which includes a responsibility of the international community in cooperation and assistance to help the affected state. Article 2 ICESCR furthermore proscribes a duty of the affected state to in fact seek that international assistance in fulfilling the rights of the ICESCR. Whilst

Article 11 ICESCR does not allow for a 'right to access' in relation to the right to food as it evolves around state consent, of course resort may be had to enforcement mechanisms should certain core rights be violated. Similarly, Article 12 Additional Protocol to the ACHR in the area of Economic, Social and Cultural Rights and 15 Additional Protocol to the ACHPR on the Rights of Women in Africa recognise an obligation upon states parties to take measures in cooperating to ensure food security and ending malnutrition. Article 12 ICESCR pertaining to the right to health does not call for the consent of the affected state, but also does not formulate a right to access. As seen in Chapter 5 pertaining to the right to water, no consensus exists regarding such a right in international treaty or customary law and hence no right to access in this regard can be discerned.[18]

Support for a duty to cooperate in the fulfilment of human rights can also be found in the UN Charter and through the perspectives of various UN bodies, adding to the argument that some *opinio juris* exists on an emerging responsibility or duty to cooperate in the fulfilment of such human rights through the provision of humanitarian assistance, as reflected also in Article 2 ICESCR. Relevantly, the ICJ has as recently as 2007 declared in the *Georgia v. Russia* case a need to refrain from impediments to humanitarian assistance, in support of a population's human rights under the ICERD; such as concerning Articles 5 (b) regarding security of persons and (e) regarding economic, social and cultural rights. Such a formulation, although focusing on the duty-bearer to allow access, also appears to presuppose a right to offer assistance by third parties. In human rights law therefore, obligations of conduct and non-impediment of assistance can be found, as well as a potential responsibility of the international community to provide assistance in the fulfilment of human rights of the affected population.

Furthermore within the UN framework, the Security Council has as a primary actor in circumstances requiring the cooperation of the international community for many decades addressed the humanitarian responsibilities of the UN as well as making appeals to the international community of states to provide assistance in circumstances where it was needed. Increasingly, towards the end of the 20th century, the Council acted under Chapter VII and called upon the global responsibilities of the international community in various country-resolutions. In its resolutions, the Council does not differentiate between circumstances of international armed conflict or of non-international armed conflict, but bases itself solely on the establishment of a potential threat to the peace, providing a more egalitarian approach. Whilst such resolutions are not 'thematic', they are an indication of the perspective of the Council, as it commenced (in Resolution 688) formulating calls to the affected sovereign to 'allow access' as well as 'safe and unhindered' access and passage for the provision of assistance from 1991 onwards. Rather than formulating a right of third parties, the Council does so by calling upon the affected state to comply with its duties under international law. In fact, by arguing that the affected state should allow access for the provision of assistance in line with its duties under international law, the Council actually somewhat foregoes

[18] 7.3 The Provision of Humanitarian Assistance by Third Parties Under Human Rights Law.

a 'right to offer' as this is presupposed in such an assertion, to the point where the 'right to access' becomes the flip side of the coin of a duty of 'allowing access'. However, although the Council calls or urges the affected state to comply with the law, it does not actually assert a right to access of third parties. The furthest the Council has gone to date, acting under Chapter VII, is 'demanding' of the affected state to 'ensure' access and safe passage in compliance with its duties under international law, as done for example with regard to Iraq in 2003. In case-specific circumstances therefore, the Council has shown its willingness to act under Chapter VII of the UN Charter and assert a duty of the affected state to allow access for humanitarian aid, culminating in its novel approach towards Syria in 2014 where humanitarian assistance was called upon without force, but circumventing the state sovereign.[19]

Similar to the Security Council, the General Assembly has assumed a need for the international community to assist. In its well-known Resolution 46/182, the General Assembly has furthermore argued the need to strengthen the collective efforts of the international community in the provision of humanitarian aid and subsequently in the Millennium Declaration, the General Assembly has expressed the view that such provision is a shared, collective responsibility. Unlike the Security Council, the General Assembly has not expressed an international legal 'duty to provide' or a right to access a territory. Although such expressions would not have been legally binding, they would have expressed broad viewpoints from member states and as such contributed to the potential formation of customary norms. With time, the General Assembly has however broadened its scope when discussing humanitarian assistance, to include more complex emergencies and circumstances of conflict. At first asserting this need primarily in times of natural disaster, the General Assembly has broadened this to include times of 'war', and has argued that such assistance is an expression of the principle of international solidarity. In the late 1990s the General Assembly commenced reiterating the stance taken by the Security Council, using similar wording in resolutions, and thereby leading to the conclusion that indeed the overall impression from these UN bodies may be that a duty exists of affected states to allow access in compliance with norms in international law, which in itself is a presupposition of a right to offer assistance by third parties.[20]

Chapter 7 has furthermore addressed the rights and duties in the external provision of assistance in specific circumstances in international law, such as armed conflict and natural disaster. In case of international armed conflicts, Article 10 GC IV proscribes a right to offer assistance of international organisations, subject to the consent of the affected state, which must merely be seen as an invitation and not entailing legal duties. Article 23 GC IV cites an obligation of the affected state that passage 'shall' be allowed for relief, save for 'serious reasons'. Article 70(1) AP I then asserts that relief 'shall' be undertaken when a territory is inadequately supplied. This provision too is subject to agreement with the affected

[19] 7.4.2 Security Council Resolutions and the Right to Access.
[20] 7.4.4 General Assembly Resolutions and the Right to Access.

state, but the state does not have unlimited freedom in this regard as Article 70 AP I must be read in conjuncture with 54 AP I concerning the duty to refrain from starvation. The 'shall' in Article 70 AP I implies an obligation, and even if read in the least stringent manner, still entails a right to offer assistance. Article 70(2-5) AP I subsequently broadens the content of Article 23 GC IV, but balances this with further control rights of the affected state. Lastly, Article 71(2) AP I addresses the safety of humanitarian personnel, a prerequisite in the delivery of assistance. Thus, in an international armed conflict, again the right to offer assistance is somewhat presupposed, as deduced from the formulations in the provisions which call for a *duty* of the affected state to allow passage of humanitarian assistance, subject to various specific control rights and in specific circumstances the right of the affected state to refuse assistance.[21]

In non-international armed conflicts, Chapter 7 has seen a similar development from the Conventions to the Additional Protocols. Common Article 3 merely states that humanitarian organisations may offer 'services', whilst Article 18 AP II (to be read in line with Article 14 regarding the prohibition of starvation), states that 'relief actions shall be undertaken' when a population is suffering 'undue hardship', but again such relief is subject to consent of the 'concerned party'.[22] AP II assumes this party to be the state, but given the non-international character of the conflict, it has been argued that this may include a non-state actor acting as an authority, or alternatively when the authority is not to be determined, consent must be presupposed. In drafting Article 18 AP II, consensus was difficult to find concerning the concept of humanitarian access, and it is regrettable that stricter wording was not agreed upon, given the amount of problems faced today in non-international armed conflicts.

Conversely, as seen in Chapter 6 also, the law concerning humanitarian assistance in times of occupation is rather explicit: Article 59 GC IV states that an occupying power 'shall' accept relief if a territory is inadequately supplied, subject to control rights, and facilitate its rapid distribution according to Article 61 GC IV. The latter Article also declares that all states have a duty to allow the transit of such assistance. As seen before, the law of occupation stems from the circumstances in World War II and in subsequent times has not been developed much: Article 69 AP I succinctly declares that civilians in times of occupation are subject to the provisions of GC IV and AP I. Hence, it can be concluded that similar to circumstances of armed conflict, an offer to provide external assistance is presupposed, the occupying force has an obligation to accept assistance when a territory is inadequately supplied, and it continues to exercise control rights over the provision of assistance.

Chapter 7 has shown that – as is the case in the legal framework pertaining to the duties of the affected state – no specific field of law is applicable in times of external provision of assistance in the aftermath of (natural) disasters. Whilst human rights law and general principles of international law are applicable at all

[21] 7.5.2.1 The Potential Right to Access in Times of International Armed Conflict.
[22] 7.5.2.2 The Potential Right to Access in Times of Non-International Armed Conflict.

times, very few conventions are tailored to address the external provision of assistance. An example includes the Inter-American Convention to Facilitate Disaster Relief, which presupposes an offer of assistance, but leaves the power to accept such an offer in the hands of the affected state, thereby not addressing a right to access. Should however the sovereign concede to access, then Article V asserts that such access shall be fully facilitated. Also, the ASEAN Agreement on Disaster Management and Emergency Response recognises a duty of states to promptly respond to the affected states' requests for aid in Article 4(c), thereby envisioning an international duty to cooperate. This duty is furthermore reflected in Article 8, asserting an obligation of states to coordinate the provision of aid amongst themselves, whilst Articles 3 and 11(2) continue to assert the right of the affected state to consent to assistance. Thus, these smaller regional conventions – although in areas of the world prone to disasters – envision a right of the affected state to consent, as opposed to a right to access for third parties. However, the ASEAN Agreement does reflect, as seen earlier in human rights law and the UN Security Council and General Assembly resolutions, a duty to cooperate for third states. A similar approach regarding cooperation and consent is held by the Convention on Assistance in the Case of a Nuclear Accident or Radiological Emergency in Articles 1 and 3. With a view to potential future regulation in times of disaster, the ILC Draft Articles explicitly formulate a right to offer assistance in Draft Article 16, and calls upon states to cooperate in Articles 8 and 9. As reflected in *lex lata*, Draft Article 14 asserts that consent continues to be required, although it may not be withheld arbitrarily, and according to Article 15 the affected state may place conditions on the provision of external assistance: a reflection of the 'control rights' as seen in international humanitarian law.[23]

With regard to the external delivery of assistance, not only circumstances but also specific *subjects* may be of relevance, such as refugees. The nature of refugee law does not exactly allow for provisions relating to the access of a territory. The Refugee Convention merely states in Article 23 that refugees in this sense must be treated as a state's national, given the fact that the third state is the *recipient* state. The regional African Kampala Convention on IDPs interestingly restricts offers from, and the seeking of assistance by, the affected state to 'international organizations', merely referring to 'other relevant actors' in Article 5(6) which could be interpreted as third states. Articles 3(1)(j) and 5(7) declare that the affected state must allow and facilitate the rapid and unimpeded access of humanitarian assistance, a duty which is also upheld for armed groups in Article 7(5)(b) and (g). Again, as other provisions have done, the Convention formulates such allowance of assistance as a duty of the affected state, rather than as a right of external parties. Furthermore, it remains problematic to the protection of IDPs – a group associated both with natural disasters and non-international armed conflicts – that only a regional binding document such as the Kampala Convention serves for their specific protection.[24] Outside of the African continent, no binding

[23] 7.5.6 The Potential Right to Access in Times of (Natural) Disaster.
[24] 7.5.10 The Potential Right to Access under the (Potential) IDP Framework.

provisions exist, although both the UN General Assembly and other UN bodies have expressed their concern in this regard.

The discussion of the legal framework on the external provision of humanitarian assistance in Chapter 7 has brought several clear gaps in the rights and duties to the forefront. A (legal) right of third parties to offer humanitarian assistance is often presupposed, and taken for granted. The law tends to commence its regulation at a 'next' step or level: access. The notion of access however is not formulated from the perspective of the external providers, but rather from the perspective of an obligation of the affected state to *allow* such access for the provision of aid. Throughout the various bodies of law, a consensus can be found to exist with regard to the initial power of the affected state to 'consent' to the delivery of aid, but no consensus exists on the threshold of such consent. Such consent can be subject to various degrees of sovereignty or freedom, depending on the 'arbitrariness' of the refusal, but consent as a concept nevertheless continues to play a crucial role. Such a role for the sovereign is also seen in the formulation in international humanitarian law that a territory must be determined 'inadequately supplied'. Yet, no definition of this, or of 'arbitrary denial' is provided, nor is the abuse of 'control rights' precluded. What however also surfaces, in a *positive* development, is the recognition throughout the various bodies of law, that an (emerging) duty of the international community exists to cooperate in the provision of humanitarian assistance. As such the UN Security Council and General Assembly resolutions contribute to the formation of *opinio juris* and state practice, in conjuncture with the various conventions. Furthermore, from the developments in the various *corpora juris*, it can also be concluded that at times, a duty to allow access exists: consent must be provided when its refusal would amount to a violation of international law such as for example the right to food.

It must, however, be noted that the proliferation of 'sectoral' regulations and codifications result in this present wide range of provisions and diversity regarding the aspect of the provision of aid by third parties in the legal framework on the provision of assistance. Each individual circumstance in which assistance may be necessary has been subject to a variety of different regulations and conventions, such as the Kampala Convention or the ASEAN Agreement. As such, the rights and duties vary greatly according to the specific circumstances, and whilst the Kampala Convention for example may serve to aid IDPs in Africa, it may hinder a more comprehensive protection internationally. A minimum level of protection is difficult to discern, as the control rights and consent thresholds vary throughout the bodies of law, the regions and the circumstances. A lack of clarity ensues concerning the responsibilities of various rights-holders and duty-bearers. To this end, the various soft law doctrines on the topic all recognise a third party's right to offer assistance, and a duty of the affected state not to arbitrarily refuse such an offer. Furthermore, the San Remo Principles and the Bruges Resolution also note an obligation to allow for safe passage, and the latter asserts an obligation of the affected state to seek assistance from third parties. In order to coerce the international community to pursue the international provision of humanitarian assistance, clarity is needed in the determination of the extent to which assistance can be 'enforced', which is what Chapter 8 has sought to deliver.

The *enforcement* of the provision of humanitarian assistance touches the very core of the relationship between humanitarian assistance and state sovereignty. Legal enforcement of assistance is possible if and when a sovereign is in violation of international law by denying those in need of the aid they are entitled to. A violation of international law exists when (1) a humanitarian crisis warranting the delivery of humanitarian assistance exists, (2) the affected state is not providing (sufficient) assistance and (3) a lawful offer of external assistance is refused for reasons outside of those allowed for in international human rights and humanitarian law. If these circumstances take place, (4) a violation of international law occurs as the affected state is obstructing or denying the provision of humanitarian assistance, resulting in enforcement possibilities. Currently in international law, such assessments are made by either the Security Council, or judicial entities such as the ICJ, ICC or human rights bodies.[25]

Chapter 8 has addressed the various methods through which the enforcement of assistance might take place, upon the establishment of state responsibility for the violation of international law. State responsibility arises under Articles 2 and 3 ARSIWA and is today no longer considered purely bilateral, as considered by the ICJ in the *Barcelona Traction*-case (amongst other cases). This assessment is particularly relevant to the establishment of responsibility by other states for the non-provision of assistance by the affected state. Articles 42 ARSIWA (invocation by an injured state) and somewhat more progressively Article 48 ARSIWA (invocation by the international community) assert a responsibility that is owed towards a larger community, such as states parties to a treaty, or responsibility for a violation of a norm of customary international law. Attribution of acts to the state is possible under Articles 4-11 ARSIWA, and although Articles 20-25 ARSIWA note circumstances precluding wrongfulness, with regard to the provision of humanitarian assistance only Article 23 may potentially be argued and it will most likely not be accepted given the nature of such provision. Relevant to the provision of humanitarian assistance, by means of enforcement through state responsibility potentially in combination with the use of force, Articles 40 and 41 ARSIWA assert a duty for states to cooperate in the ending of breaches of peremptory norms. With regard to humanitarian assistance, such violations of norms of *jus cogens* are the commission of racial discrimination, war crimes, crimes against humanity and genocide. The principle of humanity is furthermore also placed within the context of intransgressible norms of international law. Thus, the law of state responsibility distinctly places a duty not only upon the affected state not to commit such acts, but also upon the international community to cooperate in ending their commission.[26] The ICJ has supported this stance in its 2007 *Bosnian Genocide*-case, arguing an obligation of conduct to end the commission of genocide. This perspective is also voiced in Article 89 AP II, where third states are called upon to

[25] 8.3.3 The Denial or Obstruction of Assistance: a Violation of International Law.

[26] 8.2.3 State Responsibility and the Potential Duty to Cooperate in the Event of a Breach.

cooperate with a view to ending 'serious violations' of the Geneva Conventions taking place in a non-international armed conflict. Equally, with a view to the future, the ILC Draft Articles on the protection of persons in the event of disasters deduce a 'secondary role' for third states in the provision of assistance in Draft Article 12 and also reflected in Draft Article 8; although the Articles are too hesitant to assert such a role as 'responsibility'.

State responsibility can be enforced through judiciary means, largely utilised after a crisis has taken place. An alternative method of enforcement at this state *vis-à-vis* state level, is the use of force under the auspices of the UN Security Council. The use of force must naturally always be seen as an ultimate resort, upon establishment by the Security Council that a threat to the peace according to Article 39 exists (to date it is not used in cases of natural disasters), and as a potential mechanism to give effect to prior measures such as those under Articles 40 and 41 of the UN Charter. The Security Council has the role of enforcer in this regard, with a view to Articles 2(4), 25 and 103 UN Charter. A determination by this body that the use of force may be warranted to ensure the provision of humanitarian aid simultaneously functions as the determination that in fact (1) a territory is inadequately supplied at a times of crisis and (2) the affected state is not providing for those in need within its jurisdiction or not allowing aid into the territory. It remains essential when discussing the use of force as an enforcement mechanism to distinguish between those *providing* the emergency aid, and those *enforcing* it; in order to allow those providing aid to adhere to the core principles of neutrality, impartiality and humanity. The Council has alluded to the use of force by asserting a need for 'appropriate measures' in its Resolution 1265 on the protection of civilians, and equally has cautiously eased into the use of force in the early 1990s in Somalia and the Former Yugoslavia, for the purpose of the delivery of aid, although state sovereignty remained a constant factor. Over time, peacekeeping operations have been entrusted with the enforcement of humanitarian assistance and from the turn of the century, increasingly coalitions of states have been entrusted to do so too. The Security Council is comfortable asserting a need to provide assistance under Chapter VII, but this also includes measures under Article 40 as opposed to solely the use of force in Article 42. With the recognition of the doctrine of the Responsibility to Protect, and continuing with thematic resolutions pertaining to the protection of civilians, the use of force also with regard to the provision of aid, has become more embedded, such as in Somalia through troops of the African Union in 2007. The Security Council in particular has increasingly referred to violations of international law as a reason leading to these forceful actions.[27] A well-known and discussed example is Resolution 1973 (2011) where under RtoP, the use of force was asserted in particular relation to the provision of humanitarian assistance in Libya. Since then however, the Council has been hesitant, which leaves a clear line lacking in the Council's work.

It is apparent from previous country-specific resolutions that the Council is willing to use force *for the purpose of the delivery of aid*, yet in which

[27] 8.4.3 Security Council Action since the UN embracement of the Responsibility to Protect.

circumstances and with what threshold, is currently not to be distilled. Such reasoning of course also lies within the political mandate of the Council. Yet, useful on the other hand is the increasing level of specificity in the Council's resolutions, which is helpful in providing more clarity in distilling the direction of the body. Chapter 8 has concluded that the Council *does* in fact see itself fit to resort to the use of force *for the purpose of the provision of aid*, with and on occasion without, the cooperation of the sovereign. Whilst in practice a more 'standard' formulation or threshold might not be viable, it would be necessary or at least helpful to ascertain some more consistency in the work of the Council, as its inactivity in Syria (despite the more recent authorisation of humanitarian assistance without the consent of Syrian authorities) is a painful failure to act, following the assertive resolutions concerning Libya. Furthermore, should the scope of the concept 'threat to the peace' as formulated in Article 39 UN Charter be given a wide interpretation so as to not be exclusively reserved for armed conflicts, they might include for example widespread crimes against humanity. Such crimes are relevant with regard to the provision of humanitarian assistance, and although they no longer need a nexus to an armed conflict, they do by nature result in a threat to the peace. In such instances, Security Council action might in the future also be possible in circumstances of natural disaster. Again, as in the case of Syria, the Council's inaction in the face of disasters such as the one in Myanmar following cyclone Nargis make the political character of the body painfully apparent. Indeed the notion of sovereignty, changing over the decades, would also allow for a more active role of the Council in circumstances where the consent of the affected state is lacking, and the potential duty to cooperate under the law of state responsibility discussed above furthermore supports such an attitude.

From the enforcement of assistance through to the use of force, at an inter-state level, Chapter 8 has progressed to the level of enforcement of assistance through human rights law. Human rights treaty bodies such as the HRC, CESCR and regional courts like the ECtHR recognise both inter-state and individual complaint mechanisms. The inter-state mechanism, although a reflection of the concept of shared responsibility as codified in Article 48 ARSIWA, has proven too political to be used in practice. Both the HRC and CESCR have also not had the opportunity to express themselves regarding the provision of humanitarian assistance through the individual complaint mechanism, the latter due to the fact that it has only recently opened up to such a mechanism. A problem may also well lie in the 'obligation of conduct'-nature of the rights enshrined in the ICESCR, as the minimum core obligations the states parties must fulfil at all times might not be sufficiently explicit to allow for such an individual complaint mechanism. The HRC, however, has addressed its concerns regarding humanitarian assistance and Article 6 ICCPR in its own investigations. Both bodies, although legal in nature, do not have the power to create binding legal findings, but have both asserted that the non-provision of humanitarian aid may amount to a violation of the rights in their respective Conventions.[28] The ECtHR has in its case law touched upon the non-

[28] 8.5.1 Enforcement through Human Rights Treaty Mechanisms.

provision of humanitarian assistance, although not in direct correlation to a violation of a human right, but calling it a 'serious abuse'. Furthermore, rather than placing such an abuse in the context of the right to life, the ECtHR addressed it in relation to torture. Thus, the main human rights bodies have not (yet) taken it upon themselves to determine in specific cases brought before them whether or not an affected state *in casu* violated international human rights law by falling short of the obligation to ensure the provision of assistance in the fulfilment of the rights to life, food and health. Conversely, the ICJ has in the *Georgia v. Russia*-case asserted that the non-provision of assistance may amount to a violation of the rights enshrined in the ICERD.

A second human rights approach used for enforcement, rather than the legal treaty bodies, is through the more political UN mechanisms under the Human Rights Council, such as the UPR system and the Special Rapporteurs. As a political mechanism, these Rapporteurs are often very vocal and they have on many occasions asserted states' violations of human rights when denying the provision of assistance. The inter-state UPR rather focuses on recommendations, inciting states to allow or facilitate humanitarian assistance. Rather than 'naming and shaming', such a positive formulation may help in the creation of more willingness to allow for external assistance, although the political nature of these mechanisms continues to overshadow their potential value.

From a different viewpoint of enforcement, Chapter 8 has discussed two methods of individual responsibility for the non-provision of humanitarian assistance in international law. Firstly, the possibility to bring about 'targeted sanctions' towards individuals and their assets has increasingly been utilised by the Security Council in recent years following violations of international law in particular relation also to the obstruction and denial of humanitarian assistance. Specifically, the Council has opted for enforcement mechanisms such as travel bans and financial asset freezing targeted towards those individuals and entities the Council assessed as having obstructed humanitarian aid. Such sanctions provide a specific coercion mechanism to entice those involved in conflict to allow access for the providers of assistance, without resorting to force which may have an impact on society as a whole on a larger scale.[29]

Moreover, aside from targeted sanctions, individual responsibility for specific *crimes* in international criminal law – reflecting violations of human rights law and international humanitarian law, has been addressed. Two specific crimes in the ICC Statute are most relevant for the incurrence of individual responsibility for such violations that pertain to the denial of the provision of aid, namely war crimes and crimes against humanity.

The ICC Statute criminalises violations of international humanitarian law as war crimes in Article 8 of its Statute, and differentiates between provisions tailored towards an international and a non-international armed conflict. Concerning the former, several provisions within Article 8 ICC Statute are most relevant in relation to the obstruction of aid. Article 8(2)(b)(xxv) criminalises the use of starvation by

[29] 8.6.1 Enforcement through Targeted Sanctions.

depriving civilians of means for survival, Article 8(2)(b)(iii) concerns the unlawfulness of attacks on those providing humanitarian assistance, to which Article 8(2)(b)(xxiv) is closely related, concerning attacks on personnel. Furthermore, Article 8(2)(a)(iii) concerning the wilful causing of 'great suffering, or serious injury to body or health' is considered a grave breach of international humanitarian law and arguably the non-provision of humanitarian assistance, when amounting to such serious injury, would also be considered such a breach. For the above crimes, a level of intentionality and knowledge is required, which is however not required for Article 8(2)(a)(ii) concerning 'inhuman treatment' and might therefore be argued more easily concerning the withholding of humanitarian aid, although being less tailored as a provision in and of itself. Furthermore, the ICC provisions concerning attacks that result in damages to the environment (Article 8(2)(b)(iv)) or acts that lead to 'outrages upon personal dignity' (Article 8(2)(b)(xxi)), can be violated, when they lead to obstructing humanitarian assistance. Concerning the former, an assumption is made regarding the presupposition of knowledge of the extent of the damages caused, and it must be excessive in relation to military advantages, formulating a reflection of the principle of proportionality. 'Outrages upon personal dignity' can be placed within a human rights context, allowing the argument that violations of the right to life, food, or health may have occurred resulting in such outrages when humanitarian assistance is not provided, but must at least amount to humiliation, degradation or other violations of dignity. Throughout the criminalisation of war crimes in an international armed conflict, military necessity remains an argument to which those being held responsible may resort in their defence.

Such an argument cannot be made in times of non-international armed conflict. Many of the provisions of the ICC Statute are similar, but not all acts are criminalised in the same manner. In a non-international armed conflict, Article 8 ICC Statute does *not* criminalise starvation as a method of warfare, which *has* been recognised by Article 14 AP II and conviction is thus only possible should the ICC accept it as a norm of customary international law and would then be incorporated through Article 21 ICC Statute, an argument that has been made by the ICRC.[30] Also absent is Article 8(2)(b)(iv) concerning damages to the environment from the provisions of Article 8 ICC Statute with regard to non-international armed conflicts, as is Article 8(2)(a)(iii) regarding the 'grave breach' of doing wilful damage to a person's health. Yet, attacking those persons or objects involved in the provision of humanitarian assistance shall amount to war crimes (Article 8(2)(e)(ii) and (iii)) needing a level of intentionality and awareness that the objects of the attack were under protection of the Geneva Conventions, as is the case for international armed conflicts. Also the concept of 'outrages upon personal dignity' which is criminalised according to Article 8(2)(c)(ii) ICC Statute is recognised as unlawful in times of non-international armed conflicts.[31]

[30] In these circumstances, Article 22 ICC Statute regarding the principle of 'nullum crimen sine lege' must be taken into consideration.
[31] 8.6.2.1 War Crimes and Humanitarian Assistance

Conversely to the situation of war crimes, no nexus to an armed conflict is necessary for the categorisation of a crime as a crime against humanity, which allows for prosecution of such crimes under all circumstances relevant to the provision of assistance. As such, whilst both war crimes and crimes against humanity may give rise to responsibilities (amongst which the resort to the use of force) under the RtoP doctrine, this is especially relevant given that such responsibilities might now also arise outside the framework of an armed conflict. A resort may be had to the use of force should a threat to the peace in the widest sense be asserted by the Security Council, as discussed above. In practice however, this has yet to be ascertained. Key to the assessment of an act as a crime against humanity, is the fact that it must have occurred 'as part of a widespread or systematic attack', which in the context of the unlawful deprivation of humanitarian assistance means that a form of systematic or widespread targeting of a particular group must have taken place, or in the alternative, a single strategic action with the *intent* of impacting a large group of people. Article 7(1)(b) (k) and 7(2) ICC Statute criminalise the 'deprivation of access to food and medicine' as part of the 'extermination' of civilians as well as 'other inhumane acts', the latter of which are explained as an infliction of 'serious injury to body or to mental or physical health, by means of an inhumane act'. Whilst the provisions relevant to the criminalisation of the denial or obstruction of humanitarian assistance are clearly not as elaborate as the provisions concerning war crimes, it is interesting to note that the deliberate choice was made to include the 'deprivation of access to food and medicine' *within* the Statute of the ICC, rather than as an explanation in the Elements of the Crimes. Such an inclusion can only be considered as an acknowledgment of the seriousness of the violation of international law that the obstruction or denial of humanitarian assistance constitutes. Whilst intentionality is difficult to argue, and shall have to occur on a case-by-case basis, case law has given indications with regard to the notion of how 'widespread' extermination must be to amount to a crime against humanity as opposed to singular persons. As such the ICTY has argued that less than 1700 people, and in referral to the Nuremberg Tribunal, less than 800 people, may be a sufficiently large group of persons to amount to the collective and widespread element of such a crime.[32] Indeed, the notion of a *humanitarian crisis* will by its very nature affect a larger amount of persons, making it possible to 'fit the profile' of a crime against humanity.

Lastly, Chapter 8 has addressed the manner in which enforcement of humanitarian assistance might take place should a state sovereign be absent in a territory. A distinction has been made in circumstances where a level of authority exists, such as certain organised non-state actors in non-international armed conflicts, which carry responsibilities in international law that have been addressed throughout this research, and situations where in fact authorities are absent such as in failed states or even complex emergencies. Problems arise as no primary responsible actor is present, leading to a vacuum in the primary responsibility.

[32] 8.6.2.2 Crimes Against Humanity and Humanitarian Assistance.

Article 9 ARSIWA argues for a responsibility of *de facto* regimes, whereas the ICJ in its *Namibia*-Opinion is somewhat more pragmatic, arguing that actual physical control of a territory as opposed to 'sovereignty or legitimacy of title' serves as the basis for liability in international law. It is indeed generally accepted in international law today that – as established in this research – those in *de facto* control or non-state actors carry obligations under human rights law and humanitarian law. Yet, enforcement mechanisms in human rights law do not allow non-state actors to be held accountable in their courts or before their council or committee, nor can they be held responsible by the ICJ. Equally, whilst addressing individuals, Articles 7 and 8 ICC Statute assume some form of responsibility, either through a sense of authority in *de facto* regimes and armed groups or the existence of persons exercising governmental authority. These enforcement mechanisms are therefore merely relevant in the circumstance that 'some' form of authority exists. In the assumption that no request has been made to the international community welcoming the provision of aid, or that no sovereign authority is identifiable, resort may be had to the Security Council, in line with the doctrine of RtoP, as the international community takes on a responsibility in the absence of a sovereign to provide aid. The *Commentary* to Article 18 AP II envisions such action too, as it argues a level of consent is presumed in circumstances of uncertainty of a sovereign. As judicial bodies are unable to deal with circumstances of denial of aid in the absence of a responsible actor, the Security Council – as the designated authoritative body dealing with impending crises – shall therefore be considered the most appropriate enforcer of humanitarian assistance in such circumstances and when the crisis is still on-going.[33] With a potential future perspective, the ILC Draft Articles appear to follow the line of reasoning of the *Commentary* to AP II, as Draft Article 14(3) cites that the affected state shall 'whenever possible, make its decision regarding the offer known' pursuant to an external offer of assistance, which has been explained by the Drafting Committee as an acknowledgement of the possibility that consent must be implied in the circumstance a functioning sovereign is absent. This stands to reason, as in the absence of a sovereign wilfully denying aid or access for its delivery, the affected persons remain in need of assistance.

The final Chapter of this research has assessed the manner in which international law allows for the enforcement of the provision of aid, which in fact, considering the amount of gaps in the earlier stages of the research, are relatively satisfying. Although some of the provisions in the ARSIWA are considered progressive development, a responsibility (if not duty) to cooperate in the enforcement of assistance in order to end violations of humanitarian law or human rights law – general human suffering – can be discerned. Indeed, whilst none of the bodies with authority in the matter of enforcement: the ICJ, Security Council, ICC and human rights bodies are all-encompassing or infallible, their combined strength allows for enforcement mechanisms in a variety of ways. A large gap however remains in the international judicial enforcement of the denial of humanitarian

[33] 8.7 The Enforcement of Humanitarian Assistance and the Absence of a Sovereign.

assistance by non-state actors. However, such entities might be held accountable before the ICC or in national proceedings. The Security Council as a political and 'forceful' body must in fact be differentiated from legal and judiciary bodies. The various types of enforcement bodies fulfil different roles, from specific case-assessments after the fact as done by the ICJ, ICC and human rights bodies, to immediate decisions in the midst of a crisis as done by the Security Council. As such, each functions in its own merit, but the fact remains that not one 'single' high authority exists in international law, to determine enforcement in *all* circumstances of humanitarian crisis. As seen above, the Security Council restrains its actions to circumstances reflecting a threat to the international peace, which to date has meant refraining from action in times of natural disaster. Yet, as has been seen in the discussed interaction between the RtoP doctrine and the notion of a crime against humanity, such crimes no longer warrant a nexus to armed conflict and as such may now, as a core crime of RtoP as established in the World Summit Outcome Document, potentially trigger Security Council action. Lastly, it has become apparent that enforcement in the absence of a sovereign is obtained largely via inference, clearly not the strongest or most reliable method. These gaps point out the need to strengthen the law, also in this final aspect of the legal framework on the provision of humanitarian assistance.

9.2 Recommendations for Improvement of the Legal Framework Concerning Humanitarian Assistance

The above conclusions have distilled the current *lex lata* pertaining to the provision of humanitarian assistance and laid bare the gaps in the law. Prior to addressing these gaps in more depth and discussing potential solutions, it is relevant to establish which legal framework can be discerned for the provision of humanitarian assistance in times of a humanitarian *crisis*, that is to say: which rights and duties exist *at all times*, regardless of the factual circumstances on the ground, provided that the circumstance meets the threshold of the notion of a 'humanitarian crisis' as defined in this research. Humanitarian assistance need only be provided if it can be ascertained that such a *crisis* is taking place; acknowledged by all parties involved and/or a relevant authoritative body in international law. Such an assessment will prevent legal disputes concerning the status of the situation and thereby also the legality of the provision of assistance. The basic threshold for the provision of assistance therefore commences with the assessment that a humanitarian crisis is taking or has taken place.

Following on from this, it is important to assess which aspects of the legal framework result in legally binding obligations for states or other actors. This assessment firmly brings the framework regarding the delivery of humanitarian assistance from the notion of an 'imperfect obligation', not entailing binding legal duties, into the realm of 'perfect obligations' that do not allow as much leeway and oblige actors to abide by their legal duties and rights.

9.2.1 The Basic Existing Legal Framework and Problems with Fragmentation

It has become very apparent that the law varies according to circumstances, leading to much more explicit provisions for the delivery of humanitarian aid in times of applicability of humanitarian law, as well as, recently, for those falling within the scope of the Kampala Convention. How can we explain that no aid is provided because those who needed it were 'merely' victims of a natural disaster and the international community did not enforce it? Or, as argued by the UN High Commissioner for Refugees, because the persons in need of assistance lived in certain 'parts of the world'?[34] That simply will not do. It is precisely for this purpose that this research has taken a more overarching, comprehensive and integral view of the delivery of humanitarian assistance and its legal framework. In 2007, the ICRC noted how dispersed, underutilised and lacking harmonisation the law can be in disaster relief.[35] Fragmentation of the law is a serious problem in the provision of humanitarian assistance, as it leads to a lack of clarity concerning the applicable law in certain given circumstances. Regional and 'sectoral' law are the effects of such fragmentation, creating a patchwork, as opposed to a single framework. Fragmentation is furthermore exacerbated by the legal difficulties surrounding the simultaneous applicability of various bodies of law, as well as potential domestic legal regulations. Such problems continue to highlight the undesirable circumstance that certain types of emergencies or locations might result in more or less provision of aid, whilst the persons in need continue to share one single common denominator: a need for humanitarian assistance. It is precisely this *need* which should define *them* and determine the *law*, as opposed to being defined by their location in the world. Throughout this research, an attempt has therefore been made to discern those rights and duties that are continuous, regardless of the specific circumstance where humanitarian assistance may be needed.

Firstly, this research has shown that the notion of state sovereignty entails a *responsibility* of the sovereign towards all persons under its jurisdiction, which coincides with the primary responsibility in the provision of humanitarian assistance lying with the affected state itself. This duty is also recognised by the UN Security Council and General Assembly and is also embraced in the notion of the Responsibility to Protect. Indeed the legal developments concerning the provision of humanitarian assistance and those regarding the notion of state sovereignty as responsibility reinforce and mutually support each other.

Secondly, whereas no independent human right to receive humanitarian assistance exists, its provision is a vehicle in the fulfilment of the rights to life,

[34] Repertoire of the Practice of the Security Council (1996-1999), Chapter VIII, 'Consideration of questions under the responsibility of the Security Council for the maintenance of international peace and security' Section 40 Promoting peace and security: humanitarian assistance to refugees in Africa 766.

[35] ICRC Resolutions, 30th International Conference (Geneva, 26-30 November 2007) § preamble.

food and health as enshrined in the ICCPR and ICESCR that both have widespread accession. The rights to life (which is excluded from derogation in times of emergency), food and health (for which the state must continue to fulfil the minimum core obligations) continue to be applicable at all times, resulting in an obligation of the affected state to provide humanitarian assistance in times of crisis in order to fulfil its obligations under international human rights law. This includes refraining from the impediment of assistance. As such, human rights law forms a legal basis for the provision of humanitarian assistance in all circumstances amounting to a humanitarian crisis.

Thirdly, the current law can be seen to *presuppose* the right of the international community – including both international organisations and third states – to offer the provision of humanitarian assistance, provided that such delivery abides by the principles of humanity, neutrality and impartiality. The offer and provision of such neutral, humane and impartial assistance cannot be considered an infringement on the affected state's sovereignty.

Lastly, whilst no general right to access a territory exists, upon the initial consent to access by the affected state, a duty rests on said state to facilitate the passage of aid and provide a safe environment for its provision. Furthermore, consent may not be arbitrarily withheld, and the Security Council has, in line with obligations under human rights law, asserted in some specific instances that a duty to allow access exists. State sovereignty is therefore curtailed by the international legal duties under human rights law (such as Article 2 ICESCR), as well as following Security Council assertions, to allow access for the provision of humanitarian assistance.

Whilst these basic duties exist *at all times* in the law today, international law is of course ever changing, and new norms are continually emerging. Indeed, one such emerging norm is the responsibility of the international community to cooperate, based on provisions in the ARSIWA, Additional Protocol II, ICJ jurisprudence, human rights law and Security Council resolutions, in ending circumstances of denial of humanitarian assistance, as such denial is a violation of international law. In other words: an emerging responsibility exists for the international community to contribute to the provision of humanitarian assistance.

Creating *more* law is however not necessarily the solution and does not necessarily help persons facing an emergency. Proper application of the law which exists, and which can be applied *to all circumstances amounting to a humanitarian crisis*, will provide more clarity and will – relevantly – also align with the principle of human dignity. Equity and the principle of humanity can be considered as a source of law to fill lacunae. In a similar manner, the General Assembly and ILC Draft Articles on the protection of persons consider the principle of solidarity as a basis upon which a duty to cooperate might exist for the international community (although it is not explicitly incorporated in the Draft Articles).[36] For this purpose, it is relevant

[36] 7.4.3 General Assembly Resolutions and the Right to Offer Assistance.

to distil the remaining needs for the existing comprehensive and overarching legal framework. Many tools are present, and bringing them together will allow for equal protection of all those in need of humanitarian assistance. Without attempting to 'universalise' certain legal provisions into applications for which they were not designed, it is possible to assert which sources of law are available to potentially fill the gaps in the current patchwork of law pertaining to the provision of assistance. The cornerstone notion of human dignity clearly supports such an overarching approach to the provision of assistance. Furthermore, the principles of humanity and solidarity stress the importance of the need to treat all humans equally, as codified also in the UN Charter and supported by the ICJ's assertion that the principle of humanity is related to the intransgressible norms of international law. Such principles may serve as a basis upon which this framework is founded. Protection of individuals' rights, by way of the provision of humanitarian assistance, must therefore be ensured in times of a humanitarian crisis.

9.2.2 Fixing the Problems and Gaps in the Law

The above research has pointed out areas in which the law is missing necessary provisions, or areas in which fragmentation has led to other issues in protection. It must be noted that the solutions offered attempt to find a realistic and pragmatic conjoining and synchronisation between the *practical realities* faced in times of crisis, and the *legal rights and legitimate needs* of those in need of assistance. It is precisely this that Henry Dunant attempted to do nearly two centuries ago.

Firstly, this research has pointed out that a single definition of both the notion of humanitarian assistance and the concept of a natural disaster are lacking. Whilst this may not amount to legal problems *per se*, those involved in the provision of assistance both from a practical and legal perspective, may benefit from the development of one generally used and applicable definition of 'humanitarian assistance' as well as that of a 'natural disaster', such as the definitions proposed in this research.[37] Furthermore, as multiple actors in the provision of aid held diverse views as to the principles according to which such aid is provided, a common denominator in the principles of humanity, neutrality and impartiality had to be distilled. Also, the division of legal protection according to circumstances such as conflict or disaster do not enhance equal protection, resulting in the suggestion of the notion of a 'humanitarian crisis' in this research, to form a single basis upon which the legal framework can operate.

Prior to addressing the existing problems and gaps in the legal framework, such problems and gaps are therefore immediately apparent at the outset, due to a lack of synchronisation of what in fact the framework *is* and *where* its boundaries lie. A delimitation has therefore been made regarding the notion of 'humanitarian

[37] 9.1 Conclusions Pertaining to the Existing Legal Framework.

assistance', the principles for its provision and the concept of a 'humanitarian crisis'.

Secondly, regarding the existing legal framework, it is first and foremost clear that an individual human right to receive humanitarian assistance is lacking. Such an absence in the human rights framework, however, is not problematic, nor should such a right necessarily be created: the absence can well be compensated by acknowledging that provision of assistance is a vehicle in the fulfilment of the existing rights to life, food and health, as can be done in international law today.[38] Whilst these individual human rights do not contain many specificities pertaining to the delivery of aid, the ICJ has determined that at the very least, states must ensure to abide by non-discrimination measures in such provision. Ascertaining that the delivery of emergency aid functions as the fulfilment of the rights to life, food and health in times of a humanitarian crisis will allow for the elaboration of this by various human rights courts, without the need to develop new regulations. Indeed, this provision is the fulfilment of the 'minimum core obligations' that must be respected at all times, as enshrined in the ICESCR.

Thirdly, whilst humanitarian law contains various detailed provisions pertaining to aid, it lacks a *general* codification of the duty of the affected state to provide assistance in times of a crisis. In particular in the increasingly frequent circumstances of non-international armed conflicts over the past decades, such an absence is painfully visible in the realities on the ground. The result is a fragmentation of regulations that does not enhance the protection of persons in need. A solution may be sought in the approach to the *lex specialis*-doctrine in this research. It has been suggested that the most specific clause – in this field concerning the provision of assistance thereby also the most protective clause – must be adhered to as opposed to considering an entire body of law the most specialised law. In times of a humanitarian crisis, such an interpretation would allow for the assertion of duties of the affected state to provide assistance to be found in human rights law or general international law principles such as concerning state sovereignty or the principle of humanity. Indeed, the developments regarding human rights law over the past century have influenced the concept of state sovereignty, which has evolved with time to incorporate a responsibility to protect its citizens. Such a general duty to provide assistance can therefore be sought in the more overarching concept of state sovereignty and the more broadly applicable human rights law. Through this approach to the *lex specialis*-doctrine, human rights provisions concerning the right to life, food and health would function as the most protective clauses.

Fourthly, the existing legal framework does not specifically recognise a right of international organisations or third states to offer assistance. In fact as also seen in the *Nicaragua*-case, such a *bona fide* offer does not violate international law, and is generally even presupposed. Given the attitude of various bodies such as the

[38] 5.5.2 Humanitarian Assistance as a Vehicle in the Fulfilment of Existing Human Rights.

Security Council to indeed presuppose such a right, it is not necessary to establish, but again, might assist in clarification of the law, should an authoritative body decide to do so. Unequivocally establishing that such a right exists, adds to the responsibilities to cooperate in bringing humanitarian crises to an end. Problems with regard to the provision of assistance by third parties, following the circumstances in which a sovereign does not fulfil its own obligations under international law, do in fact form a large component of the issues that the legal framework on the delivery of humanitarian assistance faces. Indeed, such problems clearly flow from the initial problem of a sovereign not fulfilling its own duties. Whilst this non-provision may arise through both incapacity and unwillingness of the sovereign to fulfil its duties, it is more often than not the latter which results in problems for external or international access.

Fifthly therefore, it is key to note that no right to access a territory exists for third parties, for the purpose of the provision of humanitarian assistance. Indeed, determining whether or not such a right *should* exist is a normative question that is bound by the legal parameters of the current law. Currently, the provisions relating to provision of aid by third parties are formulated from the perspective of the obligation of the affected state to *allow* such assistance. These obligations are formulated in international humanitarian law from the perspective of a duty to allow access in relation to certain 'control rights'. The obligations are absent in circumstances of natural disaster due to the lack of a specific body of law. In such circumstances as also possible in times of armed conflict, recourse must currently be had to the obligations of the affected state to seek international cooperation as found under Article 2 ICESCR. This latter obligation is arguably not as strongly formulated as that in international humanitarian law which dictates that relief 'shall' be provided. However, fulfilment of the rights to food and health under the ICESCR *does require seeking international assistance*. Indeed, the basic provisions of humanitarian assistance are considered 'minimum core obligations'.

Whilst it may not be problematic to be lacking a 'right' to access, such access should then however be formulated from the perspective of the sovereign as an *obligation* in international law, taking into account and recognising in particular the content of the concept of state sovereignty. When state sovereignty includes a duty to provide emergency assistance to those within its jurisdiction, such a duty must be seen to include the prohibition of arbitrarily refusing external aid that might be able to do just that.

Yet, this duty proves to be lacking uniformity in international law. A general basis is currently found in human rights law, but not formulated as an obligation of result, although the minimum core obligations must be fulfilled at all times. A further obligation to allow access is furthermore only established on an *ad hoc* basis by the Security Council, given the explicit control rights that otherwise exist under international humanitarian law.

Indeed, sixthly, in the only field of law addressing an obligation to allow access (humanitarian law), such access is subject to the consent of the affected state, which then in turn may not be 'arbitrarily refused'. This consent-issue is one of the greatest concerns pertaining to those attempting to provide aid, as no clear threshold can be established regarding what precisely constitutes 'arbitrary' refusal of consent in relation to the provision of humanitarian assistance. Such attempts at a legal definition have also not been made in soft law documents, and it stands to reason that this must be determined on a case-by-case basis.[39]

Creating an exhaustive list of potential 'arbitrary refusals' by a sovereign is simply not realistic, as practice will always surpass the attempted regulation. However, determining which acts *as a minimum* would amount to such a threshold or 'arbitrariness' would be an aid in practice. Indeed, circumstances where the affected sovereign authority acquiesces, concedes or grants access without outright 'consent' are not the contested problem in international law today. Currently, the 'baseline' in humanitarian law can be found in the provisions prohibiting the starvation of civilians. Arguably, such a baseline in human rights law would be the threshold of the fulfilment of the minimum core obligations of the rights to food and health, as well as the non-arbitrary deprivation of the right to life. The risk of proliferation of definitions and of minimum standards of protection is ever-present, and thus such an assessment of what in fact amounts to an 'arbitrary refusal' of humanitarian assistance should be done by an authoritative judiciary body in international law.

Seventhly and closely related to the matter of the prohibition of the arbitrary denial of access, is the fact that the obligation in humanitarian law to allow access, resting upon the sovereign, is dependent on the assessment that a territory is 'inadequately supplied'. This law is inherently flawed, as it grants leeway to the sovereign itself to determine and interpret this 'inadequateness' of supply. Similarly outside of armed conflict, gaps exist in international legal regulation, as it is often mistakenly assumed that a sovereign will show willingness to call for assistance from abroad when it is overwhelmed. Yet here too, a margin of appreciation is left to the sovereign to ascertain whether or not those within its jurisdiction are adequately supplied.

One of the great difficulties in the current framework is determining whether or not the affected territory is 'inadequately supplied', when no legal direction is provided in this regard. Again, a case-by case analysis is currently the only viable manner in which a pragmatic solution to these difficulties may be found; the

[39] However, in an attempt at more clarity, the Resolution 'Humanitarian Assistance' (2 September 2003) Institute of International Law, Sixteenth Commission, Bruges Session Principle VIII(1) does note that: "Affected States are under the obligation not arbitrarily and unjustifiably to reject a bona fide offer exclusively intended to provide humanitarian assistance or to refuse access to the victims. In particular, they may not reject an offer nor refuse access if such refusal is likely to endanger the fundamental human rights of the victims or would amount to a violation of the ban on starvation of civilians as a method of warfare". Such clarification however is not comprehensive, as it does not address issues falling short of 'starvation' or outside the context of armed conflict.

concept is too vast to exhaustively delimitate. In proffering a solution to these two related problems concerning access, calls have been made for the creation of a new treaty.[40] Yet, states are understandably and necessarily attached to their sovereign rights, including the notion of non-intervention and that of non-interference with domestic affairs. It does not seem viable therefore that states shall be willing to forego these in an international convention and effectively address the concerns regarding the adequacy of supply of a territory and the right to refuse consent, through the codification of methods of enforcement to tackle such crucial issues. The potential new legal document addressing the provision of assistance would then be created without addressing issues of enforcement, and therefore be futile from its birth. Human rights law as a basis continues to be a constant factor that may provide guidance, as an 'inadequate' supply of humanitarian assistance amounts to violations of the rights to life, food and health, which can be ascertained through legal standards of enforcement. The focus then lies with the establishment of a violation of the rights to life, food or health, rather than establishment of the 'inadequate supply' of a territory.

This brings forward the eighth and final issue faced by the current legal framework that must be addressed. Upon deciding that the need for access must be determined on a case-by-case basis, the question is raised: who shall determine whether or not a territory is inadequately supplied, and whether or not consent is arbitrarily withheld when an offer of assistance is made? If such circumstances are affirmatively assessed, enforcement becomes possible as violations of international law arise through the unlawful obstruction and denial of assistance.

Enforcement issues in international law are not new, nor are they unique to the legal framework on the delivery of humanitarian assistance. Leaving the determination of such matters regarding the use of force solely in the hands of the Security Council, as (political) authoritative body in international law concerning the use of force, risks widening the gap between the protection in times of armed conflict and that in times of natural disasters, as the Security Council operates within the realm of peace and security and its related functions and powers under Chapters VI and VII, most notably of course the concept of a 'threat to the peace' as established in Article 39 UN Charter. Yet, handing such matters solely to international courts and tribunals shall also not provide timely, satisfactory enforcement, as such judiciaries shall not have the opportunity to act in the midst of a humanitarian crisis. With the current judiciary bodies, enforcement will occur well *after* the crisis has taken place.

An ensuing issue pertaining to having sole recourse to enforcement by means of the judiciary, is the fact that existing human rights bodies cannot enforce a situation of denial by non-state actors. Non-state actors are, given the proliferation

[40] Amongst others Yoram Dinstein, 'The Right to Humanitarian Assistance' (2000) LIII *Naval War College Review* 4, 88-89; Rohan J Hardcastle & Adrian T L Chua, 'Humanitarian Assistance, Towards a Right of access to victims of natural disaster', (1998) 38 *International Review of the Red Cross* 325, 596-597; Report of the Representative of the Secretary-General, Mr. Francis M. Deng (5 December 1995) UN Doc E.CN.4/1996/52/Add.2 § 416.

of non-international armed conflict, in reality often those denying humanitarian assistance. Equally, in the absence of a responsible authority, such as in the circumstance of a failed state, the ICJ and ICC face problems with adjudication as they are not equipped to adjudicate such actors. The absence of a sovereign, as seen from the above assessment that the existing duties all rest *upon* a sovereign, results in the need for legal recourse to immediate action for those persons finding themselves in a crisis in a 'failed state' with no sovereign.

It cannot be denied that all these authoritative bodies therefore have their limitations, as well as shortcomings and flaws. Yet, as addressing *and overcoming* these crucial enforcement issues in a potential new treaty regarding the framework on the provision of assistance does not appear viable, solutions from within the current international legal system must be sought. Granted, the International Fact Finding Committee as envisaged by Article 90 AP I exists, but aside from the fact that it is indeed in practice not being sought out in conflict resolution, it merely has authority over international armed conflicts. As such, it is currently also not a realistic enforcer, with the most pressing crises arising in non-international armed conflicts, natural disasters and complex emergencies.

In the current international legal arena, the ICJ, ICC, human rights courts and Security Council are the bodies available to address enforcement issues. A combined solution might provide the answer: the advice of a judiciary body or committee to the Security Council, in *ad hoc* circumstances amounting to a humanitarian crisis. Such an informal (*ad hoc*) judiciary body or committee would provide more judicial backing for the otherwise political decisions of the Council.

As the above shows, the law regarding the rights and duties concerning the *provision* of assistance is largely in place. Human rights law and general principles in international law allow for a broad basis to build on. Problematic is especially the situation in which an affected state does not *allow* access, and international law must dictate how to *enforce* access.

This is indeed a normative issue: *how* the denial of humanitarian assistance is enforced – either *ex post facto* by the judiciary, or immediately by the Security Council – is directly related to the manner in, and speed with which, the rights of the affected persons are fulfilled. It has been argued above that a responsibility of third states to cooperate to provide humanitarian assistance in the ending of violations of international law (the denial of humanitarian assistance) can be seen to be emerging in international law, through the combination of norms in existing human rights law, the ARSIWA, appeals of the Security Council and the General Assembly, as well as the Draft ILC Articles. These assertions must be considered the most protective clauses concerning the external provision of assistance at this time, and furthermore relate to the violation of norms of *jus cogens* as such cooperation becomes a potential duty when the affected state may violate norms of *jus cogens* in the denial of emergency aid. This emerging duty also falls in line with Security Council action as seen over the past years ranging from measures under Articles 40 and 41, to the use of force under Article 42 UN Charter regarding for example Somalia, as well as the emerging doctrine on the Responsibility to Protect, which has been embraced by the Security Council and put into practice by that body with regard to the situation in Libya.

Whilst this doctrine is by no means well-established in international law, it *does* acknowledge Security Council authorisation for the use of force in circumstances amounting to 'crimes against humanity', a circumstance that does not require a nexus to an armed conflict. The denial of humanitarian assistance may in fact, as discussed above, amount to such a crime.[41] When a state sovereign does not provide assistance and denies access to third parties wishing to do so, the result might be a humanitarian crisis that can be qualified as a crime against humanity. The scope and magnitude of such a crime can in reality often result in a threat to the peace. Indeed, whilst the Council remains bound by the text of the UN Charter, requiring the existence of a 'threat to the peace' to warrant the enforcement by means of the actual use of force, it is viable to argue that a threat to the peace may arise should crimes against humanity be committed also outside of the context of an armed conflict.

Therefore, should for instance a natural disaster occur where humanitarian assistance is not being provided, resulting in vast amounts of IDPs and/or refugees and risking for example a spill-over effect or instability in a larger area, the Security Council might find such circumstances to be a threat to international peace, and have the tools to resort to the use of force in order to enforce the provision of humanitarian assistance. Similarly, circumstances not meeting the threshold of a non-international armed conflict as considered by Additional Protocol II may nevertheless concern the Council with regard to a threat to the peace in that area, and equal recourse may be had. In such circumstances, where an armed conflict *can* however be ascertained, recourse may *also* be had to the use of force when 'war crimes' are committed through the denial of humanitarian assistance. Security Council action is thereby possible through a variety of means. Through such a view of the meaning of Article 39 UN Charter, the Security Council would remain within its mandate, yet also ensure enforcement options *at all times that the provision of humanitarian assistance may be necessary* due to the existence of a humanitarian crisis amounting to a threat to the peace, even when this does not involve a 'classic' armed conflict. The Council shall evidently remain bound by the determination that indeed a crisis exists warranting the provision of assistance. Should the provision of assistance not be initially required, then its denial also does not result in a violation of international law.

Currently, legal developments regarding the concept of 'crimes against humanity' are underway, as the ILC announced in July 2014 that it would move the topic of crimes against humanity from its long-term agenda and now include it in its 'programme of work'. This might provide more insights into the possibility to view crimes against humanity as a threat to the peace in the absence of an armed conflict

[41] 8.6.2.2 Crimes Against Humanity and Humanitarian Assistance.

and for the purpose of the provision of humanitarian assistance. Potentially, this new study might develop into greater protection for persons in times of a humanitarian crisis.

The use of force is never the first, nor the perfect solution, but sometimes it is the only option when all others fail and the international community is witness to massive human suffering. As such, the use of force must always be proportional to the goal it is serving: the relief of a civilian population in need. Naturally, all other (coercive) measures to entice a sovereign to allow access to a territory should have prior preference. These include methods of access as discussed, such as for example through diplomatic channels, to establish means of access to provide aid on a more consensual basis. Such methods may be followed by measures within Chapter VII but still exempting the use of force. Furthermore, regardless of Security Council action, judicial enforcement mechanisms shall remain open to those wishing to enforce the delivery of humanitarian assistance through other means. As argued by Schwendimann, although the norms of international law can at most represent the *minimum standards* in obtaining access, the legal framework remains a useful mechanism in the insurance that aid is delivered to those who need it most.[42]

Indeed, establishing the minimum legal framework does not withhold international actors to take further steps to protect persons in times of a humanitarian crisis. International law has developed over time to protect the interests of persons through human rights law and humanitarian law: both branches have developed parallel to each other and thus so should the protection of persons be parallel and equal.[43] It is therefore *essential* to the protection of persons in need of aid that the legal framework be addressed in this integral, over-arching and comprehensive manner, as uncertainty regarding the applicability of the law results in a *lack* of application and thereby a *lack of protection* on the ground. The existing legal framework pertaining to the provision of humanitarian assistance and its enforcement mechanisms must therefore be communicated, disseminated and endorsed in all possible manners towards all actors involved in the provision of assistance. With an increase in knowledge of the legal regulations to ensure the provision of humanitarian assistance, comes an increase in power to implement them, resulting in an increase of protection of those in need. In the end, that is the ultimate goal of this research.

[42] Felix Schwendimann, 'The legal framework of humanitarian access in armed conflict', (2011) *93 International Review of the Red Cross* 884, 1008.
[43] 3.4.1 Development of the Interaction between both Fields of Law.

Samenvatting: Humanitaire Assistentie en Staatssoevereiniteit in het Internationale Recht: Richting een Integraal Raamwerk

1 Inleiding

In een wereld met toenemende globalisering bestaat er ook een toenemende mate van mondiale betrokkenheid bij humanitaire rampen. Men ontkomt niet aan de shockerende beelden van mensen in nood, die getoond worden in internationale media bij conflictsituaties of na (natuur-)rampen. De lokale overheden zijn meestal overweldigd door de intensiteit en omvang van de ramp, en kunnen de situatie vaak niet zelfstandig oplossen. De wens om humanitaire assistentie te verlenen is dan ook groot, en deze assistentie vindt voornamelijk plaats op initiatief van derde landen of internationale organisaties. Hoewel het verlenen van humanitaire assistentie geen rampen kan *voorkomen*, kan het wel nadrukkelijk bijdragen aan de verlichting van *bestaande* rampen, en bijdragen aan de overleving van mensen in nood.

Zowel het verlenen van humanitaire hulp als het ontvangen hiervan is gebonden aan internationaal juridische regels. Veel van deze regels zijn ontwikkeld na afloop van de Tweede Wereldoorlog, met het oog op het voorkomen van een herhaling van het lot dat miljoenen mensen in deze periode trof. Door ontwikkelingen in de tweede helft van de twintigste eeuw, en aan de start van de eenentwintigste eeuw kan echter geconcludeerd worden dat de bestaande regelgeving helaas noch eenduidig, noch altijd helder is. De noodzaak tot verheldering ligt in de veranderende aard van humanitaire rampen en een toenemend aantal actoren op het internationale speelveld.

Bestaande regelgeving is veelal toegespitst op internationale gewapende conflicten en bezettingssituaties. Daarentegen zijn de hedendaagse humanitaire rampen (voortvloeiend uit een periode van dekolonisatie en het einde van de Koude Oorlog) over het algemeen het gevolg van interne gewapende conflicten en (natuur-)rampen. Men kan hierbij denken aan de huidige conflicten in Syrië, Libië en Irak, evenals rampen zoals de aardbevingen in Haïti en Nepal, respectievelijk in 2010 en 2015, of de tsunami in Japan in maart 2011. Bovendien zijn in de afgelopen jaren behalve staten, ook in toenemende mate niet-statelijke actoren, zoals gewapende groeperingen en internationale organisaties, actief welke aan regelgeving gebonden dienen te zijn. Deze ontwikkelingen gaan hand in hand met een nieuwe kijk op het eeuwenoude concept van staatssoevereiniteit. Met het oog op deze veranderende omstandigheden is er een verheldering nodig van het bestaande internationale recht, om vast te stellen of het huidige juridische raamwerk afdoende is, dan wel of er behoefte bestaat aan ontwikkeling van nieuwe regelgeving. Vragen dienen zich aan, zoals: welke rechten hebben mensen in nood om hulp te ontvangen? Welke plichten bestaan er voor de getroffen staat of derde partijen om hulp te leveren? Hoe kan hulpverlening gehandhaafd worden?

Kortom, de noodzaak tot het in kaart brengen van het huidige internationaal juridische raamwerk is bijzonder groot in de hedendaagse maatschappij. De actuele internationaal juridische vraagstukken met betrekking tot het leveren van humanitaire assistentie zijn in essentie viervoudig: allereerst bestaat er een grote verscheidenheid aan *omstandigheden* waarin humanitaire hulp verleend dient te worden, zoals bezetting, internationale en interne conflicten, en (natuur-)rampen, en daaraan gelieerde verscheidenheid in toepasbare juridische regelgeving. Deze verscheidenheid leidt tot een risico van fragmentatie in de beschermingsgraad van individuen. Dit risico bestaat doordat de bescherming van het individu in het huidige internationale recht bepaald wordt door het juridische regime dat van toepassing is in de specifieke omstandigheid. Een tweede probleem is de grote verscheidenheid aan *actoren* op het internationale speelveld, wat leidt tot een veelvoud aan rechthebbenden en dragers van plichten. Onduidelijkheid bestaat ten aanzien van (met name) de plichten van de getroffen staat, internationale organisaties, (coalities van) derde staten, niet-statelijke actoren, non-gouvernementele organisaties en individuen, al naargelang de aard van de humanitaire crisis. Deze actoren zijn niet alleen dragers van rechten en plichten, maar ook actoren in het al dan niet verlenen van humanitaire assistentie. Gelieerd aan deze eerste twee vraagstukken is het concept van *staatssoevereiniteit*, als derde component met betrekking tot het juridische raamwerk ten aanzien van het verlenen van humanitaire assistentie. De nadrukkelijke rol van de soevereine overheid en politieke wil om humanitaire assistentie te verlenen of toe te staan van buitenaf speelt een doorslaggevende rol in de overleving van getroffenen ten tijde van een humanitaire crisis. Tenslotte is de *proliferatie van regelgeving* een laatste probleem dat zich heeft voorgedaan in het bestaande juridisch kader ten aanzien van humanitaire assistentie, als gevolg van de drie bovenstaande vraagstukken. Deze proliferatie heeft gelijktijdig gezorgd voor onduidelijkheid in het bestaande recht, in plaats van verheldering hiervan.

2 Doel onderzoek & probleemstelling

Deze vier problematische vraagstukken leiden tot zowel overlappingen als hiaten in de regelgeving ten aanzien van het verlenen van humanitaire assistentie, en hebben geleid tot het opzetten van het onderhavige onderzoek. Bij gebrek aan een gemeenschappelijk, alomvattend en integraal raamwerk van rechten en plichten is onderzoek naar de mogelijkheden hiertoe van belang, evenals het in kaart brengen van de specifieke hiaten in de rechtsbescherming van mensen in nood. Het brengen van duidelijkheid in het internationale recht met betrekking tot humanitaire assistentie zal bijdragen aan de handhaving van bestaande rechtsregels en de mogelijke ontwikkeling van eventuele nieuwe regelgeving.

Het doel van dit onderzoek is: het vaststellen wat de *status en reikwijdte* is van het huidige juridische raamwerk met betrekking tot humanitaire assistentie, en om vast te stellen of *verduidelijking en verbetering* hiervan nodig en wenselijkzijn. Onderzoek naar deze vraagstukken, en de beantwoording hiervan, zal bijdragen aan de inbedding en handhaving van humanitaire assistentie in het internationale recht. Het onderzoek hanteert hierin een integrale benadering, en bestudeert de stand van het recht in alle mogelijke omstandigheden (bezetting, conflict en (natuur-)ramp)) waarin humanitaire assistentie van belang kan zijn. Op deze wijze zal het mogelijk zijn om vast te stellen wat het juridisch kader is met betrekking tot de rechten en plichten welke te allen tijde van toepassing kunnen zijn met betrekking tot het leveren van humanitaire assistentie, ongeacht of dit zou moeten plaatsvinden ten tijde van oorlog of vrede.

De algemene onderzoeksvraag van dit onderzoek luidt: *wat zijn de bestaande rechten en plichten met betrekking tot het ontvangen, leveren en handhaven van humanitaire assistentie, en is ontwikkeling of verbetering van het huidige internationale recht nodig voor het creeëren van een integraal juridisch raamwerk?* In het onderhavige onderzoek wordt deze algemene vraag beantwoord door de bespreking van drie subkwesties, namelijk: 1) wat zijn de huidige rechten en plichten met betrekking tot de ontvangst, levering en weigering van humanitaire assistentie?; 2) identificatie van ontwikkelingsmogelijkheden en/of verbetermogelijkheden van het internationale recht ter voorkoming van wederrechtelijke weigering van humanitaire assistentie; en 3) het vaststellen van een allesomvattende en samenhangende kern van het juridisch raamwerk dat kan functioneren als basis voor het verlenen van humanitaire assistentie ongeacht de specifieke omstandigheid van de humanitaire crisis.

3 Juridisch kader

Gezien het veelomvattende karakter van het onderzoek, neemt het ook een veelvoud aan juridische bronnen mee. Met betrekking tot het juridische kader worden regels van algemeen internationaal recht, zoals ten aanzien van staatssoevereiniteit en de internationale verantwoordelijkheid van staten besproken, evenals specifieke deelgebieden binnen het internationale recht. Onder andere de mensenrechten, het humanitaire oorlogsrecht, vluchtelingenrecht en regelgeving met betrekking tot natuurrampen komen aan bod. Binnen deze bespreking zijn zowel primaire als secundaire rechtsbronnen relevant, evenals *lex lata* en *lex ferenda*. In de bespreking van secundaire rechtsbronnen is de jurisprudentie van het Internationaal Gerechtshof van belang. Hoewel de nadruk ligt op de *lex lata*, wegens het in kaart brengen van het huidige juridische kader, wordt ook aandacht besteed aan de *lex ferenda* met het oog op mogelijke ontwikkelingen van en verbeteringen aan het bestaande juridisch kader.

Deel I: Het Raamwerk

Alvorens de bestaande rechten en plichten te bespreken heeft dit onderzoek een raamwerk vastgesteld waarbinnen het verlenen van humanitaire assistentie plaatsvindt. Zo is een definitie van het concept humanitaire assistentie voorgesteld bij gebrek aan een bestaande algemeen geaccepteerde definitie: 'humanitaire assistentie is assistentie welke bestaat uit voedsel, medicijnen, onderdak en de logistiek ten behoeve van de verlening van deze assistentie voor dringende doeleinden en die onmisbaar is voor het overleven dan diegenen voor wie het bedoeld is'. Drie beginselen zijn vastgesteld welke een grootst gemene deler vormen bij het verlenen van humanitaire assistentie door de grotere actoren zoals de Verenigde Naties en het Rode Kruis, te weten 'humaniteit', 'onpartijdigheid' en 'neutraliteit'. Hiernaast spelen ook andere beginselen zoals 'menselijke waardigheid' en non-discriminatie een belangrijke rol bij het verlenen van noodhulp. Statelijke actoren zijn eveneens gebonden aan deze beginselen. Als onderdeel van het raamwerk is bovendien vastgesteld dat de ontvangers van humanitaire assistentie burgers zijn, een begrip dat tevens vluchtelingen en ontheemden kan omvatten.

Zoals reeds aangegeven, gaat dit onderzoek uit van een alomvattende benadering van het verlenen van humanitaire hulp, in tegenstelling tot een benadering vanuit het perspectief van een conflict, bezetting of (natuur)ramp. Om deze reden is ook een drempel vastgesteld als graadmeter voor het concept van een humanitaire crisis: 'een humanitaire crisis is een situatie welke kan ontstaan uit meerdere oorsprongen, waaronder een natuurramp of een ramp met menselijke oorsprong, gewapend conflict en bezetting, welke ernstige schade teweegbrengt van een persoonlijke of materiële aard, waar (externe) assistentie nodig is omdat de lokale capaciteit ofwel overweldigd is, ofwel niet in staat is, danwel soms niet welwillend is om de omstandigheden te beheersen en te regelen'. Hoewel het concept van een 'humanitaire crisis' dus als gemene deler wordt aangehouden in dit onderzoek, is ook gebleken dat een definitie van het concept 'natuurramp' ontbrak binnen het juridische raamwerk. Deze is dan ook voorgesteld: 'een natuurramp is een plotselinge of langzaam groeiende natuurlijke omstandigheid of reeks gebeurtenissen welke uit verscheidene natuurlijke oorsprongen kan voortvloeien (waaronder biologische, klimatologische, geofysische, hydrologische etc.), en welke resulteert in een overweldiging van de lokale of nationale capaciteit en resulteert in een onmiddelijke noodzaak tot het verlenen van assistentie aan de burger-bevolking'.

Terwijl de specifieke omstandigheden (conflict, bezetting en (natuur-)rampen) moeten uitgroeien tot een 'humanitaire crisis' voor de verlening van humanitaire assistentie, zijn in de specifieke omstandigheden verschillende rechtsregels van toepassing. Zo is ten tijde van een natuurramp uiteraard geen oorlogsrecht van toepassing, in tegenstelling tot de onmiddellijke toepassing van dit recht ten tijde van een gewapend conflict. De rechtsregels voor het verlenen van assistentie ten tijde van bezetting gelden pas wanneer inderdaad ook is vast komen te staan dat er een zekere mate van 'controle' is over het bezette grondgebied. De toepasselijke rechtsregels staan tot elkaar in verhouding volgens de doctrine van de 'lex specialis'. Dit onderzoek stelt voor dat de *lex specialis*-doctrine inhoudt dat de meest specifieke clausule toegepast dient te worden in een bepaalde omstandigheid, in tegenstelling tot een *corpus juris* in zijn geheel. Als gevolg hiervan zal soms een bepaling uit de mensenrechten van toepassing zijn, en soms een bepaling uit het oorlogsrecht, maar de grootst gemene deler zal zijn dat de meest specifieke bepaling, en daarmee ook de meest *beschermende* bepaling, toegepast kan worden.

Tenslotte komt in de vaststelling van het juridisch raamwerk ook het concept 'staatssoevereiniteit' aan bod. Als gevolg van de ontwikkelingen in de 21^e^ eeuw ten aanzien van de mensenrechten, internationale interdependentie, de grotere rol van het individu en de internationale tribunalen die ontwikkeld zijn, is het Westfaalse beeld van staatssoevereiniteit veranderd. Wanneer de nieuwe doctrine van de 'Responsibility to Protect' hier bovendien aan toegevoegd wordt, is er nog een bestanddeel in het internationale speelveld dat het concept 'staatssoevereiniteit' aan verandering onderhevig maakt. In de 21^e^ eeuw moet het concept van staatssoevereiniteit dan ook gezien worden als een wederkerige relatie tussen de rechten en plichten van de soeverein. Hoewel traditionele beginselen als non-interventie, respect voor territoriale jurisdictie en toestemming door de soeverein blijven bestaan, heeft diezelfde soeverein ook plichten jegens burgers binnen zijnjurisdictie. Wanneer de soeverein faalt in het vervullen van deze verplichtingen, verschuift in sommige gevallen de plicht naar de internationale gemeenschap; in het bijzonder in het geval van internationale misdrijven jegens de burgerbevolking. Het leveren van humanitaire assistentie is in die zin een manier voor de soeverein om zijn plichten als staatssoeverein te vervullen.

DEEL II: PRIMAIRE RECHTEN EN PLICHTEN TIJDENS EEN HUMANITAIRE CRISIS

Deel II van dit onderzoek bespreekt de rechten van ontvangers van humanitaire assistentie, evenals de primaire plichten voor levering, welke rusten op de getroffen staat, als verantwoordelijke soeverein. Ten aanzien van de discussie omtrent het bestaan van een eventueel onafhankelijk 'mensenrecht op het ontvangen van hulpverlening' is vast komen te staan dat een dergelijk mensenrecht niet bestaat in het huidige internationale recht. Zowel gewoonterechtelijke componenten ontbreken hiertoe, als bepalingen in bestaande mensenrechtenverdragen. Daarbij is voor een dergelijk mensenrecht geen directe noodzaak, wanneer een pragmatische benadering wordt gehanteerd ten aanzien van de reeds bestaande mensenrechten op leven, voedsel en gezondheid.

Het verlenen van humanitaire assistentie functioneert als middel in de vervulling van bestaande mensenrechten. Een basis kan gevonden worden in de artikelen 55 en 56 VN Handvest, evenals bestaande rechten in het UVRM, IVESCR, IVBPR, EVRM, Afrikaanse en Amerikaanse mensenrechtenverdragen, en toegespitste verdragen zoals o.a. het Vrouwenrechtenverdrag, het Kinderrechtenverdrag en het IVERD. Het gebrek aan voorbehouden bij deze verdragen ten aanzien van de 'noodtoestand' welke uitgeroepen kan worden, draagt hier aan bij, evenals het concept van 'minimum core obligations' welke voortvloeien uit het IVESCR. Het gebrek aan een zelfstandig mensenrecht is dan ook niet per definitie een gebrek aan een recht op het ontvangen van hulpverlening *an sich*. Dit recht vloeit immers voort uit de plichten welke de soevereine staat heeft in de vervulling van het recht op leven, voedsel en gezondheid zoals vastgelegd in bovengenoemde verdragen.

Met betrekking tot het recht op leven hebben staten een positieve verplichting om dit te waarborgen door een verbod op het willekeurig ontnemen van leven zoals neergelegd in o.a. de artikelen 3 UVRM, 6 IVBPR, 2 EVRM, en Artikel 4 in zowel het Inter-Amerikaanse als Afrikaanse Verdrag voor de rechten van de mens (en volkeren). Het recht op voedsel omvat een meer actieve rol van de soeverein tot het vervullen van de 'minimum core obligations' in de artikelen 2 en 11 IVESCR, waaronder ook de verplichting valt tot internationale samenwerking. Een recht op voedsel kan ook gevonden worden in o.a. Artikel 24(2) van het Kinderrechtenverdrag en Artikel 12(2) Vrouwenrechtenverdrag. Het recht op gezondheid is o.a. gecodificeerd in Artikel 12(2)(c) IVESCR, 25 UVRM, 5(e)(iv) IVERD, 24 Kinderrechtenverdrag en Artikel 16 van het Inter-Amerikaanse verdrag. Dit recht heeft iets meer codificatieverschillen, waardoor het moeizamer eenduidig te distilleren is. Een consensus kan gevonden worden in het verlenen van humanitaire assistentie aan een behoeftige bevolking, en het voorkomen van ziektes. Een internationaal mensenrecht op het ontvangen van water is tevens afwezig, hoewel er codificaties zijn in bij voorbeeld Artikel 21(1)(c) Kinderrechtenverdrag en 14(2)(h) Vrouwenrechtenverdrag.

In het internationaal oorlogsrecht bestaan verschillende bepalingen al naar gelang de aard van het gewapende conflict. Deze bepalingen functioneren tevens vanuit de plichten van de getroffen staat om humanitaire assistentie te leveren. Artikel 54 AP I formuleert een verbod op het veroorzaken van uithongering ten tijde van een internationaal gewapend conflict. Artikel 70 AP I stelt dat hulpverlening 'zal plaatsvinden', maar daaruit kan geen direct recht op het ontvangen van humanitaire assistentie worden afgeleid. Bovendien bestaat de uitzonderingsgrond van 'militaire noodzaak' voor de getroffen staten ten aanzien van het niet (onmiddellijk) leveren van hulpverlening. Ten tijde van bezetting bestaan er verplichtingen volgend uit Artikel 55 GC IV voor de bezetter om voedsel en medische voorzieningen te leveren wanneer het bezette gebied 'ontoereikend' voorzien zou zijn. Met betrekking tot een intern gewapend conflict bestaan echter vooralsnog geen specifieke bepalingen ten aanzien van het ontvangen of leveren van humanitaire hulp, en wordt dit gedistilleerd uit Gemeenschappelijk Artikel 3 en het verbod op uithongering zoals neergelegd in Artikel 14 AP II.

Specifiek ten tijde van natuurrampen gelden de toepasselijke mensenrechten en worden ook nog bepaalde 'Draft Articles' door de International Law Commission van de VN ontwikkeld, waarin Artikel 12 een primaire taak voorziet voor de getroffen staat om hulpverlening te bieden. Voor specifieke groepen zoals ontheemden en vluchtelingen geldenook enkele specifieke bepalingen, en met name zogenaamde 'soft law' documenten hebben veelvuldig de taak van de getroffen staat beargumenteerd in het verlenen van humanitaire assistentie.

DEEL III: HULPVERLENING DOOR DERDEN

Volgend op de primaire rechten van burgers en plichten van staten ten tijde van een humanitaire crisis worden de rechten en plichten van derde partijen, zoals andere staten en internationale organisaties, besproken. In dit kader bestaat een mogelijk recht op toegang tot een grondgebied als de getroffen staat zelf geen humanitaire assistentie biedt.

Ten aanzien van de bestaande mensenrechten bevatt met name Artikel 2 IVESCR de basis voor een algemene verplichting en verantwoordelijkheid voor de internationale gemeenschap om samen te werken en assistentie te bieden aan de getroffen staat in tijden van nood, welke de getroffen staat zelf ook moet vragen. Deze interpretatie wordt tevens onderschreven door meerdere VN organen. Het Internationale Gerechtshof heeft in 2007 gesteld dat de getroffen staat zich moet weerhouden van het belemmeren van humanitaire assistentie, op basis van het IVERD.

De VN Veiligheidsraad roept de internationale gemeenschap al vele jaren op tot het leveren van humanitaire assistentie, en vooronderstelt in deze zin een 'recht op aanbod' van de internationale gemeenschap hiertoe. In specifieke landenresoluties richt de Veiligheidsraad zich op de mogelijkheid van zogenaamde ongehinderde toegang voor humanitaire assistentie van buitenaf, en de verplichting van de getroffen staat in deze context. Hoewel de Veiligheidsraad geen onderscheid maakt tussen interne of internationale gewapende conflicten, is hij gebonden aan die omstandigheden die te kwalificeren zijn als een bedreiging voor de internationale vrede en veiligheid (volgend uit art. 39 VN Handvest). De Veiligheidsraad stelt echter geen recht op toegang van derde partijen, maar formuleert eerder vanuit het perspectief van de getroffen staat een verplichting tot het verzekeren van ongehinderde toegang. In een alternatieve poging heeft de Raad met betrekking tot Syrië in 2014 de internationale gemeenschap opgeroepen tot het verlenen van humanitaire hulp buiten de toezeggingen van de getroffen soevereine staat om. Dit wellicht in verband met de omstreden status en het zwakke gezag van het Assad-regime. De Algemene Vergadering van de VN heeft eveneens al sinds de jaren '90 van de vorige eeuw gesteld dat er een noodzaak is tot internationale assistentie bij humanitaire rampen, zoals o.a. in haar bekende Resolutie 46/182. Evenwel zonder het stellen van harde plichten.

Met betrekking tot internationaal humanitair recht en hulpverlening bij conflicten stelt Artikel 10 GC IV een recht op het aanbieden van hulpverlening door internationale organisaties, hetgeen onderworpen is aan de toestemming van de getroffen staat. Een dergelijke bepaling behelst echter geen verplichtingen, en moet gezien worden als een uitnodiging aan het adres van internationale organisaties. Deze bepaling wordt aangevuld door Artikel 23 GC IV, evenals door de artikelen 70 en 71 AP I, waarin gesteld wordt dat hulpgoederen toegestaan 'zullen' worden wanneer een grondgebied ontoereikend voorzien is. Een vergelijkbare tendens is zichtbaar bij interne gewapende conflicten, waar Gemeenschappelijk Artikel 3 wordt aangevuld door de artikelen 14 en 18 AP II, die zowel een verbod op uithongering behelsen als de stelling dat de levering van hulpgoederen 'zal' plaatsvinden wanneer een bevolking lijdt. Met betrekking tot bezettingssituaties stelt Artikel 59 GC IV op vergelijkbare wijze dat de bezettende macht hulpgoederen 'zal' accepteren, en de verdeling daarvan (volgens art. 61) zal faciliteren. Evenals bij de rechtsregels ten aanzien van internationale conflicten wordt een aanbod tot leveren van hulpgoederen dus reeds verondersteld.

Een specifiek juridisch kader voor het leveren van humanitaire assistentie door derde partijen ontbreekt ten tijde van (natuur-)rampen. Derhalve wordt teruggevallen op meer algemene bepalingen, evenals bestaande mensenrechten. Enkele regionale overeenkomsten bestaan, zoals de ASEAN Agreement, waaruit volgt dat staten een verplichting hebben om samen te werken in de coördinatie van hulpverlening. Inderdaad is een dergelijk perspectief ook te zien in de ILC Draft Artikelen (artt. 8 en 9). Zo zijn er evenzeer enkele specifieke bepalingen voor groeperingen zoals vluchtelingen en ontheemden. Deze laatsten krijgen met name bescherming op het Afrikaanse continent middels de bepalingen van het Kampala Verdrag (artt. 3(1)(j), 5(7) en 7(5)(b) en (g)), waarbij vooral relevant is op te merken dat dit verdrag zich tevens richt op de verplichtingen van niet-statelijke actoren ten aanzien van het toelaten van hulp van buitenaf.

Uit bovenstaand overzicht blijkt, zoals besproken in dit onderzoek, dat er met name problemen liggen bij de mogelijkheid van de getroffen staat tot het bepalen van toestemming voor het leveren van hulp, terwijl tegelijkertijd gesteld wordt dat dergelijke assistentie geleverd 'zal' worden. De getroffen staat heeft dan ook bepaalde controlerechten ten aanzien van deze levering. De handhavingsproblematiek ten aanzien van de levering van humanitaire assistentie raakt derhalve de kern van de relatie tussen staatssoevereiniteit en humanitaire assistentie. Handhaving is mogelijk bij een schending van het internationale recht. Een dergelijke schending bestaat wanneer: (1) er sprake is van een humanitaire crisis waarbij de levering van humanitaire assistentie nodig is; (2) de getroffen staat zelf niet (afdoende) voorziet in deze levering; (3) een rechtmatig aanbod door derde partijen wordt afgeslagen om redenen welke buiten de toegestane uitsluitingsgronden liggen. Als aan deze voorwaarden wordt voldaan is er (4) sprake van een schending van internationaal recht wanneer de getroffen staat de levering van humanitaire hulp weigert of belemmert. De vaststelling van deze mogelijke schendingen vindt onder huidig internationaal recht plaats door de VN Veiligheidsraad, het Internationaal Gerechtshof, het Internationaal Strafhof of mensenrechtenorganen.

Juridische handhaving bij een rechterlijke instantie is in eerste instantie mogelijk wanneer de verantwoordelijkheid van de getroffen staat wordt vastgesteld onder internationaal recht. Met name relevant hierin zijn de artikelen 2 en 3 ARSIWA, evenals de artikelen 42 en 48 ARSIWA ten aanzien van eventuele verantwoordelijkheden jegens de internationale gemeenschap, evenals de artikelen 40 en 41 ten aanzien van plichten van de internationale gemeenschap zelf met betrekking tot het eindigen van ernstige schendingen van internationaal recht. Bij situaties waar onduidelijkheid bestaat ten aanzien van de betreffende soevereine actor bieden de artikelen 4-11 ARSIWA uitkomst(en).

Een alternatieve methode van handhaving vindt meer *ad hoc* plaats middels handelingen van de Veiligheidsraad bij de vaststelling dat er sprake is van een bedreiging van de internationale vrede en veiligheid. Tot op heden is deze mogelijkheid nog niet door de Raad benut voor natuurrampen. Met betrekking tot conflictsituaties is de Raad langzamerhand vooruitstrevender geworden in zijn kijk op het gebruik van geweld door de internationale gemeenschap met als doel het leveren van hulpgoederen ter beëindiging van een humanitaire crisis. Thematische resoluties ten aanzien van de bescherming van burgers en de omarming van de 'Responsibility to Protect' doctrine dragen hier aan bij en zijn zichtbaar in o.a. de bekende Resolutie 1973 (2011) met betrekking tot Libië.

Handhaving vindt ook plaats door middel van het stellen van schendingen van mensenrechten, in het kader van regionale gerechtshoven zoals het Europees Hof voor de Rechten van de Mens, of mensenrechtencommissies horend bij het IVBPR of IVESCR. Hoewel de mogelijkheden hiertoe bestaan, wordt er weinig tot geen gebruik gemaakt van het interstatelijke klachtenrecht. Het individuele klachtrecht met betrekking tot de niet-levering van humanitaire assistentie en daaropvolgende eventuele schendingen van mensenrechten bestaat in het IVESCR nog maar kort (sinds 2013) en heeft tot op heden tevens nog niet geleid totprocedures op dit terrein. Het Internationaal Gerechtshof daarentegen heeft in de Georgië v. Rusland-zaak gesteld dat het niet leveren van assistentie kan leiden tot een schending van de mensenrechten als neergelegd in het IVERD. Oproepen tot handhaving van het leveren van assistentie op mensenrechtelijk gebied vinden bovendien plaats in een meer politieke context middels de VN-mechanismen als de Mensenrechtenraad en de Speciale Rapporteurs.

Ten slotte bespreekt dit onderzoek handhavingsmogelijkheden op individueel niveau, zoals door gerichte sancties en individuele strafrechtelijke aansprakelijkheid. Gerichte sancties zoals het bevriezen van banktegoeden, worden de afgelopen jaren in toenemende mate toegepast door de Veiligheidsraad, in specifiek verband met de weigering van humanitaire assistentie. Individuele strafrechtelijke aansprakelijkheid is met name besproken in het kader van de specifieke categorien 'oorlogsmisdrijven' en 'misdrijven tegen de menselijkheid' zoals tegenwoordig gecodificeerd (respectievelijk art. 8 en 7) in het Statuut van Rome. Voor mogelijke vervolging voor oorlogsmisdrijven moet daadwerkelijk sprake zijn van een gewapend conflict, en het Strafhof maakt onderscheid tussen een intern en een internationaal gewapend conflict: meer mogelijkheden bestaan voor vervolging bij de weigering of belemmering van hulpverlening ten tijde van een internationaal gewapend conflict. In het geval van vervolging voor misdrijven tegen de menselijkheid is tegenwoordig geen verband meer nodig met een gewapend conflict: dit zou dus eventueel ook mogelijk zijn voor situaties waarin hulp geweigerd wordt na een (natuur-)ramp. Cruciaal is echter wel dat er een wijdverbreide of systematische aanval moet zijn geweest op de getroffen bevolking, om iets aan te merken als misdrijf tegen de menselijkheid. Het onthouden van hulp na een natuurramp zou dan dus zeer gericht moeten zijn. Het Statuut van het Internationaal Strafhof erkent ook het ontzien van voedsel en medicijnen als een mogelijkheid hiertoe, en biedt dus in ieder geval de mogelijkheid tot vervolging in de context van het weigeren van humanitaire assistentie.

Het internationale recht is, zoals blijkt, redelijk toereikend als het gaat om handhavingsmogelijkheden, maar ook hier blijven hiaten bestaan. Deze zijn vooral te zien met betrekking tot handhaving in verhouding tot niet-statelijke actoren, en situaties waarbij de soeverein afwezig is, wat kan leiden tot een vacuum in verantwoordelijkheid.

Conclusie

Uit bovenstaande verhandeling blijkt duidelijk dat het recht niet alomvattend is in situaties waar humanitaire assistentie nodig is. Dit onderzoek distilleert dan ook welke rechten en plichten te allen tijde van toepassing zijn (ongeacht of er sprake is van bij voorbeeld een conflictsituatie of een natuurramp) wanneer een crisis gaande is. Onderscheid maken in de hoeveelheid hulp die iemand zou moeten kunnen ontvangen vanwege de omstandigheid van de crisis druist immers in tegen iedere notie van humaniteit.

Dit onderzoek heeft *ten eerste* aangetoond dat staatssoevereiniteit een verantwoordelijkheid omvat van de soeverein jegens diegenen binnen de jurisdictie van de staat, welke overeenkomt met een primaire verantwoordelijkheid tot het leveren van humanitaire assistentie. *Ten tweede* is in dit onderzoek aan bod gekomen dat, hoewel er geen onafhankelijk mensenrecht op het ontvangen van hulpgoederen bestaat, het leveren van humanitaire assistentie ten tijde van een crisis in zichzelf het vervullen is van het recht op leven, voedsel en gezondheid. Als zodanig vormen de mensenrechten als *corpus juris* een juridische basis voor het leveren van humanitaire assistentie. *Ten derde* kan geconcludeerd worden dat een vooronderstelling bestaat in het huidige internationale recht ten aanzien van een recht van de internationale gemeenschap om hulp aan te bieden bij de levering van humanitaire assistentie, wanneer deze assistentie zich houdt aan de beginselen van humaniteit, neutraliteit en onpartijdigheid. *Ten slotte* is duidelijk geworden dat hoewel er geen *recht* op toegang bestaat, wanneer de getroffen soeverein daadwerkelijk toestemming geeft tot toegang, deze soeverein dan ook al datgene dient te doen dat bevordelijk is voor de doorstroom van hulpgoederen en een veilige omgeving dient te waarborgen voor de distributie hiervan. Hierbij komt bovendien dat er momenteel sprake is van een zich ontwikkelende norm ten aanzien van de noodzaak tot samenwerking in de levering van assistentie door de internationale gemeenschap ten tijde van een crisis.

Hoewel hiaten in het recht bestaan en het recht aan verandering onderhevig is, is het niet *per se* nodig om nieuwe rechtsregels te ontwikkelen. Voortbouwen op bestaande rechtsregels en deze verder uitdiepen of naar de voorgrond brengen, kan een alternatieve oplossing brengen. De geboden oplossingen in dit onderzoek trachten een realistische en pragmatische kijk te geven op de juridische rechten en plichten ten tijde van crisis.

Ten eerste stelt dit onderzoek voor dat het raamwerk verhelderd wordt, door het bieden van definities voor de concepten 'humanitaire assistentie', 'humanitaire crisis' en 'natuurramp'. Tevens dienen de actoren zich te houden aan die beginselen waarvoor een grootst gemene deler bestaat, te weten de beginselen van humaniteit, neutraliteit en onpartijdigheid.

Ten tweede is vast komen te staan dat het gebrek aan een onafhankelijk mensenrecht op het ontvangen van humanitaire assistentie niet problematisch hoeft te zijn voor de bescherming van burgers in nood, wanneer erkend wordt dat het leveren van assistentie een vervulling is van de bestaande rechten op leven, voedsel en gezondheid ten tijde van een crisis. Het Internationaal Gerechtshof vult hierbij aan dat levering dient plaats te vinden middels het beginsel van non-discriminatie.

Ten derde, hoewel internationaal humanitair recht vele specifieke bepalingen kent, ontbreekt een algemene codificatie van een plicht tot het leveren van humanitaire hulp. Fragmentatie in het recht is een gevolg van het ontbreken van een dergelijke plicht, en een oplossing kan gevonden worden in de wijze waarop naar de *lex specialis* doctrine gekeken wordt. Wanneer de meest beschermende clausule te allen tijde gebezigd wordt, hebben de getroffen burgers de grootste kans op de juiste mate van bescherming. Deze benadering strookt ook met het huidige concept van staatssoevereiniteit, welke plichten met zich meedraagt jegens de burgerbevolking.

Ten vierde is vast komen te staan dat het huidige juridische raamwerk geen specifiek recht erkent van de internationale gemeenschap (organisaties en staten) om assistentie aan te bieden. Een dergelijk recht wordt vaak verondersteld reeds te bestaan, zoals gezien in de resoluties van de VN Veiligheidsraad en ook bepaald door het Internationaal Gerechtshof in de Nicaragua-zaak. Het uitblijven van een dergelijk specifiek recht is gekoppeld aan de problematiek welke samenhangt met toegang verkrijgen tot een grondgebied.

Ten vijfde is dan ook vastgesteld dat er in het huidige internationale recht geen recht op toegang tot een grondgebied bestaat voor derden, ten behoeve van het leveren van humanitaire assistentie bij ontbreken van toestemming door de soeverein. In het huidige recht zijn de verplichtingen geformuleerd vanuit het perspectief van de plichten van de getroffen staat en niet vanuit de rechten van derden. Dergelijke plichten omvatten vanuit de mensenrechten een plicht tot zoeken van internationale assistentie (art. 2 IVESCR), en vanuit het oorlogsrecht de verplichting dat assistentie verleend 'zal' worden, onderhavig aan de controle-rechten van de betrokken staat. De normatieve bepaling of een dergelijk recht op toegang *zou moeten* bestaan staat derhalve los van de huidige internationale rechtsregels. Tevens zijn de plichten van de betrokken staat niet geheel eenduidig in de verschillende rechtsgebieden, en is er derhalve geen uniformiteit in het huidige recht, afgezien van de verplichting welke opgenomen is in Artikel 2 IVESCR.

Ten zesde komt inderdaad hierdoor duidelijk naar voren dat het concept 'toestemming' van de getroffen staat één van de grootste obstakels vormt in het huidige raamwerk, aangezien niet één eenduidige drempel kan worden vastgesteld ten aanzien van hetgeen een zogenaamde 'willekeurige' weigering is van aangeboden assistentie. Hoewel een uitputtende lijst niet realistisch is, zou een minimum drempel eventueel vast te stellen kunnen zijn, en zou deze in de praktijk van dienst kunnen zijn. In het oorlogsrecht kan een dergelijk minimum eventueel gelezen worden in het verbod op uithongering, en in de mensenrechten in het vervullen van de zogenaamde 'minimum core obligations'. Een vaststelling hiervan dient evenwel te geschieden door middel van een juridisch orgaan met autoriteit in het internationale recht.

Als zevende, en gerelateerd aan het bovenstaande punt, is het feit dat het humanitaire recht stelt dat de verplichting om toestemming tot toegang tot een grondgebied te verlenen gekoppeld is aan de vaststelling dat dit grondgebied 'ontoereikend voorzien' is. In het recht zit een inherent problem: namelijk dat het aan de soeverein *zelf* is om te bepalen of er sprake is van een ontoereikende voorziening van humanitaire hulp. Een oplossing hiervoor kan gezocht worden in het toepassen van de criteria die een schending van het recht op leven, voedsel en gezondheid kunnen vormen. Immers is vast komen te staan dat het niet leveren van humanitaire hulp kan leiden tot een schending van deze rechten. Op deze wijze zou handhaving geschieden middels de toepassing van mensenrechtenstandaarden, in tegenstelling tot het toetsen van het criterium 'ontoereikende voorziening' in weerwil van de soeverein.

Hiermee is ook het achtste en laatste punt aan de orde gekomen waar het huidige juridische kader ten aanzien van het leveren van humanitaire assistentie mee worstelt: handhaving. Wie dient te bepalen of een grondgebied ontoereikend voorzien is? Wie bepaalt of toestemming wederrechtelijk ontbreekt bij een *bona fide* aanbod van hulp? Wanneer dergelijke vraagstukken instemmend beantwoord worden, kan geconcludeerd worden dat er sprake is van het onhouden of belemmeren van hulpverlening en dat derhalve een schending van het internationale recht plaatsvindt, wat leidt tot handhavingsmogelijkheden.

Handhaving binnen het internationale recht kent zo haar eigen problematiek: de politieke componenten van de Veiligheidsraad en de traagheid van de juridische organen zoals het Internationaal Gerechtshof zijn bekend. Tevens spelen niet-statelijke actoren een grote rol in interne conflicten, terwijl handhaving met betrekking tot hun handelen niet goed mogelijk is bij bestaande gerechtshoven. Alle organen hebben derhalve hun tekortkomingen en beperkingen. Echter, het creeëren van nieuwe rechtsregels, middels een verdrag, lijkt niet levensvatbaar, en oplossingen dienen dan ook vooral gezocht te worden binnen het huidige recht.

De huidige organen met autoriteit zijn de VN Veiligheidsraad, het Internationaal Gerechtshof en het Internationaal Strafhof, en mensenrechtenhoven. Een gecombineerde aanpak biedt dan ook wellicht de oplossing: een juridisch orgaan dat advies brengt aan de Veiligheidsraad in *ad hoc* omstandigheden. Een dergelijk orgaan zou zorgen voor meer juridische onderbouwing van de politieke besluitvorming van de Raad.

In het huidige internationale recht vormt de Veiligheidsraad het orgaan dat het snelste in staat is vast te stellen of er handhavingsmogelijkheden zijn welke vallen binnen het internationale recht. Met het onderschrijven van de 'Responsibility to Protect'-doctrine is deze weg voortgezet. Tevens, wanneer de Raad zich zou richten op eventuele natuurrampen en overige scenario's waar grote groepen ontheemden uit voortvloeien met een 'spill-over' effect naar naburige landen, bestaat de mogelijkheid ook hier te concluderen dat sprake kan zijn van een 'gevaar voor de internationale vrede en veiligheid' als gesteld in Artikel 39 VN Handvest. Met de toepassing hiervan, staat het de Veiligheidsraad vrij om te handelen. Dit geldt evenzeer met betrekking tot de toepassing van het concept 'misdrijven tegen de menselijkheid' waarbij geen koppeling nodig is aan een gewapend conflict, en welke dus ook vastgesteld kan worden inclusief daaropvolgend handelen van de Veiligheidsraad, indien een soeverein geen hulpverlening biedt na een natuurramp.

Dit gezegd zijnde, moet evenwel benadrukt worden dat het gebruik van geweld nooit de eerste, noch de perfecte oplossing is voor het handhaven van het leveren van humanitaire assistentie. Het is echter in sommige gevallen de enige optie voor de internationale gemeenschap, wanneer zij getuige is van wederom een enorme humanitaire crisis. Bovendien geldt dat, ongeacht of de VN Veiligheidsraad overgaat tot handelen, de route naar juridisch handhaven altijd blijft bestaan.

Inderdaad, het vaststellen van het huidige bestaande 'minimum' raamwerk kan en mag niet afdoen aan de mogelijkheid van internationale actoren om *verder* te gaan in de bescherming van burgers ten tijde van een humanitaire crisis. Het internationale recht heeft zich in de afgelopen decennia steeds verder ontwikkeld in de bescherming van personen door middel van de geleidelijke samenkomst van het oorlogsrecht en de mensenrechten. Deze ontwikkeling dient ook tot uiting te komen in de gelijke bescherming van personen ongeacht het soort crisis waarin zij zich bevinden. Het is daarom van essentieel belang dat het raamwerk ten aanzien van het leveren van humanitaire hulp deze rechten en plichten op een integrale wijze benadert. Onduidelijkheid in het recht leidt al te vaak tot het niet (juist) toepassen ervan, en dat resulteert in het onderhavige geval in een gebrek aan hulpgoederen voor diegenen die het nodig hebben. Het huidige juridische raamwerk ten aanzien van het leveren van humanitaire hulp, en de handhaving ervan, dient dan ook verspreid en onderschreven te worden op alle mogelijke wijzen, door de verscheidene actoren in dit veld. Met grotere kennis ontstaat ook een grotere kans op bescherming van diegenen die het nodig hebben. Dat is het uiteindelijke doel van dit onderzoek.

BIBLIOGRAPHY

LITERATURE

Abril Stoffels Ruth, 'Legal Regulation of Humanitarian Assistance in Armed Conflict: Achievements and Gaps', (2004) 86 *International Review of the Red Cross* 855, 515-546.

Alston Philip & Tomaševski Katarina (eds), *The Right to Food* (Martinus Nijhoff 1984).

Alston Philip & Quinn Gerard, 'The Nature and Scope of State Parties' Obligations under the International Covenant on Economic, Social and Cultural Rights' (1987) 9 *Human Rights Quarterly* 1.

Anderson Mary B & Spelten Angelika, 'Conflict Transformation: How International Assistance Can Contribute', *Policy Paper 15* (Development and Peace Foundation 2000).

Annan Kofi, 'Two concepts of sovereignty', *The Economist* (18 September 1999) 49-50.

Annan Kofi, '"We the peoples": the role of the United Nations in the 21s century' (United Nations, 2000).

Arnison Nancy D, 'International Law and Non-Intervention: when do humanitarian concerns supersede sovereignty?' (1993) 17 *Fletcher Forum for World Affairs* 199-211.

Aspremont Jean d' & Tranchez Elodie, 'The quest for a non-conflictual existence of international human rights law and humanitarian law: which role for the lex specialis principle?' in Robert Kolb and Gloria Gaggioli (eds) *Research Handbook on Human Rights and Humanitarian Law* (Edwar Elgar 2013), 223-250.

Barber Rebecca, 'The Responsibility to Protect Survivors of Natural Disaster: Cyclone Nargis, a Case Study' (2009) 14 Journal of Conflict and Security Law 3-34.

Barber Rebecca, 'Facilitating humanitarian assistance in international humanitarian and human rights law', (2009) 91 International Review of the Red Cross 874, 371-397.

Beeckman Katrien, 'International Response to Non-Armed Conflict Disasters: Legal Challenges Encountered in light of the current Regulatory Framework', (2006) 25 *Refugee Survey Quarterly* 4, 129-137.

Beigbeder Yves, *The Role and Status of International Humanitarian Volunteers and Organizations: the Right and Duty to Humanitarian Assistance* (Martinus Nijhoff Publishers 1991).

Bellamy Alex, *Responsibility to Protect: the Global Effort to End Mass Atrocities* (Polity Press 2009).

Bellamy Alex J & Williams Paul D, 'The new politics of protection? Côte d'Ivoire, Libya and the responsibility to protect', (2011) 87 *International Affairs* 4, 825–850.

Bettati Mario & Kouchner Bernard (eds) *Le devoir d'ingérence: Peut-on les laisser mourir?* (Denoël 1987).

Benvenisti Eyal, 'International Protection of the Right to Water', (October 2010) *Max Planck Encyclopedia of Public International Law*

Benvenisti Eyal, *The International Law of Occupation* (Oxford University Press 2012).

Benvenisti Eyal 'Sovereigns as Trustees of humanity: The Concept and its Normative Implications', (2012) *SSRN* accessed 24 January 2012.

Blokker Niels, 'Is the Authorization Authorized? Practice of the UN Security Council to Authorize the Use of Force by 'Coalitions of the Able and Willing', (2000) 11 *European Journal of International Law* 3, 541-568

Blokker Niels, 'The Security Council and the Use of Force: On Recent Practice', in Blokker Niels & Schrijver Nico (eds) *The Security Council and the Use of Force: Theory and Reality – A Need for Change?* (Martinus Nijhoff Publishers 2005).

Boyle Alan & Chinkin Christine M, *The Making of International Law* (Oxford University Press 2007).

Boyle Alan, 'Soft Law in International Law-Making' in Malcolm Evans (ed) *International Law* (Oxford University Press 2010).

Broude Tomer & Shany Yuval (eds), *The Shifting Allocation of Authority in International Law: Considering Sovereignty, Supremacy and Subsidiarity* (Hart 2010).

Brownlie Ian, *Principles of Public International Law* (Oxford University Press 2008).

Buergenthal Thomas, 'The Evolving International Human Rights System', in (2006) 100 *American Journal of International Law* 783-807.

Buergenthal Thomas, 'Human Rights' in *Max Planck Encyclopedia of Public International Law* (March 2007)

Bugnion François, 'From Solferino to the Birth of Contemporary International Humanitarian Law', online publication with the ICRC (April 22nd 2009).

Bulto Takele Soboka, 'The Emergence of the Human Right to Water in International Human Rights Law: Invention or Discovery?', (2011) 12 *Melbourne Journal of International Law* 2, 290-315.

Cassese Antonio, 'On the Current Trend towards Criminal Prosecution and Punishment of breaches of International Humanitarian Law', (1998) 9 *European Journal of International Law* 1

Cassese Antonio, 'The Nicaragua and Tadic Tests Revisited in Light of the ICJ Judgment on Genocide in Bosnia', (2007) 18 *European Journal of International Law* 4, 649-668.

Chetail Vincent, 'The contribution of the International Court of Justice to international humanitarian law', (2003) 85 *International Review of the Red Cross* 850, 235-269.

Chinkin Christine M, 'The Challenge of Soft Law: Development and Change in International Law', in International and Comparative Law Quarterly, 38 (1989) 850-866.

Claude Richard Pierre & Weston Burns H (eds), *Human Rights in the World Community: Issues And Action* (University of Pennsylvania Press 2006)

Clapham Andrew, 'Human rights obligations of non-state actors in conflict situations', (2006) 88 International Review of the Red Cross 863

Cohen Roberta & Deng Francis Mading, *Masses in Flight: The Global Crisis of Internal Displacement* (Brookings Institution Press 1998).

Cohen Roberta, 'Humanitarian Imperatives are Transforming Sovereignty', (2008) 9 *Northwestern Journal of International Affairs* 1, 2-13.

Cohen Roberta & Bradley Megan, 'Disasters and Displacement: Gaps in Protection', (2010) 1 *International Humanitarian Legal Studies*, 95-142.

Conlon Justin, 'Sovereignty vs. Human Rights or Sovereignty and Human Rights?', (2004) 46 *Race & Class* 75, 75-96.

Coomans Fons, 'Application of the International Covenant on Economic Social and Cultural Rights in the Framework of International Organisations', (2007) *Max Planck Yearbook of United Nations Law* 11, 359–390.

Costa da Karen, *The Extraterritorial Application of Selected Human Rights Treaties* (Martinus Nijhoff Brill Leiden 2013).

Cortright David & Lopez George A, 'Reforming Sanctions', in Malone David (ed) *The UN Security Council: From the Cold War to the 21st Century* (Lynne Rienner Publications 2004)

Coupland Robin, 'Humanity: What is it and how does it influence international law?' (2001) 83 *International Review of the Red Cross* 844, 969-989.

Crawford James, *The Creation of States in International Law* (Oxford University Press 2006).

Crawford James, *State Responsibility: the General Part* (Cambridge University Press 2013).

Cryer Robert, Friman Hakan, Robinson Darryl and Wilmshurst Elisabeth, *An Introduction to International Criminal Law and Procedure* (Cambridge University Press 2010)

Cullen Anthony, *The Concept of Non-International Armed Conflict in International Humanitarian Law* (Cambridge University Press 2010).

Daes Erica-Irene, *Freedom of the Individual under Law: A Study on the Individual's Duties to the Community and the Limitations of Human Rights and Freedoms under Article 29 of the Universal Declaration of Human Rights* (1990).

Damrosch Lori (ed), *International Law: Cases and Materials* (West Group 2001)

Danchin Peter D and Fischer Horst (eds), *United Nations Reform and the New Collective Security* (Cambridge University Press, 2010).
Deng Francis, 'Frontiers of Sovereignty: A Framework of Protection, Assistance and Development for the Internally Displaced', (1995) 8 *Leiden Journal of International Law* 2, 249-286.
Dennis Michael J, 'Application of Human Rights Treaties Extraterritorially in Times of Armed Conflict and Military Occupation', (2005) 99 *American Journal of International Law* 1, 119-141.
De Vattel Emerik, *Le Droit de Gens: ou Principes de la Loi Naturelle*, (London 1758).
Dinstein Yoram, 'The legal consequences of infringing upon the right to humanitarian assistance', *International Colloquium on the Right to Humanitarian Assistance* (UNESCO, Paris 1995).
Dinstein Yoram, 'The Right to Humanitarian Assistance' (2000) LIII *Naval War College Review* 4, 77-92
Dinstein Yoram, *The International Law of Belligerent Occupation* (Cambridge University Press 2009).
Dinstein Yoram, *The conduct of hostilities under the law of international armed conflict* (Cambridge University Press 2010).
Diop Abdoulaye, 'Humanitarianism and Sovereignty: the State versus Human Rights', *Experts meeting on State Sovereignty, Human Rights and Humanitarian Action* (Montreal, 1-2 March 1995).
Doswald-Beck Louise, 'The right to life in armed conflict: does international humanitarian law provide all the answers?' (2006) 88 *International Review of the Red Cross* 864.
Dunant Henri, *Un Souvenir de Solférino* (self-published 1862 ; 3rd ed. Imprimerie de J.G. Flick 1863).
Dundes Renteln Alison, *International Human Rights: Universalism Versus Relativism* (Sage Publications 1990).
Dungel Joakim, 'A Right to Humanitarian Assistance in Internal Armed Conflicts Respecting Sovereignty, Neutrality and Legitimacy: Practical Proposals to Practical Problems', (2004) *Journal of Humanitarian Assistance* <http://sites.tufts.edu/jha/archives/838> accessed 24 November 2014.

Eide Asbjorn, 'State Obligations Revisited' in Eide Wenche Barth & Kracht Uwe (eds) *Food and Human Rights in Development* (Volume II) (Intersentia 2005).
Eide Wenche Barth & Kracht Uwe, 'The Right to Adequate Food in Human Rights Instruments: Legal Norms and Interpretations' in Eide Wenche Barth & Kracht Uwe (eds) *Food and Human Rights in Development* (Volume II) (Intersentia 2005).
Evans Gareth, 'From humanitarian intervention to the responsibility to protect', (2006) 24 *Wisconsin International Law Journal* 3, 703-722.

Fassbender Bardo, 'Targeted Sanctions Imposed By The UN Security Council And Due Process Rights: A Study Commissioned By The UN Office Of Legal Affairs And Follow-Up Action By The United Nations', (2006) 3 *International Organizations Law Review* 437–485

Fastenrath Ulrich, 'Relative Normativity in International Law' (1993) 4 *European Journal of International Law*, 305-340.

Feinstein Lee, 'Darfur and Beyond: What is Needed to Prevent Mass Atrocities', (2007) *Council on Foreign Relations* Special Report No 22.

Feller Erika, Türk Volker, Nicholson Frances (eds), *Refugee Protection in International Law: UNHCR's Global Consultations on International Protection* (Cambridge University Press, 2003).

Ferris Elizabeth, 'Humanitarian Perspectives on "Protection of Persons in the Event of Disasters', *Roundtable on Canada and International Law, Department of Foreign Affairs and International Trade* (Brookings 2009).

Findlay Trevor, *The Use of Force in UN Peace Operations* (SIPRI/Oxford University Press 2002)

Fisher David, 'Domestic regulation of international humanitarian relief in disasters and armed conflict: a comparative analysis' (2007) 89 *International Review of the Red Cross* 866, 345-372.

Fisher David, 'Right to Humanitarian Assistance' in Kälin Walter, Williams Rhodri C, Koser Khalid and Solomon Andrew (eds) *Incorporating the Guiding Principles on Internal Displacement into Domestic Law: Issues and Challenges* (American Society of International Law 2008).

Fischer Horst, 'International Disaster Response Law, a Preliminary Overview and Analysis of Existing Treaty Law: summary of the study on existing treaty law' (January 2003) *International Federation of Red Cross and Red Crescent Societies*.

Focarelli Carlo, 'Duty to Protect in Cases of Natural Disasters', (2010) *Max Planck Encyclopedia of International Law*.

Ford Stuart, 'Is The Failure To Respond Appropriately To A Natural Disaster A Crime Against Humanity? The Responsibility To Protect And Individual Criminal Responsibility In The Aftermath Of Cyclone Nargis', (2009) 38 *Denver Journal of International Law & Policy* 2.

Forsythe DP, 'The International Committee of the Red Cross and humanitarian assistance – A policy analysis', (1996) *International Review of the Red Cross* 314, 512-531.

Fortin Katharine, 'Complementarity between the ICRC and the United Nations and international humanitarian law and international human rights law, 1948–1968' (2012), 94 *International Review of the Red Cross*, 888, 1-22.

Franco Andrés, 'Armed Non-State Actors', in Malone David (ed) *The UN Security Council: From the Cold War to the 21st Century* (Lynne Rienner Publications 2004)

Gazzini Tarcisio, 'The Rules on the Use of Force at the Beginning of the XXI Century', (2006) 11 *Journal of Conflict and Security Law* 3, 319-342.

Gilliard Emanuela-Chiara, 'The law regulating cross-border relief operations', (2013) 95 *International Review of the Red Cross* 890, 351-380

Giustiniani Flavia Zorzi, 'The Works of the International Law Commission on 'Protection of Persons in the Event of Disasters. A Critical Appraisal' in de Guttry A, Gestri M, Venturini G (eds), *International Disaster Response Law* (TMC Asser Press / Springer 2012).

Goodwin-Gill Guy S and McAdam Jane, *The Refugee in International Law* (Oxford University Press 2007).

Grey Christine, 'Host-State Consent And United Nations Peacekeeping In Yugoslavia', (1996) 7 *Duke Journal of Comparative & International Law* 241-270.

Grey Christine, *International Law and the Use of Force* (Oxford University Press 2008).

Grey Christine, 'The use of force and the international legal order' in Evans Malcolm (ed) *International Law* (Oxford University Press 2010).

Guha-Sapir Debarati, Hoyois Philippe and Below Regina, *Annual Disaster Statistical Review 2013: The numbers and trends* (CRED 2014).

Hamilton Rebecca, 'The Responsibility to Protect: From document to doctrine – but what of implementation?', (2006) 19 *Harvard Human Rights Law Journal* 189-197.

Henckaerts Jean-Marie, 'Assessing the Laws and Customs of War: The Publication of 'Customary International Humanitarian Law', (2005) 13 *Human Rights Brief* 2.

Henckaerts Jean-Marie & Doswald-Beck Louise (eds), *Customary International Humanitarian Law (ICRC Study)* (Cambridge University Press 2006).

Hardcastle Rohan J & Chua Adrian T L, 'Humanitarian Assistance, Towards a Right of access to victims of natural disaster', (1998) 38 *International Review of the Red Cross* 325, 589-609.

Harris Rimmer Susan, 'New Issues in Refugee Research: Refugees, internally displaced persons and the 'responsibility to protect'', (2010) *UNHCR Policy Development and Evaluation Service* Research Paper No. 185.

Haslam Emily, 'United Nations Relief and Rehabilitation Administration', (2006) *Max Planck Encyclopedia of International Law*.

Heath Benton J, 'Disasters, Relief and Neglect: The Duty to Accept Humanitarian Assistance and the Work of the International Law Commission' (2011) 43 *NYU Journal of International Law & Politics* 2, 419-477.

Heinzte Hans-Joachim, 'Convergence Between Human Rights Law and International Humanitarian Law' in Hans-Joachim Heintze & Andrej Zwitter (eds) *Humanitarian Assistance and International Law: A Crosscut Through Legal Issues Pertaining to Humanitarianism* (Springer 2011).

Henkin Louis, 'That "S" Word: Sovereignty, and Globalization, and Human Rights, Et Cetera', (1989) 68 Fordham Law Review 1, 1-14.
Henkin Louis, *The Age of Rights* (Columbia University Press 1990).
Henkin Louis, 'Group Defamation and International Law' in MH Freedman & EM Freedman (eds) *Group Defamation and Freedom of Speech: The Relationship Between Language and Violence* (Greenwood Press 1995).
Hoffmann Julia & Nollkaemper Andre, 'Concluding observations' in J Hoffmann & A Nollkaemper (eds), *Responsibility to Protect: from Principle to Practice* (Pallas Publications 2012) 355-371.
Homan Kees, Klimaatverandering als veiligheidsprobleem, (2008) *Atlantisch Perspectief* 12-18.
Hunt Paul & Leader Sheldon, 'Developing and applying the right to the highest attainable standard of health: the role of the UN Special Rapporteur (2002-2008)', in Harrington John & Stuttaford Maria (eds) *Global Health and Human Rights: Legal and philosophical perspectives* (Routledge 2010) 28-62.

Iliopoulos Katherine, 'UN Debates the Responsibility to Protect', (12 August 2009) Crimes of War Project <www.crimesofwar.org/commentary/un-debates-the-responsibility-to-protect/> accessed 25 December 2014.
'International Military Tribunal Nuremberg Judgment and Sentences', (1947) 41 *American Journal of International Law* 1, 172-333.

Jackson Robert H, 'Nuremberg In Retrospect: Legal Answer To International Lawlessness' (1949) 35 *American Bar Association Journal* 813-816, continued 881- 887.
Jacobsen Trudy, Sampford Charles & Thakur Ramesh, (eds) *Re-envisioning Sovereignty: The End of Westphalia?* (Ashgate 2008).
Jakovljevic Bosko, 'Right to Humanitarian Action and State Sovereignty' in (eds) Stefania Baldini & Guido Ravasi, *Humanitarian Action and State Sovereignty; Refugees: a continuing challenge* (Institute of International Humanitarian Law 2000) 95-101.
Jansen-Wilhelm Stefanie, 'A duty to accept humanitarian assistance under the ICESCR' in Zwitter A et al (eds) *Humanitarian Action: Global, Regional and Domestic Legal Responses* (Cambridge University Press 2014).
Jennings Robert, 'Sovereignty and International Law' in Kreijen Gerard (ed), *State, Sovereignty and International Governance* (Oxford University Press 2002) 27-44.
Jemczyk Erin, 'Norms and Their Effect on Humanitarian Aid', (2005) 2 *Atlantic International Studies Organization* (online).
Joyner Christopher, 'The responsibility to protect: humanitarian concern and the lawfulness of armed intervention', (2007) 47 *Virginia Journal of International Law,* 693-724.

Kabasakal Arat Zehra F, *Human Rights Worldwide: A Reference Handbook* (ABC Clio 2006).
Kalshoven Frits, 'Impartialité et neutralité dans le droit et la pratique humanitaires', (1989) 71 *International Review of the Red Cross* 780, 541-562.
Kalshoven, Frits & Zegveld Liesbeth, *Constraints on the Waging of War: An Introduction to International Humanitarian Law* (Cambridge University Press 2011).
Keren Michael & Sylvan Donald (eds), *International Intervention: Sovereignty versus Responsibility*, (Routledge 2002).
Kiefer Thorsten & Brölmann Catherine, 'The Human Right to Water', (2005) 5 *Non-State Actors and International Law,* 183-208.
Kioko Ben, 'The right of intervention under the African Union's Constitutive Act: From non-interference to non-intervention', (2003) 85 *International Review of the Red Cross* 852, 807-825.
Klabbers Jan, 'The Redundancy of Soft Law' (1996) 65 *Nordic Journal of International Law*, 167-182.
Kolb Robert, 'The Relationship between international humanitarian law and human rights law: A brief history of the 1948 Universal Declaration of Human Rights and the Geneva Conventions', (1998) *International Review of the Red Cross*, 324.
Kolb Robert, 'De l'assistance humanitaire: la résolution sur l'assistance humanitaire adoptée par l'Institut de droit international à sa session de Bruges en 2003', (2004) 86 *International Review of the Red Cross* 856.
Kolb Robert and Hyde Richard, *An Introduction to the International Law of Armed Conflicts* (Hart 2008).
Krieger Heike, 'A Conflict of Norms: The Relationship Between Humanitarian Law and Human Rights Law in the ICRC Customary Law Study' (2006), 11 *Journal of Conflict and Security Law*, 2, 265-291.
Kuijt Emilie, 'A humanitarian crisis: reframing the legal framework on humanitarian assistance', in Zwitter A et al (eds) *Humanitarian Action: Global, Regional and Domestic Legal Responses* (Cambridge University Press 2014) 54-80.

Lahmann Henning, 'Biafra Conflict', (2009) *Max Planck Encyclopedia of Public International Law*.
Langholtz Harvey J and Stout Chris E (eds) *The Psychology of Diplomacy* (Praeger Publishers 2004).
Lee Amra, 'The Case for Strengthening Protection Frameworks in 'Other Situations of Violence' (2014) *The Journal of Humanitarian Assistance* online publication <http://sites.tufts.edu/jha/archives/2091> accessed 1 March 2015.
Lubell Noam, 'Challenges in applying human rights law to armed conflict', (2005) 87 *International Review of the Red Cross* 860.
Lauterpacht Elihu (ed), *International Law: Being the Collected Papers of Hersch Lauterpacht* (Cambridge University Press 1975) Vol. II, part 1.

Luck Edward C, The Responsibility to Protect: The First Decade' (2011) 3 *Global Responsibility to Protect*, 387-399.

Luopojärvi Katja, 'Is There an Obligation on States to Accept International Humanitarian Assistance to Internally Displaced Persons under International Law?' (2004) 15 International Journal of Refugee Law 4, 678-714.

Magnuson William, 'The Responsibility to Protect and the decline of sovereignty: Free speech protection under international law', (2010) 43 *Vanderbilt Journal of Transnational Law* 255-312.

Macalister-Smith Peter, International Humanitarian Assistance: Disaster Relief Actions in International Law and Organization, Martinus Nijhoff 1985.

Macalister-Smith Peter, 'International Guidelines for Humanitarian Assistance Operations', (Max Planck Institute for Comparative Law and International Law, Heidelberg,1991).

Mackintosh Kate 'The Principles of Humanitarian Action in International Humanitarian Law: Study 4 in: The Politics of Principle: the principles of humanitarian action in practice', *Humanitarian Policy Group* Report 5, March 2000.

Magnuson William J, 'The Responsibility to Protect and the Decline of Sovereignty: Free Speech Protection under International Law', (2010) 43 *Vanderbilt Journal of Transnational Law* 2.

Maogoto Jackson & Kindiki Kithure, 'A people Betrayed – the Darfur Crisis and International Law: Rethinking Westphalian Sovereignty in the 21st Century', (2007) 19 *Bond Law Review* 2, 102-123.

Maogoto Jackson Nyamuya, 'Westphalian Sovereignty in the Shadow of International Justice? A Fresh Coat of Paint for a Tainted Concept' in Jacobsen Trudy, Sampford Charles & Thakur Ramesh (eds) *Re-envisioning Sovereignty: The End of Westphalia?* (Ashgate 2008) 211-227.

Martin Susan F, Weerasinghe Sanjula & Taylor Abbie (eds), *Humanitarian Crises and Migration* (Routledge 2014).

Maus Sylvia, 'Human Rights in UN Peacekeeping Missions: A Framework for Humanitarian Obligations?' in Heintze HJ & Zwitter A (eds) *International Law and Humanitarian Assistance: A Crosscut Through Legal Issues Pertaining to Humanitarianism* (Springer 2011).

McCorquodale Robert, 'The Individual and the International Legal System' in Evans Malcolm (ed), *International Law* (Oxford University Press 2010) 284-310.

McGonagle Tarlach, 'International and European Legal Standards for Combating Racist Expression: Selected Current Conundrums', *Expert Seminar: Combating Racism while respecting Freedom of Expression* (2007).

Mechlem Kerstin, 'Right to Food, International Protection' in *Max Planck Encyclopedia of Public International Law* (June 2008).

Mepham David & Ramsbotham Alexander, 'Safeguarding Civilians: Delivering on the Responsibility to Protect in Africa' (The Institute for Public Policy Research, 2007).

Meron Theodor, 'The Geneva Conventions as Customary Law' (1987) 81 *American Journal of International Law* 2, 348-370.

Meron Theodor, 'The Martens Clause, Principles of Humanity, and Dictates of the Public Conscience', (2000) 94 *American Journal of International Law* 1, 78-89.

Meron Theodor, 'The Humanization of Humanitarian Law', (2000) 94 *American Journal of International Law* 2.

Mills Kurt, 'Sovereignty Eclipsed?: The Legitimacy of Humanitarian Access and Intervention', (1997) *The Journal of Humanitarian Assistance* <https://sites.tufts.edu/jha/archives/111> (online publication).

Minear Larry, *Humanitarianism under siege: A Critical Review of Operation Lifeline Sudan*, (the Red Sea Press, Inc.1991).

Moir Lindsay, *The Law of Internal Armed Conflict* (Cambridge University Press 2002).

Molier Gelijn, 'De Soevereine Staat en het Internationaal Recht: Een ongemakkelijke Symbiose' (2009) in G Molier, T J M Slootweg (eds), *Soevereiniteit en Recht. Rechtsfilosofische beschouwingen* (Boom Juridische uitgevers) 133-176.

Morris Christopher (ed), *The Social Contract Theorists: Critical Essays on Hobbes, Locke and Rousseau* (Rowman & Littlefield 1999).

Müller Amrei, 'Limitations to and Derogations from Economic, Social and Cultural Rights' (2009) 9 *Human Rights Law Review* 4, 557-601.

Muñoz Heraldo, 'The Responsibility to Protect: Three Pillars and Four Crimes', (2009) *human rights & human welfare working papers*, 53.

Nasu Hitoshi, 'Operationalizing the 'Responsibility to Protect' and conflict prevention: dilemmas of civilian protection in armed conflict', (2009) 14 *Journal of Conflict and Security Law* 2, 209-241.

Nasu Hitoshi, *International Law on Peacekeeping: A Study of Article 40 of the UN Charter* (Brill Martinus Nijhoff 2009).

Niada Laura, 'Hunger and International Law: The Far-reaching Scope of the Human Right to Food', (2006) 22 *Connecticut Journal of International Law* 1, 131-201.

Nieto Navia Rafael, 'International Peremptory Norms (Jus Cogens) And International Humanitarian Law' in Vohrah LC, Pocar F et al, (eds) *Man's Inhumanity to Man: Essays in Honour of Antonio Cassese* (Kluwer Law International 2003).

Nolte Georg, 'The Different Functions of the Security Council with Respect to Humanitarian Law' in Lowe V, Roberts A, Welsh J & Zaum D (eds) *The United Nations Security Council and War: The Evolution of Thought and Practice Since 1945* (Oxford University Press 2008).

Oakley Robert B, Dziedzic Michael J, Goldberg Eliot M (eds), *Policing The New World Disorder: Peace Operations And Public Security* (National Defense University Press 1998).

O'Connell Mary Ellen, 'The United Nations Security Council and the Authorization of Force: Renewing the Council Through Law Reform', in Blokker Niels & Schrijver Nico (eds) *The Security Council and the Use of Force: Theory and Reality – A Need for Change?* (Martinus Nijhoff Publishers 2005)

Odello Marco, 'Fundamental Standards of Humanity: A Common Language of International Humanitarian Law and Human Rights Law' in R Arnold & N Quénivet (eds) *International Humanitarian Law and Human Rights Law: Towards a New Merger in International Law* (Martinus Nijhoff Publishers 2008).

Orakhelashvili Alexander, 'The Impact of Peremptory Norms', (2005) 16 *European Journal of International Law*, 59-88.

Orakhelashvili Alexander, *Peremptory Norms in International Law* (Oxford University Press 2006).

Palumbo Michael, *Human Rights: Meaning and History* (Krieger 1982).

Paust Jordan J, 'De-Regulating Humanitarian Aid: The Need for New Norms and Interpretations' in Buffard Isabelle, Crawford James, Pellet Alain and Wittich Stephan (eds) *International Law between Universalism and Fragmentation: Festschrift in Honour of Gerhard Hafner* (Brill Martinus Nijhoff, Leiden 2008).

Pejic Jelena, 'The right to food in situations of armed conflict: the legal framework', (2001) 83 *International Review of the Red Cross* 844.

Piccin Francesca & Pusterla Elia, 'Defending eroded states' sovereignty: the European Union humanitarian aid policy' *GARNET Conference* 'The European Union in International Affairs' (22 April 2010).

Pictet Jean (ed), *Commentary on the Geneva Conventions of 12 August 1949 Volumes I-IV* (International Committee of the Red Cross 1952-1959).

Phuong Catherine, *The International Protection of Internally Displaced Persons* (Cambridge University Press 2004.

Plattner Denise, 'ICRC neutrality and neutrality in humanitarian assistance', (1996) 36 *International Review of the Red Cross* 311, 161-179.

Pommier Bruno, 'The use of force to protect civilians and humanitarian action: the case of Libya and beyond', (2011) 93 *International Review of the Red Cross* 884, 1063-1083

Ponthieu Aurelie, Vogel Christoph, Derderian Katharine, 'Without Precedent or Prejudice? UNSC Resolution 2098 and its potential implications for humanitarian space in Eastern Congo and beyond', (2014) *The Journal of Humanitarian Assistance* <http://sites.tufts.edu/jha/archives/2032> accessed 3 March 2015 (online publication).

Provost René, International Human Rights and Humanitarian Law (Cambridge University Press 2002)

Quenivet Noelle, 'Humanitarian assistance: a right or a policy? Case study: the Security Council and the armed conflict in the former Yugoslavia' (1999) *The Journal of Humanitarian Assistance,* 17 < http://sites.tufts.edu/jha/archives/category/noelle-quenivet-2> (online publication).

Pocar Fausto, 'Human Rights Under The International Covenant On Civil And Political Rights And Armed Conflicts', in LC Vohrah, F Pocar et al, (eds) *Man's Inhumanity to Man: Essays in Honour of Antonio Cassese* (Kluwer Law International 2003).

Popovski V and Fraser T (eds), *The Security Council as Global Legislator* (Routledge Global Institutions Series 2014).

Porretto Gabriele & Vité Sylvain, 'The application of international humanitarian law and human rights law to international organisations' (2006) *UCHL Research Paper Series* 1

Quénivet Noelle, 'The History of the Relationship Between International Humanitarian Law and Human Rights law' in R Arnold & N Quénivet (eds) *International Humanitarian Law and Human Rights Law: Towards a New Merger in International Law* (Martinus Nijhoff Publishers 2008).

Ragazzi Maurizio, *The Concept of International Obligations Erga Omnes* (Oxford University Press 1997)

Reeves Eric, 'On the Obstruction of Humanitarian Aid', (2011) 54 *African Studies Review* 3.

Rehof Lars Adam, 'Article 3', in Alfredsson Gudmundur & Eide Asbjørn (eds) *The Universal Declaration of Human Rights: A Common Standard of Achievement* (Martinuss Nijhoff Publishers 1999).

Reinisch August, 'Developing Human Rights and Humanitarian Law Accountability of the Security Council for the Imposition of Economic Sanctions', (2001) 95 *American Journal of International Law* 4, 851-872

Reinisch August, 'The Changing International Legal Framework for Dealing with Non-State Actors' in Alston Philip (ed) *Non-State Actors and Human Rights* (Oxford University Press 2005), 37-92.

Riedel Eibe, 'International Protection of the Right to Health', (April 2011) *Max Planck Encyclopedia of Public International Law.*

Rieff David, 'Humanitarianism in Crisis', (2002) 81 *Foreign Affairs* 6.

Roht-Arriaza Naomi & Aminzadeh Sara C, 'Solidarity Rights: Development, Peace, Environment, Humanitarian Assistance' in *Max Planck Encyclopedia of Public International Law* (2007).

Rottensteiner Christa, 'The denial of humanitarian assistance as a crime under international law', (1999) 81 *International Review of the Red Cross* 835, 555-582.

Russbach Rémi & Fink Daniel, 'Humanitarian action in current armed conflicts: opportunities and obstacles', (1994) 1 *Medicine and Global Survival* 4, 188-199.

Ryngaert Cedric, 'Clarifying the Extraterritorial Application of the European Convention on Human Rights (Al-Skeini v the United Kingdom)' (2012) 28 *Merkourios - International and European Security Law* 74.

Ryngaert Cedric, 'Humanitarian Assistance and the Conundrum of Consent: A Legal Perspective', (2013) 5 *Amsterdam Law Forum* 2, 5-19.

Salman M A Salman and Mclnerney-Lankford Siobhán, 'The Human Right to Water: Legal and Policy Dimensions', The World Bank *Law, Justice and Development Series* (2004)

Sandoz Yves, Swinarski Christophe and Zimmermann Bruno (eds), *Commentary on the Additional Protocols of 8 June 1977 to the Geneva Conventions of 12 August 1949, Protocol I and II* (International Committee of the Red Cross 1987).

Sandoz Yves, '"Droit" or "devoir d'ingérence" and the Right to Assistance: The Issues Involved', (1992) ICRC Review 32, 215-227.

Sanvik-Nylund Monika, *Caught in Conflicts: Civilians, Victims, Humanitarian Assistance and International Law* (Institute for Human Rights Åbo Akademi University 2003).

Sassòli Marco and Olson Laura M, 'The relationship between international humanitarian and human rights law where it matters: admissible killing and internment of fighters in non-international armed conflicts', (2008) 90 *International Review of the Red Cross* 871, 599-627.

Schindler Dietrich, 'The right to humanitarian assistance: right and/or obligation?', *International Colloquium on the Right to Humanitarian Assistance* (UNESCO 1995).

Schrijver Nico J, 'Begrensde Soevereiniteit: 350 jaar na de vrede van Munster', inaugural address as Professor of international law at the Law Faculty of the VU University Amsterdam (15 May 1998).

Schrijver Nico J, 'Sovereignty versus Human Rights? A Tale of UN Security Council Resolution 688 (1991) on the Protection of the Kurdish People', in: M Castermans, F van Hoof and J Smith (eds), *The Role of the Nation-State in the 21st Century: Human Rights, International Organizations and Foreign Policy. Essays in Honour of Peter Baehr* (Brill Nijhoff 1998), 347-357.

Schrijver Nico J, 'The Changing Nature of State Sovereignty', (1999) 70 *British Year Book of International Law*, 65-98.

Schrijver Nico J, 'Paving the Way Towards...One World Wide Human Rights Treaty', (2011) 29 *Netherlands Quarterly of Human Rights* 3, 257-260.

Schwendimann Felix, 'The legal framework of humanitarian access in armed conflict', (2011) *93 International Review of the Red Cross* 884.

Shaffer Gregory C and Pollack Mark A, 'Hard vs. Soft Law: Alternatives, Complements, and Antagonists in International Governance' (2010) 94 *Minnesota Law Review*, 706-799.

Shaw Malcolm, International Law (Cambridge University Press 2008).

Shawki Noha, 'Responsibility to Protect: The Evolution of an International Norm', (2011) 3 *Global Responsibility to Protect* 2, 172–196.

Shelton Dinah, 'International Law and "Relative Normativity"' in Evans Malcolm (ed), *International Law* (Oxford University Press 2010) 141-171.

Siegrist Michael, 'The Functional Beginning of Belligerent Occupation' (2011) 7 *eCahiers de l' Institut* (Graduate Institute Geneva).

Simma Bruno, 'NATO, the UN and the Use of Force: Legal Aspects', (1999) 10 *European Journal of International Law* 1-22

Slaughter Anne Marie, 'Disaggregated Sovereignty: Towards Public Accountability of Global Government Networks', (2004) 39 *Government and Opposition* 2, 159-190.

Slaughter Anne Marie, 'Sovereignty and Power in a Networked World Order', (2004) 40 *Stanford Journal of International Law*, 283-327.

Slaughter Anne Marie, 'Intervention, Libya, and the Future of Sovereignty', *The Atlantic* (4 September 2011).

Spieker Heike, 'The Right to Give and Receive Humanitarian Assistance', in HJ Heintze & A Zwitter (eds), *Humanitarian Assistance and International Law* (Springer 2011).

Spieker Heike, 'Humanitarian Assistance, Access in Armed Conflict and Occupation' (2013) *Max Planck Encyclopedia of Public International Law*

Staden Alfred van and Vollaard Hans, 'The Erosion of State Sovereignty: Towards a Post-territorial World?' in Kreijen Gerard (ed), *State, Sovereignty and International Governance* (Oxford University Press 2002) 165-184.

Stahn Carsten, 'Responsibility to Protect: Political Rhetoric or Emerging Legal Norm?' (2007) 101 *American Journal of International Law* 1, 99-120.

Stahn Carsten, 'Syria and the Semantics of Intervention, Aggression and Punishment On 'Red Lines' and 'Blurred Lines', (2013) 11 *Journal of International Criminal Justice* 955-977

Steiner Henry, Alston Philip & Goodman Ryan, *International Human Rights in Context: Law, Politics, Morals* (Oxford University Press 2007).

Stevenson Frances & Macrae Joanna, 'Legislating for humanitarian aid', (2002) 21 *Humanitarian Exchange Magazine*, 33-35.

Talmon Stefan, 'The Statements of the President of the Security Council', (2003) 2 *Chinese Journal of International Law*, 419 – 466.

Talmon Stefan, 'The Security Council as World Legislature', (2005) 99 *The American Journal of International Law* 1, 175-193.

Tams Christian J, Enforcing Obligations Erga Omnes in International Law (Cambridge University Press 2010).

Tesón Fernando R, *Humanitarian Intervention: An Inquiry into Law and Morality* (Transnational Publishers, Inc 2005).

Tesón Fernando R, 'Humanitarian Intervention: Loose Ends', (2011) 10 *Journal of Military Ethics* 3, 192-212.

Thakur Ramesh, *The United Nations, Peace and Security: from Collective Security to the Responsibility to Protect* (Cambridge University Press 2006).

Thirlway Hugh, 'The Sources of International Law' in Malcolm Evans (ed) *International Law* (OUP 2010).

Thomas Daniel C, 'International NGOs, State Sovereignty and democratic values', 2 (2001) *Chicago Journal of International Law* 2.

Toebes Brigit, *The Right to Health as a Human Right in International Law* (Intersentia 1999).

Tomuschat Christian, 'The Applicability of Human Rights Law to Insurgent Movements', in Fischer Horst, Froissart Ulrika, von Heinegg Heintschel Wolff and Raap Christian (eds), *Krisensicherung und Humanitärer Schutz – Crisis Management and Humanitarian Protection: Festschrift für Dieter Fleck, Berliner Wissenschafts-Verlag* (Berliner Wissenschafstverlag 2004) 573–91.

Tomuschat Christian, *Human Rights: Between Idealism and Realism* (Oxford University Press 2008).

Tomuschat Christian, Lagrange Evelyne & Oeter Stefan (eds), *The Right to Life* (Brill 2010).

Tsui Ed & Myint-U Thant, 'The Institutional response: creating a framework in response to new challenges' (2004) II *The Humanitarian Decade: challenges for Humanitarian Assistance in the last decade and into the future* (OCHA).

Tsui Ed, 'Analysis of Normative Development in Humanitarian Resolutions since the Adoption of 46/182', independent review for OCHA (2009).

Tucker Spencer, *Battles That Changed History: An Encyclopedia of World Conflict* (Greenwood Publishing Group 2011).

Vasak Karel, "Human Rights: A Thirty-Year Struggle: the Sustained Efforts to give Force of law to the Universal Declaration of Human Rights", *UNESCO Courier 30:11* (Paris: UNESCO, November 1977).

Vaurs-Chaumette A L, 'Peoples and Minorities' in Crawford J et al (ed) *The Law of International Responsibility* (Oxford: Oxford University Press, 2010).

Viotti Aurélio, 'In search of symbiosis: the Security Council in the humanitarian domain', (2007) 89 *International Review of the Red Cross* 865, 131-153.

Vidar Margret, 'The Interrelationships between the Right to Food and Other Human Rights' in Eide Vigny Jean-Daniel and Thompson Cecilia, 'Fundamental Standards of Humanity: What Future?', (2002) 20 *Netherlands Quarterly of Human Rights* 185–99.

Wenche Barth & Kracht Uwe (eds) *Food and Human Rights in Development* (Volume I) (Intersentia 2005) 141-160.

Vité Sylvain, 'The interrelation of the law of occupation and economic, social and cultural rights', (2008) 90 *International Review of the Red Cross* 871

Vité Sylvain, 'Typology of armed conflicts in international humanitarian law: legal concepts and actual situations', (2009) 91 *International Review of the Red Cross* 873, 69 – 94.

Vukas Budislav, 'Humanitarian Assistance in Cases of Emergency', (2007) *Max Planck Encyclopedia of Public International Law*.

Weis Paul, 'Human Rights and Refugees', (1971) 1 *Israel Yearbook for Human Rights* 35-50.
Weis Paul, *The Refugee Convention 1951: The Travaux Preparatoires Analysed With A Commentary* (UNHCR 1995).
Weiss Thomas & Hubert Don 'State Sovereignty' in *The Responsibility to Protect: Research Bibliography and Background: Supplementary Volume to the Report of ICISS* (International Development Research Centre 2001).
Wheeler Nicholas J, 'Legitimating humanitarian intervention: principles and procedures', (2001) 2 *Melbourne Journal of International Law* 2, 550-567.
Wong Jarrod, 'Reconstructing the Responsibility to Protect in the Wake of Cyclones and Separatism', (2009) 84 *Tulane Law Review*, 219-263.
Wood Michael C, 'The Interpretation of Security Council Resolutions', (1998) *Max Planck Yearbook of United Nations Law* 73-95.
Wu Daniel I, 'Reconciling Sovereignty with Responsibility: Burma and ASEAN' (2010) *CSIS Southeast Asia Program*.

Zegveld Liesbeth, *The Accountability of Armed Opposition Groups in International Law* (Cambridge University Press 2002).

TABLE OF CASES

International Court of Justice

Corfu Channel Case (UK v Albania) (Merits) 9 April 1949 I.C.J. Reports 4

North Sea Continental Shelf cases (Federal Republic Of Germany/Denmark; Federal Republic of Germany/Netherlands) Judgment Of 20 February 1969, I.C.J. Reports 1969, p. 3.

Legal Consequences for States of the Continued Presence of South Africa in Namibia (South West Africa) notwithstanding Security Council Resolution 276 (1970), Advisory Opinion, ICJ Reports (1971) p. 16.

Military and Paramilitary Activities in and against Nicaragua (Nicaragua v. United States of America), Merits, Judgment 27 June 1986 I.C.J. Reports 1986, p. 14.

Legality of the Threat or Use of Nuclear Weapons, Advisory Opinion, I.C.J. Reports 1996, p. 226.

Gabčíkovo-Nagymaros Project (Hungary/Slovakia), Merits Judgment 25 September 1997, I.C.J. Reports 1997, p.7

Legal Consequences of the Construction of a Wall in the Occupied Palestinian Territory, Advisory Opinion, I. C. J. Reports 2004, p. 136.

Armed Activities on the Territory of the Congo (Democratic Republic of the Congo v. Uganda), Judgment, I.C.J. Reports 2005, p. 168.

Armed Activities on the Territory of the Congo (New Application: 2002) (Democratic Republic of the Congo v. Rwanda), Jurisdiction and Admissibility, Judgment, I.C.J. Reports 2006, p. 6

Application of the Convention on the Prevention and Punishment of the Crime of Genocide (Bosnia and Herzegovina v. Serbia and Montenegro), Judgment, I.C.J. Reports 2007, p. 43

Application of the International Convention on the Elimination of all Forms of Racial Discrimination (Georgia v. Russian Federation), Provisional Measures, Order of 15 October 2008, I.C.J. Reports 2008, p. 353.

Application of the International Convention on the Elimination of All Forms of Racial Discrimination (Georgia v. Russian Federation), Preliminary Objections, Judgment, I.C.J. Reports 2011, p. 70

Questions relating to the Obligation to Prosecute or Extradite (Belgium v. Senegal), Judgment, I.C.J. Reports 2012, p. 422.

International criminal tribunals

Prosecutor v. Tadić a.k.a "Dule" (Appeals Chamber Decision on the Defence motion for Interlocutory Appeal on Jurisdiction) IT-94-1-AR72 (2 October 1995).

Prosecutor v. Tadić a.k.a "Dule" (Judgment Trial Chamber) IT-94-1-T (7 May 1997).

Prosecutor v. Zejnil Delalic, Zdravko Mucic (aka "Pavo"), Hazim Delic and Esad Landžo (aka "Zenga") (Celebici - Case) (Trial Chamber) IT-96-21-T (16 November 1998)
Prosecutor v. Furundzija (Trial Judgment) IT-95-17/1-T (ICTY 10 December 1998).
Prosecutor v. Tadić, (Appeals Chamber) IT-94-1A (15 July 1999).
Prosecutor v. Kupreškić et al. (IT-95-16) "Lašva Valley"(Judgment Trial Chamber) IT-95-16-T (14 January 2000).
Prosecutor v. Zejnil Delalic, Zdravko Mucic (aka "Pavo"), Hazim Delic and Esad Landžo (aka "Zenga") (Celebici - Case) (Appeals Chamber) IT-96-21-A (20 February 2001).
Prosecutor v. Krstic (Trial Judgment) IT-98-33-T (2 August 2001)
Prosecutor v. Mitar Vasiljevic (Trial Judgment) Case No IT-98-32-T (29 November 2002)
Prosecutor v. Mladen Naletilić, aka Tuta & Vinko Martinović, aka Štela (Trial Judgment) IT-98-34-T (31 March 2003).
Prosecutor v. Galić (Trial Judgment) IT-98-29-T (5 December 2003)
Prosecutor v. Vasiljevid (Appeal Judgment) IT-98- 32-A (25 February 2004)
Prosecutor v. Krstic (Appeal Judgment) IT-98-33-A (19 April 2004)
Prosecutor v. Radoslav Brdanin (Trial Judgment) Case No IT-99-36-T (1 September 2004)
Prosecutor v. Dario Kordić and Mario Čerkez (Appeal Judgment) IT-95-14/2-A (17 December 2004)
Prosecutor v. Blagojević & Jokić (Trial Judgment) IT-02-60-T (17 January 2005)
Prosecutor v. Fatmir Limaj, Haradin Bala, Isak Musliu, (Judgment Trial Chamber II) IT-03-66-T (30 November 2005)
Prosecutor v. Issa Hassan Sesay, Morris Kallon and Augustine Gbao (the RUF accused) (Trial judgment), Case No. SCSL-04-15-T, Special Court for Sierra Leone (2 March 2009)
The Prosecutor v. Abu Garda, Case No ICC-02/05-02/09 Decision on Confirmation of Charges (8 February 2010)
The Prosecutor v. Al Bashir, Case No ICC-02/05-01/09 Second Decision on the Prosecution's Application for a Warrant of Arrest (12 July 2010)

Human rights courts, committees and monitoring bodies

European Commission X v Ireland, Appl. No. 6040/73 (20 July 1973).
European Commission, Association X v UK Case No. 7154/75 (12 July 1978).

Loizidou v Turkey (Preliminary Objections) (App no 15318/89) ECHR 23 March 1995.
Bankovic and others v. Belgium and 16 Other Contracting States (Decision as to the Admissibility) (App no 52207/99) ECHR 12 December 2001.
Ilascu and others v Moldova and Russia (App no 48787/99) ECHR 8 July 2004.

Isayeva, Yusupova and Bazayeva v. Russia [Isayeva I] (App nos 57947/00, 57948/00 and 57949/00) ECHR 24 February 2005.
Isayeva v. Russia [Isayeva II] (App no 57950/00) ECHR 24 February 2005.
Öcalan v Turkey (App no. 46221/99) ECHR 12 May 2005.
Budayeva And Others v Russia (App Nos 15339/02, 21166/02, 20058/02, 11673/02 and 15343/02) ECHR 20 March 2008, Final 29 September 2008.
Sufi And Elmi v. The United Kingdom (App nos 8319/07 and 11449/07) ECHR 28 June 2011, Final 28 November 2011.
Al-Skeini and Others v The United Kingdom (App No 55721/07) ECHR 7 July 2011.
Popov v. France (App nos 39472/07 and 39474/07) ECHR 19 January 2012.
Mohammed v. Austria (App no 2283/12) ECHR 6 June 2013, Final 6 September 2013.
Benzer And Others v. Turkey (App No 23502/06) ECHR 12 November 2013, Final 24 March 2014.

Inter-American Commission on Human Rights, *Juan Carlos Abella v Argentina* ('Tablada Case') (Case no 11.137) (18 November 1997).
Inter-American Commission on Human Rights, *Coard et al v USA* (Report No 109/99 Case 10.951) (29 September 1999).
Inter-American Court of Human Rights, *Case of Las Palmeras v Colombia* (4 February 2000) (Preliminary Objections) Case no 67, Series C.
Inter-American Court of Human Rights, *Case of Bámaca-Velasquez v. Guatemala* (November 25 2000) (Merits), Series C No. 70.

Social and Economic Rights Action Center (SERAC) and Center for Economic and Social Rights (CESR) / Nigeria, African Commission on Human and Peoples Rights Case No 155/96 (27th October 2001)

European Committee of Social Rights 'Conclusions 2009' Greece: 2009/def/GRC/ (1 December 2010)

Other courts

S.S. Lotus (France. v. Turkey.), 1927 P.C.I.J. (ser. A) No. 10 (Sept. 7), The Case of the S.S. Lotus France v. Turkey Judgment September 1927.
Arbitral Tribunal *Libyan Arab Foreign Investment Company v. Republic of Burundi,* I.L.R., vol. 96 (1994).
Denmark: '*The Prosecution v. Saric*', Eastern Division of High Court (Third Chamber) (25 November 1994).
'Western Front, Aerial Bombardment and Related Claims - Eritrea's Claims 1, 3, 5, 9-13, 14, 21, 25 & 26' *Eritrea-Ethiopia Claims Commission* (Partial Award, 19 December 2005).

TABLE OF TREATIES

1899 Convention (II) with Respect to the Laws and Customs of War on Land, The Hague, 29 July 1899 (entry into force: 4 September 1900).

1907 Convention (IV) respecting the Laws and Customs of War on Land and its annex: Regulations concerning the Laws and Customs of War on Land, The Hague, 18 October 1907 (entry into force: 26 January 1910).

1943 Agreement for United Nations Relief and Rehabilitation Administration, 9 November 1943.

1945 Charter of the United Nations, San Francisco, 26 June 1945 (entry into force: 24 October 1045) *1 UNTS xvi.*

1948 Convention on the Prevention and Punishment of the Crime of Genocide, New York, 9 December 1948 (entry into force: 12 January 1951) *78 UNTS 277.*

1949 Convention (IV) relative to the Protection of Civilian Persons in Time of War, Geneva, 12 August 1949 (entry into force: 21 October 1950), *75 UNTS 287.*

1950 European Convention for the Protection of Human Rights and Fundamental Freedoms, as amended by Protocols Nos. 11 and 14, Rome, 4 November 1950 (entry into force: 3 September 1953) *ETS 5.*

1951 Convention Relating To The Status Of Refugees, Geneva, 28 July 1951 (entry into force: 22 April 1954), *189 UNTS 137.*

1965 International Convention on the Elimination of All Forms of Racial Discrimination, New York 21 December 1965 (entry into force: 4 January 1969) *660 UNTS 195.*

1966 International Covenant on Economic, Social and Cultural Rights (ICESCR), New York, 16 December 1966 (entry into force: 3 January 1976), *993 UNTS 3.*

1966 International Covenant on Civil and Political Rights (ICCPR), New York, 16 December 1966 (entry into force: 23 March 1976), *999 UNTS 171.*

1966 First Optional Protocol to the International Covenant on Civil and Political Rights, New York, 16 December 1966 (entry into force: 23 March 1976), *999 UNTS 302.*

1969 Convention on the Law of Treaties, Vienna, 23 May 1969 (entry into force: 27 January 1980), *1155 UNTS 331.*

1969 Organization of American States (OAS), American Convention on Human Rights, "Pact of San Jose", Costa Rica, 22 November 1969 (entry into force: 18 July 1978), *OAS Treaty Series No 36; 1144 UNTS 123.*

1977 Protocol Additional to the Geneva Conventions of 12 August 1949, and relating to the Protection of Victims of International Armed Conflicts (Protocol I), Geneva, 8 June 1977 (entry into force: 7 December 1978) *1125 UNTS 3.*

1977 Protocol Additional to the Geneva Conventions of 12 August 1949, and relating to the Protection of Victims of Non-International Armed Conflicts (Protocol II), Geneva, 8 June 1977 (entry into force: 7 December 1978) *1125 UNTS 609.*

1979 Convention on the Elimination of All Forms of Discrimination Against Women, New York 18 December 1979 (entry into force: 3 September 1981) *1249 UNTS 13*.

1981 African Charter on Human and Peoples' Rights, Banjul, 27 June 1981 (entry into force: 21 October 1986) *1520 UNTS 217*.

1984 Draft Convention on Expediting the Delivery of Emergency Relief, 18 June 1984, UN Doc A/39/367/Add.2 – E/1984/96/Add.2.

1986 Convention on Assistance in the Case of a Nuclear Accident or Radiological Emergency, Vienna, 26 September 1986 (entry into force: 26 February 1987), *1457 UNTS 133*.

1988 Additional Protocol to the American Convention on Human Rights in the Area of Economic, Social and Cultural Rights, "Protocol of San Salvador", 17 November 1988 (entry into force: 16 November 1999), *OAS Treaty Series No 69*.

1989 Convention on the Rights of the Child, New York, 20 November 1989 (entry into force: 2 September 1990) *1577 UNTS 3*.

1990 Organization of African Unity (OAU), African Charter on the Rights and Welfare of the Child, 11 July 1990 (entry into force: 29 November 1999), *CAB/LEG/24.9/49* .

1991 Inter-American Convention To Facilitate Disaster Assistance, Santiago, 7 June 1991 (entry into force: 16 October 1996), *OAS A-54*.

1993 Statute of the International Tribunal for the Prosecution of Persons Responsible for Serious Violations of International Humanitarian Law Committed in the Territory of the Former Yugoslavia since 1991, 25 March 1993, UN Doc S/RES/827.

1994 Convention on the Safety of United Nations and Associated Personnel, New York, 9 December 1994 (entry into force: 15 January 1999) *2051 UNTS 363*.

1996 Council of Europe, European Social Charter (Revised), 3 May 1996 (entry into force 1 July 1999), *ETS 163*.

1998 Organization of African Unity (OAU), Protocol to the African Charter on Human and People's Rights on the Establishment of an African Court on Human and People's Rights, 10 June 1998 (entry into force: 25 January 2004).

1998 Tampere Convention on the Provision of Telecommunication Resources for Disaster Mitigation and Relief Operations, Tampere, 18 June 1998 (entry into force: 8 January 2005), *2296 UNTS 5*.

1998 Rome Statute of the International Criminal Court, Rome 17 July 1998 (entry into force: 1 July 2002) *2187 UNTS 90*.

1999 Lome Peace Agreement between the Government of the Republic of Sierra Leone and the Revolutionary United Front of Sierra Leone (RUF/SL), 3 June 1999.

2000 Framework Convention on Civil Defense Assistance, Geneva 22 May 2000 (entry into force: 30 October 2001), *2172 UNTS 213*.

2002 Protocol Relating To The Establishment Of The Peace And Security Council Of The African Union, Adopted by the 1st Ordinary Session of the Assembly of the African Union, Durban, 9 July 2002.

2003 Protocol to the African Charter on Human and Peoples' Rights on the Rights of Women in Africa, Maputo, 11 July 2003 (entry into force: 25 November 2005), *CAB/LEG/66.6*.

2006 Convention on the Rights of Persons with Disabilities, New York 13 December 2006 (entry into force: 3 May 2008) *2515 UNTS 3*.

2007 European Union, Consolidated version of the Treaty on the Functioning of the European Union, Lisbon, 13 December 2007 (entry into force: 1 December 2009), *OJ C 115/47*.

2008 Agreement between the Transitional Federal Government of Somalia (TFG) and the Alliance for the Re-Liberation of Somalia (ARS), Djibouti, 9 June 2008.

2008 Optional Protocol to the International Covenant on Economic, Social and Cultural Rights, UN Doc A/RES/63/435 Annex, New York, 10 December 2008 (entry into force: 5 May 2013).

2009 African Union, African Union Convention for the Protection and Assistance of Internally Displaced Persons in Africa ("Kampala Convention"), Kampala, 22 October 2009 (entry into force: 6 December 2012), *52 ILM 397*.

UN Documents

Security Council Resolutions

UNSC Res 253 (29 May 1968) UN Doc S/RES/253
UNSC Res 513 (19 June 1982) UN Doc S/RES/513
UNSC Res 661 (6 August 1990) UN Doc S/RES/661
UNSC Res 687 (8 April 1991) UN Doc S/RES/687
UNSC Res 688 (5 April 1991) UN Doc S/RES/688.
UNSC Res 706 (15 August 1991) UN Doc S/RES/706
UNSC Res 712 (19 September 1991) UN Doc S/RES/712
UNSC Res 713 (25 September 1991) UN Doc S/RES/713
UNSC Res 721 (27 November 1991) UN Doc S/RES/721
UNSC Res 724 (15 December 1991) UN Doc S/RES/724
UNSC Res 727 (8 January 1992) UN Doc S/RES/727
UNSC Res 733 (23 January 1992) UN Doc S/RES/733
UNSC Res 740 (8 February 1992) UN Doc S/RES/740
UNSC Res 743 (21 February 1992) UN Doc S/RES/743
UNSC Res 746 (17 March 1992) UN Doc S/RES/746
UNSC Res 749 (7 April 1992) UN Doc S/RES/749
UNSC Res 751 (24 April 1992) UN Doc S/RES/751
UNSC Res 752 (15 May 1992) UN Doc S/RES/752
UNSC Res 757 (30 May 1992) UN Doc S/RES/757
UNSC Res 758 (8 June 1992) UN Doc S/RES/758
UNSC Res 761 (29 June 1992) UN Doc S/RES/761
UNSC Res 764 (17 March 1992) UN Doc S/RES/764
UNSC Res 767 (27 July 1992) UN Doc S/RES/767
UNSC Res 770 (13 August 1992) UN Doc S/RES/770
UNSC Res 771 (13 August 1992) S/RES/771
UNSC Res 775 (28 August 1992) UN Doc S/RES/775
UNSC Res 776 (14 September 1992) UN Doc S/RES/776
UNSC Res 781 (9 October 1992) UN Doc S/RES/781
UNSC Res 786 (10 November 1992) UN Doc S/RES/786
UNSC Res 787 (16 November 1992) UN Doc S/RES/787
UNSC Res 794 (3 December 1992) UN Doc S/RES/794
UNSC Res 807 (19 February 1993) UN Doc S/RES/807;
UNSC Res 813 (26 March 1993) UN Doc S/RES/813
UNSC Res 814 (26 March 1993) UN Doc S/RES/814
UNSC Res 816 (31 March 1993) UN Doc S/RES/816;
UNSC Res 819 (16 April 1993) UN Doc S/RES/819
UNSC Res 824 (6 May 1993) UN Doc S/RES/824
UNSC Res 836 (4 June 1993) UN Doc S/RES 836

UNSC Res 837 (6 June 1993) UN Doc S/RES/837
UNSC Res 872 (5 October 1993) UN Doc S/RES/872
UNSC Res 908 (31 March 1994) UN Doc S/RES/908;
UNSC Res 918 (17 May 1994) UN Doc S/RES/918
UNSC Res 929 (22 June 1994) UN Doc S/RES/929
UNSC Res 947 (30 September 1994) UN Doc S/RES/947
UNSC res 958 (19 November 1994) UN Doc S/RES/958
UNSC Res 981 (, 31 March 1995) UN Doc S/RES/981
UNSC Res 986 (14 April 1995) UN Doc S/RES/986
UNSC Res 1004 (12 July 1995) UN Doc S/RES/1004
UNSC Res 1059 (31 May 1996) UN Doc S/RES/1059
UNSC Res 1071 (30 August 1996) UN Doc S/RES/1071
UNSC Res 1078 (9 November 1996) UN Doc S/RES/1078
UNSC Res 1083 (27 November 1996) UN Doc S/RES/1083
UNSC Res 1132 (8 October 1997) UN Doc S/RES/1132
UNSC Res 1199 (23 September 1998) UN Doc S/RES/1199
UNSC Res 1258 (6 August 1999) UN Doc S/RES/1258
UNSC Res 1264 (15 September 1999) UN Doc S/RES/1264
UNSC Res 1265 (17 September 1999) UN Doc S/RES/1265
UNSC Res 1270 (22 October 1999) UN Doc S/RES/1270
UNSC Res 1272 (25 October 1999) UN Doc S/RES/1272
UNSC Res 1289 (7 February 2000) UN Doc S/RES/1289
UNSC Res 1296 (19 April 2000) UN Doc S/RES/1296
UNSC Res 1314 (11 August 2000) UN Doc S/RES/1314
UNSC Res 1319 (8 September 2000) UN Doc S/RES/1319
UNSC Res 1325 (31 October 2000) UN Doc S/RES/1325
UNSC Res 1378 (14 November 2001) UN Doc S/RES/1378
UNSC Res 1379 (20 November 2001) UN Doc S/RES/1379
UNSC Res 1430 (14 August 2002) UN Doc S/RES/1430
UNSC Res 1472 (28 March 2003) UN Doc S/RES/1472
UNSC Res 1483 (22 May 2003) UN Doc S/RES/1483
UNSC Res 1502 (26 August 2003) UN Doc S/RES/1502
UNSC Res 1509 (19 September 2003) UN Doc S/RES/1509
UNSC Res 1528 (27 February 2004) UN Doc S/RES/1528
UNSC Res 1593 (31 March 2005) UN Doc S/RES/1593.
UNSC Res 1674 (28 April 2006) UN Doc S/RES/1674.
UNSC Res 1701 (11 August 2006) UN Doc S/Res/1701
UNSC Res 1706 (31 August 2006) UN Doc S/RES/1706
UNSC Res 1727 (15 December 2006) UN Doc S/RES/1727
UNSC Res 1738 (23 December 2006) UN Doc S/RES/1738
UNSC Res 1739 (10 January 2007) UN Doc S/RES/1739
UNSC Res 1744 (21 February 2007) UN Doc S/RES/1744
UNSC Res 1769 (31 July 2007) UN Doc S/RES/1769
UNSC Res 1770 (10 August 2007) UN Doc S/RES/1770

UNSC Res 1772 (20 August 2007) UN Doc S/RES/1772
UNSC Res 1794 (21 December 2007) UN Doc S/RES/1794
UNSC Res 1801 (20 February 2008) UN Doc S/RES/1801
UNSC Res 1806 (20 March 2008) UN Doc S/RES/1806
UNSC Res 1814 (15 May 2008) UN Doc S/RES/1814
UNSC Res 1828 (31 July 2008) UN Doc S/RES/1828
UNSC Res 1842 (29 October 2008) UN Doc S/RES/1842
UNSC Res 1844 (20 November 2008) UN Doc S/RES/1844
UNSC Res 1861 (14 January 2009) UN Doc S/1861
UNSC Res 1860 (8 January 2009) UN Doc S/RES/1860
UNSC Res 1863 (9 July 2009) UN Doc S/RES/1863
UNSC Res 1866 (13 February 2009) UN Doc S/RES/1866
UNSC Res 1868 (23 March 2009) UN Doc S/RES/1868
UNSC Res 1872 (26 May 2009) UN Doc S/RES/1872
UNSC Res 1882 (4 August 2009) UN Doc S/RES1882
UNSC Res 1889 (5 October 2009) UN Doc S/RES/1889
UNSC Res 1893 (29 October 2009) UN Doc S/RES/1893
UNSC Res 1894 (11 November 2009) UN Doc S/RES/1894
UNSC Res 1906 (23 December 2009) UN Doc S/RES/1906
UNSC Res 1946 (15 October 2010) UN Doc S/RES/1946
UNSC Res 1970 (26 February 2011) UN Doc S/RES/1970
UNSC Res 1973 (17 March 2011) UN Doc S/RES/1973
UNSC Res 1980 (28 April 2011) UN Doc S/RES/1980
UNSC Res 1996 (8 July 2011) UN Doc S/RES/1996.
UNSC Res 2010 (30 September 2011) UN Doc S/RES/2010
UNSC Res 2014 (21 October 2011) UN Doc S/RES/2014
UNSC Res 2016 (27 October 2011) UN Doc S/RES/2016
UNSC Res 2036 (22 February 2012) UN Doc S/RES/2036
UNSC Res 2040 (12 March 2012) UN Doc S/RES/2040
UNSC Res 2042 (14 April 2012) UN Doc S/RES/2042
UNSC Res 2043 (21 April 2012) UN Doc S/RES/2043
UNSC Res 2046 (2 May 2012) UN Doc S/RES/2046
UNSC Res 2060 (25 July 2012) UN Doc S/RES/2060.
UNSC Res 2076 (20 November 2012) UN Doc S/RES/2076
UNSC Res 2078 (28 November 2012) UN Doc S/RES/2078
UNSC Res 2085 (20 December 2012) UN Doc S/RES/2085
UNSC Res 2093 (6 March 2013) UN Doc S/RES/2093
UNSC Res 2096 (19 March 2013) UN Doc S/RES/2096
UNSC Res 2100 (25 April 2013) UN Doc S/RES/2100.
UNSC Res 2112 (30 July 2013) UN Doc S/RES/2112
UNSC Res 2113 (30 July 2013) UN Doc S/RES/2113
UNSC Res 2118 (27 September 2013) UN Doc S/RES/2118
UNSC Res 2127 (5 December 2013) UN Doc S/RES/2127
UNSC Res 2149 (10 April 2014) UN Doc S/RES/2149

UNSC Res 2165 (14 July 2014) UN Doc S/RES/2165.
UNSC 2191 (17 December 2014) UN Doc S/RES/2191
UNSC Res 2196 (22 January 2015) UN Doc S/RES/2196

Security Council documents

'Report to the UN Secretary General on humanitarian needs in Kuwait and Iraq in the immediate post-crisis environment by a mission to the area' (20 March 1991) UN Doc S/22366.
Repertoire of the Practice of the Security Council (1996-1999), Chapter VIII, 'Consideration of questions under the responsibility of the Security Council for the maintenance of international peace and security'.
Repertoire of the Practice of the Security Council (1996-1999), Chapter XI 'Consideration of the provisions of Chapter VII of the Charter'.
Statement by the President of the Security Council (12 February 1999) UN Doc S/PRST/1999/6.
Report of the Secretary General 'Protection of civilians in armed conflicts' (8 September 1999) UN Doc S/1999/957.
Repertoire of the Practice of the Security Council (2000-2003), Chapter VIII, 'Consideration of questions under the responsibility of the Security Council for the maintenance of international peace and security'.
'Aide Memoire Protection of Civilians in Armed Conflict' UN Doc S/PRST/2002/6 (15 March 2002).
Report of the Secretary General 'Protection of civilians in armed conflicts' (26 November 2002) UN Doc S/2002/1300.
Repertoire of the Practice of the Security Council (2004-2007), Chapter VIII, 'Protection of Civilians in armed conflict'.
Repertoire of the Practice of the Security Council 16th Supplement (2008 – 2009) 'Protection of Civilians in armed conflict'.
'Report of the Secretary-General on the protection of civilians in armed conflict' UN Doc S/2009/277 (29 May 2009).
'Report of the Secretary-General on the protection of civilians in armed conflict' UN Doc S/2010/579 (11 November 2010).
'Aide Memoire Protection of Civilians in Armed Conflict' UN Doc S/PRST/2010/25 (22 November 2010).
UN Doc SC/10200 (17 March 2011) 6498th Meeting.
UN Doc SC/10403 (4 October 2011) 6627th Meeting (Night).
UN Doc SC/10536 (4 February 2012) 6711th Meeting (AM).
'Aide Memoire Protection of Civilians in Armed Conflict' UN Doc S/PRST/2013/2 (12 February 2013).
'Aide Memoire Protection of Civilians in Armed Conflict' UN Doc S/PRST/2014/3 (12 February 2014).

General Assembly Resolutions

UNGA Res 2034 (XX) (7 December 1965)
UNGA Res 2131 (XX) (21 December 1965)
UNGA Res 2435 (XXIII) (19 December 1968)
UNGA Res 2444 (XXIII) (19 December 1968).
UNGA Res 2608 (XXIV) (16 December 1969)
UNGA Res 2625 (XXV) (24 October 1970)
UNGA Res 2674 (XXV) (9 December 1970)
UNGA Res 2675 (XXV) (9 December 1970)
UNGA Res 2676 (XXV) (9 December 1970)
UNGA Res 2677 (XXV) (9 December 1970)
UN Doc. A/RES/2717 (XXV) (15 December 1970)
UNGA Res 2816 (XXVI) (14 December 1971)
UNGA Res 3244 XXIX (29 November 1974)
UNGA Res 3440 XXX (9 December 1975)
UNGA Res 33/22 (29 November 1978) UN Doc A/RES/33/22
UNGA Res 33/73 (15 December 1978) UN Doc A/RES/33/73
UNGA Res 34/127 (14 December 1979) UN Doc A/RES/34/127
UNGA Res 35/92 B (5 December 1980) UN Doc A/RES/35/92 B
UNGA Res 36/103 (9 December 1981) UN Doc A/RES/36/103
UNGA Res 36/225 (17 December 1981) UN Doc A/RES/36/225
UNGA Res 38/202 (20 December 1983) UN Doc A/RES/38/202
UNGA Res 39/367 (18 June 1984) UN Doc A/39/367/Add.2 and E/1984/96/Add.2
UNGA Res 41/128 (4 December 1986) UN Doc A/RES/41/128
UNGA Res 41/201 (8 December 1986) UN Doc A/RES/41/201
UNGA Res 42/169 (11 December 1987) UN Doc. A/42/169
UNGA Res 43/8 (18 October 1988) UN Doc A/RES/43/8
UNGA Res 43/52 (6 December 1988) UN Doc A/RES/43/52
UNGA Res 43/131 (8 December 1988) UN Doc A/RES/43/131
UNGA Res 43/202 (20 December 1988) UN Doc A/43/202
UNGA Res 44/12 (24 October 1989) UN Doc A/RES/44/12
UNGA Res 44/236 (22 December 1989) UN Doc A/RES/44/236
UN GA Res 45/94 (14 December 1990) UN Doc A/RES/45/94.
UNGA Res 45/100 (14 December 1990) UN Doc A/RES/45/100
UNGA Res 45/226 (21 December 1990) UN Doc A/RES/45/226
UNGA Res 46/91 (16 December 1991) UN Doc A/RES/46/91
UNGA Res 46/119 (17 December 1991) UN Doc A/RES/46/119
UNGA Res 46/178 (9 December 1991) UN Doc A/RES/46/178
UNGA Res 46/182 (19 December 1991) UN Doc A/RES/46/12
UN Res 47/168 (22 December 1992) UN Doc A/RES/47/168
UNGA Res 48/57 (14 December 1993) UN Doc A/RES/48/57
UNGA Res 48/141 (20 December 1993) UN Doc A/RES/48/141

UNGA Res 48/188 (9 March 1994) UN Doc A/RES/48/188
UNGA Res 48/104 (20 December 1993) UN Doc A/RES/48/104
UNGA Res 49/139 (20 December 1994) UN Doc A/RES/49/139
UNGA Res 49/169 (23 December 1994) UN Doc A/RES/49/169
UNGA Res 49/174 (24 February 1995) UN Doc A/RES/49/174
UNGA Res 51/185 (11 February 1997) UN Doc A/RES/51/185
UNGA Res 51/194 (10 February 1997) A/RES/51/194
UNGA Res 52/167 (18 February 1998) UN Doc A/RES/52/167
UNGA Res 52/168 (18 February 1998) UN Doc A/RES/52/168
UNGA Res 53/87 (27 January 1999) UN Doc A/RES/53/87
UNGA Res 53/88 (29 January 1999) UN Doc A/RES/53/88
UNGA Res 54/95 (28 January 2000) UN Doc A/RES/54/95
UNGA Res 54/192 (21 February 2000) UN Doc A/RES/54/192
UNGA Res 54/233 (25 February 2000) UN Doc A/RES/54/233
UNGA Res 55/2 (18 September 2000) UN Doc A/RES/55/2
UNGA Res 55/163 (7 February 2001) UN Doc A/RES/55/163
UNGA Res 55/164 (7 February 2001) UN Doc A/RES/55/164
UNGA Res 55/175 (7 March 2001) UN Doc A/RES/55/175
UNGA Res S-26/2 (27 June 2001)
UNGA Res 56/83 (28 January 2002) UN Doc A/RES/56/83 (corrected by UN Doc A/56/49 (Vol. I)/Corr.4)
UNGA Res 56/99 (31 January 2002) UN Doc A/RES/56/99
UNGA Res 56/103 (5 February 2002) UN Doc A/RES/56/103
UNGA Res 56/107 (7 February 2002) UN Doc A/RES/56/107
UNGA Res 56/164 (19 December 2001) UN Doc A/RES/56/164
UNGA Res 56/195 (21 January 2002) UN Doc A/RES/56/195
UNGA Res 56/217 (19 February 2002) UN Doc A/RES/56/217
UNGA Res 57/150 (27 February 2003) UN Doc A/RES/57/150
UNGA Res 57/152 (3 March 2003) UN Doc A/RES/57/152
UNGA Res 57/153 (3 March 2003) UN Doc A/RES/57/153
UNGA Res 58/25 (29 January 2004) UN Doc A/RES/58/25
UNGA Res 58/114 (5 February 2004) UN Doc A/RES/58/114
UNGA Res 58/177 (12 March 2004) UN Doc A/RES/58/177
UNGA Res 59/141 (25 February 2005) UN Doc A/RES/59/141
UNGA Res 59/202 (31 March 2005) UN Doc A/RES/59/202
UNGA Res 59/212 (3 March 2005) UN Doc A/RES/59/212
UNGA Res 60/1 (24 October 2005) UN Doc A/RES/60/1
UNGA Res 60/123 (24 March 2006) UN Doc A/RES/60/123
UNGA Res 60/124 (8 March 2006) UN Doc A/RES/60/124
UNGA Res 60/125 (15 March 2006) UN Doc A/RES/60/125
UNGA Res 60/165 (2 March 2006) UN Doc A/RES/60/165
UNGA res 60/168 (7 March 2006) A/RES/60/168
UNGA Res 60/124 (8 March 2006) UN Doc A/RES/60/124
UNGA Res 61/131 (22 February 2007) UN Doc A/RES/61/131

UNGA res 61/133 (1 March 2007) UN Doc A/RES/61/133

UNGA Res 61/134 (1 March 2007) UN Doc A/RES/61/134

UNGA Res 61/163 (19 December 2006) UN Doc A/RES/61/163

UNGA Res 62/92 (1 February 2008) UN Doc A/RES/62/92

UNGA Res 62/94 (25 January 2008) UN Doc A/RES/62/94

UNGA Res 62/95 (29 January 2008) UN Doc A/RES/62/95

UNGA Res 62/153 (6 March 2008) UN Doc. A/RES/62/153

UNGA Res 62/164 (18 December 2007) UN Doc A/RES/62/164

UN GA Res 62/168 (6 March 2008) UN Doc A/RES/62/153

UNGA Res 63/137 (11 December 2008) UN Doc A/RES/63/137

UNGA Res 63/138 (5 March 2009) UN Doc A/RES/63/138

UNGA Res 63/139 (5 March 2009) UN Doc A/RES/63/139

UNGA Res 63/141 (11 December 2008) UN Doc. A/RES/63/141

UNGA Res 63/176 (20 March 2009) UN Doc A/RES/63/176

UNGA Res 63/187 (18 December 2008) UN Doc A/RES/63/187

UNGA Res 63/308 (7 October 2009) UN Doc A/RES/63/308

UNGA Res 64/74 (7 December 2009) UN Doc A/RES/64/74

UNGA Res 64/76 (2 February 2010) UN Doc A/RES/64/76

UNGA Res 64/77 (8 February 2010) UN Doc A/RES/64/77

UNGA Res 64/159 (10 March 2010) UN Doc A/RES/64/159

UNGA Res 64/162 (17 March 2010) UN Doc A/RES/64/162

UNGA Res 64/250 (30 April 2010) UN Doc A/RES/64/250

UNGA Res 64/251 (30 April 2010) UN Doc A/RES/64/251

UNGA Res 64/292 (28 July 2010) UN Doc A/64/292

UNGA Res 64/296 (13 October 2010) UN Doc A/RES/64/296

UNGA Res 65/132 (1 March 2011) UN Doc A/RES/65/132

UNGA Res 65/133 (3 March 2011) UN Doc A/RES/65/133

UNGA Res 65/264 (21 June 2011) UN Doc A/RES/65/264

UNGA Res 65/307 (25 August 2011) UN Doc A/RES/65/307

UNGA Res 66/117 (1 March 2012) UN Doc A/RES/66/117

UNGA Res 66/119 (7 March 2012) UN Doc A/RES/66/119

UNGA Res 66/120 (7 March 2012) UN Doc A/RES/66/120

UNGA Res 66/227 (15 March 2012) UN Doc A/RES/66/227

UNGA Res 67/85 (21 March 2013) UN Doc A/RES/67/85

UNGA Res 67/87 (26 March 2013) UN Doc A/RES/67/87

UNGA Res 67/231 (9 April 2013) UN Doc A/RES/67/231

UNGA Res 68/101 (18 February 2014) UN Doc A/RES/68/101

UNGA Res 68/102 (12 February 2014) UN Doc A/RES/68/102

UNGA Res 68/103 (19 February 2014) UN Doc A/RES/68/103

ECOSOC resolutions

ECOSOC 'Assistance in cases of natural disaster' (15 August 1964) UN Doc E/RES/1049 (XXXVII).
ECOSOC 'Assistance in cases of natural disaster' (16 July 1970) UN Doc A/RES/1546 (XLIX).
ECOSOC 'Proposal for the establishment of an emergency fund for disasters' (23 July 1970) UN Doc E/RES/1533 (XLIX).
ECOSOC 'Assistance in cases of natural disaster' (30 July 1970) Res 1546 (XLIX).
ECOSOC Resolution 1612 (LI) (23 July 1971) UN Doc E/1612 (LI).
ECOSOC Resolution 2102 (LXIII) (3 August 1977) UN Doc. E/2102 (LXIII).
ECOSOC Resolution 1989/99 'International Decade for Natural Disaster Reduction' (26 July 1989) UN Doc E/1989/89/Add.1.
ECOSOC Resolution 2002/32 (26 July 2002) UN Doc E/RES/2002/32 'Strengthening of the coordination of emergency humanitarian assistance of the United Nations'.

Secretary General Reports

UN Secretary General Report 'Respect for Human Rights in Armed Conflict', UN Doc A/7720 (20 November 1969).
UN Secretary General Report 'Respect for Human Rights in Armed Conflict', UN Doc A/8052 (18 September 1970).
Report of the Secretary General to General Assembly / Economic and Social Council 'International Decade for Natural Disaster Reduction' UN Doc A/44/322 - E/1989/114 (20 June 1989).
Report of the Secretary General 'New International Humanitarian Order: Humanitarian Assistance to Victims of Natural Disasters and Similar Emergency Situations' UN Doc A/45/587 (24 October 1990).
Report of the Secretary General Pursuant to Paragraph 5 of the Security Council Resolution 955' (13 February 1995) UN Doc S/1995/134.
Report of the Secretary-General 'Protection of civilians in armed conflict', UN Doc S/1999/957 (8 September 1999).
Report of the Secretary-General 'Protection of civilians in armed conflict', UN Doc S/2001/331 (30 March 2001).
Report of the Secretary-General 'Protection of civilians in armed conflict', UN Doc S/2002/1300 (26 November 2002).
Report of the Secretary-General 'Protection of civilians in armed conflict', UN Doc S/2004/431 (28 May 2004).
Report of the Secretary General's High Level Panel on Threats, Challenges and Change 'A More Secure World: Our Shared Responsibility', UN Doc A/59/565 (2 December 2004).
Report of the Secretary General 'In larger freedom: towards development, security and human rights for all', UN Doc A/59/2005 (21 March 2005).

Report of the Secretary-General 'Protection of civilians in armed conflict', UN Doc S/2005/740 (28 November 2005).
Report of the Secretary-General 'Protection of civilians in armed conflict', UN Doc S/2007/643 (28 October 2007).
Report of the Secretary-General 'Protection of civilians in armed conflict', UN Doc S/2009/277 (29 May 2009).
Report of the Secretary-General 'Protection of civilians in armed conflict', UN Doc S/2010/579 (11 November 2010) and UN Doc S/2012/376 (22 May 2012).
Report of the Secretary General 'Fulfilling our collective responsibility: international assistance and the responsibility to protect' UN Doc A/68/947–S/2014/449 (11 July 2014).

ILC Documents

1947 Statute of the International Law Commission (Adopted by the General Assembly in resolution 174 (II) of 21 November 1947), as amended by resolutions 485 (V) of 12 December 1950, 984 (X) of 3 December 1955, 985 (X) of 3 December 1955 and 36/39 of 18 November 1981.
Commentary to the Vienna Convention (1966) *Yearbook of the International Law Commission*, Vol. II.
Report to the General Assembly UN Doc A/61/34 (18 December 2006).
Report of the Study Group on the Fragmentation of International Law: Difficulties arising from the Diversification and Expansion of International Law UN Doc A/CN.4/L.682 (16 April 2006).
Report to the General Assembly UN Doc A/62/10 (7 May-5 June and 9 July-10 August 2007).
'Protection of persons in the event of disasters, Memorandum by the Secretariat' UN Doc A/CN.4/590 (11 December 2007).
'Protection of persons in the event of disasters, Memorandum by the Secretariat' UN Doc A/CN.4/590/Add.1 (11 December 2007).
Report to the General Assembly on the work of its fifty-ninth session UN Doc A/62/66 (8 January 2008).
'Protection of persons in the event of disasters' Memorandum by the Secretariat, Addendum, UN Doc A/CN.4/590/Add.1 (26 February 2008).
'Preliminary report on the protection of persons in the event of disasters' UN Doc A/CN.4/598 (5 May 2008).
'Report of the International Law Commission Sixtieth session UN Doc A/63/10 (5 May-6 June and 7 July-8 August 2008).
'Second report on the protection of persons in the event of disasters' UN Doc A/CN.4/615 (7 May 2009).
Report to the General Assembly UN Doc A/64/10 (August 2009).
'Draft Articles 1-5 on the Protection of Persons in the Event of Disasters' UN Doc A/CN.4/L.758 (24 July 2009).

'Third report on the protection of persons in the event of disasters', Special Rapporteur Eduardo Valencia-Ospina UN Doc A/CN.4/629 (31 March 2010).
'Draft Articles 6-9 on the Protection of Persons in the Event of Disasters' UN Doc A/CN.4/L.776 (14 July 2010).
'Report of the International Law Commission' UN Doc A/65/10 (3 May – 4 June, 5 July – 6 August 2010).
Report to the General Assembly UN Doc A/65/10 August 2010.
'Fourth report on the protection of persons in the event of disasters' by Special Rapporteur Eduardo Valencia-Ospina, UN Doc A/CN.4/643 (11 May 2011).
'Draft articles on the effects of armed conflicts on treaties, with commentaries', Yearbook of the International Law Commission (2011) Vol. II Part Two.
'Draft articles on the responsibility of international organizations, with commentaries' adopted by the ILC at its sixty-third session UN Doc A/66/10 (2011).
'Statement of the Chairman of the Drafting Committee pertaining to Article 14 [11] Protection of Persons in the Event of Disasters' (2 August 2011).
'Provisional summary record of the 3102nd meeting Held at the Palais des Nations, Geneva' UN Doc A/CN.4/SR.3102 (25 January 2012).
'Fifth report on the protection of persons in the event of disasters by Eduardo Valencia-Ospina, Special Rapporteur' UN Doc A/CN.4/652 (9 April 2012).
'Sixty-fourth session (second part) Provisional summary record of the 3138th meeting, Held at the Palais des Nations, Geneva' (2 August 2012) UN Doc A/CN.4/SR.3138.
'Protection of persons in the event of disasters: Texts and titles of the draft articles adopted by the Drafting Committee on first reading' UN Doc A/CN.4/L.831 (15 May 2014).

Human Rights Commission and Human Rights Council documents

UN Human Rights Commission's Resolution 5 (XXXII) (27 February 1976).
UNCHR Res 1989/11 (2 March 1989) UN Doc E/CN.4/RES/1989/11 'Non-discrimination in the field of health'.
Report of the Special Rapporteur on the Right to Life (23 December 1992) UN Doc E/CN.4/1993/46.
Report of the Special Rapporteur on the Right to Life (7 December 1993) UN Doc E/CN.4/1994/7.
Report of the Special Rapporteur on the Right to Life (14 December 1994) UN Doc E/CN.4/1995/61.
'Report of the Representative of the Secretary-General, Mr. Francis M. Deng, submitted pursuant to Commission on Human Rights resolution 1995/57: Internally displaced persons' (22 February 1996) UN Doc E/CN.4/1996/52.
Report of the Special Rapporteur on the Right to Life (23 December 1996) UN Doc E/CN.4/1997/60/Add.1.

UNCHR, Report of the Secretary General "Promotion and Protection of Human Rights: Fundamental Standards of Humanity" (18 December 1998) § 25 UN Doc E/CN.4/1999/92.
Commission on Human Rights Res 1999/S-4/1 (27 September 1999) UN Doc 1999/S-4/1 'Situation of human rights in East Timor'.
UNCHR Res 10 (2000) UN Doc E/CN.4/2000/10 'The right to food' (17 April 2000).
Commission on Human Rights Res 2000/53, (25 April 2000) UN Doc E/CN.4/RES/2000/53.
Commission on Human Rights Res 2000/55 (25 April 2000) UN Doc E/CN.4/RES/2000/55.
UNCHR Report of the Secretary General "Promotion and Protection of Human Rights: Fundamental Standards of Humanity" (12 January 2001) UN Doc E/CN.4/2001/91.
Report submitted by the Special Rapporteur on the Right to Food 'The Right to Food' UN Doc E/CN.4/2001/53 (7 February 2001).
Commission on Human Rights Res 2001/54 (24 April 2001) UN Doc E/CN.4/RES/2001/54.
Commission on Human Rights resolution 2002/561 (25 April 2002).
Report of the Special Rapporteur on the right of everyone to the enjoyment of the highest attainable standard of physical and mental health (13 February 2003) UN Doc E/CN.4/2003/58.
Commission on Human Rights Res 2003/52 (24 April 2003) UN Doc E/CN.4/RES/2003/52.
UNCHR Report of the Secretary General "Promotion and Protection of Human Rights: Fundamental Standards of Humanity" (25 February 2004) UN Doc E/CN.4/2004/90.
Commission on Human Rights Res 19 (16 April 2004) UN Doc E/CN.4/2004/19.
Commission on Human Rights Res 2004/55 (20 April 2004) UN Doc E/CN.4/RES/2004/55.
'Report of the Special Rapporteur on the right of everyone to the enjoyment of the highest attainable standard of physical and mental health 'Addendum: Summary of cases transmitted to Governments and replies received' (2 February 2005) UN Doc E/CN.4/2005/51/Add.1.
Report of the Special Rapporteur on the right of everyone to the enjoyment of the highest attainable standard of physical and mental health (11 February 2005) UN Doc E/CN.4/2005/51.
UNCHR Res 2005/24 (15 April 2005) UN Doc E/CN.4/RES/2005/24 'The right of everyone to the enjoyment of the highest attainable standard of physical and mental health'.
Report of the Special Rapporteur 'The right of everyone to the enjoyment of the highest attainable standard of physical and mental health' (12 September 2005) UN Doc A/60/348.

'Operational Guidelines on Human Rights and Natural Disasters' by the Representative on human rights of internally displaced persons UN Doc A/HRC/4/38/Add.1 (26 January 2006).

Report of the Chairperson-Rapporteur of the Working Group on Arbitrary Detention, Leila Zerrougui; the Special Rapporteur on the independence of judges and lawyers, Leandro Despouy; the Special Rapporteur on torture and other cruel, inhuman or degrading treatment or punishment, Manfred Nowak; the Special Rapporteur on freedom of religion or belief, Asma Jahangir; and the Special Rapporteur on the right of everyone to the enjoyment of the highest attainable standard of physical and mental health, Paul Hunt (27 February 2006) UN Doc E/CN.4/2006/120 'Situation of detainees at Guantánamo Bay'.

Civil And Political Rights, Including The Question Of Disappearances And Summary Executions: Extrajudicial, summary or arbitrary executions' Report of the Special Rapporteur Philip Alston Addendum 'Mission to Sri Lanka' UN Doc E/CN.4/2006/53/Add.5 (27 March 2006).

Report of the Representative of the Secretary-General on the human rights of internally displaced persons UN Doc A/HRC/4/38/Add.2 (18 October 2006).

Report of the independent expert on human rights and international solidarity (Mr. Rudi Muhammad Rizki)' UN Doc A/HRC/4/8 (7 February 2007).

UNHRC Decision 2/104 (27 November 2006) UN Doc A/HRC/DEC/2/104 'Human rights and access to water'.

'Report of the United Nations High Commissioner for Human Rights on the scope and content of the relevant human rights obligations related to equitable access to safe drinking water and sanitation under international human rights instruments' (16 August 2007) UN Doc A/HRC/6/3.

HRC Res 6/32 (14 December 2007) UN Doc A/RES/6/32.

Report of the Special Rapporteur on the right of everyone to the enjoyment of the highest attainable standard of physical and mental health (31 January 2008) UN Doc A/HRC/7/11.

Report of the Special Rapporteur on the Right to Health UN Doc A/HRC/7/11/Add.2 (5 March 2008).

UNHRC Res 7/14 (27 March 2008) A/HRC/RES/7/14.

UNHRC Res 7/22 (28 March 2008) UN Doc A/HRC/7/22 'Human rights and access to safe drinking water and sanitation'.

'Promotion And Protection Of All Human Rights, Civil, Political, Economic, Social And Cultural, Including The Right To Development: Rights of peoples, and specific groups and individuals', Report of the Representative of the Secretary-General on the human rights of internally displaced persons (24 April 2008) UN Doc A/HRC/8/6.

'Report Of The Representative Of The Secretary-General On The Human Rights Of Internally Displaced Persons' (21 May 2008) UN Doc A/HRC/8/6/Add.4.

UNHRC Res S-7/1 (22 May 2008) Special Session 'The negative impact of the worsening of the world food crisis on the realization of the right to food for all'.

'Report of the Working Group on the UPR' (5 June 2008) UN Doc A/HRC/8/46 (Sri Lanka).
HRC Res 9/23 (8 September 2008) 'Building resilience: a human rights framework for world food and nutrition security', UN Doc A/HRC/9/23, Special Session on the global food crisis.
'The right to food', Report of the Special Rapporteur, Note by the Secretary General UN Doc A/63/278 (21 October 2008).
HRC General Comment 33 (5 November 2008) UN Doc CCPR/C/GC/33.
'Report of the Working Group on the UPR' (8 January 2009) UN Doc A/HRC/10/76 (Israel).
Report of the Special Rapporteur on the right to food 'Promotion and Protection of all Human Rights, Civil, political, economic, social and cultural rights, including the right to development' (11 February 2009) UN Doc A/HRC/10/5.
'Promotion And Protection Of All Human Rights, Civil, Political, Economic, Social And Cultural Rights, Including The Right To Development' Report Of The Representative Of The Secretary-General On The Human Rights Of Internally Displaced Persons UN Doc A/HRC/10/13/Add.1 (5 March 2009)
UNHRC Res 10/12 (26 March 2009) 'The right to food'.
'Report of the independent expert on the issue of human rights obligations related to access to safe drinking water and sanitation' (1 July 2009) UN Doc A/HRC/12/24.
'Promotion And Protection Of All Human Rights, Civil, Political, Economic, Social And Cultural Rights, Including The Right To Development Human Rights And International Solidarity' 'Report of the Independent Expert on human rights and international solidarity' Note By The United Nations High Commissioner For Human Rights UN Doc A/HRC/12/27 (22 July 2009).
UNHRC Res 12/8 (1 October 2009) UN Doc A/HRC/RES/12/8 'Human rights and access to safe drinking water and sanitation'.
'Report of the Working Group on the UPR' (4 January 2010) UN Doc A/HRC/13/13 (DPR Korea).
'Report of the Working Group on the UPR' (4 January 2010) UN Doc A/HRC/13/17 (Ethiopia).
'Report of the Representative of the Secretary-General on the human rights of internally displaced persons', UN Doc A/HRC/13/21 (5 January 2010).
Report of the Representative of the Secretary-General on the human rights of internally displaced persons, Walter Kälin, Addendum Mission to Somalia, UN Doc A/HRC/13/21/Add.2 (21 January 2010).
'Report of the Special Rapporteur on the right to food, Addendum Mission to Guatemala' UN Doc A/HRC/13/33/Add.4 (26 January 2010).
Report of the Representative of the Secretary-General on the human rights of internally displaced persons, 'Addendum Framework on Durable Solutions for Internally Displaced Persons' UN Doc A/HRC/13/21/Add.4 (9 February 2010).
Special Rapporteur on the Right to Food, Report on the Mission to Nicaragua UN Doc A/HRC/13/33/Add.5 (19 February 2010).

'Report of the Working Group on the UPR' (15 March 2010) UN Doc A/HRC/14/14 (Iraq).
UNHRC Res 13/4 (24 March 2010) 'The right to food'.
'Report of the independent expert on human rights and international solidarity, Rudi Muhammad Rizki' UN Doc A/HRC/15/32 (5 July 2010).
Report by the independent expert on the issue of human rights obligations related to access to safe drinking water and sanitation 'Human rights obligations related to access to safe drinking water and sanitation' (6 August 2010) UN Doc A/65/254.
HRC Res 14/6 (23 June 2010) UN Doc A/HRC/RES/14/6.
Report of the independent expert on human rights and international solidarity (5 July 2010) UN Doc A/HRC/15/32
UNHRC Res 15/9 (30 September 2010) UN Doc A/HRC/RES/15/9 'Human rights and access to safe drinking water and sanitation
UNHRC Res 12/10 (12 October 2010).
'Report of the Representative of the Secretary-General on the human rights of internally displaced persons' (23 December 2010) UN Doc A/HRC/16/43/Add.3l.
'Report of the Working Group on the UPR' (4 January 2011) UN Doc A/HRC/16/15 (Libya).
'Operational Guidelines on Human Rights and Natural Disasters' UN Doc A/HRC/16/43/Add.5 (31 January 2011).
'Report of the Working Group on the UPR' (16 March 2011) UN Doc A/HRC/17/11 (Georgia).
'Report of the Working Group on the UPR' (24 March 2011) UN Doc A/HRC/17/9 (Myanmar).
UNHR Council Res 16/27 (25 March 2011) 'The right to food'.
UNHRC Res 16/2 (8 April 2011) UN Doc A/HRC/RES/16/2 'Human rights and access to safe drinking water and sanitation'.
'Report of the Working Group on the UPR' (11 July 2011) UN Doc A/HRC/18/6 (Somalia).
'Report of the Working Group on the UPR' (11 July 2011) UN Doc A/HRC/18/16 (Sudan).
'The right to food', Note by the Secretary General, UN Doc A/66/262 (4 August 2011).
UNHRC Res 18/L.1 (23 September 2011) UN Doc A/HRC/18/L.1.
'Report of the Working Group on the UPR' (24 January 2012) UN Doc A/HRC/19/11 (Syria).
HRC Res 23/L.1 (28 May 2013) UN Doc A/HRC/23/L.1.
'Report of the Working Group on the UPR' (8 July 2013) UN Doc A/HRC/24/12 (Bangladesh).
Report of the Special Rapporteur on the right to food (24 January 2014) UN Doc A/HRC/25/57.

Report of the Special Rapporteur on the human right to safe drinking water and sanitation 'Common violations of the human rights to water and sanitation' (30 June 2014) UN Doc A/HRC/27/55.

Human rights treaty bodies

CCPR General Comment 5: 'Derogation of rights (Art. 4)' (31 July 1981).

CCPR General Comment 6: 'The right to life (art. 6)' (30 April 1982).

CCPR General Comment 12: The right to self-determination of peoples (Art. 1) (13 March 1984).

CCPR General Comment 14 'Nuclear weapons and the right to life (Art. 6)' (9 November 1984).

Concluding Observations of the Human Rights Committee: United States of America UN Doc CCPR/C/79/Add.50, A/50/40 (1995).

CCPR General Comment 29 pursuant to Article 4 'States of Emergency' UN Doc. CCPR/C/21/Rev.1/Add.11 (31 August 2001).

UN Doc CCPR/C/ISR/2001/2 (4 December 2001).

Human Rights Committee's Concluding Observations on the Second Periodic Report of Israel, UN Doc CCPR/CO/78/ISR (21 August 2003).

UN Doc CCPR/CO/72/NET/Add.l, (2003).

CCPR General Comment No. 31 (26 May 2004) on the nature of the general legal obligation imposed on States parties to the Covenant (art. 2) UN Doc. CCPR/C/21/Rev.1/Add.13.

Human Rights Committee 'List of issues in relation to the fourth periodic report of the Sudan' (22 November 2013) UN Doc CCPR/C/SDN/Q/4.

CESCR General Comment 3 on Article 2 (14 December 1990).

CESCR General Comment 4 (13 December 1991) UN Doc E/1992/23 'The right to adequate housing'.

CESCR General Comment 6 (8 December 1995) UN Doc E/1996/22 'The economic, social and cultural rights of older persons'.

CESCR General Comment 8 (12 December 1997) UN Doc E/C.12/1997/8 'The relationship between economic sanctions and respect for economic, social and cultural rights'.

CESCR General Comment 14 (11 August 2000) UN Doc E/C.12/2000/4 'The right to the highest attainable standard of health'.

CESCR General Comment 15 (20 January 2003) UN Doc E/C.12/2002/11 'The Right to water (arts. 11 and 12 of the International Covenant on Economic Social and Cultural Rights'.

CESCR 'Concluding observations of the Committee on Economic, Social and Cultural Rights – Israel', (2003) UN Doc E/C.12/1/Add.90.

CESCR General Comment 20 (2 July 2009) UN Doc E/C.12/GC/20 'Non-discrimination in economic, social and cultural rights'.

CESCR Statement on the Right to Sanitation (19 November 2010) UN Doc E/C.12/2010/1.

Other UN documents

Resolution XXIII 'Human Rights in Armed Conflict', adopted by the International Conference on Human Rights in Teheran UN Doc A/Conf.32/41 (12 May 1968).

Stockholm Declaration of 16 June 1972

'Further Promotion And Encouragement Of Human Rights And Fundamental Freedoms, Including The Question Of The Programme And Methods Of Work Of The Commission Alternative Approaches And Ways And Means Within The United Nations System For Improving The Effective Enjoyment Of Human Rights And Fundamental Freedoms' Note by the Secretary-General UN Doc E/CN.4/1993/35 (21 January 1993).

'Vienna Declaration and Programme of Action' UN Doc A/CONF.157/23 (12 July 1993).

Report of the Representative of the Secretary-General, Mr. Francis Deng, 'Further promotion and encouragement of human rights and fundamental freedoms, including the question of the programme and methods of work of the commission human rights, mass exoduses and displaced persons Internally displaced persons' UN Doc E/CN.4/1994/44 (25 January 1994).

'Further Promotion And Encouragement Of Human Rights And Fundamental Freedoms, Including The Question Of The Programme And Methods Of Work Of The Commission on Human Rights, Mass Exoduses And Displaced Persons', Report of the Representative of the Secretary-General (28 November 1994) UN Doc E/CN.4/1995/50/Add.2.

'Human Development Report' United Nations Development Programme (UNDP) (Oxford University Press 1994).

'Further Promotion And Encouragement Of Human Rights And Fundamental Freedoms, Including The Question Of The Programme And Methods Of Work Of The Commission Human Rights, Mass Exoduses And Displaced Persons: Internally displaced persons', Report of the Representative of the Secretary-General (2 February 1995) UN Doc E/CN.4/1995/50.

Report of the Representative of the Secretary-General, Mr. Francis M. Deng (5 December 1995) UN Doc E.CN.4/1996/52/Add.2.

'Contributing to Conflict Prevention and Post-Conflict Peace-Building', Medium-Term Strategy for 1996-2001,UNESCO General Conference 28th session, 1995.

'Human Rights Questions: Human Rights Situations And Reports Of Special Rapporteurs And Representatives: Internally displaced persons' Note by the Secretary-General (24 October 1996) UN Doc A/51/483/Add.1.

'Further Promotion And Encouragement Of Human Rights And Fundamental Freedoms, Including The Question Of The Programme And Methods Of Work Of The Commission Human Rights, Mass Exoduses And Displaced Persons Internally displaced persons' Report of the Representative of the Secretary General UN Doc E/CN.4/1997/43 (4 February 1997).

'Report of the Representative of the Secretary-General, Mr. Francis M. Deng, submitted pursuant to Commission resolution 1997/39', Addendum 'Guiding

Principles on Internal Displacement' (Guiding Principles on IDPs) (11 February 1998) UN Doc E/CN.4/1998/53/Add.2.
'The Right to Food – Note by the Secretary-General' (23 July 2001) UN Doc A/56/210.
'Specific Groups And Individuals: Mass Exoduses And Displaced Persons' Report of the Representative of the Secretary-General UN Doc E/CN.4/2002/95/Add.3 (10 December 2001).
FAO Legislative Study 'Right to Adequate Food in Emergencies' (2002).
FAO Report of the World Food Summit: five years later (2002).
UN Doc A/58/330 'The right to food' (28 August 2003).
'The Right to Food', Report submitted by the Special Rapporteur on the Right to Food UN Doc E/CN.4/2004/10 (9 February 2004).
'Report of the Representative of the Secretary-General on internally displaced persons' 'Conference On Internal Displacement In The Inter-Governmental Authority On Development (Igad) Subregion, Experts' Meeting' (17 February 2004) UN Doc E/CN.4/2004/77/Add.4.
'Specific Groups and Individuals: Mass Exoduses and Displaced Persons', Report of the Representative of the Secretary-General on internally displaced persons, Francis M Deng, UN Doc E/CN.4/2004/77 (4 March 2004).
FAO 'Voluntary Guidelines to support the progressive realization of the right to adequate food in the context of national food security' (Adopted by the 127th Session of the FAO Council November 2004).
Report of the Representative of the Secretary-General on the human rights of internally displaced persons, Walter Kälin 'Specific Groups and Individuals Mass Exodus and Displaced Persons' UN Doc E/CN.4/2005/84 (31 December 2004).
OCHA, *Glossary of Humanitarian Terms in relation to the Protection of Civilians in Armed Conflict* (2004).
'The Right to Food', Report submitted by the Special Rapporteur on the Right to Food UN Doc E/CN.4/2005/47 (24 January 2005).
UN Doc A/60/350 'The right to food' (12 September 2005).
'Operational Guidelines on Human Rights and Natural Disasters' UN Doc A/HRC/4/38/Add.1 (23 January 2006).
Promotion and Protection of Human Rights: Human rights and international solidarity' (Note by the UN High Commissioner for Human Rights) UN Doc E/CN.4/2006/96 (1 February 2006).
'The right to food', Report of the Special Rapporteur on the right to food, UN Doc E/CN.4/2006/44 (16 March 2006).
IASC, 'Protecting Persons Affected by Natural Disasters, IASC Operational Guidelines' (2006).
UN Doc A/62/289 'The right to food' (22 august 2007).
Report of the Special Rapporteur 'The right to food' (21 October 2008) UN Doc A/63/278.
OCHA/ReliefWeb, *Glossary of Humanitarian Terms* (2008).

'Implementing the responsibility to protect', Secretary General Report UN Doc A/63/677 (12 January 2009).
Secretary General's Note 'The right to food - Seed policies and the right to food: enhancing agrobiodiversity and encouraging innovation' UN Doc A/64/170 (23 July 2009).
OCHA *Compilation of United Nations Resolutions on Humanitarian Assistance*, Policy and Studies Series 2009.
OCHA *Compilation of United Nations Resolutions on Humanitarian Assistance: Reference Guide*, Policy and Studies Series 2009.
'Early Warning, Assessment, and the Responsibility to Protect', Secretary General Report UN Doc A/64/864 (14 July 2010).
Report of the UN Special Rapporteur on IDPs UN Doc A/65/282 (11 August 2010).
IASC 'Protecting Persons Affected by Natural Disasters, IASC Operational Guidelines' (January 2011).
'The Role of Regional and Sub-regional arrangements in Implementing the Responsibility to Protect', Secretary General Report UN Doc A/65/877–S/2011/393 (27 June 2011).
'Promotion and protection of human rights: human rights questions, including alternative approaches for improving the effective enjoyment of human rights and fundamental freedoms', Note by the Secretary-General UN Doc A/66/330 (30 August 2011).
'Report of the Secretary-General on the protection of civilians in armed conflict' (22 May 2012) UN Doc S/2012/376.
'Right of everyone to the enjoyment of the highest attainable standard of physical and mental health' Report of the Special Rapporteur on the Right to Health UN Doc A/68/297 (9 August 2013).
'Humanitarian Bulletin Syria' Issue 49, UN OCHA (19 Jun – 16 July 2014).

ICRC / IFRC Documents

Final record of the Diplomatic Conference for the Establishment of International Conventions for the Protection of War Victims (Geneva, 21 April - 12 August 1949) Vol. II-B.

Declaration of principles for international humanitarian relief to the civilian population in disaster situations' XXIst International Conference of the Red Cross, Resolution XXVI (Istanbul September 1969).

Code of Conduct for the International Red Cross and Red Crescent Movement and NGOs in Disaster Relief, prepared jointly by the International Federation of Red Cross and Red Crescent Societies and the ICRC (December 1995).

'Principles and Rules of the Red Cross and Red Crescent in Disaster Relief' as amended by the 26th International Conference of the Red Cross and Red Crescent (1995).

International Red Cross/Red Crescent Movement, Council of Delegates Resolution 5 'International Disaster Response Law' (11-14 November 2001).

XXVIIIth International Conference of the Red Cross and Red Crescent, 'Agenda for Humanitarian Action' (6 November 2003).

'International disaster response laws, principles and practice: reflections, prospects and challenges', *Global Study* (IFRC2003).

Thürer Daniel, 'Current challenges to the law of occupation', Speech delivered to the International Committee of the Red Cross, 6th Bruges Colloquium (20-21 October 2005).

Statutes of the International Red Cross and Red Crescent Movement, (adopted by the 25th International Conference of the Red Cross at Geneva in 1986, amended in 1995 and 2006).

Law and legal issues in international disaster response: a desk study (International Federation of Red Cross and Red Crescent Societies 2007).

'Guidelines for the domestic facilitation and regulation of international disaster relief and initial recovery assistance' (the "IDRL Guidelines"), 30th International Conference of the Movement (30 November 2007).

ICRC Resolution 1 'Together for Humanity', 30th International Conference (Geneva, 26-30 November 2007).

ICRC Resolution 30IC/07/R4 'Guidelines for the domestic facilitation and regulation of international disaster relief and initial recovery assistance', 30th International Conference of the Red Cross and Red Crescent (30 November 2007).

ICRC Opinion Paper 'How is the Term "Armed Conflict" Defined in International Humanitarian Law' (March 2008).

'The International Committee of the Red Cross (ICRC): Its mission and work', Adopted by the Assembly of the ICRC on 19 June 2008, (2009) 91 *International Review of the Red Cross* 874, 399-413.

International Federation of the Red Cross and Red Crescent Societies *World Disasters Report 2010: Focus on Urban Risk* (2010).

ICRC Customary International Humanitarian Law Study (2006 and on-going).

European Community and European Union

European Council Regulation concerning humanitarian aid (EC) No. 1257/96 (20 June 1996).
Recommendation Rec(2001)14 of the Committee of Ministers to member states on the European Charter on Water Resources (17 October 2001).
European Union Council Decision (2001/792/EC, Euratom) (23 October 2001).
'Joint Statement by the Council and the Representatives of the Governments of the Member States meeting within the Council, the European Parliament and the European Commission' (European Consensus on Humanitarian Aid) (30 January 2008) EU Doc 2008/C/25/01.
'Communication From The Commission To The Council And The European Parliament An EU Policy Framework to assist developing countries in addressing food security challenges' (31 March 2010) Doc SEC(2010)379.
European Parliament Res 'Assisting developing countries in addressing food security challenges' (27 September 2011) on an EU policy framework to assist developing countries in addressing food security challenges Doc (2010/2100(INI)).

Miscellaneous sources

'The Laws of War on Land' (9 September 1880) Institute of International Law.

International Guidelines for Humanitarian Assistance Operations, P. Macalister-Smith (Max Planck Institute for Comparative Law and International Law 1991).

'Guiding Principles on the Right to Humanitarian Assistance' (April 1993) The International Institute of Humanitarian Law in San Remo.

'Mohonk Criteria for Humanitarian Assistance in Complex Emergencies, Task Force on Ethical and Legal Issues in Humanitarian Assistance' (Fall 1993) reprinted in 17 *Human Rights Quarterly* 1, 196-197.

Statement Jean-Daniel Tauxe (Director of Operations, ICRC Geneva) at the 45th Rose-Ross Seminar (Montreux, Switzerland 2 March 2000).

'Report and Draft Declaration for Consideration at the 2000 Conference', Committee on Internally Displaced Persons, *International Law Association Conference* (July 2000).

ILA Declaration of International Law Principles on Internally Displaced Persons (29 July 2000).

'The Responsibility to Protect', Report of the International Commission on Intervention and State Sovereignty (ICISS 2001)

Resolution 'Humanitarian Assistance' (2 September 2003) Institute of International Law, Sixteenth Commission, Bruges Session.

'Humanitarian Assistance in Armed Conflict' Conference of the Luxemburg Group, Graduate Institute of International Studies (Geneva 24-25 May 2004).

The Netherlands Advisory Council on International Affairs (AIV), Report 'Failing States A Global Responsibility' No. 35 (May 2004).

International Conference on Peace, Security, Democracy and Development in the Great Lakes Region 'First Summit of Heads of State and Government' in Dar-Es-Salaam (19-20 November 2004) 'Declaration On Peace, Security, Democracy And Development In The Great Lakes Region'.

'Report of the International Commission of Inquiry on Darfur to the United Nations Secretary-General' (25 January 2005).

ASEAN Agreement on Disaster Management and Emergency Response, 26 July 2005.

'The Responsibility to Protect and the European Union', Policy Paper Oxfam International (March 2008).

'Burma – Joint Communiqué issued by the French Ministry of Foreign and European Affairs and Ministry of Defence', 25 May 2008.

Heidelberg Institute for International Conflict Research, *Conflict Barometer 2009: Crises - Wars - Coups d'État Negotiations - Mediations - Peace Settlements*, (University of Heidelberg 2009).

'Nederland en de Responsibility to Protect': de verantwoordelijkheid om mensen te beschermen tegen massale wreedheden', *Adviesraad Internationale Vraagstukken* (June 2010).

Centre for Research on the Epidemiology of Disasters, 'Annual Disaster Statistical Review 2009: The numbers and trends' (June 2010).
International Law Association, 'Final Report on the Meaning of Armed Conflict in International Law' of the Committee on the Use of Force (Hague Conference 2010).
Maastricht Principles on Extra-Territorial Obligations (ETOs) of States in the area of Economic, Social and Cultural Rights' of 28 September 2011.
'Security Council, Internal Displacement And Protection: Recommendations For Strengthening Action Through Resolutions', *Brookings Institute* (September 2011)

Online sources

<www.ifrc.org/en/who-we-are/vision-and-mission/> accessed 3 January 2011.
<http://nobelprize.org/nobel_prizes/peace/> accessed 23 June 2011.
<www.ifrc.org/en/what-we-do/disaster-management/about-disasters/what-is-a-disaster/> accessed 14 July 2011.
<www.emdat.be/glossary/9#term81> accessed 14 July 2011.
<www.who.int/hac/about/definitions/en/index.html> accessed 21 October 2011.
<www.ifrc.org/en/what-we-do/disaster-management/about-disasters/definition-of-hazard/> accessed 21 October 2011.
<www.unisdr.org/who-we-are> accessed 21 October 2011.
<www.humanitarianinfo.org/iasc/pageloader.aspx?page=content-about-default> accessed 24 October 2011.
<www.ifrc.org/en/what-we-do/disaster-management/about-disasters/definition-of-hazard/complex-emergencies/> accessed 24 October 2011.
<www.unesco.org/webworld/fed/temp/communication_democracy/conflict_resolution.htm> accessed 2 November 2011.
<www.icrc.org/IHL.nsf/(SPF)/party_main_treaties/$File/IHL_and_other_related_Treaties.pdf> accessed 7 November 2011.
<www.ifrc.org/en/what-we-do/disaster-management/about-disasters/definition-of-hazard/> accessed 10 November 2011.
<www.ifrc.org/en/what-we-do/idrl/idrl-guidelines/> accessed 29 December 2011.
<www.unocha.org/about-us/who-we-are/history> accessed 3 January 2012.
<http://ochanet.unocha.org/p/Documents/UNOCHA%20Organigramme%202011.pdf> accessed 3 January 2012.
<www.unocha.org/about-us/headofOCHA> accessed 3 January 2012.
<www.unocha.org/about-us/who-we-are> accessed 3 January 2012.
<www.beta.undp.org/content/undp/en/home/ourwork/overview.html> accessed 4 January 2012
<www.oecd.org/pages/0,3417,en_36734052_36734103_1_1_1_1_1,00.html> accessed 4 January 2012.
<www.ila-hq.org/index.cfm> accessed 5 January 2012.
<http://www2.ohchr.org/english/law/cescr.htm> accessed 19 February 2012.

<www.ifrc.org/en/who-we-are/history/> accessed 23 February 2012.

<http://treaties.un.org/Pages/ViewDetails.aspx?src=TREATY&mtdsg_no=IV-4&chapter=4&lang=en#EndDec> accessed 24 May 2012.

<http://conventions.coe.int/Treaty/Commun/ListeDeclarations.asp?NT=005&CM=8&DF=24/05/2012&CL=ENG&VL=1> accessed 24 May 2012.

<www.oas.org/juridico/english/sigs/b-32.html> accessed 24 May 2012.

<http://www2.ohchr.org/english/law/crc-reserve.htm> accessed 24 May 2012.

<http://treaties.un.org/Pages/ViewDetails.aspx?src=TREATY&mtdsg_no=IV-3&chapter=4&lang=en> accessed 31 May 2012.

<www.let.rug.nl/~usa/D/1501-1600/plakkaat/plakkaat.htm> accessed 5 July 2012.

<www.un.org/en/preventgenocide/adviser/edwardluck.shtml> accessed 10 July 2012.

<www.unhchr.ch/huridocda/huridoca.nsf/(symbol)/a.conf.157.23.en> accessed 19 July 2012.

<http://www2.ohchr.org/english/bodies/cerd/index.htm> accessed 19 July 2012

<http://www2.ohchr.org/english/bodies/hrc/index.htm> accessed 19 July 2012;

<http://www2.ohchr.org/english/bodies/cescr/> accessed 19 July 2012

<http://www2.ohchr.org/english/law/ccpr.htm> accessed 19 July 2012.

<http://www2.ohchr.org/english/law/crc.htm> accessed 19 July 2012.

<www.un.org/en/documents/udhr/> accessed 19 July 2012.

<www.echr.coe.int/NR/rdonlyres/D5CC24A7-DC13-4318-B457-5C9014916D7A/0/CONVENTION_ENG_WEB.pdf> accessed 19 July 2012.

<www.oas.org/en/iachr/mandate/Basics/convention.asp> accessed 19 July 2012.

<www.achpr.org/files/instruments/achpr/banjul_charter.pdf> accessed 19 July 2012.

<www.un.org/apps/news/story.asp?NewsID=42513&Cr=Syria&Cr1=> accessed 19 July 2012.

<www.ohchr.org/EN/HRBodies/SP/Pages/Themes.aspx> accessed 19 July 2012.

<www.un.org/womenwatch/daw/cedaw/cedaw.htm> accessed August 2, 2012.

<www.icrc.org/eng/resources/documents/update/2012/syria-update-2012-10-25.htm> accessed 9 November 2012.

<www.reuters.com/article/2011/03/02/us-libya-food-wfp-idUSTRE7214TM20110302> accessed 9 November 2012.

<www.icrc.org/eng/resources/documents/news-release/2012/23-10-libya-aid-distributed-fighting-drags-bani-walid.htm> accessed 9 November 2012.

<http://www2.ohchr.org/english/bodies/cerd/comments.htm> accessed 16 November 2012.

<http://www2.ohchr.org/english/bodies/crc/comments.htm> accessed 16 November 2012.

<www.mfa.gov.il/MFA/Government/Communiques/2010/Israel_Navy_warns_flotilla_31-May-2010.htm> accessed 3 December 2012 and <www.jpost.com/Israel/Article.aspx?id=177342> accessed 3 December 2012.

<www.icrc.org/customary-ihl/eng/docs/v2_rul_rule55_sectionb> accessed 20 August 2013.

<www.oecd.org/dac/stats/DAC%20List%20used%20for%202012%20and%202013%20flows.pdf> accessed 23 August 2013.

<www.hrw.org/news/2010/04/29/burma-after-cyclone-repression-impedes-civil-society-and-aid-0> accessed 2 October 2013.

<http://reliefweb.int/report/myanmar/myanmar-cyclone-nargis-ocha-situation-report-no-6> accessed 2 October 2013.

<www.reuters.com/article/2012/02/29/us-syria-un-idUSTRE81S20Z20120229> accessed 2 October 2013.

<http://hansard.millbanksystems.com/lords/1968/jul/15/biafra-united-nations-and-international> accessed 13 November 2013.

<http://edition.cnn.com/2005/WORLD/americas/09/05/katrina.cuba/> accessed 6 July 2014.

<http://edition.cnn.com/2008/WORLD/americas/09/15/cuba.us/> accessed 6 July 2014.

<www.reuters.com/article/2008/09/17/us-cuba-castro-usa-idUSN1740403120080917> accessed 6 July 2014.

<http://m.nos.nl/artikel/573773-somali-vraagt-hulp-vn-na-storm.html> accessed 8 July 2014.

<http://reliefweb.int/report/somalia/un-envoy-somalia-puntland-discuss-tropical-cyclone-response-and-forthcoming-elections> accessed 8 July 2014.

<www.ifrc.org/what-we-do/disaster-law/about-disaster-law/international-disaster-response-laws-rules-and-principles/idrl-guidelines/> accessed 1 September 2014.

<www.au.int/en/sites/default/files/Convention%20on%20IDPs%20-%20displaced..._0.pdf> accessed 9 September 2014.

<http://uk.reuters.com/article/2014/08/12/uk-ukraine-crisis-russia-aid-idUKKBN0GC08O20140812> accessed 9 September 2014.

<www.unocha.org/south-sudan/crisis-overview> accessed 17 September 2014.

<www.ifrc.org/en/what-we-do/idrl/model-act-on-idrl/> accessed 19 October 2014.

<www.unhcr.org/pages/49c3646c23.html> accessed 20 October 2014.

<https://docs.unocha.org/sites/dms/Documents/16%20July%202014%20Syria%20SC%20resolution_joint%20statement.pdf> accessed 21 October 2014.

<www.nbcnews.com/id/29492637/ns/world_news-africa/t/sudan-expels-aid-groups-response-warrant/#.VFETffmsWP4> accessed 29 October 2014.

<www.theguardian.com/world/2009/mar/05/sudan-aid-agencies-expelled> accessed 29 October 2014.

<www.ohchr.org/en/hrbodies/upr/pages/BasicFacts.aspx> accessed 2 November 2014.

<www.ihffc.org/index.asp?page=recognition_general> accessed 2 November 2014.

<www.icrc.org/eng/resources/documents/misc/fundamental-principles-commentary-010179.htm> accessed 24 November 2014.

<http://ec.europa.eu/commission/2014-2019/stylianides_en> accessed 15 December 2014.

<www.ifrc.org/en/publications-and-reports/code-of-conduct/> accessed 11 January 2015.

<http://ec.europa.eu/echo/who/about-echo_en> accessed 21 May 2015.

<http://in.reuters.com/article/2014/07/24/syria-crisis-un-aid-idINKBN0FT28A20140724> accessed 22 May 2015.

INDEX

CURRICULUM VITAE

Emilie Ellen Kuijt (Amsterdam, 1984) studied law at the University of Amsterdam and at the Columbia University School of Law in New York. In 2007, she obtained her Master in Public International Law, and in 2009 her Master in Information Law. While pursuing her Ph.D., Emilie worked as a lecturer & course coordinator at the department of Public International Law / Grotius Centre for International Legal Studies of Leiden University, where she taught and coordinated various Public International Law courses in the Bachelor programme and the LL.M programme, supervised theses and moot court teams, as well as other research projects. She furthermore co-organised the international conference 'International Humanitarian Assistance and International Law' (Leiden, January 2013), as well as organised and participated in various other international conferences, panels, workshops and events. During the spring of 2013, she was the Cegla Visiting Scholar at the Buchmann Faculty of Law, Tel Aviv University. At Leiden University, Emilie was a Gieskes-Strijbis-Fund Ph.D. Fellow and a Scholar in the Kalshoven-Gieskes Forum on International Humanitarian Law.

Prior to her position in Leiden, Emilie gained experience in the field of international law during a traineeship with the Permanent Mission of the Netherlands to the United Nations (Human Rights Council) in Geneva. After her 2nd LL.M. degree she worked with the Defence Counsel of a case before the International Criminal Tribunal for the Former Yugoslavia.

Publications (based on research undertaken for this book):

- 'A humanitarian crisis: reframing the legal framework on humanitarian assistance' in A. Zwitter et al (eds) *Humanitarian Action: Global, Regional and Domestic Legal Responses*, Cambridge University Press (2014).
- 'Legal Challenges in the Provision of Humanitarian Assistance: the Case of Non-International Armed Conflicts', in Vol. 17 *Yearbook of International Humanitarian Law*, Part IV, Asser Press (forthcoming Dec. 2015).

School of Human Rights Research Series

The School of Human Rights Research is a joint effort by human rights researchers in the Netherlands. Its central research theme is the nature and meaning of international standards in the field of human rights, their application and promotion in the national legal order, their interplay with national standards, and the international supervision of such application. The School of Human Rights Research Series only includes English titles that contribute to a better understanding of the different aspects of human rights.

For previous volumes in the series, please visit http://shr.intersentia.com.

Published titles within the Series:

68. Esther Janssen, *Faith in Public Debate. On Freedom of Expression, Hate Speech and Religion in France & the Netherlands* ISBN 978-1-78068-309-6
69. Stefanie Jansen-Wilhelm, *Accepting Assistance in the Aftermath of Disasters* ISBN 978-1-78068-329-4.
70. Helen Beckmann-Hamzei, *The Child in ICC Proceedings* ISBN 978-1-78068-339-3.
71. Karel De Meester, *The Investigation Phase in International Criminal Procedure: In Search of Common Rules* ISBN 978-1-78068-305-8.
72. Nelleke Koffeman, *Morally sensitive issues and cross-border movement in the EU. The cases of reproductive matters and legal recognition of same- sex relationships* ISBN 978-1-78068-349-2.
73. Roland Moerland, *The Killing of Death. Denying the Genocide against the Tutsi* ISBN 978-1-78068-351-5.
74. Andrea Broderick, *The Long and Winding Road to Disability Equality and Inclusion. The United Nations Convention on the Rights of Persons with Disabilities* ISBN 978-1-78068-358-4
75. Christina Peristeridou, *The principle of legality in European criminal law* ISBN 978-1-78068-357-7.

www.ingramcontent.com/pod-product-compliance
Ingram Content Group UK Ltd.
Pitfield, Milton Keynes, MK11 3LW, UK
UKHW051917100926
8556IPUK00021B/1232

9 781780 683669